Monarchs ar.

a (top). Building that housed the main Grand Council offices (and other offices as well) in the palace in Peking. This edifice is located on the northwest side of the Ch'ien-ch'ing Gate plaza, south of the imperial residence, the Yang-hsin Palace, which is barely visible in the distance at the far right. Grand Council subordinates such as the clerks and the archives staff usually worked elsewhere. (Photo by author, 1974)

b (bottom). Closeup of the east end of the Grand Council office in Peking. During the Ch'ing there were so many complaints against loiterers standing on the walk and peering through the windows in hopes of glimpsing state secrets that tough paper instead of glass remained in use until late in the nineteenth century. (Photo by author, 1974)

Monarchs and Ministers

The Grand Council in Mid-Ch'ing China, 1723–1820

Beatrice S. Bartlett

UNIVERSITY OF CALIFORNIA PRESS

Berkeley   Los Angeles   London

The author and the University of California Press gratefully acknowledge
support from the China Publication Subventions program.

University of California Press
Berkeley and Los Angeles, California

University of California Press, Ltd.
London, England

First Paperback Printing 1994

Library of Congress Cataloging-in-Publication Data
Bartlett, Beatrice S.
    Monarchs and ministers : the Grand Council in Mid-Ch'ing China,
1723–1820 / Beatrice S. Bartlett.
        p.   cm.
    Includes bibliographic references (p.   ) and index.
    ISBN 0-520-08645-7
    1. China. Chün chi ch'u—History.   2. Administrative agencies—
China—History.   3. Executive departments—China—History.
4. China—Politics and government—18th century.   5. China—Politics
and government—19th century.   I. Title.
JQ1508.B37 1990
354.5104'09'033—dc20   90-11068
                                                                                        CIP

Printed in the United States of America
1 2 3 4 5 6 7 8 9

The map on pp. 14–15 was prepared by Pamela Baldwin.
The index was prepared by Olive Holmes.

To the Memory of My Sister

Susan Leigh Bartlett Bull

1935–1987

Contents

Tables and Illustrative Material

TABLES

MAP

FIGURES

Acknowledgments

It is a pleasure to acknowledge the many colleagues, friends, and family members who supported this project in manifold ways over the years. After beginning graduate studies at Yale and deciding to work on the Chia-ch'ing reign (1796–1820), I asked Jonathan Spence what he most wanted to know about the period. His reply, "What had happened to the imperial power," has been at the back of my mind ever since. Although I have wandered far afield since that early conversation and in the manner of historians pressed my investigation ever backward into earlier reigns, one of my findings was that the rise of the Grand Council probably did affect the imperial power. This book may not supply the definitive answer to Professor Spence's thought-provoking question, but my work has profited from that query and many others as well. I am glad to have the opportunity to record my gratitude here.

Other special mentors and friends from whose detailed knowledge of Ch'ing history I have benefited include Chao Chung-fu of the Institute of Modern History, Academia Sinica; Chuang Chi-fa of the National Palace Museum in Taipei; Ju Deyuan of the Number One Historical Archives in Beijing; and Wei Qingyuan of the Archives Department, People's University. There is no question that without the advice of these colleagues and friends, this project would have foundered at an early date.

Studying the Grand Council's first century has involved pursuit of many strands, some of which have already led to other publications or will yield more in the future. The council's substantial documentary remains have been basic to my work. Understanding Ch'ing communications in all their permutations and combinations has been essential in using the documents as well as in comprehending the role of the inner-court communications system in the council's rise to dominance. As a result, many of the following acknowledgments are for assistance with related and subsidiary projects as well as with this one.

Previous scholarship on aspects of the vast topic of the Grand Council and its communication system has been invaluable, and I have had the privilege of discussing their work with all but one of the following: Chuang Chi-fa, Fu Tsung-mao, Huang Pei, Ju Deyuan, Liu Ziyang, the late Shan Shikui, and Silas H. L. Wu. Professor Wu was especially helpful during my early years in Taipei, when he generously shared his deep knowledge of Ch'ing documents.

I am also grateful to Dr. Chiang Fu-tsung, Director of the Palace Museum in Taipei at the time I was privileged to use its Ch'ing archives. Dr. Chiang's leadership in opening the museum's magnificent Ch'ing holdings for the use of scholars made possible the basic research presented here. My years of study at the Palace Museum brought me great happiness and many friends. At the risk of failing to acknowledge all who should be thanked, I nevertheless mention the following: Chang Lin-sheng (Leslie Chang), Ch'ang P'i-te (Peter Chang), Ch'en Chi-fu, Ch'en Chieh-hsien, Fung Ming-chu, Hou Chün-te, Lai Yung-erh, Li Ju-chen, Na Chih-liang, So Yü-ming, Su Tu-jen, T'ang Jui-yü, Wang Ching-hung, Wu Che-fu, and the late Wu Yü-chang. Others in Taiwan for whose assistance I am grateful include Jerome Cavanaugh, Chang Wejen, Hu Ying-fen, Robert Irick, Kao Wen-wen, Li Kuang-t'ao, Jean Oi, P'eng Hung Hsiao-ju, Robert Weiss, Yang Shuo-hsiang, Yin Chih-wen, and Yin Wang Chin-i.

In Beijing I was aided by Han Yuhu, Huang Xiaoceng, John Jamieson, Jiang Qiao, Lin Yongkuang, Liu Guilin, Liu Zhongying, Wu Tiqian, Yan Yongsheng, Yang Naiji, and Zhang Lizhong. I am particularly grateful to Professor Wei Qingyuan for arranging two opportunities for me to discuss Grand Council history and the communications systems with the Shan brothers, the late Shan Shikui and Shan Shiyuan. I am also grateful for the invitation of the State Archives Board of China to come to China as a state guest and participate in the Ming-Qing Research Symposium in Beijing in 1985. Fortunately that trip allowed me a further look at recently sorted Manchu as well as Chinese archival materials that had not previously been available, and which proved crucial for the book.

In Japan I was helped by Michael and Carol Freeman, Miyazaki Ichisada, Ishikure Kyoko, and the late Robert Somers. In Hong Kong I profited from contacts with Robert Lam, Registrar of the City Museum; Adam C. Y. Lui for arranging for me to see Liu Yat-wing's dissertation; and Mary and the late C. T. Yung.

Others who gave help in the United States and on encounters overseas include A. Doak Barnett, Knight Biggerstaff, Ch'en Jo-shui, Ch'en Kuo-tung, Janis Cochran, James Cole, Pamela Crossley, Natalie Zemon Davis, Jack Dull, Ulla Dydo, Robert Entenmann, John King Fairbank, Edward L. Farmer, the late Joseph F. Fletcher, Charlotte Furth, Bob Geyer, the late L. Carrington Goodrich, R. Kent Guy, Lotte Hamburger, Michael Ipson, Robert Jenks, Rick Johnston, Hideo Kaneko, Robert Kapp, Philip A. Kuhn, Hong Yung Lee,

Ruth Barcan Marcus, Tony Marr, Alynn Nathanson, Don C. Price, William and Priscilla Rope, William T. Rowe, Benjamin I. Schwartz, Stephen Shutt, Kent C. Smith, Hugh Stimson, Leonard Thompson, David Ts'ai, Tu Wei-yun, Frederic Wakeman, Joanna Waley-Cohen, Bin Wong, Edmund Worthy, the late Arthur and Mary Wright, Thomas Cheng-liang Wu, and Monica and Ying-shih Yü. Professor Susan Naquin merits special mention for sharing her information and experience derived from her wide reading and vast scanning of the Ch'ing archives. I also appreciate the late Joseph F. Fletcher's willingness to admit me as a member of his beginning Manchu class at Harvard University in 1981. My acquaintance with the Manchu language proved essential in solving certain problems connected with Grand Council development.

Those who read chapters of a work as it takes shape endure the special pain of grappling with an unpolished manuscript. I was fortunate in my readers— none of whom was burdened with the entire work—and am grateful for their willingness to comment, question, and argue. I thank Thomas C. Bartlett, Marie Borroff, Sherman Cochran, Joseph Hamburger, Emily Honig, Howard Lamar, Kenneth Lieberthal, Ann Lindbeck, Dian Murray, Elizabeth J. Perry, John Shepherd, Jonathan Spence, Lynn Struve, Wei Peh T'i (Betty Wei Liu), and Margaret Wimsatt. Some of my material was presented at the Columbia Modern China Seminar; I am grateful to Madeleine Zelin for arranging the occasion and particularly to my former teacher, Professor C. Martin Wilbur, for his incisive comments. Another presentation at the New England Historical Association brought helpful criticisms from Michi Aoki and Terry MacDougall. I further benefited from Yü Ying-shih's remarks on a paper given at the annual meeting of the New England branch of the Association for Asian Studies and the comments of my Saybrook College fellows following a presentation in the spring of 1988. None of these persons should be held responsible for errors that may remain.

I was helped immeasurably by the publications team of the University of California Press. My initial contact with the director, James Clark, was rewarding. I gained many valuable insights from the comments of the two readers, Jerry Dennerline and Madeleine Zelin. The project editor, Betsey Scheiner, was unfailingly supportive, and I was unusually fortunate in my copyeditor, Anne G. Canright. For typing various incarnations of the manu-script and for help with manuscript preparation I thank Janis Cochran, Katy Greenebaum, Ginny Guin, Joan Hill, Stephen Shutt, Florence Thomas, Karin Weng, and Gretta Yao.

I am grateful for access to the following installations possessing Ch'ing archival holdings: in Taiwan, the Institute of History and Philology (for the Ming-Ch'ing Shih-liao) and the Institute of Modern History at the Academia Sinica and, above all, the meticulously organized and indexed holdings at the National Palace Museum. On the China mainland I principally used the superb holdings at the Number One Historical Archives in Beijing, but the opportunity to consult materials at the Liao-ning Provincial Archives in Shen-yang, assisted there by Shen Wei and Wu Fuheng, was also valuable. In London I saw documents and Peking gazettes at the British Library thanks to their keeper, Howard Nelson. The principal libraries I used were the British Library, the Fu Ssu-nien Library in Taipei, the library of the Harvard-Yenching Institute, the Library of Congress, the National Central Library in Taipei, the library of the Palace Museum in Taipei, and the East Asian Collection at Yale University.

Financial support began many years ago with a Special Faculty Award from the Brearley School, a national Defense Foreign Language Fellowship, and a Fulbright-Hays grant for the initial foray to Taiwan. The Taiwan phase of the work was variously supported by the American Council of Learned Societies (for a separate but related project), the Chia-hsin Foundation, and the Inner Asia Regional Council of the Association for Asian Studies (also for a separate project). The Committee on Scholarly Communication with the People's Republic of China supported time in the Beijing archives just as those enormous vaults were being sorted and opened to foreigners. A brief return visit in 1985 was made possible by an invitation from the State Archives Board of the People's Republic of China and support from the American Council of Learned Societies and the A. Whitney Griswold Faculty Research Fund of Yale University. Manuscript preparation was financed in part by a Faculty Research Grant from the Yale Center for International and Area Studies. Although I was not able to work on this manuscript when I was at Harvard under a postdoctoral fellowship, I am nevertheless indebted to the Fairbank Center for occasional opportunities to consult with scholars and to use the libraries at Harvard University for the purposes of this book.

Finally, I was gratified to discover that my family was no less enthusiastic about intellectual pursuits than members of a Chinese clan might have been. It is with pleasure and affection that I acknowledge their support: the late Russell S. Bartlett, the late Julia M. Bartlett, William M. Bartlett, the late Susan Dwight Bliss, the late Susan B. Bull, the late Stanley and Dorothea Daggett, the late Sarah Barney Bartlett Finley, Alexander and James Finley, Carter Keane, and the late Emilie Daggett Reynolds.

July 15, 1989

Note on Technical Matters

REIGNS AND DATES

New Ch'ing reign titles began officially on the first Chinese New Year's Day of the lunar year following the death of the previous emperor. As a result an emperor usually ruled under the previous emperor's reign title while finishing the remaining months of his predecessor's final year. Chia-ch'ing (r. 1796–1820), whose reign intentionally began on Chinese New Year's Day because of the timing of his father's abdication, is an exception to this scheme. Emperors are most commonly known by their reign titles, as given below. They also had personal names, tabooed during the Ch'ing, and, except for the last emperor of the Ch'ing, posthumous titles.

Dates are rendered according to the Chinese lunar calendar, using the Chinese order—beginning with the largest unit and progressing to the smallest: year/month/day. Western equivalents are given in the same order, in parentheses.

PLACE-NAMES AND PERSONAL NAMES

Wade-Giles romanization has been used not to make a political statement but rather to allow compatibility with its use in so many of the standard references and libraries in the field. Postal spellings have been employed for some place-names, but the northern capital is referred to as "Peking" for the Ch'ing (up to 1911), "Peiping" (with a few liberties arising from the political confusion of the times) for the moments when the capital was elsewhere (1912–49), and "Beijing" for the People's Republic (since 1949). Manchu names are given in the Chinese style (Ma-erh-sai rather than Marsai, for instance) to facilitate looking them up in standard Chinese reference works.

TECHNICAL TERMS

For many, the translations of some of the Grand Council's technical terms will be one of the special interests of this book, particularly because these will amplify E-tu Zen Sun's splendid *Ch'ing Administrative Terms*, which is a translation of a Ch'ien-lung–period work (recently printed in Japan as *Rikubu seigo chūkai*) largely concerned with outer- rather than inner-court terminology. For the sake of general intelligibility, I have used Grand Council terms in translation; Chinese romanizations have been supplied occasionally to assist the specialist reader. All terms in both their romanized and translated forms may be looked up in the Glossary-Index, where characters supplement the romanizations.

I have made numerous terminological discoveries, not all limited to the eighteenth-century development of the Ch'ing inner-court system. When I first investigated the Grand Council's document register known as the Sui-shou teng-chi, I found many memorials mysteriously marked *pao* (military report). Patient sleuthing eventually revealed the probable source of this usage to be the four-character "report from the military encampments" (*chün-ying wen-pao*, occasionally abbreviated to *chün-pao* as well as more frequently to *pao*).

Other kinds of terminological discoveries revealed changes in terms over time. In the early Ch'ien-lung period, for instance, the grand councillors used *shuo-t'ieh* to identify a "memorandum" of explanation for the emperor, but this was later replaced with *tsou-p'ien*. In Yung-cheng times "secret memorial" (*mi-tsou*) meant all palace memorials, but by the Chia-ch'ing period it meant a certain type of secret memorial within the palace memorial system. The grand councillors occasionally explained unclear terminology in the documents, as when in one instance they pored over provincial finances and reported that deposits called *chi-k'u* in Yunnan were known as *wai-shou* in Hupei. For the meaning of a particularly elusive Grand Council term, *t'u-t'a-mi*, Professor Susan Naquin and I trailed mentions all through various council record books until we had assembled a file of uses that, unfortunately, told us nothing—in the circles of the term's use contemporaries knew what it meant and felt no need to write it down for future researchers. Only later did I come upon a nineteenth-century explanation. (The term proved to be derived from the Manchu *tutambi*, "to stay behind," and denoted the Grand Council duty group that remained in the capital when the emperor went on tour.) Grand Council terminology was a special eighteenth-century development, often heavily influenced by Manchu, frequently changing within a short space of time.

Reign Titles of the Ch'ing Emperors (1644–1911)

(with abbreviations used in the text and notes)

SC	Shun-chih, 1644–61
KH	K'ang-hsi, 1662–1722
YC	Yung-cheng, 1723–35
CL	Ch'ien-lung, 1736–95 (this emperor also ruled for three abdication years, 1796–99)
CC	Chia-ch'ing, 1796–1820
TK	Tao-kuang, 1821–50
HF	Hsien-feng, 1851–61
TC	T'ung-chih, 1862–74
KHsu	Kuang-hsu, 1875–1908
HT	Hsuan-t'ung, 1909–12

Principal Events Mentioned in the Text

YUNG-CHENG PERIOD (1723–35)

KH61/11/13 (1722 Dec. 20)	Death of the K'ang-hsi Emperor, age 68; the Plenipotentiary Council founded to assist the new emperor during the mourning period
YC1/4/7 (1723 May 11)	The I Prince (Yin-hsiang) appointed Superintendent of the Board of Revenue
YC1–2 (1723–24)	Lobdzan Dandzin leads a Khoshote rebellion in Ch'ing-hai; suppressed by Nien Keng-yao and Yueh Chung-ch'i while the leader escapes
YC3/2/14 (1725 Mar. 27)	Dissolution of the Plenipotentiary Council
YC4 (1726)	Plans for campaign against the Zunghars; the Board of Revenue ministers and inner deputies Prince I, Chang T'ing-yü, and Chiang T'ing-hsi in charge of planning at the capital; General Yueh Chung-ch'i in charge of the western front
YC5 (1727)	General Yueh brought to capital for consultations
YC5/12/10 (1728 Jan. 20)	Earliest surviving archival court letter (to General Yueh)
YC7 (1729)	Founding of the Board of Revenue Military Finance Section, supervised by the inner deputies and headed by Weng Tsao

YC7/J7/21 (1729 Sept. 13)	General Yueh starts to march his troops "beyond the pass" (from Su-chou in West Kansu to Barkul, in Sinkiang)
YC8/5/4 (1730 June 18)	Death of the I Prince; northwest campaign halted and General Yueh recalled for consultations
YC8/11 (late 1730)	General Yueh back on the northwest front
YC8/12 (early 1731)	Earliest appearance of the High Officials in Charge of Military Finance; earliest court letter with a roster enlarged beyond the inner deputies
YC10/3/3 (1732 Mar. 28)	Seal cast for the Office of Military Strategy
YC10 (1732)	O-erh-t'ai joins the inner deputies; General Yueh impeached, recalled, imprisoned
YC11 (1733)	High Officials' name gradually changes from "In Charge of Military Finance" to "In Charge of Military Strategy"
YC13/8/23 (1735 Oct. 8)	Death of the Yung-cheng Emperor, age 57

CH'IEN-LUNG PERIOD (1736–99)

Note: The Yung-cheng–period dates (YC) that follow are from the remainder of the year after Yung-cheng's death when Ch'ien-lung had already become the ruler. The Chia-ch'ing period dates (CC) are from the era when Ch'ien-lung ruled as Supreme Abdicated Monarch during the first three years of his son's reign. The sixty Ch'ien-lung years plus three abdication years make this reign the longest in Chinese dynastic history.

YC13/8/23 (1735 Oct. 8)	Death of the Yung-cheng Emperor; the Interim Council set up by decree of the deceased emperor to assist the new emperor, its members including two princes and the two surviving Yung-cheng deputies, O-erh-t'ai and Chang T'ing-yü
YC13/9/3 (1735 Oct. 18)	The Ch'ien-lung Emperor enthroned in the T'ai-ho Palace
YC13/9/22 (1735 Nov. 6)	The Military Finance Section disbanded; files turned over to the ministerial level of the Board of Revenue (that is, to the Interim Council)
YC13/10/29 (1735 Dec. 12)	Office of Military Strategy disbanded, responsibilities turned over to the Interim Council

CL2/11/28 (1738 Jan. 17)	The Interim Council disbanded, continues under the revived name of the Office of Military Strategy (commonly translated "Grand Council"); Chang T'ing-yü is first Chinese grand councillor
CL13–14 (1748–49)	First Chin-ch'uan campaign spurs Grand Council growth with increased personnel, new office space close to emperor; Office of Military Archives founded
CL14 (1749)	Execution of the Grand Councillor and General in Charge of the First Chin-ch'uan Campaign, No-ch'in
CL14–35 (1749–70)	Fu-heng serves as Ranking Grand Councillor
CL21 (1756)	Chao I becomes a Grand Council clerk
CL24 (1759)	End of the Mongol Wars
CL28 (1763)	A-kuei first appointed to the Grand Council
CL37 (1772)	Liu T'ung-hsun appointed first Chinese Ranking Councillor
CL38–41 (1773–76)	Second Chin-ch'uan War; many grand councillors and clerks deputed to the front
CL41 (1776)	Ho-shen first appointed to the Grand Council
CL42 (1777)	A-kuei appointed Grand Secretary
CL45 (1780)	A-kuei appointed Ranking Councillor
CL51 (1786)	Ho-shen appointed Grand Secretary
CC1/1/1	Ch'ien-lung abdicates, becomes the "Supreme Abdicated Monarch" and continues to rule from behind the scenes
CC2 (1797)	A-kuei dies; Ho-shen becomes Ranking Councillor
CC4/1/3 (1799 Feb. 7)	Death of the Ch'ien-lung Emperor, age 87

CH'IA-CH'ING PERIOD (1796–1820)

CC1/1/1 (1796 Feb. 9)	Abdication of Ch'ien-lung; Chia-ch'ing enthroned (see previous table)
CC4/1/3 (1799 Feb. 7)	Death of the Supreme Abdicated Monarch

CC4/1 (1799 Feb.)	Entire Grand Council replaced; earliest imperial denunciation of the "copies [of documents] sealed up" and sent separately to Ho-shen
CC4/1/15 (1799 Feb. 19)	Indictment of Ho-shen handed down; Secret Accounts Bureau abolished
CC4/1/16 (1799 Feb. 20)	First regulation of Grand Council clerk appointments
CC4/1/18 (1799 Feb. 22)	Imperial command that Ho-shen commit suicide
CC5 (1800)	Edict requiring increased security measures at the Grand Council premises
CC7 (1802)	Earliest Chia-ch'ing period censor's protest against the Grand Council (for monopolizing the edict drafting power)
CC23 (1818)	Publication of the first notice concerning Grand Council work in the *Collected Statutes* (*Hui-tien*)
CC25/7/25 (1820 Sept. 2)	Death of the Chia-ch'ing Emperor, age 59

Prologue

This book describes the great eighteenth-century transformation of Ch'ing (1644–1911) rule by which many of the central-government agencies were consolidated under a new supervising and coordinating high privy inner-court organization, the Grand Council (*Chün-chi ch'u*). Early Ch'ing emperors had for the most part discharged the relatively uncomplicated government affairs of their day by dealing personally and directly with the multiplicity of subordinate agencies in the capital. For most of these responsibilities the monarchs had only a few ministerial assistants and small staffs. As a result of the mid-Ch'ing transformation (1723–1820), several of the scattered groups of imperial assistants were gathered in a new body—the Grand Council—and that organization was interposed between the monarch and the central-government agencies, creating an entity able to deal with the greatly increased business of the mid-Ch'ing polity. The transformation was an important factor in the final defeat of China's ancient Mongol enemy on the northwest frontier as well as in the military successes of the Ch'ien-lung Emperor's Ten Campaigns, which pushed the boundaries of the Chinese Empire to their greatest extent in history (except for the period when China was part of the Mongol Yuan Empire, 1260–1368). After the Opium War (1839–42), the experienced council was in place to deal with the dynasty's final half-century of emergencies wrought of great rebellions, infant emperors, regencies, and the intensified western intrusion. Thus the eighteenth-century transformation from direct imperial personal rule to joint monarchical-conciliar administration enabled the dynasty to rise to greatness in its middle years and at the end prolonged its life.

The main concern of this book is to ask how and why this eighteenth-century transformation took place. What caused the formation of the Grand Council and enabled it to rise to the overlordship of almost the entire central government of the Chinese empire within such a short space of time? How was a new

1

high-level agency propelled to dominance in an administrative context that was frozen by legal codes of exhausting detail and susceptible to factional disputes between long-established ministerial and bureaucratic coalitions? Do the existing theories of Grand Council genesis, usually applied to the final seven years of the Yung-cheng Emperor (r. 1723–35), assist our understanding when we shift to the broader time frame of the council's first and formative century?

THE YUNG-CHENG THREE-STEP MODEL
OF GRAND COUNCIL GENESIS

Most accounts of Grand Council development in the Yung-cheng reign have followed the Ch'ing official view and looked back from the standpoint of the strong centralized council of subsequent reigns to describe how a supposedly wise, all-seeing Yung-cheng Emperor purposefully created the powerful, centralizing inner-court agency known in English as the "Grand Council." Although these analyses vary slightly, the usual story is that the early Grand Council—believed to have originated as an offshoot of the Grand Secretariat—developed in three precisely definable steps. It began in YC7 (1729) as the "Military Finance Section" (*Chün-hsu fang*), set up close to the emperor in the inner court to deal with the northwest campaign against the Zunghar Mongols. Next it metamorphosed through an intermediate phase as the "Military Strategy Section" (*Chün-chi fang*). And finally it became the powerful "Grand Council" (*Chün-chi ch'u*). All three of these steps are said to have been accomplished within the final seven years of the Yung-cheng Emperor's reign.[1]

This picture of a single agency growing in strength and undergoing name changes presents difficulties. As Chuang Chi-fa of the Taipei Palace Museum has pointed out, the term "Military Strategy Section" (*Chün-chi fang*) does not regularly occur in documents of the Yung-cheng era.[2] In his 1970 book *Communication and Imperial Control*, Silas H. L. Wu also questioned the standard view when he described a small tightly knit group of imperial assistants who, while not members of a single changing agency that dealt with the northwest military situation, nevertheless performed duties characteristic of the later grand councillors. These inner-court assistants to the emperor, sometimes called "inner grand secretaries" (*nei chung-t'ang*), were high-level imperial confidants who could be deputed to perform any task the emperor assigned. They were concerned with the other inner-court administrative staffs not as full-time members but as part-time supervisors.[3] With this brilliant insight Professor Wu's work supplied the essential step toward the understanding that the administrative part of Yung-cheng's inner court did not consist of a single powerful agency and thus did not precisely resemble the Grand Council of later times. Rather, the Yung-cheng inner court consisted of several informal nonstatutory groups, a design intended to facilitate imperial control.

My own subsequent archival discoveries have filled out this new framework.

At the Taipei Palace Museum in the 1970s, thinking that the Ch'ien-lung Emperor might have been briefed after coming to the throne, I unearthed a crucial memorial that revealed another flaw in the standard narrative. This document showed that after the Military Finance Section was founded subordinate to the ministerial level of the Board of Revenue, it never underwent name changes or any kind of metamorphosis at all but instead remained continuously in place, operating under its YC7 mandate and title right through to the end of the reign. In 1980–81, when I used Chinese materials in Beijing's Number One Historical Archives, I found repeated mentions of yet another inner-court group, the "High Officials in Charge of Military Finance" (*Pan-li Chün-hsu ta-ch'en*), created late in YC8 (early 1731), whose title later changed to "High Officials in Charge of Military Strategy" (*Pan-li Chün-chi ta-ch'en*, also sometimes *Chün-chi ch'u* or, in Manchu, *Cooha-i nashūn-i ba*). This proved to be yet another staff—nowhere near as strong as the later Grand Council but bearing the same name.[4] Like the other two groups, this one also had a separate existence and lasted to the end of the reign.

Finally, when I was in Beijing for a conference in the autumn of 1985, I was allowed to see some recently sorted court letter edicts and Manchu-language memorials and record books. These supplied further details about the inner-court confidants and the High Officials in Charge of Military Finance—their responsibilities, personnel, and organizational structure. These archival discoveries conclusively demonstrate that for the administrative sector of his inner court, Yung-cheng clung to the K'ang-hsi model of a divided inner court. Yung-cheng's inner court consisted of separate individuals and small staffs, not a consolidated Grand Council. This is the story told in Part One of this book. The key transformation from a compartmentalized to a consolidated inner court had to wait for the early years of the Ch'ien-lung reign (late 1735–95) and is recounted in Part Two.

THE INNER/OUTER-COURT MODEL AND GRAND COUNCIL GROWTH IN THE CH'IEN-LUNG PERIOD

In contrast with the Yung-cheng–period Grand Council genesis, which scholars have narrated in dozens of chapters and essays, the council's astonishing rise to dominance over the central government in the Ch'ien-lung period has hardly been studied at all. Yet similar developments in dynasties before the Ch'ing have been described. These have frequently been analyzed as power struggles between the so-called inner court (*nei-t'ing*), the emperor's faction, and the outer court (*wai-ch'ao*), the bureaucracy's faction.[5] On the one hand were the emperor, his palace household, and his privy council assistants; on the other were the officials who presided over the departments that administered the empire. Specific elements in the contests varied from reign to reign and indeed within reigns. Strong emperors might direct the administrators; strong bureaucrats might isolate the emperors and administer the realm independently. In some periods battles were fought entirely within the inner court, sometimes with the palace eunuchs playing a leading role. But with the notable exception of Huang Pei, who astutely grasped the significance of the council's early history as "essentially" a re-creation "of the inner court," most writing about the Ch'ing has failed to stress this kind of cleavage.[6] In fact, an inner/outer-court division did exist at the heart of the Ch'ing government. What is more, it was intimately related to Grand Council development.

The two communications systems that flourished through most of the Ch'ing period supply a good example of this bifurcation and offer an opportune means of studying it. The routine communications system inherited from the Ming flourished in the outer court. This was an open, public, regulated bureaucratic channel, many of whose documents—both the reports as well as their responding edicts—were eventually published in the Peking gazettes. To support and make further use of the routine communications system, the outer court had its own archival installations and drew on its archival holdings for official compilations such as the court chronicles (*Shih-lu*) and official histories (*Kuo-shih*).

By contrast, the palace memorial system began in the K'ang-hsi period as the emperor's private channel, with documents kept secret and limited to circulation between the inner court and provincial correspondents. The two main kinds of official responses to the palace memorials were rescripts written in vermilion, the emperor's own color that signified the source was the emperor himself, and court letter edicts. These responses were composed, dispatched, and processed entirely in the inner court. Under Yung-cheng the inner court also began to develop its own archival storage, first for the palace memorials and later of other types of documents. In the next reign the inner-court Grand Council acquired authority over its own publication projects, notably the campaign histories (*fang-lueh*), which were based on its inner-court files. The special inner-court communications system played a key role in these Grand Council developments, supplying both secrecy and access to important information for the monarchs and their inner-court ministers.

Differences between the inner and outer courts were likewise exhibited in the structure of the central-government administration. The outer-court bureaucracy consisted of the major administrative organs, most inherited from the Ming and earlier times. The chief mission of these agencies was to process the documents of the routine system—reports from all over the empire concerning nearly all the major spheres of government enterprise. Most important for understanding eighteenth-century developments was the fact that the outer court operated according to statutory prescription: the administrative code governed the outer-court staffs that ran the empire.

Unlike the inherited and largely unchanging organizations of the outer court that were defined by law, the early-Ch'ing inner court was the creature of imperial fiat and tended to change from reign to reign. Although the Yung-cheng Emperor, for instance, allowed his father's Deliberative Princes and Ministers (*I-cheng wang ta-ch'en*) and the Southern [Imperial] Study (*Nan-shu fang*) to continue, they were used less and gradually declined; in their place he conceived a new design for his inner court and appointed a top echelon of his favorites—one to four high assisting ministers—and two new middle-level staffs—the Board of Revenue's Military Finance Section and the High Officials in Charge of Military Finance (described above). When Ch'ien-lung came to the throne another major change took place as Yung-cheng's three new inner-court entities coalesced in one organization. The old name of the Office (or High Officials) in Charge of Military Strategy (*Pan-li Chün-chi ch'u*), now appropriately translated into English as "Grand Council," was revived for the new consolidated agency, which became the major central-government administrative body for as long as the dynasty lasted. This explains why for the remainder of the Ch'ing and into modern times, people believed that the powerful consolidated inner-court Grand Council of the Ch'ing had been founded in the Yung-cheng period. But we now know that this was true only in the sense of its name.

In employing English-language terminology in this book I have used the words "bureaucrat" and "bureaucracy" much as Yung-cheng himself saw these men—to refer to the large outer-court staffs. By contrast, the inner-court upper-echelon officials whom I call "ministers" (certain grand secretaries, board presidents, and vice presidents who were the focus of imperial blandishments) were the emperor's personal appointees, usually in daily contact with the sovereign. Although they had become inner-court servitors, through their concurrent outer-court positions the emperor deputized them to supervise the outer-court bureaucracy. From Yung-cheng's as well as Ch'ien-lung's perspective these men were not ordinary outer-court bureaucrats, and I have accordingly avoided using outer-court terminology to describe them.

We would be wrong to regard causation in this study (that is, the reasons for the Grand Council's founding and growth) solely as the outcome of a long-term imperial plot to develop the inner court and thereby the capabilities of the autocrats. Other factors also contributed to the council's development into a large inner-court organization of more than two hundred persons directing the government of the empire. The council's monopoly of a fully developed communications channel played an important role in Grand Council growth, as did the secrecy that hid inner-court activities and council expansion from outer-court jealousy and retaliation. Special situations of the times—Yung-cheng's fear of outer-court tendencies to malfeasance, needs of the military campaigns, Ch'ien-lung's fondness for touring—also favored a small tightly knit council directed by ministers with whom the emperors were well acquainted and in whom they had confidence. Although ministerial ambition is difficult to measure, that must also be reckoned as a factor in the council's rise.

Finally, inner-court informality—particularly as manifest in Yung-cheng's inner court—was another important element in Grand Council growth. Yung-cheng's new inner-court staffs were neither enshrined in statute law nor awarded the prestige that would have accompanied formal establishment. Instead his three inner-court entities functioned beyond the reach of the administrative code, thus gaining an advantage that I call "the extralegal dynamic." In the Ch'ien-lung period, when these groups joined together and challenged the long-established outer-court agencies, this freedom from legal constraints promoted growth. The council's extralegal status allowed it to undertake new activities and so engage in expansion of kinds that the administrative codes did not permit its competitors, the outer-court agencies. One example of this advantage is recounted toward the end of Chapter 6, where the grand councillors' concurrent posts—which arose from the lack of formal positions on the council itself—are described. Some of the outer-court responsibilities of those holding the concurrent positions were transferred into the council's purview, thereby enlarging its capabilities. Concurrent posts also supplied council members with unofficial contacts throughout the capital bureaucracy, as well as access to widely scattered sources of information. Thus paradoxically, Yung-cheng's insistence on developing his inner court while keeping it weak, divided, lacking in formal status, and subservient to his will was a major factor that resulted in a Grand Council heyday in the following reign.

At this point the reader may ask how in an autocratic situation where the monarch supposedly made the law, an extralegal dynamic could confer an advantage. If the emperor wished to change the legal arrangements for either the inner or the outer court, it might be argued that he surely possessed the power to do so.

The key fact lies in the differing statutory status of the inner and outer courts. The outer-court agencies of the government were set up under the administrative code and generally ran according to its statutes and precedents. Although the monarch could probably change these arrangements at will (and indeed in a few instances did so), for most matters imperial respect for established statutes prevailed and advice on the wisdom of proposed changes was both sought and followed. The outer-court government thus ran more by a combination of law and consensus than by the imposition of raw imperial power, even though the rhetoric of governing always strongly implied that such power existed.

By contrast, in the early eighteenth century—and at the beginning of our story—statute law did not define the inner court. At that time the imperial assistants and staffs were regarded as the emperor's own men: his to appoint, his to command. In the inner court no statutes could be summoned to confound the monarch's desire. The sovereign's will was law. The inner court was free of legal restraints and enjoyed a flexibility denied its outer-court competitors.

Where did the mature Grand Council described in Part Two of this book fit in the inner/outer-court framework? Was it an inner-court privy council that loyally served the mid- and late-Ch'ing emperors and promoted their autocratic designs? Or did it eventually develop its own concerns and become an outer-court administrative staff that ran the bureaucracy? In other words, did the council enter the nineteenth century as the emperor's pawn or as the bureaucracy's directorate? My research suggests that the council did not take sides in this struggle but seized the opportunities provided by both worlds. It remained loyal to the emperor but at the same time extended its reach to direct most of the agencies of the outer court. The result was a greatly expanded inner-court dominance, but one where both ministers and monarchs could be strong. While the framework for autocracy continued in place, the expansion of inner-court work and the ministerial skill and labor essential to accomplishing it weakened the monarchs' ability fully to oversee and direct the government. As a consequence, much of the entire central government—inner as well as outer court—and the provinces too, came under the new inner-court consolidated council.

PLAN OF THE BOOK

This book is divided into two main parts. Part One investigates the council's Yung-cheng–period origins at the hands of a monarch who distrusted organizations with plenipotentiary powers. These chapters (1–4) show how the Yung-cheng Emperor, jealous of possible alternative power centers that might rival his own, pursued a divide-and-rule policy, preferring to deal directly with selected individuals and small informal groups that were never intended to coalesce and become a single strong privy council at the heart of the inner court. In Chapter 1 I describe the inner/outer-court situation that Yung-cheng faced on coming to the throne and explain how he apparently decided that strengthening the inner court was the answer to his difficulties. Chapter 2 shows how two inner-court confidants gradually came to be used for a variety of high-level tasks. In Chapter 3 I explain how these two became the nucleus of a very small nameless high-inner-managerial echelon, which I call the "inner deputies." Chapter 4 completes the Yung-cheng period with a description of the two subordinate staffs set up to deal with the military campaign. Thus, although Yung-cheng founded the inner-court organizations ancestral to the Grand Council, he always kept them separate and strenuously avoided creating a single strong organization worthy of the translation "Grand Council."

Not all readers will be interested in the details of the first part; many will want to proceed directly to Part Two, which describes the mature eighteenth-century Grand Council. In comparison with Part One's focus on a short thirteen-year reign, the approach in Part Two, which covers a sixty-year reign plus the three years after the abdication, has had to be less detailed. The introductory Chapter 5 narrates the consolidation of Yung-cheng's three informal inner-court staffs in the single mourning-period transition council (*Tsung-li shih-wu wang ta-ch'en*), which I have called the "Interim Council," and explains how the name of one of Yung-cheng's small inner-court groups, the "Office of Military Strategy" (*Chün-chi ch'u*), was revived early in the Ch'ien-lung period and applied to the newly enlarged inner-court council, whose name is thenceforth properly translated "Grand Council." Chapters 6 and 7 then describe the council over the sixty-three years that Ch'ien-lung ruled. Some narrative of development is supplied but there has been little attempt to depict the twists and turns of council growth in detail. The main thrust of these chapters is to show the tremendous expansion of central-government paperwork and thereby of Grand Council responsibilities that took place during the long Ch'ien-lung reign.

Finally, Chapter 8 describes the Ho-shen abuses and Chia-ch'ing reforms of 1799–1820, following the height of the council's power. A few features of the council were reformed, but the reform process was limited and the council emerged largely unchanged from the Chia-ch'ing period. Although I would have liked to round out the Grand Council story with a detailed description of the effects of the new conciliar administrative and decision-making structure on central-government policy making, only a summary can be offered here. It would take another book to describe the council's nineteenth-century history and show how its influence probably did not cease with its demise in May 1911.[7] Future study may reveal ways in which council traditions have shaped Chinese government and bureaucracy in the present day.

SOURCES

The Ch'ing Grand Council is the only historic Chinese high privy council for which substantial numbers of archival materials survive. During the course of my research, the magnificent Ch'ing archives in both Beijing and Taipei were arranged and opened to foreigners. For my initial research, on a slightly different topic, I used the Taipei Palace Museum's superbly indexed Grand Council materials. But at the very moment that I was completing my work, a delegation of scholars led by Professor Frederic Wakeman was touring the mainland archives. As a result, the next year part of that treasure trove was opened to foreigners, and my application to go to Beijing found favor.

In Beijing I was confronted with an ocean of documents ten times as numerous as the holdings I had worked with in Taipei. I realized that the staggering number of new materials would make it possible to write a history of the eighteenth-century monarchical-conciliar transition, whose story had been only indistinctly visible in the Taipei archives. In the end I recast my focus and wrote an almost entirely new book.

The Beijing documents were both voluminous and difficult to use. In 1980–81 archive rules did not permit research assistants, nor were photocopying and microfilming easily available; everything that might be needed had to be copied out by hand and summarized in Chinese in a final report to the archive authorities. My report ran to 108 pages! A brief return trip late in 1985 yielded the pleasures of much-improved facilities but only a frustratingly short time to inspect the tantalizing sea of newly available documents now at my disposal. As a result, on both trips I had to limit my searches to periods of Grand Council history not well covered in Taipei—chiefly late Yung-cheng and early Ch'ien-lung (ca. 1728–60). Even these years could only be skimmed, while I reluctantly had to overlook the Beijing documentation for most other years. This concentration has resulted in an intensive examination of the council's formative years—up to approximately CL25 (1760) when the new conciliar system was being worked out—and less detail for the remainder of the reign.

Despite the importance of the Beijing materials to the final study, reliance on only one of the archival depositories would not have sufficed. Although the Grand Council had a policy of making duplicate and even triplicate (or more) copies of its documents as early as the eighteenth century, several unique items turned up in both places. The book could not have been attempted without recourse to crucial materials in both Taipei and Beijing.

Archival access is necessary to study the Grand Council. No surviving published primary sources tell the full story. The council's early growth depended in part on its being shielded by inner-court secrecy, a situation that has also shielded the facts of its development from later investigators. A policy of confidentiality appears to have prevailed well into the nineteenth century. When an official entry finally appeared in 1818 in the Chia-ch'ing *Collected Statutes and Precedents (Hui-tien* and *Hui-tien shih-li)*, the statutes provided a short description of the council, but little was supplied under precedents.[8]

Grand councillors also guarded the council's secrets. The published autobiographical writings and memorial collections of grand councillors such as Chang T'ing-yü (1672–1755) and A-kuei (1717–97) preserved confidentiality by omitting information on important council activities. Chang T'ing-yü's chronological autobiography, for example, fails to mention the new group of High Officials until YC11 (1733), more than two years after its founding, even though he had been intimately concerned with its labors throughout the period.[9] Moreover, while some eighteenth-century council clerks (Wang Ch'ang and especially Chao I) left useful descriptions of council processes, they too appear to have exercised self-censorship and avoided sensitive information. The same stricture probably applied to the extensive selection of surviving records made by the Grand Council clerk Liang Chang-chü (1775–1849) for his 1822 compilation on Grand Council history and working processes, *Shu-yuan chi-lueh.* Although Liang had access to the council's voluminous archival remains, his compendium is highly selective. In recent years some scholars have resorted to the piecemeal recollections of peripheral figures such as Hsi Wu-ao and Yeh Feng-mao, who wrote about council origins many years after their tenuous early observation of some of the activities of its forerunners, but now that comparison with archival evidence is possible these remembrances have frequently proved only partly accurate or, even downright misleading. Reliance on them has sometimes thrown modern scholars far off the track and exacerbated the difficulties of researching the Yung-cheng period.[10] My emphasis on the role of Yung-cheng's loyal younger brother, Prince I (Yin-hsiang), and the Board of Revenue ministers as significant formative elements of the Yung-cheng inner circle, for instance, derives from archival materials dating from long before the time that the authors of those hazy reminiscences got around to publishing their observations.

The documents relevant to the eighteenth-century Grand Council story probably number in the hundreds of thousands, with perhaps as many as several thousand items in Chinese and Manchu per year; needless to say, even if I had gained access to all these materials, it would have been impossible to read through them. As a result, at many points I have summarized strenuously in order to condense the material to meet the page limits of modern academic publishing. Among the multitude of state papers available for studying the Grand Council are the palace memorials—high officials' reports to the throne —preserved in their original form (*chu-p'i tsou-che*) as well as in reference copies (*lu-fu tsou-che*) and record books. All of these may now be tapped for a deeper level of detail and frankness than we have had heretofore.

For the Yung-cheng reign an even more unusual set of documents survives: the numerous holograph imperial responses (rescripts) to the memorials, inscribed in the emperor's own color, vermilion. Frequently the Yung-cheng Emperor composed these when he was off his guard, spontaneously confiding his thoughts for an audience of one or another of his most trusted favorites. Some of these imperial screeds run for several pages and amount to stream-of-consciousness letters. When we read these today we find Yung-cheng speaking to us directly and without subterfuge. We have nothing like their length and self-revelation for any other ruler of imperial China.

Yet although the Yung-cheng documentation frequently reveals what was on the imperial mind, this evidence is also difficult to use. The emperor's ruling style was chaotic at times—to deal with it I developed a card file category headed "Yung-cheng chaos." Notes from the file show that behind Yung-cheng's earnest and frenzied attention to governing there flourished an imperial preference for handling things independently and sometimes haphazardly or even capriciously. For instance, Yung-cheng frequently inscribed his decisions on memorials that were then sent back to the field without any record of what had been said being retained in the capital files. Not surprisingly, the high assisting officials soon developed methods for keeping track of the imperial detritus. Another feature that turned up in the Yung-cheng chaos file was the emperor's proclivity for using different terms to refer to the same thing, or the same term for different things. Researchers familiar with the Yung-cheng materials will have little cause to wonder why officials of the times remedied the situation by instituting strict regularization at the very outset of the Ch'ien-lung reign.

Changes in archival documentation mark the Ch'ien-lung and Chia-ch'ing periods. Although fuller than the previous period, with many more record books (*tang-ts'e*), nevertheless materials of these two later reigns lack the numerous spontaneous imperial confidences of the Yung-cheng papers. Thus in contrast with Yung-cheng's long-windedness and frankness, the Ch'ien-lung Emperor usually wrote pithy and routinized rescripts, a fact reflecting the regularization introduced at the beginning of the new reign. As a result, the researcher has to forgo the fascination of the many direct Yung-cheng holograph revelations in exchange for the pleasures of increased general information.

Another Ch'ien-lung–era phenomenon, one of many examples of the increased scope of Grand Council activities, came to light in the archival volumes of the Office of Military Archives (*Fang-lueh kuan*). These ledgers reveal the operations and development of the archives and historical compilation offices that were directly supervised by the council. The new publications office was able to censor (approve, gloss, or suppress) original archival documents before publishing the many military campaign histories (*fang-lueh*) that were issued in particularly large numbers in the Ch'ien-lung period to extol the dynasty's territorial conquests. The Grand Council also came to be in charge of some of the many publication activities bequeathed from earlier times. Other archival sources depicted the Grand Council's Manchu Division (*Man-pan*), a group whose activities have been overlooked until now, possibly as part of the general faith that what the dynasty was claiming about the existence of an evenhanded Manchu-Chinese dyarchy was true. The Grand Secretariat record books of instructions for writing the routine draft memorial rescripts (P'iao pu-pen shih) depicted the previously unimagined extent of the bureaucratization in the Grand Secretariat and Six Boards system, where thousands of details were anticipated and little was left to the possibility of independent action in routing or framing decisions. In the Beijing archives I also ran down the Grand Council's own storage records, regular inventories that suggest the changing range of council responsibilities. Grand Council daybooks containing correspondence below the imperial level opened vistas on the activities of middle-level bureaucrats, a layer of the bureaucracy that heretofore has rarely reached the researcher's eye.

For the entire period the grand councillors' own memoranda (*tsou-p'ien*), composed to convey explanations to the Ch'ing emperors, in the twentieth century performed the same service for this grateful researcher.

PART ONE

Grand Council Antecedents in Yung-cheng's Divided Inner Court, 1723–35

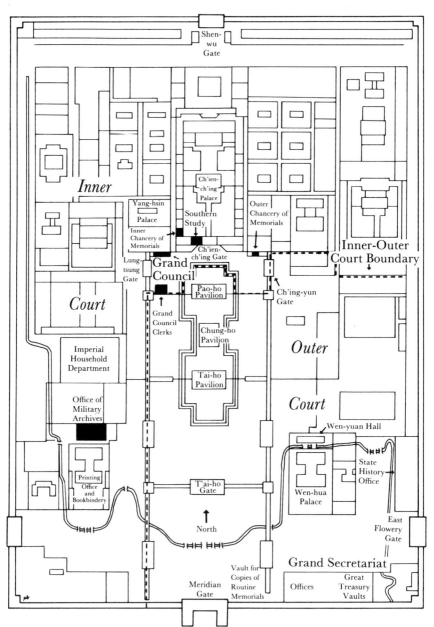

Shen-wu Gate

Inner

Ch'ien-ch'ing Palace

Yang-hsin Palace

Southern Study

Outer Chancery of Memorials

Inner Chancery of Memorials

Lung-tsung Gate

Ch'ien-ch'ing Gate

Inner-Outer Court Boundary

Grand Council

Court

Pao-ho Pavilion

Ch'ing-yun Gate

Grand Council Clerks

Chung-ho Pavilion

Imperial Household Department

Outer

Tai-ho Pavilion

Office of Military Archives

Court

Wen-yuan Hall

Printing Office and Bookbindery

State History Office

T'ai-ho Gate

Wen-hua Palace

North

East Flowery Gate

Grand Secretariat

Meridian Gate

Vault for Copies of Routine Memorials

Offices

Great Treasury Vaults

- - - - - Approximate Boundary of Inner-Outer Court

MAP I. The Peking Palace inner and outer courts in the seventeenth and eighteenth centuries. The new rooms and buildings used by the inner court after the start of the K'ang-hsi reign are shown in heavy black shading. Sites of certain outer-court offices mentioned in the text are also shown (the Six Boards were too far south to appear on this map). Although there was no fixed boundary between the outer and inner courts, the dotted line shows the approximate division. Based on Chu Hsieh, *Pei-ching kung-ch'üeh t'u-shuo* (Changsha: Commercial Press, 1938; redrawn by Pamela Baldwin).

I was first introduced to recollections about the Ch'ing palace through conversations with the late Mr. Wu Yü-chang, then a deputy director of the Taipei Palace Museum. (At the opening of the palace to the public in 1925, Mr. Wu had worked in the small building that was once the Grand Council clerks' office.) For assistance in learning about palace buildings I am also indebted to Professors Thomas Fisher and Susan Naquin. Above all, shortly after my arrival in Beijing for research in 1980, I was fortunate to meet Mr. Yang Nai-chi of the Institute of Architectural History. Mr. Yang most generously reached into his vast store of knowledge and supplied much helpful information.

Sources consulted for this map include the following, some of which also supply useful maps:

Arlington, L. C., and William Lewisohn, *In Search of Old Peking* (Peking: Henri Vetch, 1935) pp. 26–27.

Bredon, Juliet, *Peking* (Shanghai, 1931), map between pp. 196–97 (Father Hyacinth Bichurin's map of 1829).

Ch'ing-kung shu-wen, comp. Chang T'ang-jung (Repr. Taipei, 1969), 4/1 and passim.

Ch'ien-lung ching-ch'eng ch'üan-t'u (Peiping, 1940) (dated to CL14–15; 1739–40—see related article listed next).

"Ch'ing Nei-fu ts'ang ching-ch'eng ch'üan-t'u nien-tai k'ao," in *Wen-hsien t'e-k'an* (Peiping, 1935), *Pao-kao* sec., pp. 37–38.

Ch'ing Nei-ko k'u-chu chiu-tang chi-k'an, comp. Fang Su-sheng (Peiping, 1934), esp. the maps in the front of the first *ts'e*.

Hsieh Min-ts'ung, *Ming-Ch'ing Pei-ching ti ch'eng-yuan yü kung-ch'üeh chih yen-chiu* (Taipei, 1980), p. 61 and passim.

Kuang-hsu *Shun-t'ien fu chih* (Ch'ing woodblock ed., 1886), 2/7b–8.

Kung-shih hsu-pien, passim.

Pei-ching li-shih ti-t'u chi, comp. Hou Jen-chih (Beijing, 1985), passim.

Pei-p'ing Ku-kung po-wu-yuan Wen-hsien kuan i-lan (Peiping, 1932), pp. 8–9 and passim.

Yang Nai-chi, "'Ch'ien-lung ching-ch'eng ch'üan-t'u k'ao-lueh," *Ku-kung po-wu-yuan yuan-k'an* 1984, no. 3 (Aug. 1984): 8–24.

Ta-Ch'ing li-ch'ao shih-lu (Yung-cheng) 4/13b.

Note that the explanation in Fu Tsung-mao, *Ch'ing-tai Chün-chi ch'u*, p. 108, mistakenly places the inner-court boundary at the T'ai-ho Gate, too far south.

ONE

Strengthening the Inner Court
in the Early Yung-cheng Period

Just before noon on an autumn day in YC8 (1730), a mild earthquake rattled the outskirts of Peking, damaging buildings but not seriously injuring the citizenry. The Yung-cheng Emperor (r. 1723–35)[1] had been boating on a palace lake when the tremor hit, but until he saw houses sagging and people running to and fro on the distant shore, he was not aware that an earthquake was taking place. In the end, buffered by the waters, he and his ministers rode out the moment in safety.[2]

The scene might be construed as a metaphor for one of the chief accomplishments of the Yung-cheng reign: this was the development of a secure separate inner-court sanctuary where the monarch and his highest ministers would preside over as much of the central government as possible, buffered by the secrecy of the inner court and set apart from the distant activity of outer-court bureaucrats. To fortify his power, Yung-cheng shaped his inner court into a secret, cut-off place—a separate imperial demesne. His inner court was to be an imperial bailiwick where he dominated at the center and the imperial fiat was law. One of the ways that Yung-cheng accomplished this was to create new inner-court committees to serve closely at his side. But he always kept these staffs small, divided, and informal so that he would remain in charge. Thus strengthened within his inner court, Yung-cheng was able to reach out for power over matters previously not directly susceptible to his will. As many areas of government as possible were to be drawn into the inner court, where the monarch and his close assisting ministers, rather than the outer-court bureaucrats, would hold sway.

These rearrangements laid the foundation for the great eighteenth-century transformation of the Ch'ing central government that was marked by the emergence of the Grand Council (*Chün-chi ch'u*) early in the following reign.[3] In contrast with Yung-cheng's divided inner court, the high privy council

FIGURE 1. New inner-court institutions in the seventeenth and eighteenth centuries. Inner-court governing administrative institutions added in the K'ang-hsi, Yung-cheng, and Ch'ien-lung reigns are outlined in boxes. The major corresponding outer-court agencies in each category showed no comparable institutional innovation in the same time period.

Communications and Reference Archives	Policy Deliberation and Administration	Official Publications and Their Archives
	Inner Court	

Emperor
Deliberative Council

Imperial [Southern] Study (1677)

Imperial Princes

Regency (Plenipotentiary or Interim) Councils

Palace Memorial System (1693)	Inner Deputies (1726–35)	Office of Military Archives, Military Campaign History Section (*Fang-lueh kuan*) (1749)
Outer Chancery of Memorials (probably early YC)	Military Finance Section (1729–35)	
Inner Chancery of Memorials	High Officials in Charge of Military Finance (later, Strategy) (1731–35)	
	Grand Council (1735 or 1738)	

Imperial Household
Imperial Bodyguards

Office of Military Archives, Document Storage Section (*Fang-lueh kuan, Chün-chi ch'u lu-fu tsou-che*) (1749)

Superintendents of Outer-Court Offices (Begun earlier but used more beginning YC1)

Audit Bureau (1723)

Figure 1—Continued

Communications and Reference Archives	Policy Deliberation and Administration	Official Publications and Their Archives
	Outer Court	
Routine Memorial System	Six Boards and Six Sections Censors	Hanlin Academy
Grand Secretariat		State History Office
	Censorate; Nine Ministers	*Veritable Records* Office
Transmission Office	Court of Judicature	
		Diarists' Office
		Printing Office and Bookbindery
		Archives of Imperial History
		Grand Secretariat Great Treasury

of the Ch'ien-lung Emperor (r. 1736–95, plus the three abdication years 1796–98) consolidated the administrative sector of the inner court, fusing Yung-cheng's separate staffs in one powerful organization. Nevertheless, the council that dominated the Chinese government for the remainder of the dynasty was the heir to both the informal, nonstatutory, separate agencies of Yung-cheng's devising and the powerful consolidation fashioned under Ch'ien-lung. As we shall see, both features were important factors in the council's extraordinary growth over the course of the eighteenth century. The key impetus for this growth was Yung-cheng's decision to strengthen his inner court far beyond what had been accomplished in his father's reign.

Tangible evidence of more than a century of inner-court administrative changes that began under the K'ang-hsi and Yung-cheng Emperors and were completed under Ch'ien-lung is displayed in the small rooms and cramped buildings shown with shading on Map 1 and in the entities shown in boxes in Figure 1. Before the administrative reforms had taken place, with few exceptions the offices responsible for central government business had been located far from the emperor's living quarters, in the "outer court" (*wai-ch'ao*) in the southern parts of the palace and just outside. By contrast, by the end of the Ch'ien-lung reign, several new offices had been installed in the "inner court" (*nei-t'ing*), on the edge of the emperor's private apartments in the northern part of the palace. By the beginning of the nineteenth century the occupants of these new offices may have numbered as many as 250 men who were directing much of the government of the entire realm. Map 1 and Figure 1 provide a graphic demonstration that over the course of the K'ang-hsi, Yung-cheng, and Ch'ien-lung reigns a power contest between the outer and inner courts had taken place and the inner court had moved ahead.

Similar power struggles had occurred with variations throughout China's dynastic history.[4] Again and again the bureaucracy had vied with the emperor and his personal retinue. The terms "outer" and "inner" courts came to be used as metaphors to reduce various complex situations over the centuries to two sides: a bureaucratic faction and an imperial faction. Just as earlier dynasties had exhibited numerous configurations, the Ch'ing did not precisely replicate the contests of the past. In Ch'ing times the Manchu-Mongol alliance held a special position in central politics and crossed the somewhat porous inner/outer-court boundary. Other alignments and organizations—the grand secretaries, the Nine Ministers, various court factions—also served on both sides of the vaguely understood demarcation line. Nevertheless, early- and mid-Ch'ing emperors frequently stressed the inner/outer-court framework of their government and strove to correct what they regarded as an imbalance that militated against the imperial interest and favored the outer-court strength and independence inherited from the Ming.

THE EARLY YUNG-CHENG OUTER COURT

The outer court of the Peking palace, or Forbidden City, has been vaguely defined as an area in the southern part of the palace where the civil administrators worked and the great imperial public ceremonies were held. During the Ch'ing the term usually referred to the three formal public pavilions that dominated the central axis of the Forbidden City and the administrative offices clustered nearby. In the pavilions were celebrated some of the dynasty's most solemn public ceremonies: the year's Three Great Festivals' audiences at the winter solstice, the lunar new year, and the imperial birthday. The capping of the successful candidates for the examination system's highest degree (*chin-shih*), receptions for foreign envoys, and many of the large formal audiences for deciding state policy also took place here. One of the most elaborate ceremonies marked the completion of each reign's court chronicle (the so-called *Veritable Records*, or *Shih-lu*), when the editorial board members would solemnly celebrate their accomplishment with the performance of the full kowtow of nine kneelings and three prostrations. On occasion a formal examination for the promotion of officials might be held in one of these halls, with special arrangements in winter for braziers to assure that the ink necessary to the candidates' endeavors would not freeze.[5]

The other major elements of the outer court, the administrative offices housed in the nooks and crannies of the palace—in the passages between buildings or the narrow spaces in a thick wall, as well as in special rooms and buildings—were scattered in the southern and eastern parts of the palace and just outside the main gate, to the south. In the early Yung-cheng period these agencies oversaw four main areas of outer-court responsibilities: administration of government affairs, management of communications underlying all operations, preservation of government documents, and publication of the dynasty's historical record.

Administration

Administration was largely in the hands of the Grand Secretariat (*Nei-ko*) and the Six Boards (*Liu-pu*): the boards of Civil Appointments, Revenue, Rites, War, Punishments, and Works. The outer court also contained a multiplicity of other offices such as the Censorate (*Tu-ch'a yuan*), the Hanlin Academy, the Court of Mongolian Affairs (*Li-fan yuan*), the central law courts (*San fa-ssu*), the sacrificial courts, and offices where works of history and other publications were compiled. By early Yung-cheng times the staff members attached to these outer-court agencies, which were distinguished by exhaustively detailed statutory definition of personnel and responsibilities, probably numbered in the thousands.[6] The outer-court agencies generally took care of all the routine continuing business of government.

The numerous middle-level offices and departments of the Board of Revenue, for example, audited reports on one of the most essential government responsibilities: the collection of tax income. They supervised the reception of shipments of tax silver (transported in the hollowed interiors of specially prepared logs) at the state treasury in Peking and made sure that the contents matched the manifests in terms of silver quality and amounts. Payments were checked for compliance with various quotas and regulations; discrepancies were investigated. Whether the regular land tax, other dues, arrears, or fines were being submitted, the files had to be searched to make sure that collections tallied with what was owed. All this necessitated elaborate archives for looking up regulations, amendments, and exceptions as well as to store the records of the local reporting units all over the empire. Keeping track of this mass of information gave the middle-level officials of the Board of Revenue both training and eventually expertise in their various areas of specialization.[7] As a result, even the second-class board secretaries (*chu-shih*) appended their names to the recommendations submitted in reports to the emperor, for, as the best-informed and most experienced members of an agency, they were frequently essential to its deliberations. Other boards functioned in similar fashion, keeping track of changing regulations and approving or rejecting the provincial memorials in accordance with the administrative code. ("Memorial" is a nineteenth-century English translation of the Chinese term for a high official's report to the throne.)

Communications

Board work was greatly aided by the communications system inherited from the Ming—in Chinese known as "memorials of submission [of information]" (*t'i-pen*), but usually (and somewhat perplexingly) translated into English as "the routine system."[8] The routine system was monitored by the Grand Secretariat, which examined documents and distributed them in accordance with elaborate requirements set forth at length in code books of prescriptions.[9] After various outer-court agencies had processed the reported information (work that frequently involved lengthy research and deliberation), the imperially approved recommendations might be disseminated as decisions, usually with excerpts from their base memorials, in the Peking gazettes. (The Peking gazettes were court circulars that enabled officials all over the empire to keep abreast of government affairs.)[10]

Archives

To store the mass of records, every outer-court board and agency had its own reference files.[11] In addition, there were two major outer-court archival installations: the Archives of Imperial History (*Huang-shih ch'eng*) and the Great Treasury of the Grand Secretariat (*Nei-ko ta-k'u*), both first established during the Ming.[12] Although the former housed many kinds of documents, its most famous holding was one of the sets of each reign's court chronicles, the *Veritable Records*, which was interred in large chests elaborately embossed with gold dragon designs.[13] The vaults of the Great Treasury contained rare books, another set of the Ch'ing court chronicles, and large numbers of memorials— amounting to two million original documents by the end of the dynasty.[14] Thus the stewards of the outer-court archives had a complex role. In addition to overseeing the storage of precious works, these officials also supervised holdings of documents that were used for both policy reference and historical writing.

Publications

The outer court also had a number of publications offices, many of which drew on archives to compose the records of the dynasty's achievements. There was an office for the so-called Diarists (*Ch'i-chü chu kuan*), who maintained a detailed chronology of the imperial words and actions.[15] Also in the outer court was the *Veritable Records* Office (*Shih-lu kuan*), which compiled each reign's court chronicles as well as the *Edicts of Exhortation* (*Sheng-hsun*) and from time to time other works such as the collected imperial writings. The State History Office (*Kuo-shih kuan*) staffs drafted preliminary sections of the official history of the dynasty (*kuo-shih*).[16] Other publications offices periodically revised the administrative codes such as the *Collected Statutes and Precedents* (*Hui-tien kuan*) and the *Law Code* (*Lü-li kuan*). Many of these agencies were staffed by men from the Hanlin Academy (*Han-lin yuan*), the top cultural and intellectual organization of the country, whose members were chosen on the basis of grueling competitive examinations that probed their literary and scholarly skills. Thus the thousands of civil officials and staff members in the outer-court bureaucracy were chiefly concerned with processing documents not only to administer the empire but also to bequeath a glorious record of that administration to future generations.

The sprawling palace grounds with their scattered one- and two-story buildings did not promote easy communication between the monarch and his outer-court bureaucrats. Although the emperor occasionally appeared in the outer court to take part in the ceremonies staged in one of the three public pavilions or at the great Meridian Gate (Wu Men), such visits were rare. The emperor also regularly summoned outer-court officials to come to the inner court to discuss policy with him, but the distance to be covered was considerable. An aging grand secretary might take fifteen or twenty minutes to complete his stately promenade under the hot summer sun or through blustering winter winds from the Grand Secretariat to one of the intimate inner-court pavilions where the sovereign received his officials. The journey would have been even longer for a board president, who might have had to come from a building located outside the palace. Some monarchs, however, took little interest in seeing their high officials. One late-Ming ruler failed to receive his own chief minister for more than two decades, a situation that played a significant role in the development of outer-court independence in that dynasty.[17] The physical distance between the sovereign in his inner court and the outer-court agencies enhanced the gulf between these two main spheres of government.

THE EARLY YUNG-CHENG INNER COURT

The inner court, vaguely described in different texts, embraced roughly the northern third of the palace, the area running from the plaza in front of the Ch'ien-ch'ing Gate to the palace's northernmost exit, the Shen-wu Gate. In addition, the inner court occupied much of the western third of the Forbidden City, where the offices of the Imperial Household were located. In the early Yung-cheng period the inner court included both a few offices and the private imperial residential suites.[18] Much of it was guarded by palace bodyguards, who turned back all who had no good reason for entering and arranged escorts for those proceeding further. Numerous regulations also provided in reverse that inner-court personnel (particularly eunuchs) were to be strictly isolated and prevented from having contact with officials and others from beyond their precincts.[19] Thus, although the boundaries shifted slightly in various definitions, there was general agreement that the inner court embraced both the emperor's living quarters and the nearby offices of those who closely served the monarch. Consequently, the area was set off from the outer court both in the spatial organization of its territory and in the activities of its servitors.

The inner court that Yung-cheng inherited from his father was organized principally to house, feed, clothe, and guard the imperial person, his family, and his entourage. Thousands of eunuchs supervised by the Imperial Household

Department (*Nei-wu fu*) attended not only the sovereign but also his empress, the royal concubines, the royal offspring, and other imperial relatives resident in the palace.[20] The Imperial Household ran the palace and oversaw the eunuchs, cooks, maidservants, embroiderers, barbers, masseurs, and other persons necessary to the imperial comfort. Imperial Household storerooms were stocked with the best of China's local products from all over the empire: silks, porcelains, furs, precious stones, and other fine stuffs. The Household also staffed and managed enterprises outside the palace, such as the lucrative salt, ginseng, and jade monopolies and the agencies that collected both inland and foreign customs dues, whose income was deposited in Household treasuries. In the eighteenth century the Household's annual income frequently exceeded that of the Board of Revenue.[21] The activities of the Imperial Household Department were strongly in evidence all through the palace and particularly in the inner court.

Other inner-court personnel guarded the emperor and the imperial precincts. Several hundred bodyguards were said to be on rotating assignment in the inner palace at any one time,[22] and hundreds of picked Manchu and Mongol banner troops, responsible for the security of all palace gates, stood sentinel at the inner-court entrances as well.[23] But these offices and positions ministered largely to inner-court needs; they did little to govern the country. If a monarch wished to rule as well as to reign, he had to develop his own administration, both through links to civil servants in the outer court and in the provinces and through a strengthened inner court. The K'ang-hsi Emperor had maintained a small inner-court administrative component consisting partly of inherited staffs and partly of one new staff that he founded. In addition, he had inaugurated the palace memorial system, a special new communications system whose documents, mostly of provincial origin, in his day circulated only to inner-court offices at the capital. As we shall see, the Yung-cheng Emperor worked with his father's inner-court institutions but also tried several new approaches.

PROBLEMS FACED BY YUNG-CHENG AT HIS ACCESSION

The Yung-cheng Emperor, fourth son of K'ang-hsi, came to power under a cloud. Acceding to the monarchy at the age of forty-five, the new emperor had risen to this position after several decades of bitter turbulence and bickering among some of the more ambitious and favored of K'ang-hsi's numerous sons and their factions of supporters and hangers-on. Questions about the new emperor's claim to the throne were raised in his own time and have never been entirely laid to rest.[24] One story accused Yung-cheng of having changed K'ang-hsi's will so that it chose him for emperor rather than the son K'ang-hsi really wanted. According to this tale, the dying emperor had in fact bequeathed the throne to his number "ten and four [i.e., fourteenth]" (*shih-ssu* 十 四) prince, the popular frontier general Yin-t'i, but Yung-cheng, making several visits to his father on his deathbed, had managed to get hold of the will and alter the character for "ten" to the sign for an ordinal number (*ti*), so that the will read to "the fourth" (*ti ssu* 第 四) prince—that is, himself.[25] Yung-cheng was thus able to take over in Peking while Yin-t'i was still at the front. As a result, from the outset of the new reign the atmosphere at court was poisoned by the disappointment of the defeated factions, their insinuations against the new emperor, and their fear of his retaliation.

The Manchu Preponderance in Government

The doubts about the Yung-cheng accession were part of a broader problem concerning the preponderance of Manchu princely and grandee influence in the inner counsels of the realm. From the beginning of the dynasty Manchus and a few Mongols had dominated the advisory apparatus in the inner court. The Ch'ing founding emperor, Nurhaci (1559–1626), had sought to ensure a collegial decision-making process by requiring that ranking princes assist his successor.[26] The princes and other Manchu and Mongol potentates were also members of the Deliberative Council (variously *I-cheng wang ta-ch'en* or *I-cheng ch'u*), where they had a strong voice in military policy. Members of the imperial clan and other high Manchu and Mongol grandees headed the Imperial Household Department, where they worked close to the emperor and ran certain of the court's most lucrative enterprises. In the early period, too, leading princes had controlled the Manchus' main social, economic, and military units—the Eight Banners. While the strong Manchu influence at court may have been viewed as the justly deserved spoils accruing to the conquerors of the Chinese empire, it could also be a thorn in the side of an emperor. Some monarchs had tried to limit this Manchu influence by reducing—though not entirely eliminating—the princes' leading role. But the large number of K'ang-hsi's sons and the heir-apparent issue that had roiled K'ang-hsi's declining years now highlighted the divisive and potentially destructive propensities of the royal princes and their followings.

On coming to the throne, Yung-cheng attempted to master K'ang-hsi's unruly brood by conciliating one of the heir-apparent factions. To this end he appointed his half-brother Yin-ssu and one of Yin-ssu's supporters, the Grand Secretary Ma-ch'i, to the Plenipotentiary Council (*Tsung-li shih-wu wang ta-ch'en*), which was ordered to direct the government during the transition years. But Yung-cheng made no similar concessions to other disappointed and even more powerful parties among his siblings. Yin-t'i, for instance, was too much of a threat: he was widely admired, he had expected the throne to come to him, and in addition to his supporters at court he controlled thousands of frontier troops. No sop could win the support of this rival who was filled with rancor at the spectacle of his brother on the throne that he had reckoned was to be his.

But if Yung-cheng had hoped to gain support by extending the olive branch to the Yin-ssu faction, he was soon disappointed. The problem of the princes proved to be a problem not only of the individual contenders for the throne but also of large groups of adherents and hangers-on who had cast their lives for one or another of the candidates and had counted on succeeding to power. The court was filled with ruined men.[27]

Although we do not know what happened to cause the breach between Yung-cheng and Yin-ssu, the reign was hardly launched when Yin-ssu remarked that he feared he would not survive "with my head still on my neck." The emperor, annoyed on hearing this, at first limited himself to calling down Yin-ssu for having run things at the Board of Works, where he had been made superintendent, in a "muddled" (hu-t'u) fashion.[28] But later Yung-cheng devised a nasty sobriquet, "A-ch'i-na" (said to mean "cur"), and peppered Yin-ssu with insults.[29] A climax of sorts was reached at the end of the first year of the new reign, when Yung-cheng furiously responded to one of Yin-ssu's memorials with a rescript calling him as good as "dead" and underlining this terrifying threat by exclaiming "dead" (in Manchu, bucehe) twice in the two lines of the rescript.[30] In fact, Yin-ssu did eventually die in prison, probably from poisoning.[31] Yung-cheng also moved against the popular Yin-t'i, but he had to wait to consolidate his position before that brother could be placed under arrest.[32] One of the major immediate tasks facing the new emperor was curbing the danger to the Manchu realm posed by Manchus.

The Mongol Wars

In the figure of Yin-t'i the problem of Manchu influence in government became tied to another major issue of the times: the war against the Mongols. The late-seventeenth- and eighteenth-century war was part of the longer history of China's unsettled inland frontier, which for centuries had involved disputes and battles ranging from Tibet on the southwest through the various Mongol peoples to the west and north. By the time of Yung-cheng's accession, the Mongol problem had many facets. At times it was strictly a military question of pushing back tribesmen who failed to respect China's boundaries. There was also a diplomatic problem that required disrupting dangerous coalitions among the tribes or preventing Russia from supporting them. A religious aspect involved Tibet and concerned Chinese protection and on occasion sequestration of the Dalai Lama so that the dominant religion on the frontier, Yellow Lamaism, would not be used against Manchu interests. In particular, Yung-cheng had to contend with the continuing war against the Mongol Zunghar tribe (men "on the left hand," that is, in the northwest); in addition, in the first year of the reign there was a separate uprising in Ch'ing-hai perpetrated by the Khoshote Mongols, who otherwise were usually docile and loyal.

Thus the decision for war had already been made by the time Yung-cheng came to power. But the new emperor and his advisers shaped the policies by which their segment of the war—which continued into the next reign—was fought. Yung-cheng's style differed from his father's. In the 1690s K'ang-hsi had ridden to battle in pursuit of the Zunghar chieftain Galdan, and hounded him in three separate forays until Galdan slunk away and took his life.[33] Later K'ang-hsi deputed one of his sons, Yin-t'i, as one of two major generals at the front.

By contrast, Yung-cheng did not lead regiments in the front lines, but he took other measures that involved him intensely in the campaign. He devoted endless hours to the crucial business of selecting military leaders for deployment at the front. And as we shall see, he also took great pains over the manifold details of campaign plans, particularly for the Zunghar campaign, which occupied most of the reign and whose three years of advance planning amounted to a miniature campaign in itself. He wrote voluminously to his generals in the field, flattering them with attention, exhorting them to their best effort, and proffering advice. On one occasion Yung-cheng took the trouble to go through the calendar and prescribe auspicious days and hours for troops to set out on a hoped-for march to victory.[34] Other imperial writing advised on how to handle enemy depositions: even when men surrendered voluntarily, he cautioned, "artful tricks" were to be expected, and whatever such people deposed was "definitely not to be trusted."[35]

Although Yung-cheng had inherited the old Manchu inner-court Deliberative Council, which in K'ang-hsi and earlier reigns had been in charge of military policy, he soon took a dislike to the council's domineering Manchu grandees, many of whom had sided with the resentful defeated factions on the heir-apparent issue. The emperor developed other inner-court sources of military counsel, at first depending heavily on one of his brothers whom he felt able to trust, Prince I, and a few other specially picked confidants. His attempts to create an effective yet unpretentious inner-court source of military advice to replace the Deliberative Council eventually led to new staffs that were ancestral to the Grand Council.

Financial Weakness

The new emperor was also strongly preoccupied with military finance at the beginning of his reign. In fact, Yung-cheng was soon forced to grapple not only with slippage in the military supply lines but also with the wider problem of general debility in the financial health of the realm. During the late K'ang-hsi years the public trough had broadened into a cornucopia at which civil servants as well as military men of all ranks had become accustomed to helping themselves, a situation that Yung-cheng despairingly denounced as "a hundred kinds of malfeasance" that had plagued the empire for decades.[36] On coming to power he was informed that the arrears in the land tax collections alone came to a staggering 2.5 million taels.[37] Although the financial difficulties of the realm will be discussed in greater detail in the following chapters, they deserve mention here as one of the major problems that confronted the new emperor on his accession.

The preponderant Manchu princely and grandee influence in government, the Mongol wars, and the financial crisis interacted with the problems of administrative structure in the design of the inner and outer courts and intensified the difficulties that Yung-cheng had inherited. On occasion the new emperor found himself unable to have his way in either his outer or his inner court; the emperor might find himself hedged by outer-court autonomy on the one hand and inadequate staff support in the inner court on the other. The weaknesses in government structure posed a deeper threat to monarchical control than the temporary issues of vengeful courtiers, the northwest war, and economic debility. The greatest problems lay in the outer and inner courts themselves.

Problems in Outer-Court Practices

Outer-court autonomy had been building since the days of the ineffectual late-Ming emperors, many of whom were do-nothing rulers who had failed to play a strong leading role at the helm of government. The case of the Ming emperor who declined to receive his chief minister for two decades has already been cited. The Ming monarchy was weakened in its early years by regencies that transferred power from infant emperors to inexperienced regent empresses and their advisers. It was then further battered when the Mongol enemy took one of the Ming rulers prisoner and held him captive for over a decade.[38] Imperial inattention to ruling did not bring all government to a halt, however. Instead it meant that the outer court devised (and we may surmise that its bureaucrats even preferred) ways of getting along without the royal intervention. By the end of the Ming much of the ordinary business of government had come to be managed in the outer court at a distance from the emperor and without constant recourse to him for guidance.

The outer-court autonomy developed in the Ming posed problems for the would-be autocrats of the early Ch'ing. Communications arrangements were particularly vexing. The chief difficulty with the routine system inherited from the Ming was that it had favored the outer-court bureaucracy's control over central-government decision making and reduced the emperor's opportunities for taking the initiative. Most central-government policies were framed in response to the routine memorials by specialists who worked in various outer-court agencies. The purpose of sending their proposed responses, known as "draft rescripts" (*ni-p'iao*, *p'iao-ni*, or *p'iao-ch'ien*), to the emperor was not so much to obtain inner-court advice and opinion as to secure the imperial authorization (in the form of a vermilion circle on the draft rescript) for official promulgation of their own proposals.

This system put the emperor and his inner-court advisers under two principal disadvantages. First, the lack of specialists in most subject areas left the inner court without the means to conjure up its own responses; as a result, the emperor usually had to support proposals advanced by outer-court specialists for want of anything better at hand. Second, once an approved proposal was returned to the outer court it had to run the gamut of obstructionism at both the central and the provincial government levels.[39] Thus, while in theory the inner court checked and balanced the outer court, in fact the routine communications system allowed the inner court a very weak role in both decision making and implementation. To be sure, the monarchy still had its ultimate weapon of revenge against the outer court—the power to demote or dismiss officials—but doing so might only bring a new set of opportunistic bureaucrats into the outer court. Extraordinary imperial intervention seldom happened. Chang T'ing-yü's exclamation over one occasion when the Yung-cheng Emperor took up his brush specifically to change an outer-court draft rescript (kai-ch'ien) indicates the rarity of this kind of imperial action.[40] In most cases the outer-court recommendations went through without change.

Although the early- and mid-Ch'ing emperors probably objected mainly to the routine system's susceptibility to bureaucratic dominance in decision making, there were other problems as well. Delays caused by observances of ritual or by meticulous attention to document processing might ignore the need for a speedy response. Reliance on precedent (composition of many of the bureaucracy's rescripts was "guided by regulations") could be stifling. Outer-court operations were also mired in regulations that prescribed for the agencies' personnel and responsibilities in minute and sometimes exasperating detail. Particularly damaging—especially for military operations—was the lack of secrecy in outer-court document processing. Thus an eighteenth-century court clerk boasted of "the many tens of hands" that provided a kind of safety in numbers as documents were processed.[41] For in the course of its journey through the outer-court bureaucracy, a document could be exposed to many eyes, published for all to read in the court circulars (Peking gazettes), stored in archival installations that were not always properly secured, and eventually written into the official historical accounts. Although secrecy was possible despite these practices, it was achieved not as a matter of course but only through special efforts.

Outer-court independence had also allowed the growth of several practices that teetered on the edge of illegality. There was an increasingly indistinct line, for instance, between small gratuities bestowed for extra courtesies, on the one hand, and bribes that became one of the expected costs of doing business with an outer-court agency, on the other. Various sorts of advance news could gain advantages for those who purchased it either by lavish tips to the bearers or by specific payments in return for obtaining and passing on certain information. Surreptitious copying (hsiao-ch'ao) of a memorial before the moment ordained for its publication was another kind of outer-court malfeasance, as was forgery—dates or numerals in documents might be altered with a variety of advantages for the perpetrators.⁴² Board exaction of commissions (*pu-fei*)— perhaps better described as bribes—to approve provincial reports caused such difficulties that Yung-cheng created a special inner-court staff in an attempt to eliminate this practice. The traditions of independence, distance from the emperor, large size, lack of secrecy, long-established work patterns, inflexible and exhaustively detailed rules, malfeasance, and formal constraining hierarchies all made it difficult for the emperor to impose his will on the outer court. One approach was to attempt to bring the outer court more closely under imperial control; another was to build up inner-court staffs to handle certain critical areas of administration away from outer-court intervention. As we shall see, Yung-cheng tried both solutions.

Problems in the Inner Court

Yung-cheng was not satisified with the structure of the inner court he inherited from K'ang-hsi. The Manchus who dominated his father's inner court had become too accustomed to exercising power and influence. High-level Manchus and Mongols had monopolized the top posts in two of K'ang-hsi's major inner-court administrative organizations, the Imperial Household Department and the Deliberative Council, and they frequently dominated the temporary committees set up to advise on special problems. Although the high-ranking Chinese scholars appointed to another K'ang-hsi inner-court body, the Southern [Imperial] Study (*Nan Shu-fang*), might have counterbalanced the preponderant Manchu strength in the inner court, the Southern Study's ethnic exclusivity segregated the inner-court Chinese and kept them out of other important councils of the realm. Thus the presence of a new Chinese staff, even one with such important work as edict drafting, did not significantly dilute Manchu influence in the inner court.

The agencies dominated by Manchus and Mongols were formally constituted. Their members ranked among the high and mighty of the realm. As a result they were less amenable to monarchical leadership than appointees of lower status might have been. All in all they enjoyed too much prestige. The doubts and fury over the Yung-cheng accession emboldened them, making it even more difficult for the new emperor to move decisively against them.

In the face of these difficulties Yung-cheng took a prudent stance. Wisely he preferred to downgrade his father's inner-court organizations rather than dispense with them entirely. As a result, he never entirely rid himself of their presence, but neither did he allow them to get the better of him. At the same time, instead of using the established dignitaries of the factions of his father's day, he created new inner-court structures and brought in his own men. In a move of special significance that was probably part of his policy of weakening the Manchu influence in government, at the top level he abandoned the ethnic divisions of his father's inner court and assigned Chinese to work alongside

Manchus. These policies strengthened the inner court and were basic to the founding of the Grand Council in the following reign.

YUNG-CHENG'S ATTEMPTS TO CONTROL THE OUTER COURT

To win ascendancy over the outer court, Yung-cheng tried using various inner-court institutions—the Plenipotentiary Council, the grand secretaries, the board superintendents, and the Audit Bureau—to offset various difficult features of outer-court operations. In addition, he attempted a few reforms of the outer-court communications system. Apparently his experience with these approaches was disappointing, and eventually his interest in outer-court reform declined. In its place he resorted to a bypass of the outer court, developing his inner court instead.

The Plenipotentiary Council

Although the Plenipotentiary Council (*Tsung-li shih-wu wang ta-ch'en*) was the earliest of Yung-cheng's inner-court councils, having been appointed the day after the K'ang-hsi Emperor's death, it was not primarily set up as part of a policy of creating inner-court agencies as links to outer-court bodies. Instead it was established in the pattern of earlier Ch'ing regency councils, chiefly to assist the new monarch with the problems of the transition period. But the council's enabling edict endowed it with sweeping responsibilities, some of which facilitated inner-court intervention in the outer court. The Plenipotentiary Council was put in charge of "all memorialized matters" except the emperor's "private affairs" and empowered to handle "all imperial edicts." Thus it was authorized to supervise and rule on some outer-court activities.[43]

Yung-cheng himself made the four prestigious appointments to his Plenipotentiary Council, all Manchus: two imperial princes, the Lien Prince Yin-ssu and the I Prince Yin-hsiang; the Grand Secretary Ma-ch'i; and the board president Lung-k'o-to, who had also long been in charge of the Peking Gendarmerie.[44] In addition, the council's responsibilities would have required a substantial staff of both middle-level secretaries and low-level runners and errand boys. At the beginning the emperor routed many key problems— funeral arrangements for the K'ang-hsi Emperor, the vast array of new appointments, and military questions, for example—to this new inner-court body.[45] But within a short time his policy of trust had changed.

Despite the sweeping endowment of powers with which it had been founded, the Plenipotentiary Council was not permitted to become an entrenched and powerful structure; in reality it proved to have no monopoly on "all memorialized matters," or even any special responsibilities of its own. Soon after its creation Yung-cheng himself began to weaken it by ordering others— the Deliberative Council (*I-cheng wang ta-ch'en*; literally, the Deliberative

Princes and Ministers), various board directorates, and the grand secretaries—to consider subjects that had previously been assigned to the council.[46] The grand secretaries drafted some of the imperial edicts just as if that duty had never been earmarked as a Plenipotentiary Council task, and were given the authority to review the emperor's vermilion responses to the palace memorials, even being instructed to tell the emperor when he was wrong and to "memorialize explaining how."[47] In addition, before his first year was out Yung-cheng had announced that for routine system communications, "in the capital I rely on the grand secretaries."[48] The grand secretaries, not the Plenipotentiary Council, were also assigned to make recommendations on the important matter of compiling the imperially authorized biographies (lieh-chuan) for the official history of the Ch'ing, a task that touched nerves of prestige and concern in high official families all over the empire.[49] Thus the Plenipotentiary Council was by no means in charge of "all" but the emperor's private affairs. If Yung-cheng was to establish links by which to influence the outer court, this was not to be achieved by a council composed of Manchu princes and grandees.

As time went on Yung-cheng also became disenchanted with certain council members, devising insults for his brother Yin-ssu and hinting that Lung-k'o-to was not to be trusted.[50] Although the council continued to be kept busy, the circumstances surrounding its demise on YC3/2/14 (1725 Mar. 27) suggest the role it had come to play in Yung-cheng's government; it was not replaced, nor was there any announcement of a redistribution of its responsibilities.[51] The emperor had long since bypassed it.

Tainted by the presence of two henchmen who had disappointed the emperor, the Plenipotentiary Council had been granted more authority than Yung-cheng later wished to allow. It was no candidate for further development as part of Yung-cheng's experiments in restructuring the inner court. In contrast with the later Ch'ien-lung regency council of CL1–2 (1735–38), which was to survive, the Plenipotentiary Council's failure under Yung-cheng points up the special situation of early Yung-cheng times. Yung-cheng wished to create inner-court staffs to assist him in governing the country, but at the same time he feared to endow these bodies with sweeping powers that might rival his own. For this reason he eventually resorted to a divided inner court composed of low- and middle-ranking individuals and informal groups. The Plenipotentiary Council, with its excessive grant of authority and unreliable members, was too difficult for the emperor to control.

The Grand Secretaries and the Grand Secretariat

Like certain of the other groups to be described in this chapter, the grand secretaries (ta hsueh-shih) held an anomalous position that straddled the outer and inner courts. Their subordinate staff organization, the Grand Secretariat (Nei-ko), was distinctly an outer-court body, located far from the emperor in the distant southeastern corner of the palace. By contrast, the grand secretaries who headed this agency were high-ranking dignitaries of both the outer- and inner-court worlds, a situation best understood in the light of their historical background.

The grand secretaries had a long history before Yung-cheng days. After abolishing the prime ministership in 1380, the first Ming emperor, Hung-wu (r. 1368–98), had created these positions as an alternative source of inner-court advice. Although the Ming grand secretaries had held a low civil-service rank (5A), in fact they usually possessed concurrent titles and duties that greatly enhanced their prestige and authority.[52] Many came to the grand secretaryship from the Hanlin Academy, another honor indicating that they had been specially selected from the flower of their *chin-shih* class. By the end of the dynasty their power had swelled to a point where the Ming official history, ignoring the strong role of eunuchs late in the dynasty, declared with some exaggeration that by the seventeenth century all "government had been delegated to the Grand Secretariat."[53] Among the keys to the grand secretaries' great influence during the Ming were their supervisory responsibility for communications, their large outer-court staff, and the fact that some Ming emperors heightened their usefulness to the sovereign by employing them in the inner court both as links to outer-court communications processing and as a means of bypassing the outer court.[54] Thus the grand secretaries' organization that was passed on to the Ch'ing was a powerful one.

During the early Ch'ing the Grand Secretariat had an uncertain history. Sometimes its very strength was daunting. It is not surprising that some early Manchu administrations allowed it to languish, at times replacing it with other organizations.[55] In the early years the Manchu grand secretaries outranked the Chinese, and both groups rose and fell or moved back and forth between the inner and outer courts depending on whether or not various monarchs and regencies desired to use them as close imperial assistants. When the young K'ang-hsi Emperor personally took over the government in KH9 (1670) he refounded the Grand Secretariat and equalized the ranks of all grand secretaries (both Manchu and Chinese) at the second level (2A) of the civil-service hierarchy.[56] Under K'ang-hsi's personal rule (KH9–61 [1670–1722]), the number of grand secretaries varied between five and nine, averaging 5.5 per year.[57] Nevertheless, K'ang-hsi failed to support equality for Chinese at lower levels in the Grand Secretariat, and as a result during his reign the imbalance of Manchus in that staff developed further.

Yung-cheng's policy was to strengthen the grand secretaries without allowing them continuous dominance over crucial areas of government. Like other monarchs before him, Yung-cheng moved some grand secretaries into the inner court for high-level assistance, an arrangement that brought some control over the routine system into the inner court.[58] In addition, during his reign eleven grand secretaries were appointed superintendents (posts higher than the board presidencies) of outer-court organizations, a considerable increase compared with only six over the course of the much longer K'ang-hsi reign. As time went on, the grand secretaries whom Yung-cheng had selected became increasingly useful in the inner court, and additional secretaries had to be appointed to handle the outer-court and routine system work. A new post of assistant grand secretary (*hsieh-pan ta hsueh-shih*), of which there were to be one or two drawn from the board presidents, was created to relieve the grand secretaries of some of their increasingly heavy work load, particularly the burdens of outer-court routine communications. In a move typical of his fondness for keeping his high officials off balance by playing with their titles, Yung-cheng called two of the early incumbents of this post "Acting Grand Secretary" (*Shu ta hsueh-shih*) and "Associate Grand Secretary" (*Hsieh-li ta hsueh-shih*). The increase in central government paperwork, plus Yung-cheng's selection of a few grand secretaries for the inner court, meant that the average number of grand secretaries rose to 7.38 per year, a considerable increase over his father's 5.5 per year.[59]

At mid-reign in YC8 (1730), Yung-cheng capped his support of the grand secretaries by elevating them to rank 1A, an action that catapulted them to the apex of the civil service. By this time all grand secretaries additionally possessed high-sounding palace or pavilion titles, and many were honored with one of the dozen honorary ranks.[60] The grand secretaries' new high civil-service designation and other honors appeared to raise them to the very pinnacle of the central-government administration.[61] But Yung-cheng's award of the highest civil-service rank probably had a special political purpose and was perhaps designed to compensate the outer-court grand secretaries for their loss of authority at the very moment that the Zunghar campaign and expanding palace memorial system were leading not to increased outer-court power but to inner-court expansion.

With its dominance of the routine communications system, trained staff-members, long experience, and established patterns of work, the grand secretaries and the Grand Secretariat seem likely candidates for a leading part in Yung-cheng's policy of strengthening the inner court. But in the end Yung-cheng did not emphasize these men in his reorganization. He treated the grand secretaries and their agency in much the same way that he treated the inner-court groups he had inherited from his father. On the one hand he followed a policy of using and not alienating them, while on the other he undercut them and made sure they were not able to exercise significant inner-court power as a group. Most of the grand secretaries were shunted aside in the outer court, with more and more of the significant edicts coming to be drafted by the specially selected imperial confidants and committee members—only a few of whom were grand secretaries—in the inner court.

Several considerations may have caused the emperor to overlook this imposing and experienced agency when reorganizing his inner court. The secretariat's physical location in the outer court and its connection with the outer-court bureaucracy—including the possibility of involvement in that bureaucracy's corruption—militated against its suitability as a private imperial inner-court staff. The openness with which its outer court operations were handled may also have been cause for concern, especially when secrecy was crucial. Although the secretariat's control of the principal channel for provincial communications might have made it attractive for imperial co-optation, again the threat of outer-court dominance ruled it out. Indeed, the Grand Secretariat's outer-court connections and experience, together with its history of monopolizing the routine communications system, meant that such a well-developed organization composed of high-ranking grand secretaries and a large staff might under certain conditions threaten the imperial power. As a result, Yung-cheng left the Grand Secretariat as a body to concentrate on outer-court activities. Occasionally a grand secretary might be invited to assist in the inner court, but the emperor was careful to ensure that he, not an inner-court grand secretary, remained in charge. Eventually he decided to bypass outer-court operations and create the means for inner-court autocratic control. The outer-court Grand Secretariat was not the appropriate vehicle for that policy.

The Inner-Court Superintendents

From the outset of his reign, Yung-cheng attempted to assert control over the outer court by reviving the early-Ch'ing board superintendency (*tsung-li*) post, which he used to place trusted high level inner-court personnel in top management positions over certain outer-court agencies, chiefly the Six Boards. The imaginary line across the middle of Figure 2 shows how a board was divided in two, with its lower administrative departments (located in the outer court) at the bottom, and above them a ministerial or directorate level. Many or all of the ministers would probably be well known to the emperor; sometimes they would be assigned to work in the inner court. The superintendent was positioned above all these people, at the highest level, and enjoyed a vantage point from which he might oversee all board work.

In line with the Manchu policy of dyarchy, the six top board posts of president and vice president were strictly apportioned between Manchus and Chinese. After the superintendencies were revived in the eighteenth century, however, these topmost positions were usually held by inner-court figures such as imperial princes and especially trusted Manchu and Mongol grand secretaries. Although there were some important Chinese superintendents, in general the use of the post weakened the Ch'ing tradition of evenhandedness between Manchus and Chinese in government appointments.

Not much is known about the superintendency position.[62] The post is difficult to study—it was neither listed in the *Ch'ing Statutes and Precedents* nor identified in the board tables of the Ch'ing official history.[63] The post may have been inherited from the Ming practice of having grand secretaries serve concurrently as board presidents. At the beginning of the Ch'ing, its use was

FIGURE 2. The structure of a typical board, showing the divisions between the ministerial and the departmental levels and the superintendent's relation to other personnel.

The Ministerial or Directorate Level of a Board (t'ang)

Superintendent (not always appointed):
Manchu or Chinese, but more often Manchu

Two presidents:
one Manchu, one Chinese

Four vice presidents:
two Manchu, two Chinese

Dividing line between ministerial and department levels

Administrative Departments

Department directors

Assistant department directors

Second-class secretaries

Department staffs:
clerks, copyists, errand runners, etc.

This diagram offers a greatly condensed sketch of the upper levels of board structure. The line dividing the diagram separates the lower administrative departments from the upper ministerial or directorate level. Although the Six Boards were part of the outer court, their ministers were usually personally known to the emperor and frequently worked in the inner court.

In line with the Manchu policy of dyarchy, the six top board posts of president and vice president were strictly apportioned between Manchus and Chinese. The superintendent post, however, was usually held by a Manchu or Mongol. The superintendent post was not always filled. Yung-cheng and Ch'ien-lung were the first to make frequent use of the post, but they nevertheless often allowed certain boards to function without superintendents. The eighteenth-century superintendents were usually inner court figures, imperial princes and high level imperial confidants such as grand secretaries. In the century's later years some grand councillors were appointed.

During the early nineteenth century the situation changed as inner-court links to the ministerial level of the boards were frequently achieved not with superintendent appointments but instead by means of grand councillors, regarded as inner-court appointees, serving concurrently as board presidents. Later in the century superintendency appointments became less frequent and sometimes went to princes.

SOURCES: H. S. Brunnert and V. V. Hagelstrom, *Present Day Political Organization of China*, translated by A. Beltchenko and E. E. Moran (Shanghai: Kelly and Walsh, 1912), pp. 97–102; Derk Bodde and Clarence Morris, *Law in Imperial China: Exemplified by 190 Ch'ing Dynasty Cases (Translated from the "Hsing-an hui-lan"); with Historical, Social, and Juridical Commentaries* (Cambridge, Mass.: Harvard University Press, 1967), pp. 123–24.

sporadic and mostly limited to first-, second-, third-, and fourth-degree princes of the blood (*ch'in-wang*, *chün-wang*, *pei-le*, and *pei-tzu*), who at the time of the boards' founding in 1631 were appointed to act as the highest-level board heads.[64] The use of princes lasted to the 1640s, when Dorgon, the prince regent for the Shun-chih Emperor (r. 1643–60), abandoned it.[65] Although the superintendency was shortly reinstated, K'ang-hsi made only limited use of such appointees, with only six appointments—most from the ranks of the grand secretaries rather than princes—in the fifty-three years of his personal rule.[66] Yung-cheng appointed many more superintendents, but after learning to distrust many of his royal relatives, he shortly turned to other figures, such as grand secretaries, to fill these posts.[67]

The Yung-cheng Emperor's intensified use of the early Ch'ing superintendency position did not precisely resemble the traditional form. He added several features, putting his own stamp on the practice. Ambiguity marked his use of the post.[68] His terminology was capricious, employing a variety of verbs—"superintend" (*tsung-li*), "direct" (*kuan* or *kuan-li*), "manage" (*liao-li*), and "concurrently [head]" (*chien* or *chien-li*)—in a hierarchy of meaning that possibly only the emperor himself understood. (For examples of this variety, see Table 1.) Thus Yung-cheng might withhold the very highest of this high designation from all but a select few, with one hand conferring esteemed rank and power, yet with the other retaining the allure of future honors that might be conferred with just a slight shift in nomenclature.[69]

Yung-cheng used both Manchus and Chinese in the superintendency posts, but in the early years there were more Manchus, with an emphasis on Manchu princes. Perhaps the Manchu preponderance was the reason that the superintendencies had to be omitted from the official lists. These posts skewed the balance supposedly achieved through dyarchical appointments at the ministerial level of the boards (dyarchy being the Ch'ing practice of balancing equal numbers of Manchus and Chinese in appointments). A cover-up was necessary lest the defect in this much-touted government objective be revealed. As a result, these appointments were kept unofficial. Of course they were known in high circles of the bureaucracy; nevertheless, lists of board presidents dated YC? and YC6 (1725, 1728), for instance, neglect to mention any superintendents, even though we know such appointments existed at the time.[70] These officials were shadowy inner-court figures with undefined ties to both the monarch and the outer court, possessing an awesome power somehow derived from closeness to the sovereign. Their position was at once unclear and yet somehow had to be considered.

Some of the superintendent appointments—like that of the highly favored I Prince at the Board of Revenue—were designed to use inner-court personnel to oversee a key outer-court agency. But some had a double edge, illustrating Yung-cheng's willingness to deal with his high officials in a purposefully ambiguous fashion. Thus, in addition to using the superintendency post to exercise

TABLE 1. Early Yung-cheng superintendent appointments. This table shows some of the Yung-cheng Emperor's early superintendent appointments to Six Board and other outer-court posts and in particular displays the sovereign's changing and apparently capricious use of varied terminology for what must have been virtually the same kinds of responsibilities.

Date	Name	Presidency	Term Used
61/12/13[a]	Lien Prince Yin-ssu	Court of Colonial Affairs	*kuan*
61/12/13	Fu-ning-an (grand secretary from this date)	Board of Civil Office	*chien*
61/12/15	I Prince Yin-hsiang	Board of Revenue Three Treasuries	*tsung-li*
61/12/18	Pai Huang (grand secretary from this date; dismissed YC3/7/27)	Board of War	*jeng-chien*
1/1/19	Lü Prince Yin-t'ao	Board of Works	*liao-li*
1/2/2	Chang P'eng-ko (grand secretary from YC1/2/2; died YC3/3/15)	Board of Civil Office	*chien*
1/2/17	Lien Prince Yin-ssu	Board of Works	*pan-li*
1/2/17	Yü Prince Pao-t'ai	Court of Colonial Affairs	*pan-li*
1/4/7	I Prince Yin-hsiang	Board of Revenue	*tsung-li*
1/10	Pei-tzu Yin-t'ao	Board of Rites	*kuan-li*
2/6/5	Yü Prince Pao-t'ai	Board of Rites	*pan-li*
3/4/24	T'ien Tsung-tien	Board of Civil Office	*chien*
3/9/20	Chu Shih	Board of Civil Office	*jeng-kuan*[b]
4/2/28	Chang T'ing-yü	Board of Revenue	*jeng-kuan*
4/8/16	La-hsi (demoted as of this date)	Court of Colonial Affairs	*pan-li*

SOURCES: Yung-cheng *Shih-lu*, passim; *Ch'ing-shih* 4:2461 (grand secretaries tables) and 2609–13 (board tables); memorials of period.

[a] The dates supplied above are from the Yung-cheng period; those that begin with the year 61 denote the last six weeks of K'ang-hsi 61 (late 1722 and up to Chinese New Year of 1723) after the old emperor had died (on KH61/11/13 [1772 December 20]) and Yung-cheng had come to the throne. Dates in the table do not necessarily represent the date of appointment to the position. Because of the secrecy surrounding the superintendent posts, these appointments were not always clearly recorded; as a result the dates supplied indicate only the earliest mention that I have been able to find—in the absence of other sources some dates have had to be culled from memorials where the appointees inscribed their own ranks.

[b] Chu Shih's promotion to grand secretary is cited in the board tables, but as his name was omitted as concurrent board president for the following year I take this to be a superintendency post.

control over an outer-court agency, Yung-cheng might also employ such appointments to reduce powerful inner-court figures whom he did not entirely trust but could not get rid of.

Such was apparently the case with the powerful and well connected imperial "Uncle" Lung-k'o-to. The reign was but a month old when Lung-k'o-to was appointed Board of Civil Office president, a move that acknowledged the necessity of rewarding him with a key post. But at the same time, Yung-cheng checkmated him by appointing the Manchu grandee Fu-ning-an grand secretary yet ordering him to continue concurrently (*chien*) to head the Board of Civil Office.[71] Fu-ning-an thus acquired an uncertain position that seemed to cut into Lung-k'o-to's power: he was no longer listed in the board tables as president, and Lung-k'o-to had replaced him in the Manchu board presidency; yet although he was elevated above Lung-k'o-to, he was ordered to continue his board president duties. A few weeks later Yung-cheng again fortified himself against Lung-k'o-to when he raised Chang P'eng-ko, another former Board of Civil Office president (this time a Chinese) to another grand secretaryship, while ordering him too to continue "concurrently" to take care of Civil Office president matters.[72] As a result, for a while the Board of Civil Office was in the ambiguous condition of having one Manchu president, Lung-k'o-to, and two superintendents, one Manchu and one Chinese. By such means Yung-cheng added the superintendent post to the ruler's repertoire of ranks that might be conferred both to run the empire and to check and balance members of the highest circle of officials. In Yung-cheng's hands the superintendency was useful in controlling both the outer-court agencies and, on occasion, an imperial courtier in the bargain.

Yung-cheng made a number of other superintendency appointments in the early years of his reign (see Table 1). The I Prince Yin-hsiang, a man who figures importantly in this story and who will be discussed in detail in Chapter 2, was first given a superintendency at the Board of Revenue Three Treasuries (*Hu-pu San-k'u*) and a few months later, still within the first year of the reign, was designated the full superintendent of that board. In the early years other superintendencies went to other princes as well as grand secretaries. But although Yung-cheng steadfastly supported Prince I at the Board of Revenue, he later abandoned the use of other royal siblings and cousins for this kind of command.

Yung-cheng's most significant step in superintendent appointments came when close to mid-reign he created a second superintendency at the Board of Revenue and appointed the grand secretary Chang T'ing-yü to serve alongside Prince I, with another grand secretary, Chiang T'ing-hsi, being given the board president position just below. These three stalwarts later became the nucleus of Yung-cheng's highest inner-court echelon, an informal group of inner deputies that was to last and was eventually transformed into the highest level of the Ch'ien-lung Grand Council.

Did the superintendency involve real work or was it, as appears in the case of the Board of Civil Office arrangements blocking Lung-k'o-to, granted for other purposes? This is difficult to assess. There are many memorials signed by the superintendents; for example, Yin-ssu submitted a number in the course of his tenure as head of the Board of Works. Nevertheless, Lung-k'o-to jealously guarded his rights as board president at the Board of Civil Office and appears to have ignored any claims to preeminence that his superintendents might have sought.[73] The work probably varied with the man. In the next reign, when the grand secretary and superintendent of the Board of Civil Office, Chang T'ing-yü, reached old age, he entreated the Ch'ien-lung Emperor to release him from what he had found to be an excessive responsibility as board superintendent. Stating that he had superintended (*chien-kuan*) the Board of Civil Office for eleven years, he pointed out that others had not been weighed down with such heavy responsiblities for so long. "Now I am the age of a [worn-out] dog or horse—sixty-seven—and feel my energy and mental agility are not what they used to be. Many matters slip my mind. I eat less and less. I am approaching the age of seventy and at the same time I am in charge of an important post. Moreover, if I cannot go to my office and oversee its affairs, I fear that errors may be unavoidable." Adding the disclaimer that although his personal reputation might not matter, Chang insisted: "I cannot afford to make mistakes in official business." He concluded with a poignant warning of how seriously he feared an inability to carry on: "When I contemplate this [burden]," he wrote, "I perspire and the water runs down my back."[74] Chang's view of the superintendency suggests that it placed a considerable burden on the incumbent and therefore that it really did facilitate inner-court control of outer-court processes.

Chang correctly realized that because superintendencies, like most other high posts, were held concurrently, a high minister could be distracted by many responsibilities. The possibility for error was considerable. Yung-cheng had acknowledged this several times when he assured superintendents such as Chang T'ing-yü and another of his important inner-court figures, O-erh-t'ai, that they would not be punished for slipups. The lines of this compassionate policy were laid down in YC6 (1728) when Yung-cheng told Chang:

> Of all my most trusted high officials, the duties given to you are the most numerous. [Your] days are without repose. At first I was unwilling to give you yet another task—of handling Board of Civil Office affairs—but on thinking it over there was no one else. You are only to deal with general principles and need not concern yourself personally with details. If there is an instance of carelessness, I will forgive you—it will not be your responsibility.[75]

In YC12 (1734) there was a recommendation that both the Board of Revenue directorate and the middle-level officials be punished for a slight administrative error. Yung-cheng's response was to be lenient to Chang, the board superintendent, but to let the others' punishments stand: "The Grand Secretary Chang

T'ing-yü is in the inner court every day. The things he handles are numerous. How would he have time to deal with this sort of petty board matter? He is not to be punished with a fine or loss of salary."[76] This same treatment was reaffirmed the following year and applied to an entire board's directorate, as well as to O-erh-t'ai and Chang:

> In this instance of the Board of Civil Office directorate being [recommended for] punishment, let them all be forgiven. As for the Grand Secretary Chang T'ing-yü, he is most assuredly without any cause for punishment. I cannot bear that anyone should utter the two words "permit forgiveness" [*k'uan-mien*; in other words, there is nothing to permit forgiveness for].... He and the Grand Secretary O-erh-t'ai handle a great many matters, working from sunrise to dark without a moment's respite. Considering one person's limited energies, [I ask] how can they oversee all the petty details of board affairs? In the past there was an edict ordering that when transgressions in the banner office were being considered [for punishment], O-erh-t'ai not be included. At present [we ought to proceed] according to this precedent so that for the future, when O-erh-t'ai and Chang T'ing-yü concurrently are in charge of board directorate matters and there is likely to be punishment, they are not held responsible.[77]

Following Yung-cheng, in his early years the Ch'ien-lung Emperor continued this policy of leniency for his high inner-court officials.[78] He even forgave O-erh-t'ai and forbade that he be questioned when his son was accused of leaking Grand Council secrets.[79]

Yung-cheng's interest in the early Ch'ing superintendency position and his special methods of using it not only facilitated inner-court control of certain outer-court agencies but also formed part of the emperor's experiments with new organizational structures for the inner court. The use of superintendents was so successful that as early as the second decade of the following reign an edict proclaimed this method of board overlordship to be an established dynastic practice. Nearly a century later Yung-cheng's grandson, the Chia-ch'ing Emperor, by that time equipped with a full-scale inner-court Grand Council, was able to discard the superintendency post and instead place grand councillors over each board in much the same way by appointing them concurrently to the board presidencies. In fact Chia-ch'ing boasted of this solution, advocating grand councillors for all the boards, but at the president, not the superintendent, level.[80] Thus this inner-court method of control of outer-court agencies, used occasionally by K'ang-hsi and intensified by Yung-cheng, laid the basis for a lasting pattern in Ch'ing government by which the outer-court boards and other agencies became hierarchically linked to the monarch through inner-court figures.[81]

The Audit Bureau

Having the outer-court agencies overseen by inner-court superintendents was only one of Yung-cheng's methods of linking himself to the outer court. Another was to set up an inner-court investigative staff to deal with particularly vexing outer-court problems. In his second month on the throne, Yung-cheng created the Audit Bureau (*Hui-k'ao fu*) to attack the problem of illicit outer-court "board fees" (*pu-fei*) or bribes, which had become a conspicuous example of bureaucratic malfeasance.

The board fees were demanded by the boards in return for approval and clearance of the annual provincial financial reports. Operating under regulations requiring that boards reject faulty or inaccurate reports and return them for revision, corrupt board officials sometimes sent back accurate and honest reports that had been submitted without the requisite illegal payment. As Frederic Wakeman has written of the outer-court bureaucracy in the early Ch'ing, "Scratch a clerk and you would find a felon." Provincial officials could not ignore the demand for money—their promotion or transfer could be held up pending board acceptance of all cases and accounts. As a result, bribery had become not only a requirement of doing business with the boards but also an essential for further career prospects.[82]

The YC1 (1723) edict establishing the Audit Bureau described the questionable board handling of reports on land tax collection and appointed four men, two Manchus and two Chinese—Prince I, "Uncle" Lung-k'o-to, the grand secretary Pai Huang, and the senior president of the Censorate Chu Shih—to serve at the agency's top level. When Yung-cheng ordered this panel to consider how the new organization should proceed, the subsequent recommendations (*hsun-i*) specified a twenty-one–member staff to consist of two each of Manchu and Chinese department directors and assistant department directors, three second-class secretaries, and ten clerks. Provincial tax (*ti-fang cheng-hsiang*) and military supplies (*chün-hsu*) reports were to be the principal subjects for investigation. Thus the bureau was to take over the boards' monopoly of investigating certain financial reports and accept or reject all reports itself, cutting the boards out of their traditional opportunity to collect illicit fees.[83]

The Audit Bureau labored mightily against bureaucratic obstructionism in the financial reporting system. In its three years of existence it handled 550 reports, of which almost one-fifth were returned for correction. Yung-cheng took great interest in the bureau's work, sometimes providing detailed instructions on how rejected accounts were to be explained and insisting that malefactors' names be revealed to him.[84] But the new agency soon ran into difficulties. There were conflicts over procedures, such as which provincial financial accountings were to go to the boards (where they would be scavenged for bribes) and which to the new bureau. Despite the Audit Bureau's existence, the boards continued to extort commissions and reject with impunity memorials arriving without them. A new regulation was drawn up to forestall this practice: from then on all board rejections of memorials had to have Audit Bureau authorization. But the boards ignored this injunction too, and in addition refused to send over their own materials to assist the bureau's investigations. There were complaints that the agency was not functioning properly and failing to meet reasonable time limits, so new time limits were set.[85] Each instance of board recalcitrance was checked with a new regulation.

An ironic verdict on the Audit Bureau is visible in the acts of those provincial officials who, so accustomed to the rapacity of capital staffs, entirely misunderstood the reform nature of the new agency and proceeded in customary fashion to reach into their pockets to forward what they believed to be the commissions necessary to do business with the new bureau.[86] But Yung-cheng delivered the coup de grace when after three years he suddenly abolished the Audit Bureau, giving no clear reason for his action and publicly announcing only that it had become "one more agency and one more matter [to be dealt with]."[87]

As an experiment in restraint of outer-court malfeasance, the Audit Bureau was a failure. A chief reason may have been that the outer court was able to obstruct imperial purposes because communications practices then in force delivered many of the financial reports necessary to the bureau's inquiries directly to the boards and not to the new inner-court investigative body. Later this situation would be remedied by transferring many crucial financial responsibilities to the palace memorial system. The emperor may also have had other reasons for abandoning the agency. The presence of the wily Lung-k'o-to on the panel may have hastened its demise—Lung-k'o-to himself fell from favor in the same year that the bureau was abolished.[88]

The Audit Bureau illustrates several features of Yung-cheng's experiments in restructuring the inner court. It was probably physically located in the secrecy of the inner court (most likely in Prince I's offices), away from prying outer-court eyes. It was an ad hoc, temporary committee, the creature of the imperial will and dissolvable by that same will.[89] Its actions created no precedents. It was flexible and informal, designed to further the emperor's— rather than the bureaucracy's—goals. It may also have offered the emperor a way of trying out new high-level people under close supervision. In later years Yung-cheng was to create another inner-court agency for investigating and checking financial malfeasance, this time in the military financial accounts. This was the Board of Revenue's inner-court Military Finance Section (*Chün-hsu fang*), a staff that was connected with the development of the Grand Council and which in many ways resembled the Audit Bureau. But one important difference lay in the realm of communications, for by mid-reign the military finance reports that had to pass muster in the new office were being written in the palace memorial system. No longer would routine system procedures hinder imperial desires.

Remedies for Problems in the Outer-Court Communications System
The routine communications system of the outer court was another candidate for imperial interest. Although outer-court staff members made nearly all decisions concerning preparation of the throne's responses to routine system memorials, there were several methods—employed in earlier reigns as well as

by Yung-cheng—by which the inner court might intervene. Chief among these were the reviews of certain routine system documents in the formal Imperial Gate audiences (*Yü-men t'ing-cheng*) and the opportunities that the emperor had to make changes (*kai-ch'ien*) in the draft rescripts submitted for imperial approval.[90] In addition, grand secretaries working in the inner court served as links to the outer-court communications system, sometimes bringing their routine system responsibilities with them into the inner court and sometimes extending their supervision to outer-court document processing. Nevertheless, as has been explained earlier, these traditional opportunities for inner-court control over the routine system did not suffice. Yung-cheng made other changes to deal with the routine system's problems.

One of Yung-cheng's changes was to reduce the number of large formal open audiences of the sort at which K'ang-hsi had conversed with his ministers and made decisions on many of the problems raised in the routine memorials. Although Yung-cheng continued to hold occasional Imperial Gate audiences, by nature he preferred to communicate in writing rather than by conversation and as a result increasingly based his work on written documents and intimate conversations with a few trusted confidants at court. Apparently he disliked the openness and constraining formality of the large audiences, once declaring that his audiences were to be private interviews with only one or two others present and that no one else, "not even a three-foot child," was to be admitted.[91]

In keeping with his dislike of open audiences, Yung-cheng also took steps to reduce the openness of the outer-court communications system. The emperor complained that so many copies of routine documents were made that sometimes "urgent matters are already circulating to the people before they come to my attention." Things had come to such a pass that government strategies for the pursuit of criminals were being divulged to the very miscreants who were being tracked. Although secrecy had always been possible (yet not common) in the routine system, Yung-cheng now decreed that routine documents on "sensitive" (*chin-yao*) topics were to be sealed up (*mi-feng*) for transmission and circulation at the capital "in order to prevent leaks."[92] The emperor struck another blow for secrecy when he railed against the fact that state secrets were appearing in the Peking gazettes (*t'ang-pao*). The solution was to require that information copies (*chieh-t'ieh*) of important routine documents be held up for five days before being sent to the gazette offices for further dissemination[93]—a measure intended to reduce the timeliness of certain kinds of secrets that had previously appeared too early in the gazettes.

By means of the somewhat unusual form known as "changing the draft rescript" (*kai-ch'ien*), the emperor might deal with another unsatisfactory feature of the outer court: the procedures whereby its draft rescripts nearly always had to be accepted. In most instances, imperial acquiescence followed a draft rescript proposed by the outer-court bureaucracy because the rescripts were known to be drawn up strictly in accordance with earlier imperially approved precedents and the monarch and his advisers in the inner court seldom had access to well-researched alternatives. But inner-court intervention was possible. The emperor generally accomplished this by personally inscribing the new rescript on the rescript slip (*p'iao-ch'ien*). Thus the Yung-cheng favorite, Chang T'ing-yü, proudly reported that on one occasion, when his request for dismissal (submitted in accordance with the Metropolitan Inspection [*Ta-chi*] regulations) had come over from the Grand Secretariat with an approving draft rescript, the emperor took up "his own brush and revised it." Changed rescripts could also be recommended by the high officials in charge of inner-court communications—grand secretaries in the early era and grand councillors later on.[94] In this way the drafts were monitored at the very highest level, not only by the emperor but also by his close inner-court assistants. Thus although inertia and tradition ordinarily paved the way for automatic imperial authorization of routine system draft rescripts, special inner-court moves could impose changes.

A few moves against the Transmission Office (*T'ung-cheng ssu*) reduced its dominance over communications. In the Ming this organization had been extremely powerful, possessing the authority to scrutinize all incoming memorials (even, it has been said, top secret ones) and reject those whose further circulation to capital authorities it wished to delay or prevent. Although it is not entirely clear how this agency operated in the Ch'ing, apparently some of its powers to reject routine memorials—usually for matters of form—persisted in the early years of the dynasty. As a result, even this practice was prohibited in the Yung-cheng period. In addition, Yung-cheng's expansion of the palace memorial system and the establishment of the Chancery of Memorials (*Tsou-shih ch'u*), which probably took place early in the Yung-cheng reign, also weakened the Transmission Office.[95] In later reigns the agency was further impaired when some of its powers were transferred to the Grand Secretariat.

Other routine communications reforms included requirements clarifying the distinction between the two major types of provincial routine memorials of the time (*t'i-pen* and *tsou-pen*), the length of the routine memorial summaries (*t'ieh-huang*), the information necessary for a memorial guaranteeing a person for appointment, and the methods deemed suitable for organizing policy deliberations to be reported in the routine system.[96] In addition, some imperial edicts laid down strictures concerning methods of record keeping and archival storage of routine memorials. Archivists, for instance, were carefully monitored lest they become habituated to practicing frauds.[97] Another regulation, following a fire that destroyed large numbers of Board of Civil Office archives, required that copies of routine memorials be filed separate from the originals. Additional strictures mandated several copies for certain papers in order to have enough for various types of reference and also "to guard against the malefaction of... surreptitious altering [of documents]."[98] Because of certain incomplete routine-system archival holdings, clerks frequently had to visit several different document depositories to assemble reference copies of all the varied state papers that might be needed for an investigation. As a result, further specifications for keeping proper routine system records all together in one place were laid down.[99] But the outer-court communications problems were too well entrenched to be uprooted and reformed. Yung-cheng's edicts did not attempt to grapple with the problems of outer-court dominance over routine system policy drafts. As we shall see in the next few chapters, the Yung-cheng Emperor's main thrust against excessive autonomy and other difficulties in the outer court was to focus on the inner court, creating one staff to counter another and strengthening the new palace communications system to counter the old outer-court one. Thus, although Yung-cheng continued to employ traditional methods to reach into outer-court decision making—the "change-the-draft rescript," occasional discussions at Imperial Gate audiences, special investigatory panels and agencies, and the use of inner-court grand secretaries and superintendents as links to the outer court—eventually his answer to problems in the outer court was to circumvent them with his own new inner-court arrangements.

YUNG-CHENG'S INNER-COURT BYPASS OF THE OUTER COURT

At the beginning of the Yung-cheng reign, the principal entities of the administrative side of the inner court consisted of the grand secretaries and superintendents on duty there, the mourning-period Plenipotentiary Council, the Southern [Imperial] Study, the Deliberative Council, occasional temporary committees of high dignitaries, and the palace memorial system. Except for the Plenipotentiary Council, created only after K'ang-hsi's death, K'ang-hsi had employed all of these (some more than others) as instruments of government. In particular K'ang-hsi used the Southern Study, the Deliberative Council, temporary inner-court deliberative committees, and the palace memorial system to bypass the outer court and accomplish certain kinds of administrative tasks—deliberations on military strategy and the handling of problems associated with the western missionaries at Canton and Peking, for instance. Yung-cheng continued these bypass methods, but made several changes. On the one hand, his father's two assisting and deliberative bodies of high prestige were allowed to continue, but they were downgraded and gradually given less important work. On the other hand, Yung-cheng stressed the palace memorial system and expanded its uses. In what follows I shall describe the decline of the Southern Study and the Deliberative Council and Yung-cheng's intensified use of the palace memorials. Because K'ang-hsi's temporary committees did not function continuously, they will be described in Chapter 3 in connection with a similar committee established by Yung-cheng.

The Southern [Imperial] Study

The Southern [Imperial] Study (*Nan Shu-fang* or sometimes *Nan-chai*) was established in KH16 (1677) to discharge certain inner-court literary tasks.[100] These included drafting sensitive or important edicts, selecting the questions for certain central-government examinations, preparing fine calligraphy, serving as tutors for the imperial princes, and composing poetry for the emperor.[101] At the outset the study was given high prestige by being enrolled in the administrative statutes of the empire and having important work (including some edict drafting) to do. Office space was allotted at the heart of the inner-court administrative compound, on the west side of the Ch'ien-ch'ing Gate.[102] Appointment to high literary and administrative responsibilities so close to the imperial quarters was a coveted assignment. During the K'ang-hsi period, forty-eight Chinese and one Manchu were honored with elevation to the prestigious body.[103] Many of the appointees were drawn from the Hanlin Academy. Chang T'ing-yü's father, the grand secretary Chang Ying, was one of the high-level and well-known scholars of the day who served in the study. The Southern Study was particularly effective because its office was secreted away in the inner court—on one occasion even a board president was denied admittance. This location gave the monarch swift access to the study's erudites whenever he required their services and assured confidentiality for policy discussions and edict drafting.[104]

At the beginning of his reign, Yung-cheng continued his father's policy of appointing Chinese of high distinction to the Southern Study.[105] But this soon changed as the emperor began to undermine the study's exalted position in the government by staffing it with middle-level personnel, young sons of favored officials, and even new examination graduates. One man was described as being appointed "to gain experience"—hardly the kind of man K'ang-hsi would have selected for his most trusted inner-court body of high Chinese officials.[106] The Southern Study office space came to be used for other purposes; Chang T'ing-yü was said to have sat alone in its western part discharging his duties as an inner grand secretary. In the following reign it was employed as a general-duty office for inner-court personnel, and for a while it was the site where certain revised *Veritable Records* (for the reign of the Ch'ing founding emperor Nurhaci) were copied. In the last third of the Yung-cheng period the study's Summer Palace office was also converted for use by the inner grand secretaries and another inner-court body, the new informal group known as the "High Officials in Charge of Military Strategy" (*Pan-li Chün-chi ta-ch'en*). The study's important responsibility of drafting edicts in inner-court precincts dwindled away and was gradually passed to new inner-court individuals and groups specially appointed by Yung-cheng. In the Ch'ien-lung period this responsibility passed to the Grand Council, even while the study continued to exist.[107]

Yung-cheng managed the Southern Study in line with a policy that eventually became characteristic of much of his inner-court reorganization. Although in the beginning he cautiously retained the study as part of the government structure inherited from his father, at the same time he gradually undermined it. The study continued to exist, but with diminished lustre and responsibilities. Yung-cheng wished to set up his own inner-court staffs and appoint his own personnel to them. If there were to be any important inner-court staffs, he wished to create them. An organization possessing a half-century's experience of closeness to the K'ang-hsi Emperor, distinguished high-level personnel, and statutory status conferred more prestige than Yung-cheng could tolerate.

The Council of Deliberative Princes and Ministers

From his father, Yung-cheng had also inherited the prestigious inner-court Deliberative Council (*I-cheng wang ta-ch'en*; literally, Council of Deliberative Princes and Ministers, sometimes abbreviated to *I-cheng ch'u*), a largely Manchu group of notables and middle-level staff, with roots running far back in Manchu tradition.[108] The council was informally convened without statutory status— a condition typical of some early Ch'ing inner-court committees that made it susceptible to imperial control. During the K'ang-hsi period the council had assumed special responsibility for military policy and deliberated other matters of Manchu interest such as appointments, preservation of customs, assistance to the Eight Banners' poor, and whether or not Manchus should be allowed to engage in overseas trade.[109] But the new emperor's drive to reduce Manchu princes' and banner influence required that the Deliberative Council be diminished.[110] To this end, Yung-cheng simultaneously pursued both the positive and the negative policies that were characteristic of the way he dealt with the inner-court bodies inherited from his father. As a result, although he may appear to have been vacillating and indecisive, in fact his approach was similar to his treatment of the Southern Study, as he attempted both to downgrade the council and yet avoid alienating its powerful Manchu grandee members. Thus the council was retained, appointments to it were made, and during the early part of the reign it was given numerous assignments to deliberate military matters such as appointments and troop allocations.[111] At the same time, however, it was slowly undermined. Where the high Manchus of the Deliberative Council were concerned, the emperor had to move with caution.

Yung-cheng's dissatisfaction with the council was made clear as early as the first year of his reign, when he berated it because a decision "not yet in effect had nevertheless been divulged, so that everybody knew it." This imperial tirade was followed by the dismissal of certain council members. Later the emperor promised an important court military appointment to a provincial official, but in the same breath he confided that he was not entrusting the Deliberative Ministers with the information.[112] Yung-cheng also used check-

and-balance tactics against the council, refusing to allow it to monopolize topics, information channels, or files. His favorite method was to employ the imperial routing power that permitted him to switch discussers, a kind of "competitive administration."[113] During the first two years of the reign, the Deliberative Council frequently shared discussion responsibilities with the Plenipotentiary Council and the Board of War. Occasionally two of the three groups were ordered to serve together, but generally a problem would be assigned to one group to consider alone, with responsibility for the same issue later passing to a different group.[114] This course differed significantly from late K'ang-hsi times, when the Deliberative Council had been continuously in charge of discussions of military policy. The stratagem of switching discussion groups assured the emperor that no one of his inner-court government bodies would be able to monopolize important areas of policy. At the same time, improprieties were discouraged because of the expectation that subsequent different deliberators might uncover the malfeasance.

But the Deliberative Council was not entirely in eclipse: occasionally it had important work to do. In YC7 (1729) it was assigned joint responsibility with the Board of Punishments for an important sedition case, a topic not precisely within the military scope of the council's usual past endeavors. Furthermore, during the early Yung-cheng period its expertise and experience required that it be regularly consulted on Tibet.[115] But apparently the emperor found the council's Manchu preponderance and high prestige unpalatable; he was thus led to a search for new inner-court structures to deal with military problems. During the final two-thirds of the reign, in order to run the Zunghar campaign without resorting to the Deliberative Council, he turned to a new high inner-court echelon of inner deputies and staffs subordinate to them, the Military Finance Section and the High Officials in Charge of Military Finance (later Military Strategy). His new arrangements better satisfied his requirements that his staffs be informal, lack tradition, and enjoy only diminished prestige.[116]

The Use of the Palace Memorial System to Manipulate the Outer Court

Another institution that Yung-cheng inherited was the new inner-court communications system known as the palace memorial (*tsou-che*) system. This second Ch'ing communications system was designed to bypass the outer court and ensure that the emperor and his personal staff would handle certain crucial government business entirely in the inner court.[117] The K'ang-hsi Emperor had created the palace memorials to assure himself of his own private channel of communication that would yield information on local matters—unrest, administrative problems, weather, harvest prospects, and the like. In the early years, in contrast with the routine system's openness and domination by the outer-court bureaucracy, secrecy was the palace memorials' outstanding feature. These memorials were carried by a private transmission channel that used personal memorial servants to deliver the documents directly to the inner court, forestalling preliminary scanning or intervention by outer-court agencies. Imperial control was further ensured by having the emperor write his replies in vermilion, a color reserved for imperial use, directly on these memorials, instead of having the throne's responses drafted in the Grand Secretariat in the manner of routine system documents. The memorials were sent directly back to the field so that the memorialist might read his sovereign's responses. The K'ang-hsi system was characterized by this private imperial channel, a limited number of provincial correspondents, infrequent reporting, lack of regularization, and laconic imperial responses. It met the needs of those times for prompt, informal, and secret reporting, particularly on the possibility of local unrest, but was greatly altered during the following reign.

Yung-cheng continued to use the palace memorial system to bypass the outer court. Like his father before him he stressed the new system's secrecy and frequently called these documents "secret memorials" (*mi-shu tsou-che*, usually shortened to *mi-tsou* or *mi-che*), emphasizing their confidentiality by requiring memorialists to be alert for spies and to prepare their reports themselves. Even the secretaries of high provincial officials were not to assist.[118]

But under Yung-cheng the palace memorial system was greatly changed to enhance inner-court opportunities to play a decisive role in the central government. Numbers of documents in the system greatly increased. Estimates for the last thirteen years of the K'ang-hsi reign compared with the thirteen-year Yung-cheng period suggest at least a tenfold increase, from approximately 2,500 to 25,000, statistics that indicate a change of substantial magnitude.[119] The increase arose partly from the fact that new topics were being handled in the palace system. For example, because routine system rules required assembling all of a province's harvest information before reporting the results of any one administrative subdivision, it was often more convenient to use the palace system to obtain a quick look at a crucial spot.[120] (It may have been for this reason that K'ang-hsi had asked for harvest reports in the new system.) Some of Yung-cheng's new topics may likewise have compensated for delays caused by other routine system rules.

Yung-cheng also employed the palace memorials for questionable or tentative matters that might have been either turned into law or rejected in the course of outer-court processing. The silver-meltage fee reports (*hao-hsien*), for instance, were of this type. As Yung-cheng admitted in an edict, "Adding a silver-meltage fee to the land tax initially was something that ought not to be." According to an imperial edict on the subject, the fee's dubious legality meant that this topic "should be reported only in a palace memorial and that the information should be sent to the [inner-court directorate of the] board to keep on file. It ought not to be revealed in a routine memorial [that would go to the outer court]." If information on the silver-meltage fee regularly reached the outer court, its illegality might eventually cause collections to be halted. But it was also possible that if the outer court regularly accepted such reports for processing, soon the proposed temporary and tentative payments might become "fixed quotas" with the status of unalterable regulations.[121] Yung-cheng detested the fact that the routine system empowered the outer court to manufacture a precedent from any imperially authorized government action in the routine system or to call on other precedents to dismiss one of his cherished proposals. The palace memorial system helped rectify this situation by transferring certain issues to the inner court to ensure that they would be handled according to the emperor's liking.

Under Yung-cheng the court also expanded the palace memorial system by allowing more officials to use it and by encouraging frequent use. At the capital the censors were invited to submit palace memorials bearing information that the emperor might not otherwise hear about. Additional provincial officials given the palace memorial privilege included the lieutenant governors (financial commissioners), judicial commissioners, and circuit intendants of the civil ranks, and provincial commanders-in-chief (*t'i-tu*) and brigade generals (*tsung-ping*) on the military side.[122] Some of these privileges may not have offered the emperor as much as he hoped. Provincial officials below the highest ranks tended to be overshadowed by their superiors and were rarely able to use the palace memorial system to circumvent those in charge of their work and recommendations of their own promotions.[123] Nevertheless, this expansion of the palace memorial system strengthened the inner court by drawing new groups of provincial officials into that network.

During the Yung-cheng reign the palace memorial system was also enhanced by increased use of certain document forms—the capital officials' deliberation memorial (*i-fu tsou-che*) and the new kind of edict, the court letter (*t'ing-chi*, *chi-hsin*, or *tzu-chi*). Use of these promoted inner-court secrecy by ensuring that the responses to the palace memorials would stay within the inner court. (Details concerning these forms will be provided in Chapter 3.) As the new system expanded, archival records and reference copies of both provincial and capital memorials were developed to bring order to the mass of state documents now being handled close to the emperor. There were also stacks of new record series (mostly albums of copied documents), at first chiefly in the Manchu language; by the end of the Yung-cheng reign these Manchu record books numbered more than one hundred *ts'e*. Later when the history of the great Ch'ing military campaign against the northwest Zunghars was compiled under inner-court supervision, these archival records would be carefully screened and used as a basis for telling the Yung-cheng portion of the story.

The surge of activities represented by the increase in documents was partly responsible for new organizational and personnel arrangements to process the flood of papers now engulfing the inner court. The Chancery eunuchs (*tsou-shih t'ai-chien*) that Yung-cheng inherited from his father were transformed into a new office for receiving the palace memorials, the Chancery of Memorials (*Tsou-shih ch'u*), with an outer section (*Wai tsou-shih ch'u*) manned by officials and an inner complement (*Nei tsou-shih ch'u*) staffed by eunuchs.[124] Two new informal groups of officials—the inner deputies and the High Officials in Charge of Military Finance—also had as part of their duties the responsibility for scanning certain of the palace memorials and drafting responses. (These activities will be described in Chapters 3 and 4.)

Yung-cheng saw that the secret system could serve many imperial aims. Under his administration K'ang-hsi's relatively simple new communications form for provincial reporting became a sophisticated instrument for preserving inner-court secrecy, allowing imperial intervention in outer-court administration, facilitating imperial dominance of the policy formulation process, and, through the imperial rescript feature, permitting the emperor to cultivate provincial officials by means of a personal imperial correspondence. The palace memorial system thus accomplished several of Yung-cheng's most cherished purposes, assuring secrecy and winning influence in both the outer court and the provinces. Most significantly, this inner-court communications system also put power and influence into the hands of the emperor's highest inner-court advisers, who frequently scanned the palace memorials and counseled the monarch on problems raised. In the Yung-cheng period these were the inner deputies; in the following reign they were the grand councillors.

Secrecy.   Palace memorial secrecy sheltered certain imperial thoughts and activities from publicity, in particular from the dangers of outer-court scrutiny. The emperor was enabled to write frankly, committing whatever was on his mind to paper without fear of disclosure. This was especially useful for personnel matters but of course could conceal any imperial view. One can imagine the difficulties that might have ensued had the publicity of the routine system attended such caustic vermilion comments as the following: "Ho Ching-wen is a good-hearted, hard-working old hand. I think he's very good. But he's a bit coarse. By nature he is just like Chao Hsiang-k'uei, except that Chao Hsiang-k'uei is intelligent."[125]

In similar vein, the emperor once dismissed what he regarded as an unworkable and idiotic proposal (requiring extra summaries of routine memorials) with a withering blast addressed to the proponent: "You are one of those mediocre provincial officials appointed on a trial basis because I couldn't find anyone better."[126] Even a provincial official's frank appraisal, such as one governor's plain-spoken denigration of a subordinate as "scatter brained," might have stirred the wrath of the man's factional associates and caused endless difficulties for the governor had it been revealed. As it was, many of the Yung-cheng–period palace memorials with their forthright, even sarcastic personnel evaluations lay hidden in the inner-court archives for two hundred years. Although some innocuous documents were published in the multivolume edition of the Yung-cheng palace memorials, concealment was possible and was practiced to cloak dubious imperial maneuvering. The secrets of Yung-cheng's unrehearsed and candid scribblings on the palace memorials and his provincial officials' responses were strictly secured.[127]

The Prohibition Against Wide Circulation for Inner-Court Documents.   Strict inner-court secrecy for the palace memorials also had other advantages, for the system permitted Yung-cheng to work out proposals before they reached the boards. This was possible because of a prohibition against allowing these inner-palace documents to circulate to the Grand Secretariat and Six Boards bureaucracies. Yung-cheng was adamant that the outer- and inner-court information channels be strictly separated, scolding and even punishing memorialists who ignored this restriction and leaked palace memorial secrets to the outer court.[128] In addition, any kind of response to a palace memorial had to be treated as a "secret edict" (*mi-yü*) and likewise handled in the inner-palace system rather than the routine system.[129] This meant that vermilion rescripts on the palace memorials could not be passed around to other high officials, not even to those stationed in the same provincial administrative office.[130] The strict separation of communications channels supplied the emperor with the informality, secrecy, and privacy that he desired. But at the same time this imperial concern created difficulties when palace memorial information had to undergo official processing.

The proscription on sending a palace memorial to the outer court meant that if the topic necessitated outer-court handling, an entirely new document had to be composed for routine system submission. This involved a cumbersome process. First the emperor would return the palace memorial to its author with the order "Resubmit in a routine memorial" (*Chü-t'i lai*).[131] Then the provincial memorialist would write up the same information (sometimes with bowdlerized content) in the form of a routine memorial and send it to the capital a second time. Although this could cause considerable delay, it gave the emperor time to consider proposals at length and in some cases have them revised before they were fed into the outer-court machinery.[132] Thus, on one occasion Yung-cheng responded to a governor's plea for a year's extension to make up provincial treasury shortages by granting the desired permission, but he additionally instructed the memorialist to "remove all improper passages that should not be included in a routine memorial [and thereby be revealed to the board] and submit this in a routine memorial."[133] On another occasion Yung-cheng counseled a governor-general on handling shortages in payments for regular salt quotas. The problem was whether or not it would be permissible to alter the amounts of the "special surplus" (*ying-yü*) fund's annual payments. Again the emperor knew that the information had to be reported to the outer court but wished to prevent unnecessary information from going beyond the inner court. "What should be sent in a routine memorial," he advised, "report in a routine memorial."[134] Inner-court secrecy kept certain kinds of information from ever reaching the outer-court bureaucrats.

The strictures on resubmission proved particularly useful in deciding personnel matters. On one occasion, for example, Yung-cheng instructed O-erh-t'ai (at the time still a governor-general in the southwest) on the differences in the information that was to go to the outer-court board vis-à-vis the frank personnel evaluation that was to be reserved for a palace memorial report that would go directly to the emperor: "Chang Kuang-ssu is also a very talented person; I never expected him to possess such ability. It is surely auspicious. When you send in a routine memorial [destined for the board], you should stress his good points. [At the same time] you should also tell me by palace memorial [i.e., by writing more frankly in the secret system] which man [of two being considered] is suitable for placement in each of the two provinces."[135]

Although in the absence of further information these instances of imperial advice are difficult to interpret with certainty, some seem designed to protect specific local interests—perhaps in some cases the concerns of officials and local gentry whom Yung-cheng wished to cultivate—and others appear intended to protect special inner-court operations. The emperor's candid mandates for obfuscation reveal that one imperial use of the palace memorial system was to circumvent the outer-court agencies and concentrate privileged information and decision making in the inner court. Behind-the-scenes maneuvers were necessary to bypass both outer-court openness and corruption. If an outer-court board was susceptible to bribes that might influence an appointment recommendation or a tax arrears payment, for instance, then appointments and tax arrears would have to be decided in the inner court.

Using the Inner-Court Communications System to Circumvent the Boards.   The palace memorial system's imperial exclusiveness also allowed the emperor to ignore the regulations and precedents that were supposedly defended by the outer-court agencies. Archival evidence reveals an instance of imperial connivance with a provincial official to get around board regulations, a tale that was carefully excised from sources circulated at the time. In YC1 (1723) the emperor forthrightly instructed a provincial memorialist on how to evade an unwanted board verdict on a proposed appointment: "If you have the right man for a position [but] his candidacy is not in accordance with [board] regulations [so that you cannot] recommend him in a routine memorial [which the board would have to reject], there is nothing to prevent your secretly reporting this [to me] in a [palace] memorial." Nor was this all. In the same vermilion rescript Yung-cheng advised against waiting too long, for soon it might be too late to intervene to protect his favorite provincial officials' choices.[136]

Three years later in another palace memorial rescript, Yung-cheng gave different orders on how an anticipated board denial of his wishes could be circumvented, for by now the emperor was willing to confront the boards directly with a veto:

There is no need to stick to regulations; just send in a routine memorial [that would go directly to the board] asking to have a position filled. But you must in that memorial clearly point out whatever is inconsistent with regulations. If the board deliberates and recommends not permitting [what we want], then I can hand down a special decree [*t'e-chih*; a means of making an exception to precedents] granting permission. Let all [board] regulations remain the same so that they will not have to be revised. Not only is there this instance of handling without adhering to regulations—there are many. I have my special way of considering these cases.[137]

Thus the palace memorial system allowed the emperor to bypass not only the outer court but also the law. It seemed that at times rules were to be respected only so long as they allowed Yung-cheng to do what he, rather than the boards and their regulations, deemed necessary. Although the emperor possessed the power to change the law as he wished, as we can see by the previous quotation, in many instances he preferred to direct matters according to his will in the inner court and leave the outer court to deal with issues not of intense concern, all the while avoiding a direct challenge of the outer-court bureaucracy.

Yung-cheng's dislike of outer court regulations took another form when he employed the character "exception" (*t'e*, sometimes *t'e mi-yü*), meaning that he was specifying—at the end of imperial edicts or one of his vermilion commands —that what he had decided or written was not to become a precedent. Although Yung-cheng was not the first to withhold his own decisions from becoming part of administrative precedent law, he made greater use of this maneuver than is observable in older sources. For instance, his edicts allocating funds for the military fronts were likely to be marked "exception" because such allocations were made on a one-time basis and were not automatically to be enshrined in the body of precedent law and at a later date summoned forth as an argument for similar future allocations. On one occasion an imperial exception tag permitted holding certain imperial rescripts in a provincial office until their commands had been fulfilled instead of returning them quickly in obedience to the usual requirement, but this was also declared not to be a precedent for future action.[138]

Thus, Yung-cheng's palace memorial bypass of the outer court allowed him many advantages. With the palace memorials he was able to keep secrets in the inner court and hence deny the outer court the opportunity to influence related decisions. In addition, he was able to use the palace system to have his own way instead of submitting to the regulations of the administrative code. Although he could have put through changes in the code, he preferred to avoid this, letting "all board regulations remain the same." In his hands the palace memorial system could be used as a finely tuned instrument for promoting his autocratic aims without mounting a direct challenge to his outer-court bureaucrats.

Use of the Palace Memorial System to Cultivate Provincial Officials

In addition to employing the palace memorials to maneuver around outer-court regulations and recommendations that he disliked, Yung-cheng also used them to reach out to provincial officials, thereby bypassing the old outer-court provincial correspondence in the routine system. Under the rules of the routine system, the imperial calligraphy did not usually appear on the memorials. In the rare instances when the emperor changed a draft rescript with his own brush (*kai-ch'ien*), the imperial alteration was recorded on the rescript slip (*p'iao-ch'ien*), but the memorialist never received it.[139] Instead the routine memorialist in the provinces usually learned the court's response to what he had written by reading it in the Peking gazette. By contrast, the personal imperial-rescript feature of the palace memorial system introduced an important new element, for it allowed direct imperial intervention, in particular permitting the emperor to conduct a personal correspondence with provincial officials. Yung-cheng was adept at wielding his vermilion brush to cultivate high military and civil officials in the provinces; he was shrewdly aware of how flattered an official would feel on receiving a lengthy vermilion confidence or even a single line of imperial praise in the emperor's own handwriting. The palace memorial system offered a monarch who was willing to do the necessary writing the opportunity to forge links with his provincial officials.

Although the archives teem with examples of Yung-cheng's vermilion provincial-palace memorial rescripts in which he wheedled, coaxed, and praised his provincial officials, with one exception I shall here depend only on the correspondence with General Yueh Chung-ch'i (1686–1754). Yung-cheng's responses to General Yueh's memorials contain examples of the full range of the emperor's positive relationships with most of his high provincial officials: encouragement, praise, concern for an official's well-being, comments on contacts with family members, gifts, and of course policy directives. In addition, Yung-cheng's vermilion writing to Yueh includes long imperial letters of the sort that Yung-cheng reserved for his top favorites. The correspondence with General Yueh has also been chosen because he was in charge of the western front of the northwest campaign in YC4–10 (1726–32), the crucial years when Yung-cheng created the new inner-court agencies for campaign staffwork that eventually became the Ch'ien-lung Grand Council. Accordingly, Yueh's activities in the northwest are relevant to Grand Council history, and the imperial vermilion confidences that he received illustrate another use of the palace memorial system: the Yung-cheng Emperor's attempt to cultivate his provincial officials and run a military campaign with his vermilion brush—a kind of ruling through writing.

The Ch'ing campaign against the Zunghar Mongols had begun in KH29 (1690) and was to conclude more than sixty years later in CL20 (1755), the twentieth year of the reign of Yung-cheng's son and heir. During the early years of his reign, Yung-cheng's efforts to deal with the Zunghar menace became increasingly fervent. Finally late in YC5 he wrote one of his provincial officials that he intended "to make a big stand [on this matter] once and for all."[140]

General Yueh's career occupied only two segments of the contest. In YC2 (1724) he had assisted General Nien Keng-yao in the pacification of the Khoshote rebellion led by Lobdzan Dandzin (Lo-pu-tsang Tan-chin) in the western area of Ch'ing-hai. And during the years YC4 to 10 (1726–32) he was the general in charge on the western front against the Zunghars. The two campaigns were tied together by the fact that after the failure of the uprising, the Zunghars took the side of the Ch'ing enemy by giving asylum to Lobdzan Dandzin, thus asking for trouble with the Ch'ing.

Yueh's participation in the preparations for a new thrust against the Zunghars began in YC4 or 5 (1726–27). According to two edicts issued later by the Yung-cheng Emperor, this phase of the campaign was secretly inaugurated with provisioning for the northern front in the hands of the I Prince, Chang T'ing-yü, and Chiang T'ing-hsi at the capital and western-front logistical arrangements being handled by General Yueh in the field.[141] Although dispatches went back and forth with astonishing rapidity (depending on where the general was, a week or ten days usually sufficed for a one-way transit), face-to-face discussions at the capital were sometimes necessary, with the result that General Yueh was occasionally brought to the capital for consultations.[142] The general may have been only a frontier military figure, but he was the key to one of Yung-cheng's most cherished hopes: a final victory over the Zunghars.

Yung-cheng's particular fondness for and trust in General Yueh Chung-ch'i date from the middle of the reign. There had been some early admiring edicts, such as the YC1 (1723) rescript in which the emperor beguilingly told him: "As far as military matters are concerned, I have complete confidence in you."[143] But in YC7 (1729), just as the general was embarking on the journey that was to take him to the far west in fulfilment of plans for Yung-cheng's "big stand," the emperor issued an edict praising him handsomely, saying that he was a man of great experience who had "applied his whole heart" to the management of military logistics over the years.[144] On YC7/J7/21 (1729, Sept. 13), General Yueh led twelve contingents of troops "beyond the pass"—that is, beyond Su-chou in Kansu province—reaching Pa-erh-k'u-erh (Barkul) in Sinkiang six weeks later.[145] Yung-cheng solicitously rescripted the memorial bearing this news, expressing concern for the welfare of both Yueh and his troops: "I am very well. You have now been beyond the frontier for ten days. Is everything proceeding the way you want? How are you after riding on a horse through wind and snow? Are the officers, troops, and the animals in good condition?"[146] Such imperial pleasantries were not uncommon in Yung-cheng's correspondence with other provincial servitors besides Yueh. But the planning for the increased military effort of YC7 (1729) resulted in intensified imperial expressions of concern for the favorite general. Once Yueh was preparing to march, the correspondence was additionally marked by the bestowal of imperial largesse and the long imperial rescripts that really amount to personal letters.[147]

After Yueh reached distant Barkul, the emperor initiated a new phase of the relationship by dispatching culinary delicacies and medicines. One shipment included a basin and two leather purses, two caskets of bottles of milk, two caskets of "lama biscuits," one basket of deer tails, and one of smoked pork.[148] Herbal medicines were also conveyed, together with imperial instructions on their use. One concoction was forwarded on the recommendation of the imperial favorite T'ien Wen-ching, governor of Honan province, although the emperor added that he himself had also "often used it, with excellent results."[149] Another vial of medicine was dispatched with the emperor's prescription that one hundred days of use would be necessary before it could be truly effective.[150] The emperor also sent Yueh several caskets of fans that he had inscribed (as a kind of decoration) when a young prince. Confidingly Yung-cheng admitted in an accompanying note, "For the past six years I have not had the time to write on fans—occasionally I might do one or two—but then I would feel that my calligraphy was not up to the polish of past years."[151] A gift of a prized imperial possession such as this, coupled with the disarming admission of imperial weakness, was a terrific mark of imperial favor. Although the gifts may have been in sorry condition after jogging the long leagues out to Barkul, any shortcoming in quality would have mattered much less than the psychological uplift of being honored with such high marks of imperial solicitude. With blandishments such as these a provincial servitor toiling on the frontier might be won for the imperial cause.

Yung-cheng also lavished praise on the general. Several times the emperor complimented Yueh on his handling of his responsibilities. On one occasion the emperor called Yueh "well informed on the officials and staff members [in the northwest]" and ordered him to make recommendations on promotions, an opportunity for patronage not offered to all frontline generals.[152] On another occasion he was ranked in tandem with the I Prince, an extravagant statement that the emperor could justify as part of his campaign to win the general's loyalty.[153] Yung-cheng even liked Yueh's son Yueh Chün: "the moment I saw him," he wrote, "I knew this son of yours was a man of integrity who would be a fine official and do things extremely well."[154]

Some of the rescripts addressed to Yueh may seem humdrum today, but in reading them we must remember that we are studying a society in which filial remembrances, auspicious omens, and weather that might water crops in the dry plains of north China were of deep concern. Thus in one note the emperor describes at length a tomb visit honoring his father, the K'ang-hsi Emperor:

> On the tenth day of the second month I began the journey and on the thirteenth
> reached the imperial tomb. The same day I started back. At the tour encampment

on the fourteenth I received your memorial. The entire trip going and returning was exactly to my taste. Today the weather is calm, as before rain or snow, all expressing the concern of [the K'ang-hsi Emperor's] spirit in Heaven and giving me the greatest happiness. I specially write [*t'e-yü*] this to let you know.[155]

Other imperial jottings—addressed to various provincial favorites as well as to Yueh—commented on whatever came to the royal mind. A greetings memorial today bearing a circular stain that looks as if the imperial teacup had been set down on it brought forth a vermilion apology: "This got stained on my table. I worried you might be afraid [that later you could be accused of desecrating an imperial document]." As Pei Huang has remarked, Yung-cheng was like a schoolmaster correcting papers with a red pen. Mistakes and misunderstandings might equally be the focus of the imperial zeal. On one occasion the emperor-schoolmaster even admonished a memorialist not for what he had written but for leaving too many unused extra folds at the end of his report![156]

In an unusually long note from the winter of YC7 (1729), the emperor confessed to Yueh that he had felt "very apprehensive" because of the lack of snow. But, he added, "at the *tzu* hour [11:00 P.M. to 1:00 A.M.] on the 19th the clouds suddenly gathered, and at the *ch'ou* hour [1:00 A.M. to 3:00 A.M.] there was a great snowfall. By the *wu* hour [noon] we had about five or six inches of snow, and as I now write [*yü*] to you, the snow still has not stopped falling." It is "the benevolence of Heaven!" exulted the emperor. "Why has this great happiness come to me? I specially write [*t'e-yü*] to share this happiness with you."

As usual, a spate of imperial afterthoughts followed:

> I have made a selection of auspicious days for you to start on your journey from Sian to the front and am sending it to you. Another point [*tsai*]: [Your son] Yueh Chün is completely recovered. Chung Yüan-fu told me he could take the pills for balanced health and that there would be no point in increasing or reducing the dosage. Accordingly I have ordered Yueh Chün to leave the capital on the 21st to return to his post [in Shantung].

Finally this haphazard series of notes was terminated with yet another afterthought: "Another point. If you will take care of yourself for a few months, [I] can stop worrying." With a redundant flourish the emperor came to a halt: "I have written these [thoughts] as they came to me to let you know."[157] The freedom to set down his thoughts as they came to him was one of the palace memorial system features that strongly appealed to Yung-cheng.

Most striking in the collection of Yueh Chung-ch'i memorials are long letters from the emperor to Yueh. These resemble the palace memorial rescripts— vermilion ink was used and the writing was intended for one person—but their length puts them beyond what is usually regarded as a rescript. Inscribed on sheets of paper with lines ruled to guide the placement of the characters, they could be as long or as brief as the emperor wished. Some are only two or three lines; others stretch in accordion folds for one or two feet and contain twenty or thirty vertical lines of writing. Most follow the classical style and are not punctuated, but the emperor frequently placed small circles at the phrase breaks. These letters are informal, rambling, and spontaneous. They reveal the emperor as uncertain as to what to do, weighing alternatives, seeking Yueh's counsel, and even depending on the general to make high policy decisions and pull off victory. Owing to the emperor's musing half-thought-through ideas, full accurate translations are probably impossible. The two renderings excerpted here attempt to reflect both the tentativeness and the spontaneity of the originals. They illustrate another way that Yung-cheng, a writing emperor, used the new communications system to extend the range and privacy of the inner court to military officers and civilians all over the empire.

The first such letter, probably dating from late YC5 (early 1728), was appended to the draft of a court letter edict based on conversations between Yung-cheng and Prince I. Apparently not completely satisfied with the draft, the emperor continued to think about the problem as he added further comments at the end. He filled the available space on the paper unused by the draft and then went on scribbling on extra sheets of paper. Prince I's draft had described several recent Zunghar cruelties—poisonings, cutting out of eyes, and confinement of enemies to underground dungeons—along with the court's difficulties in figuring out the Zunghars' intentions. The problem now was how to manipulate the Zunghar leadership into giving the Ch'ing the pretext they desired for reopening hostilities. Timing was crucial. The Ch'ing needed to mount their campaign at a moment that would allow their armies the time both to make adequate preparations (a full year was thought desirable) and to set out and carry their march through to victory before the onset of the harsh winter in the Zunghars' homeland.

The Ch'ing search for a pretext focused on the fact that the Zunghars were guilty of harboring Lobdzan Dandzin, the Ch'ing-hai Khoshote rebel of YC2 (1724). The court's plot was to release a Zunghar envoy in Peking with a message demanding that the Zunghars surrender the rebel. But it was difficult to anticipate how the Zunghars would respond. Perhaps they would do as the Ch'ing hoped and refuse to surrender the Khoshote leader, thus providing the excuse for war that Yung-cheng sought. But perhaps they would meekly comply with the Ch'ing demand and send Lobzan Dandzin to Peking, in which case the pretext would collapse. Nonetheless, Yung-cheng hazarded a guess that even if the Zunghars complied, matters could be saved by arranging for the surrender to take place too late. So the first of the problems was how to time the envoy's return.

This letter shows Yung-cheng in an optimistic but indecisive frame of mind, at the start of the first massed thrust against the Zunghars in his own reign. In the letter we may see how the emperor seized the opportunity of the correspondence with Yueh to hold a kind of written conversation, arguing back and forth and contradicting ideas of others (the I Prince, for instance). But in the end he left things up to General Yueh and admitted that he had not in fact firmly made up his mind. The following translation begins in the middle of Yung-cheng's writing.

On the other hand, if [the Zunghar envoy in Peking] sees the great power of our armies and [as a result the Zunghars] surrender Lobdzan Dandzin, the situation will be difficult to deal with [because there will be no pretext for war]. It would be better to let him [the envoy] go back soon and [then] if they do not surrender [Lobzan Dandzin], that would be the best thing possible. In the year after next when our armies arrive [in the northwest], even if they do surrender him [at that late hour], we would [still] have a pretext [for war].... It is my guess that they will not surrender Lobzan Dandzin....

Another point. If we let [the envoy] return early, and if they perceive that my decree is uncompromising and it does not seem that we are talking peace, and possibly they hear of our military preparations, they might plan to take advantage of [us] when we are [still] not fully prepared and in the autumn ravage the frontier.... I have not made up my mind and want to discuss [these matters] with you....

Another point.... I propose that in the early autumn of next year [YC6] we secretly marshal forces in the Altai [Mountains] and in the early spring of [YC7] move forward directly to the E-erh-ch'i-ssu [the Kara Irtysh River]—this will be very easy [because troop strength will not be divided between two fronts].

The I Prince says that these two steps [massing in the Altai one year and then moving forward the next] will only waste a lot of money. Furthermore, he is afraid that [the Zunghars] will make their own preparations on hearing of ours. [According to the I Prince], if we have all rations, camels, and horses ready at the Altai next year when the troops arrive, we can exchange [old animals for new ones] and move forward.... All this can be accomplished [marching straight through] without a long halt. I think what the I Prince said is right. But I think that our troops would reach the E-erh-ch'i-ssu in the seventh or eighth months [1729 July 26–Oct. 21—that is, earlier than the prince estimates]. I hope that we could catch the [Zunghar] harvest [to replenish our supplies], but the prince says we cannot depend on that. [He thinks] if they should hear [of our moves] in advance, they might be unwilling to plant or to leave [their crops in the ground]. [Even if] our troops carry their own seeds for planting, they will have to wait until the next year before they can sow them [and reap a harvest]. What the prince has said is very sound. In my view [the problem] is only that proceeding straight through the Altai to the E-erh-ch'i-ssu [on one long foray instead of a two-stage march] will be difficult. But these are not my unalterable views.

One point: it is not a good idea to discuss this with others—especially [because there are] men sent by the Zunghars [eager to spy out information]. I am exceedingly fearful that at the capital our plans are not secret. Moreover, [here at the capital] I have no informed, sincere men to deal with the empire's affairs—they just listen to me and repeat what I say, or only gauge the direction of my thinking and go along with it. To hold [court] discussions is useless. Accordingly, [you] are to write out all your thoughts on these three problems and send me your views. Think them over carefully, make detailed plans, and memorialize. I will again discuss them with the I Prince and reach decisions.

Another point. How should our armies proceed to the Zunghar area? How should we plan for military colonies on the two fronts? How do these scoundrels wage war? What is the likelihood [of the Zunghars'] fleeing? What methods of entrapment do they employ? What are the chances of their suing for peace? Are their adherents likely to come over to us? How is the pursuit of these scoundrels going? According to your understanding, tell me how we ought to assess the situation. Send me a report in the second or third month [of YC6; 1728 March 11–May 8] so that I may forward instructions to the generals on the northern front as to how the two fronts ought to cooperate.... I don't mind reading whatever comes to your mind. Report [everything] item by item. Even if you first send in a report and then afterward, on thinking it over, feel that it was not exactly right, there is nothing to prevent you from changing.

There was also a hurried afterthought: "Find out Chou K'ai-chieh's eight characters [that is, the characters by which a man's horoscope was analyzed: birth year, month, day, and hour] and send them to me at your convenience—the sooner the better."[158]

A second letter shows the emperor in defeat, in anguish as he contemplates battle losses. Although this letter lies next to the preceding in the archives, it was of a much later—but not identified—date. There is no mention of taking up problems with Prince I, who must have died in the meantime. Together with the tale of Zunghar depredations, this suggests that the letter may have been written late in YC8 (1730). Here the emperor once again opens his heart to his favorite general:

From last year until now, everything has gone awry. I am very nervous, very afraid. It is so painful that I have turned to self recriminations. Item by item everything can be blamed on you and me [chün-ch'en; literally, ruler and minister]. In terms of military tactics it may be said that our overconfident troops have been defeated and we underestimated the enemy's strength—these and our ignorance have been the causes of our defeat. Our side has perpetrated these bad things....

In the period of time in which we made preparations on the two fronts, victories occurred so long ago that I can no longer remember them. In addition to facing Heaven and acknowledging my transgressions, what else can I do...? It is something that, considering what I had seen and heard in the past, I never expected. To undertake the task of campaigning and exterminating the enemy is not merely a matter of brute strength.... As I observe the situation, [it is obvious that] Heaven has not looked favorably on what has happened. Even so, the odds are against us. If you and I again embark on another campaign, our transgressions may be even more unforgivable. But let's just keep this between you and me—the generals need not be told. It is possible that the enemy would take advantage [if they knew of our desperate situation].... If there is any chance for us to take revenge, we don't know about it yet.

These days I only regret my mistakes and beg that the mercy of Heaven will forgive me, [that it will] regard protecting me as important.... But as far as this matter is concerned, even though it was originally your idea, I gave my approval, and I did not do that carelessly. Furthermore, this undertaking is the unfulfilled project of my late imperial father and the great sorrow of this country. You, after all, are a loyal [official] and want to exert your strength [on behalf of the nation] and accord with my ideas. Furthermore, I have no other people except you to take responsibility. Fortunately, I have you and [your] loyal and valorous sincerity, and that is why I have appointed you. If there is any mistake, it is that I did not figure the whole thing out. I have sinned against the clear pronouncements of Heaven and Earth. How could I shamelessly put all the responsibility on you? These truly are words from deepest in my heart. I am afraid that you might not know my feelings. I also am afraid that you might, viewing the present difficulties, be ashamed that your previous promises cannot be fulfilled. Keep doing the best you can—don't lose your head and make a bad mistake.... If you want to do something to repay me, then keep up your strength—don't make any bad move. Hold where you are.[159]

The fact that such imperial letters (the two supplied here are only a selection from a large number in the archives) could be written in the new palace memorial–court letter system shows how the Yung-cheng Emperor had solved one of the problems related to the outer-court autonomy inherited from the Ming. Yung-cheng's development of the inner-court palace memorial system allowed him easily to bypass his bureaucrats and the statutes governing routine system documents and communicate independently, directly, and even at great length with his provincial correspondents. But if an emperor was to write freely on a palace memorial, his spontaneous jottings, musings, and comments had to be strictly locked up in the inner-court files. Outer-court dissemination of defeatist views such as those in the second letter above might have sapped the country's nerve just as battle loomed. It would not have done for the empire to learn that their sovereign felt "nervous and afraid." K'ang-hsi's and Yung-cheng's strengthening of the inner-court communications system supplied the confidentiality that allowed these emperors, and Yung-cheng in particular, to cultivate provincial officials and work out policies in secret.

These letters also provided an answer to the age-old dilemma of frontier generals who had to be kept in check and yet at the same time allowed freedom of independent action at the scene of battle. Yung-cheng's solution was to cast his hopes on Yueh's loyalty, but he first went to great lengths to cultivate that loyalty through his palace memorial correspondence with Yueh. Yung-cheng used the new memorial system to identify prospective servitors and allow them free rein on distant frontiers, doubtless hoping all the while that they would not go off on their own and form new frontier coalitions to plague the dynasty as had happened so often in China's history. Thus these refinements were another way that Yung-cheng fashioned the new inner-court communications into the instrument essential to his vision of autocratic rule.

The Yung-cheng Emperor's search for new government forms grew from the difficulties that the early Manchu emperors had encountered when they attempted to rely on the outer court to discharge the main business of government. The early Manchu monarchs had used only a small coterie of inner-court advisers to deal with secret sensitive issues and otherwise had administered the realm through direct personal dealings with the outer-court boards and agencies. Yung-cheng was dissatisfied with these arrangements. But at the same time his inner court, which was dominated by Manchus and riven by the factionalism of the late K'ang-hsi years, was not adequate to shouldering many additional burdens. New approaches were needed both to deal with these problems and to fight a victorious campaign against the Zunghars.

Yung-cheng's solutions stressed the inner court in two major ways: he expanded that area of government and intensified the role of the monarch as administrator. He threw his energies into the hurly-burly of governing, his long days and half his nights consecrated to the mission of ruling. In this chapter we have seen how hard he worked to take care of details: writing out auspicious days for the start of the military campaign, arguing with Prince I over the timing and routes of march, and examining appointees with care. The emperor even took charge of teacup stains on memorials. Recalling the earthquake scene described at the beginning of the chapter, one is astonished to learn that he had time for boating in the middle of a morning.

But the monarch's frenzied devotion to hard work was not enough. Additional effort was needed. Yung-cheng's inner-court innovations were shaped by the emperor's exasperation with outer-court shortcomings, his dissatisfaction with Manchu princely and grandee dominance in government, and pervasive outer-court corruption. The result was new inner-court bodies that in the early years responded to these imperial requirements and later became the framework for the dynasty's new high privy council.

TWO

Yung-cheng's Inner-Court Assistants: Prince and Grand Secretary

Like his father before him, Yung-cheng did not wish to rule mainly through the distant and unmanageable outer court. Even his direct personal links to the outer court in the form of audiences, responses to documents processed in the outer court, superintendents, grand secretaries, and investigative agencies such as the Audit Bureau were not strong enough to control that vast bureaucracy. In acknowledgment of the difficulties in outer-court governance, both K'ang-hsi and Yung-cheng developed a limited inner-court administration designed to compensate for the outer-court shortcomings of bureaucratic dominance, lack of confidentiality, subservience to administrative regulations, and the conniving and malfeasance they found so unpalatable. But Yung-cheng's approach to a strengthened inner court was different from his father's. K'ang-hsi had chiefly used groups of exalted tradition and statutory authority in his inner court, conferring honor and rank on his inner-court servitors through membership in high-level groups such as the Deliberative Council or the Southern [Imperial] Study. In addition, K'ang-hsi's inner-court organizations had been divided by ethnic group as well as by assigned responsibilities. In contrast, Yung-cheng discouraged and even undermined the statutorily constituted and traditional inner-court entities that he had inherited from his father and in his early years avoided long-established organizations, in their place sometimes appointing ad hoc panels to deal with a particular issue or emergency. But his main early inner-court structural preference was to turn to one or two trusted individuals—men who were close, able confidants on whom he could depend for the utmost in service and loyalty. By this means Yung-cheng expected to rule autocratically, coordinating high policy in his own hands with the assistance of a select handful of inner-court advisers.

Although Yung-cheng tested several individuals at the beginning of his reign, only two, one Manchu and one Chinese, held the emperor's esteem over

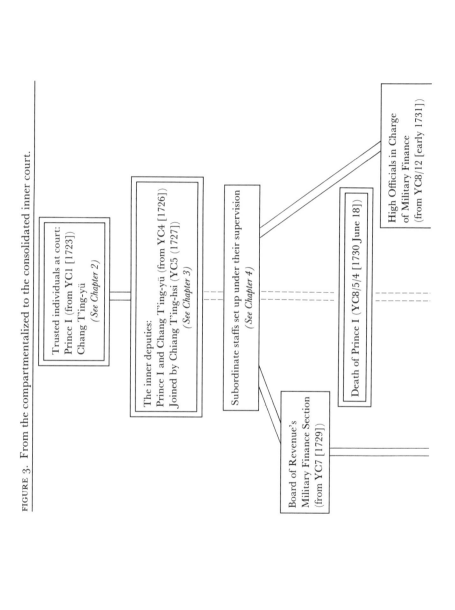

FIGURE 3. From the compartmentalized to the consolidated inner court.

Trusted individuals at court:
Prince I (from YC1 [1723])
Chang T'ing-yü
(*See Chapter 2*)

The inner deputies:
Prince I and Chang T'ing-yü (from YC4 [1726])
Joined by Chiang T'ing-hsi (YC5 (1727])
(*See Chapter 3*)

Subordinate staffs set up under their supervision
(*See Chapter 4*)

Board of Revenue's
Military Finance Section
(from YC7 [1729])

Death of Prince I (YC8/5/4 [1730 June 18])

High Officials in Charge
of Military Finance
(from YC8/12 [early 1731])

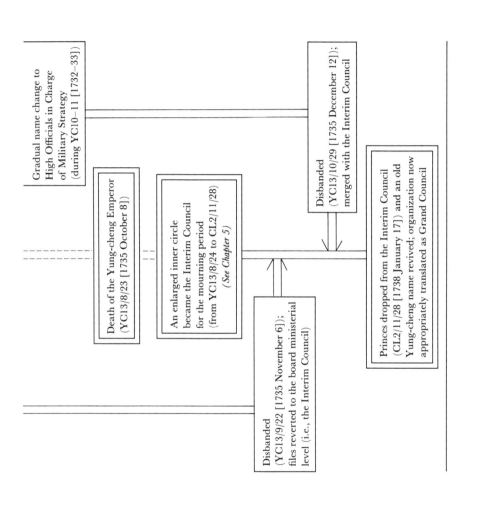

Gradual name change to **High Officials in Charge of Military Strategy** (during YC10–11 [1732–33])

Death of the Yung-cheng Emperor (YC13/8/23 [1735 October 8])

An enlarged inner circle became the Interim Council for the mourning period (from YC13/8/24 to CL2/11/28) (*See Chapter 5*)

Disbanded (YC13/10/29 [1735 December 12]); merged with the Interim Council

Disbanded (YC13/9/22 [1735 November 6]); files reverted to the board ministerial level (i.e., the Interim Council)

Princes dropped from the Interim Council (CL2/11/28 [1738 January 17]) and an old Yung-cheng name revived; organization now appropriately translated as Grand Council the first half of the reign. These were Prince I (Yin-hsiang), a younger half-brother of the emperor, and Chang T'ing-yü, the son of one of K'ang-hsi's grand secretaries. At first Yung-cheng used these two men intermittently and for a variety of tasks. Later they came to assist regularly with general policy-making and supervision of various staffs and committees. Soon they were helping with three of the most pressing problems of the day: finance, the northwest military campaign, and communications. This chapter will describe their contributions and show how for a while they and their small staffs sufficed for most of Yung-cheng's inner-court management needs. No new long-term organizations were set up in the early years. Only when the planning for a renewed northwest military campaign necessitated inner-court labors too great for these two men did they join together as an informal inner-court team that eventually became the nucleus of the Grand Council's top echelon. This development led in turn to the new inner-court organizations that many historians regard as the Grand Council and which I identify as Grand Council antecedents (see Figure 3).

THE I PRINCE, YIN-HSIANG

Prince I (1686–1730) stands out from Yung-cheng's other brothers because of his loyal service at the center of government.[1] As was described in Chapter 1, the Yung-cheng Emperor sparred with many of his brothers in order to end the factional divisions at court and achieve a permanent reduction in the royal princes' influence in government. In the early years of the reign several imperial siblings died under suspicious circumstances, possibly of poisoning. Prince I was an exception to this pattern. He won Yung-cheng's confidence and served with loyalty at the heart of the inner court for the first half of the reign. During these years the emperor depended on this brother more than on any other courtier. The prince provided frank advice as well as administrative talents. Although he never formally held a Grand Council title, some have regarded him as the earliest grand councillor.[2]

   This prince died young, in the middle of the reign, at the age of forty-three. But his contributions to his brother's rule had already been so crucial in his eight years as the emperor's right-hand man that at his death the emperor succumbed to a fit of grief at the loss of his closest confidant. Business at court was suspended for three days.[3] Yung-cheng wrote General Yueh Chung-ch'i that he was so upset he could not write down his feelings about the tragedy in brush and ink. The emperor moaned of his "terrible sorrow," stating that his heart was "adrift."[4] A series of edicts poured forth to mourn the loss; in one the distraught emperor cried that the prince's final illness "has tied my heart in knots and dominated all my waking hours." Other edicts numbly summed up the emperor's anguish with repetitions of the phrase "Eight years have passed as one day."[5] In his turmoil the emperor waxed maudlin, claiming that even the weather had cooperated whenever the prince assisted him—it had been "warm and clear" and "everything went smoothly." Yung-cheng recalled the prince's extreme modesty and suggested that his virtues must now be recognized, for if no one did so, that "would put an end to the prince's goodness." Indeed, the emperor went so far as to ponder the possibility of his own complicity in the prince's death. "Could it be," he mused, "that I have committed a crime against Heaven or against my late father and as a result my loyal and assisting prince has been snatched away so suddenly?"[6]

The final illness and death of the man who bore the princely title "I" ("Harmonious," pronounced *ee*) were a major turning point of the reign. For the seven years before the onset of his illness the prince had been Yung-cheng's chief factotum, "handling all central government affairs," taking on crucial responsibilities, and debating high policy with the emperor. Yung-cheng's own words enumerated the many areas of government with which the prince had been concerned: "state policy, state finance, water conservancy, leadership of the imperial bodyguard, and all internal palace affairs."[7] Moreover, as we saw in Yung-cheng's letters to General Yueh in Chapter 1, the emperor frequently debated military strategy with his brother. In this chapter we shall see how from the beginning the prince was the driving force behind certain financial policies and their implementation. Then Chang T'ing-yü joined him in the ministerial level of the Board of Revenue and brought his talents to bear on some of the pressing financial problems of the day. But Chang was not a beloved, trusted brother of the monarch. Moreover, he was a Chinese. His relationship with the emperor had to be more formal and less confiding than the prince's. This fact alone suggests the extent of Yung-cheng's loss at his brother's death. After that sad event, the emperor appears to have lost his bearings for a time. He was distraught and even suffered ill health. For several months Chang held the central position at court, taking charge of such diverse responsibilities as the emperor's medical treatment and edict drafting.

Although the first half of the reign had been characterized by many new high-level committees and staffs, in general these had been only temporarily set up to handle a specific problem or a facet of a long-term question. Such ad hoc committee assignments continued after Prince I's death, but during these later years, when at first Chang dominated in the inner court, two of the earlier inner-court groups—the inner deputies and the subordinate Military Finance Section—became more solidly established. Later another staff, the High Officials in Charge of Military Strategy, was convened to make recommendations on campaign policy. Finally the great Manchu governor-general O-erh-t'ai was recalled from his post in the southwest to serve at the head of the inner court. Thus, the intensified needs of the northwest campaign, coupled with the loss of the prince who had done so much to help the emperor cope with the campaign, forced a restructuring of the inner court.

Prince I served Yung-cheng in many ways that an ordinary official who was not a close relative could not have done. This was apparent, for instance, in the prince's handling of the touchy questions of intrigue and treachery at court. One of Yung-cheng's long funeral eulogies on the prince described how at the beginning of the reign "A-ch'i-na [Yung-cheng's derogatory name for his despised brother Yin-ssu] harbored evil designs to disrupt the country,"[8] while at the same time "Lung-k'o-to [a high Manchu official and imperial relative] made use of his prestige and fortune to monopolize power and overuse his authority. So," the emperor continued, praising Prince I's handling of these difficulties, "it fell to the prince alone in his magnificent way to bring about an atmosphere of unity in the midst of their wrangling. The result was that in the end these traitors did not attain their goals."

The same eulogy also described how the prince had turned his back on Lung-k'o-to's schemes to impede General Nien Keng-yao's management of the campaign. The prince, said the emperor, had recommended acting "in accordance with the principle of total authority for those in command," throwing full support to the man in charge at the front—in this case, General Nien. Accordingly, said Yung-cheng, "I heeded the prince's advice and thus Lung-k'o-to was unable, from his vantage point in the palace, to impede the campaign any further. As a result Ch'ing-hai was pacified."[9] Introducing "unity in the midst of [the princes'] wrangling" was no small service to the strife-ridden court of the early Yung-cheng years.

Debating high policy with the emperor was another of Prince I's contributions in the early years. The two brothers argued freely and challenged each other's ideas. Yung-cheng several times described how the prince had questioned his thinking or persuaded him to change his mind. For example, when the emperor later recalled the palace intrigues marshaled against General Yueh Chung-ch'i when he was considered for the overlordship on the western front, the edict read:

> Yueh Chung-ch'i is an outstanding official, but [in the early years of the reign] Ts'ai T'ing [a court official] and others with malice insinuated that he had been in the clique of Nien Keng-yao [who had been dismissed under suspicion of disloyalty]. Over and over again they assured me that he could not be counted on. But the prince pleaded with me, arguing that Yueh Chung-ch'i's great abilities and single-minded love of country would not [allow him] to turn his back on the imperial benevolence or ignore what was right. [The prince even] wanted to guarantee him with his own life and property.[10]

These quotations from one of Yung-cheng's mourning edicts show some of the ways the emperor depended on the prince. The edicts, together with many of the handwritten imperial commentaries and other sources of the time, make clear that during his early years Yung-cheng leaned heavily on the prince for advice, help in working out policies, troubleshooting, and a myriad other inner-court tasks.

Prince I, the thirteenth son of the K'ang-hsi Emperor, did not attain prominence until Yung-cheng came to power. Eight years younger than his imperial brother and thirty-seven years old at the death of his father, he had not been given important responsibilities during his father's reign.[11] The day after K'ang-hsi's death the new emperor raised him to a first-degree princedom[12] and gave him his first of several inner-court appointments, a place on the four-member Plenipotentiary Council (set up to assist during the mourning period).[13] A month later the prince was given his first high responsibility when he was put in charge of the Three Treasuries (*San-k'u*), a key post at the Board of Revenue.[14] In this capacity, as well as in two other posts that he shortly took over—head of the Audit Bureau (*Hui-k'ao fu*) and superintendent (*tsung-li*) of the Board of Revenue—the prince dealt with the depleted imperial treasury, malefactions in the Board of Revenue, and decades of unpaid taxes.[15]

Prince I and the Financial Crisis

At the beginning of the reign Yung-cheng was challenged by an array of financial problems ranging from mismanagement to outright corruption. One area—the tax arrears inherited from the late K'ang-hsi years—will illustrate Prince I's assistance to the emperor in the thorny realms of state finance.[16] The tax crisis consisted of a very large shortage—some say as much as 2.5 million taels—in the Board of Revenue accounts.[17] Early in the reign, problems of this type had been handed to the Plenipotentiary Council, which would then frequently hold discussions with the appropriate outer-court boards. But soon the emperor turned his back on these organizations, taking the financial weakness of the realm out of their jurisdiction. Increasingly he came to depend on the I Prince acting either alone in his capacity as Board of Revenue superintendent or jointly with a small number of specially designated high-level officials.

According to Yung-cheng's own description of how the tax arrears policies were decided and administered in the early years of the reign, the prince sought ways to replenish the state treasury without overburdening the debtor-officials or their families and descendants. One of his proposals was that the central government gradually pay off the shortages by tapping parts of two tax surcharges: the silver-purity fee (called *p'ing-yü* in Yung-cheng's description) and the food money payments (*fan-shih yin*).[18]

But Yung-cheng objected to the prince's proposals. They were too lenient and failed to punish the miscreants who had caused the shortages. The emperor thought it only fair that the accounts be cleared by either the defaulting taxpayers themselves or their descendants. In a long edict dating from after the prince's death Yung-cheng recalled his disagreements with the prince on this issue:

> My view was that for many years those officials who had been in charge [of provincial finances] had eaten away the national treasure and treated with contempt the laws of the land; if we did not force them to make restitution, why

should they obey the financial [regulations] and how would we ever get rid of corruption? Therefore, I did not approve what the prince had sought, but ordered that he draw up a report [with the details of those who owed money] so that they would be forced to repay.

At first [as we discussed this] the prince changed his expression [*pien-se*, meaning he was visibly upset]. But afterward, he obeyed my decree and fully carried it through. As a result, people at the capital and in the provinces only knew that the Board of Revenue had had unpaid debts for many years and that these had been brought to light by Prince I. There were uninformed small-minded persons who said that the prince had gone to excess in seeking out [those who owed money—that is, he had been too harsh] and who did not realize that the prince had asked that men be spared repayment and requested that he pay instead [with the purity fee and food money fund]....

Now for several years [in accordance with my will, not the prince's] the debts have been traced to the names of the [defaulting] officials. [But these payments have accounted for] less than ten or twenty percent [of the total], and Prince I, using the purity fee and food money fund, has paid up eighty or ninety percent for them.

Toward the end of this recollection the emperor revealed his negative view of his provincial officials and their greed and irresponsibility in failing to pay what they owed; he also described how Prince I's arguments had influenced policy even when the two men were not in agreement:

As for this money that the officials ought to have paid over and which had not been paid, how could we just forget it? As for these crimes, how could we forgive them?

This spring [YC8; 1730], when I saw that the prince was ill and not getting well, I thought of what the prince had so earnestly beseeched in the past and handed down a special edict forgiving the debts of those officials who had not yet repaid, in accordance with what the prince had wanted from the beginning....

In the past the prince had told me, "Your Majesty's methods are rather severe." My response was that men's disposition is to shirk responsibility, a hundred kinds of malfeasance have been with us ere long, multiplying in abundance. If at the present time we fail to punish [these miscreants], in the future there will be no end [to our problems]. Thus, although I did not [always] follow the prince's advice at the time, nevertheless, the prince's generous and loyal intentions were never even for a day not held in my heart.

The emperor concluded this part of his soliloquy by affirming that "bribe seeking, taking from the treasury, and acting in a traitorous fashion are all gradually disappearing among the lower bureaucrats." Although Yung-cheng clearly believed in stern taxation methods, these changes, he admitted, had been brought about by the prince's policies at the Board of Revenue.[19] The edict bears witness to the prince's high-level role in serving at the head of the Board of Revenue, debating policy alternatives with the emperor, and implementing the policies that eventually replenished the treasury reserves. It also shows how occasionally the prince persuaded the emperor to change his mind.

Many of Prince I's surviving memorials also affirm his central role in the financial problems of the day. As superintendent of the Board of Revenue he was in charge of policy discussions undertaken by the board directorate and middle-level staff. (A board directorate consisted of officials at the three highest levels—superintendent, presidents, and vice presidents; see Figure 2). The memorials that carry the prince's name at the head of the list of discussers took up many financial problems, including various tax arrears cases—payments, punishments, promotions, and leniency.

One of these, a joint Manchu–Chinese-language (*Man-Han ho-pi*) memorial of YC2 (1724), for example, was produced in concert by the boards of Revenue and Civil Office, the latter having been brought in because some of the unpaid taxes threatened promotion chances for the responsible officials still in office. The conclusion was that since the arrears were of fairly recent date (KH58; 1719) the time limit for payment had not yet been reached and the taxes were not technically in arrears; the matter was postponed for reconsideration should formal impeachment become necessary.[20] A similar deliberation of YC4 (1726) considered a provincial governor's insistence that a district magistrate be denied promotion because he had exceeded the time limit for handing over his district's back taxes. The board directorate lightened the governor's harsh stand and recommended that the man be restored to his career because the taxes for KH60 and 61 (1721 and 1722) had been paid and only those of YC1 (1723) remained; most of the money could easily be forwarded to the capital, they thought, and the only appropriate punishment would be a small fine deducted from his salary.[21] One memorial on a financial topic went into such detail that it ran on for eighty-six folds—more than fifteen feet of writing in the Chinese half of the document alone.[22]

These memorials and others like them display the accomplishments that Yung-cheng attributed to his brother—painstaking consideration of each case, leniency rather than the harshness that the emperor desired, mild penalties when necessary, and deft arrangements to get the missing sums repaid. Gradually, through a combination of rigor and compassion coupled with the banking of small fees, the Board of Revenue arrears were cleared. Indeed, the financial wizardry of the prince and his staff was so successful that according to a laudatory edict, the problem of the K'ang-hsi tax arrears had been resolved by mid-reign; in the process the prince had even amassed an extra ten million taels to help finance the northwest campaign against the Zunghars.[23]

In addition to tax arrears, the prince's memorials show his concern with other aspects of the economic life of the realm. One proposal urged punishments for two kinds of improper connivances between provincial and board officials known as "adding the weight" (*chia-p'ing*) and "adding the touch" (*chia-se*). The former functioned by having the board ignore shortages in tax shipments in return for a cut of the illegal spoils; the latter resulted in excess touch being required for the silver sent to the capital. In both kinds of malefaction the provincial and board officials split the illegal take.[24] In another memorial, the prince urged the reduction of the old heavy taxes on Kiangnan and Chekiang rice and silk that had been imposed as long before as the fourteenth century.[25] Still another memorial wrestled with problems arising from Ch'ing bimetallism, pondering which coinage, copper or silver, should be required for tax payments; in the end the deliberation rejected the argument that the very poor should be given the option of paying their taxes in copper rather than silver (because copper was not as good a store of value as silver).[26] Another position paper considered the complexities of interest owed on government money invested at Chin-chiang.[27]

Most of the early Prince I financial memorials were submitted as Board of Revenue deliberations, listing many middle and high board members as authors—one document had seventeen names at the end and reached deep into the board's departments for contributors to the discussions. Although the prince may not have thought up all the solutions presented in these documents, as the highest-ranking board member he guided the deliberations and may have drafted some of the recommendations himself. Deservedly, these position papers won the emperor's esteem for the man who had so adroitly managed the deliberations. Thus, it was for his early work in finance that the prince first gained the new emperor's trust.

Prince I and Water Conservancy

In YC3/12 (early 1726) the prince was given the title "Managing Water Conservancy Matters in the Capital Area" (*Tsung-li chi-fu shui-li shih*) and put in charge of the long-standing problem of the Yung-ting River floods near the capital.[28] Once again he was a success. The situation was investigated, proposals submitted and approved, channels dug. Chihli province survived the following year's rainy season with floods and landslides appreciably diminished.[29]

After Prince I took over the management of Chihli's water conservancy problems, Yung-cheng began to ignore the boards and other established organizations that might have dealt with this kind of problem, relying instead on his favorite brother to handle all matters connected with the post. On one occasion even a low-level appointment in the water conservancy project was referred to the prince rather than to the responsible board. This happened in YC4 (1726), when the Chihli governor-general submitted a palace memorial asking for a decision about applying the rule of avoidance to a man posted to a water conservancy project.[30] The imperial rescript ordered the material rewritten in a routine memorial. When it arrives, wrote the emperor, "I will see what the I Prince has to say." Thus Yung-cheng planned to follow the proper procedures: the board would receive the memorial and go through the motions of preparing its views; but at the same time he anticipated that he might decide to ignore the board recommendation and accept the prince's advice instead.[31] Once again, in water conservancy as in other areas, the emperor revealed his predilection for relying on high-level inner-court assistants, especially a top trusted favorite, rather than statutory outer-court organizations.

Honors for Prince I

Yung-cheng's appreciation of his brother's loyalty, rectitude, and financial acumen stood out in contrast with his anguished relations with most of his other brothers. At the end of the first year of the reign, for example, the emperor held up Prince I as a model, at the same time disparaging the behavior of his other siblings: "Among my brothers are several men lacking in self-restraint. When my late father was alive, they neither stopped nor stayed [in their pursuit of] manifold plans to plunder the national treasury.... I desire to set the prince's goodness before all and shame my worthless brothers."[32] As a result, the emperor attempted to lavish honors on his good brother. In YC4 (1726), the emperor bestowed a horizontal tablet (*pien-e*) on the prince, eulogizing him as "loyal, upright, prudent, and incorruptible." The accompanying widely promulgated edict named nine specific areas in which the prince had "given his utmost to serve with loyalty and devotion." At the top of the list was "counsel on government affairs of the highest importance." This was followed by the prince's work at the Board of Revenue and the Three Treasuries and in the Chihli water conservancy post. The last five items together showed how the prince was given one of the most sacred'trusts of the realm: the guarding of the imperial person. This included responsibilities for imperial bodyguards, matters affecting the royal princes, the emperor's residence before he came to the throne, Summer Palace (*Yuan-ming yuan*) guards, and the supervision and remodeling of the imperial residence in Peking (the Yang-hsin Pavilion). The edict added that the prince had "alone planned and administered" this great variety of responsibilities "from the broadest scope down to the smallest detail."[33] In another edict issued after the prince's death, the emperor described the prince's services with a verb generally employed for prime ministers (*fu-pi*), adding that on occasion the prince had even "substituted for me" (*tai-chen*).[34] Such imperial eulogizing was rare.

How was the I Prince able so successfully to thread his way upward through the thickets of court gossip and conspiracies and at the same time win the respect of a ruler often regarded as suspicious and mistrustful? Probably most important was the fact that the prince had played little or no part in the succession struggles that had clouded the end of his father's reign. The Yung-cheng Emperor admired this circumspect behavior, saying: "During my father's time [the prince] respectfully [conducted himself] with self-discipline and integrity and did not take part in any schemes for his own private interest or join in cliques ... not like my other brothers who in various ways troubled my late father's heart."[35]

In addition, the prince adroitly forestalled the imperial suspicion by refusing all honors and awards and cultivating a posture of lack of personal ambition. The historical record on these matters is full of Yung-cheng's satisfaction with such rectitude. Although it was good Chinese practice to refuse an honor three times, acceptance was permissible on the fourth offer. But no matter what money or honors were at stake, Prince I continued adamantly to refuse. There was one instance at the end of the first year of the reign when he finally but most reluctantly agreed to accept part of a large gift of money that the emperor was distributing to all first-degree princes. But other subsidies were "most earnestly" declined.[36] On occasion even honors conferred on his son were not found acceptable.[37] In one of the mourning edicts, the emperor praised the simplicity of his brother's life, pointing to the frugality of his household accounts and the fact that his residence possessed only three gates and five pavilions and halls, circumspectly in agreement with regulations.[38] Such upright behavior, coupled with the prince's lack of desire for gain, won the emperor's confidence. The prince seems to have known that it was not enough to cast his lot with the new monarch; faced with an emperor who had reacted strongly to those brothers who had challenged him for the throne, he seems to have cultivated as unthreatening an appearance as possible. He was rewarded with the highest possible encomium: the emperor's satisfaction that he had "wholeheartedly" supported him, always playing "the proper role of an official or younger brother."[39] In the politics of the day this course of action was probably the best one to follow.

Prince I and the Northwest Military Campaign

As we saw in Yung-cheng's epistles to General Yueh at the end of Chapter 1, the prince was also concerned with another of the pressing problems of his times—the northwestern military campaign. Plans for the foray against the Zunghar Mongols intensified only in late YC4 (1726), when, as the emperor later recollected,

> [the problem of] military provisions for the northern front was turned over to the late Prince I and others to handle, and western-front military supplies were put under the charge of General Yueh Chung-ch'i to supervise. All of this began in YC4 [1726] ... and was carried on for several years without either the officials or the people knowing that troops were being marshaled. Then when the military crisis came in YC7 [1729], we were [able to] ship supplies [to the front].[40]

Prince I's role in discussing the campaign with the emperor is attested in a long undated edict to General Yueh written in Yung-cheng's vermilion script probably sometime during late YC5 (early 1728). In this document (which is extensively quoted at the end of Chapter 1 above), the prince was cited as having advocated a quick surprise swoop on the Zunghar Mongols in preference to lengthy, costly, and obvious preparations that the Zunghars would be sure to hear about in advance. The prince was also said to have warned that the plan of depending on Zunghar harvests to support Chinese troops on campaign in the far west might meet with disappointment, especially if the surprise element of the campaign was lost and the enemy was foresighted enough to destroy crops before fleeing. Toward the end of this letter Yung-cheng asked General Yueh to send in his own detailed plans for the campaign, adding: "I will then take them up with the I Prince." From the earliest days, the prince's talents for strategic planning as well as financial management won him a central role in the campaign.[41]

In the middle of YC7 (1729), military preparations were intensified and became openly discussed in the capital. The prince was given the title "In Charge of Military Affairs on the Northern and Western Fronts" (*Pan-li hsi-pei liang-lu chün-chi*) and now directed the campaign from the capital. At the same time, the Board of Revenue Military Finance Section (*Chün-hsu fang*) was established as an independent unit responsible to the ministerial level of the Board of Revenue, with Prince I, in his capacity as Board of Revenue superintendent, serving as the new section's topmost but part-time supervisor (see Figure 3).[42] These titles and posts meant that in addition to discussing campaign policy with the emperor, the prince now directed a staff of subordinates at the capital who were specially concerned with military supply.[43] In addition, he took charge of many deliberations on campaign matters, and his name headed the list of deliberators in those memorials. Had his death not intervened he would probably have continued in this central role.

Prince I and Communications Management

The prince may also have had a hand in the development of inner-court communications management. Part of the assault on tax arrears and financial malfeasance, for instance, included new communications management procedures for accounting and filing at the Board of Revenue. In YC2 (1724), the prince had petitioned for an additional second-class secretary at the board to handle archives, note down figures, and help check the year-end financial reports from the provinces—activities designed to reduce malefactions in financial reports.[44] The prince's organizational work at the Board of Revenue may also have been responsible for the improvement in financial statistics that is observable beginning with figures for the Yung-cheng period.[45]

Prince I was also concerned with some of the developments in the palace memorial system that took place during the early part of the reign. When the provincial reporting net was broadened to include provincial lieutenant governors and treasurers, the prince's office was frequently designated as a marshaling point for the new reports.[46] The prince may have had a role in confidential imperial audiences, for one of Yung-cheng's handwritten comments recalled a top-secret audience conversation at which the prince had clearly been present.[47] Prince I was also involved with the inauguration of the court letter (chi-hsin or t'ing-chi) system, a secret method developed to help the emperor respond to palace memorials. The imperial vermilion calligraphy on the earliest surviving archival example of an actual court letter names the prince as having noted down the emperor's words; other early examples of this new type of edict carry his name at the head of the rosters of those who discussed edict content with the emperor.[48] The prince also took charge of transmitting certain imperial directives, some of which were regarded as too confidential to be committed to writing.[49] We know too that he organized numerous discussions involving Board of Revenue and other court officials and was thereby concerned with the expansion of the discussion memorial (i-fu tsou-che) feature of the palace memorial system.

Prince I also oversaw the editing and publishing of Yung-cheng's Grand Secretariat edicts (the work known as Shang-yü Nei-ko).[50] In later years editorial work on many of the dynasty's official publications became an important inner-court task, and the grand councillors not only headed but also frequently dominated the editorial boards of the major official productions of their day. Inner-court concern with the official publications process was not well advanced during Prince I's tenure as unofficial adviser to the throne; this was another facet of inner-court strength that was only beginning to develop during the K'ang-hsi and Yung-cheng years.

The I Prince did not live to assist his brother beyond mid-reign. The untimely loss of the royal sibling, friend, and high minister led to a broken-hearted imperial eulogy: "There was nothing, no matter how great or small, that the prince did not take charge of and manage, nothing that he did not attend to in all detail and deal with in such a satisfactory fashion that my heart was completely at peace."[51] Historians have usually written eagerly about Yung-cheng's brothers in terms of the lurid tales of their wrangling for the throne. Now from archival records of the emperor's own composition we have an imperial tribute to one prince's devoted service.

The prince had two chief inner-court successors: the Chinese official Chang T'ing-yü, who had played an important role in the inner court from the beginning of the reign; and the Manchu O-erh-t'ai, who was recalled to the capital service from the provinces only late in the reign, in YC10 (1732). Because of his longer inner-court service, Chang will be the focus of the remainder of this chapter. His story shows one way that Yung-cheng attempted to fill the gap left by Prince I's death and how once again the emperor was fortunate in his highest associates. Chang could not replace Prince I; he could never be as close to Yung-cheng or speak as frankly to him. But in his moment at the top he made a different kind of contribution, for several significant organizational changes were made during Chang's tenure. In the end his achievements may have been even more lasting than Prince I's.

CHANG T'ING-YÜ

During the early years of his reign Yung-cheng tried out several inner-court associates, winnowing out those who would not do and promoting the others and increasing their responsibilities. Of these, the one who served the longest and in the highest capacity was Chang T'ing-yü (1672–1755). Chang had an unusual career. A Chinese who won the confidence of three Manchu emperors, he held several top inner-court posts. Yet he was very different from Prince I. There is no evidence, such as the enthusiastic imperial affirmations that attest Prince I's central role, that Chang approached parity with the prince or was ever able to act as forthrightly when face to face with his sovereign. Yet for several years following the death of Prince I—until O-erh-t'ai was summoned back from the southwest to the capital in YC10 (1723)—Chang was Prince I's chief successor in the inner court. For a few years Chang was even the major means by which Yung-cheng further developed his inner court.

Relatively few documents survive to help us tell Chang's story. Because Chang was at the emperor's beck and call in the inner court he was not, like General Yueh, the recipient of long vermilion imperial confidences. Moreover, although imperial writing occasionally refers to and even praises Chang's services and his name appears on many of the court letter rosters, nowhere do we find the equivalent of Yung-cheng's frequent mentions of Prince I's conversations and even arguments with the emperor. There is also a shortage of Chang's own writing. The palace memorials of all capital officials were excluded from the great compendium of memorials of his day, the *Imperial Vermilion Rescripts* [*on the Palace Memorials*] (*Chu-p'i yü-chih*).[52] As for Chang's writings that do survive, of necessity they were swathed in formality and clouded with deference. Even his chronological autobiography (*tzu-ting nien-p'u*) strictly adhered to the stultifying form of an official autobiography and lacks spontaneous comments and personal insights. In what follows I have employed these scattered sources to piece together Chang's role at court, a subject worthy of study because for several years after Prince I's death Chang worked alone at the head of the inner court and was involved in most of the major problems of the day.

Chang T'ing-yü During the K'ang-hsi Reign

Chang T'ing-yü's family background was the springboard of his career. He came from a prominent Anhwei landholding and literati family who in the preceding generations had begun to do well in the civil-service examinations and achieve high office.[53] His father, Chang Ying, had served the K'ang-hsi Emperor closely, was a member of the prestigious inner-court Southern Study, and at retirement held the post of grand secretary. Chang T'ing-yü made an unpromising start on his career by achieving a low examination score for the highest degree (*chin-shih*)—215th, which placed him in the third and lowest group of his KH39 (1700) class of 305 men. Such a score would ordinarily have meant that he would have been rusticated as a district magistrate, but because of his illustrious family connections he immediately won the opportunity for further study and a prestigious position as a Hanlin Academy corrector.[54] In the two decades remaining in the K'ang-hsi reign he advanced steadily, receiving appointments as a member of the Southern Study, diarist, Hanlin expositor, subchancellor of the Grand Secretariat, official lecturer on the classics to the emperor, and, at the very end of the reign, vice president on the boards of Civil Office and Punishments.[55]

Chang T'ing-yü's Official Posts During the Early Yung-cheng Reign
Immediately following the death of the K'ang-hsi Emperor, Yung-cheng began to use Chang, who was his senior by six years, in a variety of assignments. He drew on Chang's literary abilities and Hanlin experience by appointing him to the editorial boards of official publications, supervisory examination posts, and the roster of princely tutors.[56] Chang's editorial positions included being vice-director of the Veritable Records Office, director-general of the Ming History Project, and director-general of the State History Office.[57] Because he was a member of the Southern Study, Chang was thus being used as an inner-court link to certain outer-court publications agencies. These assignments were important. Through historical publications the dynasty promulgated its own interpretation of events and determined how its achievements would be understood by future generations. The *Veritable Records* of the K'ang-hsi reign, for example, is said to have suppressed details of Yung-cheng's dubious maneuvers to attain the throne, an editorial assignment that was masterminded by Chang T'ing-yü.[58]

Family background may have given Chang his high start, but Chang also possessed genuine abilities. One of the emperor's edicts of YC7 (1729), for instance, praises Chang's excellent memory: "Ever since Chang T'ing-yü became a grand secretary [in YC4; 1726] he has listened to what I say and has been able to note it down entire, copying it out and sending it up for me to go over. [What he writes] tallies with what I have said." The remainder of this edict makes clear that the emperor's other edict writers were not so accomplished.[59] As we shall see in the next chapter (and particularly in Table 2 there), Chang's name appeared more often than any other official's in the draft court letter rosters of the time. There is also evidence that Chang enhanced his usefulness to the throne by taking the trouble to learn Manchu well. The Ch'ien-lung Emperor occasionally rescripted the Manchu half of Chang's board memorials, writing in Manchu to do so, something he did not usually do for other Chinese officials. And under both Yung-cheng and Ch'ien-lung, Chang was appointed to several editorial posts that required Manchu (the imperial clan genealogy, the Manchu terminology section of the official Chin history, and the Nurhaci *Veritable Records* that chronicled the history of the dynasty's founding leader).[60] Such positions were usually filled by Manchus and were unusual for a Chinese.

Chang's rise in the top levels of the central government began as early as the first year of the Yung-cheng reign. His first board presidency—at the Board of Rites—was conferred less than a month after the K'ang-hsi Emperor's death. Toward the end of the first year he was elevated to the much more important presidency of the Board of Revenue. In this capacity Chang, rather than Prince I, was sometimes in charge of the financial policy debates that led to memorialized recommendations prepared under his aegis.[61] Later Chang became part of the top Board of Revenue team that masterminded preparations for the northwest campaign. In YC3 (1725), the emperor appointed Chang to the newly created office of assistant grand secretary (*hsieh-pan ta-hsueh-shih*); at the same time, however, to set him apart from two others who were also promoted to the same rank that year, Yung-cheng further awarded him the more prestigious designation of "acting grand secretary" (*shu ta-hsueh-shih*).[62] These were trial appointments, some with new titles probably invented by the emperor—favorite imperial devices designed to try out new men slowly and prevent ambitious and gifted officials from rising too fast. The award of such titles to Chang T'ing-yü suggests that early in the reign Yung-cheng had identified Chang as an official to be brought along with care in the hope that he would prove both talented and loyal. As we shall see, these imperial hopes were to be fulfilled.

Chang's early promotions were soon followed by a progress through the ranks of the grand secretaryship: first, in YC4 (1726), he became grand secretary of the not so prestigous Wen-yuan Pavilion; next he was awarded the slightly higher title of Wen-hua Palace Grand Secretary; finally, in YC6 (1728), he was honored with the highest possible appellation, Grand Secretary of the Pao-ho Palace.[63] Shortly after this Chang was observed at work in the inner court rather than at the distant Grand Secretariat premises far away in the southeastern corner of the palace. One eighteenth-century observer later recalled the time he had been sent to serve briefly in the inner court in YC8 (1730), and described Chang as an "inner grand secretary" (*nei chung-t'ang*) and even as "prime minister" (*shou-k'uei*).[64] As an inner-court confidant, Chang dealt chiefly with palace memorials and the court letter edicts (*t'ing-chi*) rather than with the outer-court routine memorials. As a result, a special appointment of an extra assistant grand secretary ensured that Chang's outer-court responsibility for reading the routine memorials would not be ignored.[65]

At this juncture (after YC4; 1726), Chang's tenure at the Board of Revenue presented a complex situation. Ordinarily a board directorate (*t'ang*) consisted of two presidents, one Manchu and one Chinese, and four vice presidents, two

FIGURE 4. Anomalies in the Board of Revenue directorate after it acquired its second superintendent in YC4 (1726).

Superintendents

Prince I
(from YC1/4/7)

Chang T'ing-yü
(from YC4/2/28)

Presidents

Manchu president: Hsu-yuan-meng	Chinese president: Chiang T'ing-hsi (from YC4/2/28: appointed grand secretary "concurrently as before to be in charge of the Board of Revenue presidency")

Vice Presidents

Ch'ang-shou	P'ei Shuai-tu
Sai-te	Wu Shih-yü

This diagram shows an unusual situation at the head of the Board of Revenue after Chang T'ing-yü was elevated to grand secretary on YC4/2/28 (1726 Mar. 31). Although commanded at the time to continue his board president duties, his name no longer appeared in the board tables, a signal that he had risen to the level of board superintendent. A similar situation occurred two years later when Chiang T'ing-hsi was likewise elevated to grand secretary and also ordered at the same time to continue his former board president duties. But in the latter case, Chiang's name was not removed from the board presidency list in the official board tables, so his superintendency—if as grand secretary he had one—was of a level different from Chang's, just as Chang's, with its use of the identifying verb "to direct" (*kuan*), was different from Prince I's post, which was identified with the verb "to superintend" (*tsung-li*).

   SOURCES: *Ch'ing-shih* 4:2609ff.; *Ch'ing-tai chih-kuan nien-piao* 1:204–9.

Manchu and two Chinese, in fulfillment of the dynastic principle of dyarchy, or evenhandedness, in balancing Manchu and Chinese influence in government. Evenhandedness at the Board of Revenue, however, had been in abeyance since the first year of the reign because a strong Manchu board superintendent, the I Prince, had been superimposed above the two board presidents. But things changed again after Chang was appointed grand secretary in YC4 (1726) with the order to "continue as before in charge of [*jeng-kuan*] the Board of Revenue presidency."

At this point, even though he still had board president responsibilities, Chang's name disappeared from the official board president list, to be replaced by Chiang T'ing-hsi.[66] The Board of Revenue now had three heads with three different designations: Prince I was the "superintendent" (*tsung-li*); Chang T'ing-yü held the anomalous post that was variously known by the characters for "to direct" (*kuan* or *li*) or to deal "concurrently" (*chien*) with "board president affairs" (*shang-shu shih-wu*); and Chiang T'ing-hsi was identified with the title ordinarily used for board president.[67] (There was also a Manchu board president, but he seems not to have played a strong role.) As Figure 4 shows, this unusual structure was not a triumvirate of equals but rather a finely tuned hierarchy of Manchu superintending overlord at the top, an ordinary Chinese board president below, and Chang T'ing-yü floating somewhere in between. If the situation seems perplexing, that may have been just what Yung-cheng desired.

Honors for Chang T'ing-yü

Chang's upward rise to posts at the center of government was accompanied by imperial honors and gifts. Like Prince I, he regularly refused many of these; nevertheless they were usually awarded anyway following the required displays of reluctance and modesty. Thus over his protests he received a pawnshop, a residence (the Ch'eng-huai villa), honorific horizontal plaques, and on several occasions substantial gifts of money (the records show enormous gifts of ten, twenty, and even thirty-five thousand taels).[68] In YC8 (1730), when an imperial award of twenty thousand taels was "earnestly refused," the emperor declared he was "not to refuse again."[69] Yet because of his privileged position close to the throne, it may have been better for Chang to avoid the appearance of being an imperial favorite and forgo as many imperially bestowed honors as possible. In YC11 (1733) Chang was given another honor—special permission for a trip to his native place, T'ung-ch'eng in Anhwei province (his first in twenty-three years)—to take part in ceremonies in memory of his father. In addition to a handsome sum for travel expenses, the emperor granted him the privilege of using imperial post-service horses and grooms and ordered local troops and officials to protect and greet him at suitable points along his journey—rarely bestowed marks of imperial favor.[70]

Yung-cheng's congratulatory eulogizing words, sometimes in his own hand, were another sign of imperial favor frequently bestowed on Chang. In his autobiography, Chang describes how at the time of the triennial Metropolitan Inspection in YC7 (1729) he handed in his resignation as required. The Grand Secretariat drafted the responding decree (*p'iao*) approving the dismissal, but, as Chang proudly relates, the emperor "did not make use of it." Instead "the emperor took up his own brush to write the response." The resulting edict praised Chang as "calm and upright, of broad scholarship," and added that ever since his appointment he had "toiled from dawn to dusk to deal with the myriad affairs of state to render assistance [to the emperor]."[71] Another imperial gift was a horizontal plaque (*pien-e*), whose four characters complimented him on his "fine service."[72] Even though Yung-cheng held tight the reins of government, fostering competitiveness and dispensing promotions sparingly, he was well aware of the great ability that underlay Chang's service and used his power of reward appropriately.

The importance of refusing imperial honors, especially those that might be publicly promulgated, is illustrated by Chang's audience conversations concerning the *chin-shih* examination rank of his eldest son, Chang Jo-ai. At the top of every *chin-shih* examination graduation list was a small, specially honored class of the three men who had placed the highest in all the empire that year. In YC11 (1733), Jo-ai won the third place in that top class for the year, the so-called *t'an-hua* rank.

Faced with this high honor for his son, Chang carried the ritual of refusals far beyond the prescribed three. Chang's autobiography records that when the eunuch first came to announce the good news, Chang immediately sought an audience with the emperor and, "taking off his hat and kowtowing," asked that his son be excused this honor. The debate proceeded, Chang earnestly and modestly wishing to avoid the honor—"to put him in the second class would be sufficiently generous"—and the emperor assuring Chang that when judging the examinations he had not known it was Jo-ai's paper he was assigning to the third place of the top class. As the autobiography relates: "T'ing-yü again knocked his head on the ground [in a kowtow] begging [to be excused], but as before [the emperor] refused and instead picked up the examination and wrote his decision on the cover, ordering the examining officials to announce it with the posted results." But this was not the end of the matter. In yet another audience on the subject, the emperor bestowed a scepter on Chang. Chang thanked his sovereign "and as before took off his hat and kowtowed," but the emperor remained adamant in his refusal to lower Jo-ai's examination rank. Once again the father argued: "These great examinations take place only once every three years.... Several tens of thousands took the preliminary *chü-jen* examinations, and only a thousand or so passed; of those who came to the capital for the metropolitan examination little more than three hundred passed. To attain the third place in the top class [of three] ... is too much." Finally the emperor relented. Jo-ai was demoted to fourth place, being denied membership in the top class of three examination honorees and instead listed at the head of the large second class.[73]

This tale of ritual courtesies and entreaties is significant not so much for what it tells us about Chang Jo-ai's scholarly ability as for what it reveals about Chang's relations with both his sovereign and other court officials of his day. The son's demotion from such a high honor was a small price to pay to deflect the jealousy of other officials. Chang could accept private eulogies and unpublicized gifts from the emperor; he could not risk a great public honor without the dangerous appearance of being an imperial favorite who took advantage of his position to win undeserved preference. Moreover, in the same year another high inner-court official, O-erh-t'ai, had a son and a nephew in the same *chin-shih* class. For Chang to gain such a high honor for someone in his own family while O-erh-t'ai's relatives placed lower might have led to difficulties with the man who was his chief colleague as well as his rival in the inner court.

Chang T'ing-yü's High Role After the Death of Prince I

During YC8, 9, and 10 (1730–32) Chang T'ing-yü received another informal promotion and imperial recognition of his great talents. At this point the vacuum in administration following the death of the I Prince was intensified by the emperor's own indisposition—an illness that may have been exacerbated by the loss of the prince. Chang was called on to step into the breach and describes the situation in his autobiography: "From spring to autumn [of YC8; 1730] the emperor was not feeling well; he ordered myself, with the Grand Secretaries Ma-erh-sai [Marsai, a new inner-court servitor] and Chiang T'ing-hsi, to take charge of all government matters. In addition, we were to discuss prescriptions for the [emperor's] recovery with the imperial doctor. Occasionally, if there were any secret edicts, I was to stay [and handle them] alone."[74]

The following year offered other occasions when Chang single-handedly assisted Yung-cheng. Beginning late in YC8 (early 1731), for instance, when the northwest campaign was renewed, "The emperor was extremely careworn and ordered [me] to be on duty in the inner court. From morning till evening, I did not dare leave. Sometimes I waited on the emperor until the first or second drum [8:00–10:00 P.M. or 10:00–12:00 P.M.]. This continued until the ninth month [of YC9; 1731], when the military affairs became quieter."[75]

Yung-cheng depended so greatly on Chang T'ing-yü that once when Chang fell ill the emperor joked that because he had previously called Chang "his arm and his leg," now that Chang was sick he, the emperor, was stricken too.[76] A Grand Secretariat clerk briefly on duty at the Summer Palace later recalled that in YC8 (1730) Chang had sat "alone in a room in the western part of the Southern Study," close to the imperial quarters, instead of working in other chambers with a group of high inner-court officials.[77] Thus for two to three years in the middle of the reign Chang appears to have been closer to the emperor than any other high privy imperial assistant of the day. He had already for several years (since YC4; 1726) been in charge of the capital management of military supplies with Prince I, and since YC7 (1729) he had also been one of the supervisors overseeing the work of the new Military Finance Section attached to the Board of Revenue directorate. Although at the time of Prince I's illness Yung-cheng had appointed another grand secretary, Ma-erh-sai, to inner-court service, apparently Ma-erh-sai was not a success. After only a short tour of duty in the inner court he was given a command at the front in the autumn of YC9 (1731). As a result, Chang dominated the emperor's inner circle, and Ma-erh-sai may have shouldered very few burdens. This explains why Chang described himself as alone in the inner court over a considerable period of time, even when Ma-erh-sai was on hand. For a few years Chang fulfilled the top central role in the inner court—a Manchu-speaking Chinese at the head of the Manchu administration.

Chang T'ing-yü and Communications Management

Although Prince I was probably concerned with communications developments during the early years of the reign, Chang T'ing-yü has been credited with "fixing the forms" of the new court-letter edict system. Chang probably acted as inner-court edict drafter more than anyone else. His name appears more than any other inner-court servitor's on the Yung-cheng–period rosters of court letter drafters (see Table 2). Chang's edict-drafting duties probably meant discussing policy content with the emperor, writing out the first drafts, and submitting them for imperial approval. Thus Chang's influential position at court, particularly during the middle years of the reign, involved him in communications at the highest level, and policy discussions brought him in on the full range of problems confronting the emperor.[78]

We know that Chang was probably also concerned with creating and maintaining sound document storage procedures. Early in YC6 (1728) he suggested that decrees on Eight Banners matters be noted for inclusion in the court diaries, along with Grand Secretariat and Six Board affairs (which were already being noted), "to facilitate keeping a record."[79] Chang may also have been involved with the development of document storage in what later became the Grand Council reference collection (Chün-chi ch'u lu-fu tsou-che), which dates from YC7 (1729).[80] Although Yung-cheng himself occasionally took an interest in working out sound archival curatorship methods, the many mid-reign memoranda on the subject—short notes to assure the emperor that the new filing procedures were being properly followed—were probably composed by the three inner-court stalwarts of the time: Prince I, Chiang T'ing-hsi and Chang himself.

Like Prince I, Chang was also used to receive and forward certain palace memorials. When the palace memorial reporting privilege was expanded to include provincial lieutenant governors and judicial commissioners, the privilege did not operate in exactly the same way as for higher provincial officials. Instead of having their reports go directly in to the emperor, these secondary personnel were required to submit their memorials to a high inner-court official who then passed them along to the emperor (chuan-tsou).[81] The fact that Chang's was one of the offices used for this purpose underscores his concern with palace memorial development. In communications as in other areas, Chang discharged a great variety of tasks for the emperor. Because he was not attached to a statutorily constituted office with a defined mission, he could be asked to take on any responsibility that the emperor desired.

Chang T'ing-yü and Official Publications

Chang was also entrusted with official compilations and publications. Early in the reign he had held high editorial posts in the offices for compiling the *Veritable Records* and the Ming History. Later he dealt with other works, such as the *Huang-Ch'ing wen-ying*, a collection of court writings that included contributions from both emperors and high officials.[82] When the edict ordering the compilation of the Collected Statutes (*Hui-tien*) was handed down in YC2 (1724) and Chang was just winning Yung-cheng's favor, his name had been second highest on the list of editors-in-chief (*tsung-ts'ai*). When the work appeared in YC11 (1733), Chang's name was fourth on the list of editors, after two Manchu princes and the aging Manchu grand secretary Yin-t'ai, but the three Manchus may not have contributed substantially to the work. With O-erh-t'ai, Chang was one of the two top editors of the collection of memorials and imperial vermilion responses of the time, the famous Yung-cheng *Chu-p'i yü-chih*. The Yung-cheng reign was not marked by strong attention to official publications; nevertheless, many of the official works that did appear carried Chang's name on the editorial rosters and probably his influence in the editing as well.[83]

Although Prince I was closer to the emperor than Chang and probably suggested many policies that were eventually put into effect, Chang has been better known in history. Until the archival revelations about the prince came to light, the full extent of his crucial role at the center of Yung-cheng's government was not known. Official historians may have suppressed the facts about the prince because he had to take responsibility for the unpopular policy of tracking down official indebtedness—for, as the emperor admitted, there were "small-minded persons" who attributed the government's drastic new toughness on tax arrears to the prince alone. The prince may indeed have been hated in his own time.[84] The fact that Chinese rather than Manchu historians shaped many of the accounts of the period may also have helped emphasize Chang. In addition, Yung-cheng's attempt to reduce princely influence in his own government, as well as later declarations to the effect that Manchu dynastic law did not permit strong administrative roles for the imperial princes, would have made it undesirable to emphasize Yung-cheng's dependence on a brother. As a result, Prince I's contributions have not been well understood, while Chang was honored for the remainder of the dynasty. Chang was the only Chinese whose posthumous spirit plaque was placed in the Imperial Ancestral Hall (*T'ai-miao*). Years later another Chinese who came close to attaining this honor was denied it because, as the Ch'ien-lung edict announced, "He cannot be rewarded in the way that Chang T'ing-yü was."[85]

Archival access now allows us to compare the achievements of the two men.

Both were informal and unofficial servitors, without legal status or statutory authorization in the administrative code of the empire. In this guise they were not only the ultimate tool of the autocrat—available to do the emperor's bidding without fear of interference from any statute—but also the embodiment of a substantial informal influence at the heart of the central government. Most of K'ang-hsi's inner-court servitors had been enrolled in legally constituted organizations such as the Southern Study and the Imperial Household or in traditional bodies of high prestige such as the Deliberative Council. By contrast, Yung-cheng's unofficial use of the prince and Chang T'ing-yü (and later others, such as O-erh-t'ai) heightened the inner court's informality and served the emperor's autocratic vision. As we shall see in subsequent chapters, this extralegal character of Yung-cheng's inner court created a new dynamic in the central government. The absence of legal limits became a significant stimulus in the following reign that allowed the inner-court servitors and staffs a swift and exponential growth.

The differences between the prince and the grand secretary were also significant. Yung-cheng appears to have used Prince I as a close confidant to achieve an autocratic governing style. With the kind of loyal and devoted assistance that the prince provided, Yung-cheng could hope that he would be able to direct the government of the entire realm by himself. In contrast, Chang T'ing-yü could not meet Yung-cheng's desire for a close confidant. He could not talk back to his sovereign or speak in the straightforward manner of Prince I. Although Yung-cheng trusted Chang and relied heavily on him, the two did not have as close and frank a relationship as did the emperor and the prince. Chang could not be the emperor's alter ego or "substitute" for him as had the emperor's brother. Yet at the same time, the fact that Chang was Chinese may have given him the advantage of being less threatening to the emperor than members of the royal Manchu circle and their grandee retinues at the capital. This consideration, along with Chang's administrative skill and experience, may have led the emperor to turn to Chang after the loss of the favorite. As a result, Chang was elevated to a position unique in the dynasty up to that point—a lone Chinese presiding at the apex of officialdom in the Manchu Ch'ing government.

THREE

The Inner-Court Imperial Deputies

During the early years of the Yung-cheng reign the emperor most frequently turned to Prince I for discussion of policy, supervision of subordinates, and implementation of major inner-court responsibilities. Until the prince suffered his final illness and died in YC8 (1730), he was Yung-cheng's right-hand man. No one else ever achieved the same stature at court, and after his death the prince was never fully replaced. Nevertheless, Yung-cheng did not rely exclusively on one person. For inner-court assistance in the early years he also frequently turned to a Chinese official who had won his trust, Chang T'ing-yü. In addition, Yung-cheng also occasionally appointed temporary committees to handle specific issues.[1] But as time went on, he found that he could not singlehandedly govern the entire realm through such ad hoc assignments to individual inner-court confidants and temporary committees. Some problems required sustained time and energy beyond the capacities of the lone man at the helm or of individuals to whom he delegated tasks on a shifting basis.

In YC4 (1726) the emperor departed significantly from previous organizational methods and deputed three members of the Board of Revenue directorate—Prince I, Chang T'ing-yu, and Chiang T'ing-hsi—as a high-level inner-court team to be continuously in charge of overseeing the northwest campaign preparations. Together these three men shouldered the burdens of analyzing military policy, producing recommendations to be authorized (or occasionally disputed) by the emperor, and supervising subordinate staffs. Although at first their teamwork focused on what was then called "military finance" (*chün-hsu*) but in reality concerned all aspects of military preparations, and eventually the military campaign itself, soon they branched out into other areas as well, together handling the varied range of topics that the two top men had previously been assigned on an individual basis. Study of these imperial confidants is important because of their leadership role all through the Yung-cheng period and into the following reign. Eventually this top echelon became the top layer of highest officials in the early Ch'ien-lung–period Grand Council.

One extraordinary fact about this new high-level inner-court echelon was that it was so lacking in organizational status that it had no name. At first Yung-cheng dealt with this lacuna by issuing commands to "Prince I and the grand secretaries," a designation that the emperor frequently abbreviated to "Prince I and the others." After the prince's death the preferred nomenclature became simply "the grand secretaries," even though only the inner-court grand secretaries were meant. Yung-cheng also sometimes referred to these three early favorites as "the board," meaning the Board of Revenue.[2] Although the lack of a consistent terminology occasionally makes for uncertainty in reading the documents of the day, the emperor's failure to bestow an official name is important because it highlights the informality of Yung-cheng's inner court, which contained entities significantly different from the impressive establishments of K'ang-hsi's day.

Thus Yung-cheng's inner-court imperial deputies were not a single statutorily established committee of a prescribed number of men with grandiloquent titles and a defined organizational mission. There was no personnel roster of places to be filled and replacements to be appointed as vacancies occurred. Although in most years two men sufficed, during the middle years of the reign there were three and occasionally four. And as we saw in Chapter 2, there were also moments when Chang T'ing-yü was in charge alone.

These men were personal instruments of the autocrat. They discharged burdens of policymaking and administration that in simpler days the emperor himself might have shouldered. Indeed, in one of the mourning edicts praising Prince I, Yung-cheng went so far as to say that the prince had frequently "substituted for me [the emperor]" (*tai-chen*).[3] The emperor held one of his later inner deputies, O-erh-t'ai, in similar high regard and is reported to have exclaimed, "I trust O-erh-t'ai completely." In YC10 (1732), when General Cha-lang-a wanted to come to Peking for face-to-face discussion of military plans with the emperor, Yung-cheng instead deputed O-erh-t'ai to journey to meet Cha-lang-a in Su-chou in the far west, averring that "when O-erh-t'ai personally discusses the myriad affairs with Cha-lang-a, it is the same as if I the emperor were personally speaking with Cha-lang-a." In further remarks on the same point Yung-cheng wrote that when the general talked with O-erh-t'ai in Su-chou, it would be "the same as speaking with me in audience."[4] Not many officials in the empire could claim to substitute for or speak for the emperor. A small, flexible inner circle of one or two completely trustworthy and capable deputies who could act for the emperor suited Yung-cheng's need for high-level assistance without loss of control.

THE DEVELOPMENT OF THE INNER-COURT
IMPERIAL DEPUTIES

The Board of Revenue Directorate

The earliest inner deputies were probably first drawn together as members of the Board of Revenue directorate, the prince and Chang T'ing-yü in YC1 (1723), with another experienced inner-court official, Chiang T'ing-hsi (1669–1732), added in YC2 (1724).[5] As directors they would have cooperated on deliberations on whatever financial subjects the emperor ordered them to consider. For example, late in YC3 (early 1726), a provincial memorial on Yunnan salt taxes that was sent for deliberation "to the board" (*fa-pu*)—by which Yung-cheng meant to the board directorate—was considered by the six Board of Revenue ministers, the superintendent, the Chinese president (there was no Manchu president at the time), and the four vice presidents.[6] Apparently of all of Revenue's directorate, Prince I, Chang T'ing-yü, and Chiang T'ing-hsi made the greatest impression on the emperor, for later they were separated from the rest of the board directorate to work on the finances of the early military buildup for the northwest campaign.

Although the three began to cooperate on military finance beginning in YC4 (1726), the emperor continued to use these favorites both individually and as a group on other projects.[7] In addition to the late YC3 (early 1726) discussion of the salt tax, evidence of other teamwork on financial matters can be dated to late YC5 (1727) when the three served jointly as drafters—and therefore advisers on content—for a court letter on a provincial official's nourish-honesty (*yang-lien*) payments.[8] But the earliest surviving archival court letter is an example of their continued service on an individual basis, for this document on northwest policy, probably dating from late YC5 (early 1728), was handled by the I Prince alone. Another example from about the same time is Chang T'ing-yü's dealing alone with one of Yüeh Chung-ch'i's memorials on troop rations. And another instance is found in a YC6 (1728) rescript that ordered the I Prince to take care of a matter of cart prices.[9] Finally, a court letter roster from the middle of YC6 contained the names of only two of the three: the prince and Chang.[10] Nevertheless, when in the middle of YC7 (1729) Yung-cheng desired to honor those who had overseen the early capital management of the military campaign, he named all three men, saying that Prince I, together with Chang and Chiang, had handled everything "exceedingly well."[11]

Thus their display of competence at the Board of Revenue led Yung-cheng to select his three most competent financial viziers to serve concurrently as the inner-court team dealing secretly with the northwest campaign plans and accounts. As a result, following the dissolution of the Audit Bureau and the Plenipotentiary Council in YC3 (1725), Yung-cheng's earliest continuous inner-court team had a twofold origin: in the Board of Revenue directorate and in the individual inner-court aides. Occasionally the emperor convened other committees, usually for specific problems, but for his most confidential inner-court handling he greatly preferred to call on the inner three.

From Board of Revenue to Grand Secretaries

Early in YC7 (1729), the nature of this informal group changed when a former imperial bodyguard and newly appointed grand secretary, the Duke Ma-erh-sai (Marsai), also began to serve as an inner-court imperial deputy.[12] Ma-erh-sai had no Board of Revenue experience. His arrival on duty and Prince I's subsequent illness and death in YC8/5 (June 1730) ended the inner deputies' exclusive Board of Revenue connection. The two Chinese deputies were also grand secretaries, so Ma-erh-sai's appointment resulted in a top inner-court team of grand secretaries.

Looking back on the situation many years later, Yeh Feng-mao, a Grand Secretariat clerk (chung-shu) who tells us in his memoirs that he "came on duty at the Summer Palace in the spring of YC8 [1730]," observed not the inner circle's Board of Revenue connections but three grand secretaries on duty in the inner court. Yeh described them as "inner grand secretaries" (nei chung-t'ang), who, he said, were in reality so august that Chang T'ing-yü was a "prime minister" (shou-k'uei) and Chiang T'ing-hsi a "vice prime minister" (tzu shou-k'uei). Yeh's use of the character "inner" (nei) emphasized the inner-court duties of these men, in contrast with those he called "outer grand secretaries" (wai chung-t'ang), who continued to perform regular Grand Secretariat work at their outer-court offices.

Yeh also distinguished the inner deputies from yet another group, referred to only as "high officials" (ta-ch'en), whom he identified as sitting to the west of the inner deputies in their Summer Palace offices. These were probably men of another inner-court staff, the Board of Revenue Military Finance Section (Chün-hsu fang). Unfortunately for the prospects of an accurate historical account of these personnel shifts, Prince I's early death led many to ignore both the prince's role and the earliest inner deputies' Board of Revenue connections. Instead, the grand secretaries' prominence in Yung-cheng's inner court following Prince I's death and the fact that their duties were later handled by the Grand Council laid the basis for the widespread perception that the council in fact originated in the Grand Secretariat. But Yeh Feng-mao was not an inner-circle staff member. Moreover, he had arrived on the scene too late to observe Yung-cheng's earliest inner-court arrangements for handling northwest military finance. The kind of testimony that Yeh offered, which was subsequently used as the basis of nearly all accounts of Grand Council genesis, did not fully describe the inner deputies' origins.[13] Yeh Feng-mao and other observers of YC8 never saw the I Prince and the other two Board of Revenue directorate members working together.

In the years YC8–10 (1730–32), Yung-cheng lost the services of three of his inner deputies: Prince I died in YC8 (1730), Ma-erh-sai was deputed to the front in YC9 (1731), and in YC10 (1732) Chiang T'ing-hsi died.[14] Another temporary setback took place in YC8 (1730) when the emperor himself became ill, worked into a frenzy of despair over the prince's death. At this point Chang T'ing-yü sometimes found himself in the remarkable position of being the most experienced official at the helm of the Manchu government. Even when Ma-erh-sai and Chiang T'ing-hsi were on duty, Chang was nevertheless the emperor's favorite—in Yung-cheng's words, now "only the one man at court." Eventually in YC10 (1732), the emperor promoted the Yun-Kuei governor-general O-erh-t'ai to grand secretary and brought him to the capital for inner-court service. After O-erh-t'ai arrived, the emperor confidently remarked with a tone of satisfaction, "Now I have two men."[15] Thus at this juncture, two trusted confidants sufficed for the highest echelon in Yung-cheng's inner court. The inner-court imperial deputy group had to be small. Yung-cheng's highest-level appointments indicate that he had no intention of establishing a large, prestigious organization staffed with high-ranking officials who might threaten his dominance in government.

Although the exact role of one other man, the chamberlain of the imperial bodyguard, Feng-sheng-e (Fengshengge), is not clear, he may also have been an inner deputy, even though he was not a grand secretary.[16] The chief evidence for this is the positioning of his name at the head of discussion memorial (*i-fu tsou-che*) and court letter rosters, in the same fashion as other inner deputies. As the ranking Manchu after Ma-erh-sai left for the front and before O-erh-t'ai arrived, Feng-sheng-e headed the rosters for the Manchu-language discussions of military affairs recorded in the many volumes of Manchu recommendations. Later, on the few occasions O-erh-t'ai was away from the capital, Feng-sheng-e was also listed first in the Chinese-language discussions, as well as at the head of many court letter edicts (*t'ing-chi*).[17] Thus although Feng-sheng-e has not generally been acknowledged as an early inner-court deputy, he did perform some of the same duties as the others. Perhaps he fulfilled a requirement that as many deliberations as possible be managed by a Manchu rather than a Chinese. (But for the fact that he was a Chinese, Chang T'ing-yü would surely have been named first in the documents.) Moreover, Feng-sheng-e continued to hold an important place in the inner court right through to the end of the reign. In YC10 (1732) he was appointed to the Deliberative Council.[18] In YC13 (1735), as Yung-cheng lay dying, Feng-sheng-e was one of only seven men not related to the emperor to be summoned to the royal deathbed when the emperor took a turn for the worse.[19] Shortly after the emperor's death he was given the title "Military Strategist" (*Pan-li chün-chi*) and put in charge of arranging imperial audiences for men being rewarded for their service in the northwest.[20] But he was shortly dropped from candidacy for the new interim regency council. His position in

Yung-cheng's inner court is thus not entirely clear; perhaps he held one of those anomalous appointments of the sort that Yung-cheng so preferred.

This account of the inner deputies differs from most other analyses, which variously list several additional individuals as having served on what has been viewed as the early Grand Council of the Yung-cheng years. But those tabulations fail to distinguish between the highest echelon of inner deputies—Yung-cheng's "two men" (or occasionally three or four)—and the group of advisers just below them, the "high officials" in the Office of Military Finance (later Strategy) (*Pan-li Chün-hsu ch'u*, later *Chün-chi*). A notice that a man had been ordered "to be attached to the Office of Military Strategy" (*tsai Pan-li Chün-chi ch'u hsing-tsou*) made him only a military adviser, not a high imperial confidant with authority to handle a broad variety of subjects. There is no evidence that the Manchus and Mongols named in the retrospective lists of Yung-cheng–period grand councillors—men such as Ma-lan-t'ai, Fu-p'eng, No-ch'in, and Pan-ti—ever held the exalted post of inner deputy. They had important tasks, but they served as specialist advisers to the throne and did not shoulder the broad range of responsibilities of their more distinguished colleagues.[21] Only in the Ch'ien-lung period were they and their successors in the Office of Military Strategy amalgamated with the inner deputies in the organization that became the Grand Council.

To understand the high-level role of the inner deputies, we shall now examine two of the principal tasks that they performed for the emperor: policy deliberation and edict drafting.

WRITTEN DELIBERATIONS

During the Yung-cheng period, the inner-court system of written deliberations greatly expanded over what it had been in K'ang-hsi's days. Although written deliberations had occasionally been composed in the K'ang-hsi palace memorial system, most such writings were submitted in the outer-court system where they openly made the rounds of outer-court offices, were sometimes published in the Peking gazettes, and were eventually stored in the Grand Secretariat archives.[22] The routine system contained provision for protecting the secrecy of a memorial's contents if necessary, but this was not the usual method of processing. If inner-court and other capital officials were going to consider problems raised in the secret palace memorials, then those deliberations had to be kept secret too. Yung-cheng, a writing emperor, made less use of open audiences for decision-making purposes and depended more on written reports than his father. This was best accomplished by using the new confidential inner-court channel for all topics raised in the palace memorials.

Under Yung-cheng there came to be two chief types of inner-court deliberations composed in response to palace memorials: formal palace memorials of recommendation (*i-fu tsou-che*) and short memoranda (*i-p'ien*). For both, the usual processing pattern was to have the inner deputies read an incoming provincial palace memorial, compose a recommendation, and fold and insert the piece of memorial paper containing the recommendation into the memorial. Both documents—the provincial report and the capital officials' recommendation—would then be submitted to the emperor.[23]

At that point the emperor might reject the recommendation outright. But if he liked it or had no better idea (as was frequently the case), he had several courses of action: he might accept the recommendation and incorporate it in his vermilion rescript; he might approve it and send it back with the memorial to the original memorialist; or he might have the findings drafted into a formal edict. Whatever happened, the processing was confined to the inner court and its provincial correspondents, a fact that supplied several advantages. The new deliberation forms protected confidentiality—neither the summary of the base provincial memorial nor the recommendations were exposed to outer-court scrutiny. Moreover, because these documents were limited to the inner court, their contents were not added to the precedent-building machinery of the routine system. Getting advice in writing instead of through audience conversations also gave Yung-cheng a shortcut for dealing with the increasing press of government business, for once the memorialized recommendations had received imperial approval, they were frequently directly circulated in that form, without being rewritten as edicts, to the appropriate provincial officials. Thus they served as an efficient substitute for detailed instructions that the emperor would otherwise have had to handle more formally.[24]

This expansion of the inner-court communications system favored the inner deputies' influence. Although outer-court advisers could be consulted, the management of the major central-government deliberations, including many board discussions assigned to the inner-court superintendents, was now firmly in the inner court. Thus these new forms constituted another form of board bypass: the board directorates and particularly the superintendents and grand secretaries continued to participate in many discussions, but frequently the middle- and lower-level board personnel in the outer court—the very civil servants who in the past had demanded the illicit board fees (*pu-fei*)—were cut out or drawn in only for the limited purposes of contributing to specific deliberations.

The Archives' Casket of the Early Inner Deputies' Advice

Although Yung-cheng could tap large numbers of people for advice, after the middle of the reign he most often turned to the imperial deputies for help with problems raised in the palace memorials. A remarkable wooden casket probably constructed in the eighteenth century to store a large number of "recommendation slips" (*i-p'ien*) for the years YC6–10 (1728–32) and now held by the Palace Museum in Taipei supplies many clues to the nature of this counsel. Covered in satin of imperial yellow, the box is labeled: "Containing the Secret Discussion Memorials and Memoranda of the Prince [I] and the High Ministers [chiefly Chang T'ing-yü, Chiang T'ing-hsi, and later Ma-erh-sai]" (*Wang Ta-jen mi-i che-p'ien tsai-nei*).[25] The 118 items in the box are a varied assortment: some are lengthy detailed considerations of a problem, others are only three- or four-line notes informing the emperor about some minor matter. Most are not dated, the dates having been clear at the time because the recommendations were originally inserted in dated provincial reports and have only subsequently become separated from the base memorials that they analyzed.

Although presented in elegant calligraphy, most of the notes lack formal opening and ending phrases and the requisite homage to the imperial compassion and all encompassing perspicacity, or favorable comparison with the ancient mythological rulers Yao and Shun, that frequently decorate the provincial memorials. Usually they open with the single word "investigated" (*ch'a*), then briefly summarize the provincial base report. At the end, the deputies would give their own views.

The documents in the satin-covered box show the wide range of problems that the imperial deputies considered. Many of the memoranda deal with military matters: the northwest campaign, for instance, or the Miao battlefront (where another war was being fought in southwest China).[26] Economic topics such as prices, taxes, water conservancy, grain shipments, and nourish-honesty payments, matters appropriate to the financial expertise of the three high Board of Revenue officials who were also the earliest inner deputies, were also debated.[27] The box contains recommendations on many miscellaneous topics as well: a sea god temple, tomb sacrifice costs, local district-magistrate appointments, and examination travel expenses, for instance.[28] Taken together, the documents in this box as well as the similar deliberations found elsewhere in the archives display the inner deputies' great versatility. These memoranda show that the emperor's inner-court aides were keeping track of the issues, retrieving relevant documents from files, pondering the questions raised, and producing knowledgeable recommendations—all on a broad spectrum of topics.

Although some of the deputies' notes were very short, simply reminding the emperor that an edict had already been dispatched or informing him that the report was being copied for inner-court files, many at greater length approved, disapproved, or revised the recommendations of the base memorials. For instance, in one communication the deputies assured the emperor that they had meticulously gone over the provincial memorialist's figures and argument and could therefore approve a scale for tax-rice shipping payments that O-erh-t'ai had worked out when he was lieutenant-governor in Kiangsu.[29] Another palace memorial on the technicalities of digging new channels in the Grand Canal was read with care before the deputies—and as a result the emperor—approved.[30] The deputies also closely scrutinized wearying numbers of reports on purchases and the health of draft animals for the supply trains of the northwest campaign. One of their most difficult responsibilities was to negotiate the fine line between forestalling malpractices such as excessive purchases and misreported high prices while giving permission for procurement sufficient to ensure uninterrupted shipments to the front lines. In one instance—unusual amid the government's attempts to cut down on military expenses—General Cha-lang-a's reluctance to maintain enough animals in reserve resulted in his being firmly ordered to make more purchases.[31] The casket's contents display the inner deputies' virtuosity in supplying authoritative advice on a wide range of subjects.

Other Recommendation Memoranda

In addition to the casket, many other imperial deputies' recommendations are still to be found in the archives, paired with the palace memorials that they considered. I shall describe two examples of this type; both are short considerations of a Yueh Chung-ch'i memorial of YC6 (1728) that are still enclosed in Yueh's original memorial. Today we can trace the capital handling of Yueh's memorial because Yung-cheng took the trouble to explain it to the general in a rescript: "I took this memorial of yours," he wrote, "and turned it over to the I Prince and others for secret deliberations. [Now] I am sending the deliberations to you so that [you] may proceed accordingly." The two inner deputies' memoranda also received imperial rescripts, "[Proceed] as recommended" (*I-i*) on one, and "Right! [Proceed] according to the recommendation" (*Shih. Chao-i*) on the other.[32]

In the base memorial, General Yueh reported that after he had written directly to the I Prince (*ch'i*) and received the prince's reply (*chi-tzu*), his scouts had been able to obtain only 15,000 of the planned 45,900 camels required for transporting supplies to the front, and that even the most diligent effort would probably not turn up as many as an additional 5,000 animals, for an eventual total of less than 20,000. "Cartage is urgently needed before the end of the year," Yueh exclaimed; "Time is pressing!" He accordingly advocated abandoning the search for camels and now proposed to fall back on a type of light horse- and mule-drawn Kansu cart that had been successfully used in the past. Yueh calculated that four carts could do the work of ten camels. "So, if we currently are short approximately 25,000 camels," he reckoned, "I recommend constructing 12,000 carts and [purchasing the necessary] 12,000 horses and mules [to go with them]." In addition, Yueh presented cart, horse, and mule prices, estimating that the totals would "save one-third of the cost of [using] camels."

The capital discussers of Yueh's memorial politely refrained from calling attention to the inadequacies of the great general's mathematics (at a ratio of four to ten, 10,000, not 12,000, mule carts were all that would have been necessary to replace 25,000 camels). From their files they assembled different figures, asserting that the western front, where Yueh was in command, would be short only 19,614 camels. Therefore, being able to work ratio problems, they concluded that the correct figure for the number of light carts required would be 7,846, not 12,000, with an equal number of horses and mules.

Yueh's memorial ran for seven folds, each fold having seven lines (for a total of thirty-eight inches).[33] Although the two discussions were not much shorter, they usefully summarized the original so that the emperor did not have to wade through Yueh's convoluted reckonings; in addition, they improved on Yueh's plans with different mule prices and purchase arrangements. Twelve, not ten, taels would probably have to be spent per mule, the deputies thought, for otherwise "funds would be insufficient and the local governments would be forced to make up the difference."

The deputies' responses to Yueh's memorial show that the press of documents associated with the military campaign had forced efficiencies in document processing. Apparently Yung-cheng read Yueh's memorial only after the deputies had prepared their deliberation slips, at which point the emperor authorized all counts of the recommendations and had them sent to the front; no additional imperial reply was found necessary. As campaign preparations increased and hostilities loomed, Yung-cheng often resorted to this kind of shortcut—getting advice before seeing the memorials, writing shorter rescripts, and circulating the informal recommendation memoranda instead of having formal edicts drafted. Documents were still being addressed to him, but he was now forced to seek more assistance than before and to trust recommendations that came from others who had time to carry out the necessary research and administrative work.

The Relation Between the Recommendations and the Imperial Rescripts

Sending the inner deputies' memoranda to General Yueh in the northwest was one solution to the paperwork created by the military campaign. The handling of other sets of memoranda and their base memorials illustrate other solutions. The four following examples of the deputies' memoranda paired with memorials submitted by the acting Chihli governor-general Yang K'un during YC7/4 (1729 Apr. 28–May 27) are significant because they show the extent to which Yung-cheng depended on his inner deputies' recommendations. Comparisons reveal that in three of these four instances, the emperor's handwritten rescript on the memorials was a close copy, sometimes of the ideas alone, sometimes of the exact words of the discussion. Although the fourth instance exhibits an imperial departure from the recommendations, this rescript also incorporated the main points of the deputies' recommendation.

One of the four Yang K'un memorials was accompanied by a yellow register (*huang-ts'e*) reporting nourish-honesty payments for Chihli officials. The deputies gave this a substantial going-over. They found that Yang K'un's "computations seemed to be right" and that the money ought to be "distributed according to the figures" he had listed, with "the original [yellow] register turned over to the board to keep on file." They offered one improvement on the provincial schedules, however, stating that because the "salaries of lower officials such as the assistant district magistrates were meager, [these men] should also be given" an opportunity to share in the imperial largesse. Although Yang K'un had excluded these minor officials, the deputies argued that "of the entire province's meltage fee of approximately 300,000 taels, the [provincial] recommendations had allotted ... [only] 220,000 taels, so that some is still left over.... The lower district personnel might [well] be given 100 taels or several tens of taels [apiece]."

Apparently when Yung-cheng perused these comments he was fully persuaded, for he lifted all the phrases quoted above directly from the deputies' memorandum into his rescript. His only contribution to his own rescript was to order Yang K'un to produce a new schedule for the omitted ranks. Thus from the deputies' memorandum of fourteen lines (212 characters), Yung-cheng selected three lines (60 characters) for his rescript—all but one of the ideas in the rescript and more than three-quarters of the characters were directly derived from the recommendation.[34]

The imperial rescript on another Yang K'un memorial shows a similar correlation with the recommendation, with no significant new ideas of imperial origin. Office expenses were the subject of the provincial report, which was accompanied by another yellow register explaining how a large sum of more than ten thousand taels had been almost entirely swallowed up by the costs of running the governor-general's yamen. Yung-cheng's response was in line with the well-known imperial concern for frugality. It opened by pointedly asking why there was a charge on public money (*kung-yung yin*) for the office expenses of officials who had already received disbursements of nourish-honesty payments intended to cover the same costs. An item of wages and food for yamen clerks and sedan-chair bearers was also found to be unsuitable for deduction. "These four items marked with vermilion circles [in the yellow register]," declared the emperor, "will not be authorized; [instead the responsible officials] are to repay them immediately." The rescript closed with the command that wrongly disbursed items were to be repaid tenfold by the responsible officials.

The appearance that this document gives of intense imperial creativity in decision making belies the fact that the same ideas had first been conveyed in the inner deputies' memorandum of advice. Although the rescript expressed Yung-cheng's zealous opposition to any whiff of malfeasance in dealing with public finance—a favorite imperial hobbyhorse—in fact all the ideas in the rescript were derived from the imperial deputies' investigation. The substance of the rescript lifted fifty-five characters verbatim from the recommendation, with only four one- or two-character substitutions of equivalent characters. Moreover, the emperor also copied a dozen other characters, with the result that more than four-fifths of the rescript was directly appropriated from the inner-circle review.[35] Where the discussers approved the provincial requests, the emperor followed their lead; where they disapproved, he copied their suggestions and even their wording.

The third memorial of this group was on meltage fees "already collected, as well as what has not yet been received." Yang K'un assured his imperial reader that delayed collections were being pursued with zeal. The deputies' discussion memorandum ruthlessly boiled Yang's fifteen lines into a single summarizing phrase identifying the year and topic of his accompanying yellow register, and then commented that the register's figures had been checked and found to be "without error." The remainder of the recommendation advised the emperor about office processing procedures. With only a one-character change Yung-cheng compliantly copied those seven characters into his rescript, ordering that the register be sent to the board to be retained on file.[36]

A close reading of the first three memoranda and rescripts on these Yang K'un memorials suggests how much pressure the military campaign had generated at court, requiring the emperor to get help in dealing with the complex provincial financial reports and their yellow registers, just as he had had to do with General Yueh's military finance reports. They also show how, were there to be an overtrusting monarch, the imperial authority might be susceptible to being misused to back improper recommendations from close associates. Under Yung-cheng's watchful attention this does not appear to have happened, but the possibility always lurked.

The fourth Yang K'un rescript shows, however, that Yung-cheng did not always follow his inner deputies. In this case most of the advisers' recommendations did not get copied into the imperial rescript. Instead the base memorial's suggestions on nourish-honesty payments struck an imperial nerve. Yung-cheng bridled at the thought that a man he despised, Wei Ching-kuo, would be one of those eligible for Yang K'un's proposed disbursements. "Not a single *fen* of the provincial commander-in-chief subsidy is to be given to Wei Ching-kuo," scribbled the emperor. "Wei Ching-kuo is only a military official of the most vile type; his life hangs in the balance beneath the [executioner's] knife. He gives no thought to honest effort to repay the imperial grace.... This post has been given him to allow opportunity to atone for his crimes; if there is the slightest transgression, I will have him executed as a warning."[37] This tirade strikingly departed from the memorialized recommendations, although after giving vent to his feelings about Wei the emperor appears to have calmed down, for he continued with a milder statement permitting Yang K'un's request to use surplus funds for office expenses, precisely as the discussion had seconded. Thus even in this instance the rescript's technical information depended on the inner deputies' analysis.

The four matched Yang K'un memorials and their inner-circle memoranda illustrate one pattern of advice by which "secret discussions" (*mi-i*) were not part of the regular work of the full Board of Revenue and other agencies far away in the outer court, but rather were confined to the palace memorial system, where questions, plans, and schedules could be carefully worked out beyond the reach of the middle and lower officials of the outer-court staffs. These matched sets also show how dependent on his adviser-managers the emperor had become. Lacking time to attend to the increasing minutiae of governing, he required not only detailed advice but also memorial summaries. Thus, although most provincial recommendations were accepted, it was usually the inner deputies' views, and not the provincial requests, that in the end persuaded the emperor.

Most surprising is the fact that the imperial assistants' analyses served as a source for the vermilion rescripts. One of the elements of Yung-cheng's reputation for zeal in the cause of governing has been his lengthy vermilion rescripts, which have been taken to signify a conscientious and knowledgeable ruler. Indeed, the vermilion writing produced by the Yung-cheng Emperor surpasses in length, variety, and technical knowledge that known of any other emperor in the entire history of the celestial empire. One feature of this picture must now be modified. The emperor's use of so many of the ideas and words of others in some of his rescripts flies in the face of his repeated assertions that he worked without assistance on the palace memorials. In his prefatory edict for the first edition of palace memorials and rescripts of his reign, for instance, Yung-cheng assured his readers that "these palace memorials were all sealed by the original writer and came before me [directly, without being seen by others en route]. I myself read them and personally with my own brush wrote the comments on them and then sent them on. Every character and every phrase came from myself alone."[38] Now we have contrary instances in which the technical details of the vermilion rescripts can be shown to have sprung directly from the deputies' recommendations. The fact that on occasion Yung-cheng copied the deputies' recommendations word for word into his rescripts alters our understanding of how the palace memorial system operated in his time.

Formal Deliberations Submitted by the Inner Deputies

In contrast with the short notes (*p'ien*) described above, during the Yung-cheng period the inner deputies also researched and wrote longer more substantial deliberations. These were known as "palace memorials of discussion composed in response [to provincial palace memorials]" (*i-fu tsou-che*). Amid the flux of the developing Yung-cheng communications forms, I have discerned two principal subtypes of this memorial, differentiated according to their outer- or inner-court origins. When the deputies wrote as board superintendents heading board directorate deliberations, the memorials greatly resembled the old outer-court routine-system forms: their full list of participants was inscribed at the end of these documents and the memorials were submitted in two languages, as "joint Manchu- and Chinese-language [documents]" (*Man-Han ho-pi*). (The emperor might rescript either half.) They also followed the pattern of outer-court board and agency memorials by first summarizing the base provincial memorial, then presenting their research, and finally closing with recommendations. A number of these board memorials with the names of inner-court board superintendents listed first in their discussant rosters now repose in the Taipei Palace Museum archives.

The other kind of lengthy inner-court deliberation from these years was simply an informal extension of the deputies' memoranda described earlier in this chapter, a simplified form that named only the official who had headed the research and, unfortunately for the modern cause of understanding eighteenth-century decision making, omitted the names of all other parties to the deliberations. The largest assemblage of this type is held in the Beijing Number One Historical Archives, which has more than one hundred Manchu- and Chinese-language record books of deliberations (I-fu tang), the former for YC8–13 (1730–35), and the latter for YC11–13 (1733–35). For our purposes here the most significant question concerning these documents is, who or what group was responsible for their recommendations?

Although it seems that the inner deputies were ultimately responsible for these documents—because nearly all had a deputy's or a superintendent's name attached (and after mid-reign most superintendents were deputies)—this point is open to question, in that the entire Beijing assemblage of record books that I was able to examine narrowly concerned the northwest campaign. With a multitude of specific details on strategy, procurement of supplies, quality, shipping, prices, expenditures, accounts, and so forth, these records seem to depend not on the inner deputies but on inner-court specialist staffs. Probably the imperial deputies managed these deliberations—giving orders for staff research, examining the reports, and steering any discussions that took place—but the work of research and maintaining files was carried out at the staff level. If the contents of these record books reflected only or mainly inner-deputy work, they would have embraced the full range of the deputies' concerns rather than being narrowly focused on the military campaign. Our preliminary conclusion must be that this large group of *ts'e* was produced not by the inner deputies but by subordinate inner-court staffs responsible for various aspects of the military campaign. Nevertheless, the inner deputies were generally in charge of the work of the subordinate staffs.

Other deputies' deliberations that were formerly in the Ch'ing archival holdings but are apparently now lost supply a further clue to understanding the pattern of inner-court deliberations. One was a set of nonmilitary records held (according to the Ch'ing Grand Council inventories) in Manchu-language *ts'e* bearing the title "Records of Deliberations Categorized as Ordinary" (Hsun-ch'ang i-fu tang). Although it is hazardous to guess the content of archival records not available for examination, I believe that these documents, as well as others in the "ordinary" (*hsun-ch'ang*) category (chiefly palace memorials, edicts, and lateral communications), were drawn up by another staff subordinate to the inner deputies—perhaps by their own clerks—working under the deputies' supervision much in the way other staffs did.

The inner deputies were also responsible for other formal memorials of deliberation, writing sometimes as members of ad hoc committees convened to investigate a specific problem, sometimes as the highest-ranking members of a board directorate. The pattern of these memorials was similar to those in the record books described above. The inner deputies were named ahead of other deliberators and therefore probably directed the production of the recommendations and took overall responsibility for them. But the large amounts of technical information in these memorials suggest that even if the deputies were in charge, they must have relied on agency, board, or committee staffs for much of the analysis presented.

Although there were prototypes in the K'ang-hsi period, the two types of inner deputies' deliberations on the palace memorials described in these pages greatly increased in number during the Yung-cheng reign. This was part of the emperor's attempt to run much of his government from the inner court, using inner-court officials to advise him on problems raised in the provincial palace memorials. But not all provincial memorials were turned over for written recommendations. Some were answered more directly by means of edicts. Under Yung-cheng a new kind of edict was developed to respond to the palace memorials. Like the deliberations just described, the new edict form also depended on inner-court deliberation.

THE COURT LETTERS

We have seen that palace memorial confidentiality required that the deliberation memorials be composed and preserved in secrecy in the inner court. Not suprisingly, a new type of edict was also developed to respond to these memorials. This was the so-called court letter (*t'ing-chi*, among other terms). From the beginning, the imperial deputies were involved at the heart of this new system.

The earliest original court letter to come to light in the Ch'ing archives is an undated document that was drafted by Prince I and dispatched to General Yueh Chung-ch'i, probably on YC5/12/10 (1728 January 20).[39] Although this may not have been the very first court letter to have been written, its irregular form and the fact that the emperor took pains to write an explanation for its addressee—"This is a [court] letter [*tzu*] that I ordered the I Prince to send to you"—suggest that this was the earliest court letter sent to General Yueh and therefore probably one of the earliest documents of the new type. The considerable number of other early archival examples and references occurring just after this one (but not before) confirms a beginning at about this time.[40]

The court letter was another solution to the increased imperial burdens arising from the military emergency. It could replace both the emperor's long, handwritten vermilion rescripts and the elaborately drafted, publicly promulgated Grand Secretariat edicts, thus conserving the emperor's energy and maintaining the secrecy of the communications. As Yung-cheng wrote to Yueh Chung-ch'i, "Because I have so many edicts, there is no time personally to write on the memorials. [I just] orally tell the grand secretaries [that is, those on duty in the inner court] [what] to send in a court letter."[41]

Several features mark the mature form of the court letter that developed soon after its tentative beginning. Most unusual was the fact that in addition to the term "court letter," the new edict form was also known by the contemporary word for "personal letter" (*chi-hsin, tzu-chi,* and sometimes *chi-tzu*) and was dispatched in the form of a letter from one or a group of officials, opening not with the word for edict or any indication that it was to contain one, but with a roster of the officials' names and titles (see Figure 5). After writing the edict into their letter, the officials would then conclude with the words "Respectfully received, in obedience to the imperial decree this letter is dispatched."[42]

As with other edicts, the emperor was free to add his vermilion comments to the final draft, a process known as "going over with vermilion" (*kuo-chu*). This suggests that in some senses the court letters were extensions of the former lengthy vermilion rescripts. In the case of a single addressee or a pair of officials stationed at the same place, it was this vermilioned version that was dispatched, a practice that of course had to be altered for multiple addressees.[43] As a result, the provincial recipient sometimes received what must have seemed like an edict in two parts, one written in the black characters of the draft and one in the vermilion of the imperial additions. Yueh Chung-ch'i treated these vermilion additions the same as the imperial comments on his memorials, frequently quoting them back to the emperor in his next memorial and thanking the emperor for what he had written.[44]

Because the court letters were part of the palace memorial system, they were handled with the same strict confidentiality accorded the rescripted palace memorials, dispatched with their base memorials in locked memorial boxes, and returned for storage in the inner court along with the memorials.[45] Like the palace memorials, they were treated as inner-court documents and not put into general circulation: they did not appear in the Peking gazettes, nor were they made available to most of the bureaucracy. Very few found their way into the Diaries. Only a small number appeared in the Yung-cheng *Veritable Records.* Conveying an imperial edict in the form of an insert in a letter from officials deprived the missive of high formal status. Thus the court letters were yet another imperial device for operating beyond the precedent-making machinery of the outer-court bureaucracy, rarely being cited in the Ch'ing *Collected Statutes and Precedents* (*Hui-tien* or *Hui-tien shih-li*). They offered the emperor confidentiality, independence, and maneuverability.[46]

FIGURE 5. Excerpt from the opening lines of a Yung-cheng–period court letter, showing the roster of officials involved in the draft (shown at 74 percent of original size).

上諭

又據格梅爾文稱有準噶爾投降之奔楚克口
濟爾卡倫賊勢甚眾盜去馬匹隨即撥兵應援
爾文稱十二月十二日有準噶爾賊眾圍住哈
上諭據達鼐奏稱接到駐防柴達木副都統格梅
雍正九年正月初四日奉
大臣理藩院尚書特字寄 大將軍岳
軍兵部尚書查 內大臣步軍統領阿 內
大學士公馬 大學士張 蔣 尹 副將

Reading from right to left, the seven participants in the drafting deliberations are named in the first three lines, along with the addressee, General Yueh. Following the date in the fourth line, the edict itself begins with the two characters for "imperial edict" (*shang-yü*) elevated above the body of the edict. The document concerns the Zunghar depredations that had taken place in the middle of the twelfth month of the previous year and the fact that Zunghar spies had obtained information on the deployment of Ch'ing troops.

SOURCE: *Kung-chung tang* (Taipei) YC000455, YC9/1/4 (1731 February 10). Reproduced by permission of the Taipei Palace Museum.

Many of the Yung-cheng court letters were concerned with the outstanding problem of the last two-thirds of the reign: the northwest military situation. But the new edict form was by no means limited to this subject. Two of the earliest court letters, from late YC5 and YC6 (1728), dealt with topics far removed from the battle front: nourish-honesty payments for a Shantung official and local brigandage in Shansi.[47] Later court letters also ranged widely, from Westerners' use of the Canton and Macao anchorages to local appointments. One carried a reprimand to the Manchu general-in-chief in Canton for spending too much time reading Buddhist sutras. (Sending the reproof by court letter was the gentlest possible way of administering an imperial rebuke; at the capital the content was heard and drafted by Chang T'ing-yü alone, and the system's secrecy ensured an absence of unfavorable publicity for the recipient.) As Table 2 shows, harvest reports, an impeachment, taxes and tax relief, and even imperial concern for a frontier official's aging parents—in short, anything coming before the emperor—could be taken up in a court letter edict. This fact suggests that the officials ultimately responsible for the court letters were not the High Officials in Charge of Military Strategy (*Pan-li Chün-chi ta-ch'en*), as has often been contended, but rather the inner deputies whose names appeared first in the rosters.

The Court Letter Rosters

All of the surviving Yung-cheng court letter rosters place one or more inner deputies at the head of the lists (see Figure 5 and Table 2). Even when the majority of roster members came from outside the deputy circle, an inner deputy was invariably listed first. The names of all six deputies appear in the sixty-three surviving archival court letters of the Yung-cheng period; no court letter lacks at least one of them, and each of the six is represented at least twice.[48] Chang T'ing-yü's name appears the most frequently (forty-five times), but he headed a roster only eighteen times, doubtless because he was a Chinese official in a Manchu government (see Table 2). We know that Chang was Yung-cheng's favorite edict drafter; the frequent appearance of his name in the court letter rosters is in line with other evidence of his high competence.[49]

The other roster members, particularly those who were not deputies, were summoned to contribute their expertise to the discussions that preceded the drafting of one of these edicts. They were invited to take part at the behest of the emperor (or possibly the deputies) and could easily be dropped at the next round. A chance imperial remark in the middle of one of Yung-cheng's court letters reveals that the roster members not only drafted edicts on the basis of imperial instructions, as has long been thought, but also contributed to the discussions of policy alternatives. "As for reconstituting the original quotas of troops [in certain units in the northwest]," stated the emperor, "your [*erh-teng*, the plural form] recommendation was to make these up either from the Shensi and Kansu battalions or from the regiments and battalions of Szechuan or from new recruitments."[50] Here the plural "your" refers not to the addressee (who was not plural, but only Yueh Chung-ch'i) but to the roster officials whose thinking was being summarized in the text of the edict.

Thus the roster members who were not inner deputies—Cha-pi-na, A-ch'i-t'u, T'e-ku-t'e, Mang-ku-li, Hai-wang, and perhaps others who will be revealed in documents not yet come to light—were named in the rosters of court letters on military matters because of their experience with northwest affairs or with military finance. Cha-pi-na, for instance, had long been involved with Russia and Tibet: he and T'e-ku-t'e were two of the three delegates who represented China at the signing of the Treaty of Kiakhta with Russia in YC5 (1727), and for a time in YC8 (1730) he had been posted to the northwest in a supervisory capacity.[51] A-ch'i-t'u, a member of the imperial bodyguard, had been in Ch'ing-hai in the late K'ang-hsi period; in YC3 (1725) he had been given a post of enormous trust as commandant of the Peking Gendarmerie. He was occasionally sent back to the northwest on temporary missions; in YC5 (1727), for instance, Yueh Chung-ch'i was instructed to take up the question of troop deployment in An-hsi with A-ch'i-t'u, when the latter was on a mission at the front. In YC9–10 (1729–30), in the course of leading a group of loyal Mongols to the front, A-ch'i-t'u's units created a disturbance for which he was cashiered. His name is also recorded as principal signer of certain Manchu-language discussion memorials on the campaign.[52] As for T'e-ku-t'e, by the middle of the Yung-cheng reign he had served more than fifty years in the Court of Colonial Affairs (*Li-fan yuan*), becoming vice president in KH56 (1717) and serving as president from YC3 to 11 (1725–33). He thus brought to the court letter conferences long experience in dealing with China's borderlands, particularly Russia and the nearby independent khanates and tribes.[53]

The names of Cha-pi-na, A-ch'i-t'u, and T'e-ku-t'e were listed in the rosters following the names of the inner deputies. Two other men—Mang-ku-li and Hai-wang—appear occasionally in the court letters that have survived. Mang-ku-li came from an old family of the Bordered Yellow Banner; his grandfather had made distinguished contributions in the conquest era. Mang-ku-li began his own career as a scribe (*pi-t'ieh-shih*) in the Court of Colonial Affairs; later, as salt censor in Tientsin, he submitted a number of worthy suggestions. He moved around a lot, never rising very high, and was briefly involved in Tibetan affairs in YC6 (1728). His inclusion in two discussion rosters in YC9 (1731) and again in YC10 (1732) is difficult to explain on the basis of available evidence. After K'ang-hsi's death, Mang-ku-li was asked to draw a portrait of the deceased emperor from memory; he did so, and the result was hung in Yung-cheng's residential palace.[54] Possibly filial appreciation led the emperor to attempt to work Mang-ku-li into the high-level discussions. As for Hai-wang, he was junior to these others—his years of prominence in government finance came in the early Ch'ien-lung reign. But his career began under Yung-cheng, when he was first entrusted with financial responsibilities in the Imperial Household and at the Board of Revenue.[55] He was included in the court letter deliberations because of his profound understanding of finance.

Thus, three of these five Manchus who contributed to court letter discussions possessed direct experience in Tibetan and Mongol territories that the inner deputies lacked, and another was knowledgeable in finance. These men belonged to yet another informal inner-court cluster put together in late Yung-cheng times—the High Officials in Charge of Military Finance (*Pan-li Chün-hsu ta-ch'en*), a group that emerged at the time of the first court letter bearing an expanded roster.[56] Admittedly, the use of the term "military finance" (*chün-hsu*) in the new group's title fails to convey their broad range of expertise and concern, but at the time the term had long stood for the entire campaign effort, shaped as it had been in the early marshaling of animals and supplies many years before hostilities had begun.

The Yung-cheng–period court letter rosters offer evidence not only of court discussion of edict content, but also of a felt need to announce that such consultations had in fact taken place. The practice of adding experienced older soldiers to the discussion rosters, which previously had included only inner deputies, seems to have begun at the end of YC8 (1730), when plans for the renewal of the military campaign were being laid (see Table 2). Perhaps Yung-cheng (and the inner deputies as well) felt that Yueh and other generals in the field needed to be reassured that capital planning was now more thorough and drew on more experts than had been the case when so much high policy had been resolved in the debates between the emperor and Prince I. The court letter rosters not only assured the recipients that experts were being consulted, but underlined that fact by supplying their names.

The Yung-cheng court letter rosters also yield clues to the puzzle of Grand Council origins. The new inner-court cluster who are personally named in the rosters—the High Officials in Charge of Military Finance—first appeared in the *Veritable Records* for YC10/3/3 (1732 Mar. 28), when their organization was granted a seal "for imprinting [*yin-hsin*] the closure on matters being secretly transmitted [*mi-hsing shih-chien*]."[57] Because the *Veritable Records* edicts subsequently entered under this organization's changed name (*Pan-li Chün-chi ta-ch'en*, or High Officials in Charge of Military Strategy) were focused on military problems—the oft-supposed concern of the embryo Grand Council—and because this organization later bequeathed its name to what became the Grand Council, this first appearance has frequently been taken as the council's beginning.[58] But the revelations of the early court-letter rosters tell a different story. The court letters were not solely the responsibility of the high officials; indeed, they antedated the high officials. Moreover, the subject matter ranged far beyond the military campaign concerns of the high officials. Some court letters were dispatched in the name of only one or two deputies; others went out under the names of many discussers, who included but were never drawn exclusively from the high officials group. The high officials did come to have a connection with the court letters, but this happened long after the new edict form had been established. Initially, like so much else, the court letters were an inner-deputy responsibility. The new court letter system was not tied to the military situation; it was tied to the high inner clique who helped Yung-cheng with edict drafting on any topic he chose. The YC10 (1730) announcement signified not a new organization but only a new seal being used for transmission.[59]

Analysis of the Court Letters

Were the Yung-cheng court letters truly an innovation, or had there always been arrangements whereby this type of edict could be dispatched? The best approach to this question is to examine the two main types of edicts of the times—the bureaucratic and the imperial. Most of the machinery for processing bureaucratic edicts was bequeathed from the late Ming when the government had run with a minimum of recourse to the imperial person. Ch'ing bureaucratic edict drafting took place in the various outer-court capital agencies and was followed by submission to the emperor for authorization (or occasionally for correction or rejection). The Grand Secretariat "draft rescript" (*p'iao-ni*) system is a good example of this type, whereby the drafts were usually produced as a result of agency consultation or reference to books of instructions and established precedents.[60] Other outer-court agencies might also be called on to draft edicts; Hanlin academicians frequently performed such tasks. Outer-court edicts were public and open, often published in one or more of the Peking gazettes; they could be enrolled in the *Collected Statutes and Precedents* (*Ta Ch'ing Hui-tien*) and used as precedents. Although secrecy was possible, it was not often invoked or deemed necessary.

In contrast, imperial-edict drafting was derived directly from the emperor and his inner-court advisers and edict drafters. Oral edicts (*k'ou-ch'uan*) were the most direct and most secret, announced to couriers who memorized them for oral transmission without writing them down.[61] Another type that emanated directly from the emperor was the decrees written in vermilion. These included the "vermilion rescripts," inscribed directly on the palace memorials (*chu-p'i, chu-p'i yü-chih*), and "vermilion brush edicts" (*chu-pi yü-chih*, later known as *chu-yü*), usually longer screeds written on separate pieces of paper but frequently dispatched as enclosures in the documents being sent to the field. There were also edicts known as "transmitted decrees" (*ch'uan-chih*); although these could take many forms, most were an informal means by which the monarch might have attendants note down his commands and then forward them, usually in writing, to any named addressee.

A K'ang-hsi example of this last type, dated KH49 (1710), was concerned with the problems of Westerners at Canton who were to learn Chinese before being permitted to take up residence in Peking. Four inner-court officials hastily noted this edict on thin, cheap paper still visible in its archival original. The edict was dispatched to the Canton governor-general, advising him of the throne's concern and asking for a reply.[62]

Although this document did not conform to the later regulations for court letter form, it is closer to the developed court letter of the Yung-cheng period than other early surviving archival edicts because its edict roster makes clear that consultation with specialists had taken place. The four inner-court attendants named at the head of the edict—in a position similar to the later court-letter rosters—were high Manchu ministers of the Imperial Household. Scattered information about their responsibilities and experience shows that they were often concerned with problems relating to the church in China, including missionaries in both Canton and Peking, and that the emperor frequently had these men draft edicts to be sent to Canton officials, as well as interview the Catholic priests in Peking and occasionally relay imperial commands to them.[63] One of the officials present for the discussions of the edict of KH49 was the current superintendent of Maritime Customs at Canton, the Hoppo.[64] The four men at the roster's head appear to have constituted a flexible informal committee for dealing with missionary problems; indeed, their titles included the phrase "concurrently in charge of the Westerners' affairs." Committee membership was fluid—an expert from Canton found to be on hand could be summoned to participate, and others could just as easily be dropped.[65] As we have seen, this is similar to the way that Yung-cheng and his inner deputies later drew on the expertise of northwest specialists known as the "high officials" to create policies relayed in edicts on the northwest campaign. Thus, several features of this edict were close to the later court letters.

But although the court letters of the Yung-cheng era were inner-court and imperial documents, they differed from our K'ang-hsi example and other prototypes in several significant ways. The mature Yung-cheng examples possessed a developed and prescribed form: a roster of drafters and deliberators, places where the date and addressees were to be written, and certain terms and phrases that were invariably employed.[66] The Yung-cheng court letters were also expressed as insertions in lateral communications sent by one official to another, a fact that kept these documents informal—they were not official pronouncements to be enrolled in the dynasty's precedents. Most important, the Yung-cheng court letter drafts were without exception managed by the inner deputies (see Table 2). The emperor's high inner echelon of trusted confidants took on all the crucial supervisory responsibilities for policy formulation and management of edict deliberations and drafting. They also dealt with certain other kinds of edicts in addition to the court letters.[67] Here we can see a significant difference from the K'ang-hsi inner court, where tasks were compartmentalized and separate committees of changing membership dealt with the major problems of the day—an Imperial Household committee for foreign churchmen, the Deliberative Council for the military campaign, the Southern Study for certain other edicts—all in a multitude of separate arrangements that left the emperor to act as grand coordinator. Although Yung-cheng had begun with a multiplicity of staffs and committees, after mid-reign the inner-court deputies offered continuity and stability, with the management of edict drafting—and much else—uninterruptedly in the hands of the same small high-level group.

The informal group that I have called the inner deputies came into being in response to Yung-cheng's autocratic vision. Although in the early years the emperor expected to rule autocratically by coordinating a congeries of separate inner-court servitors and ad hoc committees, he soon abandoned this approach in favor of a small team of two or three absolutely trustworthy high-level advisers. The characteristics of the inner deputies constituted a particular Yung-cheng solution to the problem of inner-court assistance. This monarch sought skilled courtiers but had no intention of empowering them. In contrast with much of K'ang-hsi's inner court, most of Yung-cheng's servitors were informally organized without statutory basis or titles of high prestige. The emperor could use them flexibly, as he saw fit, and they could lay no claim to continuous control over any area of government concern. By the end of the mid-reign period and the renewal of the northwest campaign late in YC8 (early 1731), the increasing press of government business that now fell to the monarch and his assistants had forced further new arrangements in the inner court, among which were new communications forms and new inner-court clerks and subordinate staffs. The inner deputies also promoted the emperor's autocratic plans by assisting Yung-cheng in his battles with the outer court. The deputies were able to offer a measure of control over the outer court. In addition, they worked in secrecy, locked away from the outer court's corrupt profiteering and loyally immune to its blandishments. With the inner deputies at hand Yung-cheng could be sure he had taken steps to defend the national treasury. Thus Yung-cheng attempted to define the relationship of monarch and ministers as that of autocrat and obedient servitors.

Yung-cheng's autocratic vision was assisted by two kinds of inner-court communications: the inner-circle recommendations (*i-p'ien* and *i-fu tsou-che*) and the court letters (*t'ing-chi* or *chi-hsin*). These conveyed counsel ultimately derived from the same source—the new deputies and their subordinates and contacts. Development was a matter of mutual reinforcement: as inner-court communications flourished, they promoted the growth of the official groups that dealt with them; and as the official groups expanded, they were able to improve the new communications, coming to terms with such matters as efficient transmission, archival storage, and use of archival materials as a basis for historical compilations.

Because Yung-cheng's drive to impose autocracy ruled out legal specifications for his inner-court assignments, the deputies had to be drawn from other bodies (usually the Grand Secretariat, which paid their salaries) and frequently held many other concurrent posts as well. This gave them the advantage of contacts and access to files elsewhere in the capital. Although the inner-deputy circle was too small to make much use of these opportunities in Yung-cheng times, in the following reign these were to become important factors in Grand Council growth.

TABLE 2. Surviving archival originals of Yung-cheng–period court letters. The capital participants in the edict discussions are listed in the order that their names appeared in the original document, and each document's roster is listed in two groups with the inner deputies set apart at the beginning. Court letter edicts that appeared in the *Veritable Records* (*Shih-lu*), even in summary form, are preceded by an asterisk (*). Additional numbers in the left-hand column give the Taipei Palace Museum's retrieval numbers. (The Beijing court letters do not correspondingly possess individual numbers.) The table is probably not complete—more court letter originals may in future come to light.

Document Site and Date	Addressees	Topic	Roster
Early Court Letters with Roster Officials Only from the Deputies			
(T) Undated (5/12/10?) 592	Yüeh Chung-ch'i	Zunghar conditions	I Prince[a]
(B) 6/5/6	Shih-lin	Shansi local violence	I Prince, Chang T'ing-yü
*(T) 7/11/18 469	Yüeh	Northwest provisions	I Prince and others[b]
(T) 8/12/19 467	Yüeh	Loyalty problems among troops fighting in NW	Ma-erh-sai, Chang T'ing-yü, Chiang T'ing-hsi
Beginning of Court Letters with Roster Officials from Beyond the Inner Deputies			
*(T) 8/12/28 470	Yüeh	Provisions for northwest	Ma-erh-sai, Chang T'ing-yü, Chiang T'ing-hsi / Yin-t'ai, Cha-pi-na, A-ch'i-t'u, T'e-ku-t'e[c]
(T) 9/1/4 455	Yüeh	Troop allocations	Ma-erh-sai, Chang T'ing-yü, Chiang T'ing-hsi / Yin-t'ai, Cha-pi-na, A-ch'i-t'u, T'e-ku-t'e

Continued on next page

Table 2—Continued

Document Site and Date	Addressees	Topic	Roster
(T) 9/1/6 466	Yueh	Enemy movements	Ma-erh-sai, Chang T'ing-yü, Chiang T'ing-hsi Yin-t'ai, Cha-pi-na, A-ch'i-t'u, T'e-ku-t'e
(T) 9/1/8 459	Yueh (Emperor added Cha-lang-a)	Campaign plans	Ma-erh-sai, Chang T'ing-yü, Chiang T'ing-hsi Yin-t'ai, Cha-pi-na, A-ch'i-t'u, T'e-ku-t'e
(T) 9/1/13 457	Yueh	Troop movements	Ma-erh-sai, Chang T'ing-yü, Chiang T'ing-hsi Yin-t'ai, A-ch'i-t'u, T'e-ku-t'e[d]
(T) 9/1/24 458	Yueh	Rumors concerning enemy	Ma-erh-sai, Chang T'ing-yü, Chiang T'ing-hsi Yin-t'ai, A-ch'i-t'u, T'e-ku-t'e
(T) 9/1/28 460	Yueh	Shipping grain	Ma-erh-sai, Chang T'ing-yü, Chiang T'ing-hsi Yin-t'ai, A-ch'i-t'u, T'e-ku-t'e
(T) 9/2/3 456	Yueh, Cha-lang-a	Battle	Ma-erh-sai, Chang T'ing-yü, Chiang T'ing-hsi Yin-t'ai, A-ch'i-t'u, T'e-ku-t'e
*(T) 9/3/6 463	Yueh	Troop movements	Ma-erh-sai, Chang T'ing-yü, Chiang T'ing-hsi Yin-t'ai, A-ch'i-t'u, T'e-ku-t'e

(T) 9/3/17 464	Yueh	Question of using Kazakhs in a pincer movement against the Zunghars	Ma-erh-sai, Chang T'ing-yü, Chiang T'ing-hsi Yin-t'ai, A-ch'i-t'u, T'e-ku-t'e
*(T) 9/6/9 465	Yueh	Response to Zunghars surrounding Turfan	Ma-erh-sai, Chang T'ing-yü, A-ch'i-t'u, T'e-ku-t'e
(B) 9/6/20	Yueh	Enemy depredations	Ma-erh-sai, Chang T'ing-yü, Chiang T'ing-hsi A-ch'i-t'u, T'e-ku-t'e
*(B) 9/7/27	Yueh	Western front strategic considerations	Ma-erh-sai, Chang T'ing-yü, Chiang T'ing-hsi T'e-ku-t'e
(T) 9/9/8 462	Yueh	Enemy depredations, reprimanding Yueh	Feng-sheng-e, Chang T'ing-yü, Chiang T'ing-hsi T'e-ku-t'e, Hai-wang, Mang-ku-li
(T) 9/9/18 461	Yueh	Enemy depredations and counter measures	Feng-sheng-e, Chang T'ing-yü, Chiang T'ing-hsi T'e-ku-t'e, Hai-wang, Mang-ku-li
*(B) 10/1/24	Yueh	Battle strategy	Feng-sheng-e and others
(B) 10/1/26	Yueh	A-ch'i-t'u's recent return to capital with report on troop training	O-erh-t'ai and others
*(B) 10/1/28	Yueh	Troop allocations	O-erh-t'ai and others[e]

Continued on next page

Table 2 — Continued

Document Site and Date	Addressees	Topic	Roster
		10/3/3 Seal cast for Office of Military Strategy	
(B) 10/5/24	Yüeh	Enemy depredations	O-erh-t'ai, Chang T'ing-yü, Chiang T'ing-hsi T'e-ku-t'e, Feng-sheng-e, Hai-wang, Mang-ku-li
		Death of Chiang T'ing-hsi	
(B) 10/8/1	Cha-lang-a	O-erh-t'ai being sent to discuss military situation with Cha-lang-a in Su-chou	Chang T'ing-yü and others
(B) 10/8/3	Cha-lang-a	Northwest	Chang T'ing-yü T'e-ku-t'e, Hai-wang, La-(?)[f]
(B) 10/8/6	Ch'ang-lai, Chang Kuang-ssu	Zunghar raids	Feng-sheng-e and others
(B) 10/8/8	O-erh-t'ai	Troop deployments in northwest	Feng-sheng-e and others
(B) 10/8/10	O-erh-t'ai	Troop deployments in northwest	Chang T'ing-yü and others
(B) 10/8/14	Po-chih-fan[g]	Reprimand for spending time reading Buddhist sutras	Chang T'ing-yü (alone)
(B) 10/8/18	O-erh-t'ai	Northwest personnel	Chang T'ing-yü and others
(B) 10/8/21	O-erh-t'ai	Northwest personnel	Chang T'ing-yü and others
(B) 10/8/21	O-erh-t'ai	Northwest campaign	Chang T'ing-yü and others

(B) 10/8/24	O-erh-t'ai	Northwest campaign	Chang T'ing-yü and others
(B) 10/8/28	O-erh-t'ai	Northwest campaign	Feng-sheng-e and others
(B) 10/8/28	O-erh-ta	Macao anchorage use by Westerners	Chang T'ing-yü Hai-wang
(B) 10/9/2	O-erh-t'ai	Guessing enemy plans	Chang T'ing-yü and others
(B) 10/9/18	Cha-lang-a	Troops on march	Feng-sheng-e, Chang T'ing-yü Hai-wang, Mang-ku-li
(B) 10/10/7	O-erh-ta, Yang Yung-pin	Anchorages for foreign ships coming to Canton	Chang T'ing-yü Hai-wang
(B) 10/10/11	Cha-lang-a, Chang Kuang-ssu, Ch'ang-lai	Plans for march to Turfan	Chang T'ing-yü Hai-wang
(B) 10/11/11	Hao Yü-lin, Chao Kuo-lin[h]	Fukien nourish-honesty payments and local case	Chang T'ing-yü (alone)
(B) 10/11/11	Huang T'ing-kuei, Hsien-te	Inquiry re questionable imperial appointee now serving in Szechuan	Chang T'ing-yü (alone)
(B) 10/11/14	Wei T'ing-chen	Exhortation to be careful	O-erh-t'ai, Chang T'ing-yü
(T) 10/12/3 3898	P'an Shao-chou	Miao areas official corruption	O-erh-t'ai (alone)
(B) 11/1/19	Hao Yü-lin	Fukien naval commander-in-chief	O-erh-t'ai, Chang T'ing-yü
(B) 11/2/5	Cha-lang-a, Chang Kuang-ssu	Moslems who escaped the Zunghars	O-erh-t'ai and others
(B) 11/2/20	Shih-lin	Difficulty collecting land tax arrears in frontier areas	Chang T'ing-yü (alone)

Continued on next page

Table 2—Continued

Document Site and Date	Addresses	Topic	Roster
(B) 11/3/4	Cha-lang-a, Chang Kuang-ssu[1]	Two who fled Zunghars	Feng-sheng-e and others
(B) 11/4/4	Shih-lin	Shansi nourish-honesty payments	Chang T'ing-yü (alone)
(B) 11/4/8	Cha-lang-a, Chang Kuang-ssu	Enemy troop strength	Chang T'ing-yü and others
(B) 11/4/15	Cha-lang-a "and others"	Defenses	Feng-sheng-e and others
(B) 11/6/13	K'ang Hua-ling (brigade-general in Kiangsi)	Kiangsi military training funds	O-erh-t'ai, Chang T'ing-yü, and others
(B) 11/6/14	Hsu Pen	Reprimand for excessively detailed harvest report	O-erh-t'ai, Chang T'ing-yü
(B) 11/7/14	Wang Shih-chün	Possible sources of interest bearing funds for Shantung Ch'ing-chou Hsien Manchu garrison troops	O-erh-t'ai, Chang T'ing-yü
(B) 11/7/19	Wei T'ing-chen	Proposed new regulations for natural disaster tax relief	O-erh-t'ai, Chang T'ing-yü
(B) 11/8/3	Chin Hung	Kwangsi bandit pursuit	O-erh-t'ai, Chang T'ing-yü
(B) 11/10/4	Cha-lang-a	Dealing with western front captured enemy	O-erh-t'ai (alone)
(B) 11/11/11	Hao Yü-lin	Questioning Hao why he gave a high rating to a man others rated low	O-erh-t'ai (alone)

(B) 11/11/20	Mai-chu	Miao frontier problem	O-erh-t'ai (alone)
(B) 11/11/21	Wang Shih-chün	Pursuit of local brigands	Chang T'ing-yü (alone)
(B) 12/3/9	Hao Yü-lin	More on the Ma Shao-nan case (see 11/11/11)	O-erh-t'ai, Chang T'ing-yü
(B) 12/3/26	Wang Shih-chün	Imperial concern for a frontier official's aging parents	O-erh-t'ai, Chang T'ing-yü
(B) 12/4/11	O-ch'ang	Impeachment of a major in Szechuan	O-erh-t'ai, Chang T'ing-yü
(B) 12/4/25	O-erh-ta	Gift of ivory to the emperor	O-erh-t'ai, Chang T'ing-yü

SOURCES: (B) *Kung-chung T'ing-chi* packets YC1–20; *Kung-chung tang* (T) YC000455-7, 459–63, 466–67, 469–70, 592.

[a]This early document was not composed in the proper court letter form that developed later. Dated only the tenth day of the twelfth month, its internal evidence suggests late YC5 (early 1728). Earlier court letters may have been written in Manchu; if these existed, the Beijing archives staff has not yet been able to locate them. They may not have survived. For an earlier edict that may have been a court letter prototype probably drafted by the inner deputies (described only as "Board of Revenue"), see *Ta-Ch'ing li-ch'ao shih lu* (Yung-cheng; YCSL) 88/17–18. [b]This is one of the few of these early court letters to appear in the *Veritable Records*; see *Ta-Ch'ing li-ch'ao shih lu* (Yung-cheng; YCSL) 88/17–18. In fact, it may not have been a true court letter. On the original version it is said to have been heard by Prince I, but in YCSL it is headed "Edict to the Grand Secretariat" (*Yü Nei-ko*), probably an editing error. It was sent to Yueh Chung-ch'i and returned to the capital by him with other court letters. In some respects its form is exceptional, possibly because it is an early example. When Cha-lang-a quoted it in *Kung-chung tang* (T) YC016724, YC7/12/15, he referred to it as a "Board of Revenue court letter" (*Hu-pu tzu*). [c]This edict, *Kung-chung tang* (T) YC000470, is also in the *Veritable Records*; see YCSL 101/19b–20, there listed as "Edict to the Grand Secretaries" (*Yü Ta-hsueh-shih teng*), an epithet appropriate once Ma-erh-sai had succeeded the I Prince as one of the inner deputies. [d]The original of this court letter had an additional yellow slip with vermilion calligraphy pasted on at the end but not reproduced with the document in *Kung-chung tang tsou-che Tung-cheng ch'ao* 17:469–70; see *Kung-chung tang* (T) YC000457. The slip appears to have accompanied an imperial gift for General Yueh, for it read: "This I have carried on my person and am sending to you as a remembrance." [e]*Ta-Ch'ing li-ch'ao shih-lu* (Yung-cheng) 114/15a–b has this but entered as "Edict to the Grand Secretaries" (*Yü Ta-hsueh-shih teng*). [f]Unidentified individual listed as a member of the Imperial Bodyguard. This may be La-sche; see *Shang-yü tang* (Beijing) YC1/1/24, p. 117, where he is described as having worked with T'e-ku-t'e on a Mongol matter. [g]Listed as Kwangtung Manchu general-in-chief. [h]The court letter gives Chao Kuo-lin's title as Fukien governor, but in the *Ch'ing-shih* (CS) tables he is listed as holding this post only beginning in YC12; see *Ch'ing-tai chih-kuan nien-piao*, he in fact did hold the Fukien governorship from YC8 on; see CS 4:3059–60. According to the *Ch'ing-tai chih-kuan nien-piao*, he in fact did hold the Fukien governorship from YC8 on; see 2:1585–87. [i]The Beijing court letter packets contain one more document than are listed here; its front fold with names of hearers and date is missing. It was sent to General Yueh and concerns Zunghar depredations near Turfan. It has been omitted because the roster members' names are not available.

FOUR

The Inner-Court Subordinate Staffs Set Up for the Zunghar Campaign

For the Yung-cheng Emperor, the middle of his reign was a turning point from the early preoccupations of establishing his authority to active pursuit of the Zunghar War during the remainder of the reign. At the beginning, Yung-cheng had been absorbed in winning the throne and keeping it, with concerns as diverse as triumphing over his treacherous brothers and other disloyal courtiers, quashing the Ch'ing-hai rebellion and settling the Tibet situation, and prodding local officials all over the realm to repay their tax collection arrears. By mid-reign the emperor had identified new loyal servitors on whom he could depend, and Prince I had replenished the state treasury and even amassed a surplus.[1] The problems of the early years seemed solved. The emperor was ready to embark on what he had called the great "unfulfilled project of my late imperial father": a decisive strike against the Mongol threat that had menaced China's land frontiers for centuries.[2]

The magnitude of the campaign led to administrative changes at court. We already saw in Chapter 3 how the three inner deputies were drawn together beginning in YC4 (1726) to direct the early secret preparations. Their collaboration and the fact of the campaign probably first became public in the middle of YC7 (1729), when in a large court ceremony Yung-cheng thanked the inner three for their services.[3] Shortly afterward, General Yueh Chung-ch'i led his forces along the Kansu Corridor and into the vaguely charted territory that would become first a newly conquered area and then, in the late nineteenth century, the province of Sinkiang. To meet the needs of this active phase of the campaign, two new informal inner-court organizations appeared at moments that paralleled surges in campaign intensity. First the Board of Revenue's Military Finance Section (*Hu-pu Chün-hsu fang*) came into being in YC7 (1729), just as the campaign was being transformed into the visible fact of thousands of troops on the march into the northwest territories. More than a year later, after the military campaign had been temporarily halted and then renewed following Prince I's death in YC8 (1730), a group emerged known first as the "High Officials in Charge of Military Finance" (*Pan-li Chün-hsu ta-ch'en*), and later as the "High Officials in Charge of Military Strategy" (*Pan-li Chün-chi ta-ch'en*).

The new organizations resembled the Audit Bureau (*Hui-k'ao fu*) of Yung-cheng's first year in that they were temporary and fragile, existing only at the emperor's behest. Informally established, they lacked legal status or officially defined jurisdictions.[4] The similarity with the Audit Bureau was especially pronounced in the case of the Military Finance Section, because one of the new staff's missions was to forestall or uncover corrupt dealings in the military supply lines. Like the Audit Bureau, the two groups were also part of the inner court, operating under the emperor and his deputies and designed to bypass the mistrusted outer-court agencies. The Military Finance Section dealt with military accounts and the high officials separately advised on strategy. Sheltered by the strict boundaries that kept the inner court apart from the rest of the government, the two worked in secrecy. Indeed, so little is known about Yung-cheng's inner court that other shadowy agencies and committees about which we are not informed may also have passed in and out of existence in those early days. Few documents survive to describe the Miao Council (*Pan-li Miao-chiang shih-wu wang ta-ch'en*), for instance, that appeared briefly toward the end of the reign. And by the time Ch'ien-lung came to the throne, the Military Finance Section was so little understood that the new emperor's interim mourning-period council found it necessary to submit a memorial of explanation to brief the new sovereign.

The significance of these two groups for inquiries into Grand Council origins lies in their parallel existences, which continued to the end of the reign. This contradicts previous assertions that during the Yung-cheng period the Grand Council developed into a single strong organization worthy of its successor in an orderly three-stage metamorphosis from "Military Finance Section" (*Chün-hsu fang*) through "Office of Military Strategy" (*Chün-chi fang*) and finally to "Grand Council" (*Chün-chi ch'u*).[5] In fact, during the last five years of Yung-cheng's reign there were three major inner-court groups: the inner deputies, the Board of Revenue's Military Finance Section, and the High Officials in charge of Military Finance (or, later, of Military Strategy), all co-existing simultaneously. Early in the next reign these three entities coalesced to form the high privy council—the Grand Council—that was to direct the government of the entire Chinese empire for the remainder of the dynasty.

The Zunghar War that led to the inner-court reorganization had troubled the court since the late seventeenth century. Although Yung-cheng had determined to settle the Zunghar nuisance "once and for all,"[6] final victory was to come only during the reign of his son, in CL24 (1759). Enormous sums were committed to the enterprise; one estimate put the cost of the seven-year Yung-

cheng segment of the campaign at nearly 130 million taels.⁷ During the years
that battle was joined, dozens of units of frontline fighters, cavalry, and farmer-
soldiers as well as more than one hundred thousand garrison troops made the
three-month march to the front. Because both sides practiced scorched-earth
tactics, the war zone was an unreliable source of supply; food crops could not
be planted with the expectation that they could be left in the ground and
harvested to feed the army.⁸ Every material need of the frontline armies had
to be anticipated and transported out to the far northwest. The job of arranging
for all this fell to a large number of officials at the capital and in the provinces
who were given new titles that frequently included the designation "in charge
of military finance" (*pan-li chün-hsu*).

To support the front line, these military procurement officials had to produce
a continuous pipeline of supplies: one report enumerated thousands of bows
and hundreds of thousands of arrows; another spoke of two hundred heavy
cannon that were lugged out to their emplacements at the front.⁹ Shipments
of rice, vegetables, salt, meat, noodles, "dried lamb slices," "snake medicine,"
and even traditional Chinese "herbal medicines" had to be hauled hundreds
of miles.¹⁰ Protein for troops en route to the front was assured by allotting one
live sheep to accompany each man on the march.¹¹ Military finance staffs at
the capital and in the provinces had to estimate, price, locate, purchase, and
oversee the transportation of tents, cooking pots, clothing of all kinds (chiefly
of sheepskin and felt), boots, gloves, helmets, saddles, saddle pads, spades,
shovels, and animal fodder.¹² Horses, mules, bullocks, and camels had to be
bought, marshaled, and fed during their labored journeys to the northwest.¹³
The military finance officials repeatedly reviewed cartage and porter fees. A
transport proposal had to consider that although camels cost more initially,
they covered the distance faster and needed less sustenance than other dray
animals, whereas bullocks were relatively cheap but had to be allowed long
detours for grass and water.¹⁴ Horses (two, three, or four, variously, per
mounted soldier) were prized for battle, but horses and mules were difficult to
herd and frequently proved unsatisfactory because of the number of animals
that sickened and died of exhaustion on the journey. Complaints about paying
for unhealthy and deceased animals filled thick piles of correspondence from
both capital and provincial officials. Detailed regulations governed reimbursements. Only limited numbers of horses could be claimed as losses within any
one year, and the permissible losses varied according to the type of unit.¹⁵ At
times it seemed that prices and purchasing figured more importantly in the
reports than did fighting.

The responsibilities falling in the category of "military" had a wide range.
Northwest generals found themselves in the business of erecting military post
roads, post stations, and even hostels, all to satisfy the requirements of both
transport and security.¹⁶ At one point funds were awarded to help build a
lama temple, part of an initiative to win the support of local tribesmen.¹⁷

The meticulous attention to detail was carried so far that on one occasion a memorialized request for extra rations for a unit containing a hundred "big eaters" (*yu fan-liang tsui ta-che*) was duly considered and approved.[18]

Right up front after the military there marched another army, composed of "unscrupulous yamen clerks and lower officials" eager to get what they could out of the situation, their own profiteering activities raising fresh problems that threatened the entire enterprise.[19] The possibility of other kinds of malfeasance lurked in the vast capital and provincial bureaucracy, where "board commissions" (*pu-fei*) and other illicit practices could interfere with or reverse the effects of victories hard won at the front. Inflation and price gouging also took their toll. One comparison of prices of military goods reveals the high cost of failing to maintain control: at the end of the K'ang-hsi reign, grain prices at the front had run as high as forty to one hundred taels per picul (*tan*), whereas six years later Prince I was strictly holding the line at only twenty-five taels.[20]

Although an elaborate and experienced administrative apparatus for handling a war was already in place in the capital and provinces, the entire military effort seemed threatened by a fatal hemorrhage of funds and supplies. A succession of edicts lamented the situation—"The officials embezzle, the lower-level runners take their bite, and treasury shortages multiply"—and warned that profiteering from the military emergency was a crime so heinous it could not be forgiven. One of Yung-cheng's solutions was to remove the supervision of military supply accounts from outer-court board control, thus ensuring (or so the emperor appears to have thought) upright inner-court handling under the watchful eyes of himself and his closest partners.[21]

THE BOARD OF REVENUE'S MILITARY FINANCE SECTION

In the summer of YC7 (1729), General Yueh Chung-ch'i marched his troops "beyond the pass" (*ch'u-k'ou*) west of Su-chou and out to the "New Frontier" (*Hsin-chiang*, present-day Sinkiang province) to be poised for the long-awaited strike against the Zunghars the following year.[22] Troops on the march meant additional responsibilities for the three capital planners: campaign expenditures for YC6 (1728), for instance, were almost twenty times the previous year's, and the YC7 (1729) outlays doubled this again.[23] While the generals prepared to grapple with the enemy at the front, the campaign administrators at the capital did battle with the paperwork arising from the attempt to control supply-line profiteering. A subordinate staff, the Board of Revenue's Military Finance Section, came into being as a result.

Few descriptions of this new office and its work have come to light. The office's own records seem to have disappeared.[24] Thinking that Ch'ien-lung might have been briefed on the administrative history of his father's reign after he came to the throne, I checked the archival documents for the period following Yung-cheng's death and turned up a short memorial composed late in YC13 (1735) that summarized the organization's six-year history. This document, submitted by the imperial brother Yin-li and the two high finance ministers of the day, Chang T'ing-yü and Hai-wang, will forever alter our notions about Grand Council origins. It is so important that the essentials of its text must be quoted in full:

> ... during YC7 (1729) when troops were dispatched on campaign to the western and northern fronts, all the military affairs were extremely urgent. The Board of Revenue set up the Military Finance Section [*Chün-hsu fang*] and selected middle-level officials [*ssu-kuan*], scribes [*pi-t'ieh-shih*], and messengers [*shu-li*] to work full-time [*chuan-pan*], with the Board of Revenue superintendent, the late I Prince, and one or two other members of the Board of Revenue directorate having [part-time] supervisory responsibilities [*kuan-li*]. At the present time the fighting on the western and northern fronts has diminished and cannot be compared with the urgency at the beginning of the campaign. It is appropriate to ask for an imperial decree ordering the Board of Revenue directorate [*t'ang-kuan*] to handle all the dossiers on financial matters together, so that finance will receive careful attention and cases will not be delayed. To this end we respectfully seek imperial authorization.[25]

The imperial rescript was brief: "As recommended [*I-i*]," wrote Ch'ien-lung, "but proceed with the greatest caution." The document corroborates Yeh Feng-mao's long-ignored recollection that in the midst of the military campaign "the Board of Revenue separately established the Military Finance Section with the middle-level official Weng Tsao in charge."[26] Further corroboration is supplied in documents at the Number One Archives in Beijing, where the "Board of Revenue's Military Finance Section" was cited throughout the late years of the reign. Moreover, some of these citations make clear the important fact that the Military Finance Section was separate from but contemporary with the High Officials in Charge of Military Finance, because in some documents the high officials recommend forwarding or turning matters over (*chiao*) to the section.[27] Thus from this key memorial and other sources we learn that the Military Finance Section was created as part of the Board of Revenue and supervised by the top three imperial deputies in the board directorate: Prince I, Chang T'ing-yü, and Chiang T'ing-hsi.[28] Contrary to the claims of most historical writing on the period, it was never transformed into anything else; it was founded in YC7 (1729),[29] continued for six years, and was disbanded after Yung-cheng's death, its files and duties reverting to the Board of Revenue directorate at the beginning of the Ch'ien-lung era.

These are important points, for they affirm that the Board of Revenue's Military Finance Section was by no means an outer-court department of the Six Board bureaucracy. By being subordinated not to the Board of Revenue but to its directorate, the Military Finance Section was always an inner-court organization. Growing out of Prince I's inner-court office for the Board of Revenue directorate and attached to the ministerial level of the board, it enjoyed inner-court secrecy and protection. Even though its connection with the Board of Revenue led the emperor occasionally to refer to it loosely as "the board," this did not mean that it operated in the outer court.[30] As we shall see, the section was established in the inner court not only to take advantage of secrecy in the logistical planning necessary to fight the war, but also to combat official malfeasance by removing surveillance responsibilities from the outer court.

The Work of the Military Finance Section

Why was an inner-court Military Finance Section needed, and what work did it do? In general it was in charge of processing records—copying, filing, and checking—rather than making plans or determining policy. Such processing might have been appropriate for a regular outer-court department of the Board of Revenue but for two reasons: the need for secrecy for documents related to military planning (even giving out the destinations of large quantities of military goods might have aided spies in the capital) and the need for efficiency and honesty in military procurement and submission of accounts. Had the outer-court Board of Revenue been permitted to impose its board commissions and other dubious tactics on the reporting process, the crucial matter of reimbursements might have become bogged down in outer-court malfeasance. Bitter memories of earlier difficulties survived. For four years in a row (YC2–5; 1724–27), the Board of Revenue had rejected the annual Kiangning troop rice-distribution reports,[31] possibly in an effort to gain commissions. Early in YC7 (1729), board obstructionism had resulted in delays in releasing funds for returning troops. A military campaign offered a myriad opportunities for profiteering—even this one proved not to be immune.[32] Far better that as many operations as possible, including the laborious but crucial task of checking accounts, be confined to the inner court where these activities could be monitored by the emperor and his trusted deputies.

The Board of Revenue's inner-court Military Finance Section appears to have functioned in much the same way as the outer-court middle-level staffs—that is, it received provincial reports on prices, purchases, and shipments and kept them on file so as to be prepared to audit the final accounts. Price records were maintained with particular care to ensure that military operations went forward with minimal concessions to official rapacity. Yung-cheng ordered that every two months provincial authorities submit reports on the costs of rice, beans, and fodder—the three staples of human and animal life at the front—to the Military Finance Section.[33] Harvest reports for the various provinces were likewise assembled at the capital to assist with purchase decisions.[34] Transport expenses—the costs of horse, mule, camel, and cart purchases, and porterage fees—figured heavily in the official correspondence of the times. Yet these prices were not always readily available. General Yueh reported that prices rose and fell so rapidly that he could not always provide accurate lists. Other itemizations suffered from the existence of a variety of scales—the seasonal price (*shih-chia*) versus the fixed price (*ting-chia*), for instance.[35] Such problems led to capital deliberations and further correspondence on how to handle the situation. A set of transactions and related deliberations in a single military-supply dossier could quickly become a thick pile of documents.

A typical "military-supply dossier" (*chün-hsu an*) usually consisted of four principal transactions. The first was an expenditure memorialized by someone responsible for military finance at the front when matters were still in the planning stage, as when in YC12 (1734) the Kansu governor, Hsu Jung, reported not only on bean prices but also on shipping costs, amounts, destinations, and how a needed consignment might be financed. Hsu further suggested funds could be advanced to pay for immediate needs that could be reported later.[36]

At the second stage a proposal was reviewed at the capital. In the early days, Yung-cheng took a great interest in working out procedures for capital processing. On one memorial that reported wages for different categories of troops he wrote detailed orders: "Turn [this] over to the board [that is, the Board of Revenue's Military Finance Section] to copy and keep on file, so that this can be referred to when the total accounting arrives in a yellow register next year."[37] Later, the emperor ignored this kind of detail, leaving it to the inner deputies to handle the reviews and compose the deliberation memorials that evaluated the provincial requests.

At the third stage, a palace memorial would itemize actual expenditures, frequently with the exact amounts spent accounted for in accompanying ledgers of exhaustive detail, the "Military Finance Accounts Registers" (*Chün-hsu tsou-hsiao huang-tse* or, variously, *Chün-hsu tsou-ts'e*, *Tsou-hsiao ts'e*, and once, in Yung-cheng's hasty abbreviation, simply *Tsou-ts'e*). The accounts were then sent to "the board" so that figures could be checked (*ho-hsiao*, *ch'a-ho*, or *ch'a-tui*) against the numbers for planned and approved expenditures and previously reported prices already on file.[38]

Permission for reimbursement was granted at the final stage. In the early days Yung-cheng dealt with such minutiae, inscribing vermilion instructions directly on the requesting memorials. On one memorial, for instance, he took the trouble to write out the command, "Take the items of expenditure and enter them in the Military Provisions File. The items may be reimbursed."[39] As time went on, however, the job of reviewing the final expense accountings devolved on the inner deputies and later on another high-level group, the High Officials in Charge of Military Finance.[40]

Thus the Military Finance Section operated in much the same way as a middle-level department at the outer-court Board of Revenue, keeping track of figures and approvals and checking the final reports, yet it was an inner-court organization close to the emperor and supervised by the inner deputies. Inner-court secrecy protected the military intelligence in its files; its proximity to the monarch and his respected high associates assured effective monitoring of expenditures. From the inner court, the section helped to wage Yung-cheng's two-front war against both corruption and the Zunghars.

Relations with Outer-Court Agencies

We might expect that the demarcation between inner- and outer-court communications would have easily determined the allotment of tasks to the various capital staffs. Typically, reports submitted in the outer-court routine system would have been routed to outer-court board and agency departments; palace memorials would have gone to the new inner-court staffs for processing. But there is some evidence that in the years when court officials were working out new procedures, the distribution did not proceed in so clear-cut a manner. Instead, the provincial military-finance memorials (*t'i-pen*) of the outer-court system appear somehow to have been routed first to the inner-court grand secretaries, to be forwarded to the outer court only if appropriate.[41] Similarly, routine-system capital discussions on military matters headed by such inner-court figures as O-erh-t'ai and Chang T'ing-yü may also have stayed in the inner court.[42] The lines between the two main central-government areas became blurred as prickly questions—such as how to pay for broken equipment —might be passed back and forth between a board and the inner court over the course of several months.[43] The precise treatment of the routine-system documents so many years after the formative period, when new administrative structures were being worked out by a secretive and suspicious central administration, was difficult to determine at the time and is hard to assess today.

Thus the fact that Prince I, the other inner deputies, and the Military Finance Section were overseeing the campaign did not result in a complete inner-court bypass of the outer-court bureaucracy. The inner-court staffs were too small to take on all outer-court campaign responsibilities. The Board of War, for instance, maintained Green Standard army records; hence it was their job to monitor the expiration of scheduled terms of service, locations of Green Standard military units all over the empire, and appointments, promotions, demerits, demotions, and awards for each man in service.[44] Similarly, the Board of Civil Office kept track of civilian personnel, including those deputed to frontier areas. Even the outer-court middle-level staff at the Board of Revenue had a role in the campaign when it arranged for funds from the board treasury to be dispatched to the front.[45] Nevertheless, when the Board of Works was asked to check provincial accounts for building a city wall and providing food for the workers in a town near the front, it refused the assignment because it had received none of the inner-court documents necessary to audit such reports.[46] The outer-court agencies could not be kept out of the campaign entirely: they alone possessed staffs and files large enough to cope with many of the details. They were now mainly cut out of tasks that in the past had allowed them to collect illicit fees. In sum, outer-court agencies had a role in the campaign, but exactly how they functioned and what changes they underwent are questions awaiting further research and possibly the discovery of new materials.

THE HIGH OFFICIALS

A third inner-court group, whom I shall call the "high officials," was convened as part of the administrative expansion accompanying the renewal of the Zunghar campaign late in YC8 (early 1731). Following the death of the I Prince in YC8/5 (1730 June), the military effort had faltered as, distraught over the loss of his brother, the emperor halted the campaign and recalled General Yueh for consultations. By the end of the year, however, spirits had been restored. Late in YC8 (1730) General Yueh was sent back to the front and a concentrated thrust against the Zunghar menace was planned for the spring of YC9 (1731).[47] The new battle plans required additional capital support.

As was related in Chapter 3, the renewal of the campaign was accompanied by the enlargement of the court letter rosters to include advisers from beyond the inner circle of imperial deputies. The small number of capital-based ministers who had usually advised the emperor on campaign (and other) edicts was now expanded to include men with long experience in Mongol and other border affairs. The new men were an informal group of Manchus and Mongols, at the beginning known as the "High Officials in Charge of Military Finance" (*Pan-li Chün-hsu ta-jen*), later as the "High Officials in Charge of Military Strategy" (*Pan-li Chün-chi ta-ch'en*).[48]

The group's changing nomenclature reflects its unofficial status. For a little more than a year it operated exclusively under the "Military Finance" title (see Appendix B).[49] In YC10 (1732) its name began to shift to the slightly different "Military Strategy" wording. Both titles were then employed interchangeably during the next two years (YC10–11 [1732–33],[50] but by late YC11 the new name—the one that was to last almost until the end of the dynasty and that will be recognizable to Western readers in its customary English translation, "Grand Council"—had supplanted the earlier one. The fact that in the early years the group operated with a changing name as well as a fluid membership underscores its informality and flexibility, qualities characteristic of Yung-cheng's inner court.

Early Membership

The new organization drew on three levels of personnel. At the top were the Manchu inner deputies. Their names—Ma-erh-sai, Feng-sheng-e, and O-erh-t'ai—nearly always headed the rosters of the high officials' deliberation memorials. Apparently the inner deputies had part-time supervisory responsibilities similar to those they discharged in organizing the court letter discussions; here too they supervised and managed while others contributed specialized knowledge. Thus, despite the fact that the inner deputies' names headed the court letter and deliberation rósters, strictly speaking they did not belong to the high officials' group.[51] Next below the deputies were the "high officials" themselves, the cluster that at the beginning had probably consisted of the four specialists in Mongol affairs who had participated in the early expanded court letter deliberations.[52] The membership of this group is difficult to trace. Precise identifications are doomed by the fact that both the Manchu and the Chinese record book copies of their discussion memorials invariably named only the leading memorialist—an inner deputy (most often O-erh-t'ai) rather than a member of the high officials—frequently followed by the character for "and others" (*sei* in Manchu, or *teng* in Chinese); and neither the Manchu nor the Chinese originals, which would probably usefully list all parties to a deliberation, appear to have survived in the archives. As far as can be ascertained from the available evidence, in the five years of the high officials' existence, only about a dozen men served in this group. (See Appendix C). It is possible that one member was the future Ch'ien-lung Emperor, who may have participated in deliberations of either the high officials or the Miao Council (or perhaps both) when he was a prince.[53]

At the bottom level were clerks, copyists, and proofreaders. For the last month of YC8 and the entire year of YC9 (1731), sixteen scribes and proof-readers—all with Manchu or Mongol names—can be identified in the record book copies of the high officials' Manchu-language discussion memorials. Although many were also named in the most reliable published list,[54] their backgrounds and banner affiliations were not recorded, and they appear to have lacked both examination experience as well as civil service ranks and concurrent positions. They were new men, brought into inner-court service without prospects elsewhere in the bureaucracy, a fact that might have been expected to intensify their devotion to inner-court work. The names of others, who are also sometimes known as early "Grand Council clerks," can be garnered from other lists; it is likely, however, that these men did not serve the high officials but instead assisted the inner deputies or the Military Finance Section.[55] (See Appendix D.) Thus at the beginning, the more than twenty individuals connected with the group known as High Officials in Charge of Military Finance consisted exclusively of Manchus and Mongols. Although not all organizational connections can be traced, it seems that Chinese joined this group only later, perhaps in YC11 (1733), when the high officials' earliest surviving Chinese-language record books appeared and Chang T'ing-yü's son, Chang Jo-ai, was appointed.[56]

Despite the group's early title, financial matters were not its sole or even its principal preoccupation. From the campaign-planning years, when the three high Board of Revenue ministers secretly laid the groundwork for the entire campaign, the two characters "military finance" (*chün-hsu*) had come to stand for all aspects of the campaign, including strategy, appointments, and battle reports far removed from a strict interpretation of the rubrics of finance and supply. Yet these two characters continued to be employed, and civil and military officials assigned to the northwest provinces were given "military finance" titles, even though they coped with many more aspects of the campaign than its supply and payment problems.[57] Thus in YC9 (1731) a "governor-general for Military Finance" (*Chün-hsu tsung-tu*) was set up in Szechuan, and a military official, the former Szechuan provincial commander-in-chief (*t'i-tu*), was appointed to the new post while continuing to command troops.[58] Another indication of the broad meaning of the term at this time appears in different texts of the same notices, where "military finance" (*chün-hsu*) and "military affairs" (*chün-wu*) were frequently interchanged.[59] The high officials' earliest title, then, was derived from a time when the campaign had chiefly concerned planning for supply purchases and shipment. Over the years the term acquired its later broadened meaning.

At the beginning, the new group appears to have worked exclusively in Manchu. With the exception of the Chinese-language court letters, which were managed by the deputies and probably drafted by Chang T'ing-yü in Chinese,[60] almost all of its documents in its first two years (YC8/12 to the end of YC10; early 1731 and 1732) were in Manchu. Late-eighteenth-century Grand Council inventories for the last five years of the Yung-cheng reign variously list about 110 record books in Manchu and only ten or fewer in Chinese, none of the Chinese albums deriving from before YC11 (1733).[61] Although not all of these can be ascribed with certainty to the Military Finance Officials or their successors, much of the early Manchu records' coverage— edicts, provincial memorials, and deliberations on "military affairs" (*chün-wu*) generally, as well as on "Zunghars," "Russia," and "northern front military affairs"—reflects the high officials' concerns.[62] In CL21 (1756), when plans were made to compose a history of this great campaign, the compilers found so many important edicts and memorials in Manchu (without Chinese translations) that they had to ask for special personnel to cope with the materials.[63] The group's Manchu preponderance is underscored by the fact that when O-erh-t'ai was away another Manchu, Feng-sheng-e, rather than Chang T'ing-yü, who was next in line in the inner clique, directed the high officials' discussions.[64] The group's early Manchu exclusiveness was in significant contrast to the approximate ethnic balance achieved in the personnel of the emperor's close confidants and elsewhere in the government. Such a preponderantly Manchu inner-court staff prefigures the "Manchu Division" (*Man-pan*) of the Grand Council in the following reign.

Although there was a certain logic that advisers for the northwest campaign against a Mongol tribe would themselves be Manchu or Mongol, their selection at this time may also have been a politically dictated choice designed to meet objections to Yung-cheng's harsh treatment of his brothers and of other

Manchus in their cliques who had opposed him for the throne. Moreover, there may have been murmurings against Yung-cheng's downgrading of the Manchu and Mongol Council of Deliberative Princes and Ministers (*I-cheng wang ta-ch'en*), following K'ang-hsi's heavy reliance on it. A new exclusively Manchu and Mongol body in the inner court might have helped win the cooperation of influential Manchus. Nevertheless, the new group differed from K'ang-hsi's Deliberative Council. Its status was not exalted by the presence of princes, and its membership was not announced as an honor in the fashion of Deliberative Council appointments (which K'ang-hsi used not only to gather military advisers but also to celebrate those appointed). Thus despite the fact that both groups deliberated military policy, the second was a quite different successor to the first.

The Seal

One of the earliest official notices employing the high officials' new title appeared in an inner deputies' deliberation dated YC10/3/3 (1732 Mar. 28). The notice read:

> Concerning the seal needed for the matters that are to be secretly transmitted by the Office of Military Strategy [*Pan-li Chün-chi ch'u*], we respectfully recommend using a seal with the characters "in Charge of Military Strategy" [*Pan-li Chün-chi*]. [We also recommend] sending a lateral communication to the Board of Rites to have it cast, storing it at the Office of Military Strategy, and deputing an official to be in charge [of safeguarding it]. In addition, notices should be sent to the [administrative offices in the] various provinces as well as to military encampments on the western and northern fronts.[65]

This notice, which some have taken to indicate the Grand Council's founding, suggests nothing so momentous. This was not the earliest seal—secret matters had certainly been transmitted long before, probably under the seal of the inner grand secretaries. Rather, the seal notice merely concerns an administrative rearrangement: a transfer of the responsibility for dispatching court letters and lateral communications (the "secretly transmitted" matters) from the deputies' to the high officials' office. Perhaps the volume of paperwork (campaign activity was said to have intensified about this time) necessitated the change.[66] The new responsibility is borne out by the presence of a great many lateral communications (now transmitted by the high officials) in the Chinese-language record books that date from shortly after this announcement. There was also a corresponding change at this juncture in the *Veritable Records* nomenclature for dispatching court letters. Previous notices had specified the grand secretaries (that is, the inner deputies), but thenceforth the *Veritable Records* presented the court letters as edicts to the High Officials in Charge of Military Strategy.[67] Now that we can examine the archival court letters from before and after the new seal we realize that there was no change either in document form or in the drafting and discussion rosters at this point; apparently the new seal marked only a change in the administrative responsibility for dispatching certain types of communications.

Duties of the High Officials in Charge of Military Strategy

By the final years of the reign the high officials' responsibilities had expanded from the early days when the first four consultants had been summoned to participate in the northwest court letter deliberations. At the beginning, the members of the new group had been called on chiefly to give their views, either in the court letter discussions or in the deliberation memorials. Gradually, however, a process of devolution set in whereby the new group fell heir to some of the inner deputies' duties. For instance, the inner deputies had been in charge of processing inner-court communications, and even the emperor himself had formerly taken an interest in such mundane problems as how to preserve palace memorial secrecy, make necessary copies, and set up files.[68] Although the evidence is elusive, it appears that once procedures were worked out at the highest level and routinized, responsibility for communications was shifted downward to the high officials' group. Thus after the casting of their seal in YC10 (1732), the high officials' communications management responsibilities ranged widely while in the sphere of rendering advice they seem to have been limited to military subjects.[69]

The high officials also inherited certain other inner-court responsibilities for the northwest campaign. A YC11 (1733) communication on cavalry troop deaths in the course of an earlier march to the front stated that in YC9 (1731) the grand secretaries (or inner deputies) had handled the matter, whereas now the high officials were to take care of it.[70] There may also have been some overlap with the Military Finance Section, with the staff keeping records, and with the high officials exercising the inner deputies' former responsibility for policy related to the section's work. The organizational arrangements for these various levels of the inner court permitted flexibility and shifts in work assignments, important administrative concerns for the Yung-cheng Emperor right through to the end of his reign.

The high officials were further characterized by having new office space allotted for their work, their staff, and their files in the Imperial Household area, to the west of one of the main inner-court gates. One late-eighteenth-century source called this the "outer Office of Military Strategy" (*wai Chün-chi ch'u*) and claimed that its establishment in YC8 (1730) made possible the keeping of files.[71] This office was different from that occupied by the inner grand secretaries, who may sometimes have worked in the inner-court building that the grand councillors were later to occupy. Although new quarters were outfitted early in the Ch'ien-lung reign, the old site continued in use all through the dynasty as a place for archival storage, the site of some of the clerks' work, and the locus of the publication activities of the Office of Military Archives (*Fang-lueh kuan*).[72]

The high officials' voluminous documentary remains—record books filled with deliberation memorials and lateral communications and the court letters that dealt with the military campaign—inform us of the range of subjects they covered: all the usual campaign problems of provisioning (pricing; procurement; shipping, including endless debate on transport and transport animals; rationing and distribution), personnel (expenses, wages, quarters, nourish-honesty payments for officials, transfers, promotions), training and deploying battle-ready units and relieving troops that needed respite, dealing with local people (Tibetans, lamas, Moslems), official peculation, and of course, battle strategy. The thorny problems of Ch'ing finance received close attention in these records, including different pricing arrangements in various localities, accounting procedures, deductions, surcharges, imposts, conversions into grain, conversions into silver, conversions tallied as if measured in grain, various measures for grain, and so on through the murky permutations and combinations whose understanding conferred considerable authority on those who knew how to manipulate such figures.[73] Small wonder that experts had to be called in and that, in addition to the initial four with their background in Mongol affairs, financial specialists like the Board of Revenue vice president Hai-wang had to be summoned to contribute views.

The Yung-cheng Emperor's attempts at autocratic control of decision making may be divided into two phases: the first occupying the first four years of his rule and the second dominating the remainder of his reign. Up to YC4 (1726), the emperor ran a competitive administration that was generally marked by the use of a kaleidoscope of shifting ad hoc committees for many deliberations. The I Prince was unusual in being permitted to retain continuous charge of certain major problems; in general Yung-cheng attempted to dominate the highest level of inner-court policy, particularly by rotating research and discussion assignments and coordinating the various top-level elements of government by himself.

Change came in YC4 when the emperor allowed the inner-court team of Board of Revenue stalwarts—the I Prince, Chang T'ing-yü, and Chiang T'ing-hsi—to assist with the burdens of management. Thus Yung-cheng followed his father in introducing high-level assisting staffs into his inner court, but like his father he was careful to do this without abandoning the autocratic style. To this end the YC4 team was kept informal and unofficial; it worked under imperial supervision and took up problems only at the emperor's behest. The three men were Yung-cheng's first new continuous staff.

After this, the emperor created two other inner-court staffs, one in YC7 (1729) and one late in YC8 (early 1731). These are the two reviewed in the present chapter. Other inner-court staffs whose records have since disappeared may also have existed; the Miao Council, for instance, was organized late in the reign and apparently functioned similarly to the High Officials.

The indefatigable Yung-cheng may have been hinting at what was coming when in YC4 he exclaimed that "one man's strength is not sufficient to run the empire."[74] But this statement merely heralded the abandonment of competitive administration and signified his willingness to accept close high-level assistants; it did not signal the end of autocracy. Yung-cheng maintained autocracy through to the end of the reign. One of his chief methods was to keep the inner-court staffs weak and unofficial.

Despite the fact that the Yung-cheng Emperor has been renowned for the founding of the Grand Council, we now know that the inner court remained divided throughout the reign, possessing nothing so grand as a Grand Council.[75] The continuity of the same Chinese name used for two dissimilar inner-court bodies masked striking organizational differences. Although an organization known by the Chinese term for "Grand Council" (*Chün-chi ch'u*) existed during Yung-cheng's last five years, it was but one of several inner-court staffs. For the late–Yung-cheng phase of this organization's history its name is properly translated "Office of Military Strategy" (or one of the variants specified above). The inner-court consolidation and use of the translation "Grand Council" are appropriate only for the following reign.

Nevertheless, over the course of the Yung-cheng reign there were changes in the inner court. Gradually the arrangements inherited from the Ming and early Ch'ing were reshaped to facilitate strenuous imperial intervention in governing. The first steps had been taken earlier, but by the end of Yung-cheng's thirteen years on the throne the inner court was substantially stronger in comparison with the late K'ang-hsi era. The framework for the early–Ch'ien-lung transformation had been laid.

PART TWO

Grand Council Founding and Expansion in Ch'ien-lung's Consolidated Inner Court, 1735–99

FIVE

Inner-Court Transformation
Under the Interim Council, 1735–38

In CL14 (1749), shortly after the conclusion of the first of Ch'ien-lung's ten great campaigns to extend the boundaries of the empire (the first Chin-ch'uan campaign, fought in west Szechuan), a censor proposed changing the name of the Grand Council to the title of the T'ang (618–906) and Sung (960–1279) dynasties' high central government council, *Shu-mi yuan*.[1] The suggested name recalled the powerful inner-court councils of the distant past that had advised emperors, managed governments, and overseen communications—frequently at the expense of the imperial power.[2] Although today we may view the censor's idea as appropriate because the Grand Council had just undergone an unprecedented expansion, in fact the proposal was probably a warning that history might be repeating itself and that a new powerful inner-court council might be emerging in Ch'ing times.

The censor's view did not find favor at court. The ancient title was summarily rejected. The responding edict piously declared that the late Yung-cheng Emperor's modest "Office of Military Strategy" (*Chün-chi ch'u*), whose responsibilities had been limited to "edict drafting and the management of state business," was still in existence and "was definitely not an organ of high power."[3]

In the light of the inner court's rapid expansion immediately after the Yung-cheng Emperor's death and the intensification of the council's mission in the years that followed, the censor's proposal and its swift rejection suggest two contradictory impulses at work in the early Ch'ien-lung government. One, possibly the source of the censor's protest, expressed a fear of the overweening ambition that lay behind the current expansion of inner-court influence and strength. Men of this persuasion may have been outer-court grandees who had observed their agencies losing ground to the inner court. The others—probably

137

men of the inner court—knew that caution was necessary. Power and influence might be sought, but the seekers must not advertise their intentions. If inner-court influence was to increase, it would have to do so quietly. The censor's suggestion gave dangerous publicity to these subterranean plans. Even though this view may have accurately reflected what was happening, it had to be quashed.[4]

By the time of this proposal, fourteen years after Yung-cheng's death, inner-court expansion had long been under way. Advances had been made under K'ang-hsi and particularly under Yung-cheng, but those emperors had been wary of consolidated inner-court power and had taken care to keep their inner-court staffs small, informal, and divided, leaving themselves in control. At Yung-cheng's death on YC13/8/23 (1735 Oct. 8), there was little to suggest the wholesale transformation of the central government that was to come. The several acts that laid the basis for the new order occurred in the first three months of the new reign. By the time of the first lunar year that was to be known by the new reign title, "Lasting Prosperity" (*Ch'ien-lung*), Yung-cheng's carefully nurtured inner-court compartmentalization had been abandoned and the informal groups created during the previous reign had been swallowed up in the new Interim Council (*Tsung-li shih-wu wang ta-ch'en*). The result shortly made the eighteenth-century title for the Grand Council, *Chün-chi ch'u*, as worthy of a high-sounding translation as had been its T'ang and Sung predecessor, the *Shu-mi yuan*.

Before proceeding further we must consider two matters of nomenclature and translation. First, because Ch'ien-lung's Interim Council had the same name in Chinese, *Tsung-li shih-wu wang ta-ch'en*, as the similar mourning-period group formed at the beginning of the Yung-cheng reign, I have employed different translations to distinguish the two.[5] The reader is already familiar with the translation "Plenipotentiary Council" used in Chaper 1 for the mourning-period council that assisted the Yung-cheng Emperor at the begin-ning of his reign. In this chapter I shall use "Interim Council" for the similar inner-court council with the same Chinese name that was established for Ch'ien-lung. The Interim Council dominated the central government during the three-year period of mourning for the late emperor: the remaining months of YC13 (1735) after Yung-cheng's death and the years CL1–2 (1736–early 1738). After it was disbanded on CL2/11/28 (1738 January 17), the old title of Yung-cheng's Office of Military Strategy (*Chün-chi ch'u*) was revived and applied to the organization that continued the Interim Council's work.

The second problem of nomenclature and translation concerns the fact that from this time on "Grand Council" is an appropriate rendering of the Chinese title *Chün-chi ch'u*, because the continuing council was no longer merely one of several informal inner-court staffs. Rather, during the Interim Council era it had become an enlarged amalgamated organization that dominated the inner court.[6] Although the council bore the same name as one of the old Yung-cheng inner-court bodies, the different translation clarifies in English what was obscured in the Chinese.

HISTORICAL BACKGROUND OF CH'ING
TRANSITION COUNCILS

The Ch'ien-lung Interim Council was in the tradition of transition councils reaching back to the early years of the dynasty. The appointment of interim or regency councils to assist new or baby emperors at the beginnings of reigns was initially designed to ensure an orderly succession. Moreover, the first Ch'ing ruler, Nurhaci (1559–1626), had desired the advantages of collegial rather than autocratic government, which a top-level council would provide.[7] The emperors usually determined the membership of their successors' councils; generally they chose imperial princes and other imperial relatives, some from the empresses' side. Up to Ch'ien-lung's accession, with the exception of the regency council for the K'ang-hsi Emperor, most of whose members were not of the imperial bloodline and which instead represented a court faction, the Ch'ing mourning-period councils had been composed exclusively of Manchus related to the emperor (see Table 3).

The councils were set up to endure either for the "three-year" mourning period (actually twenty-seven months)—in which case they assisted or ruled in tandem with a new adult emperor as he learned his imperial role—or, as had been the situation in two seventeenth-century regencies, for the entire minority of an infant monarch.[8] These councils possessed sweeping powers —almost as sweeping as those of the throne itself. In some instances they were prizes to be fought over by the deceased emperor's survivors. We know that in at least one situation—the succession from the Shun-chih Emperor (r. 1644–61) to the child K'ang-hsi—an imperial will had been forged by the dominant faction at court so that these sweeping powers might be enjoyed by others than those intended by the late monarch.[9] Yung-cheng's deathbed choices for his son lacked the drama of a disputed inheritance. Instead these appointments were significant for a far more worthy reason, one that was to have a lasting effect on Ch'ing governance. For the first time, a Chinese was appointed to a Manchu transition council.

Following Ch'ing tradition, Yung-cheng named some imperial relatives to the council. His selections consisted of the two surviving younger members of the faction that had supported him during the late K'ang-hsi struggles for the throne: the first-degree Chuang Prince Yin-lu, who headed the new council, and the Kuo Prince Yin-li. At ages forty and thirty-eight, these uncles of the new emperor were scarcely a generation older than the twenty-four-year-old Ch'ien-lung.[10] And all three were considerably younger than the holdover stalwarts of the Yung-cheng inner court, Chang T'ing-yü and O-erh-t'ai, who at sixty-three and fifty-five, respectively, were also to continue to serve.

TABLE 3. Members of the early and mid-Ch'ing mourning period and regency councils. Shows the gradual broadening of mourning period and regency council members from the exclusively royal basis of the two earliest regencies to the inclusion of Manchu commoners and finally, in the second of two councils named by the Yung-cheng Emperor, a Chinese member. (Only the top echelon of the Ch'ien-lung Interim Council is given.)

Council Dates	Council Members	Relationship to Emperor by Blood or Marriage
Huang T'ai-chi 1626–29	Tai-shan (Daisan)	Brother
	A-min (Amin)	First cousin on male side
	Mang-ku-erh-t'ai (Manggultai)	Brother
Shun-chih 1643–51	To-erh-kun (Dorgon) (d. 1650)	Uncle on father's side
	Chi-erh-ha-lang (Jirgalang)	Cousin once removed on father's side
	To-to (Dodo) (d. 1649)	Uncle on father's side
K'ang-hsi 1661–69	Ao-pai (Oboi)	None (Guwalgiya clan)
	Su-ni (Soni) (d. 1667)	None (Hesheri clan)
	Su-k'o-sa-ha (Suksaha) (d. 1667)	Mother an imperial princess
	O-pi-lung (Ebilun)	Related on mother's side
Yung-cheng	Yin-ssu (Prince Lien)	Brother
	Yin-hsiang (Prince I)	Brother
	Ma-ch'i	None at the time of the Plenipotentiary Council; in YC5 (1727) his brother's daughter married the future Ch'ien-lung Emperor
	Lung-k'o-to (Lungkodo)	Known as "Uncle" because his aunt was K'ang-hsi's mother; he was first cousin once removed to Yung-cheng
Ch'ien-lung	Yin-lu (Prince Chuang)	Uncle
	Yin-li (Prince Kuo)	Uncle
	O-erh-t'ai	None
	Chang T'ing-yü	None (first Chinese)

SOURCES: Arthur W. Hummel, ed., *Eminent Chinese of the Ch'ing Period, 1644–1912* (Taipei reprint, 1967), passim; Robert B. Oxnam, *Ruling from Horseback: Manchu Politics in the Oboi Regency, 1661–1669* (Chicago: University of Chicago Press, 1975), esp. pp. 17–23; Fu Tsung-mao, *Ch'ing-tai Chün-chi ch'u tsu-chih chi ch'i chih-chang chih yen-chiu* (Taipei, 1967), pp. 40–41.

Unlike most of the dynasty's earlier transition-council members, Yung-cheng's deathbed choices for his own heir additionally reached beyond the circle of imperial-family connections and placed illustrious members of the elite who had no blood or marriage ties to the throne on the new council. One was the prominent Manchu grand secretary O-erh-t'ai. Although the choice of a high-ranking Manchu official was in line with the KH61 (1722) choice of another Manchu, the grand secretary Ma-ch'i, with the exception of the faction-determined appointments of the Oboi Regency (1660–69) these were the first occasions when Manchus entirely lacking imperial-family connections had been selected for a Ch'ing transition council.

But Yung-cheng's decree was even more unusual because it honored a Chinese, Chang T'ing-yü, with a place on the council, making him the first Chinese ever to be deputed for this type of assignment in the Manchu government.[11] What is more, in his will Yung-cheng conferred on these two the dynasty's highest encomium, the promise of a place in the Manchu Imperial Ancestral Temple—an award that raised them as close to princely status as possible and acknowledged their highly unusual achievements. Indeed, Chang was the only Chinese to be so honored during the entire Ch'ing.[12]

The appointments of O-erh-t'ai and Chang T'ing-yü were in line with Yung-cheng's other efforts to break the hold of Manchu princely and grandee influence in government and indicate that continuity in the central-government administration was thought desirable. Above all, these choices were significant because they paved the way for the growth of ordinary official influence of both Manchus and Chinese working together in the consolidated inner court.

CONSOLIDATION OF YUNG-CHENG'S INNER-COURT AGENCIES

After the Interim Council's founding, an astonishing set of changes took place as the council was swiftly consolidated and enlarged in a fashion that Yung-cheng had surely not envisaged (see Figure 3, at the beginning of Chapter 2, and Table 4). Within two days of the emperor's death a new intermediary echelon of "adjunct members" (*hsieh-pan*) was inaugurated with two men—the imperial son-in-law Pan-ti and the experienced minister So-chu—brought over from the High Officials in Charge of Military Strategy. Shortly after, another new member and a second Chinese, the grand secretary Chu Shih, came on in an "adjunct" status (*hsieh-t'ung*).[13] Yet another shift took place a month after the emperor's death when the Board of Revenue's Military Finance Section (*Hu-pu Chün-hsu fang*), which had been created in YC7 (1729) to monitor military disbursements, was disbanded, its files, and possibly some of its person-nel, reverting to the ministerial level of the Board of Revenue, now headed by that board's two superintendents on the Interim Council, the Kuo Prince

TABLE 4. Inner-court amalgamation in the three months immediately following the death of the Yung-cheng Emperor (October 1735–January 1736). Shows the rapid-fire sequence of appointments and disbanding of organizations that transformed the inner court at the beginning of the Ch'ien-lung era. By the end of this period, the Interim Council had at least eight and perhaps more members, divided between two top echelons. In addition, there were clerks (not shown) who had come over from the disbanded agencies, and probably runners and messengers from the same source as well. In this chart, the names of the three Chinese members are underlined.

Date	Top Echelon	Adjunct Echelon	Organizations disbanded and joined to the Interim Council
	Death of the Yung-cheng Emperor		
	Original Four Interim Council Members Appointed		
	(YC13/8/23)		
YC13/8/23	Yin-lu (Prince Chuang)		
	Yin-li (Prince Kuo; removed YC13/11/19)		
	O-erh-t'ai		
	Chang T'ing-yü		
	Individuals and Former Inner Court Staffs Added		
	(YC13/8/25–YC13/11/24)		
YC13/8/25		Pan-ti	
		So-chu	
YC13/9/4		Chu Shih	
YC13/9/22			Military Finance Section (*Chün-hsu fang*)
YC13/10/16		Hsu Pen[a]	
YC13/10/29		No-ch'in	High Officials in
		Hai-wang	Charge of Military
		Na-yen-t'ai[b]	Strategy (*Chün-chi ch'u*)
			Miao Council
YC13/11/24		Fu-p'eng	
		(Prince P'ing)	

SOURCES: *Kung-chung tang* (T) YC020499, YC13/9/22, Yin-li and others; *Ch'i-chü chu* (T) YC13/10/16; *Chu-yuan chi-lueh*, compiled by Liang Chang-chü, 6/1–2b; *Ch'ing-shih*, 1:128.6; Ch'ien-lung *Shih-lu* 1/9a–b, 1/18b, 2/14, 5/421a–b, 7/10a–b, 7/25b; Fu Tsung-mao, *Ch'ing-tai Chün-chi ch'u tsu-chih chi ch'i chih-chang chih yen-chiu* (Taipei, 1967), p. 149.

[a] The sources date Hsu Pen's appointment differently; compare (T) Ch'i-chü chu YC13/10/16 and *Ta-Ch'ing li-ch'ao shih-lu* (Ch'ien-lung) 5/42a–b (YC13/10/29). Earlier appointment to *Chün-ch'i ch'u*.

[b] In one source Na-yen-t'ai's appointment was equated with Pan-ti's (and others, presumably So-chu's) and distinguished from the appointments of No-ch'in, Hsu Pen, and Hai-wang; *Ch'ing-shih* 1:129.2.

Yin-li and Chang T'ing-yü.[14] (By this move the work of that former staff was bequeathed to the inner court and did not revert to the outer-court board.) One month later, the adjunct echelon was further augmented when the Office of Military Strategy (the old high officials' staff), which thus far had had a parallel existence with the Interim Council, was discontinued and most of its members, including the board presidents No-ch'in and Hai-wang and the vice president Na-yen-t'ai, were ordered to assist in the Interim Council.[15] Another appointment went to a third Chinese, the assisting grand secretary and Board of Punishments president, Hsu Pen.[16] At the same time, the Miao Council (*Pan-li Miao-chiang shih-wu wang-ta-ch'en*), which had been in charge of military policy to counter the uprisings in the southwest, was deemed unnecessary and was abolished, its responsibilities also absorbed by the new inner-court organization.[17] Finally, toward the end of the lunar year a change in the princely composition of the council occurred when Yin-li (Prince Kuo) was removed and the P'ing second-degree prince, Fu-p'eng, a man with considerable experience on the northwest battle front, was brought in at the adjunct level.[18] Thus within barely three months the several formerly compartmentalized inner-court groups were combined in the new council.

The Interim Council's rapid enlargement meant that it now possessed four informal echelons and that its size had swelled from Yung-cheng's initial four appointees and their staff of assistants and runners. At the top was the old inner-deputy echelon.[19] Although this group had been augmented with two imperial princes, it nevertheless continued to be dominated by the two grand secretaries, O-erh-t'ai and Chang T'ing-yü, who functioned much as before, continuing their former duties of policy deliberation, edict drafting, and general oversight of inner-court staffwork as well as of certain outer-court agencies. The next level, now composed of eight men, was based on the former High Officials in Charge of Military Strategy (*Pan-li Chün-chi ta-ch'en*) and for a while also continued that agency's former duty of debating military policy. These two top echelons comprised the ministerial level of the council. They were further bolstered by a third echelon of clerks transferred into the new organization from various posts in the disbanded component parts of the old Yung-cheng inner court. At the bottom was a fourth layer of messengers and errand runners. Although it is difficult to tally the exact numbers involved, by the beginning of the lunar new year of CL1 (1736) there were eleven ministers and perhaps thirty to forty clerks and runners, making a total of around fifty in Ch'ien-lung's new council. The military campaign had slackened, but the inner court had been consolidated and expanded.[20]

INTERIM COUNCIL PERSONNEL ASSIGNMENTS

Superintendents

Immediately at the beginning of the new reign, inner-court control of outer-court agencies was secured in the hands of both imperial relatives and Interim

Council members by means of superintendencies (see Chaper 1). The earliest such appointment under Ch'ien-lung was the Lü Prince (Yin-t'ao), who on the day after Yung-cheng's death was put in charge of the Board of Rites so that a member of the imperial family would direct the royal funeral.[21] At the same time, Chang T'ing-yü continued in his superintending posts at the boards of Civil Office and Revenue, persevering with the duties of appointments made far back in the Yung-cheng period.[22] A week later the remaining boards were brought under Interim Council supervision, with O-erh-t'ai returning to the Board of War after an illness, Prince Kuo (Yin-li) at the Board of Punishments, and Prince Chuang (Yin-lu) at the Board of Works. A second superintendent, Prince Kuo, was additionally placed over the Board of Revenue.[23] Except for Prince Lü at the Board of Rites, all of these board superintendents were Interim Council members. Like the others, Prince Lü, an imperial family member, was also of the inner court.

The Six Boards were not the only agencies and staffs overseen by princes and Interim Council members. The Kuo Prince, who during the Yung-cheng period had already been successful at the Board of Revenue, was additionally given control of the Board of Revenue's Three Treasuries (*San-k'u*). The Chuang Prince assumed the leadership of the Imperial Household (*Nei-wu fu*).[24] The Imperial Clan Court was put variously under the Kuo Prince, the Lü Prince, and the third-degree Prince Yin-hsi. Yin-hsi was also put in charge of the Imperial Library (*Yü-shu ch'u*) but shortly afterward was withdrawn. In addition to his duties at the two boards, Chang T'ing-yü was also responsible for the overall direction of the Hanlin Academy.[25] Some of these assignments were holdovers from Yung-cheng days, while some were added by various early Ch'ien-lung edicts. The effect was to create a new inner-court layer (for the most part composed of Interim Council members) of board and agency managers above the regular inner- and outer-court staff hierarchies. Although dynastic organizational policies later came back to this kind of structure, at this time these arrangements were not to last.

The Special Position of the Imperial Princes

About two months into the new reign, with two important exceptions, the princes were relieved of their superintendencies. The edict ordering these further changes pointed out the new government's initial difficulty in identifying good candidates for the top posts and explained that the princes had been called on to help only for that emergency. Also cited was the inadvisability of having "one man in charge of three or four offices and five or six matters." Only Prince Kuo was left at the Board of Punishments and Prince Lü at Rites;[26] even these two proved only temporary, the former lasting only another month, the latter until the funeral obsequies were ended.[27] But the nonprincely superintendents—O-erh-t'ai at the Board of War and Chang T'ing-yü at the boards of Revenue and Civil Office—kept their posts, even though these two were concurrently handling five or six jurisdictions. The dismissal of the princes still left three of the most important boards under the supervision of the two former high-inner deputies, an arrangement that supplied both inner-court control and continuity from the previous reign. In addition, the dismissal of most of the princes put firmly to rest any doubts that the Manchu princes' former strong influence in government was not being revived under the new emperor (see Table 5).

Although the Manchu princes had once enjoyed influence, both K'ang-hsi and Yung-cheng had made inroads on princely power by separating the princes from the banner military units that they had traditionally controlled. Moreover, the princes' role as board superintendents and members of the important central government advisory body, the Deliberative Council (*I-cheng wang ta-ch'en*), had also gradually been curbed during these reigns.[28] The dismissal of the Interim Council princes from the board superintendencies after only a few weeks in these offices at the beginning of the Ch'ien-lung reign reinforced the trend against the princes. After these dismissals, only Prince Chuang (Yin-lu) remained in place at the head of the Interim Council until its term ended in CL2/11 (early 1738), with the second-degree P'ing Prince (Fu-p'eng) at the adjunct level. Then they, too, were excused from the government. If inner-court influence over the outer court was to be accomplished, it would not be by means of the old early-Ch'ing princely superintendencies. We shall see later in the Ch'ien-lung reign that the emperor made considerable use of superintendencies, but at the same time, like his father, he strictly kept the princes out of policymaking most of the time.

Thus most princes were removed from the board superintendencies and did not play a leading role in the Interim Council years. Archival versions of the court letter edict-drafting rosters and many deliberation memorials from the period show that the two former inner deputies, O-erh-t'ai and Chang T'ing-yü, and not the princes, were managing the edict drafts and the deliberations. Even vague headings suggesting that the full Interim Council had been responsible for certain documents frequently turn out to mean, once the archival originals have been examined, that O-erh-t'ai and Chang T'ing-yü had drafted the documents.[29] Yung-cheng's inner deputies in Ch'ien-lung's council continued to perform the same type of work as for their late sovereign. Princely appointments at the top of the Interim Council did not mean that the work was dominated by princes.

During the Ch'ien-lung period, after the princes' privy council service was over, princes did still occasionally serve the government, but rarely in discretionary posts. Whenever the emperor was on tour, for instance, they headed the group known as "Princes and High Officials Left in Charge at the Capital" (*Tsai-ching tsung-li shih-wu wang-ta-ch'en*). Given Ch'ien-lung's predilection for going on tour, there were a great many such appointments. But here again the princes appear to have played only a circumscribed role. For in addition to the

TABLE 5. The declining role of princes in the Interim Council period. Although princes had a leading role in the early years of Ch'ing rule, by the Ch'ien-lung period their influence had declined substantially. This table shows those princes involved in government at the beginning of the Ch'ien-lung reign. Most were uncles of the young emperor—a relationship exhibited by the "Yin" character in their names (Ch'ien-lung had very few brothers). While many ordinary Manchu and Chinese officials were awarded long-term appointments in the new government, as this table shows, most of the princes were soon relieved.

Date	Prince and Appointment	Cut-off Date	Length of Service
YC13/8/23 CLSL 1/9a–b	Yin-lu (Prince Chuang), head of the Interim Council	CL2/11/27	2 + years
YC13/8/24 (B) SYT-FP CL3/1/20, p. 23	Yin-li (Prince Kuo), on the Interim Council	YC13/11/19	3 months
	Yin-t'ao (Prince Lü), superintendent of the Board of Rites	CL3/1/20	2 + years
YC13/9/1 CLSL 2/1b–2	Yin-li (Prince Kuo), superintendent of the Board of Revenue	YC13/10/18	1 1/2 months
YC13/9/1 CLSL 2/1b–2; 5/12–13	Yin-lu (Prince Chuang), superintendent of the Board of Works	until shortly after Lai-pao's return to the capital	2 months
YC13/10/4 CLSL 4/16, 5/12–13	Yin-li (Prince Kuo), in charge of the Imperial Clan Court	YC13/10/18	2 weeks
YC13/10/4 CLSL 4/16, 5/12–13	Yin-t'ao (Prince Lü), in charge of the Imperial Clan Court	(?)	(?)

Name and position	Date	Duration	Source
Yin-li (Prince Kuo), superintendent of the Court of Colonial Affairs	CL1/9/7	(?)	(?) CLSL 26/15a–b
Yin-li (Prince Kuo), superintendent of the Board of Revenue's Three Treasuries	CL1/9/7	10 months (?)	(?) CLSL 26/15a–b
Yin-li (Prince Kuo), superintendent of the Board of Punishments	CL1/9/7	11 months	YC13/10/18 CLSL 2/1b–2, 26/15a–b
Yin-hsi (*pei-le*), in charge (*kuan*) of the Imperial Clan Court	(?)	(?)	YC13/10/18 CLSL 5/12–13
Fu-p'eng (Prince P'ing) on the Interim Council (adjunct level)	CL2/11/27	2 + years	YC13/11/24 (B) SYT-FP, p. 123
Yin-li (Prince Kuo), head of the Council of Princes and High Officials Left in the Capital	(?)	Length of tomb visit tour (one week?)	CL1/1/12 CLSL 10/10b
Yin-lu (Prince Chuang), head of Princes and High Ministers in Charge of Affairs When Accompanying the Emperor on Tour	(?)	Length of tomb visit tour (one week?)	
Yin-t'ao (Prince Lü), member of above group	(?)	Length of tomb visit tour (one week?)	
Fu-p'eng (Prince P'ing), member of above group	(?)	Length of tomb visit tour (one week?)	

SOURCES: Ch'ien-lung *Shih-lu* (CLSL) 1/91a–b, 2/1b–2, 5/12–13, 10/10b; *Ch'ing-shih* 1.128:5; Shang-yü tang (Beijing) YC13/11/24, p. 123; Shang-yü tang (Beijing) CL3/1/20, p. 23. Not all information sought was available.

princes, the committees left at the capital frequently had two or three grand councillors with long experience in state affairs—often O-erh-t'ai and Chang T'ing-yü in the early years of the new reign—who worked alongside their royal peers.[30] Administrative procedures had grown complicated and needed the attention of experienced full-time ministers. Aside from their concern with matters of Manchu and imperial interest, there was little place in government for princes.[31]

At first glance the gradual reduction in the royal princes' influence in government may seem to fit S. N. Eisenstadt's views on the importance for the growth of bureaucratic empires of the ruler's independence from traditional and aristocratic groups.[32] Unquestionably a significant reduction in princely influence did take place in the mid-Ch'ing. But at the same time, the emperors continued to conciliate and make use of their royal relatives. The princes were frequently given final responsibility for the safety of the imperial palace when the emperor was on tour. They were often appointed in emergencies. Even when they held no official positions monarchs consulted with them. Finally, as we shall see in Chapter 6, the Ch'ien-lung Emperor frequently gave high-level Grand Council appointments to relatives from his mother's and the empress's side while shunning men with royal blood who might have seriously challenged his leadership. And in the emergency at the beginning of the Chia-ch'ing reign after Ho-shen's downfall, two princes were summoned to temporary places on the Grand Council. Thus the royal relatives in the early and middle Ch'ing did not continuously lose influence. The princes were reduced but not entirely in eclipse. On occasion the emperors sagaciously fell back on a variety of family connections.

Interim Council Clerks

As we have seen, because most inner-court appointments conformed to the will of the emperor and were not legally constituted in the law code, the Interim Council ministers had to hold concurrent positions elsewhere in the bureaucracy. O-erh-t'ai, Chang T'ing-yü, and Chu Shih, for instance, were grand secretaries, and Hsu Pen was an assisting grand secretary; No-ch'in and Hai-wang were presidents of the boards of War and Revenue. The remaining ministers held other concurrent posts, frequently as vice presidents, in other outer-court agencies. Interim Council clerks were also appointed concurrently and had to be brought into the inner court from substantive appointments elsewhere in the capital bureaucracy.[33]

In CL1 (1736), a challenge was mounted against the validity of the inner-court concurrent posts. The complaint was cleverly limited to those metropolitan and circuit censors (*k'o-tao*) who had other posts and asked that the censors withdraw from all secondary assignments. When the memorialized proposal reached the Ch'ien-lung Emperor, it swiftly found favor. The emperor enthusiastically rescripted it: "The suggestion is correct. Let the appropriate board [Civil Office] investigate thoroughly and report back." Indeed, Ch'ien-lung was so delighted that he ordered that the propounder of this idea be sent up for a reward.[34]

Apparently the doyens of the Interim Council did not relish either the proposal or the imperial response. Stripping the Interim Council of those who held middle-level posts in the Censorate would remove four of the council's most experienced clerks, men who for the most part had begun their service as Grand Secretariat secretaries and assistant readers and had later been promoted to censor. And once the validity of concurrent posts at the Censorate was destroyed, the same arguments could be turned on the rest of the Interim Council's structure of concurrent appointees. The councillors concocted a brief for the emperor to spell out the difficulties caused by both the memorial and the precipitate imperial action. "The Interim Council," explained the councillors, "does not possess any middle-level officials of its own. In this respect it differs from the boards and offices [of the outer court]." Praising the service and accomplishments of the four, the writers closed humbly, asking the emperor to decide "whether [these men] ought to remain to tend to their duties [at the council] or whether they should withdraw to their original office." The Interim Council did not go so far as to put in writing the specter of the imminent loss of all unofficial inner-court assistance to the throne, but the emperor apparently got the point. Reversing his previous approval, he agreed that the censors should stay.[35] With the exception of one censor whose promotion had already been arranged, the others continued to work at the council. This complaint against concurrent posts for inner-court clerks may at bottom have been another outer-court strike against the behemoth growing in the inner court. If so, it did not succeed. The fact that the council had successfully defended itself strengthened its position at the emperor's side.

INTERIM COUNCIL RESPONSIBILITIES

At the end of a little more than a year on the throne, the Ch'ien-lung Emperor declared that he had turned "everything" (*i-ch'ieh shih-wu*) over to the Interim Council to handle, a statement similar to the claim made for the Plenipotentiary Council set up at the beginning of the Yung-cheng reign.[36] Indeed, the council's mission expanded as soon as the capacity of the new consolidated organization was able to cope with broader projects and deeper research. No longer was there only a small number of inner deputies (two or three persons for most of the Yung-cheng period, and at times only one) who had had to stop in the midst of their other duties to think up solutions to the enormous variety of problems flowing to the throne. Now there were many more ministers available for general work of all kinds. By Ch'ien-lung times, too, the military campaign no longer demanded the full attention of the inner-court staffs and as a result the enlarged council, increased supporting staff, and improved record-keeping systems could be directed to fresh problems. That the council's work was substantial is attested by the end-of-year report on amounts of paper used during the first year—more than seven thousand sheets.[37]

The Interim Council's labors are best studied with the aid of that body's numerous surviving records—particularly the copies of their written advice submitted to the throne. The nature of much of the high-level advice that was orally delivered to the monarch in conversation is lost forever, but increasingly, because ministerial advice had come to be researched at length rather than being offered on the spot, it was written down. Owing to sound archival preservation practices, many of these documents are still available for study, one of our main sources of information about inner-court administration.

Not surprisingly, the Ch'ien-lung Interim Council's position papers continued the inner-court forms used in the Yung-cheng era (described above in Chapter 3). During that reign many inner-court recommendations had been presented as brief slips (*i-p'ien*) inserted in the provincial memorials, but there had also been full-scale memorials of deliberation (*i-fu tsou-che*), with copies in the Manchu or the Chinese record books. In addition, the courtiers named in the court letter rosters indicate other high-level inner-court sources of advice, initially presented in conversation.

The enlargement of Interim Council support staff and files deepened the possible sources and kinds of advice available to the emperor. From this time on advice could be backed by wide-ranging research of a sort rarely undertaken in the less developed and compartmentalized inner court of the Yung-cheng years, when so much inner-court effort had had to be devoted to the military campaign. For instance, toward the end of the council's first year the emperor asked for recomendations on the problem of low central-government salaries. The salaries of high- and middle-level provincial officials had been increased some years earlier, when nourish-honesty (*yang-lien*) payments had been added to the basic stipends. Yung-cheng had similarly awarded board presidents and vice presidents a doubling (*shuang-feng*) of their stipends.[38] But other capital officials still languished with incomes that one imperial edict admitted were "inadequate to cover the costs of daily life." As a result, the Ch'ien-lung Emperor now ordered a full-scale survey of the situation.

The Interim Council was to assemble information on the outer-court offices' work loads, draw up a schedule of the number of officials and staff members in each agency, and identify any existing financial resources and regularly available sources of funding. The background facts were to be reported to the emperor together with recommendations on revised disbursement scales. The enabling edict ordered a broad investigation: even organizations such as "the Hanlin Academy and the Supervisorate of Imperial Instruction," it said, "although they do not have many responsibilities, ... are likewise to be the beneficiaries of the imperial benevolence."[39]

When the emperor charged the Interim Council with researching this prospecive bonanza, he specifically gave the council members license to find out exactly what was going on in all the varied offices of the outer court. And because salary increases for all—even for offices with insignificant work loads— were at stake, the agencies' full cooperation was assured. High would be the prestige of the government organization that could simultaneously bring reasonable recommendations to the sovereign and unprecedented largesse to the outer-court offices. The eventual decision to double the remaining capital officials' salaries must have brought satisfaction all around, winning support for the new emperor, the emperor's support for his Interim Council, and heightened prestige for the inner-court staff that had made it all possible.[40] This single piece of research and deliberation on capital salaries illustrates one way that the Interim Council expanded at the very beginning of the new reign. Its enlarged and consolidated structure increased its capacities; increased capacities found more problems to research and solve—with more details, greater order, and a wider range than before. Despite secrecy, the increased activity made the council more visible in the central administration than had been its secret, shadowy Yung-cheng–period predecessors. Each new assignment added something: experience, prestige, a favor for others, patronage, or simply further imperial confidence in the new assisting group. The advisory role was a crucial factor in the council's early expansion.

Most instances of Interim Council advice began with the responsibility for scanning all incoming provincial and capital palace memorials. Only extremely secret information could be reserved, sealed up (*mi-feng ch'en-tsou*), and sent directly to the emperor without the council's intervention.[41] Through their scanning responsibility, council members acquired a peek at all but the most confidential business of the entire empire. Archival evidence shows some of the several ways they dealt with the incoming tide of paper.

Many palace memorials in the Taipei Palace Museum holdings, for instance, still have thin slips of paper enclosed, counseling the emperor on appropriate action. A favorite tactic was to pigeonhole a memorialized suggestion with the succinct phrase of dismissal "No recommendation advised" (*Wu-yung-i*).[42] Many proposals—particularly those of censors—received this treatment. For example, in CL1 (1736), a junior metropolitan censor at the Board of Works submitted a palace memorial proposing that all instruments of punishment and torture throughout the empire be of standardized measurement. He complained that some cangues, for instance, were heavy, some light, some large, some small. Similar variations were to be found in bamboo canes and wooden pincers. The Board of Punishments had already stipulated some required measurements. A cangue, for instance, was to be three (Chinese) feet long, nearly three feet wide, and made of dry wood that would weigh twenty-five catties. But the censor protested that these regulations were being widely ignored; he wanted rigorous enforcement of the official standards. The Interim Council considered the complaint but found it unworthy. Today we can read

the slip with the response they advocated—"No recommendation advised"—
tucked in the archival original of this memorial where it was initially placed
as part of the council's responsibility for advising the monarch.[43]

Sometimes the "No recommendation advised" decision arrived in the form
of a lengthy report resulting from what must have been a substantial deliberation of the proposal. In the first year of the new reign, for instance, a censor
took up the ever fascinating topic of official salaries and advocated that portions
of the salt and customs surplus be stored separately according to whether they
were earmarked for civil or military officials. The Interim Council deliberation
ended with "No recommendation advised," but on the way to that conclusion
the proposal was faithfully weighed, with previous references and similar
actions cited so that the emperor would have a full picture.[44] Other inserted
slips informed Ch'ien-lung of earlier action. One reminded him, "There has
already been an imperial edict [composed to respond to] this memorial."[45]
Another presented the ministers' own draft response, embodying their views
on what should be done, together with a memorandum explaining and summarizing its content.[46] The Interim Council's advisory responsibility meant
that the council ministers guided the emperor on the vast range of topics
encountered in the palace memorials.

On occasion the Interim Council responded to a palace memorial with a
full-scale deliberation, as in the several memorials that led to the capital
officials' salary increase described above. Interim Council members examined
pros and cons, cited background and precedents, weighed proposals, and
offered their own conclusions as to what should be done. Sometimes they
supervised the development of recommendations by lower staffs. Although
the historical background researched for these memorials usually did not
reach back very far, there were exceptions. One consideration of the proposed
reinstatement of abandoned horse farms in China proper, for instance, provided an unusually long historical view on how Ming military readiness had
been assisted by having pastures in four northern provinces (Chihli, Shantung,
Honan, and Shansi), while over subsequent years grazing opportunities had
been destroyed by opening the lands to cultivation (*k'ai-k'en*). The deliberation
concluded that unless cultivated fields were confiscated, there was no place for
raising horses in these four provinces except on the Shensi frontier, where
enough space could now be obtained; as a result use of territory in Manchuria
was urged.[47] But such a lengthy historical perspective was the exception. Most
Interim Council deliberations dealt thoroughly with a problem but did so
mainly in terms of the immediate issues and relevant precedents in the current
and perhaps previous one or two reigns.

The topics covered in these deliberations ranged widely, embracing much
more than the heavily military proportion of topics in the late Yung-cheng
years. Inner-court discussions now touched on such questions as the imperial
name taboo, empresses' titles, a vice presidential candidate for a board, audi-

ence procedures during the mourning period, lamas who were privately buying up people's houses in the city of Peking, excessive interest being charged in local pawnshops, high rice prices in the capital area, granaries in various provinces all over China, the failure of certain capital officials to attend properly to their work, remedies for the rise in the price of copper, improper provincial surcharges being collected on the land tax, the necessity of punishing high government sponsors of appointees who committed some sort of malfeasance after obtaining office, distributing relief after a poor harvest, water conservancy repairs in the capital area, and impeachments of local officials.[48] In addition, the Interim Council jointly deliberated some topics with the boards: an examination case with the Board of Punishments, the need for experienced staff members with the Board of Works, and so forth. The subjects taken up in the palace memorial system were expanding at this time, and Interim Council advice kept pace with that growth.

In addition to the Interim Council's deliberations that commented on provincial requests, there were also some that responded to the emperor's need for information or views. For example, shortly after coming to the throne, Ch'ien-lung noted his father's attempt to identify good candidates for civil service appointments in the first year of his reign and concluded that he should do the same thing. In YC1 (1723), board ministers had examined their middle-level officials and out of every ten selected two for promotion; Ch'ien-lung suggested that this would again be an appropriate procedure. But this imperial proposal was not enthusiastically received by the Interim Council; instead the ministers foresaw that such action would crowd the imperial audiences and lead to a surplus of candidates. As an alternative they suggested that each office send names and evaluations (*k'ao-yü*) to the Board of Civil Office and that the board be ordered to arrange audiences as vacancies arose.[49] Another imperial query asked the Interim Council to deliberate how members of the royal entourage ought to be rewarded for service on an imperial tour. The resulting recommendation spelled out who was to be rewarded and with how much.[50]

Such responses to direct imperial orders accomplished more than simply supplying the researched views of experienced administrators. In the first example cited above—the question of bringing many candidates up for appointment—the emperor had to be contradicted and gently presented with a different way of proceeding, an object that may have been more easily accomplished in writing than in face-to-face confrontation. The second deliberation, on imperial tour awards, gave the council members an opportunity to display their own rectitude, for at the beginning of their memorial the council members earnestly disavowed all intention of seeking rewards for themselves, and their subsequent recommendations omitted anything that might be construed to be of personal or private interest. Putting both forthrightness and unselfishness on display in writing to the emperor could only enhance their reputation for probity as they sought to win their new sovereign's trust. Thus the councillors walked a difficult tightrope between developing a relationship of trust, on the one hand, and guiding and leading the new monarch, on the other.

Not all council deliberation responsibilities were discharged by the council acting alone. Problems could also be routed to other groups, and special bodies could be empaneled to consider a particular question. In fact, on occasion the interim councillors scanned a memorial and recommended external sources of advice. In many of these cases they would eventually review the conclusions and be in a position to add their views either orally or in writing.

The Interim Council also took a leading role in the deliberations of the so-called Nine Ministers (*Chiu-ch'ing*), an ancient body of the principal high capital officials that by Ch'ing times numbered forty or fifty members. One example of a joint deliberation will suffice to indicate the special features of this kind of advice. In the third month of the new reign, Prince Chuang, the ranking member of the Interim Council, headed a discussion of appropriate tax remissions for the people of Shensi and Kansu, who had suffered so much in the course of the northwest campaign. Signing the resulting memorial were forty-four officials, the "Nine Ministers" of the day: the eight Interim Council members (listed first), the twenty-four presidents and vice presidents of the Six Boards, six officials from the Censorate, four from the Transmission Office (*T'ung-cheng ssu*), and two from the Court of Judicature and Revision (*Ta-li ssu*). The deliberations took place over the course of a full month. The result recommended that Kansu province's land-tax quota be entirely remitted for CL1 (1736) and that Shensi be spared one-half.[51] The advantage of such a large-scale consideration was that the very strength of these numbers would have helped to smother any jealous grumblings about the outcome—particularly delicate in instances of a tax remission favoring only one area. At the same time, a full-dress recommendation signed by such a large number presented the emperor with a virtually unanswerable challenge; he would have been hard put to question the result even had he so desired. The Interim Council gained authority and prestige from its position as the leader and organizer of the Nine Ministers' deliberations.

Another example of Interim Council deliberations is seen in their assistance in resolving certain sedition cases, which differed from others by the number of levels of consideration they received. A case from CL1 (1736), for instance, was first discussed in the originating province before it came up to the capital. In Peking, the case first went to the Interim Council and the Nine Ministers. After the recommendations resulting from this consultation had been presented, the Three High Courts of Judicature (*San-fa ssu*) deliberated. The verdict was immediate decapitation, a penalty that Ch'ien-lung lightened. Eventually the miscreant was allowed to return to his native place.[52] Later in the Ch'ien-lung period the Interim Council's successor, the Grand Council, was also frequently to handle sedition cases, part of the expansion of its responsibilities that began shortly after Yung-cheng's death.

Other kinds of early administrative work at the council included appointments. At one point the council was ordered to review civil candidates at the prefect level (4B) and above, and military candidates at the rank of lieutenant colonel (3A) and above.[53] In CL2 (1737), the Interim Council drafted an edict on exceptional appointments—the "large numbers" of positions filled when the candidates did not meet legal requirements. The edict ordered the officials who submitted appointment recommendations (*t'i-pu jen-yuan*; usually provincial governor-generals and governors) to note clearly in their proposals any discrepancy between the candidates' qualifications and official regulations, so that there would be "a basis for the emperor's consideration."[54] Although research on appointments had traditionally been the concern of the boards of Civil Office and War, the fact that these agencies were now directed by the superintendents O-erh-t'ai and Chang T'ing-yü, who had the expanded resources of the consolidated inner court at their disposal, meant that many responsibilities devolved on those superintendents, who then directed the work of both the inner-court clerks and the appropriate outer-court board staff.[55]

Interim Council administrative work was thus not limited to either the inner or the outer court but reached out to both of those areas of central-government operations. Nor were all the outer-court offices equally affected. At the present state of our knowledge it does not appear possible to gauge the extent to which an Interim Council member such as Chang T'ing-yü, who had many concurrent responsibilities, was able to influence the details of the work in the boards he superintended. Nevertheless, inner-court influence over both inner- and outer-court operations was now being accomplished by an enlarged, consolidated, experienced inner-court council. The capital salaries investigation is an example of their force. In Yung-cheng times a similar salary revision with the nourish-honesty schedules for provincial officials had been painstakingly drawn up piecemeal, province by province, with debates and correspondence on the subject drawn out over several years. For the parallel revision of the salaries of employees in the capital agencies at the beginning of the new reign, the directors of the consolidated inner court were able to frame the imperial orders instigating the revision, mastermind the necessary research, draw up schedules, recommend the doubling of salaries instead of nourish-honesty payments, and get the job done within just a few months.

CHANGES UNDER THE INTERIM COUNCIL

An ancient precept in the early writings of Confucian theorists required three years of mourning following the death of a father. The same admonition forbade changes for three years after the death of an emperor, an injunction often cited by new emperors.[56] Yet this precept was repeatedly ignored during the opening years of the Ch'ien-lung reign. One of the most striking features of the Interim Council era, therefore, is the number of changes instituted in a period that was supposed to respect and preserve the deceased emperor's accomplishments. The number and speed of these changes in a royal mourning period was in itself a change so momentous that it calls for explanation.

This chapter opened with a description of what was probably the most significant innovation of the times: the reordering of central-government structure by which the inner-court mourning-period council was consolidated and enlarged. This was a departure from the pattern of earlier transition councils, in which small groups of princes and ministers had wielded power. In addition, the winding down of the military campaign freed those who before had been preoccupied with military supply and campaign planning. The council amalgamation meant that the members of the inner-court administrative groups whose energies had previously been trapped in the endeavors of small specialist staffs were now released to work together on large projects.

Another change lay in the fact that past transition councils had been temporary, intervening only while a new emperor struggled to work out his own patterns of leadership. When this council's time was up, however, the usual disbanding did not take place. Instead, a momentous break with tradition occurred and the temporary amalgamated council was continued.

Because these structural changes have already been discussed, I shall now give examples of some other, lesser changes of the times. Those I have chosen took place in the area of Interim Council handling of communications. I shall describe four: the increase in the number and range of topics handled in the palace memorial system; the ending of the old practice of rewriting the palace memorials that had to be handled in the routine system; innovations in archival curatorship; and the new emphasis on official publications. Description of other new Interim Council and Grand Council activities will be postponed to later chapters, when trends over the course of the entire Ch'ien-lung reign will be discussed.

Increased Number and Range of Topics in the Palace Memorial System

We have already observed the steady enlargement of the palace memorial system during the Yung-cheng reign, when such new concerns as the nourish-honesty supplements to provincial officials' salaries came to be worked out largely by palace memorial correspondence.[57] As was mentioned in Chapter 1, topics such as the silver-meltage fee (*hao-hsien*), which operated beyond a strict interpretation of the law, were also candidates for palace memorial treatment because only in the inner court could outer-court scrutiny of their dubious legality be evaded.[58] In addition, during the Yung-cheng period many matters that properly belonged in the outer court had received inner-court treatment by first being reported confidentially to the emperor. The surge in palace memorial scope continued in the new reign. The amalgamated inner court's increased capability for handling government business encouraged expansion.

The precise extent of this increase in difficult to measure. Topics in the surviving palace memorials of the new reign covering the period immediately following Yung-cheng's death (YC13/8–12) and the early years of the Ch'ien-lung era (CL1–2)[59] included all the provinces of China Proper and sometimes territories beyond the northwest passes and all levels of people from officials and wealthy merchants down to local yamen runners and peasant farmers. Of course, many palace memorials of this time were still concerned with the military campaign, particularly military personnel questions such as rewards for those who had distinguished themselves and special payments to the families of the martyred. The problem of horse losses continued to rankle. Miao frontier strategies could also be raised as could any kind of local unrest. As always finance was a heavy preoccupation: copper coinage, prices, harvests, taxes, tax remissions, and special problems such as what local treasury was to be tapped to pay certain expenses. Another large area pertained to personnel issues: appointments, promotions, transfers, arrangements for imperial audiences, demotions, and punishments. Even judicial matters—an amnesty for criminals, cases, and details concerning the use of torture—could be reported by palace memorial. Weather continued to be reported as it had been since K'ang-hsi times.[60] Matters concerning the imperial family—empresses, concubines, princes—appear to have been kept out of the palace system except when these persons were involved in state affairs or criminal cases. But even without these, every day the emperor and his ministers faced an enormous variety and range of reports cascading into the inner court.

Many of these subjects had already been submitted in the palace memorial system during the previous reign. But at that time there had been only a small number of executives to deal with the influx: the emperor himself plus the handful of inner deputies—sometimes two or three persons and sometimes Chang T'ing-yü alone. As long as the northwest war preoccupied the inner court, detailed research and deliberation had been impractical; now, however, the inner-court consolidation permitted expansion.

End of Rewriting the Palace Memorials for Outer-Court Processing
Another immediate change was the end of the requirement that in order to receive board processing a palace memorial had to be recopied—sometimes reformulated—and submitted in the routine memorial system. The old Yung-cheng command, "Submit in a routine memorial" (*Chü-t'i lai*; described in Chapter 1), is only occasionally observed in documents of the Ch'ien-lung and later periods. When appropriate, palace memorials could now be sent directly to the outer court. Sometimes the emperor gave the order for this procedure, but high officials such as O-erh-t'ai and Chang T'ing-yü might also issue the necessary commands. A new series of record books was inaugurated in the very first year of the reign to keep copies of the palace memorials turned over to the outer court (Wai-chi tang).[61]

The end of the toil by which palace memorials had to be rewritten for submission in the routine system was an important step. It introduced greater efficiency into palace memorial handling, for these memorials and their vermilion rescripts might now be sent directly to the outer court without being delayed for rewriting. From this time on the outer-court agencies regularly processed palace as well as routine memorials. Soon the palace memorials could be disseminated in the Peking gazettes. The decisions on the memorials that went to the outer court could also now be cited as precedents in the *Collected Statutes and Precedents* of the dynasty (*Hui-tien* and *Hui-tien shih-li*). Moreover, copies of the documents themselves could be filed in outer-court archives and drawn on for outer-court historical compilations. Although at first only a few documents were sent for outer-court treatment, a gradual increase ensued. The significance of this innovation was that the palace memorial system was no longer a private communications channel for the emperor and the inner-court circle at the capital and in the provinces. With the exception of a few specially earmarked memorials, the system now became less secret and official.

Changes in Record Keeping

Another set of communications changes took place in the Interim Council's methods of keeping records. Although many of the Yung-cheng inner court's forms continued—the storage of the hastily written cursive ("grass writing," *ts'ao-shu*) copies of the palace memorials for reference (*lu-fu tsou-che*) and the use of record books, for instance—some changes were instituted right at the beginning of the new reign. In the Yung-cheng period the High Officials in Charge of Military Strategy had maintained Chinese-language records of inner-court deliberations (I-fu tang), which, because of that group's mission, had been limited to the northwest campaign. As soon as Yung-cheng passed from the scene, however, a new series specifically concerned with northwest—a record book on "the frontier" (Pien-pei i-ch'ing tang)—was set up just for campaign matters; meanwhile, the old deliberation series was expanded to embrace the wide range of topics now flowing into the inner court. Indeed, this change was all the more remarkable in that it probably began with the very day of Yung-cheng's death. From that moment all kinds of topics coming before the highest Interim Council–level members were copied into record books of a series that in the previous year had focused exclusively on military problems.[62]

The Manchu-language record books were also changed at the beginning of the new reign, with some of the old Yung-cheng–period titles discontinued and the introduction of several new titles.[63] Still other record-keeping changes can be observed after the end of the Interim Council era; possibly some of those, such as the inauguration of the document register (Sui-shou teng-chi), had Interim Council roots that have disappeared. The Interim Council's inner-court coordination of the palace memorial system and its ramifications gave the council privileged access to information not generally available throughout the bureaucracy. In addition, the responsibility for these communications awarded council members regular access to the emperor.

Interim Council Administration of Publications

One final communications change inaugurated at the beginning of the new reign fell in the area of official publications. In the past, many of the official publications had been the responsibility of outer-court agencies such as the Hanlin Academy, frequently with a grand secretary (himself probably a Hanlin man) having an overall supervisory role.[64] But under Yung-cheng the inner deputies—most of whom were usually grand secretaries as well—had also supervised editorial work, particularly when delicate questions of glossing over or eliminating undesirable facts in the official record arose. Thus it has been suggested that Chang T'ing-yü's directorship of the K'ang-hsi *Veritable Records* resulted in an account that obscured certain questionable machinations that had marked Yung-cheng's pursuit of the throne.[65]

The Yung-cheng reign, however, was not known for a large publications program. The military campaigns and the concern with shaky finances, princely opposition, and other rifts in the body politic did not permit a strong focus on literary pursuits. During the reign, although editorial work on the numerous and lengthy Yung-cheng rescripts and edicts was begun, most of these works eventually appeared early in the Ch'ien-lung period under such titles as the "Yung-cheng Rescripts [on the Palace Memorials]" (*Yung-cheng chu-p'i yü-chih*), "Edicts Issued Through the Grand Secretariat" (*Shang-yü Nei-ko*), and "Edicts to the Eight Banners" (*Shang-yü Pa-ch'i*).[66] In the last year of the reign the printing of the entire "Dragon Edition" (*Lung-tsang*) of the Chinese Tripitaka was undertaken, a project so massive that it too could only be completed under Ch'ien-lung.[67] Some Yung-cheng–era projects, such as the compilations on laws (*Lü-li* and *Hui-tien*) and imperial-clan genealogy (*Yü-tieh*), were parts of series that were occasionally brought up to date and reissued. Some, such as the work on the official Ming history, were continuing projects left over from the K'ang-hsi reign. But relatively little publication work was carried to completion during the Yung-cheng period; the flood of publications that was to become one of the hallmarks of the high Ch'ing thus became strong only during the Ch'ien-lung reign. Indeed, the beginning took place as early as the Interim Council period, well before the end of the prescribed three years of preserving and honoring the practices of one's father.

Although an exact tabulation of publications of the Interim Council years is beyond the reach of available documentation, one early memorial (which I date to CL4 or 5 [1739–40], just after the end of the Interim Council period) itemized the projects under way at the time. The memorial gave the astonishing figure of twenty-six separate bureaus for official publication projects in existence in the early years of the reign, six of which had just finished their work and were closing their doors with twenty still in operation.[68] Because many offices, such as that for compiling the *Veritable Records*, produced more than one work, and some works, such as the board regulations, were put together in the boards themselves, the total number of editing and compilation projects under way during these years was in fact even greater than the memorialized figure.[69] At least ten of the projects can be identified as having been newly instituted at the very beginning of the new reign, with some of the others continuing from before. The high-level members of the Interim Council were heavily concerned with many of these projects—drafting publication proposals, seeking imperial authorization, preparing the enabling edicts, drawing up procedures, and selecting personnel.

Another significant fact about the Interim Council–era publication effort was the membership of the editorial committees. (See Appendix E.) Interim Council members—chiefly O-erh-t'ai and Chang T'ing-yü—headed nearly all the new publication boards. Although this meant that they exercised only supervisory authority and were not involved on a day-to-day basis in the work of compilation, nevertheless their supervisory posts gave them the authority to set policy as well as to intervene. Publishing was a steadily enlarging area of government operations. The inner-court Interim Council was not only keeping pace with that enlargement but directing much of it as well.

Changes in the editorial committees appointed to compile the *Veritable Records* (*Shih-lu*) over the early- and mid-Ch'ing period will illustrate the shift that had taken place (see Table 6). In the early Ch'ing, the outer court had dominated much of the dynasty's official publication effort. Hanlin grand secretaries, some of whom may have also been temporarily and informally attached to the inner court or close to the emperor in some way but without the benefit of the substantial amalgamated organization that came later, had frequently been appointed to the two top echelons of the *Veritable Records* editorial boards for the delicate task of editing the chronicles of the previous reign. But over the course of the middle Ch'ing, the topmost appointees came to be inner deputies (in the Yung-cheng period) and Interim Council members and grand councillors (in the Ch'ien-lung reign). Thus, although many of the men designated for the second echelon continued to be drawn from the ranks of the Hanlin and the outer-court grand secretaries, changes began when Yung-cheng appointed his two top-ranked, full-time imperial deputies, Chang T'ing-yü and Chiang T'ing-hsi, to the top supervising echelon (just after the grand secretary Ma-ch'i) for the K'ang-hsi chronicle. (Indeed, the inner deputy Chang T'ing-yü is said to have been the de facto director of that work.) In the following reign, the panel appointed in YC13/12 (early 1736) for the Yung-cheng *Veritable Records* consisted of Interim Council member O-erh-t'ai as chief overlord and, at the next level, four men, two of whom—Chang T'ing-yü and Hsu Pen—were from the Interim Council.[70]

As Table 6 shows, later *Veritable Records* editorial boards were also served by

TABLE 6. Chief compilers of the early and middle Ch'ing *Veritable Records*. Shows the editors-in-chief (*chien-hsiu tsung-ts'ai*) and the head compilers (half a dozen or so *tsung-ts'ai*) for the early and middle Ch'ing *Veritable Records* (*Shih-lu*), with each man's highest official positions. Because the information is taken from the *Veritable Records* themselves, only the final list of editorial board members is shown. The table shows how the nature of the top-level editorial committees changed from grand secretaries in the earlier reigns to inner deputies, Interim Council members, and Grand Council members later. Names of imperial inner deputies (for the Yung-cheng reign), Interim Council members, and grand councillors are underlined. The reader is reminded that some of the early grand secretaries may also have been inner-court grandees but that they differed from the later Grand Council in that they were not part of a large organization that dominated the inner court.

Reign and Work's Date of Completion	Head Compilers	Position
Shun-chih[a]	Pa-t'ai	Grand Secretary
KH11 (1672)	T'u-hai	Grand Secretary
	So-e-t'u (Songgotu)	Grand Secretary
	Li Yü	Grand Secretary (Ranking)
	Wei I-chieh	former Grand Secretary
	Tu Li-te	Grand Secretary
K'ang-hsi[b]	Ma-ch'i (Maci)	Grand Secretary (Ranking)
YC9 (1731)	Chang T'ing-yü	Grand Secretary, inner deputy
	Chiang T'ing-hsi	Grand Secretary, inner deputy
	Chu Shih	Grand Secretary
Nu-erh-ha-ch'ih	O-erh-t'ai	Grand Councillor
revision CL4 (1740)[c]	Chang T'ing-yü	Grand Councillor
	Hsu Pen	Grand Councillor
Yung-cheng	O-erh-t'ai	Grand Councillor
CL6 (1741)	Chang T'ing-yü	Grand Secretary (Ranking), Grand Councillor
	Fu-min	Grand Secretary
	Hsu Pen	Grand Secretary, Grand Councillor
	San-t'ai	Assisting Grand Secretariat Subchancellor

Continued on next page

Table 6—Continued

Reign and Work's Date of Completion	Head Compilers	Position
Ch'ien-lung CC12 (1807)	Ch'ing-kuei	Grand Secretary (Ranking), Grand Councillor (Ranking)
	Tung Kao	Grand Secretary, Grand Councillor
	Te-ying	Chamberlain of the Imperial Body-guard, former Grand Councillor
	Ts'ao Chen-yung	Board of Works President, future Ranking Grand Councillor (Tao-kuang period)
	Wang Chieh	former Grand Secretary, former Grand Councillor
	Chu Kuei	former Grand Secretary
	P'eng Yuan-jui	Chancellor of the Grand Secretariat
	Na-yen-ch'eng	former Grand Councillor
Chia-ch'ing TK4 (1825)	Ts'ao Chen-yung	Grand Secretary (Ranking), Ranking Grand Councillor
	Tai Chün-yuan	Grand Secretary, former Grand Councillor
	Pai-ling	former Grand Secretary
	Ying-ho	Chancellor of the Grand Secretariat, former Grand Councillor
	Wang T'ing-chen	Board of Rites President
	Sung-yun	Senior Vice President of the Censorate, former Grand Councillor

SOURCES: *Ta-Ch'ing Shih-lu*, introductory lists of compilers, passim; *Ta-Ch'ing Hui-tien Shih-li* (Kuang-hsu edition) 1049, passim.

[a] The choice of leaders to supervise the compilation of the Shun-chih *Veritable Records* turned into a contest between the Oboi and the emperor's factions at court. In the end the young K'ang-hsi Emperor won, so his choices are listed here. See Robert B. Oxnam, *Ruling from Horseback: Manchu Politics in the Oboi Regency* (Chicago: University of Chicago Press, 1975), pp. 192–99.

[b] For an earlier set of appointees for the K'ang-hsi *Veritable Records*, see *Ta-ch'ing Hui-tien shih-li* (Kuang-hsu edition) 1049/11a–b.

[c] This edition of the *Veritable Records* for the Ch'ing founding emperor, Nurhaci, was revised early in the Ch'ien-lung period; see *Ch'ing T'ai-tsu Nu-erh-ha-ch'ih shih-lu*, 1933 typeset edition (preface CL4/12/10 [1740 January 8]).

grand secretaries, but the top supervising official was always an inner-court figure—at least a grand councillor, and frequently the head of the Grand Council. The same was true of the *Imperial Exhortations* (*Sheng-hsun*), which were compiled at the same time as the *Veritable Records* and by the same office.[71] Emperors had to appoint their most reliable and responsible officials to take final editorial responsibility for works as important as these official historical records of each Ch'ing reign. By the Ch'ien-lung period the officials of choice were men of the Grand Council.

Interim Council members also held high concurrent supervisory posts in the State History Office (*Kuo-shih kuan*), the agency that was responsible for producing draft sections of the official history of the dynasty (*kuo-shih*). Early in the first year of the new reign there was a request that the editing of the standard history be continued. Interim Council members researched the previous compilation history for the emperor and found that K'ang-hsi had inaugurated work on the "Official History of Three [Nurhaci, Huang T'ai-chi, and Shun-chih] Reigns" (*San-ch'ao kuo-shih*) and that Yung-cheng had followed this with an order to add the K'ang-hsi era and create an "Official History of Four Reigns" (*Ssu-ch'ao kuo-shih*). The Interim Council report explained that as a result of the Yung-cheng–period labors, all four major elements of the standard history—imperial annals, essays, tables, and biographies—were in draft form (*kao-pen*) by the end of the reign, but revisions were still necessary. Now, concluded the memorialists, would be the appropriate time to begin the Yung-cheng sections of the official history.[72]

Later in the same year, the head of the State History Office, O-erh-t'ai, and his associates submitted the final version of the *Imperial Annals* (*Pen-chi*) for the Nurhaci reign (the first part of the "Official History of Four Reigns"). In the accompanying memorial they outlined their proposal for completing the drafts, planning to proceed first with all of the imperial annals and then go on in turn to the essays, tables, and biographies. But Ch'ien-lung objected. He wanted everything to move along together, with drafts of all four elements being undertaken at once so that History Office personnel would "on the one hand" do the imperial annals and "on the other hand" produce the rest.[73] As a result, official-history drafts appeared continuously over the course of the Ch'ien-lung reign. Even biographies of deceased figures who had served the current emperor were drafted and revised in his lifetime, all supervised by the council.

In addition to overseeing these compilations, the Interim Council was concerned with the government's ambitious program of printing the thirteen classics and the twenty-one official histories, also undertaken at the beginning of the new reign. The Interim Council deliberated many of the problems that arose in connection with this effort, weighing the expense of publication and the need to publish other works against the desirability of bringing the previously unavailable classics and histories within the reach of scholars, particularly to assist those preparing for the examinations.[74]

For many reasons publishing was a desirable area of government activity. Sponsoring new editions of the classics and standard histories put the state squarely behind the empire's huge amount of scholarly enterprise, which ranged from examination preparation to philological and philosophical study.[75] Publication offices also provided patronage opportunities for scholar-officials as well as jobs for some of the graduates of the country's examination system— composing, copying, proofreading, and the like. In addition, when Yung-cheng's government tentatively and Ch'ien-lung's more strongly pushed Buddhist and Manchu publication interests, they conciliated large constituencies.[76] A strong publication effort appealed to many important groups in the empire.

Editorial control over historical writing was particularly important for disseminating approved versions of events and building the historical consciousness to support government policies. Once the earlier problems of governance had been solved and the decades-long campaign of fighting the northwest tribes was winding down, it is not surprising to find that the government eagerly embraced a large number of publishing enterprises, or that the Interim Council was behind these activities. Nevertheless, it is significant that a strong push for additional publications beyond those already under way was inaugurated at the outset of the new reign, without the standard mourning-period respect for previous policies. This intensified attention to publications compared with the Yung-cheng period's relatively light interest constitutes another notable change initiated remarkably soon after the death of the former emperor.[77] Like the Interim Council consolidation of the formerly separate inner-court staffs, these changes were introduced within half a year or less. It is clear that the instigator of these speedy innovations was not the new, young, inexperienced emperor but rather his high-level ministers, who had been waiting a long time with just such plans for change.

OPPOSITION TO INNER-COURT GROWTH

The many changes and the attendant publicity by means of edicts that announced much of the Interim Council's consolidation and growth roused outer-court opposition. In Yung-cheng times the secrecy enveloping inner-court activities and the heavy focus on the military campaign had been attended by a lack of awareness of the important changes taking place in the inner court. But once Ch'ien-lung came to the throne and the inner court's administrative activities were more on display than in earlier years—in matters such as the salary question, for example—inner-court expansion and the parallel decline in outer-court influence were challenged. We have already seen how the inner court was indirectly attacked by the proposal to do away with certain clerks' concurrent posts. Other evidence suggests that during the Interim Council period an attempt was made to wrest control of certain aspects of the palace memorial communications system out of the hands of the new inner-court body.

Early in the Ch'ien-lung reign, the Interim Council studied and rejected a proposal that the palace system's harvest reports be transferred to the routine system. The Interim Council deliberation argued that although the openness of the outer-court communications system would "obstruct deceptions" and act as a restraint on malfeasance in harvest reporting, the delays that were part of the routine system—particularly the requirement that memorialists assemble all relevant information from all over a province before reporting any of it—ruled out the desired change. It is likely that the proposal was planted by outer-court men opposed to inner-court growth, and there is a hint in the document that Interim Council opposition to the proposal was based on a desire to monopolize important palace memorial information that was at the time flowing exclusively into the inner court. No ground could be yielded lest the principle of inner-court confidentiality for all palace memorials—and thereby one of the keys to inner court strength—come under attack. Still, on this occasion council members were attentive to outer-court protests. Even though they advised that harvest reports continue in the inner-court palace memorial system, they made a concession to the outer court and recommended that the provincial authorities also submit summer and autumn harvest information in two regular routine memorials that would go to the boards and their censorial sections for investigation.[78] Thus in this instance the inner court retained control, but outer-court concerns were not entirely ignored.

Another proposal presented a little later advocated that after receiving the throne's decision, the capital palace memorials be processed by the Grand Secretariat instead of by the scattered board and other capital offices as had been done in the past. The proponent, who was the senior vice president of the Censorate, sought particularly to combat various kinds of communications malfeasance committed by outer-court yamen underlings who changed figures or altered circumstances in the course of copying documents. No one, he said, outside the office where these acts were being perpetrated possessed the reliable original of the document in question to check this kind of activity and the heavy press of board business prevented corrective measures. The high Censorate official wanted the capital palace memorials handled in much the same way as the routine system memorials from capital offices—with seals stamped on copies, greater circulation for the documents, and the Grand Secretariat, not the originating offices, in charge of storage and further dissemination of the documents.[79]

It is difficult to analyze this bill without access to all the relevant documents and behind-the-scenes conversations that must have taken place at the time. On the surface, the proposal appears to be of little consequence. But precisely because the suggestion appeared innocuous, there was a chance it would win approval and then become the entering wedge by which the originals of the provincial palace memorials would also have to be treated like routine memorials and deposited in the outer court. The secret inner-court communications system was in jeopardy.

Despite the argument's plausibility, the Interim Council was not taken in. The council recommendation, which the emperor accepted and authorized, did not transfer new powers to the Grand Secretariat. A few small concessions were made by requiring that a capital office immediately submit a summary of each document returned from the inner court and within three days follow that with a stamped, sealed copy for the Grand Secretariat. But document originals and the responsibility for dissemination remained at the capital offices.[80] Board responsibilities were preserved intact and there was no transfer to the Grand Secretariat. The threat to inner-court monopolization of the provincial palace memorials—and indeed, to the very existence of the second separate inner-court communications system—melted away.

Thus, during the Interim Council era some opposition to the council did arise, including sinister insinuations of inner-court misuse of secrecy and power. Moreover, some of the attacks on the council focused on the council's control of the palace memorial system, highlighting inner-court communications as a key to council power. But the Interim Council stoutly defended itself against these challenges, a fact which suggests that this council, unlike earlier Ch'ing transition councils, thought it was going to last.

FROM INTERIM COUNCIL TO GRAND COUNCIL

On CL2/11/27 (1738 January 16), the Interim Council members sought permission to disband. Opening with the reminder that the same request put forward the previous year—when Yung-cheng's coffin had been escorted to its tomb—had met with an imperial refusal, they pointed out that they had now served continuously for "three years" (actually twenty-seven months), as ritual required, since Yung-cheng's death and were again following the traditional formalities for bringing their inner-court service to an end so as to allow the new emperor to take over the leadership of government himself.[81] Instead, at this fateful moment in Ch'ing history the government veered in an entirely new direction. The council received orders not to disband but to continue, only under a new name.

The edict's explanation for this break with tradition began with a comparison of the emperor's present circumstances with those of his father. At the close of the transition period, he was young—only twenty-six—and inexperienced, unlike his father, who had succeeded to the throne in his forties, "sage and intelligent." The edict praised the father's ability: "Of all the affairs in the empire . . . , there were none of which he did not know, nothing of which he was not informed. At the present jucture, how should I," asked the neophyte, "presume to compare myself with the late emperor?"[82]

Ch'ien-lung then praised the Interim Council, saying, "Of all the government affairs turned over, there was nothing that the council did not wholeheartedly attend to." Nevertheless, the emperor admitted he could not refuse the request to disband. The eight members (in two echelons) who were still in office were thanked and their names sent to the appropriate groups for rewards.[83]

The next day the crucial step was taken. A second edict explained that military exigencies on the two fronts (northern and western) still threatened and that the emperor was mired in dealing with "the myriad affairs [of government]." The ruler required assistance. Even though the late emperor had had no similar continuing council, the edict recalled Yung-cheng's High Officials in Charge of Military Strategy, who had served as assistants. Accordingly, six Interim Council members were now retained and given the former High Officials' title. Heading the list were the two old stalwarts, O-erh-t'ai and Chang T'ing-yü.[84]

Thus was the Ch'ing "Grand Council" founded. With an apparently filial act said to revive his father's governing arrangements but that in fact ignored the compartmentalization of Yung-cheng's inner court, the young Ch'ien-lung, in the third year of his reign, announced the administrative innovation that transformed the government for the remainder of the dynasty. This stroke was the final step in the reorganization of Ch'ing high-level governance that had begun in K'ang-hsi times.

Innovation was the most striking feature of the Interim Council years. The period opened with the consolidation of the three inner-court staffs—the inner deputies, the Military Finance Section, and the High Officials in Charge of Military Strategy—plus the absorption of the recently formed Miao Council. This was a significant departure from the precedent of Yung-cheng's separate staffs. A second break with the established structure of government came at the end of the Interim Council era, when what had been a transition council was converted to a permanent entity and allowed to persevere in a consolidated form quite unlike Yung-cheng's compartmentalized inner court. All through the period there were other rejections of the Yung-cheng past: in administration, the communications system, archival curatorship, and publications. The mourning period that was supposed to hallow the ways of the recently deceased father was incongruously marked by change.

The changes instituted in this period were not merely the temporary experiments of a new and immature monarch struggling to put his own stamp on his reign. The innovations were well thought out. They transformed the structure of the inner court. Moreover, they lasted. The fact that many were instituted in the early weeks of the new reign suggests that they had been planned well in advance of Yung-cheng's death. Perhaps for this reason they should be attributed not to the new emperor but to his inner-court advisers. The emperor, after all, did not have to make changes right away and in fact should have been restrained by the ancient Confucian mandate against change for three years. But if the ministers were hoping to put across their ideas, this could best be accomplished at the very beginning, when they were dealing with a grieving and inexperienced monarch. Some of the innovations—such as the end of the rewriting of the palace memorials submitted to the outer court—were so technical that they bear the unmistakable stamp not of an inexperienced emperor but of knowledgeable officials. Moreover, the Interim Council members' spirited defense of their organization in their deliberation memorials makes it clear that these officials were ambitious to have their new organization persevere. Although it will probably forever be impossible to draw a clear line between ministerial advocacy and imperial agency, the Interim Council's survival owes a great deal to its members' determination.

That determination was solidly backed by ability. The Interim Council was able to work effectively, delivering sound recommendations—such as those that doubled capital salaries. Efficiency was also a hallmark of their labors. In the report on Interim Council work submitted when the changeover from Interim to Grand Council took place, unfinished council business left over from the twenty-seven months came to only three items, all deliberately postponed.[85] The ministers had made themselves indispensable to the monarch.

Above all, the informality mechanism introduced in the K'ang-hsi and earlier Manchu inner courts, and insisted on by Yung-cheng, promoted inner-court development. Although under Yung-cheng informality had kept the early inner-court staffs fragile and flexible, depending for their very existence on the will of the sovereign, under Ch'ien-lung this fragility proved to be the advantage that was to allow growth unfettered by law and precedent.

SIX

The Structure of the
Eighteenth-Century Grand Council

The revival of the title of the High Officials in Charge of Military Strategy
(*Pan-li Chün-chi ta-ch'en* or *Chün-chi ch'u*) on CL2/11/28 (1738 January 17)
constituted an exception to dynastic policies, but the records do not portray
this as the momentous event that it was. The enabling edict played down the
departure from precedent and stressed that Yung-cheng's high military advisers' office was being revived to assist the emperor with the unfinished business
of the military campaign.[1] Internal documents also failed to depict the change:
the council's record books referred to the Interim Council (*Tsung-li shih-wu
wang ta-ch'en*) on one day and without a hitch made the transition to the Grand
Council (*Chün-chi ch'u*) on the next.[2] Even most of the personnel continued to
serve, with only a slight reordering as royal princes and a few others were
dropped. But despite these continuities, the moment was significant. Previous
transition councils had not been continued beyond the mourning period or the
time needed for an infant emperor to mature. The Interim Council's power
and influence were now extended beyond the emergency of a new emperor's
adjustment to his imperial role. A plenipotentiary council with both Manchu
and a small number of Chinese members had become a permanent part of the
Ch'ing inner court. This chapter will examine the structure and responsibilities
of this new organization during the last two-thirds of the eighteenth century.

Limitations of both space and sources affect the content of this chapter and
the next. Although a step-by-step account of Grand Council expansion and
occasional reverses during the Ch'ien-lung reign might be desirable, the narrative of turning points and stages of development has been held to a minimum.
One reason is lack of precision in the sources. It has not always been possible
to pinpoint the exact moment that the council acquired a new responsibility or
added a subordinate agency; subordinate offices frequently began with the
delegation of a task to one or two men and were only given names and separate

work space years after their shadowy beginnings. First mentions may signify a turning point, or they may indicate a process that had long been under way before being cited in the records.[3]

A similar difficulty in describing the stages and phases of the council's development concerns the most detailed published description of Grand Council history and procedures, a Tao-kuang–period (1821–50) compilation of documents on the eighteenth- and early-nineteenth-century council.[4] The work is valuable because its contents were assembled out of the Grand Council's own files and the compiler, the council clerk Liang Chang-chü, frequently drew on his own experience at the council to introduce his selections with useful explanations and comments. Although dates are supplied for many of the documents that Liang quotes, his own observations have none. Should we assume that the latter describe only the situation of his own day? In many instances, archival documents as well as the recollections of earlier clerks such as Chao I suggest that much of the elaborate organization depicted in Liang's compendium, particularly in his editorial comments, may already have been in place in the Ch'ien-lung period. But because the Chia-ch'ing reforms had occurred by the time Liang wrote, some topics, such as his discussion of Grand Council clerks, may reflect only the early-nineteenth-century situation. Thus the sources have to be used with care. In general I have relied on Liang as an authority for both the council's expansion and its later reform.

What follows, then, has been condensed to focus generally on the council as it developed over the entire Ch'ien-lung reign, the key period of expansion. I shall show how certain inherited features embedded in the council's structure, as well as events and personalities of the times, were responsible for the council's rapid development. Further research will be necessary before we acquire a detailed picture of the changes that took place during the reign.

THE GRAND COUNCIL HEYDAY IN THE CH'IEN-LUNG REIGN

The Ch'ien-lung reign was the Grand Council heyday, the period in which the council had its greatest spurts of growth and acquired the shape it would retain for the remainder of the dynasty. The reign was the longest in the two millennia of China's dynastic history for which accurate records survive—sixty-three years (CL1–60 plus CC1–3 [1736–99]) if Ch'ien-lung's abdication years are counted, as they should be.[5] As we have seen, the council was newly reorganized and consolidated at the beginning of the reign, when it came to direct much of the government work at the capital and in the provinces. It was able to expand chiefly because of its vantage point in the inner court, prestige of closeness to the emperor, secrecy, and inherited unofficial status. These freed it of the traditions, administrative rules, and openness to scrutiny that at the same time constrained the older outer-court agencies. Council members' participation in the great work of the day—the military campaigns that pushed China's borders to an extent second only to the vast territories held by the

Mongols under the Yuan (1280–1368), for example, and the unprecedented government patronage of literary enterprise—supplied the psychological push that inspired growth. A new order for a self-confident age was being created at the capital. The Grand Council stood at the center of that order.

Numerical indexes of council growth indicate that paperwork handled at the council more than doubled over the Ch'ien-lung period. From an average of 5.7 incoming Chinese-language provincial palace memorials (*tsou-che*) per day and 172 per month in one sample month early in the reign, ever increasing numbers of documents coursed through the council. By the end of the reign the comparable figures had almost tripled to 16 per day and 480 per month.[6] The document register (Sui-shou teng-chi) devised to log these incoming memorials and the official responses displayed a parallel increase, with one relatively slim volume per year before CL16 (1751), one or two variously until CL34 (1769), and then, generally, two large volumes per year through the end of the reign.[7] Bundles of Chinese-language memorial copies (Chün-chi ch'u lu-fu tsou-che) more than doubled from an average of less than one packet per month in the final years of the Yung-cheng reign to more than two packets per month, each packet one-third or more larger than the early ones, by the beginning of the Chia-ch'ing reign. The figures for packets of memorial copies written in Manchu also jumped. The numbers of Manchu record books, already high before the start of the reign because so many Yung-cheng records had been kept in Manchu, showed an increase too, albeit a smaller one.[8] Chinese-language record books spurted from only three or four per year in the last years of the Yung-cheng reign to more than eight per year in the same series under Ch'ien-lung.[9] The storage space required to deal with the increased paper flow is another index of the council's growth. Figures for palace memorial storage show that fifteen crates were needed to hold the Yung-cheng–period documents, or a little more than one crate per year, whereas 184 crates, or more than three per year, proved necessary for the memorial production of the sixty years of the Ch'ien-lung reign. The *Veritable Records* reflect this burgeoning of paperwork. The average number of subsections (*chüan*) per year multiplied from 1.7 in the Shun-chih reign (1644–60) and 1.1 for K'ang-hsi (1661–1722) to 3 per year for Yung-cheng and 6.2 for Ch'ien-lung.[10]

Periodic orders for supplies were another sign of expansion. Twelve cabinets and twelve hand trunks for carrying documents were requisitioned for Grand Council use in CL2 (1737), while in CL43 (1778) thirty-five pieces of furniture —cabinets, tables, and settees for the council offices—were commanded at one fell swoop. That same year five catties (*chin*) of Anhwei ink, thirty inkstones, and two hundred fine and three hundred large writing brushes were ordered.[11] These high figures reflect the fact that more areas of government work were being monitored in the inner court than before. Some topics were now handled jointly with outer-court agencies, some were transferred outright into the inner court, others were new areas being subjected to central-government attention for the first time.

Coping with the council's flood of paperwork required an increased personnel complement. Although it is difficult to calculate the exact number of persons attached to the Ch'ien-lung Grand Council, some idea of size may be ascertained from the council's daily food allotments. An early-nineteenth-century account reported twelve tables served each day at the council premises, a figure that might be calculated as 144 persons (reckoning 12 men per table).[12] Although a large part of the council personnel complements would have been on rotation and so off duty each day, those dining at the twelve tables would have included the day's duty groups of each of the following bodies: the 32 Manchu and Chinese clerks, the Military Archives Office (*Fang-lueh kuan*) personnel of about 150 persons,[13] the staff of the Inner Translation Office (*Nei fan-shu fang*), and numerous underlings such as scribes, copyists, filers (*kung-shih*), and errand runners.[14] The councillors themselves, averaging seven per year during the Ch'ien-lung reign, would not have dined with the others.[15] Accordingly, a minimum rough guess for the total number of persons connected with the late Ch'ien-lung Grand Council, including both those on and off duty (and we do not always know exactly how many members of each group were on duty), might run to well over two hundred. This was a small number compared with the thousands serving in the outer court, but was nevertheless a huge increase relative to Yung-cheng days.[16]

Although inner-court consolidation and the transition council's continuation beyond the standard mourning period following Yung-cheng's death constituted the initial steps in the council's growth, several other forward spurts may be identified later in the reign. In CL12 (1747), for example, a decision in the council's favor affirmed that high-level secret papers would continue to be stored in the Grand Council archives and not in the more accessible outer-court files.[17] This stroke both strengthened the council's power to monopolize secret information and permitted a small victory in its continuing strife with certain outer-court agencies.

Other boosts derived from the Ch'ien-lung Emperor's fondness for travel. The peripatetic monarchy that was one of the hallmarks of the Ch'ien-lung reign repeatedly confirmed the council's usefulness as a small, highly efficient centralized managerial body that for an imperial tour could reduce itself to a skeleton staff, work on the basis of only essential files brought along on the tour, and execute major government functions in the course of a royal progress. Thus the government was able to continue running from anywhere in the empire as well as beyond the passes of China proper. Each occasion of an imperial tour—and in some years there were several—reinforced the council's indispensability as a disciplined body able to provide efficient management and sound advice when on the march.

Above all, the late-eighteenth-century military campaigns also generated bursts of council expansion. In CL13–15 (1748–50), the council directed the capital management and was active at the front of the first Chin-ch'uan campaign against the west Szechuan aborigines. During the first year the number of councillors grew from eight to twelve as three Manchu members were deputed to positions of command in the southwest and another was sent on an investigative mission to Shantung.[18] Twenty-four new clerks (seventeen Manchus and seven Chinese) were taken on.[19] At about the same time, the council acquired new office space close to the imperial work area, the "Northern Quarters" (*Pei-wu*) for the councillors and the "Southern Quarters" (*Nan-wu*) for the clerks.[20] In CL14 (1749) the council's first subordinate organization to be set up in Ch'ien-lung times, the Office of Military Archives (*Fang-lueh kuan*), was established on a permanent basis to oversee both the burgeoning files of campaign and other documents and the publication of the new reign's first campaign history.[21] The Yung-cheng inner court, chiefly preoccupied with maintaining supply lines and thwarting malfeasance, had had nothing so elaborate as this.

THE GRAND COUNCIL NAME AND SPECIAL TERMINOLOGY

The Grand Council's Chinese name (*Chün-chi ch'u*) had a double meaning, capitalizing on the fact that the two descriptive characters, *chün-chi*, may mean both "military affairs" and "affairs of state."[22] As we saw in Chapter 4, during YC11 (1733) the title of the High Officials in Charge of Military Strategy had shifted gradually from the old term in use for the Yung-cheng–period northwest campaign, *chün-hsu*, meaning "military finance," to another term, *chün-chi*, which in those days meant "military planning" or "strategy." Now at the end of the Interim Council, the revived term was employed in its second sense of "affairs of state" to refer to the new council's amalgamated mission, which involved much more than a military campaign. For this, modern historians have generally abandoned the military connotation of the Chinese term and instead emphasized its broader meaning with the translation "Grand Council."[23]

THE GRAND COUNCILLORS

Hierarchies at the Ministerial Level of the Grand Council

Following the dismissal of the Interim Council princes and the restoration of the name of Yung-cheng's High Officials in Charge of Military Strategy late in CL2 (early 1738), the councillors' level in the new organization consisted of the former two top echelons of the Yung-cheng era. These were Yung-cheng's inner deputies, the grand secretaries O-erh-t'ai and Chang T'ing-yü, and the former high officials group, men such as Hai-wang and Na-yen-t'ai. At first the shadows of these two ancestor staffs persisted to keep the new council divided. For example, when a new record book of court letters was set up in CL3 (1738), it described its secret inner-court edicts (*mi-chi*) as emanating from both the "Grand Secretariat" (that is, the former inner deputies) and the

"Office of Military Strategy."[24] Another holdover from the compartmentaliza-tion of Yung-cheng days persisted in the distinction between high-level and nonmilitary matters on the one hand, which were frequently assigned to the grand secretaries, and military topics on the other, which tended to be handed to the group still sometimes known as the "high officials." In fact, many early Ch'ien-lung–period documental references to "grand secretaries" signified the topmost echelon of grand councillors, a point that has frequently led researchers to misidentify Grand Council work and accomplishments in this period as those of the grand secretaries. The persistence of these divisions is found, for example, in the CL8 (1743) record of deliberations that shows the high officials debating security issues such as the Miao frontier, coast and river patrol, weapons production, pursuit of Annam brigands, and troop assign-ments, while the inner-court grand secretaries (that is, those on the council) deliberated domestic concerns such as water conservancy, imperial tombs, drought in Chihli province, and some military appointments.[25] During the council's second decade these divisions slowly disappeared.[26] Instead, a different kind of internal organization developed in the councillors' ranks.

During the eighteenth century (we do not know exactly when, but certainly by mid-reign), the council acquired a formal hierarchical ordering. At the top was the ranking grand councillor or council leader (*ling-pan*).[27] This man was usually a Manchu, but Chinese served as leaders for eight of the sixty years of the Ch'ien-lung reign.[28] Except for the transition councils set up when Ch'ien-lung and Chia-ch'ing came to power, princes were not used, though relatives on the distaff imperial side, such as No-ch'in, who was ranking councillor in CL11–13 (1746–48), and Fu-heng, leader for more than two decades in CL14–35 (1748–70), were sometimes appointed to this post.[29]

The leading grand councillor was executive manager of the group. He supervised most edict drafting and on his person carried the key (*yin-yao*) to the official seal, responsibilities that gave him control of many aspects of inner-court communications management.[30] In addition to participating in the morning audiences when the full Grand Council usually met to discuss the day's memorials, he might also be recalled later in the day for informal meetings with the emperor known as "late conversations" (*wan-mien*).[31] The Ch'ien-lung Emperor took care to see that his ranking councillors could accomplish what he expected of them. In CL14 (1749) he issued an edict lightening Fu-heng's duties so that this top minister would not have to be fully responsible for drafts produced in the boards he supervised: Fu-heng now needed only to affix his seal, thereby satisfying the formality of having a top inner-court official in charge.[32]

Under Ch'ien-lung the ranking councillor was acknowledged to possess the highest civil office in the realm. On one occasion when Ch'ien-lung reminisced about No-ch'in's high position as ranking councillor he declared that "among the high officials, no one had surpassed No-ch'in." The ranking councillor's importance in central administration was attested in a substantial edict of CL13 (early 1749) issued shortly after Fu-heng, the leading councillor of the day, had left to take up a position of command on the Chin-ch'uan front. As a result of Fu-heng's departure, said the edict, "most of the matters handled by the Grand Council could not be satisfactorily [discharged]." The edict then gave an example of the council's disarray when "not one man among the grand councillors" could recall the previously memorialized background of a Shantung request for emergency grain shipments. "I had to remind them," declared the emperor, "and only then could it be looked up and included in the deliberation." But this was not all. There were other items of missing information, continued the emperor, "on which I had to give instruction one by one." Even when matters were put to right, complained Ch'ien-lung, "I was exhausted." Things had changed greatly "compared with when [Fu-heng] was at the capital, when so many details were satisfactorily handled without troubling me." The edict then outlined the difficulties of finding and training a man for the high position of ranking councillor and the importance of obtaining a good man for the sake of the imperial peace of mind:

> Formerly when the Grand Secretary O-erh-t'ai was at hand [serving as ranking councillor], I trained and nurtured No-ch'in. And when No-ch'in was here [as leader], I trained and nurtured ... Fu-heng. To all of them I gave instruction and experience.... Men of talent are difficult to obtain—they cannot be produced between morning and evening. Now [Fu-heng] has gone to the front. In the past [he] was truly the only man I consulted and I neglected to take the precaution of cultivating [his replacement] from among the [remaining] high officials in order to have someone to continue the [central work of] administration. As a result, during the past few days the many matters of state have not failed to involve me.[33]

Ch'ien-lung's dependence on his leading councillors brings to mind his father's gratitude for the services of Prince I years before—"so that my heart was completely at peace." Later in the century, at the end of the reign, when on A-kuei's death Ho-shen succeeded to the post of ranking councillor, Ch'ien-lung used the long-discarded title of "prime minister" and is reported to have told him, "You may now be called prime minister [*shih-hsiang*]."[34] Although the ranking grand councillor was not a prime minister in the sense of being able to authorize final policy decisions, nevertheless he was the single top official responsible for steering much of central-government decision making and implementing many of the policies that resulted. Particularly under Ch'ien-lung, who, unlike his father, detested the details of governing, the official who held this post had to function effectively.

During the Ch'ien-lung period the selection of the ranking councillor was determined first by the date of the man's appointment as grand secretary and then by his Grand Secretariat palace or pavilion rank. Because the emperor was responsible for these designations, it was possible to advance a favorite by bestowing a promotion within the grand secretary ranks.[35] Even so, Ch'ien-lung never saw fit to jump his supposed favorite Ho-shen ahead of A-kuei, who had received a grand secretary appointment nearly a decade before Ho-shen. As a result, A-kuei served as ranking grand councillor for the last two decades of Ch'ien-lung's life, predeceasing his sovereign and so making way for Ho-shen only two years before Ch'ien-lung's death.[36] This etiquette of precedence must have been developed over the course of the Ch'ien-lung reign, for at the beginning of the reign the fact that Chang T'ing-yü had been appointed grand secretary several years before O-erh-t'ai did not win him precedence on the council. Thus O-erh-t'ai served as leader until his death, whereupon he was succeeded by other Manchus, first No-ch'in and then Fu-heng. Even though Chang T'ing-yü had often served as de facto leader of the inner-court council, in his day the time had not yet arrived when a Chinese could be the officially designated leader.

There were other instances of a concern for hierarchy. For example, at the end of a lateral communication (a document sent between officials rather than to the emperor), the councillors' ranks might be written according to the order of precedence decided for the council at the time. One such document placed the name of the council leader, A-kuei, in the center, followed by an alternating pattern of Liang Kuo-chih second (at the left), Ho-shen third (at the right),

FIGURE 6. Order of precedence at the ministerial level of the Grand Council.

4   2   1   3   5

This excerpt from the end of a Grand Council lateral communication sent to officials in another agency illustrates the attention to order of precedence that prevailed in the Grand Council by late in the Ch'ien-lung reign. (The numbers on the illustration have been added to guide the readers of this book.)

SOURCE: *Shang-yü tang fang-pen* (Taipei) CL50/4/4, p. 28; cf. *Ch'ing-shih* 4:2495. Reproduced at approximately original size with the permission of the Taipei Palace Museum.

Fu-ch'ang-an fourth (again at the left), and Tung Kao fifth (at the right; see Figure 6).[37]

The deference due the upper reaches of the official hierarchy was also reflected in council documents in the epistolary practice of designating councillors only by their surname character and leaving a respectful blank or supplying the appropriate title but omitting the personal name characters. This gave a kind of imbalance to some lists, where the councillors would be recorded only with surnames while others, even grand secretaries who were not on the council, had their full names written out.[38] Such distinctions in rank and ceremony, so important in the rank-conscious society of eighteenth-century China, are examples of the rationalization and elaboration that were part of the council's growth.

Appointment of Grand Councillors

Little is known about how the grand councillors were appointed. Although many appointment edicts exist, no records explain the selection process. Nor is any light shed by procedures for appointing grand secretaries, which by the middle of the eighteenth century were formalized with the requirement that a vacancy was to be followed with a Grand Council request for a new appointment and a list of appropriate candidates.[39] There were no parallel rules for the grand councillorships: in true inner-court fashion the emperors jealously safeguarded their right to choose these closest advisers and refused to subject the process to any sort of regulation.[40] Nevertheless, from the appointments that resulted we may trace some of the considerations that probably influenced the imperial choices and guess at the kind of advice the monarch may have received while pondering the candidates.

The imperial autonomy in this matter is important to remember. The emperor could choose anyone, as the sudden elevation to the council of the Grand Council clerk Wu Hsiung-kuang in CC2 (1797) attests. Wu was the only servitor on hand in Jehol who responded to the imperial summons in the middle of the night after others, including some of the councillors, failed to appear. As a reward for this faithfulness, Ch'ien-lung proposed elevating Wu to a councillorship, doubtless with a view to reminding the others of their failure to serve their sovereign in the expected manner. Despite Ho-shen's objections to Wu's lack of qualifications and insufficiently high rank, the emperor went ahead with the appointment, and Wu served for half a year before being fobbed off with a slightly lower post at a level commensurate with the point he had reached in his career.[41] The appointment stands recorded in Wu's official biography as a reminder that the monarch exercised final control over Grand Council appointments and dismissals. At the same time, the official record of Ho-shen's remonstrance also survives to demonstrate that a high minister need not shrink from offering advice, even at this level of what was supposed to be the personal imperial choice.

Although there were some exceptions, councillors' appointments were generally limited to civil officials at the capital with a rank of 2A or higher—usually grand secretaries (1A), board presidents (1B), and board vice presidents (2A)—although occasionally high levels at other agencies were tapped for councillor appointments.[42] The Ch'ien-lung Emperor also frequently drew on imperial distaff connections. (Figure 7 shows some of the imperial family connections among Ch'ien-lung's grand councillors.) Sometimes the emperor appointed relatives of the empress who had no claim to the throne but who might be counted on to render loyal service out of family interest. Through his beloved first empress, for instance, Ch'ien-lung was related to four of his most important grand councillors: Fu-heng, brother of the empress, and Fu-heng's three sons, Fu-lung-an, Fu-k'ang-an, and Fu-ch'ang-an, who together served a total of sixty-five years on the council, including Fu-heng's two decades as leader.[43] Another grand councillor, Chao-hui, was a grand-nephew of the empress who had been mother of the Yung-cheng Emperor.[44] Pan-ti was an imperial son-in-law.[45] The objection to princes of the blood later translated into the oft-repeated statement that the dynasty had a tradition of not allowing princes to serve on the Grand Council.[46] This precept was broken briefly at the beginning of the Chia-ch'ing reign and at much greater length at a moment of supreme crisis in the mid–nineteenth century, when Prince Kung was appointed to council membership and later as council leader. Afterward, at the end of the dynasty, other princes also served.[47]

In addition to appointing suitable imperial relations, Ch'ien-lung sometimes turned to the sons of especially trusted grand councillors, as in the case of three of Fu-heng's sons. The Grand Council father and son Yin-chi-shan and Ch'ing-kuei also exemplify this policy: in CL20 (1755), Ch'ing-kuei first became attached to the council as a clerk; several years later, less than half a year after Yin-chi-shan's death, Ch'ing-kuei was named to fill his father's place on the council. In the next reign, following the Ho-shen debacle at the beginning of CC4 (1799), he became the leading councillor and served for more than a decade, to CC17 (1799–1812).[48] The Mongol bannermen Na-yen-t'ai and Ch'ang-ling were another example of father and son who served as grand councillors. A number of councillors were also drawn from men whom Ch'ien-lung had previously known as clerks, although usually with an intervening period of service elsewhere.[49] A family connection with the imperial inner circle could assist a man's rise.

The Ch'ien-lung Emperor also preferred Manchus over Chinese. Manchus of the Imperial Household represented on the council usually held the high post of adjutant general (*yü-ch'ien ta-ch'en*),[50] although the appointment of Imperial Household personnel appears to have halted in the Chia-ch'ing reign. According to the calculations of a recent student of Grand Council history, the number of Manchus on the Grand Council exceeded Chinese in forty-four years of that sixty-year reign (75 percent of the time), while Chinese exceeded

FIGURE 7. Imperial family connections of some Ch'ien-lung grand councillors.

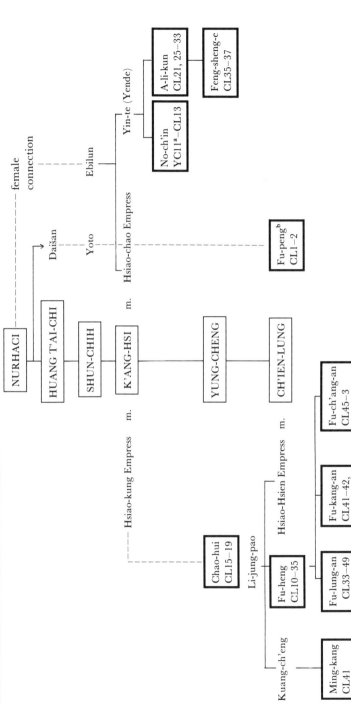

Although imperial princes did not regularly hold Grand Council appointments over a long period of time except in the late Ch'ing, some of Ch'ien-lung's grand councillors were drawn from the emperor's female relatives. In this figure, councillors' names are shown in heavily outlined boxes, and the dates below the names show each man's period of council service. Not all relationships could be clearly traced.

SOURCES: *Ch'ing-shih* 3: 2206; Arthur W. Hummel, ed., *Eminent Chinese of the Ch'ing Period (1644–1912)* (Taipei, 1967), passim.

[a] No-ch'in's YC11 appointment may have been in the Office of Military Strategy.

[b] Fu-p'eng was a sixth-generation descendant in the male line from Nurhaci. Despite his distant relationship, however, he did hold a princedom.

TABLE 7. Years of service on the Grand Council for Manchu and Chinese during the Ch'ien-lung reign.

	Total Numbers of Councillor Duty Years	Manchu Duty Years	Chinese Duty Years
1st decade, CL1–10	68	49 (72%)	19 (28%)
2nd decade, CL11–20	85	56 (66%)	29 (34%)
3rd decade, CL21–30	75	44 (59%)	31 (41%)
4th decade, CL31–40	73	42 (58%)	31 (42%)
5th decade, CL41–50	73	47 (64%)	26 (36%)
6th decade, CL51–60	63	41 (65%)	22 (35%)
Total duty years	437	279 (64%)	158 (36%)

SOURCE: *Ch'ing-shih* 4:2487–96.

NOTE: The source tables do not list the two imperial princes who headed the Interim Council at the beginning of the reign (CL1–10); if these were added the figures for Manchu dominance would be increased slightly. Chu Shih has also been omitted because he is not in the source table, although he is regarded by some as having served. Note too that Ch'ien-lung's abdication years have not been counted; only the years of the Ch'ien-lung reign are included, with the Interim Council months calculated as if they were Grand Council. Mongols and Chinese bannermen are counted as Manchus.

Manchus in only two years (3 percent). In the remaining thirteen years the two groups were equally balanced. The Manchus' dominance does not appear quite so strong, however, if the computation is figured in terms of each councillor's number of years on duty during the reign. As Table 7 shows, for the entire reign roughly a two-thirds Manchu to one-third Chinese distribution prevailed (279 years versus 158). Thus Manchus and Mongols predominated even though they did not have a strong record in the examinations, with only two *chü-jen* and two *chin-shih* holders among the thirty-eight members of this favored group appointed by the end of the reign.[51]

The number of Chinese grand councillors grew slowly. When the council was first established after the end of the Interim Council in CL2 (1738), it had only one Chinese member, Chang T'ing-yü. By the end of CL3, Hsu Pen, who had been dropped the previous year, was reinstated. Subsequently the number of Chinese on the council gradually increased. By mid-reign the emperor appears to have accepted the principle that an attempt should be made to approach dyarchy in council appointments, although exact parity was rarely reached.[52] Thus Chinese membership reached its high point in the fourth decade, after which it fell off slightly. This was also the decade in which the Grand Council acquired its earliest Chinese leading councillors: first Liu T'ung-hsun, who served two years, followed by Yü Min-chung, who served six. The slowly mounting numbers of Chinese on the council may have constituted another way of weakening the old, exclusively Manchu Deliberative Council and other Manchu preponderances of the K'ang-hsi and early Yung-cheng years.

Many Grand Council appointments reached into the board directorates and promoted board presidents and vice presidents to the council. Frequently these men retained their board posts while serving on the council. In other instances a councillor-appointed grand secretary would be elevated to a board superintendency and from that vantage point would continue "concurrently to oversee" (*chien-kuan*) board policymaking. Because of the difficulty of assembling information about the board superintendencies, we cannot be sure that Ch'ien-lung aimed to control all of the Six Boards by means of his Grand Council appointments, but at several times during the reign he approached this ideal, which under his son, the Chia-ch'ing Emperor, was later enunciated as policy.[53] Efficient management at the center made council ties to the boards desirable.

Even if not all the boards and outer-court agencies could be covered with connections leading into the council, Grand Council appointments were sure to include the Board of Revenue. Indeed, at times it appears that, because so many members of the Board of Revenue directorate were moved into the council, the emperor sought less to create a link between the inner court and that board than to have the high-level Board of Revenue work carried out in the inner court and under Grand Council supervision. In CL41/9 (late 1776), for example, five of the six Board of Revenue directorate members were also grand councillors.[54]

Indeed, by this time so much of the board's work had been drawn into the inner court that special arrangements had to be made for remaining board activities to be taken care of in the outer-court offices. This was accomplished not by removing any of the Board of Revenue grand councillors or by making a new appointment at the board but by deputing one of the board's grand councillors to "go every day to the Board of Revenue office especially to take care of Board of Revenue affairs." Even when the emperor was at the Summer Palace this councillor was to stay behind and tend to board business, nevertheless remaining on the council.[55] Thus, most of the Board of Revenue directorate carried out both their board and their Grand Council work in the inner court. Later in this chapter I shall show how, in addition to facilitating efficient governance, the council's ties to outer-court agencies through such concurrent appointments as these promoted council growth.

A preponderance of the Chinese grand councillorships came from the four middle-southern provinces of Kiangsu, Anhwei, Chekiang, and Kiangsi—a change from the large number of northerners in the government in the early Ch'ing. Fully thirteen men, or 77 percent, of the seventeen Chinese appointed in the Ch'ien-lung reign were from these provinces; this preponderance fell slightly under Chia-ch'ing and Tao-kuang (see Table 8). These provinces occupied the most prosperous area of China in the mid-Ch'ing and possessed the wealth to pay for the books, tutoring, and leisure necessary to high-level examination performance; their success in winning Grand Council appointments is therefore not surprising.[56] As we shall see in Chapter 7, this standard of achievement and the patronage generated from examination success appear

TABLE 8. Home provinces of Chinese grand councillors. Shows the home provinces of the forty-two grand councillors appointed up to the beginning of the Kuang-hsu reign (1874). For nearly a century and a half the four central coastal provinces (outlined in box) plus Shantung and Chihli were the leading source of council appointments. (Source does not go beyond 1874.)

Province	Ch'ien-lung (incl. CC1–3)	Chia-ch'ing (from CC4)	Tao-kuang	Hsien-feng	Tung-chih	TOTAL
Shantung	2	1		2		5
Chihli	1		1	1	2	4
Shansi			1			1
Shensi	1		1			2
Kansu						0
Honan					1	1
Kiangsu	4		3	2		9
Anhwei			2			2
Chekiang	6	1		2	1	10
Kiangsi	3	1	1		1	6
Hupei						0
Szechuan						0
Fukien						0
Kwangtung						0
Kwangsi						0
Hunan	1	1				2
Kweichow						0
Yunnan						0
Total	17	4	9	7	5	42

SOURCE: *Shu-yuan chi-lueh*, 15/5–7b. For a list of top examination candidates by province, see *Ch'ing-tai ting-chia lu*, comp. Chu P'ei-lien, pp. 21–29; Kiangsu placed first on this list.

to have carried over into Grand Council clerk appointments, which exhibit the same middle-southern preponderance.

Although descriptions of traditional Chinese governance have asserted the primacy of the civilian over the military, nevertheless at times the Grand Council of the Ch'ien-lung era possessed a decidedly military cast.[57] Many military men served on the council during the period, some being dispatched to the front as councillors, others being rewarded for their valor with council appointments on their return. Still others lost their Grand Council posts when leaving for the front but were reappointed on their return. Ch'ien-lung named only four men Military Commissioner (*Ching-lueh*) during his reign; three of these were grand councillors (Fu-heng twice received this appointment).[58] In a major military expedition, several grand councillors might be sent to the front together. This happened in the first Chin-ch'uan campaign, when both No-ch'in and Pan-ti proceeded to the front; and after No-ch'in was disgraced, Fu-heng succeeded to the Military Commissioner title and went out to the front.[59] Toward the close of the second Chin-ch'uan campaign in CL14 (1776), four of the eleven grand councillors of that year were on record as having been stationed in Chungking sometime during the campaign.[60] In addition, four other former and current councillors served in the battle area in that war.[61]

A-kuei's career demonstrates how a grand councillor could spend almost as much time in the provinces as on duty at the capital. His first appointment to the Grand Council in CL28 (1763) was almost immediately followed by commissions that thrust him into positions of military command in difficult tribal areas in Szechuan and Turkestan. He so distinguished himself when deputed to the second Chin-ch'uan front that on his return to Peking the emperor observed an ancient tradition and honored his great general by journeying to the outskirts of the city to greet him. After this A-kuei, though reinstated on the Grand Council, was sent to Yunnan to prepare for the Burma campaign. Even after he was elevated to ranking councillor in CL44 (1779), he was deputed to Kansu to pacify the Moslems and was often out of the capital on many nonmilitary investigative and trouble-shooting missions.[62]

The use of the Grand Council as a pool of military and investigative personnel extended beyond the councillor level when Grand Council clerks were permitted to accompany councillors assigned to the front. For instance, nine clerks went out to Szechuan in the entourage of one or another of the Grand Council generals in the course of the first Chin-ch'uan war.[63] Thus a military campaign frequently enlarged the lists of both grand councillors and clerks, as new appointments had to be made at the capital to replace the substantial number dispatched with the armies. The Ch'ien-lung Emperor followed the military campaigns with keen interest and once remarked that sending No-ch'in to Szechuan had been "the same as going myself" (*yü Chen ch'in-wang wu-i*).[64] The emperor's many military appointments to the Grand Council and the extensive use of grand councillors to fulfill important military assignments probably reflected this intense imperial interest.

The reverse side of the imperial appointment power was that the emperor might also dismiss his councillor appointees, again without regard to regulations. But emperors were not likely to indulge themselves with wholesale or arbitrary dismissals: the government had to be run without destroying the morale of the monarch's high ministerial associates. Ch'ien-lung's use of his Grand Council appointment and dismissal powers reflects the need to satisfy certain requirements and constituencies—the desire for reliable and loyal courtiers, the need for financial and military technical expertise, the securing of links to the Six Boards and other outer-court agencies, and the advisability of finding some Mongols as well as Chinese to participate in what at the beginning of the reign had been a largely Manchu group. The appointments also reflect a capital-based outlook behind the selection process: men with predominately provincial experience were not frequently elevated.[65] The judicious mixture of these elements suggests that the emperor may have received counsel in making these appointments. But whether or not the emperor chose to accept that advice was another matter, for the final choice was indubitably his. The grand councillors were his personal appointees, sometimes deputed to function "the same as" the emperor: to carry out tasks that the emperor, confined to Peking, could not accomplish alone.

The Grand Councillors' Political Reliability

An estimate of the integrity of the emperor's Grand Council appointees (both councillors and clerks) was doubtless a factor in the emperor's choices. Once appointed, those attached to the council had to be absolutely reliable men who could be entrusted with the highest secrets of the realm. Not only did they read, summarize, record, and store all but a top secret handful of the palace memorials; sometimes they worked with the top secret materials as well. The councillors and certain of their staff members were frequently the only men with access to the depositions and other memorial enclosures, some of which contained rebel confessions conveying deeply seditious views.[66] Sensitive documents with circulation limited to the inner-court administrators and the high-level provincial correspondents could be sanitized in the course of being copied for the outer court, with the councillors and their clerks assuming responsibility for identifying the "inconvenient phrases" (*pu-pien yü-chü*) that were to be expunged.[67] In addition, the grand councillors and their clerks were the chief capital officials who assembled and scanned the books proscribed in the Ch'ien-lung literary inquisition. Once the books had been sent in from the provinces, the councillors examined them and recommended which should be burned and which spared. After the emperor authorized the destruction, the councillors supervised the book burning.[68]

Political reliability was also evident in the grand councilors' being made responsible for high level supervision of publications. As mentioned in Chapter 2, the historian and biographer Fang Chao-ying has assessed Chang T'ing-yü's services to Yung-cheng in producing an acceptable version of the K'ang-hsi *Veritable Records* as the equivalent of "a military victory in support of the throne."[69] Through their control of the Military Archives Office, its compilation work on its campaign histories and other works, and their various high-level supervisory editorial assignments, the grand councillors continued to achieve similar "victories" in the Ch'ien-lung period. The Yung-cheng inner deputies and the Ch'ien-lung grand councillors also oversaw other kinds of censorship, such as that governing the selection of memorials published in the collected memorials and rescripts of the Yung-cheng period (*Yung-cheng Chu-p'i yü-chih*). For that work memorials were divided into three main groups according to whether publication had already occurred in the first edition (*i-lu*), was planned for a follow-up edition (*wei-lu*), or was to be prohibited (*pu-lu*). Some of the surviving second-edition memorials show that they were copied over by a method that in certain instances permitted extensive revision.[70] The inner-court officials and later the grand councillors were the politically trustworthy officials responsible for overseeing this process.

The grand councillors' political reliability was further enhanced by strict compartmentalization. Councillors are reported to have regularly refused to receive gifts, entertain guests, or have any social contact with other officials— even to the point of committing the discourtesy of not returning calls. In this way they kept apart and avoided the slightest appearance of any questionable involvement. Chao I lauded the councillors' probity, affirming that even though Chang T'ing-yü had received substantial imperial largesse during the Yung-cheng period, "yet at his door there were no letters [asking for favors], and presents worth thirty pieces of gold were unceremoniously rejected." Writing about No-ch'in as ranking councillor, Chao I reports that "he was the most trusted court official, but as a person rather straitlaced. His gate and courtyard were firmly closed. There was no one who could interfere [in government affairs] for private reasons." This passage also remarks on the purity of the Grand Council clerks, "who were even less involved" in accepting presents in return for special favors. Chao I tells us that in his day the council premises were physically set apart, guarded by two stalwarts "in correct dress." Should outsiders seek admission, these gatekeepers would ward them off saying, "This is a place of secrecy—the public may not enter here." Compartmentalization was carried so far that some council clerks were reprimanded merely for holding conversations with board officials. Of these, Chao I reports, "those who were scolded did not dare say a word [in their own defense]."[71] Of course, Grand Council work was already compartmentalized—cut off from the large bureaucracy and incarcerated in the inner court. The physical compartmentalization of the councillors themselves, their preference for remaining aloof and eschewing any sort of dubious official or social contact, constituted an extension of this policy and increased the organization's reliability.

Many council memoranda in the archives show how the grand councillors worked hard to merit the emperor's confidence. In edict drafting, for example, when the councillors found it advisable to change a point already agreed to in discussions with the emperor, a note of explanation would be attached to the new version for the emperor to read when going over the final draft. Usually the changes concerned small matters—additional information might be sought of a provincial investigator, or a provincial appointment might require a shift because of dyarchical considerations. Whatever the change, the researcher who scans the eighteenth-century archives is left with the impression that the councillors informed the emperor whenever their edict drafts veered in a direction not previously authorized. The emperor must also have been left with that impression. Because councillors could not use the authority of an imperial edict to issue orders that they alone desired, such care maintained the inviolability of the edict channel and confirmed their probity in the monarch's eyes.

Finally, there seems to have been an unwritten expectation, carefully observed in the eighteenth and early nineteenth centuries, that the councillors were not to publish information about council deliberations or procedures.[72] As a result, few memoirs supply meaningful details about council work. Chang T'ing-yü's own autobiography scarcely mentions Yung-cheng's compartmentalized staffs or the later Grand Council, and it carefully omits all description of council deliberations.[73] A-kuei's published memorials, which were collected by his grandson Na-yen-ch'eng (who also served on the council), exclude the position papers submitted under A-kuei's name during the years he served as ranking councillor.[74] The fact that the eighteenth-century councillors failed to bequeath memoirs teeming with gaudy revelations of inner-court processes is a testament to their integrity.

The Grand Councillors' Concurrent Positions

Because the Grand Council was an unofficial body, there were no exclusive council appointments; all middle- and high-level council posts were concurrently held, with salary and rank determined by a man's other major positions. Such combining of responsibilities was not new with the Grand Council, or even with the Ch'ing—the Ming grand secretaries had also held concurrent appointments.[75] But the practice appears to have expanded considerably with the Ch'ing grand councillors, who frequently had long lists of concurrent titles. For example, in CL13 (1748) Fu-heng listed his several concurrent posts and titles: Lecturer on the Classics, Grand Guardian of the Heir Apparent (*T'ai-tzu t'ai-pao*), Assistant Grand Secretary, Deliberative Minister, Chamberlain of the Imperial Bodyguard, Superintendent of the Imperial Equipage Department, [Official] Concurrently in Charge (*chien-kuan*) of the Board of Civil Office Board President Affairs, [Official] Temporarily in Charge of the [Board of Revenue] Three Treasuries, and Minister of the Imperial Household. In line with the principle of inner-court informality, Fu-heng's grand councillor position, being unofficial, was omitted. Four years later, in CL17 (1752), after Fu-heng had been made a grand secretary and had become the leading councillor, some of these titles were dropped and in their place were added the posts of Grand Guardian (*T'ai-pao*), Grand Secretary with the Pao-ho Palace Title, [Official] Concurrently in Charge of the Board of Revenue, Adjutant General, and [Official] Concurrently Superintending the Court of Colonial Affairs.[76] But this list too failed to mention his Grand Council post. Thus a long list of concurrent responsibilities was typical of an eighteenth-century grand councillor, but a position on the council remained unofficial and was only informally acknowledged.

Of course, a grand councillor could not possibly have fulfilled all the duties of his concurrent posts; nevertheless, these posts were important because they provided a wide range of areas should a councillor desire to act. For example, in CL23 (1758), the acting Kiangsi governor submitted a memorial on grain shipments that received the vermilion rescript, "Let the appropriate board [the Board of Revenue in this instance] speedily deliberate and report" (*Kai-pu su-i chü-tsou*). But the resulting deliberation was headed not by a Board of Revenue president but by the grand councillor Fu-heng. Although Fu-heng was not a regular member of the Board of Revenue directorate at that time, he held that board's superintendency post, a concurrent title that authorized him to take charge of the board's deliberations.[77] A similar instance occurred in CL16 (1751) when the emperor rescripted a memorial with figures on the Shansi silver-meltage-fee income to be sent to the concerned board for its information (*Kai-pu chih-tao*). But the result was that the grand councillors—not the board officials—took up the subject in a short deliberation memorial and presented the emperor with the results of their investigation.[78] Here again the council members' concurrent titles gave them access to information and allowed them to deliberate and frame recommendations for the emperor without a specific imperial authorization. Many instances of this kind of maneuver appear in the Grand Council record books.[79] Even some memorials that open with "We [your majesty's] board officials" (*Ch'en-pu*) prove on examination of the archival evidence to have been composed in the Grand Council, probably under the supervision of a grand councillor who was also the board superintendent.[80]

Other concurrent posts enabled the grand councillors to move into areas beyond the Six Boards. Many councillors were Hanlin Academy members and thus carried some of their Hanlin responsibilities into the council purview. We have already seen in Table 6 how the grand councillors gradually moved into editorial duties formerly dominated by grand secretaries and Hanlin Academy members. In addition, in the first year of the Ch'ien-lung reign the Interim Council took action on a matter concerning the Diary office (*Ch'i-chü chu kuan*), even though in the previous century Diary affairs had been subordinated to the Hanlin.[81] In similar fashion the responsibility for managing the *chü-jen* and *chin-shih* examinations as well as the testing process for promotions of officials, previously handled variously by the Board of Rites, the Hanlin Academy, and the grand secretaries (or in certain cases by other bodies), in the eighteenth century frequently devolved on the grand councillors. The grand councillors gradually took on such duties as coordinating deliberations on examination problems and helping the emperor select the questions for the *chin-shih* examinations. Sometimes they even served as examination readers.[82] During the eighteenth century other Hanlin duties, particularly in the area of publications, also came to be handled at the Grand Council or involved council personnel and the inner-court archives. This was especially true of the Ch'ien-lung–period military campaign histories (*fang-lueh*), which drew on the palace memorials and other records stored in the inner court and were compiled under council supervision (see Chapter 7). The Hanlin Academy and particularly its grand secretaries had also traditionally supervised the work of the State History Office (*Kuo-shih kuan*), but in the eighteenth century Hanlin grand secretaries who were also grand councillors came to hold the highest directorships in that body.[83]

Council duties were also augmented by some of the councillors' concurrent posts as grand secretaries. In the early Ch'ing, responsibility for processing routine-system documents had been in the hands of the grand secretaries, some of whom had held temporary assignments in the inner court. Thus in that early period the processing of routine-system documents might take place either in the inner court, where a grand secretary who was also an imperial assistant might mull over a draft rescript, or far away at the Grand Secretariat premises in the southeastern corner of the imperial palace, where the outer-court grand secretaries and their subordinates might process other routine memorials. The vague inner/outer-court division of tasks pertaining to the routine documents was also characteristic of the Ch'ien-lung Grand Council, which handled many routine documents. It is not unusual, for instance, to come across a Grand Council memorandum like the one from CL16 (1751) informing the emperor that "we [the grand councillors] have as usual [*chao-ch'ang*] drafted the [routine memorial] rescript."[84] In CL13 (1748), five Grand Secretariat officials were punished because of an error in preparing a routine-system draft rescript; three of the five were concurrent grand councillors.[85] By CC8 (1803), two grand councillors who were also grand secretaries were serving at the top of the office for registering routine-system edicts (*Chi-ch'a ch'in-feng shang-yü shih-chien ch'u* or, more briefly, the *Chi-ch'a ch'u* or *Shang-yü ch'u*).[86] Although inner-court officials had been able to interfere in the routine system in earlier days, one difference between the Ch'ien-lung and earlier periods was that by now a consolidated force was in place in the inner court to coordinate both routine- and palace-system documents. Concurrently held grand secretaryships gave the grand councillors supervisory authority on various boards and offices dependent on the routine system; thus the council acquired a firm grip on that system.

Other grand secretary responsibilities that were carried into the Grand Council via concurrent positions included the management of the Nine Ministers' deliberations (see Chaper 5). For example, toward the end of the Ch'ien-lung reign the emperor marked a provincial memorial on the possibility of corruption in a public works project for discussion by "the grand secretaries and the Nine Ministers." The resulting deliberation, however, is to be found in a Grand Council archival record book, a fact indicating that the transaction fell in the council's purview.[87] A similar transfer took place in the responsibility for marking the names of criminals scheduled for execution on the autumn assizes lists (*kou-tao*). This had been a duty of the grand secretaries, but one year when the emperor found himself on tour with only a small group of officials he declared, "The grand councillors are rather experienced in handling this" and ordered the task to be shared by grand secretaries and grand councillors.[88]

Of course, the councillors won some of their assignments not because of their concurrent posts but because the emperor had come to trust and rely on them for discharging all manner of tasks. Under routine-system regulations, for instance, state papers were routed to the appropriate committees and offices by precedents that long before had decided who should handle the various topics that regularly arose in the system. In fact, lengthy routine-system rule books existed to guide the distribution of documents.[89] But the emperor himself routed the palace memorials to officials, writing his selection in vermilion at the end of each memorial. Increasingly in the Ch'ien-lung period and after, whenever the Grand Council rode high in the imperial favor—and that was the case during much of the Ch'ien-lung period—the emperor tended to route the palace memorials to grand councillors more than to others. The councillors' concurrent posts played an important role in transferring some duties into the council, but in addition the councillors' own achievement in responsibly performing their duties and repeatedly proving their trustworthiness improved the likelihood that the monarch would assign them further responsibilities.

Because of the concurrent posts and the emperor's trust, the council now frequently acted as an intermediary between the outer-court agencies and the emperor, conducting investigations and relaying information in documents of their own creation rather than by forwarding the outer-court memoranda. The archives contain numerous examples of the councillors' summaries and rewritings of outer-court agency reports.[90] This practice tended to place the outer court at a greater remove from the monarch and bring his inner-court ministers closer. Although it may appear that the council thrust itself into this intermediary role in order to be in a position to gloss over or conceal certain outer-court information in their own interest, in my view this kind of malefaction was probably extremely rare. The main purpose of the summaries was to highlight points for the convenience and enlightenment of a busy monarch. If discovered, malfeasance would have swiftly brought severe penalties and would have run counter to the councillors' goal of winning the emperor's trust. Moreover, in most cases the information in question was fairly routine; the council could have gained little or nothing from rewriting or misrepresenting it.

Thus, the concurrent posts that the grand councillors held because of the unofficial nature of their organization were an important factor in the council's eighteenth-century expansion. Because of the concurrent posts the council acquired an enormous range of responsibilities during the Ch'ien-lung period, gathering into its own hands many strands of what had previously been handled by several outer-court bodies. In some respects it could be said that council development took place at the expense of the outer-court agencies. Ultimately the emperor became increasingly isolated from the outer court and depended on his inner-court councillors.

GRAND COUNCIL ADMINISTRATIVE RESPONSIBILITIES

During the eighteenth century the Grand Council's numerous and ever-expanding administrative responsibilities also promoted growth. Although the old outer-court bodies continued to attend to regular business, during the Ch'ien-lung period the areas subject to Grand Council management increased. The Ch'ien-lung Emperor's preference for delegating tasks to the grand councillors rather than to others quickly expanded their responsibilities. The councillors could be authorized to read, process, study, or make recommendations on almost any subject of interest to the throne or on any topic in either of the government's two main communications systems. Examples of their prodigious sweep can be found in every month of the reign.

One instance from CL49 (1784) shows how a council research task could even relate to an event in the emperor's personal life. In that year, at the age of seventy-three, Ch'ien-lung achieved the ideal of five living generations in the male line when he became a great-great-grandfather for the first time. The councillors were ordered to find out how many other similarly blessed great-great-grandfathers were living in the celestial empire. Their investigation (limited to members of the gentry class) ranged over all the provinces of China proper and turned up twenty-seven men in their seventies, ninety-nine in their eighties, sixty-two in their nineties, and four over the age of one hundred. The council presented its findings to the emperor in a listing tabulated by province, and the individuals were celebrated for their achievements. Another unusual council research assignment dispatched investigators (probably Grand Council clerks and not the councillors themselves) to the countryside to question farmers about local crop conditions. Still other council research took up the miscellaneous concerns of those commoners who attempted to circumvent their local government offices and interrupt imperial tours to present personal requests (k'ou-hun). These could vary from the petitions of the unbalanced, which had to be so judged and dismissed—as in the case of a man who protested to the emperor against fellow villagers because, he claimed, they had led his wife astray—to the plea of a man who had given his only son for adoption and now wanted him back. The councillors investigated each case, frequently obtaining a deposition, and made a recommendation to the emperor.[91] Although these particular research questions were not in the ordinary run of council business, archival records show that the council frequently handled such unusual topics —as well as many of the expected ones. Many problems that came to the attention of authorities at the capital could ultimately become subjects of council attention.

The council's chief administrative task was to run the executive office of the inner court. We know about this today because enormous numbers of archival records—daybooks, registers, indexes of various kinds—furnish details of how the council imposed order on what might have become a chaotic flood of paper and problems.[92] The archives even possess a bundle of blank green-headed audience tallies (*lü-t'ou ch'ien* or *p'ai*) that were employed in the management of imperial audiences. An examination of how the council handled these responsibilities will assist in defining its relationship both with the outer-court bureaucracy and with the monarch.

The Green-headed Sticks

The green-headed sticks supply a good example of the Grand Council's administrative responsibilities in that the system had come down from earlier times and involved traditional participating government bodies in addition to the council, a situation typical of much Grand Council work. The sticks were probably made in a palace workshop. Those that I examined in the Beijing archives were thin wooden strips painted white with a green hiltlike decoration at the top. Most were less than a foot long, their length providing space for inscribing the name of an official who was in charge of bringing men to audience or the name and pertinent information about a man whom the emperor was to interview for possible appointment or promotion. Some tallies were inscribed with a vacancy to be filled; after the imperial audience the name of the designated official would be added.[93]

Various organizations had the responsibility for preparing the information required for the tallies—sometimes the Chancery of Memorials, sometimes the board whose presidents or vice presidents brought men to audience, sometimes other groups.[94] Because the system was an old one derived from times before the founding of the Grand Council, the administrative regulations do not specify the details of the grand councillors' role. But we know the councillors were involved because at times they were punished for mistakes in handling the tallies, and on other occasions they brought men to audience or sought other imperial decisions for which they prepared tallies.[95] They also drafted edicts implementing decisions resulting from the use of the tallies (writing up appointment announcements, for instance) and conducted investigations when something went wrong in the operation of the tally system.[96] Thus where the green-headed sticks were concerned, the council role ranged from distant supervising, as long as other organizations functioned smoothly, to taking direct action when assigned duties or an emergency so required.

Tracking Paper and Problems

A chief management task of the council was to keep track of the large numbers of documents that were sent to or created in the council. Over the course of the Ch'ien-lung and Chia-ch'ing reigns several Grand Council record series were set up principally to monitor the inner-court paper flow. The document register (Sui-shou teng-chi tang; see Chapter 7), for instance, noted the arrival of all palace memorials, summarized them, and supplied other pertinent information about them—such as whether a copy had been made for an appropriate outer-court agency. Once the official response was issued, that too was entered in the register. Other records tallied how and when the palace memorials had been returned to the field, together with their responding edicts—specifying when a packet had been turned over to the Board of War dispatch service or whether it had been sent in a memorial dispatch box (*pao-hsia*) or wrapped in boards (*chia-pan*). Later, when memorials were lent to the office in charge of compiling the *Veritable Records*, another record series noted those loans—when the documents went out and when they were returned. Thus although the council had developed complex management procedures, rarely did these operate independently or without the cooperation of outer-court bodies. The success of many of the council's managerial methods depended on effective outer-court practice.

The council also developed a system for keeping track of special problems. Sometimes the emperor would postpone action on a certain matter until further information was available or the man in question could be summoned to audience. In such cases the Grand Council might be ordered to "keep [the pending item] on hand" (*ts'un-chi*) for retrieval as needed or keep the matter in mind in order to "remind" (*t'i-tsou*) the emperor at the appropriate time. An example of the use of the councillors' pending and remind files dates from a mid-reign occasion when the emperor saw a capital official in audience and ordered that a reminder of the man's record was to be forwarded after the following year's *chin-shih* examination. A year later the council retrieved the relevant documents from the pending file and reported that the man had not passed the examination. Nevertheless, on seeing the previous year's documents Ch'ien-lung was apparently reminded of his previous intention to allow the man, who had an excellent job record and presumably good connections, to take the palace examination section of the *chin-shih*. As a result, the man won a place in the second class and was awarded the highest degree. The remind file had allowed the emperor to give a special opportunity to a man he wished to favor.

The council also used its pending and remind files to hold the documents or information on a problem while an outer-court agency was consulted. In most such instances the emperor ordered that if the board failed to recommend the action he desired, his wishes were nevertheless to be carried out. Because the board had been given the chance to present its arguments, there could be no accusation that the outer court had been bypassed.

Occasionally the council failed to carry out its responsibility to remind the emperor, in which case the imperial intentions might go unfulfilled. A rare instance of such a Grand Council neglect of duty occurred in CL9 (1745), when the councillors relied on the Board of Civil Office to send the imperially ordered reminder to let them know when a certain job candidate reached Peking for audience. But the board slipped up, and no reminder arrived. As a result, the man went through the audience without the expected documents and received a substantive appointment to a district magistracy rather than being deputed on an acting basis as originally intended.[97] In spite of such an occasional lapse, however, most of the time the Grand Council's pending and remind files smoothed the path of inner-court decision making and made the council's services essential to the emperor.

The council also smoothed the path to imperial understanding when it clarified complex problems for presentation to the emperor. Some of the memorials surviving in the archives contain the slips on which the grand councillors (or the clerks) summarized or explained content, much as the inner deputies had done for the Yung-cheng Emperor.[98] Other records show that the councillors marked documents with inserted slips or labels (*chia-ch'ien, nien-ch'ien*) containing advice or comment.[99] Yellow tabs (*huang-ch'ien*) that guided the emperor to material of special interest are still attached to certain provincial palace memorials in the archives that the council prepared for imperial inspection. Three tabs marked with three names were used in one such document to help the emperor turn quickly—probably in the middle of an audience—to the beginnings of biographic information on the three job candidates described.[100] Similar labels were attached to a set of financial reports to suggest which persons should be subjected to audit and who might be spared.[101] The councillors also helped the emperor select examination questions by placing labels in a set of the Four Books (that is, the four Confucian classics that were usually drawn on for testing) to mark the topics previously used in the metropolitan and the Shun-t'ien prefecture examinations.[102] Through a myriad arrangements the council was able to digest, store, and retrieve a mass of information.

Edict Drafting: The Fill-in-the-Blank Edicts

As was explained in earlier chapters, the inner deputies of Yung-cheng days were responsible for drafting many kinds of imperial edicts. At the beginning of the Ch'ien-lung reign this duty passed to the Interim Council and shortly thereafter to the Grand Council. The council's early edict-drafting responsibilities involved mainly two types of document: the publicly promulgated edicts and the court letters. During the Ch'ien-lung reign there developed not a third form but rather a streamlined form for handling certain types of edicts. I have not discovered a general Chinese term for this new form, so I call it the "fill-in-the blank" edict.

This kind of edict draft, which was probably derived from an earlier Grand Secretariat form still in use in the eighteenth century and appropriate only for short, uncomplicated announcements, consisted of a draft containing all the particulars except the one requiring the imperial decision. A blank would be left in which the emperor would inscribe his vermilion choice: a man's name for an appointment, for instance, or a sum of money for the distribution of imperial largesse. One of these forms, known as "edicts with blanks for [the emperor to write] names" (k'ung-ming yü-chih), will serve as an example of how these drafts simplified council work. The blank name edicts would be fully written out with all appropriate information—the date, type of edict, and the position rank and place—except for the name of the imperial designee. Frequently the draft would be accompanied by a list of candidates and a Grand Council memorandum of explanation. On having the edict draft placed before him the emperor would fill in the blank with vermilion calligraphy. An eighteenth-century comment on this system expatiated on the pride that new appointees felt on knowing that their sovereign had personally inscribed their names on these forms with his own hand.[103] The edict drafts with blanks had several advantages, for they saved steps in the drafting process and preserved a vermilion record of the imperial selections. They were one of the several ways developed by the Grand Council to discharge its administrative work with efficiency and dispatch.

Advising and Correcting the Monarch

The Grand Council designed its administrative methods not only to simplify matters but also to advise and guide the emperor. Using labels to mark individuals who should be traced for additional payments of funds owed the government, for instance, gave the councillors a strong discretionary role. The Ch'ien-lung Emperor—who was rarely in a position to know more on that kind of topic than his grand councillors—usually followed their advice. Moreover, the councillors did not always present the emperor with only a fill-in-the-blank edict draft accompanied by a memorandum of explanation; frequently they wrote full recommendations and sought (ch'ing-chih) the emperor's authorization (ch'in-ting) of their plans. As the emperor was rarely aware of solidly based alternatives, he was likely to approve such proposals, particularly if they originated with his trusted and favored grand councillors. Furthermore, he frequently sent recommendations from other sources to be checked with the council before giving his assent.

The councillors also frequently corrected the monarch, both when he inadvertently made a mistake and when they perceived an error of judgment. For instance, following an imperial tour in CL16 (1751), the councillors apparently realized that a man who had impressed the emperor in the course of an imperial tour interview and had forthwith been appointed to the important prefecture of K'ai-feng city was not sufficiently experienced to handle such a complicated post. Their solution was to compose a memorandum (tsou-p'ien) gently supplying details of the man's career and suggesting that someone who had already had the experience of serving elsewhere as prefect be sent to handle the difficult affairs of K'ai-feng. The man who had seemed so impressive could then receive a simpler prefectural post. Faced with the councillors' memorandum of explanation, the emperor compliantly approved this plan.[104]

On another occasion, the grand councillors guided the emperor to revise an appointment that had resulted in an inadvisable dyarchical imbalance. After inspecting a blank name edict with the name of a Chinese filled in for Anhwei judicial commissioner, they composed a memorandum pointing out that because this appointment would place a third Chinese in the three high provincial offices for Anhwei (governor, treasurer, and judicial commissioner), they had searched other provinces for an excessive Manchu preponderance and found that both Shensi and Kueichow fitted that requirement. As a result, the man originally slated for Anhwei was instead sent to Shensi, and the Shensi judicial commissioner was transferred to Anhwei, a process known as "exchanging equals" (*tui-tiao*).[105] Similarly, when the emperor wrote incorrect or inadvisable amounts in the financial blank-spaced edicts, the councillors might prescribe changes.[106] Although it was not always a simple matter to advise the emperor or to correct an imperial error, the numerous council memoranda in the archives show not only that this was done over and over again but also that generally the Ch'ien-lung Emperor followed his councillors' advice. Perhaps the council's success should be attributed in part to the fact that much of their guidance was offered in writing rather than in conversations that might have led to impassioned on-the-spot argument.

Plans and Arrangements

Some of the council's proposals were too low level to require the emperor's involvement in working out details, but his final approval was still often necessary. Thus in CL55 (1790) the council drew up a schedule of activities and entertainments for the king of Annam's visit to the Summer Palace at Jehol. A delightful five weeks of operas, feasts, fireworks, river lanterns, and travel was envisioned, presumably with some of the known imperial enthusiasms taken into account. Ch'ien-lung might tinker with such a schedule, but in general in matters of this sort he would approve what was presented to him.[107]

The council also worked out the details of the imperial tours, a responsibility that was particularly taxing during the Ch'ien-lung reign because of that emperor's fondness for travel. A tour could mean a large-scale imperial progress with a retinue of thousands, a temporary halting place on a simple imperial journey away from the capital, or a stay in the Summer Palace outside Peking or in Jehol. The complexities of protocol, terrain, and arranging for the portage of sufficient materials to get the work of government done while on tour resembled the challenges of a military campaign. More than one tour had a cast of over three thousand, with an intimate circle of forty-five or fifty servitors— mainly Manchus and Mongols—who included imperial bodyguards, princes, some of the grand councillors, those attached to the imperial suite, and a few favorites. Board personnel were frequently represented on the larger tours, but one tour prospectus dispensed with men from the two most important boards, Civil Office and Revenue, and arranged instead that the Grand Council would "concurrently be in charge."[108] Transportation presented its own problems. One estimate envisioned the need for six thousand horses to carry some members of the throng (fresh relays had to be allowed for each man), while carts (requiring draft animals and grass and water spots) were requisitioned for the others. There were also several occasions when members of the inner circle traveled on boats, to which they were admitted by special red tickets distributed in advance. Tents and cooking and dining facilities had to be smoothly in place at the end of each day. A striking clock was a necessity, even when the retinue proceeded by water.[109] Special imperial-post arrangements had to be set up for the tours, not only to deliver the provincial palace memorials to the changing imperial encampment sites but also to facilitate correspondence with those left in the capital who had access to the full files of the entire capital bureaucracy.

Advance plans for a tour also involved what the emperor would see and do along the way. Local offices assisted the imperial pleasure by dispatching specially prepared materials to Peking. Maps depicting the scenery that might pass before the imperial eye were drawn and marked with labels to explain whatever was expected to interest his majesty—water conservancy works on one map or military posts on another. There were also little fold-out booklets, about four inches tall and executed in the form of a Chinese scroll painting, continuously unfolding to reveal a journey's prospective scenes of mountains, hills, villages, military encampments, and even houses and trees. One, prepared for an imperial tour on the Grand Canal, also depicted the towns that the entourage would pass, complete with their city walls and four gates.[110] On some tours the emperor interviewed appointment candidates, or honored retired officials and local grandees with audiences, or held a special examination (*chao-shih*), or questioned dismissed officials (*fei-yuan*) living in a locality with a view to restoring some to their careers.[111] Although the council could draw on other palace and central-government offices as well as local resources for help, it bore ultimate responsibility for coordinating all these arrangements.

Appointments and the Grand Council Noted Names Lists

Of the numerous tasks in which the council coordinated its own management activities with those of the outer court, one of the most sensitive concerned appointments. Because all major government appointments required the authorization of the emperor, the lists of persons summoned for audience interviews and the edicts announcing the imperial choices were largely handled in the Grand Council, even though in most cases the council based this work on background information furnished by the Board of Civil Office or, for military officials, the Board of War. One striking eighteenth-century addition to the appointment process, however, was the Grand Council's acquisition of certain exclusive patronage rights. This occurred when the council was allowed its own "noted names" (*chi-ming*) lists, in addition to the board's own lists of the same kind. These lists recorded candidates who had done sufficiently well in audience interviews to be put on the expectant list for job openings at their level. As vacancies occurred the lists were consulted and the appropriate man—Manchu or Chinese as needed—was chosen. When one list was used up, another round of audience interviews would be held to produce a new list.

Although we do not know how the council managed to develop its own patronage sources, there is evidence that by the middle of the Ch'ien-lung reign the council was being allowed to put some candidates on its own noted names lists for positions such as brigade-general (*tsung-ping*) and colonel (*fu-chiang*).[112] Moreover, it seems that the council's noted names lists—and indeed, the very information that such lists existed—were carefully kept secret from outer-court eyes. This is revealed in two imperial decrees of CL54 (1789), both purporting to describe the results of the same audience in which the Board of War had presented several job candidates recommended by a governor-general. According to the decree copied into the Grand Council's own record book prepared for confidential storage in the Grand Council archives, three of the men successful in the audience interview—one lieutenant colonel and two majors—were cited as having been "turned over for the Grand Council to note the names." But the same day's publicly promulgated decree recorded in the court diary described the same audience results without mentioning any special Grand Council list. Instead, the three council nominees were described simply as having been "noted." All mention of their Grand Council sponsorship was suppressed.[113]

A possible reason for such concealment is made clear in a strident Board of War memorial from the following reign that complained that because the Grand Council was in charge of submitting name lists to the emperor, when the time came to make appointments the lists brought to the emperor's attention were chiefly the council's and not the board's. Men who had served loyally and for many years in the provinces but who had the misfortune to come up for promotion under board rather than council patronage were being passed over in favor of more recent candidates who had won places on the council's lists. Board sponsorship meant little.[114] The effectiveness of Grand Council support is made clear in the CL43 (1778) case of a colonel who was brought to audience late in CL41 (1776) and put on the Grand Council noted names list for promotion to brigade-general. By the middle of the following year he had received the expected promotion, and at the beginning of CL43 (1778) he was again advanced, this time to an "important" (*chin-yao*) brigade-general post.[115] Such speed—exceptional in the clogged career ladder of the eighteenth-century bureaucracy—demonstrates the efficacy of the Grand Council list.

Thus, Grand Council administration embraced a number of complex tasks.

The council served as the executive managerial office for the government side of the inner court, smoothing the path of imperial action by keeping track of problems and documents and overseeing a myriad arrangements, some of which gave it a subtle influence over decisions. Moreover, the council accomplished all this with a laudable efficiency that is regularly displayed in the document register, which in most instances shows that action was taken on the same day that the documents reached the council.[116]

The council had a complicated relationship with the outer-court agencies, competing with them yet at the same time dependent on them. The council was a small, efficient organization and had to rely on the agencies to carry on the mass of work involved in processing the routine-system documents—checking provincial reports for such matters as accuracy of figures and compliance with precedents. The agencies also maintained records based on the documents they processed and were expected to produce information when requisitioned by the council. Even palace memorials turned over to the outer court (usually with the rescript ordering that a board be informed, *Kai-pu chih-tao*) might be included in the information base.

Yet the outer-court agencies could not be permitted to replace or outshine the council. Through its monopoly of the palace memorial system the council controlled access to all the documents in the secret information channel, retaining many documents—and certainly the most crucial ones—in the inner court. On occasion the council also took advantage of inner-court secrecy and informality to expand its topics of interest or maneuver around the boards—creating its own noted names lists or rewriting board memoranda. Thus where the Yung-cheng Emperor had frequently used his deputies and other inner-court servitors to bypass the outer court for his own purposes, the late-eighteenth-century heirs of those officials sometimes themselves bypassed the outer court to build their influence in the inner court.

Moreover, the councillors indubitably had their own concerns. Their aggressive use of their own noted names lists is but one indication of how they pushed their own interests, calibrating their power with both the outer court and the monarchy. At the same time, administering the realm did not give them license to run matters for their own benefit. In Chinese government circles of the times, a proven accusation of misuse of the public trust on behalf of private interest could be a potent weapon in bringing about the miscreants' downfall. The Grand Council's rise to a central position of power risked exciting jealousy and reprisal from the dispossessed. Although at times the councillors probably successfully pushed their own interests, they had to proceed with caution. Much of the work of administering the realm was just that and no more.

The Grand Council's rise to dominate the administration not only of the inner court but also of the outer court and the provinces was the major achievement of the council's eighteenth-century heyday. The consolidation of the inner-court staffs early in the Ch'ien-lung reign, their being made permanent at the end of the mourning period, and the council's growth during the eighteenth century allowed a transformation from the autocracy of earlier reigns to the monarchical-conciliar form of government that persevered for the remainder of the dynasty.

The emperor no longer dealt directly with many of the problems arising in connection with the outer court. Through the concurrent positions the grand councillors now supervised many aspects of outer-court work, intervening actively when necessary. Research inquiries directed to the outer court were mediated and sometimes rewritten at the council. A new layer of administration —the Grand Council—was now interposed between the emperor and the outer court.

Relations with the provinces were also now handled differently. In some areas the outer-court communications system lost ground to the new palace system as many topics were transferred into the Grand Council purview. In addition, by the Ch'ien-lung period all routine as well as palace memorials were being monitored in the inner court—the grand councillors were scanning and frequently advising the emperor on all major document traffic on provincial affairs.

The councillors' role in the inner-court administration is less clear. During the Ch'ien-lung era many Manchu councillors simultaneously held Imperial Household posts, a fact that probably led to cooperation between the two major inner-court bodies of that epoch. A separation took place in the Chia-ch'ing reign, however, by which grand councillors were no longer appointed to concurrent Imperial Household posts at the level of adjutant-general (*Yü-ch'ien ta-ch'en*). This may well have strained the former patterns of cooperation.

The Grand Council's ascendancy in administering the inner and the outer courts as well as the provinces meant that the new body now coordinated many government affairs that had previously been handled separately. Some matters had formerly been routine business and independent operations of the outer-court bureaucracy. Some had been directed by the monarchs alone. The rise of the Grand Council imposed a new inner-court hegemony on the government of China.

SEVEN

Grand Council
Subordinate Organizations

Following the founding of the Interim Council and then its successor, the Grand Council, at the beginning of the Ch'ien-lung reign, the new agency underwent exponential growth. The consolidation of the separate groups of Yung-cheng's old inner court allowed effective use of existing personnel, but the staff complement also increased as new members were brought on as councillors, clerks, and messengers. As the council increased its capability for handling complex assignments, it acquired new responsibilities. And these new areas of responsibility led in turn to the proliferation of the council's subordinate groups and elaboration and rationalization within them. Leaders were appointed, sections (*pan*) defined, suboffices named—all to keep pace with the burgeoning of council concerns. Three of the major newly defined bodies were the council clerks, a special staff known as the "Manchu Division" (*Man-pan*), and an archives and publications office usually known in English as the Office of Military Archives (*Fang-lueh kuan*) but whose work was concerned with editing certain official publications as well as the storage of documents. With the exception of the additional office for handling foreign affairs (*Tsungli Yamen*) that was set up in 1861 after the sacking of the Summer Palace,[1] the Grand Council structure of high-level officials and subordinate staffs that was laid down over the course of the Ch'ien-lung reign remained in place for the rest of the dynasty. The council's subgroups are worth attention because they illustrate additional facets of the council's structural change and growth beyond what was depicted in the study of the grand councillors themselves in Chapter 6.

THE GRAND COUNCIL CLERKS

The usual English translation, "clerks," for the Chinese *ssu-yuan* and the Manchu *chang-ching* does not accurately convey the quality of these men and their work.[2] The Grand Council clerks were not counting-house drudges, as the English translation might imply, but young and middle-aged officials who had reached the middle levels of the civil service ranks. The translation "clerk" might better be equated with the law clerks selected from the best young law school graduates in the United States to assist and learn from superior court judges. Like these individuals, the Grand Council clerks were entrusted with high-level discretionary tasks. They saw nearly all the documents that passed through the council, frequently drafted edicts, and occasionally presented their views on policy to the emperor.[3] Many clerks had distinguished government careers in which their early service on the council figured importantly by supplying crucial on-the-job training and experience. Indeed, the smooth running of the Grand Council was greatly facilitated by the network of former clerks, many of whom were strategically positioned in important posts all over the empire.

Like the Grand Council itself, during the Ch'ien-lung reign the body of clerks was left largely unregulated to operate on the basis of its inherited unofficial status. As a result, the clerks' organizational arrangements, duty schedules, and office procedures were worked out free of formal regulation. Only in the Chia-ch'ing reign (1796–1820), and particularly after the Chia-ch'ing Emperor's personal accession to power in CC4 (1799), did reforms lay down detailed specifications for the clerks. Many of these reforms simply formalized or refined existing eighteenth-century practices; but several exceptions to the later requirements also obtained during the earlier period.

Qualifications and Appointments

In the eighteenth century, Grand Council clerk appointments were made simply and informally, usually originating in the councillors' nominations, with the emperor supplying the final authorization.[4] Like the grand councillors' posts, the clerks' positions too were held concurrently; thus, a clerk depended on his original post for salary and rank. Clerks were chiefly drawn from middle-level positions in the capital bureaucracy (generally 5A to 7B, with some Manchus also entering the council from the eighth and ninth ranks). Usually clerks came from the Grand Secretariat or one of the Six Boards, but sometimes their careers began in other metropolitan offices, such as the Imperial Clan Court (*Tsung-jen fu*), the Court of Colonial Affairs (*Li-fan yuan*), or the Diarists' Office (*Ch'i-chü chu kuan*).[5] Board connections and the ability to deal with board work were particularly esteemed. Indeed, several clerkships were earmarked for men from certain boards or other outer-court agencies.[6] Even though the clerks worked full time at the council, their concurrent posts allowed an advantage to the council similar to that brought by their superiors: namely, their links to the outer-court bureaucracy broadened the council's access to information and yielded valuable connections with men working elsewhere in the capital bureaucracy.

The eighteenth-century clerks came from more diverse backgrounds than were later permitted by the Chia-ch'ing rules. During the Ch'ien-lung reign, for instance, some clerks came in at higher entry levels than were later allowed.[7] Among such exceptions were two men appointed clerks while they were serving as board vice presidents (rank 2A), three from the post of subchancellor of the Grand Secretariat (*Nei-ko hsueh-shih*, rank 2B), and four from senior and junior vice president posts at the Censorate (*Tso* and *Yu fu-tu yü-shih*, 3A).[8] According to the later reforms, such high-ranking persons could not have served; but under Ch'ien-lung, when rules had not yet been formalized, such arrangements were permissible. One informal rule that appears to have already been in force during the Ch'ien-lung period, however, was the practice of not appointing Chinese bannermen to clerkships.[9]

Another kind of diversity permitted in the eighteenth century but supposedly eliminated in the nineteenth was the personal factor of the topmost councillors being allowed to name junior relatives to be attached to the council. Thus in YC11 (1733), Chang T'ing-yü's son Chang Jo-ai and two of O-erh-t'ai's relations, his son O-jung-an and his nephew O-lun, had been designated attached to "the Office of the Military Strategists [*Pan-li Chün-chi ch'u*]" in order to "take instruction from their fathers."[10] Later several instances occurred of councillors' or clerks' sons serving as clerks.[11]

There were probably other kinds of personal interventions in clerk appointments, for such was the style of the day. An early Ch'ien-lung–period Grand Council memorandum described how for other kinds of appointments a new class of *chin-shih*s would be gone over personally by the Nine Ministers (*chiu-ch'ing*, a group of board directorate, censorate, and other high-level members of capital agencies) "to identify those they knew." These acquaintances would then be the lucky ones who would take a further examination and win an audience interview that might well lead to a good metropolitan appointment.[12] It would be surprising if Grand Council clerk selection methods differed markedly from the prevailing fashion. One of the Chia-ch'ing reforms dealt half-heartedly with the personal factor in clerk selection by putting the initial recommendation in the hands of the originating agencies rather than leaving it up to the grand councillors.[13] Even so, the councillors were empowered to scrutinize all candidates, with the result that they probably could block candidates they did not like.[14] Moreover, the councillors indubitably had ways of ensuring that a candidate they desired did receive his original office's recommendation.[15]

The role of personal connections in eighteenth-century clerk choices is also suggested by the evidence in Table 9, which shows that large numbers of the council's Chinese clerks came from the provinces of the middle south, particularly Kiangsu and Chekiang. During the Ch'ien-lung period, these also happened to be the home provinces of a substantial number of the Chinese grand councillors, Chekiang accounting for 35 percent and Kiangsu for 24 percent (on which see Table 8).[16] The figures for the clerks complement the figures for

TABLE 9. Home provinces of Chinese Grand Council clerks appointed to 1861. The four provinces of the middle south, which generated so many clerks, are outlined. Over the course of the five reigns shown, of the eighteen provinces of China proper, these four provinces' share of the 336 appointments of Chinese Grand Council clerks came to 69 percent. (Home provinces for the T'ung-chih reign and after are not given because the source on which this table is based for that reign lists only thirty men and is not complete. Yung-cheng figures refer to the council's antecedent staffs.)

Province	Yung-cheng	Ch'ien-lung	Chia-ch'ing	Tao-kuang	Hsien-feng	TOTAL
Shantung	0	4	4	3	1	12
Chihli	0	8	3	7	2	20
Shansi	0	2	4	1	2	9
Shensi	0	0	2	2	1	5
Kansu	0	0	0	0	0	0
Honan	0	0	1	4	3	8
Kiangsu	3	53	10	20	8	94
Anhwei	2	17	2	6	2	29
Chekiang	3	40	21	10	9	83
Kiangsi	1	10	4	6	4	25
Hupei	0	1	2	4	2	9
Szechuan	0	0	2	1	1	4
Fukien	0	3	1	4	2	10
Kwangtung	0	0	1	3	4	8
Kwangsi	0	0	3	0	4	7
Hunan	0	3	1	4	0	8
Kweichow	0	0	0	2	0	2
Yunnan	0	1	0	0	0	1
No province given	1	1	0	0	0	2
Total	10	143	61	77	45	336

SOURCE: *Shu-yuan chi-lueh* (SYCL) 18/1–19/8. Although the SYCL clerks' list has a few mistakes, it is the best list available.

the councillors, with 37 percent of the clerks coming from Kiangsu and another 28 percent from Chekiang. Together the four middle south provinces (outlined in Table 9) accounted for 84 percent of the clerk selections in that reign. After the Chia-ch'ing reforms a considerable reduction took place, but the four provinces were still heavily represented, accounting for 61 percent of the clerk choices in the Chia-ch'ing reign, although now Chekiang (34 percent) rather than Kiangsu (16 percent) predominated. Over the five reigns shown in the table, the four provinces dominated the clerkships with 69 percent of the 336 Chinese-clerk appointments. The high numbers of clerks from these four provinces are indubitably more than a coincidence. They parallel the figures for councillors and suggest that personal connections, as well as the wealth of the area, may have influenced the choice of clerks.

In addition to personal connections, there were other routes to a clerkship. Examination achievement was important for Chinese but not for Manchus, and there was not much difference between the eighteenth- and nineteenth-century selections in this respect. In the sixty-eight years from the first clerk appointment in YC8 (early 1731) to the last full year of Ch'ien-lung's rule in CC3 (1798), of the 223 Manchu clerks appointed, only 4 achieved degree status; over the next sixty-eight years, from CC4 (1799) to TC6 (1867), out of 147 Manchus appointed, only one achieved a degree. But for Chinese, the situation was just the opposite. Of 153 Chinese appointed in the first period, only 6 (4 percent) had no degree status, while 38 (25 percent) won the *chü-jen* and 83 (54 percent) the *chin-shih* degree. During the next sixty-eight years there were 183 new Chinese clerks, of whom many more—137 (75 percent)—had the *chin-shih* and 34 (19 percent) the *chü-jen*.[17] Among these men were several who had won one of the three highest places in the triennial examinations.[18]

In the absence of written stipulations from the council's early years it is difficult to tell what other requirements were applied in eighteenth-century clerk selections. Perhaps some of the considerations later required for these appointments by the Chia-ch'ing reforms applied in the eighteenth century as well.[19] One reform specified that the clerks were to possess "upright moral character, robust health, [and] good calligraphy." In CC18 (1813), a censor proposed that the names on the clerks' examination papers be pasted over so that readers could not identify the authors and judge on the basis of prior acquaintance. The responding edict disparaged the suggestion, explaining that judgments had to take personal character as well as qualifications such as handsome calligraphy into account.[20]

Nevertheless, the idea has persisted that clerks were selected for important positions on the highest privy council of the realm on the basis of the beauty of their calligraphy. Early in the Tao-kuang reign (1821–50), a Grand Secretariat secretary, Kung Tzu-chen, who had been bitterly disappointed in his attempt to follow his father into a Grand Council clerkship, assailed the council's selection system, claiming that it esteemed calligraphic skill above all else in selecting men who were to handle the empire's most important affairs. Kung satirized the situation as follows:

> I was examined for the Grand Council but was not given a post there.... So I have withdrawn to my home and have reproached myself, and have written a book in self-criticism. Its contents consist of twelve sections discussing the principles of selecting a fine brush-tip, five sections on the proper method of grinding the ink and impregnating the brush, ... one hundred and twenty sections on fine points in the drawing of the dot and in the execution of the sweeping downstroke, twenty-two sections on the framing of characters, twenty-four sections on the spacing of characters in [a] column, three sections on quality of spirit, and seven sections on natural temper. Having finished the work, I have entitled it *A New Treatise on Gaining Office*, and am entrusting it to my descendants.[21]

The fine, clearly formed characters of the Grand Council record books that make them a joy to read suggest that Kung's complaint may have had some basis in fact and that calligraphic skill was indeed a factor in selecting Grand Council clerks. But given the faith of those times that regular morning practice of calligraphy built character by tempering a man's outlook and producing balance and perspective, the belief that cultivation of this talent might assist the highest affairs of state cannot be viewed as off the mark.

Internal Organization

The informality and lack of specifications in the eighteenth-century council also affected the numbers of clerks, as under Ch'ien-lung the size of the body of clerks was unregulated and frequently fluctuated when extra men were taken on to deal with a crisis or to replace those who accompanied councillors to the various battlefronts of the times. At the end of the Interim Council in CL2 (1737), the council had had only eighteen clerks.[22] The earliest substantial enlargement was put through to meet the demands of the first Chin-ch'uan campaign in CL13–14 (1748–49) and resulted in twenty-nine clerks serving at once: twenty-one at the capital and eight away on campaign.[23] In CL36 (1771) there was another increase to cope with the second Chin-ch'uan war; one notice spoke of "about forty clerks" at that time.[24] Thus in the council's early years the numbers of clerk appointments fluctuated (see Table 10).

By the Chia-ch'ing period the number of clerks was prescribed by law and stabilized at thirty-two men.[25] Nevertheless, there could be supernumerary (*e-wai*) additions to meet unanticipated situations. In fact, the earliest exception to the new ruling was put through only seven years after its promulgation, and during the nineteenth century other additions responded to other emergencies, such as the need for expanded management of the campaign against the Taiping rebels.[26]

The relative numbers of Manchu and Chinese clerks also fluctuated (see Table 10). Although during the Yung-cheng era there was an imbalance of 71 percent Manchu to 29 percent Chinese, the next two decades saw changes that

TABLE 10. Grand Council clerks added in each five-year period in the Yung-cheng and Ch'ien-lung reigns.

	Manchus	Chinese	Total
YC8–13	25	10	35
YC13-CL5	8	11	19
CL6–10	9	8	17
CL11–15	24	12	36
CL16–20	19	14	33
CL21–25	18	14	32
CL26–30	11	13	24
CL31–35	18	10	28
CL36–40	25	19	44
CL41–45	25	14	39
CL46–50	8	11	19
CL51–55	21	9	30
CL56–60	12	8	20
CC1–3	0	0	0
Total	223 (59%)	153 (41%)	376

SOURCES: *Shu-yuan chi-lueh* 16/1–14b, 18/1–12b; I-fu tang (Beijing) CL2/12/11, pp. 353–55.

moved toward the more balanced proportions of later years, 61 percent to 39 percent. By the time of the Chia-ch'ing reforms the two groups were evenly balanced, with four ethnically compartmentalized duty groups, two Manchu and two Chinese, all the same size.

The clerks probably acquired an internal rationalization of their group during the eighteenth century. Each clerk duty group had its own leader (*ling-pan*) and assisting leader (*pang ling-pan*), the first also being known by the Manchu term *ta-la-mi* (from the Manchu *dalambi*, to be the head or leader). Not much is known about the leaders, but in the nineteenth century they were keeping certain financial accounts and checking the edict drafts before those went up to the grand councillors for final vetting.[27] The leaders may also have dispensed work assignments. There is some evidence that the two ethnic groups, Manchu and Chinese, carried out their work in separate offices; nevertheless, their assignments were not necessarily based on language,[28] and moreover, on many occasions they joined together on projects.

It is not clear how many clerks were on duty at any one time. Chao I, who became a clerk in CL21 (1756), later recollected a figure of ten, but this may have been high because of wartime exigencies.[29] In peace the numbers may have been smaller.

By the nineteenth century and perhaps earlier, rotation of duty groups was prescribed in precise detail. For example, Liang Chang-chü described the situation in his day, late in the Chia-ch'ing reign:

Whenever [the Grand Council] is in the city [of Peking], two subgroups of clerks rotate duty on alternate days, with each subgroup having two men [that is, a total of four, two Manchus and two Chinese] and dividing the duty each time. When the rotation has gone through [all the men, thirty-two at the time], then it starts over. A duty day includes the following night. After the work is finished [the clerks] withdraw to dine at the Office of Military Archives, and the next morning at the *yin* hour [3:00–5:00 A.M.] they return to the inner court and await the arrival of the next duty group. [The eight men of the two shifts then] attend to the [newly arrived] palace memorials [*chieh-che*], after which the [first four] are allowed to turn over their responsibilities [to the next shift].[30]

Although it was possible to rest during a round on duty, hours were long and a man could be on call for more than twenty-four hours at a stretch. Chao I felt the rigors of night duty, yet "it was not permitted to have no one there." He wrote of the early shift (*tsao-pan*), which began at the fifth drum (4:00 A.M.), and of how hard he found getting up at that hour: "Half asleep and half awake, I would lean against a pillar and doze. But through my half-closed eyes I would see a thin beam of light coming through the Lung-tsung Gate as the princes would enter their study. We [Grand Council clerks] were all poor scholars, who depended on learning for our food and clothing, but we could not get up early. Yet the scions of the imperial house did this every day."[31]

Chao I also noted the contrast between the clerks' rotation of work that placed them on duty only once every few days and the Ch'ien-lung Emperor's early rising habits and his "diligent" daily attention to his responsibilities. "In the long days of summer the sky would already be light" when the emperor arose, Chao I comments, while in winter, "ordinarily we did not know when the emperor got up." But toward the end of the last month of the year as the emperor proceeded along the path toward his study firecrackers would be set off (to ward off the evil spirits left to wander freely on earth in the period when the deities had ascended to heaven), and from the noise the clerks would know that their sovereign had arisen and was approaching. "Sometimes," adds Chao I, "it would be so early we would have to light a candle and use it until dawn."[32] The clerks roused themselves reluctantly on their early-duty days, but there was no rotation of duty for the monarch.

Instead of resting, some clerks used the night shift to do council work or read the files. Liang Chang-chü, who started as a Grand Council clerk in CC23 (1818), put his night-shift hours to good use "scanning the old [council] records" and noting materials for his compendium on Grand Council history and procedures, the *Shu-yuan chi-lueh*.[33] In fact, the clerks were not the only ones who found themselves hard at work at the dawn's first light. Huang Yueh, one of the first grand councillors appointed after the Tao-kuang Emperor succeeded to the throne, boasted that on the days he was at court, "as dawn came up I would be reading the small characters of the palace memorials without benefit of lamplight." Inner-court staff members had to get an early start on the day's work in order to be ready when the emperor began his day.[34]

The clerks also rotated duty whenever the emperor was on tour. As at the capital, head clerks supervised each section of clerks, with two men taking the duty each day. [35] Tour rules for duty rotation at the beginning of the nineteenth century exhibit considerable refinement and may well have been worked out during the days of the Ch'ien-lung Emperor's frequent excursions away from Peking. According to Liang Chang-chü:

> If [the clerks] are at the Summer Palace, then four days are one turn of duty, called "the Summer Palace tour of duty" [*kai-yuan pan*]. Two men [from each section, Manchu and Chinese] share the work on each turn of duty, and the rotation is the same as in the city. When they have finished their day's work they live at duty quarters outside the palace.... Those on duty are called "the base section" [*pen-pan*]; those not on duty are called "the assisting section" [*pang-pan*].[36]

As at the capital, tour rules specified that the group supervisor and the two men on a shift stay on duty until after the next shift's arrival, a practice picturesquely known as "not cutting off the tail" (*pu-chieh wei*).[37] Other terminology, some from the Manchu and some from the Chinese, described other features of the tours. The three Chinese characters *yin-te-mi* (from the Manchu *indembi*, to take a break on a journey, to stop for the night) denoted an imperial-tour encampment. Another Manchu term, *t'u-t'a-mi* (from *tutambi*, to remain behind), was the name for the relief group that stayed behind in the capital and did not accompany the tour. This group would go out to greet the returning entourage and then would serve several days in a row to compensate those who had been on call continuously while away. Although *t'u-t'a-mi* had a Chinese equivalent (*cho-chih*), the Manchu sounds could be written in three Chinese characters, and so the relief groups were usually thus noted in the council's log books.[38] The fact of so many Manchu special terms for these activities suggests that they had been in use a long time, perhaps ever since Yung-cheng days, when the body of clerks had been predominately Manchu. (See Appendixes C and D, which show how proportionately more Manchus than Chinese were attached to the Yung-cheng inner court.)

Concern for Time

The development of duty group rules that provided for work and rest schedules and the optimum employment of men's energies were part of the eighteenth-century process of refinement and elaboration at the Grand Council. As early as the eighteenth century, the Grand Council clerks' working style demonstrates an awareness of time and a concern for efficiency. For example, the clerks were responsible for writing up a document register that listed all incoming and outgoing documents at the council each day. The literal meaning of the register's title, "registering the work as it came to hand" (Sui-shou teng-chi), suggests a drive for efficiency behind council work. The register's concern for time is evinced in its noting the arrival hours of important memorials and the imperial post speeds at which those memorials and their responding edicts were to be carried back. Although later responses were possible, and often were necessary in the case of formal written deliberations, the fact that delays beyond one day were noted in the register exhibits a concern for prompt disposal of the business coming before the inner court.[39] The register embodied the ideal of clearing the imperial in-box each day.

There is other evidence of careful attention to the use of time. For example, the reference copies of certain memorials were made before the emperor saw the originals in case an immediate response should be required. Edict-drafting descriptions show that speed was of paramount importance, with delays in handling often noted on the record book copies.[40] On one occasion, Ch'ien-lung was so prompt in responding to a memorial, scolding the author for failing to supply all the necessary information, that a follow-up edict had to be sent off the very next day when the additional facts arrived in a supplementary report.[41] All this was in sharp contrast to outer-court practice, where numerous ritual occasions were permitted to interrupt the handling of government business; indeed, matters were allowed to reach almost a complete halt during the lunar new year month, when the seals necessary for processing documents could not be used, owing to the custom of "closing the seals" (*feng-yin*).[42]

Concern for time at the council may have been given a boost by one of the early leading councillors, Fu-heng, who took up the use of personal timepieces. The Grand Council clerk Chao I described Fu-heng's infatuation with these new arrivals from the West and, with a mixture of affection for Fu-heng and open-mindedness toward this higher technology, portrayed the use of time-pieces in Fu-heng's household:

> Self-striking clocks and watches that [hang from one's neck and] tell the time all come from the West. A clock can strike according to the hour. A watch has a needle that moves as time passes and can express twelve hours. They are both extremely ingenious.
>
> At the present time the imperial astronomers, when they observe the stars and make calendars, all employ Westerners, and from this we may deduce that [the Westerners' methods] may be said to be finer than the old methods used in China.... Now the Westerners' [land] is distant by ten thousand *li*, but their methods are better. From this we can know that the world is vast—no matter where you go there are clever men who invent things. We were not the only ones to have a Fu-hsi and a Yellow Emperor....
>
> [But] clocks and watches often have to be repaired. Otherwise the gold thread inside will break, or they go too fast or too slow, and then you cannot get the correct time. Therefore, among the court officials there are some who possess these things, but they still forget meetings—or, [to put it another way,] those in the court who never miss meetings are the ones who do not own clocks.
>
> Fu-heng's house is one that has clocks and watches, so much so that among his servants is not even one who does not hang one on his body. They can mutually check the time against each other and never be off the mark. One day when there

was a formal imperial audience, [Fu-heng's] watch still had not noted that the
time [for the audience] had arrived, but the imperial retinue had already gone
in and the emperor had taken his seat. Suddenly [Fu-heng] appeared in a great
state of agitation and kowtowed at the foot of the throne. For the rest of the day
he went around in a most upset and untranquil frame of mind.[43]

This story illustrates a growing interest in the accurate measurement of time
both at home and at the council. Fu-heng, who was the ranking councillor for
two decades early in the Ch'ien-lung reign, may have been one who led the
way.[44]

Working Conditions

In the early years, the clerks' working conditions were far from luxurious.
Chao I described the clerks'offices in the Peking palace as comprising only one
and a half "cramped and dark" rooms. After he had left the council, the clerks'
office was moved to slightly better quarters: a small low building of three rooms,
with windows only on the front, facing north. Cold in winter, it had low ceilings
that would make it stifling in summer. The windows were covered with a
special tough "Korean" paper (kao-li chih), which could be oiled to keep out
wind but not light.[45] Perhaps some of the lumps of coal (for braziers) ordered
annually for various Grand Council offices were used to improve the clerks'
premises in winter. Ice was brought in to cool the areas in summer.[46]

   At their office the clerks had to ensure the security of their files. Only records
for the current month—the document logbook, record books, and packets of
memorial copies—were kept on hand, stored in cupboards when not needed
for work. The clerks on duty were responsible for sealing the cupboards at day's
end.[47] Fortunately, the three rooms did not have to accommodate all the
documents that coursed through the clerks' hands. Additional space in the
western part of the palace was available for the Grand Council archives as well
as for special publication and copying projects, and the clerks often worked in
those other buildings.

   The working conditions of an imperial tour could tax the ingenuity of a
clerk charged with making a neat copy of a deliberation memorial or preparing
an edict for immediate dispatch. In the early days, no writing tables or other
furniture embellished the staff tents. As Chao I related: "We had to squat on
the ground to make our drafts and use a [narrow] yellow memorial box as a
table, writing without having anything on which to rest our wrists." At night
"there were no proper lampstands, but only lampholders made of iron strips.
We would hang the lamps above us and write our characters in a thin beam
of light. When we cut the candle wick, the wax would suddenly splutter all
over us."[48] Under Ch'ien-lung's peripatetic monarchy, tours were a regular
feature of government life. One hardship a clerk had to face was being away
from the capital and coping with such privations for several months of the year.
But during the council's early years, little attention was paid to the clerks'
working environment. As we shall see, improvements came later.

Responsibilities

The clerks' work ranged from routine copy work to responsibility for drafting all but the most confidential imperial edicts, with newcomers (*hsiao pan-kung*) given the easier archival supervision and copy work and old hands (*lao pan-kung*) dealing with discretionary tasks such as memorial scanning, edict drafting, and research for the councillors' deliberations.[49] Some clerks also answered the private letters sent to the grand councillors for whom they worked.[50] Others were frequently given small investigative errands and other commissions in Peking.[51] Many accompanied their councillors on missions that could take them far from the capital for many months. Through the clerks' tasks of scanning memorials and writing up the daily logbook, almost all the secrets of council work were open to them. The fact that in the nineteenth century the clerks were also charged with keeping the records of the use of the council's seal shows that they were trusted as much as the councillors, who had formerly discharged that responsibility.[52]

There is evidence that some of the clerks' division of labor reflected the specialties of their concurrent appointments or, in some cases, a special expertise they had developed on the job. For instance, a Board of Revenue subordinate with a concurrent Grand Council clerkship might handle finance memorials for the council.[53] In CC18–19 (1813–14), when the Eight Trigrams uprising was being suppressed, a clerk compiled a briefing book showing troop postings together with the names of generals and lower officials stationed at each point. Whenever the emperor inquired about strategic places in the provinces involved in the uprising, the clerk would produce his notebook. The emperor was so impressed that the man shortly won promotion to Anhwei treasurer. Another clerk is said to have given advice at the front in the course of the Eight Trigrams suppression and, in addition, to have provided policy guidance on the Moslem uprising in the northwest in the Tao-kuang period. Nevertheless, in the face of emergencies, specializations had to be put aside. During military campaigns, all the clerks worked together to cope with the flood of field reports and responding instructions. They were rewarded after victory, just as if they had been part of the march.[54]

Indeed, the clerks' responsibilities paralleled those of the councillors they served, and as the councillors became ever busier with the increasing press of business the clerks got more and more to do. The clerks could make policy suggestions on any topic with which they were familiar. They might carry out research and write drafts of important documents—both edicts and deliberation memorials. They handled many of the fussy details concerning communications, particularly scanning memorials, writing summaries, and copying documents.[55] They supervised the Grand Council archives, overseeing storage of state papers and writing up the logbook used to retrieve documents. Finally, many clerks held concurrent appointments as proofreaders and overseers in the Grand Council's publications office and as a result were concerned with council-sponsored publication projects. During the eighteenth century, as the councillors became increasingly concerned with the immense and burgeoning variety of inner-court responsibilities, the clerks' position as personal aides to the councillors involved them in a similar range of work.

Archives. Although the Yung-cheng Emperor and his inner deputies were initially responsible for working out methods for monitoring the new inner-court communications, including archival storage procedures, during the Ch'ien-lung reign the Grand Council clerks gradually assumed these burdens, and they continued to discharge them to the end of the dynasty. For instance, the clerks had to be sure that copies of all important documents that might be required for policy background were available on the council premises. This meant not only making copies of palace memorials that were returned to their authors but also providing the means for locating these and other documents in the files. A major key to their system was a logbook whose name might be translated "Register [of Documents] as They Came to Hand" (Sui-shou teng-chi tang).

This logbook's pages were crammed with information, so much so that the book can be used for substantive research today. The large square pages gave prominent place (by means of characters written bold and black near the top of the page) to the memorialists' names; second in importance were the contents of the palace memorials, whose summaries also began at the top of the page. The placement of these heavy black headings page after page facilitated quick scanning for memorials (as long as the name of the author could be recalled) and gave rise to a poem rhapsodizing on the register, whose headings were fancifully likened to "eyebrows."[56] Imperial rescripts appeared only in the middle of a page, below the document summaries and set off by a respectful space the size of one character rather than the elevation that usually marked an item of imperial origin—thus satisfying the need for efficient use of space. The problem of suitable respect for the imperial words was adroitly circum-vented by heading each notice of a memorialist's packet with the characters for "imperial rescript" (*chu-p'i*); the entire entry, then, would begin: "Imperially rescripted memorials of so-and-so" (see Figure 8). Thus, a ritual homage to imperial centrality was maintained in a logbook devised to facilitate scanning according to the users' needs.

Although the register was an index to stored inner-court state papers, it was not an index in the modern sense—that is, it did not guide the user by means of retrieval numbers to the site of the document. Instead, the clerk who was scanning the register had to obtain the desired document's date of arrival in the capital (sometimes the date of dispatch was also shown, but this was irrelevant for retrieval purposes), whereupon the full text of a document could be run to ground. Provincial palace memorial copies—which the clerks had hastily scrawled in "running script" (*ts'ao-shu*)—could be retrieved from the Grand Council reference collection (*Chün-chi ch'u lu-fu tsou-che*) stored in the

Office of Military Archives. Scanning might also locate copies of capital documents—the councillors' memorials (*i-fu tsou-che*) and memoranda (*shuo-t'ieh* or *tsou-p'ien*), as well as imperial edicts—which were bound chronologically into thick record books.[57]

Because of the large number of inner-court documents that it indexed, the document register bared the secrets of inner-court work to those who consulted its pages. The logbook's pages, crammed with the summaries of the state secrets set forth in the palace memorials and responding edicts, presented all this information to the clerks and perhaps even to lower council attendants as well. As a result, there had to be a way to preserve secrecy even while keeping a faithful record of document traffic. This was accomplished, usually on the order of a grand councillor, by the simple expedient of writing the heading but then only drawing a line to indicate that an item had arrived, the space for the summary being left blank. Alternatively, an uninformative summary might be supplied or a summary might omit sensitive details. For example, personnel reports arrived sealed as "secret memorials" (*mi-tsou*) and went directly to the emperor; the document register clerks noted only their arrival and the number of evaluations enclosed. A mid-nineteenth-century document register recorded a censor's memorial, its contents unhelpfully described merely as "respectfully presenting views."[58] Such measures were not often necessary, for council personnel were assumed to be loyal and reliable. Council work had to be carried out with the confidence that details of reports on enemy actions and rebel plots would be safeguarded even if set down in the register.

As time went on there was a proliferation not only in the numbers and types of matters reported in the palace memorials and their enclosures but also in the numbers and varieties of copies made for the council's files. Imperial edicts as well as all sorts of other materials—memorials of deliberation and recommendation, memoranda, depositions (*kung-tan*), lists (*tan*), and in some cases summaries of documents—were copied on large square sheets of paper and bound into record books (*tang-ts'e*). The provincial palace memorials were handled a little differently; in the eighteenth century the chief copies were deposited in the Grand Council reference collection, although a few record books of provincial palace memorials were also turned over to the outer court (Wai-chi tang). In the nineteenth century there were monthly and more frequent assemblages (Yueh-che tang). In addition to the several files compiled chronologically according to type of document—the "Record Book of Deliberations" (I-fu tang) and the "Record Book of Court Letters" (Chi-hsin tang), for example—there were also general assemblages such as the misleadingly titled "Record Book of Imperial Edicts" (Shang-yü tang), into which were bound many types of documents, not just imperial edicts.

There were also specialized records (for which the modern term is *chuan-an tang*), which held relevant documents of many different types, each record book covering one subject. Although such albums were most commonly compiled

一會議廣東省洋盜李複全一案　旨依議　　交

一覆議陳淮徐午一案　旨隨　交

一覆議豐城攔漕一案　旨依議　交

和等摺一件

一駁滇省年辦京銅等由　旨隨　交

論旨三道

一張繼辛補授四川按察使　交

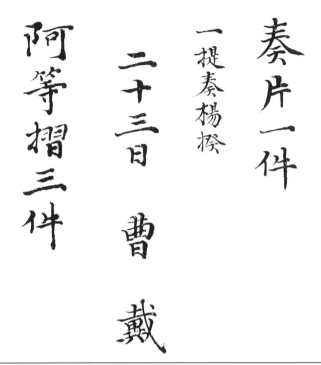

Four memorials submitted by two grand councillors, as well as other items, are depicted here, with notices (*chiao*) below that some were turned over to the outer court. Two of the memorials specifically received the imperial approval; the other two were circulated with specially drafted decrees (*chih*). In this period the emperor usually did not write in vermilion on the grand councillors' palace memorials; this explains why the term "Imperial rescript" (*Chu-p'i*) does not appear above these entries. The heavy blackened characters show the date, the types of documents (memorandum, grand council memorials, imperial edicts), and the names of the two grand councillors. Reproduced at about three-quarters of actual size.

SOURCE: Sui-shou teng-chi CC2/1/23, pp. 44–45. Reproduced by kind permission of the Palace Museum, Taipei.

on military campaigns, and for that reason were categorized as "urgent" (*chin-yao*) materials, special books were also put together on water conservancy emergencies, officials scheduled for promotion, and many other topics.[59] Anything that the councillors or clerks deemed necessary could be held in such files.

When the Grand Council archives were unpacked in the 1920s, no less than 150 types of Chinese-language Grand Council record books were unearthed, a total of eight or nine thousand fascicles (*ts'e*).[60] In addition, there were large numbers of Manchu-language records, more than sixteen hundred such albums for the Yung-cheng and Ch'ien-lung reigns alone and almost four thousand for the dynasty through TC11 (1872), the date of the last Manchu archival inventory.[61] The clerks were responsible for this prodigious labor of compilation and copying.

The clerks also supervised the periodic copying of important archival records that were in danger of disintegrating from frequent use. Copying probably began in CL43 (1778) and was carried out every five years. The additional copies could be carried on tours or left at the Summer Palace and ensured that there would be at least one duplicate set to guard against loss or deterioration.[62] The clerks' responsibility for maintaining and copying the records of the privy council gave them access to nearly all the major document traffic of the realm. Only occasionally was a document denied them.[63]

Assignments out of the Capital. In the eighteenth century, the clerks served the councillors personally, with the result that when councillors were sent out of the capital on an investigative or military assignment clerks were frequently deputed to accompany them. A CL11 (1746) notice sending a grand councillor to Manchuria to inspect a newly dug river channel ordered several Grand Council clerks to accompany him, and the entire group was awarded the privilege of traveling by imperial-post facilities.[64] On the occasion of an imperial tour, clerks were likely to accompany the councillors in the retinue.[65] As we have seen, a military campaign could also draw many clerks away from capital service.[66] Other journeys involved "handling cases." In CL43 (1779), a clerk and a Board of Punishments official accompanied a grand councillor on a journey to Sheng-ching in Manchuria. On the councillor's return to the capital, the two subordinates—the technically qualified representative from the board and the Manchu Grand Council clerk—stayed behind.[67]

Sometimes clerks were deployed on discretionary tasks without supervising councillors. The details of an instance in CL49 (1784), when a Grand Council clerk and two Board of Punishments officials journeyed to Kansu to take down the confessions of Moslems captured after a recent uprising, will show the kind of high discretionary responsibilities a clerk might have had to take on far from the capital, alone, and without the advice of his superiors or the companionship of his peers.[68] In interrogating the Kansu Moslems, a clerk had to struggle with unfamiliar territory, local dialects, Moslem vocabulary, and the confusion of rumor and fact in the rebels' defense of their antistate activity. Within a short time the clerk had to inform himself on the details of the situation and be able to pursue an evasive response and pin down the facts, separating the leaders who had rebelled with malice aforethought from those who had simply followed along. He had to get the facts on such matters as the reasons for the rebellion ("Basically, why did you rebel?—answer truthfully," began the first question preceding the Moslem rebels' depositions, to which the deponents ingenuously argued lack of intention, claiming, "We never thought the thing would snowball into the present situation"), advance preparations ("Why did you repair the fort so recently [that is, so close to the time of the rebellion]?"), sources of supply ("Where did you get your tents and weapons?"), and the deeply disturbing intelligence that the rebels had flaunted antidynastic symbols ("Why were you wearing white jackets?").[69] If a deposition's veracity was questioned, the clerk got the man to go over the same ground again. The reports and confessions were eventually sent to Peking, where they were used to decide which rebels were to be spared punishment and which were to be punished for sedition. The clerks involved in these interrogations were dealing with both the lives of individuals and the security of the empire.

Clerks who accompanied grand councillors on military assignments could find themselves off to war for several years at a time. At the front they were in charge of the highest-level campaign paperwork, researching the responses to questions sent out from the capital, drafting memorials, and keeping track of troop allocations and campaign finances. Several clerks wrote accounts of the campaigns in which they had participated, or assisted with the drafting of the official campaign histories. Other clerks edited or wrote other types of accounts derived from their Grand Council assignments.[70]

Many of the clerks were highly intelligent men who had benefited from and done well in the educational system of their times. It is not surprising that in addition to taking on unusual responsibilities in both the capital and the provinces, they might use their privileged access to documents to write about their experiences. In doing this their behavior differed from that of their superiors, the councillors, most of whom refrained from writing that was based on their knowledge of the Grand Council. Nevertheless, rarely did the clerks' eyewitness recollections or editorial work reveal council secrets. In this respect, like their superiors they doubtless exercised a kind of self-censorship.

Edict Drafting.   Edict drafting was a major Grand Council responsibility. In Yung-cheng times as well as during the early years of the Ch'ien-lung reign it was usually carried out by the councillors, who were charged with making drafts on the basis of their policy discussions with the emperor. Edict drafting was an exacting task. Chao I tells us that when No-ch'in was the leading councillor (early in the Ch'ien-lung reign), because he was slightly deficient in literary skill he had another councillor whose writing ability he admired,

Wang Yu-tun, do the actual drafting. But then says Chao I, "No-ch'in would would be afraid that [the draft] would not be quite right, so he would have [Wang Yu-tun] write it out again, and then after several revisions he might very well use the first draft. A draft would just be completed and then there would come another imperial decree to be drafted and revised in this fashion. It was all very hard on Wang Yu-tun. But he did not dare complain."[71]

Gradually much edict drafting devolved on the clerks.[72] Chao I himself is said to have been responsible, as a clerk, for most of the Grand Council documents dispatched during the final and victorious campaign against the northwest Mongols.[73] Military reports might arrive at any time of the day or night. No matter when one came in, the reply would be discussed and a responding edict drafted as fast as possible, sometimes being dispatched within a few hours. According to Chao I's recollection,

> Sometimes when [the emperor] was on tour, along the road he would suddenly hand down an edict. After Fu-heng had received it he would have a clerk dismount and compose a draft, so that when they reached that day's encampment the [draft would be ready for submission]. . . . Sometimes there were seventy or eighty *li* between one encampment and the next, and it would be half a day before everyone arrived. If [the imperial entourage] halted for lunch in order to give the emperor a short rest, the clerks would want to brag of their speed, and in great hurry and excitement would make their copies and rush eagerly to the halt to turn in their drafts. This was called "catching up at the lunch halt". This shows the speed with which these affairs could be handled, but because of the short snatch of time, the drafts often contained errors and then had to be revised.[74]

Of course, the clerks also wrote out the revisions.

The Ch'ien-lung Emperor was so engrossed with the progress of the mid-century campaign in Sinkiang that he left orders that he be wakened whenever an important report arrived from the front. Chao I's memoirs, written many years later, recall his own part in these nighttime drafts: "Even if it was the middle of the night, [the emperor] would read [the military report] himself and then summon the grand councillors to express his views. . . . At that time I would write out the draft, and then from the hastily written draft I would write it out again in neat characters to be handed in to the emperor. The whole process might take as much as one or two hours. The emperor would just wait for me in his heavy coat."[75] Rarely, however, did a clerk take dictation directly from the emperor. The clerks may have written the drafts and even selected the phrasing, but the ideas usually came from policy deliberations between the emperor and the councillors. Although a clerk might occasionally note the emperor's words directly or draft an ordinary document, the clerks did not regularly contribute to the crucial policy deliberation step of edict drafting. The councillors kept firm control over this important responsibility right through to the end of the dynasty.[76] On occasion, if secrecy or other considerations warranted, the councillors would write out the draft of an important edict themselves, just as they had in the early days.

Error, Malfeasance, and Punishment

Although little publicity was given to the subject, the archives yield some information on the clerks' inadvertent errors, intentional malfeasance, and punishment. Sometimes a clerk would himself discover an unintentional mistake, report it, and receive a light administrative punishment. This happened in CL40 (1775), for instance, when a clerk wrote an incorrect imperial rescript on the copy of a memorial being sent to the Board of Civil Office. When the memorial was returned to the Grand Council it was checked against the document register, at which point the clerk learned that where the original rescript had instructed the board "to deliberate and memorialize in reply" (*kai-pu i-tsou*), the copy he had made had specified only that the board "take note" (*kai-pu chih-tao*). Since the man discovered the error himself, the punishment was light.[77]

Sometimes another official discovered and reported an error. In CL22 (1757), for example, the clerk Chao I neglected to make an archival copy of a palace memorial reporting suspicious student activity in connection with the examinations. When the missing memorial copy could not be found, Chao I's carelessness came to light and he was recommended for light administrative punishment.[78]

More serious than mistakes of this sort were the cases where the clerks or their subordinates were found to have removed state documents from the council premises. In CL46 (1781), more than ten pages were discovered missing from the end of a record book dated four years earlier; after investigation a copyist admitted taking the pages home and then losing them when he was set upon by thieves. Of course he was punished; moreover, his supervising Grand Council clerk and others believed to have been derelict in their duty of checking the situation at the time were penalized as well.[79]

Far more serious were instances when clerks disseminated Grand Council secrets, sometimes in return for bribes, sometimes because there was a relationship between the clerk and the man to whom he divulged forbidden information. Late in the Ch'ien-lung period, a clerk whose duties included monitoring salt matters at Yangchow gave advance information to the Yangchow authorities that, according to the imperial edict on the subject, enabled a local grandee to take steps to corner the market. When this breach came to light the miscreants were severely punished—the clerk with exile to Ili.[80] Taking advantage of one's access to council secrets was far more heinous a crime then errors of copying or even such a suspicious loss of documents as that described above.

An important fact about these instances of malfeasance and punishment is that while the clerks were punished, their supervising grand councillors, whom we might expect also to take responsibility, were usually exonerated. The fact that the clerks were held fully accountable suggests that they were given considerable independence.[81] Another point of interest is that in some cases the councillors' reports to the emperor concealed the offending clerks' names in an attempt to protect these aides.[82] Generally, however, the clerks' errors and malfeasance were reported to the emperor; this was essential in order to assure his majesty that, despite occasional lapses, the councillors were keeping a watchful eye on their clerks. Above all, the confidence of the sovereign had to be maintained.[83]

Advantages of Being a Clerk and the Clerks' Careers

Through edict drafting and other tasks, the clerks were in frequent touch with the emperor, a fact that brought them immense prestige in capital circles. One clerk wrote about how closeness to the monarch meant imperial gifts: "fine textiles, cakes, and fruits," with delicacies of "fish and deer meat" bestowed at the end of each year.[84] The clerks had other sources of prestige as well. Like the grand councillors, when the clerks went on missions out of the capital they were allowed the favor of travel by imperial post.[85] At mid-reign they acquired the sumptuary privileges of wearing sable jackets and large red hats.[86] Wherever they went, they could be identified as clerks of the emperor's high privy council.

As the Ch'ien-lung reign wore on, attention was given to improving the facilities used by the clerks on imperial tours. Chao I wrote of visiting the council tents in CL45 (1780), after he had retired. At that time, he tells us, "I saw the Grand Council quarters [set up] for that imperial tour, with clear windows, clean tables, and fancy decorated mats. Those who had to write were made comfortable with plump cushions."[87] The clerks now enjoyed both the trappings of glory and the reality of doing important work at the center of the government.

Service as a clerk provided valuable on-the-job training for an ambitious middle-rank official. In CL25 (1760), Pi Yuan, who had served as a clerk for three years and had just passed the two main parts of the metropolitan examination, received an unexpected advantage that helped him the rest of his life. Stuck with the night shift the day before he was to sit for the final round of the tripos, the palace examination (tien-shih), and lacking pressing duties, he whiled away the time by scrutinizing a memorial on the Sinkiang military colonization policy that had just come out (fa-hsia) from the imperial quarters. The next day the emperor, who had himself been pondering policies for the newly conquered area of Sinkiang (Hsin-chiang, the "New Frontier"), put a question on that topic on the examination. Ch'ien-lung was said to have been so impressed with the grasp of the situation that Pi Yuan displayed that the clerk's examination rank was forthwith changed from fourth to first place (chuang-yuan).[88] Another Grand Council clerk who took the same examination won second place. As a result of their achievements, the two were immediately promoted to the Hanlin Academy and left the council.[89] On occasion, then, privileged access to important documents gave the clerks policy background and insights that were denied their fellow examinees from outside the council.

An important feature of the Grand Council clerkship was the assurance that good performance would probably serve as a springboard to a good provincial or capital post and lead to a rewarding career. Pi Yuan, for instance, had a long career in high provincial posts, with several governorships and one round as governor-general. The man who placed second in the same examination rose to prefect. Grand Council records are filled with memoranda seeking rewards and good promotions for the clerks.[90] The situation created by this policy worked to the council's advantage when, through the promotions of former clerks, the council put its men into strategic posts and gained contacts and loyal experienced assistance all over the empire. Liang Chang-chü's name list of council clerks underlined this aspect of the clerks' service by noting the highest post each man achieved after leaving the council.[91] A good later career was an expected part of a clerk's experience on the Grand Council.

It is difficult to tell how many years of service were necessary before a clerk would move on. In ordinary times the grand councillors reviewed the clerks and recommended the most able for promotion at three-year intervals—yet this did not mean that three-year terms at the council were the rule.[92] Some men served twenty years or more; others served a short while, were sent into provincial posts, and then later returned to council service.[93] One difficulty in keeping men a long time was that because of the concurrent post rule and growing limitations on how high a man could rise and remain a council clerk, good clerks faced the dilemma of forgoing the higher wages of a provincial post if they wished to remain on council service. As a result, the councillors sometimes had to seek a promotion at his concurrent capital office for a man they wished to keep.[94]

Was this a clerks' government (*k'o-yuan cheng-chih*), in which the clerks possessed the significant policy background facts, while the councillors simply rubberstamped proposals and drafts that came up from below? There is, indeed, some evidence for this view. The reminiscences of some former clerks suggest that the clerks' role was central to the entire Grand Council enterprise. Chao I explained how middle-level officials (that is, clerks) were the pivotal achievers at the council as well as in the boards, drafting edicts, for instance, in the fashion of high officials of earlier dynasties.[95] A former eighteenth-century clerk concocted a convoluted tale of why the clerks were of central importance: the councillors were reluctant to get involved, he asserted, lest they be accused of appropriating too much power to themselves, so they let their staffs make the drafts and do other important work.[96] One Chia-ch'ing edict suggested that clerks decided what to write and then got the councillors to agree.[97]

But if the reminiscences of Chao I and other former clerks smack of clerks exalting the role of clerks, we need only turn to the documentary evidence. There we may see that the clerks were indeed playing a pivotal role, not only managing the immense communications traffic but also on occasion influencing policy. The hundreds of volumes of their logbook, with its thousands of closely written pages, record the documents that the clerks scanned, abstracted, copied, evaluated, filed, and retrieved for briefing purposes. The register epitomizes the clerks' accomplishment as masters of the circulation of documents, their fingers on the communications pulse of the empire.

Yet there was another side to the story. The eighteenth-century grand councillors were close to their clerks, supervised their work, and held daily discussions with them. Moreover, even when the clerks had done the research, it was the councillors, not the clerks, who every day discussed policy with the emperor and submitted the memorials of deliberation and recommendation. The councillorship position was not a sinecure. The clerks did play a central role, but not a decisive or discretionary one. Most of the discretionary responsibilities below the imperial level were in the hands not of the clerks but of the hardworking councillors. By overseeing the many details of communications management, the clerks provided the essential support for the councillors' work.

THE GRAND COUNCIL MANCHU DIVISION

During the Ch'ien-lung period another subordinate organization of the Grand Council, known as the "Manchu Division" (*Man-pan*), handled matters of a special Manchu interest as well as the documents written in Manchu or other frontier languages. There is not much information about this group—we do not know when it began, nor can we be sure of its personnel and duties. It may have been composed of Manchu councillors and clerks, or perhaps of clerks alone. But there are many references to it. I first came across the Manchu Division in the frequent Grand Council logbook statements that a certain document had been "turned over to" or "come out from" the Manchu Division (*chiao Man-pan* or *Man-pan chiao-lai*).[98] At the time no scholar I consulted could tell me what the Manchu Division was. It has not been described in the literature and at this stage of our knowledge it is still not possible to supply a definitive description.

Although the Manchu Division's Chinese name appears to refer to one of the ethnic sections of clerks, the character for "division" (*pan*) was written differently when the group of Manchu clerks was meant (班), rather than the Manchu Division (伴); hence, the Manchu Division was probably not the same as the Manchu Section of the Grand Council clerks.[99] It may have consisted of some of the Manchu clerks, but it was probably supervised by one or more Manchu grand councillors.

Despite the vagueness of the references to the Manchu Division, we can describe it in a general way. First, we can use the document logbook statements concerning matters turned over to or sent out from it to see what the division was handling. Random selections from this source describing document contents include: Manchu-language documents; translating edicts into Manchu; translating or summarizing Manchu memorials in Chinese; appointments, promotions, and dismissals of banner personnel; punishment of palace bodyguards; cases involving Manchu officials; a mourning requirement for a Manchu official; customs post fines; banner finance and investments; the Hei-lung-chiang harvest figures; and escapees from exile in a frontier location.[100] Although these descriptions are succinct and unrevealing, they suggest that the division was handling matters relating to affairs affecting the banners, certain Manchu personnel, and the northern frontiers.

Another source of information about the Manchu Division consists of what I have identified as retrieval guides for Manchu-language palace memorial storage copies in the Grand Council reference collection (*Chün-chi ch'u lu-fu tsou-che*). I have been able to examine only two early-Ch'ien-lung–period records (known as Tsou-che hao-pu), which were an approximate Manchu counterpart of the document register maintained for the Chinese storage copies (the Sui-shou teng-chi). Like the document register, these Tsou-che hao-pu also listed topics that can be used to ascertain the concerns of the Manchu Division.

Appendix F reproduces in translation one month's storage list taken from the longest month available in this index. This list shows that most of the men submitting Manchu-language memorials were posted in frontier areas—Manchuria, Sinkiang, Tibet—with some reporting from the Manchu garrison areas inside China proper; a few—some princes, an occasional board staffmember, or a censor—were located at the capital. The topics they covered chiefly concerned frontier areas, banner affairs, and Manchu personnel administrative matters, usually reported in Manchu because that language came most easily to those writing the memorials.[101]

Banner finance looms large in these lists. One of the most elaborate summaries stated that the Grand Secretary No-ch'in (then the ranking grand councillor) and others had discussed withdrawing certain capital funds from "interest-bearing [banner] investments" at the capital and in the provinces. Beside this entry were listed four groups of enclosures with similar specific statements for certain named places in the empire.[102] Other memorials were concerned with preserving Manchu traditions. One sought greater strictness in the matter of intermarriage between Manchus and Chinese, for example.[103] The available volumes of this index further reveal that some of the entries concerned documents in languages other than Manchu. One noted "a communication in [an unidentified] barbarian language" (*fan-tzu wen-shu*). Elsewhere other languages—the written language of the Hui people and even Chinese— were cited. Some documents were very likely in Tibetan.[104] Thus the Manchu palace memorial filing and retrieval lists, compiled in the Manchu Division, also give a general idea of some of the subjects being handled by the division. We do not yet have enough information to know exactly what the division was doing with these documents—whether its responsibilities were limited to translation[105] or embraced more discretionary action.

There was an organizational logic, however, in providing that inner-court documents in languages other than Chinese be given separate treatment by speicalists in Manchu and other frontier languages. The necessity of dealing with large numbers of reports written exclusively in Manchu was particularly an inner-court rather than an outer-court problem. Regulations did not generally permit the submission of routine-system reports composed only in Manchu without a complementary Chinese copy.[106] Most outer-court work was based on Chinese-language documents, either the Chinese originals or the required translations that accompanied submissions. Moreover, the old outer-court Manchu requirements were in decline. By the middle of the Yung-cheng period, for example, the Manchu copy of a document required in the original submission no longer had to be copied for separate archival storage. In CL5 (1740), the question of whether to circulate Grand Secretariat publicly promulgated (*ming-fa*) edicts in both Chinese and Manchu was decided in favor of abandoning the old Manchu requirement, "since everyone now understands Chinese."[107]

The inner court, however, was different. Despite the slim gains made by Chinese in the Grand Council itself, Manchus still outnumbered Chinese at the councillor level, and dyarchy eventually existed only among the clerks. Taken in general, the officials of the inner court, with large numbers of bannermen in the Imperial Household and the bodyguards, remained predominately Manchu through the Ch'ien-lung period and to the end of the dynasty.[108] Furthermore, owing to the palace memorial system's preference for spontaneity, directness, and informality, inner-court communications permitted submissions in whatever language came most readily to the writer; there were no palace memorial rules requiring duplicate submissions in another language.[109] This meant that in areas where Manchu personnel predominated—the frontiers, the banner garrisons, and the Imperial Household, together with all its representative offices in customs as well as in the ginseng, jade, and other government monopolies throughout the empire—many if not most documents in these areas were written only in Manchu. As an early Chia-ch'ing–period Grand Council deliberation memorial on internal customs posts explained, little could be done about the situation: the fact that the documents and files of these areas were in Manchu meant that only Manchus should be appointed, while the fact of exclusively Manchu appointees resulted in the continued use of Manchu in the resulting reports. The councillors threw up their hands and admitted, "It is not convenient to appoint Chinese."[110]

Whether the Manchu Division served only as a translation service or dealt with other aspects of the documents cannot be answered from the evidence available at present. But despite the continued use of Manchu in so many areas of government activity, the increasing presence of Chinese personnel on the Grand Council meant that policy deliberations soon came to receive something approaching dyarchical consideration. For example, the Grand Council deliberation on internal customs posts just mentioned was submitted by four councillors, two of whom were Chinese. Thus, although an initial report may have been only in Manchu and the topic an Imperial Household preserve, the council included its Chinese members when meeting with the emperor to discuss related matters of policy. Thus, despite the Manchu Division, dyarchy prevailed at the topmost levels of the inner court.

The Manchu Division was probably derived from the predominately Manchu personnel of Yung-cheng's inner-court administration. The new, previously unknown Manchus in that administration had replaced the old ascriptive forces of Manchu princes and grandees who had held sway in earlier Ch'ing inner courts. As late as the Ch'ien-lung period, then, the Grand Council's Manchu Division helped preserve a strong Manchu presence in government, perhaps in part to console for other Manchu losses, in part as necessity to deal with certain Manchu topics.

THE OFFICE OF MILITARY ARCHIVES

The Office of Military Archives (*Fang-lueh kuan*) was another major inner-court organization that was founded and developed subordinate to the Grand Council during the eighteenth century. Like the Manchu Division, the Military Archives Office has not been properly described. Moreover, both the Chinese term and the English translation generally used for this office are misnomers. The English title emphasizes the fact that the office stored (among other items) the secret documents of the many Ch'ing military campaigns, while the Chinese term conveys the idea of a responsibility not for archives but for a certain kind of official publication: the military campaign histories (*fang-lueh*).[111] In fact, however, the Office of Military Archives attended to both these concerns. On the one hand it oversaw the maintenance of the inner court's principal archival installation; on the other hand it compiled the official histories of the major military campaigns of the Ch'ien-lung reign—and many more official publications as well. Moreover, the two activities were intimately related, for the campaign histories consisted mainly of secret war documents held in the Grand Council archives.

Thus the Office of Military Archives developed out of two separate inner-court activities, one concerning archives, the other, publications. Archival preservation probably got the earlier start, with a few highly sensitive records—those on K'ang-hsi–era relations with Russia, for instance—probably secured deep in the recesses of the inner court.[112] But few inner-court records were maintained on file during the K'ang-hsi era. Moreover, ordinary palace memorials were not collected at all: after the emperor rescripted these they were returned to the field and their authors were allowed to keep them. The relatively few K'ang-hsi palace memorials in the archives today are there as a result of orders given as soon as Yung-cheng came to the throne—that, except for the documents of a few exempted individuals, all palace memorials be returned for storage in Peking. From this requirement was generated what eventually became the "Palace Archives" (Kung-chung tang), the stored vermilioned originals of hundreds of thousands of documents.[113] A few years later—in the middle of the Yung-cheng period—another requirement was laid down that copies of most palace memorials be made before the originals were sent back to their authors, so that a record of what had been reported as well as the throne's response would be on hand at the capital while the document was making its journey back to the provinces. This was the beginning of the Grand Council reference collection.[114] At about the same time the High Officials in Charge of Military Finance (Pan-li Chün-hsu ta-ch'en) began making record book copies of important edicts, memorials, and lateral communications related to the northwest military campaign, a set of hand-copied ledgers that for the late Yung-cheng period alone came to more than one hundred albums.[115]

Inner-court sponsorship of official publications got an even later start. The three K'ang-hsi–era campaign histories were probably compiled in small campaign publications offices—perhaps amounting to only a couple of rooms occupied by a high-level editor and a few scribes. In those early years there was no permanent inner-court publications agency, and very little was preserved in the way of archival records that might have contributed to campaign histories.[116] No history of the Yung-cheng segment of the campaign against the Zunghars was published at the time; only much later, after the final victory in the Ch'ien-lung period, was that story included in the comprehensive narrative of the campaign as it had been pursued over the course of three reigns.[117]

The inner-court archives and publication activities were permanently joined in CL14 (1749), when two grand councillors, Chang T'ing-yü and Lai-pao, petitioned to establish the Office of Military Archives in order to produce the history of the first Chin-ch'uan campaign.[118] The new office had several ties to the Grand Council: it was headed by a grand councillor, and much of its middle-level supervisory personnel was drawn from grand councillors and clerks. The grand councillors appointed other staff members, most of whom were drawn from the Grand Secretariat clerks (chung-shu). Grand councillors supervised all the work and, whenever an appropriate segment was completed, submitted it to the emperor.[119] The Military Archives Office was further connected with the Grand Council by being physically located in the western section of the palace; access to council offices located nearby, just inside the Lung-tsung Gate, was therefore fairly easy.[120]

The eighteenth-century history of the Office of Military Archives paralleled the growth of its sponsoring organization, for it also soon grew in numbers and kinds of inner-court servitors—revisers, translators, copyists (specializing in either Manchu or Chinese), lower-level clerks, paper artisans, and runners—and spawned several subsections. Two Grand Council Archives offices were created at some point during the second half of the eighteenth century, one for Manchu (*Ch'ing-tang fang*) and one for Chinese (*Han-tang fang*) documents.[121] In addition, there was a Communications Section (*Wen-i ch'u*) in existence during the eighteenth century, its purpose being to send and receive lateral communications concerning lending and borrowing archival materials, to which end there was maintained a "Record Book of Lateral Communications sent out by the Grand Council [Military Archives Office]" (Chün-chi ch'u wen-i tang).[122] The Military Archives Office also had a special group of staff members known as the "Officials for Translating into Chinese" (*I-Han kuan*). Working under the supervision of Grand Council clerks, these men were responsible for keeping the Manchu archival records and working on those materials.[123]

Offices and suboffices also proliferated to deal with the Military Archives Office's publications projects. We do not know exactly when these other subsections came into being, but by the middle of the nineteenth century there were a Compilation Office (*Ts'uan-hsiu ch'u*), Copying Office (*T'eng-lu ch'u*), Transfer of Documents Office (*Wen-i ch'u*), Proofreading Office (*Chiao-tui ch'u*), storehouse (*ta-k'u*), library (*shu-k'u*), and paper warehouse (*chih-k'u*).[124] Some of these offices may have come into existence during the eighteenth century, beginning with a handful of men and occupying only one or two rooms in one of the buildings in the western part of the palace.

The eighteenth century was the era of greatest productivity for the Office of Military Archives. Archival preservation was developed so that the office was continuously occupied both with management of the storage facilities and with creating copies of documents to replace originals that either had deteriorated or had to be sent elsewhere. In addition, beginning with the Ch'ien-lung period a very large number of official campaign histories was compiled out of those archives, with the result that we now have document-based accounts of nearly all the major Ch'ien-lung and Chia-ch'ing campaigns as well as compilations on many other topics such as the Ch'ing palace history; the histories of the Liao, Chin, and Yuan dynasties; the great geographical work on the Ch'ing empire, *Ta Ch'ing i-t'ung chih*; and the official gazetteer for Jehol.[125] The founding of the Grand Council Military Archives facilitated an inner-court publications enterprise based on the secret inner-court correspondence generated chiefly by the palace memorials and court letters and edited and censored by Grand Council personnel. The old publications services continued their accustomed work in such outer-court offices as the Veritable Records Office (*Shih-lu kuan*), History Office (*Kuo-shih kuan*), and the Hanlin Academy—with many of these editorial offices headed by grand councillors. But in addition to these old

outer-court facilities there was now a second archives and publications enterprise in the inner court, allowing the Grand Council to have their own
section devoted to a crucial area of government activity.

The CL14 (1739) founding of the Military Archives Office on a permanent
basis made an important contribution to Grand Council prestige. Although
earlier Ming and even Ch'ing outer-court publications had been based on
documents, the Military Archives Office was now able to tie its editorial work
far more closely to its capacious files of stored state papers than had previously
been the case. Many of the Ming campaign histories had consisted principally
of eyewitness accounts written up by individuals; some of this tradition continued in the Ch'ing.[126] The very thin K'ang-hsi–era campaign history of
relations with Russia (*P'ing-ting Lo-ch'a fang-lueh*), for instance, seems only
loosely tied to archival documents—many of its entries are not specifically
dated, something that would have been likely in the originals.[127] By comparison
with such early efforts, the high-Ch'ing military campaign histories frequently
contained full texts of dated documents and ran for hundreds of chapters
(*chüan*), emphasizing texts in keeping with the new spirit of eighteenth-century intellectual life.[128] As a result, these new inner-court literary productions won for
the Grand Council the cachet of contributing to the scholarly life of the realm.

The organizational complexity achieved by the Grand Council's eighteenth-
century growth reflects the expansion of responsibilities that in some cases
caused growth and in others resulted from it. As we saw in Chapter 6, certain
structural characteristics, in particular the informality mechanism, were crucial
to the council's extraordinary expansion. The informality mechanism likewise
influenced the growth described in this chapter. The requirement that the
clerks be appointed from concurrent posts supplied the council with knowledgeable, experienced recruits from outer-court agencies. These appointees
then brought to the council their access to former colleagues and information
all over the capital. The extralegal dynamic also allowed the proliferation of
subordinate inner-court organizations such as the Manchu Division and the
Office of Military Archives; these could easily be set up without exposure to
full-scale debate in the capital bureaucracy. As long as the emperor could
be persuaded that inner-court expansion was desirable, he would authorize
expansion.

The particular patterns of inner-court elaboration described in this chapter
are also worth noting, for in general the organizational preferences that were
laid down in the inner court were not new. Instead, the Grand Council's own
expansion ran in the form traditional in the outer court, replicating several subordinate organizations that dealt with the four principal outer-court work categories: government administration, communications management, archives,
and publications. When change took place, it was likely to occur in traditional
ways.

PART THREE

Denouement

EIGHT

The Chia-ch'ing Reforms of the Grand Council, 1799–1820

By the beginning of the Chia-ch'ing Emperor's personal assumption of power (CC4 [1799]), the Grand Council had achieved the dominating position in the government of the empire. The council had expanded structurally, adding several subordinate organizations and refining its leadership hierarchies. The personnel complement grew; procedures were elaborated and rationalized; the number and variety of issues handled at the council increased greatly. The council was now in charge of a deluge of paperwork that continued to mount as the government was faced with numerous new projects, particularly the Ch'ien-lung military campaigns. Management of both the inner-court palace memorial system and the outer-court routine communications system was in council hands. The council also shouldered the principal responsibility for policymaking, carrying out background research, preparing position papers (*i-fu tsou-che*), holding discussions with the emperor on all manner of topics, and drafting edicts. Properly maintained files became important both for policy deliberations and for many aspects of the official publications program, which had intensified greatly during the Ch'ien-lung reign.

The council's supervisory responsibilities multiplied to embrace supervision of the Six Boards as well as many other outer-court agencies. These supervisory roles allowed several kinds of intervention. In some cases—as in choosing questions for and managing the top-level examinations—the council used its concurrent posts to take over areas that had previously been the purview of other agencies. For other tasks, such as keeping personnel records, the council assumed a more distant supervisory posture, allowing the lower agencies such as the boards of Civil Office and War to maintain the files and add new information.

The demarcation line between the Grand Council and other capital and provincial agencies was highly porous on the council's side—that is, the council easily moved into areas not its own. Generally, though, the outer-court agencies exercised little influence in the council and could not easily win back responsibilities that had been carried off to the inner court.

The concentration of so many major central-government tasks in one central inner-court body negated the old checking and balancing of former days when many of these responsibilities had been apportioned among the various outer-court agencies as well as the inner court. Not surprisingly, the situation soon became the focus of calls for reform. But as we shall see, in the end many of the demands for reform were easily ignored because the council itself drafted and secured the emperor's authorization for the reform edicts. Thus the Grand Council was able to resolve the issues resulting from its growth yet preserve its own high dominance.

Above all, it is important to remember that at the end of the Ch'ien-lung years the Grand Council was still an informally constituted and largely unregulated body. Although the council had developed its own internal practices and generally agreed-upon ways of doing things, few rules of edicted and codified force prescribed or limited its operations. As a result of the reforms of the Chia-ch'ing reign (1796–1820), however, this situation changed and new rules regulating certain Grand Council practices were announced. In what follows we shall consider the reasons for the reforms, how they took place, and the extent to which they affected the council's position at the center of the government.

CAUSES OF THE CHIA-CH'ING REFORMS

Abuses of Grand Council practices perpetrated by Ho-shen, a grand councillor of the last two decades of the Ch'ien-lung era, have frequently been cited as the chief catalyst for the Chia-ch'ing reforms. But in fact, while some of the reforms seem designed to correct Ho-shen's malefactions, others appear only vaguely connected and were probably more closely related to other Grand Council features thought unsatisfactory, particularly the dominating inner-court hegemony that the council had achieved by the end of the eighteenth century. In addition, some of the reforms dealt with the financial problems of the empire, for after the imperial treasury had become depleted as a result of heavy Ch'ien-lung–era expenses, including the costs of the military campaigns, the government responded with a miscellany of petty economic reforms.

The Chia-ch'ing–era attempts at imposing frugality will not be taken up here. Instead we shall limit this discussion to the reforms of the Grand Council itself. Here it will be useful to approach the problem of causes in terms not only of the Ho-shen case but also of the thrust of the reforms that resulted. When this is done we shall see that many of the reforms were probably designed to correct not only Ho-shen's malfeasance but also the imbalance resulting from the tremendous eighteenth-century inner-court expansion. Analysis is greatly complicated by the fact that the Ch'ing government did not publicize all the details of the Ho-shen mischief (probably for fear of disseminating a model of badness). Nor were all details of Grand Council work fully disclosed. Thus council procedures that had permitted certain of Ho-shen's malefactions or might in the future have given rise to similar problems had to be reformed without being revealed. In studying the Chia-ch'ing reforms we have to be aware of these nuances.

The Ho-shen Case

Although he was the grandson of a prominent Manchu grand secretary who had rendered faithful service to the Ch'ien-lung Emperor, Ho-shen himself began his official service with only low-level posts in what seemed destined to be an undistinguished career. But in CL40 (1775) he was promoted to be an imperial bodyguard at one of the inner-court gates deep in the palace, and that contact with the emperor led to one of the most astonishing public careers in all of Ch'ing history. Ho-shen's meteoric rise to the very summit of power was followed a quarter-century later—in CC4 (1799)—with a denouement of imprisonment and death.[1] During that quarter-century Ho-shen was frequently accused of improprieties, but for reasons that are not entirely clear the charges against him were never successfully pursued, and as long as the Ch'ien-lung Emperor was alive he was not penalized. It is widely believed that he enjoyed imperial protection.

Ho-shen had been a long-standing member of the Grand Council (since CL41; 1776) and the ranking grand councillor (*ling-pan*) since CC2 (1797). His execution by means of an imperially ordered suicide could be regarded as one of the very first of the Chia-ch'ing reforms. Although the Ho-shen case had many ramifications, only three major elements may have been connected with the Grand Council's eighteenth-century expansion: fantastic wealth supposedly accumulated by Ho-shen during his term as grand councillor and perhaps because of his high rank and influence; abuses committed by the Secret Accounts Bureau (*Mi-chi ch'u*), which Ho-shen headed; and certain dubious communication practices. These elements may also have been tied to the work of the Grand Council's Manchu Division (*Man-pan*). Several other minor charges—such as that Ho-shen had allowed himself to be carried into the palace by sedan chair and that he had taken palace serving maids as his concubines—were also included in the imperial fulminations against him, but these accusations are difficult to investigate today. Ho-shen's most villainous dealings—those pursued through the Secret Accounts Bureau—were completely covered up and received no attention at all in the published edicts of the day. Moreover, the misuse of communications was so warped in the public announcements that it could be precisely understood only by those already privy to the situation. Several monographs may be necessary before the mysteries of the Ho-shen fracas are fully unraveled.

Ho-shen's Wealth.   Contemporaries impressed with Ho-shen's avarice and successful accumulation of wealth concocted several fables about the man. One concerned a supposed weakness for fine pearls, a condition that resulted in hopeful purveyors presenting themselves at Ho-shen's gates every day with the most luminous examples available. Another story held that Ho-shen ate a large pearl for breakfast every morning, which enabled him to remember whatever passed before his eyes for the remainder of the day.[2] At Ho-shen's downfall, the twenty-count indictment of his crimes included several accusations relating to acquisitiveness, and to pearls in particular: two hundred pearl bracelets hidden in his residence—"several times as many as those possessed by the imperial palace"—with one extremely large pearl "even larger than that worn by the emperor himself." The accusations also enumerated piles of expensive clothing, receipts for investments, and precious metals and money hidden in the walls, cellar, and private treasury of his house.[3] One writer has estimated that the figures alleged for Ho-shen's confiscated estate, over two hundred million silver taels plus three times that amount in gold, would have been sufficient to pay off a debt four times the size of the entire Boxer indemnity.[4]

Fabulous wealth led to accusations of presumption: that Ho-shen had far exceeded the limits permissible for a man of his rank. The precious stones set in his hats were said to be more magnificent than those of the emperor. His family cemetery was reported to be laid out "with tunnels dug underground [in the manner of imperial tombs]." His own residence was said to contain columns of the scarce and fragrant cedar wood (*nan-mu*), appropriate for use only in imperial buildings. One accusation claimed that a structure in Ho-shen's villa was modeled on a royal pavilion in the Forbidden City.[5] A piece of hearsay evidence that came to light only later in a servant's report averred that Ho-shen had possessed a string of pearls of imperial style: at night when he thought "no one was around," he would take them out and "walk to and fro in front of a mirror, laughing and talking to his reflection [as if perceiving a monarch in what he saw reflected]."[6] Ho-shen's presumed wealth was his most conspicuous fault, and much was made of it at the time of the case as well as in subsequent writings. At present, however, although illicit transfers of enormous sums may readily be imagined, we have no hard evidence that conclusively links any kind of Grand Council peculation to his supposedly vast accumulations.

The Secret Accounts Bureau.   The Secret Accounts Bureau (*Mi-chi ch'u*) was created in the waning years of the Ch'ien-lung reign to oversee certain officials' fines. Although the archival records of this office were inventoried during the Ch'ing as part of the Manchu Grand Council materials,[7] in fact the office was set up separately from the Grand Council and was probably connected as much with the Imperial Household as with the council. We know, for instance, that those fined by the bureau were Imperial Household servitors and that the money collected was turned over to the Household, not to the council.[8] Nevertheless, two Manchu grand councillors, Ho-shen and Fu-ch'ang-an, both of whom also held Imperial Household posts, headed the office and reported the office's activities to the emperor in Grand Council documents.[9] The bureau should therefore probably be regarded as one of the council's anomalous hybrid offshoots, principally concerned with Imperial Household matters but supervised by council personnel who held concurrent positions in the Household.

The chief purpose of the Secret Accounts Bureau was to require miscreants who operated chiefly in the Imperial Household purview of internal customs collections to bring their crimes to light themselves and suggest appropriate amounts for fines they should pay (*tzu-hsing i-tsui*).[10] Although the two grand councillors masterminded the correspondence on this subject, the Ch'ien-lung Emperor's complicity is frequently attested by rescripts in his own hand in which he not only approved the transactions but also indicated (perhaps on the basis of advice) which officials were to be spared repayment or have their fines partly remitted.[11] The fines comprised extraordinary sums: some ran to tens of thousands of taels, with a few instances of more than a hundred thousand taels.[12] The fact that the Secret Accounts Bureau was abolished as soon as the new emperor came to power suggests that something was greatly amiss in its operation.

Two of the Chia-ch'ing reforms concerned the Secret Accounts Bureau. One was the abolition of the bureau itself; the other was a separation that took place between the Grand Council and the Imperial Household after the Chia-ch'ing Emperor came to power in 1799. Not much is known about this separation. I have observed it chiefly in the fact that Imperial Household communications were no longer recorded in the Grand Council's document register,[13] which meant that in these years the councillors were probably not seeing Household memorials submitted to the emperor. This suggests that something had gone awry in the Grand Council and Imperial Household collaboration that had earlier allowed certain grand councillors to hold concurrent positions in the Secret Accounts Bureau.

Ho-shen and Communications.   Some of the accusations against Ho-shen concerned his misuse of communications, but study of the exact nature of the finagling is seriously handicapped by a lack of verifiable details in the published indictments. One imperial edict denounced Ho-shen for delaying military reports;[14] another found fault with one of the decrees that Ho-shen had transmitted, implying that he had not properly conveyed the emperor's intent but instead had altered the meaning to suit his own purposes.[15] One of the most serious accusations denounced Ho-shen for assuming an imperial prerogative in insisting that he receive his own copies (*fu-feng*) of the palace memorials in order to be apprised of memorialized information before the emperor saw it.[16] Other complaints included Ho-shen's rejection of a memorial about Ch'ing-hai bandits attacking the Dalai Lama's merchants and improprieties in correspondence about jade shipments from Yarkand.[17]

These accusations are difficult to verify. Because the military reports (*pao*) were usually transmitted more rapidly than ordinary palace memorials and their transmission times were recorded, I attempted to use the document logbook to investigate the question of delays. But except for the interference of winter snowfalls, I found no sustained evidence of unusually slow deliveries at this time. Nevertheless, faulty relaying of an imperial edict—either unintentionally or with malice aforethought—was always a possibility in Ch'ing and earlier times, and for that reason the Ch'ing edict-drafting procedures included an imperial review of the final drafts before dispatch, a procedure known as "going over with vermilion" (*kuo-chu*).[18] Usually, though, the emperor could trust his own grand councillors to relay accurately the deliberated and agreed-upon content of the edicts—if matters were revealed to be otherwise, then obviously new councillors would have to be chosen.

Other safeguards concerning the content of edicts included monitoring the use of the imperial seal[19] and the practice that had earlier become a Grand Council tradition of informing the emperor when even slight changes had been made in the content of an edict between the time of deliberation and the drawing up of the draft.[20] The archival evidence I have seen does not support the charge that Ho-shen was able to wreak substantial havoc in the edict system, but fresh evidence may come to light in the future.

The veracity of the most serious communications accusation, that Ho-shen was illegally receiving copies of the provincial palace memorials, is also open to question. Although he probably was receiving illegal information from certain provincial authorities, this intelligence probably was not reaching him via illicit copies of documents intended for the emperor. In the first place, we have much evidence that all through the eighteenth century and into the nineteenth the grand councillors regularly saw all but a tiny fraction of the most secret palace memorials immediately after the emperor had read them.[21] Separate copies for Ho-shen might have given an advantage of only a couple of hours, if that, and as a serious accusation simply does not make sense. Moreover, the illegality of requiring second copies would have made many provincial officials reluctant to comply. The scheme would soon have been discovered, creating difficulties for all involved.

One of the terms the edicts used for Ho-shen's supposed palace memorial copies, "copies sealed up" (*fu-feng*),[22] was not a communications term in common use and does not necessarily refer to copies of the palace memorials, as it has usually been taken to mean. Rather, the term was more likely an intentionally vague concoction, perhaps a code signal designed for those who would not understand as well as for those who would. In this way the uninitiated would be led to assume that some provincial officials had sent illegal second copies to Ho-shen. But those in the know would have had a different understanding and would have realized that the practice of sending any sort of special missive illegally bearing information to the Grand Council was to be halted for all time.

If the term *fu-feng* did not mean palace memorial copies, what did it refer to? I believe that Ho-shen was not making illegal use of the carefully monitored palace memorial system. Instead he had found an entirely legal means of securing the special information he desired by tapping into a little-used and only lightly monitored communications system. This could have been accomplished through using lateral communications, a means by which high-ranking government personnel sent official letters to each other. Unlike the regular edicts and the palace memorials, during the Ch'ien-lung period most lateral communications were not checked by high officials, reviewed by the emperor, registered in the council's logbooks, or copied for the council's records. Even a Grand Council clerk who copied one of these documents for dispatch would have had no reason to question an order emanating from the ranking grand councillor. Using lateral communications rather than more official and higher-level documents would have enabled Ho-shen to correspond in official forms while bypassing the emperor and evading the existing monitoring arrangements.

This analysis is further bolstered by two important facts. First, a number of edicts and lateral communications drafted in Ho-shen's day (but rarely in other times) bear the concluding tag "There is no need to reply by palace memorial" (*pu-pi chuan-che chü-tsou*, and variants).[23] In other words, a simpler form of reply—perhaps by lateral communication—was sought. Second, we can tell that something had gone wrong in the lateral communications system, for one of the subsequent Chia-ch'ing communications reforms improved the monitoring of those arrangements by setting up special record books to keep track of such documents. Thus it is likely that the second copies the Chia-ch'ing Emperor found so heinous but did not wish to describe more accurately were missives sent in the lateral communications channel. We do not yet know what kind of information was being transmitted by this means—possibly it was news of local prices or imminent government purchases, changes in the copper-silver ratio, or other tidings that would have allowed insiders to profit through early trades.

The focus of certain counts of the indictment on communications about frontier areas—Yarkand jade, Ch'ing-hai bandits—makes these items appropriate subjects for reporting in Manchu and handling by Manchus in the Grand Council, perhaps by the Manchu Division. The document register that recorded Chinese-language but not Manchu correspondence did not list these items, Manchu materials usually being omitted unless they arrived with Chinese documents or had been sent for translation. Accordingly, these counts of the Ho-shen indictment may have been obliquely attacking something amiss in the management of the Manchu Division. As we shall see, this possibility is also borne out by the fact that certain of the Chia-ch'ing reforms tightened controls on the Manchu Division's work.

It seems that Ho-shen may have misused his authority as grand councillor. At the present state of our knowledge, however, his exact purposes and the precise nature of any money-raising schemes remain beyond our grasp. We can perceive some of the details, particularly those associated with Grand Council operations, but we do not yet have the whole picture.

Ho-shen's Demise

On the third day of what might well have been noted in the inner-court style as the year "Ch'ien-lung Sixty-four," CC4/1/3 (1799 February 7), the old emperor died at the age of eighty-seven.[24] With this event Ho-shen lost his protector. Immediately the court decided that an emergency existed and that the situation had to be dealt with without delay. The Chia-ch'ing Emperor ignored the Confucian precept of waiting until the three-year mourning period had passed before making changes in his father's ways. Within five days, the Earl Ho-shen, grand secretary, head of the Grand Council, and superintendent of the boards of Revenue and Civil Office, was summarily stripped of his ranks and cast into prison.[25] By CC4/1/18 (22 February) Ho-shen was dead, having been granted the privilege of committing suicide by hanging in his prison cell—a preferred form of execution because it left the body intact.[26] Ho-shen's supposed henchman in crime, the grand councillor Fu-ch'ang-an, was given the nightmarish punishment of being escorted to the cell, there to kneel and watch his erstwhile companion do away with himself. Afterward Fu-ch'ang-an was returned to his cell to await his own execution, which had been postponed until after the autumn assizes.[27] At the time he did not know that he would in the end be allowed to survive.

These were tumultuous days. Ho-shen had earlier reduced the Grand Council to only three members. Now with the two top members suddenly thrust into prison, the membership of that body was suddenly rotated. The third surviving councillor was permitted to retire, leaving the entire body open to replacement. At the top, the new emperor's brother Prince Ch'eng (Yung-hsing) was appointed ranking councillor and superintendent of both the Board of Revenue and its Three Treasuries (San-k'u). The Manchu grandee Ch'ing-kuei, scion of a family known for its loyal service to the two previous emperors (he was a grandson of the grand secretary Yin-t'ai and son of the grand secretary and grand councillor Yin-chi-shan), was recalled to council service and shortly succeeded Yung-hsing as leader. Four others who had been dismissed or gone off the council in the Ho-shen heyday of the previous two years were also restored.[28] As a signal that a serious emergency existed which called for intervention by the imperial family, no fewer than four princes were drafted to serve in the new emperor's government. In addition to Prince Ch'eng, another imperial brother, the I Prince (Yung-hsuan), was made superintendent of the

Board of Civil Office. A third relative, the Jui Prince (Ch'un-ying), became superintendent of the Court of Colonial Affairs, while a fourth, the Ting Prince (Mien-en), was given the superintendency of the Peking Gendarmerie.[29] New appointees suddenly appeared in other board and office directorships as well. In the first month of the new emperor's accession more than twenty out of almost fifty top capital positions in the boards and other agencies received new officials.[30]

Although the government made a drastic sweep when it dismissed so many top central-government leaders, further punishment of the malefactors was limited. An imperial edict declared that the case was not to be pursued to the bottom; there was to be no "tearing things up by the roots" (*pu-yü chu-lien*) that might further unsettle the bureaucracy and delay restoration of normalcy.[31] Instead, a twenty-count indictment of high crimes and misdemeanors attributed to Ho-shen alone was handed down on CC4/1/15 (1799 February 19).[32] High officials debated the indictment and recommended death by slow-slicing.[33] The emperor lightened this sentence and permitted Ho-shen to commit suicide in his cell by hanging. The other surviving principal, Fu-ch'ang-an, was shortly released and rusticated to serve at the Ch'ien-lung Emperor's tomb, about a day's journey east of Peking—a mild punishment and a common form of internal exile for disgraced courtiers.[34] Thus, despite the supposedly intricate and extensive network of cronies involved in Ho-shen's schemes, only one man—Ho-shen himself—lost his life in the debacle. While others were deprived of their official ranks, only one other—Fu-ch'ang-an—suffered so much as a short prison term. Except for the investigation and confiscation of Ho-shen's estate, the entire Ho-shen case was disposed of in just half a month. The Grand Council reforms that followed, however, were instituted gradually over the course of the entire Chia-ch'ing reign. Many of these appear to have had little direct connection with the Ho-shen case.

Protest Against the Grand Council's Eighteenth-Century Expansion
In addition to the Ho-shen mischief, a major cause of the Chia-ch'ing reforms appears to have been outer-court opposition to what was perceived as the Grand Council's relentless aggrandizement of power over the course of the Ch'ien-lung reign. Although not a great deal of evidence exists on this point, nor can we identify a strong and outspoken outer-court faction concerned with the issue, a few instances of outer-court alarm at the council's extraordinary expansion survive. In what follows I offer three examples of Chia-ch'ing–period criticisms of the council that appear to be inspired by outer-court opposition.

Opposition to Council Domination of Edict Drafting. One early instance of opposition to the Grand Council was set forth in a CC7 (1802) censor's memorial. This questioned the council expansion that had deprived various outer-court agencies of some of their former responsibilities and lodged so much power—the crucial power of edict drafting in particular—in the Grand Council. The throne did not take kindly to the censor's assertions. The responding edict rejected the suggestion that the council now threatened the dynasty's earlier, more equitable balance of powers between the inner and outer courts. The edict-drafting authority was defended as being derived not from the Grand Council but from the emperor, who was—it was averred—the only proper legitimating source of this responsibility. The Grand Council's centralized control over all edict drafting had in no way been intended "to take [other] officials' responsibility for assisting in government and hand it to these few men [the grand councillors]."³⁵ As we shall see, the Chia-ch'ing Grand Council reforms made no meaningful attempt to deal with this criticism. Since the council itself was probably responsible for discussing most of the reform edicts with the emperor and then drafting them, this lack of action suggests that both the council and the emperor were satisfied with the concentration of edict-drafting and other powers in Grand Council hands.

Opposition to Council Methods of Clerk Selection.   Another censor's proposal, presented in CC10 (1805), urged greater attention to examination achievement in selecting the Chinese Grand Council clerks and at the same time proposed that because of the danger to state secrets high officials' sons and younger brothers not be permitted to serve as clerks.³⁶ Although these complaints constituted an attack on the Grand Council's authority to choose its own clerks, the councillors found both worthy: we shall see them adopted in the course of the Chia-ch'ing reforms to be described below. Complaints of this sort may have reflected outer-court dissatisfaction with the operation of its own patronage lines and ability to obtain good placements for its own trusted personnel in the much-valued Grand Council posts.

Opposition to Grand Council Domination of Patronage.   In CC12 (1807) another instance of outer-court opposition, this time from the Board of War, questioned the grand councillors' monopolization of patronage lines to win appointments for military men sponsored by the council. The Board of War protested that its own career men who had served with distinction for many years in the field were being passed over at promotion time in favor of the Grand Council's own candidates. Those on the Grand Council's noted names (*chi-ming*) lists were being moved up the career ladder faster than the regular Board of War sponsorees; the board's own noted names list was not being taken seriously.

Once again outer-court complaints were turned aside. The responding edict, doubtless drafted by the Grand Council and authorized by the emperor, made no concessions to the board's protest. "What the board has requested would be too generous," intoned the inner court's response. "In the future, let this be handled according to the old regulations."[37] Thus did Grand Council patronage practices triumph and the board lose its bid for recognition of its claims.[38]

Apparently no concerted or continuous opposition could be mustered in the face of Grand Council dominance of the throne's responses. The idea of checks and balances between the inner and outer courts or between various competing agencies, so important at other periods of Chinese history, was almost entirely in abeyance now. The Grand Council was drafting the very edicts in which it defended its own concentration of power.

Indeed, in CC14 (early 1810) the council's close association with the monarch, whose support it clearly enjoyed, was acknowledged in a memorial that elevated the characters for the council's name, a courtesy usually strictly reserved for words associated with the emperor and august entities such as the imperial ancestors.[39] Although the throne swiftly produced a reprimand, the incident shows that in some quarters the council was perceived as an attachment of the monarchy itself. The jealousies excited by this high position and expanded powers may have been as important a cause of the Chia-ch'ing reforms as was the Ho-shen case.

THE CHIA-CH'ING REFORMS OF THE GRAND COUNCIL

Chia-ch'ing's personal accession to power following the death of the Supreme Abdicated Emperor (*T'ai-shang Huang-ti*) at the beginning of the fourth year of his reign began with the swift and decisive resolution of the Ho-shen case. But there were more reforms to come. These did not involve further executions, closing of offices, or replacement of discredited personnel. No reform was thoroughgoing or deeply upsetting to the established order of things. Apparently the court was anxious to put through a few reforms to silence potential critics and at the same time allow the Grand Council's long-established patterns of efficient inner-court operation to get back to normal. Thus most of the reforms were quietly put into effect without fanfare.

Although one rescript in the Chia-ch'ing Emperor's handwriting scolded an official for sending information privately to Ho-shen, nearly all the reforms were promulgated as edicts drafted in the emperor's name. Perhaps the term "Chia-ch'ing reforms" is a misnomer. By the end of the eighteenth century the Grand Council had waxed strong with well-established and highly elaborated procedures. A new, inexperienced monarch would hardly have possessed sufficient power, let alone acumen, to carry out reforms on his own. In view of what we now know about the development of edict drafting since the middle of the Yung-cheng reign and the Grand Council's central role in the discussion, drafting, and promulgation processes, it seems likely that the council was responsible for the reform edicts—even those that reformed its own procedures.[40]

The reforms that affected the Grand Council concerned the grand council-

lors themselves, the clerks, the Manchu Division, and the council's management of communications, particularly the lateral communications and certain
new record books. When these four categories have been examined we shall be
able to analyze further the particular direction of the reforms and explain why
the council was willing to allow a few changes.

Reforms Affecting the Grand Councillors

Beyond the abolition of the Secret Accounts Bureau and Ho-shen's imperially ordered suicide, probably the most significant feature of the Ho-shen
backlash was a slight change in the position the Grand Council occupied in
the government. This began in the months immediately following Ho-shen's
demise and was accomplished in a series of small steps that slightly reduced the
councillors' prestige as well as the scope of some of their only marginally
important activities. Thus although the grand councillors' privileged position
close to the emperor was not tampered with—they continued to advise on
incoming memorials, to draft edicts, to store and retrieve documents, and to
be concerned with official publications—their high position relative to the rest
of the bureaucracy suffered a slight downgrading.

Under the Chia-ch'ing reforms the board superintendencies previously held
by certain councillors who were placed over the board presidents were discontinued.[41] Although generally each board was still represented on the council
by one of its presidents or vice presidents, the higher prestige of superintendency
(tsung-li) ranks was now denied the grand councillors.[42] Grand councillors were
also excluded from other prestigious posts. They were no longer assigned to the
group of high functionaries who remained in the capital in charge of the
government when the emperor was on tour.[43] Beginning in the Chia-ch'ing
period the Manchu councillors no longer received concurrent appointments as
adjutants general (yü-ch'ien ta-ch'en) attached to the imperial suite.[44] At the
same time, the path to a grand councillorship was slightly narrowed for
Manchu and Mongol members when Chia-ch'ing's appointments included a
search for men qualified not by military heroics but rather by the chin-shih
degree and even occasionally by Hanlin membership, which had not been the
practice in the previous reign. Of the thirty-six Manchus appointed before the
Chia-ch'ing period, only four (11 percent) had held any degree at all, and
only two (6 percent) had attained the chin-shih. But from the Chia-ch'ing
period the percentages climbed in each reign: four chin-shihs out of ten (40
percent) under Chia-ch'ing; four out of eight (50 percent) under Tao-kuang;
and five out of eight (62.5 percent) under Hsien-feng.[45] Gradually an effort
was being made to work toward requiring the same standards for Manchus
that the Chinese grand councillors candidates had long had to meet, an effort
that meant conformity to generally accepted norms as well as the customary
reliance on a man's purely personal relationship with the emperor.

Following Chia-ch'ing's personal assumption of power, the number of grand councillors was sharply reduced. During the Ch'ien-lung reign Grand Council membership had burgeoned, occasionally reaching as many as ten, eleven, or, once, at the beginning of the first Chin-ch'uan campaign (CL13; 1748), twelve persons in one year. (Council membership dropped at the end of the reign and in the early Chia-ch'ing years, but this reduction appears to have been in part caused by Ho-shen's attempt to prune the council of his enemies.) Even if membership is reckoned not by the total number of councillors serving in any one year but rather by the lower figure of the maximum on duty (both at the capital and on missions in the provinces) at any one time, the Ch'ien-lung–period average of nearly 7 is significantly higher than the Chia-ch'ing figure of 4.5; the latter figure, moreover, approaches the standard quota of 4 men that had been set of the body of grand secretaries early in the Ch'ien-lung reign.[46] Although the number of grand councillors was never officially specified during the Ch'ing period, such an informal reduction in the direction of the standard for grand secretaries suggests the statutory quotas that regulated the tables of organization in the outer-court bureaucracy.

Another change was manifested in the numerous petty and mildly humiliating punishments meted out to Chia-ch'ing's grand councillors. The emperors had not always punished their highest officials for minor infractions. In a rescript to one of his provincial officials, for instance, the Yung-cheng Emperor had written, "If I punish you, who in the future will dare [to serve me]?"[47] As has been shown, both Yung-cheng and Ch'ien-lung specifically exempted their board superintendents from administrative punishment (reduction in rank and small forfeitures of salary increments) for petty carelessness or minor infractions committed by subordinates. Although there were exceptions to this policy, by and large the imperial magnanimity appears to have prevailed during the Yung-cheng and the Ch'ien-lung periods and to have applied to the grand councillors as well as the board superintendents.[48]

During the Chia-ch'ing period, however, the throne—in edicts probably drafted as a result of consultation with the grand councillors—took little note of this former policy. A CC7 (1802) edict sternly warned that the grand councillors would be punished for "small errors in language or writing" and affirmed the view that if "there were mistakes, then [the councillors] themselves ought to ask for punishment." The edict went on to promise leniency if the situation warranted.[49] In actuality, once threats had been issued, leniency frequently won the day.

Administrative punishment of the grand councillors and members of the various staffs worked according to established procedures. When it was appropriate to discipline a high official, the error would be designated in an edict and the case would be sent to the Board of Civil Office with a tag indicating the severity of punishment advisable. "Investigate and recommend" (*ch'a-i*) was the phrase that indicated a light case, "recommend administrative punishment" (*i-ch'u*) was used for more serious ones, and "recommend severe administrative punishment" (*yen-chia i-ch'u*) specified the most heinous of infractions.[50] During the Chia-ch'ing period, instances meriting the lightest possible punishment for a grand councillor included a mistaken character in the Chinese rendition of a Manchu name, a character left out of the final draft of an imperial edict, and the careless omission of the character *li* from the phrase "four hundred *li*" (*ssu-pai li*) in the dispatch instructions at the end of an imperial edict.[51] In the more serious category of punishable offenses were mistakes such as one that occurred in CC13 (1808) when a man's name appeared on the wrong appointment list. In this situation—a case where a good appointment might have gone to an unsuitable candidate and a councillor might have been suspected of taking a bribe—the grand councillors memorialized asking for the middle-level administrative punishment (*i-ch'u*). The emperor agreed that a punishment was merited but lightened it to "investigate and recommend." The grand councillors, knowing that this imperial directive would lead eventually to forgiveness, next effusively memorialized their gratitude for the imperial solicitude, closing with the assurance that "in the future we will take special pains [not to allow this kind of thing to happen] in order to deserve this imperial benevolence and compassion."[52]

A most unusual piece of evidence of the changed position of the Grand Council as a result of the Chia-ch'ing reforms comprises three long lists of punishments (*ch'u-fen*) accumulated by members of the inner court on the council, the Imperial Household, and the Southern [Imperial] Study in CC23 (1818). Between them the five grand councillors of that year had more than seventy instances of small oversights and petty lapses. For some of these errors they received fines varying from one month's to two years' salary; for others the councillors were reduced in grade. Some of the mistakes included the failure to catch errors in a Board of Punishments routine discussion memorial, a small error in edict drafting, a delay in dispatching a lateral communication, an error in an audience tally (*lü-t'ou p'ai*), and a failure to attach yellow labels to some poetry submitted to the emperor (marking passages for his attention).[53] Although punishing or rebuking the grand councillors had not been unknown in the past, such a meticulous bill of complaints (three months' fine for such-and-such an error, loss of one grade for another, and so forth) was new. Nevertheless, the punishments were not significant in themselves; dismissals did not take place, and the fines and demotions did not amount to much.

These new practices are difficult to interpret. They suggest a change in the grand councillors' relationship with both the emperor and the rest of the capital bureaucracy. As a result of being subjected to regular bureaucratic discipline, the councillors would have become more distant from the emperor and closer to the outer-court bureaucrats. Such a move would have reduced the exclusiveness of the councillors' inner-court position and softened criticism that they were imperial favorites who enjoyed special privileges and exemptions. Regular administrative punishments would have made them appear more like the men of the outer court and therefore less vulnerable to complaints that they were members of an extralegal organization that was operating beyond the law.

Despite the reduction in the councillors' number and the application of administrative punishments, the Grand Council remained strong, its larger interests—control of information, edict drafting, and supervision of publications—in no wise imperiled by the reforms. The council's secret inner-court preserve remained in place. In fact, two of the Chia-ch'ing reforms pertaining to the council were concerned with preserving secrecy. Both were outlined in an edict of late CC5 (1801) that described how people from other offices had been wont to hang around on the council steps, peering in the windows and, sometimes, on the pretense of conducting official business, spying out privileged information. Thenceforth, announced the edict, new rules were to go into effect: only those attached to the council—the councillors, their clerks, and the messengers—could enter the council's offices; when there, they were to deal with council business alone—matters pertaining to their boards were to be handled elsewhere to keep middle-level board personnel away from the Grand Council building. In addition, the edict enumerated other people—princes, other royal relatives (pei-le), and other high officials—who were not to loiter near the steps of the Grand Council office. Edict drafting was to be carried out only at the office. Moreover, if edicts were to be transmitted to the princes and high ministers, this was to be done not at the Grand Council itself but a little to the east, on the steps of the Ch'ien-ch'ing Gate. Finally, the edict instituted a second reform: a surveilling censor was posted every day to the Imperial Household office next to the Grand Council to monitor the human traffic at the council premises and make sure that outer-court personnel did not approach.[54]

These were neither the first nor the last attempts to grapple with the problem of secrecy in the inner court. The Yung-cheng Emperor's cautions had been so stringent that many details of his government's operations appear to be forever lost. Isolation of the council for the sake of confidentiality continued to be enforced in the Ch'ien-lung period, with gate guardians posted at the Grand Council offices to drive board staffmembers away.[55] Strictures providing for secrecy had to be periodically renewed and revised.

Apparently the Chia-ch'ing Emperor's surveilling censor did not dispose of the problem once and for all. Half a century later, at the beginning of the Hsien-feng reign, a decree allowed Grand Secretariat personnel to come to the Grand Council clerks' office to pick up documents being transferred to outer-court agencies; but, the edict continued, "As in the past, those who have nothing to do are not permitted on their own to enter the [clerks'] office." The same edict proclaimed that staffmembers were not to resort to the trick of coming over ahead of time to get their documents so that they might pick up information while waiting. The edict closed stridently with a final warning: "It is strictly forbidden for the personnel of the various [outer-court] offices to hang around and eavesdrop on the steps of the Grand Council office or the Grand Council clerks' office or in the area.''[56]

In the problem of maintaining the secrecy of Grand Council proceedings, the fault appears to have lain more with the inquisitiveness of outer-court personnel than with indiscretions committed by Grand Council staffmembers. Nevertheless, the grand councillors and clerks were penalized by being permitted only small windows covered with paper rather than glass, which prevented outsiders from seeing what was going on inside. At the beginning of the Kuang-hsu period (1875–1908), permission to install glass was sought, but even at that late date Prince Kung allowed only a few small pieces. Only after he stepped off the council was the council's window paper removed.[57]

Another reform altered the council's exclusivity by permitting publication of information about it. Whereas the previous edition of the dynasty's *Collected Statutes*, the *Ch'ien-lung Hui-tien*, compiled between CL12 and CL32 (1747–67), had had no section on the Grand Council in either its statutes or its precedents, the new edition of the *Collected Statutes*, the *Chia-ch'ing Hui-tien*, completed in CC23 (1818), contained a special section (*chüan*) devoted almost entirely to the council. At about the same time other publications on the council were also compiled and published: the clerk Wu Hsiao-ming worked on a list of clerks, and another clerk, Liang Chang-chü, put together his more ambitious and substantial assemblage of name lists, regulations, and councillors' and clerks' poetry.[58] Although these efforts were not printed until the following reign, the two clerks probably began their labors during the late Chia-ch'ing period, when they served the council and would have had access to its files.

Despite the new publicity, however, it must be admitted that matters stopped short of full disclosure. So far as we know, Wu Hsiao-ming's work was limited to only a name list, and Liang Chang-chü's compendium was highly selective. The new section on the council in the *Chia-ch'ing Collected Statutes*, moreover, consisted of only twelve Chinese pages (twenty-four sides). This was probably designed not so much to reform and restrain Grand Council growth by delimiting council activities as simply to enroll the council in the administrative statutes of the realm—another way of helping the council take its place as part of the regular bureaucracy. A truly meaningful addition on the Grand Council to the *Collected Statutes* would have included a precedents section, but neither nineteenth-century edition had one of these. Further, what was published stuck to general procedures and revealed few details of the most significant Grand Council operations. Seven closely printed Chinese pages of the section described the Grand Council's roles in drawing up lists of presents to be bestowed on officials and requirements for such lists: how odd that almost one-third of the information provided on the council should concern this relatively unimportant task, while the major but secret responsibility of edict drafting received the comparatively minor attention of two pages.[59] Nevertheless, bureaucratic agencies ran by statute; the emperor's private staff had been informal, unregulated, and beyond the reach of those statutes. Inclusion in the *Chia-ch'ing Collected Statutes* gave the council the legal status of an established government organization. This made it seem more like the outer-court agencies and, at the same time, would have supplied some protection against moves to disband it.

Reforms Affecting the Grand Council Clerks

The Grand Council clerks (*chang-ching*) were one of the focal points of the Chia-ch'ing reforms. Beginning in CC4 (1799) the clerks' numbers were limited and their methods of appointment regulated for the first time. In the Ch'ien-lung period there had been no quotas for clerks, no special examinations, and no audiences (although there had been both examinations and audiences when many of the clerks were first appointed to their earlier concurrent posts).[60] Many clerkships had been secured through the patronage of grand councillors, who often arranged for their own relatives, sons of friends, or examination protégés to make their careers at the council.[61] The council clerks were also given special marks of prestige. By the late Ch'ien-lung period, for instance, they were permitted to wear a special costume that marked their association with the council. When dispatched to the provinces on confidential missions for the emperor or as secretaries to grand councillors deputed outside the capital they traveled in the best style with access to the same facilities awarded to high officials. Although these were not problems of major importance, the reforms instituted to control the clerks after Chia-ch'ing's accession to power suggest that it was thought advisable to cut the clerks down to size.

The Chia-ch'ing reforms of the Grand Council clerks were instituted early. On CC4/1/16 (1799 February 20), less than two weeks after the new emperor had come to power, an edict announced that clerk appointment procedures would thenceforth be regulated. "Since the matters handled by the Grand Council clerks are fairly important," it stated, how is it "that there is no regulation requiring that they be brought to audience [prior to appointment]?" The edict pointed out that even the lowest-level scribes of the boards and banners were appointed only after an imperial audience. It was unthinkable that the much higher ranking Grand Council clerks should not be subjected to the same scrutiny.[62] As a result, prospective clerks thenceforth had an audience interview with the emperor. We shall shortly consider the extent to which this may have affected the clerks' appointments.

For the future the clerks' number was fixed at thirty-two (sixteen each of Manchus and Mongols on the one hand and Chinese on the other, ethnically divided into four duty groups).[63] They were to be chosen from middle-level board personnel (*ssu-yuan*), Grand Secretariat secretaries (*chung-shu*), and scribes (*pi-t'ieh-shih*) at the Grand Secretariat, Six Boards, or the Court of Colonial Affairs. Diarists and men from other offices might also occasionally be brought on board as well. Prospective clerks were to be recommended not by the grand councillors but by high-level capital officials at their original agencies. Qualifications included "upright moral character, robust health, and good calligraphy."[64] Later in CC4 (1799) another qualification, that a clerk could not concurrently serve as a censor, was specified.[65] Still another requirement was added in CC11 (1806), when a preference was decreed for clerks with experience in one of the Six Boards on the grounds that they were more useful than those ignorant of board procedures. Such individuals were to be recommended and selected ahead of others.[66]

In CC11 (1806), the methods of selecting Grand Council clerks from those personally recommended (*pao-sung*) by high officials in Peking was again changed to include written examinations. The expectations remained almost the same as before: upright behavior (*p'in-fang*), persons in the prime of life (*nien-fu*), an [elegant] style of writing (*wen-li*), and clear, legible calligraphy (*tzu-hua tuan-k'ai*).[67] But when in CC18 (1813) it was suggested that the names on the clerks' examinations be sealed so that the papers could be judged without prejudice, this notion was rejected, "[If] we paste over the name on the examination," declared the responding edict, "then we shall be able to see only the [candidate's] calligraphy. As for a man's deportment [*ts'ai-p'in*], how shall we then evaluate that?"[68]

It is significant that these changes did not substantially alter the basic principle of a determining role for the grand councillors in selecting clerks. The requirement that high officials of the prospective clerks' original agency make the initial recommendations could be circumvented by the fact that grand councillors frequently served concurrently as the high officials of those very agencies. Although the requirement of an examination appeared to inject fairness into the selection process, in practice the grand councillors went over the examination results and themselves selected the candidates for audience. Finally, although the newly introduced audience interviews may have appeared to take the matter out of the grand councillors' hands, the emperor would hardly have been in a position to use his audience interviews regularly to challenge his councillors' choices. The few records we have of clerk selections during the early nineteenth century suggest that the emperors depended on and went along with their grand councillors' recommendations.

An account of Manchu clerk selection in a diary of a Manchu grand councillor for TK24 (1844), for instance, shows that the councillors continued to get their way in most clerk selections. In that round of appointments, nine of the councillors' ten candidates chosen from a field of eighteen did in the end become clerks.[69] (The absence of the tenth from the list of appointments made over the next half-decade does not necessarily indicate a significant imperial rejection—the man might have become ill or decided to take to another post in the meanwhile.) The important point is that despite the reforms' safeguards of recommendations by other agencies, examinations, and audience interviews, the councillors were still determining who was chosen for clerkships. An earlier record of clerk selection after the early reforms shows that the emperor tended to follow his councillors' recommendations or alter them only slightly.[70] Thus, reforms in the clerk selection process did not significantly reduce Grand Council influence in the appointments. Standards were tightened, and choices were based a little less than formerly on personal relationships and connections between the grand councillors and the prospective clerks.

Another reform in the qualifications of Grand Council clerks dealt with the Ch'ien-lung–period practice of bringing grand councillors' sons and brothers into the council in the clerk positions.[71] But in CC10 (1805), sons and brothers of all high officials, not just the grand councillors, were ruled out of consideration "lest," in the words of the censor making the proposal, "they communicate privately and divulge state secrets." The new regulation required that sons and brothers of capital or provincial officials promoted to the rank of grade three or higher would have to withdraw. Even if a man was already attached to the Grand Council clerks, the promotion of a close relative to any high post could end his career there.[72] Apparently this restriction impinged too harshly on the basic interests of ambitious families, for after the Tao-kuang Emperor came to the throne it was quietly rescinded.[73]

There were a few other reforms that only mildly affected the clerks but which gave the impression that the clerks were being cut down to size. A very small nick in clerk prestige was taken right after the Ch'ien-lung Emperor's death, when it was decreed that clerks accompanying the councillors to assist in edict drafting at the Southern Study might no longer use the convenient Inner Right (Nei-yu) Gate.[74] This change involved no more than a three-minute detour, but in circles where closeness to the emperor and the use of special inner-court gates and corridors conferred cachet, the denial of the privilege of using the gate closest to the imperial reception hall in the Yang-hsin Pavilion signified a slight downgrading.

Another slight loss of status for the clerks occurred in CC5 (1801) when they were forbidden to go on missions as secretarial assistants to officials not directly connected with the Grand Council. In the Ch'ien-lung period the clerks had been commonly used as a talent pool, serving not only the grand councillors but other officials as well; indeed, they may have been sought as much for their Grand Council connections as for their talents. "This," trumpeted the Chia-ch'ing edict, "is not deputing high officials on missions; it is deputing Grand Council clerks on missions." The edict also expressed concern lest "the clerks' former attitudes reappear," although what exactly those former deplorable attitudes consisted of was not specified.[75] The thrust of the reform was to reduce the scope of the clerks' opportunities for activities outside the Grand Council.

In CC9 (1804) it was further decided that the Grand Council clerks were no longer to assist the officials left in the capital (when the emperor was on tour) with preparation of memorials and other matters. Since the grand councillors were no longer part of the official group left in charge at Peking, it was not appropriate for their clerks to be working for officials from other offices.[76] Another small change deprived the clerks of part of their financing, a loss of five thousand taels per year.[77]

But these changes were peripheral to the clerks' main responsibilities of assisting with edict drafting, copying documents, maintaining files, and overseeing publications. The Chia-ch'ing reforms tampered with none of these central tasks, nor was the clerks' access to national secrets affected by the reforms. Moreover, the clerks continued to be rewarded for special labors—in military campaigns, for instance—just as they had been in Ch'ien-lung's day.[78] Thus although several of the Chia-ch'ing reforms affected the Grand Council clerks, ultimately no crucial changes in the clerks' selection process or in their central responsibilities were instituted. These continued as before. The clerks as a body remained a pivotal inner-court group right through the remainder of the dynasty.

Reforms of the Manchu Division and the Lateral Communications System

As remarked earlier, three and possibly four counts of the Ho-shen indictment concerned transgressions that may have been committed in the Grand Council's Manchu Division (*Man-pan*). Other malefactions, concealed rather than publicized in the Ho-shen downfall, concerned misuse of the lateral communications system. There is some evidence that internal Grand Council reforms attempted to mend these loopholes by inaugurating new office records to control or keep track of the potentially dubious activities.

Two of these new Manchu Division ledgers were the "Record Book of High Officials' Sons and Brothers" (Ta-yuan tzu-ti tang)[79] and the "Record Book of Messages Turned Over" (Chiao-p'ien tang). The former contained lists of relatives of Manchu officials who themselves held official positions, sometimes with the favors they received appended. For example, one list showed the four younger brothers of the Chihli treasurer Ch'ing-ko and their positions:

1. Board of Revenue Coinage Office scribe, Chi-te, age 43 *sui*;
2. Grand Council clerk and Board of Punishments second-class secretary, Chi-hsiang, age 42 *sui*;
3. Board of Revenue scribe, Chi-ch'eng, age 37 *sui*; and
4. Board of Revenue scribe, Chi-ch'ang, age 30 *sui*.[80]

All these younger brothers had good positions, so we may surmise that the purpose of this part of the record was not to have them considered for appointment or other favor but rather to monitor family influence and reduce it if necessary.[81]

Other lists in this record book were probably drawn up both to keep track of family relationships and to see that appropriate favors—but not too many— were distributed to relatives of deserving Manchu officials. For instance, one list of CC16 (1811) shows that 105 men selected in the category of sons and brothers of high officials were brought to audience over the course of four days. Of the 105, twenty received favors: one became a third-class bodyguard, ten became junior bodyguards, and nine were given the menial post of errand runner (*pai-t'ang-a*).[82] Similar lists are scattered in various Ch'ien-lung–period record books, which suggests that the Chia-ch'ing series represents not a new ruling so much as an effort to consolidate and keep track of this type of personnel data.[83]

The "Record Book of Messages Turned Over" (Chiao-p'ien tang) was another Grand Council Manchu record new in the Chia-ch'ing reign.[84] Most of the messages were short directives issued as lateral communications—seeking information, ordering men to appear for examinations or interviews, assigning clerks to new duties, arranging personnel to accompany the imperial tours and hunts, and the like. Some messages were backed by citations of short imperial edicts.[85] Because the documents in these books probably emanated from the Manchu Division, usually there were no related notices in the document register (Sui-shou teng-chi). It seems, therefore, that this series was inaugurated to keep track of Manchu-language lateral communications, perhaps those of the same sort that Ho-shen had been able to use for his illegal purposes and that were later obliquely referred to as the "sealed copies."

There is a hint of still another reform affecting Manchus and the Manchu Division by which the council's connection with Imperial Household activities was severed. Namely, beginning in CC5 (1800) the Imperial Household Chinese-language memorials no longer appear in the document register. The fact that Manchu grand councillors were no longer granted the Imperial Household title of adjutant general may also have been part of this separation of interests, as was the council clerks' loss of Imperial Household funds. Further research may clarify this separation of the two inner-court organizations.

Communications Reforms

A number of the Chia-ch'ing reforms took place in the area of communications. One, involving the new controls over the lateral communication system, has just been described above. Another, instituted in CC4 (1799) at the beginning of the Chia-ch'ing Emperor's personal assumption of power, was "to open the avenue of words" (*kuang-k'ai yen-lu*). This meant that officials might submit memorials on topics not directly related to their sphere of responsibilities and that officials of rank lower than previously permitted might themselves address the throne.[86] But the avenue of words fell short of expectations. Before the end of the year the court had expressed disappointment with the selfishness of the suggestions. "Seldom was there anything worth noting," sighed the edict on the subject, which continued: "Now and then there were [memorialists who sought] imperial rewards or entreated riches through my benevolence. Subsequently they viewed this as a step to self-advancement and memorials poured in from all sides ... but the requests were all in private interest. None had any advantage for national affairs." With this the avenue of words was abruptly closed. "In the future," concluded the edict, "those who ought not to use the palace memorial system are not permitted to submit memorials on their own." The views of men outside the circle of approved memorialists were to be forwarded first to a privileged official who would then decide whether to pass them on to the emperor.[87]

At the beginning of the reign, sources of information were also broadened by permitting circuit intendants (*taotais*) to use the palace memorial system. Of several ranks—prefects, subprefects, magistrates—mentioned in the edict, only the intendants were now authorized to submit palace memorials, "in accordance with the rules for provincial treasurers and judicial commissioners."[88] It is difficult to imagine what the court hoped to gain by this arrangement, for modern researchers who have used the archives can attest that, in the Chia-ch'ing period at least, an intendant's memorial was a rare object indeed.[89] In fact, memorials from the provincial lieutenant governors (treasurers) and judicial commissioners were almost as rare. Furthermore, most intendants' reports were passed upward in lateral communication form and summarized or occasionally enclosed in the memorials submitted by the governors and governor-generals. It would have been almost unthinkable for an intendant to memorialize over the head of or in opposition to his superiors, the men who controlled his future promotions and career prospects.[90] The reform of permitting intendants to memorialize, therefore, apparently did not mean much at the time (although John Fairbank has found that during the Opium War the intendants did report directly and occasionally send in important news from sites distant from the location of their superiors).[91]

Another small communications reform took place in CC5 (1800), when it was decided that certain topics that had come to be reported in both the routine and palace memorial systems would thenceforth be limited to one, the palace system. The instance that brought the duplication to the court's attention was the fact that a Manchu general-in-chief had temporarily turned over his seal to a subordinate while he himself went on campaign; both men reported this action in both communications systems, with the result that four missives were used to relay a relatively insignificant piece of information that could easily have been handled in one or at most two. An edict was issued to halt the redundancies, but instead of assigning the topic to the routine system, where it had originally been placed, future reports of this kind were now to be submitted as palace memorials. "Let this be done," concluded the edict ambiguously, "in order to return to a simpler way of doing things."[92] Of course, the new way of doing things offered not only simplicity but also more exclusive sources of information for the inner court. The example cited in this edict, which was low level and not particularly important, was perhaps designed to deflect attention and forestall criticism. The instance is symptomatic of the trend that was bringing more and more topics into the palace memorial system, thereby enhancing the Grand Council's exclusive access to certain sources of information.

One Chia-ch'ing–period communications change affected the way the palace memorials were handled when they were brought before the emperor. Ordinarily when the Grand Secretariat had presented routine memorials, those from the Board of Rites or the Court of Sacrificial Worship concerning solemn imperial ceremonies (at the Altars to Earth and Heaven or at the great Ancestral Temple) were positioned ahead of other memorials for the day so that his majesty would read them first. Moreover, the eunuchs in charge would prepare a basin so that the emperor could first wash his hands; "Only then," exclaimed the edict on the subject, "would I [the emperor] respectfully open and read them."[93] But because the palace memorials were secret, they could not be similarly sorted in advance of submission to the emperor. Instead, the eunuchs of the Chancery of Memorials had customarily been content to divide the palace memorials into two groups: provincial documents and capital documents. Any that concerned the great sacrifices would therefore have been haphazardly mixed in with the rest.

In CC7 (1802) a change in this practice was announced. The old system, said the edict, did not

> exhibit sufficient respect. In the future, except for the [secret] sealed memorials
> [*feng-tsou*, which were sent directly to the emperor], palace memorials from the
> Board of Rites, the Court of Sacrificial Worship, and other capital offices shall
> all be submitted as usual, but those that concern that great sacrifices to Heaven,
> to Earth, or to the Ancestors, whether they be palace memorials [*tsou-che*] or
> audience tallies [*lü-t'ou-p'ai*] ... are all to be placed at the head [of their group of
> memorials] and handled according to the precedents for routine memorials.[94]

The edict is significant for two reasons: first, it displays an esteem for ritual that, although it had long prevailed in many routine-system matters, now appeared for the first time in the handling of the palace memorials. Second, it reveals that the contents, or at least the topics, of the capital palace memorials, except for those secretly sealed up, were no longer being kept confidential until after they were released by the emperor. In order to pull those memorials that concerned sacrifices, the chancery eunuchs had at least to know the topics covered in them. No longer were the ordinary palace memorials' contents being kept secret until after the emperor had finished with them.

The main battles of the Chia-ch'ing reform era were fought over the council's eighteenth-century gains and how the council would in future relate to both the monarch and the outer-court bureaucracy. The council's growth had reduced the former checks and balances in government and roused the ire of some in the outer court whose loss of power gave them a reason for opposing the council. The council had stolen away some of their prerogatives. On top of this, the Ho-shen malfeasance sat as a horrifying extreme example of what one inner-court agency could do when protected by secrecy and unfettered by law.

Accordingly, the reforms deprived the council of some of its imperial and inner-court exclusivity. Although two of the reforms—the abolition of the Secret Accounts Bureau and the new record book that monitored lateral communications—corrected certain Ho-shen abuses, and a few altered the clerk selection process, the major reforms tinkered with the Grand Council's position in the government in small ways. The publicity given the council in the nineteenth century, particularly the description in its own *chüan* of the *Chia-ch'ing Collected Statutes*, appeared to endow the council with a new mantle of legitimacy. Even though it was of the inner court, the council had now become a statutory agency. The petty administrative punishments to which the councillors now submitted were another indication of a willingness to appear to operate within the framework of the administrative code. Other standardizations of the councillors' positions—the loss of board superinten-dencies, the reduction in their number, and the preference for Manchus who held advanced degrees—reinforced the notion that the council had now be-come a body that operated in a fashion similar to other central-government agencies.

But at the same time, the councillors clearly continued to enjoy their former powers and privileges, stoutly backed by the emperor's confidence in them. For example, when in CC11 (1806) the Imperial Clan Court and the Censorate took more than forty days to produce recommendations on the simple question of how many grades should be added to the ranks of those who had presided over a recent set of examinations, the draft of the edict of reprimand for the delay suggested that "ten or twenty days" would have been sufficient to carry out the necessary investigation and produce a full report. Beside these words in the draft Chia-ch'ing himself added a vermilion correction further reducing the necessary time to "eight or nine days." This was followed with yet another vermilion addition: "Just think, when the grand councillors draft an edict for me it takes only three or four hours. For [other capital] offices to drag things out in this fashion is disgusting."[95] Despite the reforms, the Grand Council retained the imperial trust and the emperor's support for the council's retention of its most crucial responsibilities.

Faced with outer-court attacks, during the reform era the council drew on its inner-court advantages and successfully defended its high ground. The council was responsible for drafting the reform edicts and obtained the emper-or's authorization to promulgate them. Under these circumstances it is not surprising that only those reforms that the councillors desired emerged from this process. The council's most important tasks—communications monitor-ing, policy deliberation, edict drafting, archival storage, and publications supervision—remained intact. Except for the fact that edicts were now to be drafted only on Grand Council premises, no reform measure significantly revised the council's central responsibilities. Indeed, the most notable feature of the Chia-ch'ing reforms of the Grand Council is precisely the large area of centrally vital tasks that were not reformed.

In sum, the Chia-ch'ing reforms show that by the beginning of the nineteenth century the Grand Council could no longer be seriously reformed. Its central position had long since been worked out and solidly established. The emperor was convinced of its loyalty and efficacy. The outer-court bureaucracy was unable to mount an effective challenge to the council's hegemony achieved over the course of the middle and late eighteenth century. Neither the emperor nor the country could get along without it.

Epilogue

The subject of the Grand Council is a large one, with many facets. Now that the council's archives in both Beijing and Taipei are open, the researcher is invited by a myriad topics. In this book I have used the archives chiefly to investigate the aspect of Grand Council history that had to be tackled first: the momentous Yung-cheng– and Ch'ien-lung–period changes in inner-court structure and responsibilities. Related topics such as factionalism, the biographies of individual grand councillors, the council's subsequent nineteenth-century history, and case studies of how certain major issues were handled have of necessity been alluded to only in passing or entirely ignored. The future will surely bring forth other monographs on the Grand Council. Its documentation is almost fathomless and its possibilities for research varied and challenging.

THE PROBLEM OF THE GRAND COUNCIL FOUNDING DATE

In the light of the analysis presented in Chapters 1–5, demonstrating that the weak staffs of the late Yung-cheng inner court were scarcely comparable to the mature Grand Council, the council's founding date has to be reformulated. There are several possible approaches to this problem. If the council is viewed in terms of personnel—that is, the high inner deputies who served closely at Yung-cheng's side—then the Grand Council might be regarded as having begun with Prince I's advisory role. This would date the founding to the first year of the Yung-cheng reign. Indeed, although a different date is used, the tables of the official history of the dynasty list the prince as the earliest grand councillor.[1]

If the council is thought of in terms of the earliest continuing informal inner-court group or staff that eventually contributed to the council's formation, then the starting date should be placed in YC4 (1726), when Prince I,

Chang T'ing-yü, and Chiang T'ing-hsi began working together on military preparations and related problems. This starting date has been urged by others.[2]

If the council founding is regarded as coincident with the first use of its Chinese title, *Chün-chi ch'u*, then a point in YC10 (1732) would be indicated (when the earlier title, High Officials in Charge of Military Finance, *Pan-li Chün-hsu ta-ch'en*, began to change). A thorough archival search for early uses of the Manchu equivalent of this title might result in slight tinkering with this conclusion. Although he argued along different lines, Silas Wu also advocated a YC10 date.[3]

If we take the existence of the principal characteristics of the mature Grand Council to be a requisite part of the council's founding, then the features acquired during the Interim Council era at the beginning of the Ch'ien-lung reign must be regarded as crucial. These include the council's permanent consolidation as the single inner-court privy administrative body with broad powers, a condition achieved only with events following Yung-cheng's death, and the edict of CL2/11/28 (1738 January 17) that continued the transition council beyond the mourning period.

Apparently there was no single formal event or announcement that may be taken as the one moment of the establishment of the Grand Council. Accordingly, the best alternative might be not to seek a single founding date but instead to identify a founding era. Thus the Grand Council founding might be defined as having taken place gradually over the course of the fifteen years from the Yung-cheng accession to the end of CL2 (1723–38). The founding era might then be subdivided into two periods, the first characterized by relatively weak staffs under the strong Yung-cheng Emperor, the second by the inner-court transformation under the young and inexperienced Ch'ien-lung.

The remainder of this epilogue will analyze the major trend described in the second half of this book—the Grand Council's first century of growth—and speculate on its effects on the imperial power. By the end of this period, had the relationship between the mid-Ch'ing monarchs and the Grand Council ministers become one of cooperation or competition?

KEY STAGES IN THE INNER-COURT TRANSFORMATION

The inner-court transformation from monarchical rule to ministerial administration took place in three phases. First came the alterations of the ethnically distinct and separate inner-court bodies of high status established by K'ang-hsi, by which Yung-cheng preserved his father's compartmentalization but set up weak staffs, thereby ensuring that they would be in thrall to his will. In his early years Yung-cheng practiced competitive administration, shifting assignments and appointing ad hoc committees in order to allow no group—only himself—to monopolize a problem or manipulate information. Eventually, however, Yung-cheng took a new tack and in YC4 (1726) permitted a continuing inner-court team consisting of his three Board of Revenue favorites—Prince I, Chang T'ing-yü, and Chiang T'ing-hsi—to take over the military campaign plans, a commission that soon developed in other directions as well. Although the late Yung-cheng inner court had a staff called by the name soon to be used for the Grand Council (*Chün-chi ta-ch'en* or *Ch'ün-chi ch'u*), as only one of the several inner-court staffs it focused on the northwest campaign and managed communications, but lacked the broad range of concerns that characterized the consolidated Grand Council of the following reign. Yung-cheng's inner court was organized on an unofficial informal basis, a situation that generated the extralegal dynamic that became so important in the later phase of inner-court expansion.

The second set of important structural changes began late in YC13 (1735) with the rapid consolidation of Yung-cheng's separate inner-court staffs in the three months following the emperor's death. The newly consolidated staffs were further strengthened by falling heir to the Interim Council's plenipotentiary powers. Finally, late in CL2 (early 1738), their extended lease on life resulted in a new powerful inner-court body, the Grand Council of the Ch'ien-lung period. These changes paved the way for the expansion that took place over the remainder of the century.

The final phase of council growth consisted chiefly of an intensification of the gains won by the end of the Interim-Council era in CL2. Some slight further changes in structure did occur when new subordinate bodies, such as the Office of Military Archives (*Fang-lueh kuan*), were added. But the Ch'ien-lung era was marked less by significant organizational development and more by varieties of expansion within the existing inner-court framework.

Past explanations of Grand Council founding and growth have not stressed inner- and outer-court differences. Instead, this delineation has only been hinted in terms of communications. The outer-court routine system has been said to deal with ordinary matters as well as those that could be handled by reference to precedent, while emergencies and unprecedented situations were defined as the province of the inner-court palace memorial system operated by the Grand Council. We now know that this dichotomy does not tell the entire story, for the council handled many matters that might well be classified as ordinary, and the routine system was on occasion, particularly before the rise of the palace memorials, capable of dealing with both secrets and special situations. Moreover, connecting the Grand Council's founding and growth with communications, while important, has obscured the structural changes that were also responsible for the council's rise. Thus in addition to communications, the analysis presented in this book has also emphasized the inner-court transformation from K'ang-hsi's and Yung-cheng's separate small staffs to the consolidation and elaboration of the Ch'ien-lung age and after.

FACTORS FAVORING GRAND COUNCIL GROWTH DURING THE EIGHTEENTH CENTURY

The nature of the traditional Chinese inner court was crucial in bringing about the changes described here. In the eighteenth-century inner court, the imperial will rather than the administrative code was law. This gave latitude for many factors in council growth such as secrecy, the extralegal dynamic, concurrent posts, networks, access to information, increased responsibilities, the supervision of communications, and freedom from ritual. In addition, there were conditions peculiar to the times: the Ch'ien-lung military campaigns, for instance, and the emperor's fondness for going on tour. The mixing of the empire's two major ethnic groups—Manchus and Chinese—in the primary ruling body reduced the influence of ascriptive Manchu forces that had threatened the early emperors. Finally, although the evidence is slender, it is worth speculating on ministerial ambition as an important element in the council's expansion. In what follows I shall further describe the factors important in the council's Ch'ien-lung–period growth.

Secrecy

Secrecy was important, for it meant that council activities were hidden in the inner court. In the early days, most of the council's accomplishments were not on view, not generally known, and not published in the Peking gazettes. Council communications were closed to outsiders. When the council added a new topic for investigation or took on a new responsibility, these moves were not necessarily observed by the outer-court bureaucracy. Because so little was known about what was going on, the council and its activities generated little opposition and rarely drew fire.[4] Moreover, within the secret confines of the inner court, the council was able to supervise and control important responsibilities, particularly the two communication systems. Secrecy was maintained even though many of the formerly top-secret palace memorials now circulated to the outer court and no longer had to be rewritten (*chü-t'i-lai*), for a special determination was nevertheless needed to release them.[5] The council had its own archives, to which only persons connected with the council had access, and its own publications staff in the Office of Military Archives. The council's patronage was kept secret by means of its separate lists of noted names (*chi-ming*) of candidates for office. Inner-court secrecy surrounded and safeguarded the Grand Council world and drew a sheltering mantle of invisibility over the council's growth.

Inner-Court Informality and the Extralegal Dynamic

Once the weak Yung-cheng inner-court staffs were consolidated early in the Ch'ien-lung period, their fragility was translated into an advantage, for while most of the rest of the bureaucracy was subject to the administrative code statutes prescribing duties and specifying personnel complements, the inner court remained unregulated. Although the statutory outer-court organizations could and did change over time, innovations were not granted easily, and those of any importance were usually instituted only after deliberations that frequently were argued at more than one level in the central government. For an inner-court body such as the Grand Council, however, change was a simpler matter. Reforms were usually discussed only in the inner court and could be immediately authorized by the sovereign provided he was won to the cause.

The early growth of the body of Grand Council clerks is a case in point. During the eighteenth century the emperor usually authorized the appointment of each new clerk in response to a short councillors' memorandum (*tsou-p'ien*) making the request. But these memoranda made no effort to brief the emperor or to reveal for general discussion with other ministers and bureaucrats the full facts of the situation—that there were no rules prescribing limits on the number of clerks or requiring imperial audiences for middle-level officials at the council as at other agencies, for instance, or that the overall number of clerks was being increased, or that the number of Chinese was expanding faster than Manchus—information that might well have come out in outer-court written or audience deliberations. After the Chia-ch'ing reforms had specified that there would be only thirty-two Grand Council clerks, the councillors' petitions for more clerks were written differently, calling attention to the new legal limit and defending each request.[6] But so far as we can tell, expansion of the inner-court clerk staff was still not widely debated. Even then, the essentials for inner-court change were simply a Grand Council proposal followed by imperial authorization. In this way inner-court informality eased change and growth. An arrangement that Yung-cheng had used to control his inner-court staffs, keeping them divided and weak, in Ch'ien-lung times and later functioned as an extralegal dynamic that aided council expansion.

Concurrent Posts

Immunity from outer-court objection to inner-court expansion was partly aided by another feature of the council's structure: the fact that the council possessed few substantive posts of its own. Its middle- and top-level members were appointed concurrently and instead of relinquishing their concurrent ranks at other agencies, councillors and clerks continued to hold these posts when on duty at the council. (As we saw with Chang T'ing-yü and others, there was an occasional exception for councillors elevated to grand secretary in that those men were frequently promoted to a higher concurrent post, a board superintendency.) Silently, because of the mechanism of the concurrent posts, certain board and other outer-court responsibilities floated into the inner-court purview where officials who had been appointed to the council continued to discharge some of their concurrent agencies' work in their new offices. Concurrent posts thus aided council growth in yet another way—by disguising the transfer of tasks to the council and the council's relentless aggrandizement.[7]

Links All Through the Bureaucracy

The combination of concurrent posts and the large loyal body of former clerks gave the growing council valuable contacts throughout the metropolitan and provincial bureaucracy. By late in the Ch'ien-lung reign, the councillors and clerks probably held well over fifty concurrent positions at the capital. In addition, most of the clerks who completed their terms of service on the council won promotions to good provincial posts at the level of prefect or higher. The practice of promoting the clerks after only a few years of on-the-job training at the capital may seem shortsighted—as if the council were thereby depriving itself of an experienced body of middle-level servitors—but by this means the council placed men with inner-court experience in important provincial posts and acquired contacts all over the empire. The alumni clerks became part of the Grand Council's network, providing connections that could be drawn on as needed. Through these contacts important lines reached out laterally into several levels of the bureaucracy, in part compensating for the ever-present vertical tendencies in the government.

Access to Information

The Grand Council concurrent posts supplied many advantages, one of the most important being access to information. Capacious as the inner-court files were, they could not accommodate all the information processed by the capital bureaucracy, nor was the council's hardworking staff able to deal with all the details of the documents handled principally in the outer court. Despite Grand Council growth, much central-government work continued to be discharged at the traditional agencies and boards, with the contents of outer-court files open to members of the emperor's privy council on request. The Grand Council record books are filled with memoranda reporting information obtained from various capital agencies. Because of its concurrent posts, the council was assured access not only to its own teeming files of information but to everyone else's as well.

The Council's Responsibilities

Without question, the council's acquisition of an enormous number of new responsibilities was a sign of its growth and in turn generated further development. This is difficult to analyze in specific terms, however, because many areas of governance were variously elaborated rather than being transferred whole or newly created. Moreover, research is obstructed by the fact that because the inner-court privy council was an informal organization without legal standing, the administrative code frequently continued to list certain duties under outer-court agencies even when they had been transferred to the inner court. For

example, many of the grand councillor's responsibilities for supervising publications continued to be listed under the Hanlin Academy in the *Collected
Statutes and Precedents*.[8] Thus although it might be desirable to compare the
responsibilities acquired by the council's antecedent staffs in the Yung-cheng
reign as well as by the council itself under Ch'ien-lung with the earlier situation
in the late K'ang-hsi inner court, such an assessment cannot be fully carried out.

The role of the grand secretaries and others in supervising official publications is a case in point. During the K'ang-hsi era there were several publication
projects, particularly in the classics category, whose editorial boards included
grand secretaries. Moreover, some of these men held inner-court assignments.
As was shown in Chapter 7, however, once the Grand Council had come into
existence grand councillors were frequently given oversight of official publications. Thus in both periods, much of the supervision of official publications
was dominated by inner-court figures. Real change seems to have been only
semantic.

In fact, though, there were significant differences. Unlike the grand secretary
editorial board members, some of whom were never brought into full-time
inner-court service, the Grand Council was a strong consolidated inner-court
body. When the grand councillors supervised publications they did so from
their vantage point of playing a coordinating inner-court role as members of the
emperor's high privy council. Moreover, in addition to the changes in inner-
court publications supervisors, the strengthened council introduced changes in
both the categories of publications and the kind of cooperation given the
outer-court agencies. During the Ch'ien-lung reign, for instance, the Grand
Council paid increasing attention to a revived and expanded category of official
publications, the military campaign histories (*fang-lueh*), which were compiled
out of the inner-court archives. In addition, the councillors now oversaw the
preparation of the drafts of the dynastic history (*kuo-shih*) and also attended
zealously to Manchu historical publications.[9] Thus although certain K'ang-
hsi–era inner-court figures had sometimes been involved in official publications
in their outer-court Hanlin capacities, or even from the vantage point of being
inner-court servitors, by Ch'ien-lung times the inner-court effort in this area
had been greatly and variously elaborated. Many works were now supervised
from the inner court, some had inner-court editors, and the entire editorial
process of some works was fully secured and carried out within the inner court,
all these activities being backed by a large consolidated organization.

The transferral of responsibilities worked differently in other situations. To
revise the law code (*lü-li*), for instance, in YC1 (1723) the emperor had sought
recommendations from a mixture of inner- and outer-court staffs. In the end
he chose one inner-court servitor, Chu Shih, and three board presidents not
known for inner-court service, to form a committee to oversee revisions. At
the beginning of the following reign, however, the new emperor designated the
inner-court Interim Council for this task. As a result this inner-court body

continuously deliberated proposals on this topic and prescribed the further revisions of the code initiated at the time.[10] In similar fashion many other responsibilities likewise passed to the inner court in this period.

Expansion and Regularization of Communications

Communications management was another council responsibility of critical importance in the council's growth because this was another way of moving new topics into the inner court and gave the councillors access to all but the most secret high-level documents in the realm. In addition, the inner-court staffs probably had a voice in determining the communications changes that strengthened their influence in policy formation. By the Ch'ien-lung period, inner-court communications consisted of much more than the old K'ang-hsi channel of a few high provincial and capital officials who occasionally used palace memorials to correspond with their ruler. There was an explosion of incoming provincial reports, which may have tripled over the course of the Ch'ien-lung reign or increased tenfold since the late K'ang-hsi years. The impetus to regularization was an important factor in the palace memorial system's enlargement, as regular reports on new topics came to be required, many in the interest of "uniformity" (*hua-i*).

Expansion also occurred as the council coped successfully with the mass of paper flooding the inner court. A record-keeping system was created that embraced a reference collection of palace memorial copies and enclosures as well as hundreds of record books for preserving imperial edicts, capital memorials, and memoranda. Files subjected to heavy use became the objects of a regular copying program instituted at mid-reign. These activities required extra personnel: sometimes Grand Secretariat secretaries (*chung-shu*) were brought over for the record book copying. Other kinds of expansion took place at the beginning of the Ch'ien-lung period when the palace memorial system became official; documents no longer had to be rewritten for the outer court, and the boards were no longer bypassed as a matter of course—efficiencies that made the system more useful and thereby encouraged its growth. By the beginning of the Ch'ien-lung reign the council was also monitoring the documents of the routine system.

The many topics that came to be covered in the two major systems for reporting to the throne allowed access to large masses of information and required that the councillors and clerks carry out research and develop specializations in many fields. Most important was the crucial task of management of policy formulation, which included research, deliberation, and edict drafting, activities that enabled the councillors to influence policy. The expansion of paperwork thus aided the council's rise, as did its competence in coping with the deluge. At the same time the emperor—a single human being, after all was no longer able to stay on top of the paper flow, an impingement on the imperial power that redounded to the cause of Grand Council growth.

The newly organized Grand Council archives were soon put to effective use, not only for policy background but also for publications. Through concurrent editorial posts and the council's own publications unit, the Office of Military Archives (*Fang-lueh kuan*), many councillors acquired cultural prominence as leaders of the archive-based literary effulgence of the Ch'ien-lung period. With this accomplishment the council succeeded in replicating in the inner court the four constituent elements of traditional outer-court concerns—in administration, communications, archives, and publications.

Freedom from Ritual

Growth was also propelled by the fact that in the early years the council's activities were not regulated by ritual. In the interest of facilitating efficient scans, for instance, the pages of the daily logbook (Sui-shou teng-chi) departed from the ritual observance of imperial centrality that dominated the parallel routine-system register (Ssu-lun pu). Had the council's logbook remained faithful to ritual, all characters connected with the emperor (entries for "vermilion marginalia," for instance) would have been elevated to top place on the pages, and the names of the memorialists—probably the information most needed in a scan—would have appeared in less easily observed positions, as was the case with the outer-court register. But in the council's logbook, the imperial rescripts and marginalia were noted in the middles of the pages, and the memorialists' names were headlined in hold characters near the tops of the pages. As explained in Chapter 7, a concession to imperial centrality was retained by heading all entries "Imperial rescript [of so-and-so's memorial]." Even so, the effect was to play down old ritual forms by emphasizing the memorialist as well as the emperor.

Another freedom from the constraints of ritual lay in the palace memorial system's absence of seals. This meant that palace memorials could be used for government business during the Chinese New Year season, when the seals were closed (*feng-yin*) and most routine memorials, which required seals for processing, could not be dealt with. For example, although in mid-afternoon of the CL14 (1749) New Year's Eve Ch'ien-lung "put away [his] brush," his respect for this custom did not have to stay his hand in the face of an urgent military palace memorial from the front that shortly arrived during the night.[11] There were several other occasions during an ordinary year when the inner-court communications system did not bow to the ritual halts that obstructed the continuity of routine memorials.[12] The newness of the inner-court communications system had allowed it to grow free of the imposition of such formalities. Although the routine system had had ways of meeting emergencies, the freedom from ritual made the palace memorials especially useful in crises such as military campaigns, when delays could not be tolerated.

The Ch'ien-lung Military Campaigns

Exigencies of the times also furthered Grand Council growth. Of all government concerns during the eighteenth century, war was one that most required an efficient inner-court staff working in secret. Each of the numerous military involvements of the period reaffirmed the need for an efficient inner-court council that could oversee campaign strategy, personnel allocations, the peregrinations of military units, procurement, postal services, supply lines, and policy research. The council staff discharged many of these tasks itself and coordinated the others. Some council members were deputed as generals in the field. Thus the Ch'ien-lung era's numerous and far-flung military expeditions to the tribal and border territories on the perimeter of the empire—Taiwan, Annam, Nepal, west Szechuan, and the northwest—repeatedly renewed the council's utility. In addition to military heroics at the fronts, the success of each campaign depended on the council's sure managerial grasp at the capital.

The Peripatetic Monarchy

The Ch'ien-lung Emperor's fondness for touring forced another kind of growth in the inner court. When the imperial retinue moved away from Peking, the council had to streamline its processes and carry on with diminished personnel and files. There had to be accurate calculations of what would be needed for the tour and what could be left at home. Files taken along had to be adequate to run the government without overburdening transport facilities. Similar choices determined a personnel complement sufficient to discharge the work without crowding the tents, carts, and boats of the royal progress. Plans had to be made for a skeleton staff left on duty at the capital so that it could discharge its own work assignments and manage the necessary correspondence.

The Ch'ien-lung Emperor usually went on tour several times a year. Although many of these tours were only short-range forays to the Summer Palace or the nearby southern hunting park, others—such as those to the coastal provinces of the middle south—were major expeditions involving two or three thousand persons in the imperial retinue. They required considerable advance planning. The Grand Council's moderate size, informed personnel, and efficient work methods were entirely suited to the requirements of Ch'ien-lung's peripatetic monarchy. Each new successfully managed imperial tour reaffirmed the council's usefulness and was yet another spur to its growth.

The Mixing of Manchus and Chinese on the Council

The mixing of Manchus and Chinese in the empire's top ruling body also contributed to growth by reducing the old Manchu princely and grandee preponderance in government and allowing new scope for the influence of Chinese officials in policymaking. Although inner-court ethnic divisions were still prominent in organizations such as the imperial bodyguards and the Imperial Household, they were nevertheless diminished in the council itself. Manchu and Chinese grand councillors went into imperial audiences together every morning and worked together during the day. During the Ch'ien-lung period two Chinese served as ranking councillors (*ling-pan*), and others, of whom the earliest and best known exemplar is Chang T'ing-yü, were highly influential. The old exclusive power of the Manchu and Mongol Deliberative Princes and Ministers (*I-cheng wang ta-ch'en*) to serve as the chief source of advice on war and peace was replaced by the ethnically mixed Grand Council. The council's Manchu Division was left with control over lesser matters of a purely Manchu interest such as Banner investments, honors and decorations, personal leaves, and the like. The strengthened Chinese presence in the inner court greatly facilitated many council responsibilities, particularly the large Chinese-language publishing program and the supervision of the vast outer-court staffs whose members were predominately Chinese. Most important, Chinese officials now had a voice in nearly all top-level decisions, including those in the military sphere. A powerful body dominated by only one ethnic group might have attracted factional hostility; a mixed body might grow without drawing the fire of the opposing ethnic alliance.

Ministerial Ambition

It is difficult to penetrate throne-centered documents to assess the precise role of ministerial ambition in the Grand Council's growth, for the grand councillors' own contributions are rarely made explicit. Yet there are several indications of a strong ministerial push behind the council's rise to power. For example, the swift inner-court consolidation following Yung-cheng's death—exhibiting untimely haste in a court that was supposed to respect a deceased monarch's arrangements during the mourning period—seems to have sprung from ministerial eagerness to take advantage of the emperor's demise to realize long-standing plans. Moreover, during the transition era, the inner-court staffs were consolidated, instead of being allowed to continue their separate existences as in past mourning periods, and Interim Council members acted as if they were confident of a long-range future for their organization, enlarging the scope of activities and developing procedures that would have been difficult to dismantle at the end of the official mourning.

On this point, we may supplement the meager revelations of the contemporary sources with what may have been a conscious pursuit of an earlier pattern of changes of the sort described in this book. For there are distinct similarities between Grand Council growth in the mid-Ch'ing and the transformation of the Ming grand secretaries from their position as informal inner-court servitors appointed by the Ming founding emperor (r. 1368–98) to the well-developed organization of the middle and late years of the Ming. History did not precisely repeat itself. But the Grand Council's use of certain formerly successful procedures with which their historical studies must have familiarized them presents striking parallels with the Ming experience. Was this a conscious effort to copy successful maneuvers used in the previous dynasty? We cannot be sure, but this remains a possibility.

For instance, like the Ch'ing grand councillors, the Ming grand secretaries had also started as informal inner-court appointees. Moreover, like the earliest civil service members of the Grand Council antecedent staffs they also retained concurrent posts, which allowed them to reach into the metropolitan and provincial bureaucracies. By the middle years of the Ming, one of the grand secretaries' key powers was supervising the chief Ming communications system, the routine system.[13] Further study may reveal other ways that the Ch'ing replicated the Ming experience.

During the Ch'ing, ministerial plans for council expansion may have accounted for the enormous amounts of trivia that crowded the emperor's work schedule, impinging on the imperial capacity to deal with significant issues. The archives teem with correspondence on insubstantial matters carried out at the imperial level. Each instance of distribution and replacement of palace memorial transmission caskets (*pao-hsia*), for example, was still being submitted for imperial approval more than halfway through the Ch'ien-lung reign, even though by that time the council and one of its antecedent Yung-cheng staffs had more than three decades of experience coping with such an ordinary matter.[14] Moreover, the most unimportant details of imperial tours were regularly referred to his majesty at every stage of the planning.[15] New and unsuitable topics were also frequently added to the list of what had to be reported in the palace memorial system—and therefore read by the emperor: in YC11 (1733), for example, an edict asked for discussion of how various offices' use of red ink (for seals) should be reported for the imperial perusal. The responding discussion specified that not only the ink use be reported but also the amounts received annually, a suggestion that would surely increase unnecessary paperwork at the imperial level.[16] In one instance the emperor had to authorize a formal court letter edict for something so minor as a request for clarification of two map place-names. Many edicts led to palace memorial responses that in turn required a vermilion rescript; his majesty thus had no alternative but to read, or at least scan, lengthy missives and affix some sort of laconic comment on each. In other situations the emperor's in box was crowded with enormous piles of reading—all the chapters (*chüan*) of inner-court materials proposed for publication, for instance, for which the councillors sought the emperor's approval.[17] Indeed, the councillors may have been deliberately flooding the imperial desk with unnecessary make-work so that the monarch could not stay on top of important issues.

FACTORS THAT MAY HAVE RETARDED
THE COUNCIL'S GROWTH

Not all circumstances were propitious for council development. The Yung-cheng Emperor's governing style—in particular his lack of interest in transforming his small, divided, and informal inner-court staffs into a single large and powerful body—was an obstacle. As long as Yung-cheng was alive, full inner-court consolidation was out of the question. The possibility of a damaging imperial caprice also loomed and at times materialized, resulting in dismissals of officials or a royal veto of their plans.

The other capital agencies sometimes undermined the council with factional behavior and disruptive moves as they saw interesting work and significant policy decisions being removed from their purviews.[18] Moreover, Yung-cheng had weakened the circuit censors, who might have been expected to rail against the changes. But none of these elements was able permanently to interfere with the council's preponderant position. Even the Chia-ch'ing reforms, probably the most significant achievement of the council's opposition, failed to revive the outer court's former glory or to reduce significantly the emperor's dependence on the Grand Council. The factors retarding growth were far outweighed by the many promoting it.

THE GRAND COUNCIL AT THE END
OF THE CHIA-CH'ING REIGN

The final question posed at the beginning of this book asked about the Grand Council's situation in the early nineteenth century. By that time, where did the council fit into the inner/outer-court framework? Did the council follow the pattern of certain inner-court councils for earlier dynasties and challenge the imperial power by shifting to direct the outer-court agencies? Or did the council remain an inner-court body, continuing to act as personal imperial servitors, faithfully advancing the interests of the monarchy?

The Ch'ing Grand Council's solution to this age-old dichotomy was not to choose between inner-court subservience and outer-court autonomy but instead to consolidate its position on both fronts. On the one hand it convinced the emperor that it was indeed the faithful servant of its imperial patron, while on the other it submitted to some regulation and as a result was able to assert its leadership of the outer-court bureaucracy. The council's concurrent outer-court posts allowed supervision of the boards and other agencies. And in the inner court, the personal autocratic rule of Yung-cheng yielded to a more balanced collaboration between monarchs and ministers.

RELATIONS BETWEEN THE GRAND COUNCILLORS
AND THE MONARCHY

The emergence of the Grand Council as a force to be reckoned with led to many changes. In the space remaining I shall speculate only on those that took place in top central-government decision-making procedures. The inquiry will be difficult. One can scarcely pierce the verbiage of imperial centrality in which decisions were expressed and which the Grand Council was always careful to employ, even in those documents that were merely its own imperially approved recommendations. Nevertheless, a study of the eighteenth-century Grand Council would be incomplete without a preliminary evaluation of the council's influence on policymaking. The oft-used model of a despotism that increased as the eighteenth century wore on and which is sometimes employed as back-

ground for our understanding of China's government in the present day needs
to be re-examined.

That the grand councillors should have attempted to gain influence over
policymaking and impose constraints on the despotic tendencies of emperors is
not surprising. The possibility of serious imperial error was the single great
defect in the theory and operation of autocracy. Unchallenged imperial power
could exterminate a family line, impoverish a province, endanger the defense
of the realm, or surrender the empire to barbarians. Over the centuries, high
ministers of the Chinese state had developed ways of limiting the potential for
damage by untrammeled imperial caprice. In ancient dynasties, for instance,
there flourished a cosmological theory of imperial responsibility for order in
the natural world; ministers are said to have used adverse natural signs and
portents to restrain undesirable imperial behavior. (Vestiges of this theory
survived in the Ch'ing.) Another method was to threaten a monarch with an
unflattering posthumous reputation. Whether or not the well-known tale of
T'ang T'ai-tsung's (r. 627–49) desire to read (and possibly thereby censor) the
court diaries of his own time is to be believed, the story suggests that imperial
advisers might use such tactics to counter unwanted imperial actions.[19] Even
the K'ang-hsi Emperor seems to have absorbed the lesson of imperial responsibility when he understood that an imperial misjudgment could "lead to
thousands of years of wretchedness."[20] Not surprisingly, in the eighteenth
century, ministers of the Peking central government likewise attempted to
impose limits on the sovereign. The fact was, ruling was too important to be
left to the ruler.

In what follows I shall analyze the possibility of mid-Ch'ing ministerial
influence on imperial policy in terms of three government decision-making
opportunities: (1) the provincial palace memorials, (2) the court letter deliberations, and (3) the memorials of deliberation and recommendation. I shall show
that although the eighteenth-century monarchs retained all the powers that
we ordinarily think of as imperial powers, in these three areas the emperors
preferred to consult and most of the time tended not to exercise their decision-
making authority alone. Although ministers were dependent on imperial authorization of their objectives, ministerial cooperation was also essential to most
imperial plans. Each side checked and balanced the other. Emperors might
dash officials' hopes, but the less studied fact is that the ministers could likewise
limit the imperial autonomy.

Decision Making on the Provincial Palace Memorials

Under the K'ang-hsi and Yung-cheng Emperors, the palace memorial system
had been an informal private imperial channel for correspondence between
the high provincial officials and the emperor. K'ang-hsi had used this channel
chiefly as a direct source of information on local conditions that he might
otherwise not hear about or else learn of too late. Yung-cheng expanded the
system. He used it to build bridges to his favorite provincial officials, persua-

sively writing to them from the heart. He also used the palace channel to shape proposals before having them rewritten for presentation to an outer-court agency. Yung-cheng even took an interest in how the palace memorials were processed at the capital, sometimes troubling to write out meticulous instructions for copying and filing. As we have seen, he took charge of everything, once even apologizing to a memorialist for an imperial teacup stain on a memorial.

But the vermilion detritus of Yung-cheng's surging tide of scribbling— pieces of paper of all sizes and shapes covered with vermilion thoughts and afterthoughts and slipped into the secret memorial envelopes as they were being returned to their senders—caused immense difficulty for inner-court officials charged with keeping track of what had been said to whom in these unrecorded imperial directives. With Yung-cheng insisting on personally running the inner court and writing what he pleased, it was difficult to bring order to the chaos that his ruling style created. Under these circumstances it is not surprising that important changes took place in the inner-court communications system. Some of these changes—the introduction of court letter edicts and inner-court copies of imperial directives and memorials returned to the field—were instituted under Yung-cheng; others were begun in the next reign.

Immediately following Yung-cheng's death, the palace memorial system was transformed from the private, unofficial, personal channel of communication it had been for the K'ang-hsi and Yung-cheng emperors to an official, regularized, and institutionalized system for reporting and deciding much of the business of the realm. Most striking of all these changes was the simplification and routinization of the imperial rescripts. Where Yung-cheng had written at length and frequently put down whatever came to his mind, most of Ch'ien-lung's rescripts were couched in succinct formulae of one to four or five characters. The emperor still read through the memorials alone and decided how to respond. But for most situations the range of imperial responses was now sharply narrowed to about a dozen standard phrases.

This imperial succinctness contrasted sharply not only with Yung-cheng's lengthy vermilion correspondence but also with routine-system practice in which outer-court processing of the memorials depended on exhaustively detailed prescriptions by which middle-level bureaucrats composed the draft rescripts (*p'iao-ni*). Grand Secretariat minions who drew up these rescripts had constantly to refer to instruction books to be sure that they had both analyzed each memorial for the correct category of its concern and found the exact rescript prescribed for the particular situation.[21] Of course, the Ch'ien-lung Emperor could not be expected to sit in his study thumbing through similar volumes for instructions on how to rescript each day's palace memorials. Accordingly, a manageable number of brief imperial responses was developed to assist the emperor as he wrote replies on the increasing numbers of palace memorials.

Palace memorials that needed only to be filed in the inner court, for instance, received a laconic notation such as "Read" (*Lan*) or "Noted" (*Chih-tao-le*); a missive bearing auspicious news might additionally merit an appreciative "I have read this with pleasure" (*Hsin-wei lan-chih*). Information that had to be registered at an outer-court board was routed with the instruction "The appropriate board is to take note" (*Kai-pu chih-tao*). There were special formulae to be employed when a memorial enclosure was to accompany its covering report to the outer court: "The enclosure is also to be sent" (*Tan ping-fa*). An enclosure that was regarded as too secret for deposit even in the usual inner-court files might be marked, "I have retained the enclosure" (*Tan liu-lan*).

Other phrases were used to command policy deliberations on questions raised in the memorials. For a deliberation followed by an edict, the emperor would use the rescript "There is a separate decree" (*Ling-yu chih* or variants). Or a discussion memorial could be ordered with the instruction "Let the appropriate board consider [this] and memorialize" (*Kai-pu i-tsou*) or, more specifically, "Let the grand councillors [or other designated discussers] deliberate and report" (*Chün-chi ta-ch'en i-tsou*).[22] There were many variations and embellishments on these basic formulae, but beginning in Ch'ien-lung times nearly all of the provincial memorials received one of these short phrases. Even though there was nothing to prevent a long rescript, seldom did the Ch'ien-lung Emperor write more.

Usually Ch'ien-lung was able to select the appropriate phrase. If he failed to, the grand councillors might write him a memorandum asking him to make the necessary addition that would ensure correct handling of the memorial. I have seen instances where Ch'ien-lung mistakenly anticipated that a formal drafted edict would be necessary and wrote this, using the rescript "There is a separate decree" (*Ling-yu chih*) on a memorial, only to have a full decree later prove unnecessary and a simple "Noted" (*Chih-tao-le*) be the appropriate response. In such cases a correction was required lest the memorialist be alerted to look for the promised decree and then write—as was mandated—to report that it had failed to arrive.[23] On other occasions of imperial carelessness the grand councillors might on their own ignore an inadequate imperial rescript and act in accordance with the requirements of the situation, as when they deliberated a proposal that the emperor had marked only for recording. But these instances were exceptions in the vast flood of paper that engulfed Ch'ien-lung's table. For the most part the emperor became an accurate, hardworking purveyor of appropriate rescripts, part of the Grand Council system for processing the newly official and expanding inner-court communications system.

What powers did the emperor possess to impose his will on the palace memorials? Clearly an emperor had the power to write whatever he pleased. But the perfunctory and routinized imperial responses to the palace memorials that became standard after Yung-cheng show that in most situations the mid-Ch'ing monarchs did not attempt to rule alone. Independent imperial action, although possible, was rare.

Where the palace memorials were concerned, an emperor had two chief courses of independent action. First, he held the routing power—that is, he could choose which of his courtiers would prepare a capital memorial that deliberated a problem raised in a provincial communication (*i-fu tsou-che*), a method that could bypass the grand councillors or other individuals or groups, thus denying them the opportunity to study and make recommendations on the issue. The routing power armed an emperor with the means to select discussers who would make the recommendations that he would probably authorize. Although in his early years Yung-cheng had used the routing power autocratically, to impose his competitive style of administration, under Ch'ien-lung many of the discretionary assignments of this sort went to the grand councillors or to other groups likely to include grand councillors such as the Nine Ministers or the Six Boards. Rarely did the emperor use the routing power to bypass all his grand councillors.

The other chief course of independent action was the power by which an emperor might directly approve a proposal memorialized in the palace memorial system. By this means the monarch might make decisions independently and in private, without the interference of ministerial advice. The standard formula for such approval was the vermilion rescript "[Let it be] done in accordance with the request" (*Chao so-ch'ing, hsing*), a phrase that a true autocrat might be expected to employ with considerable frequency. Contrary to this expectation, however, this rescript was most rare—by my scattered counts in the eighteenth-century document register (Sui-shou teng-chi) usually awarded to fewer than 5 percent of the documents (not all of which contained requests). By Ch'ien-lung times the emperor was not regularly employing the provincial palace memorial channel for direct resolution of problems reported. Instead, he usually sent a memorialized request for deliberation—"[Let] the grand councillors speedily investigate and report" (*Chün-chi ta-ch'en su-i chü-tsou*)—or noted that a document was to be brought to the next daily session at which he and the grand councillors framed the policy edicts—"There is an immediate decree" (*Chi-yu chih*). Generally Ch'ien-lung and Chia-ch'ing gave direct permission for only the simplest provincial requests, and even these had to come from favored officials well known to them.

Finally, implementation could be a problem for an emperor who decorated a palace memorial with an unworkable or ill-advised scheme. My experience reading the eighteenth-century memorials and the document register that recorded both the imperial comments and the documents' disposition indicates that officials who wished to circumvent or revise an unwanted or mistaken imperial comment could easily do so. Moreover, from early in the Ch'ien-lung reign the very pithiness of the palace memorial rescripts embodied such vagueness and latitude that the terse routing commands contained much scope for varying interpretation. As we saw at the end of Chapter 6, even an imperial assignment of a deliberation responsibility was occasionally twisted in the course of implementation.

Thus the Ch'ien-lung palace memorial system differed greatly from Yung-

cheng's. It was now an official, institutionalized system with a simplified
rescript feature that was rarely used autocratically to order the emperor's own
desires on policy. Instead, the vermilion rescripts and office procedures in the
Grand Council regularly forwarded the palace memorials for deliberation or
other kind of action to others, frequently to the grand councillors or to bodies
that they dominated. The emperors still possessed the power to behave autocratically and write whatever they pleased on the palace memorials, but they
seldom inscribed their own policy instructions on those documents. The early
Ch'ien-lung–period changes in the palace memorial rescript system facilitated
imperial involvement in the business of governing without encouraging autocratic decision making.

Decision Making in the Court Letter Edicts

The court letter edicts are the second major area where the rise of the Grand
Council resulted in informal limits on imperial action.[24] To understand the
drafting process for this type of edict we have to go back to the undated
Yung-cheng vermilion comment, quoted earlier in this book, that was probably
sent to Yueh Chung-ch'i sometime in YC7 or 8 (1729–30). Although we can
no longer tell exactly what prompted the emperor's reaction, it appears that
one of Yung-cheng's and Yueh Chung-ch'i's major forays against the Zunghar
Mongols had gone down to serious defeat. In a vermilion scrawl the emperor
poured out his heart to Yueh: "Everything has gone awry," he wrote. "I
am very nervous, very afraid. It is so painful that I have turned to self-
recriminations. Item by item everything can be blamed on you and me."[25]
These words from Yung-cheng's private, most frank correspondence with
General Yueh not only reveal that a military debacle had taken place but also
show that the emperor felt he had no recourse but to shoulder the blame. He
had not made use of the many opportunities for consultation and expert
planning at the capital and instead had gone off on his own. With a side thrust
at Yueh for failing to carry through, the emperor could only face his "self-
recriminations."

Probably shortly after this was written, the court letter edict rosters were
enlarged to record sizable panels of experts consulted in framing policy directives. Although earlier court letters had named the inner deputies who had
assisted in the consultation and drafting process (chiefly the I Prince and Chang
T'ing-yü), now many of the rosters—and therefore the consultations—were
expanded to include others, particularly the High Officials in Charge of Military Finance (*Pan-li Chün-hsu ta-ch'en*), who were first convened late in YC8
(early 1731) to advise on the Zunghar campaign (see Table 2). No longer
would Yung-cheng run a military campaign by taking matters up with one
court confidant (such as Prince I) or, in the end, having to blame "everything"
on only himself and Yueh Chung-ch'i. Henceforth recipients in the field might
proceed with the assurance that the imperial orders were based in part on

contributions from specialists in whose advice and experience they had confidence. The empire now had an edict form in regular use that appeared to be of imperial origin yet was labeled to show that it had also been based on consultation.[26]

Of course, Yung-cheng participated in the edict-drafting conversations and could insist on having his way on any point he desired. Moreover, since the court letters were framed in conversation, courtiers may have found it difficult to challenge the emperor to his face and he may easily have been able to dominate these conversations. Nevertheless, as was frequently the case with the palace memorials, in many instances the emperor had little opportunity for independent investigations of his own and as a result had to depend on ministerial advice.

Ministerial participation in the court letter discussions continued under Ch'ien-lung—usually by his summoning the grand councillors to bring to audience the day's memorials marked for "a separate decree." During the Ch'ien-lung reign, however, a new practice arose of listing only the ranking minister, or sometimes two top ministers, in the court letter rosters. And in CC2 (1797), when Ho-shen became ranking minister of the council on A-kuei's death, all grand councillors' individual names were dropped from the court letter rosters and replaced simply with the notice that "the grand councillors" had drafted the decree. On the occasion of these latest changes the Ch'ien-lung Emperor told Ho-shen that since the councillor's names would no longer appear, "the provinces will not realize that all planning of [state] affairs will emanate from you, so much so that you may be called prime minister."[27] Thus, although edicts that conveyed only the ideas of the autocrat might still be issued, and although we cannot identify for sure all the sources of the ideas expressed in the court letters, we know that consultation with the grand councillors had become an established tradition and that Ch'ien-lung himself had admitted that the ranking grand councillor, Ho-shen, was to be the key planner of "all" state affairs. In the tide of instructions spewed forth every day in the name of the throne, consultation—most often with the grand councillors—had become the rule.

Decision Making and the Deliberation Memorials

No one who studies mid-Ch'ing decision making can fail to be impressed by the care with which major policies were researched and deliberated. A final example of this process (which should receive more detailed treatment than I can provide here) was the memorial of deliberation (i-fu tsou-che), a subtype in the palace memorial system. This kind of memorial involved the monarch in document processing in a way different from the provincial palace system, for the discussions were based on provincial memorials that had come in earlier and had been assigned by the emperor to one group or a combination of groups for consideration. Most of the discussion memorials were produced by various specialist agencies in the capital, frequently in consultation with or under the leadership of the Grand Council. Although occasionally alternatives were presented, usually the discussers offered only one recommendation; if this was not deemed satisfactory, the problem might be reassigned. The deliberations that reached the emperor were carefully considered, often argued with references to previous documents and precedents. When a number of committees had participated in the deliberations the result might be signed by the top members of several important capital bodies.

The emperor had several options where the deliberations were concerned. He might approve them, he might amend their recommendations, or he might reject their findings outright. The system even allowed the emperor to veto or change part of a recommendation—as when a punishment was lightened. What is most significant is the record of Ch'ien-lung's (and later emperors') actions on these memorials, for nearly all were approved, about 98 or 99 percent. Occasionally one was amended, but although outright rejection was always possible, this imperial action was rare. Thus, like the palace memorials, written deliberations of the Ch'ien-lung era also exhibit a low imperial decision-making rate. Ch'ien-lung retained the power to intervene but rarely did so.[28] As with the provincial palace memorial rescripts, what the high officials of the eighteenth century sought and were getting was not so much the imperial views but rather the imperial authorization of their own projects and plans. In effect, decisions were being made not by the monarch but by those who drew up the recommendations. Thus policymaking appears to have been carried out in the manner of the presidential clerkship propounded by Richard Neustadt in his book on the U.S. presidency, *Presidential Power*, as "service for themselves [the Washington bureaucrats], not power for the President."[29] The emperor's rescripts were sought not for their originality or fresh contributions to policy but rather for their authorization of the ideas, plans, and hopes of others. The imperial vermilion was employed chiefly to legitimize what others had proposed.

Why was this? Do we have in the Ch'ien-lung Emperor a particularly indecisive figure? My forays into the Chia-ch'ing and Tao-kuang records indicate a similar imperial reluctance to reject the formal deliberations of high capital officials. Imperial prudence will suggest one reason, for we may well ask where—outside of the occasional divisiveness thrown up by court factions— emperors would have acquired the information on which to base sound alternatives to their ministers' carefully researched recommendations.

Another argument against regular assertion of the imperial views lies in the emperors' need for ministerial cooperation. Frequent vetoes would have lowered morale and upset the ministerial cohesiveness so necessary to the smooth running of the government. Should the monarch have regularly gone further and dismissed officials simply on the basis of small disagreements, he might have jeopardized the loyalty of those who remained.

Finally, imperial independence in dealing with the recommendation memorials was also unlikely because disagreements among the officials were nearly always bartered away or papered over in the course of the deliberations, with the result that views were presented unanimously. Although an emperor might sometimes suspect or even identify divergences, he usually faced an apparently solid phalanx of officials lined up behind a recommendation signed even by those who had initially objected.[30] Even if a monarch had the power to overrule the products of such deliberations, for the reasons cited above this was not often done.

Readers may object to this line of thinking on the grounds that since the emperors appointed their own grand councillors, it is not surprising that the emperor's own appointees' recommendations regularly received the imperial approval. Moreover, it might be argued that the government was operating under conditions that penalized—perhaps even with dismissal—those with divergent views, a situation that would have mandated compliance with the imperial stance for the sake of retaining an official post. Undoubtedly such pressures did sometimes influence policy recommendations, particularly when the emperor's own position was defined early.

At the same time, other reasoning suggests that the strong factionalism of the eighteenth-century Ch'ing court was presumably accompanied by the clashing views of different faction members. Moreover, if we look at analogous situations in which other rulers—be they presidents, premiers, or prime ministers—have appointed cabinet members and other high ministers, we shall find that selection by one man is no bar to wide disparity of views among those selected. It was the palace memorial deliberation system developed in the Yung-cheng and Ch'ien-lung periods, particularly its practice of offering a single unanimously backed recommendation, and not the fact of the emperor's choosing his own inner-court associates, that gave the advantage to those who researched and discussed policy, ironed out differences, and presented a unanimous front to the emperor. The emperor was frequently left with no alternative but to acquiesce and authorize the proposals of others.

Thus although the evidence for full-blown Ch'ing autocracy is strong, careful reading of the decision documents requires a reassessment of the state of the monarchy after the founding and early growth of the Grand Council. Throughout the dynasty, if an emperor took a position on policy he could usually prevail in the formulation of decisions and the drafting of edicts. There are numerous well-known instances of successful imperial intervention in policy-making. But in a great many instances the emperor held no particular policy views at all. Moreover in other situations we may be confusing decision and authorization, or misreading the imperial emphasis of the Ch'ing epistolary style, or misunderstanding the effect of official unanimity on decisions, or ignoring bureaucratic obstructions to implementation. Although in many cases a mature Ch'ing autocrat could impose his will if he so desired, there were indubitably a great many more occasions when the much vaunted powers of

Ch'ing autocrats were successfully thwarted by official coalitions or simply not exercised at all.

In fact, instead of supporting what has been viewed as the increasing imperial despotism of the eighteenth century, the rise of the Grand Council created a government that could run effectively whether or not a strong monarch prevailed in Peking. The changes of the early Ch'ien-lung years produced a privy council that as it grew in strength reduced the necessity for active imperial intervention. This fact became a virtue in the late nineteenth-century epoch of debilitated and infant emperors when the abbreviated imperial rescripts (now solemnly respresented as views "received [from the monarch]" by the grand councillors yet created by those same councillors) and the dependence on high ministers for management of policy deliberation became safeguards that prolonged the life of the dynasty despite the ascendancy of figurehead emperors. The Grand Council's mainstay, the new secret inner-court communications system (palace memorials), which has been viewed as having been an important prop for eighteenth century autocrats, in fact had chiefly enhanced the power of only the K'ang-hsi and Yung-cheng emperors, after which time it came as much to enhance the influence of its managers, the Grand Council.

The mid-Ch'ing was not the first epoch in Chinese history in which officials mounted successful attempts to broaden their influence in government. Other examples have been cited earlier in this book. The late Ming routine memorial draft-rescript system, for instance, sometimes functioned to empower outer-court bureaucrats with a determining voice in policy decisions. Although most draft responses to the memorials were perfunctory and formalized, on occasion the men of the outer court shaped policy responses that were then authorized by the throne. The middle Ch'ing emperors, particularly Yung-cheng, sought to counterbalance this rise in outer-court influence and reinvent autocracy. And in turn the mature Grand Council was a response to Yung-cheng—another swing of the pendulum—propelled in part by ministerial objection to monarchical privilege.

It would be astonishing if over the course of their history the Chinese had not attempted to solve the problems of untrammeled autocratic caprice. It would also be a surprise to find that history had precisely repeated itself and that the Chinese had developed Western-style written constitutional limits on monarchical power of the sort that sprang from the acts of the barons who challenged King John at Runnymede. In the absence of the formally enacted restraints characteristic of Western governments, once again—this time through an inner-court privy council—China's ministers developed numerous devices for informally asserting their own influence and limiting the monarchs' opportunities for independent intervention in the decision-making process.

APPENDIX A
Analysis of "The Board" Notices
in Yung-cheng–Period Documents

Unraveling the meaning of Yung-cheng–period documents is greatly aided when certain puzzling references to "the board," generally indicating the "Board of Revenue," are properly understood. The chief problem is that some imperial edicts and rescripts responding to the secret provincial palace memorial speak of "turning [a palace memorial] over to the board [*chiao-pu*]," as if secret communications were being casually transferred to an agency in the large, open outer-court bureaucracy.[1] Despite what appears to be an imperial breach of confidentiality, there is no evidence that these memorials were actually sent to the outer court. Moreover, we know that transferring documents from one communications system to the other was not in accordance with procedures in force during most of the reign. Palace memorials that had to be referred to the outer court were usually resubmitted in the routine system (*chü-t'i lai*).[2] Other perplexing uses of "the board" appear in documents which suggest that an edict containing secret information had been drafted by an outer-court board, when we know from other evidence that it was in fact drafted in the inner court. What, then, did these "board" references mean?

One of the best answers to these questions is provided by the Yung-cheng Emperor himself in a rescript from YC4 (1726). In this the emperor approved the recommendations on certain Yunnan salt problems put forward by the Board of Revenue directorate, Yin-hsiang (Prince I), Chang T'ing-yü, Chiang T'ing-hsi, and three vice presidents. The imperial rescript did not respond directly to the discussers but instead was addressed to the author of the base report, the Yun-Kuei governor-general O-erh-t'ai, to whom the board directorate's recommendations were now being sent. The rescript explained: "This was turned over to the board for secret discussion. What you memorialized was correct. What the board has recommended is even better."

Because in this document we have two pieces of evidence available for cross-checking, we learn that Yung-cheng's "board" meant only the Board of Revenue directorate, the six men (three of whom were inner-court figures) who had composed the recommendations.[3] Moreover, the emperor's next words further distinguished the directorate from the larger board staff and, in particular, from the outer-court middle-level department that might have been expected to deal with the report's technical details, by counseling O-erh-t'ai to rewrite his memorial with a view to making it available to those subordinate levels in the outer court: "What should be sent in a routine memorial [that would go to the board], send in a routine memorial [*chü-t'i*]."[4] Had the correspondence already been scheduled for circulation to outer-court middle-level and lower-board members, this last injunction would have been inappropriate. Thus in this case, the emperor's assignment of a palace memorial to "the board" did not mean that the problem was to be transferred to the outer court. The need for confidentiality mandated secret handling for such a document. This deliberation was carried out entirely within the inner court by Yung-cheng's favorites, the three deputies who were also high Board of Revenue officials, on this occasion assisted by the other members of the directorate. This small group was Yung-cheng's "board."

Another example appears in the rescript of a slightly earlier consideration of Yunnan salt income by the Board of Revenue directorate. The rescript, also addressed not to the discussers but to the provincial memorialist who had originally investigated the problem, cited a "base report that had been sent to the board for secret discussions" (*fa-pu mi-i chih che*). But again the memorialists were not the outer-court board staff but only Prince I, Chang T'ing-yü, and four Board of Revenue vice presidents, including Chiang T'ing-hsi—in other words, once again the Board of Revenue directorate.[5] Thus, this instance was similar to the previous one in that Yung-cheng's use of "the board" in fact meant only a group with strong inner-court ties.

In some instances a reference to "the board" meant something even narrower than the foregoing, not the full Board of Revenue directorate but only the inner deputies within the directorate. Cross-checking of court letter originals with later references to the same documents reveals that edicts we know were drafted by the inner deputies were sometimes called "Board of Revenue communications" (*Hu-pu tzu*). In one instance a reference to a board in another document can be shown to refer only to "Prince I and others," a shorthand expression frequently used for the three inner deputies who were also the top members of the Board of Revenue directorate.[6]

These four examples date from the middle of the reign. At a slightly later date similar terminological confusion appears in references to "the Board of Revenue" when in fact "the Board of Revenue's Military Finance Section" was meant. A good example of this is found in a late YC11 (early 1734) deliberation on a memorial concerning horse purchases. Part of the recommendation approved the provincial official's request that his palace memorial reporting horse purchases and expenditures be "turned over to the board for auditing [*chiao-pu ho-hsiao*]." The deliberators then added their own stamp of authorization to the transaction: "In accordance with the memorialized request," they wrote, "this ought to be turned over to the Board of Revenue for investigation and checking." But the ultimate actual destination of the entire matter was made clear in an attached processing note that instructed, "Turn over to the Board of Revenue's Military Finance Section [*Hu-pu Chün-hsu fang*]." [7] Thus, three usages in one document equated turning a document over to "the board" with sending it to "the Board of Revenue" and to the "Board of Revenue's Military Finance Section." Even though some early uses of "the board" meant the Board of Revenue directorate or the three Board of Revenue inner deputies, other uses, particularly later on, might designate the board's Military Finance Section, an office supervised by the Board of Revenue inner deputies.

The evidence suggests a chronological division in the use of "the board." Before the founding of the Military Finance Section in YC7 (1729),[8] either the three inner Board of Revenue deputies or the full six- or seven-member Board of Revenue directorate seems to have been meant. Once the Military Finance Section came on the scene usage is clouded: sometimes the inner deputies were intended and sometimes their subordinates on the new Military Finance staff. Although not always made specific, at this stage commands for secret deliberations were probably destined not for the full board or even the directorate and the appropriate department but only for the inner-court superintendent and other members of the directorate, while commands ordering that "the board" investigate and hold on file were probably sent to the Military Finance Section.

The evidence makes it possible to decipher other usages of the times that have up to now seemed too vague to clarify. For instance, in YC6 (1728) Yung-cheng rescripted a palace memorial with the explanation, "I had Prince I and others secretly discuss this memorial. Now I am taking the recommendation ... and together [with the base memorial] am sending it to you [Yüeh Chung-ch'i, the original memorialist]." The recommendation is so abbreviated in form that the authors were not identified at beginning or end—but in the middle they twice referred to themselves as "officials of the board" (*ch'en-pu*).[9] From other documents we know that authors who cite themselves in this fashion were usually either the three Board of Revenue inner deputies or its full directorate. By contrast, when a YC7 (1729) edict ordered "the matters of military finance accounts" (*chün-hsu tsou-hsiao shih-chien*) that were being submitted by palace memorial turned over to "the appropriate board" (*kai-pu*) for "investigation and checking" (*ch'a-tui*), this can also now be clarified. Although before the Military Finance Section was set up the inner deputies had done this work, after the middle of YC7 (1729) the Military Finance Section took over this responsibility.[10] The new office was set up to operate under the direction of Prince I "and one or two other members of the Board of Revenue directorate" and take care of the military campaign "dossiers on financial matters."[11] Given that its full name contained the words "Board of Revenue," that in its adjunct capacity it discharged certain tasks previously carried out by men known as "the board," and that it still operated under their supervision, it is not surprising that the new office too became known by this terminology.

No single document or even pair of documents can solve this conundrum. The conclusions presented here are derived from a concatenation of several understandings:

1. that by the mid-Ch'ing there were two distinct systems for document processing: the old routine-system, whose documents circulated in the outer court, and the new palace memorial system, whose documents (during the Yung-cheng period, at least) were handled exclusively in the inner court (Chapter 1);

2. that the Yung-cheng Emperor was mightily concerned about finance and official malfeasance and that his three most trusted and earliest favorites scored some of their earliest successes as Board of Revenue officials (Chapters 2 and 3);

3. that these Board of Revenue officials were successful in their handling of early northwest campaign preparations and that their work gradually expanded to take in any topic that might be covered by a court letter or reported by palace memorial (Chapter 3);

4. that although the Military Finance Section was established as part of the Board of Revenue, this did not mean that it was an outer-court agency; instead it was strictly subordinated to the board's inner-court high ministers, Prince I and "one or two directorate officials" (*t'ang-kuan*) (Chapter 4); and

5. that cross-checking of different usages identifying the same groups demonstrates that Yung-cheng's "board" could refer both to the inner-court Board of Revenue directorate (or sometimes more narrowly its three inner deputies) and, later by extension, to the "Board of Revenue's Military Finance Section," which the deputies supervised; moreover, references to "the board" can frequently be traced to mean the Board of Revenue alone, not any other board. This fits in with what we know about the edict-drafting and deliberation roles of the earliest inner deputies who rose to high positions as imperial favorites from their start as members of the Board of Revenue directorate.

This information will be useful for understanding certain *Veritable Records* and other edict notices that name a board, or specifically the Board of Revenue, as having been involved (as in phraseology such as "Edict to the Board of Revenue," *Yü Hu-pu*). From what we now know of the Board of Revenue directorate role in discussions and the Revenue inner deputies' role in edict drafting, we may conclude that in the Yung-cheng period such notices indicate not these edicts' addressees but rather the men who discussed the edicts' content with the emperor and composed the drafts that the emperor authorized.

References to the High Officials in Charge of Military Finance, *Pan-li Chün-hsu ta-ch'en*

The following chart gives some representative references to the High Officials in Charge of Military Finance (*Pan-li Chün-hsu ta-ch'en*, abbreviated below as PLCHTC) that appeared in contemporary sources. References to the name of this group began in the first month of YC9 (1731), close to the time of their first documented appearance in YC8/12, when several of them appeared in the roster of a court letter on the military campaign. In YC11 (1733) there was a decline in the use of this title, with the title High Officials in Charge of Military Strategy (*Pan-li Chün-chi ta-ch'en*, PLCCTC) increasingly being used in its place. The first contemporary primary-source citation of the new title is to be found in IFT YC11/1/5, pp. 1–2. (For comments on certain early dates that were only specified later, see Chapter 4, note 49.) From YC11 on references to the new title are so numerous that there is little point in tabulating them.

In the chart below, the retrieval document is cited at the left, information about the citation in the middle, and the topic of the citation on the right. Abbreviations used are, in addition to those mentioned above:

(T)	document located in the Taipei Palace Museum
(B)	document located in the Beijing Number One Historical Archives
Diary	the archival Ch'i-chü chu ts'e
PLCH Ch'u	alternative title for the high officials: Office [of the High Officials] in Charge of Military Finance, *Pan-li Chün-hsu ch'u*

Document numbers in the Retrieval column (e.g., [T] 11808) reference the palace memorials in the Taipei Palace Museum holdings.

Retrieval	Activity	Topics
(T) Diary 9/1/11	PLCHTC receive edict	Northwest personnel matters
(T) Diary 9/1/13	PLCHTC named as roster officials for edict	Yin-ch'a-na and clerks deputed to Ch'ing-hai
(T) Diary 9/1/14	PLCHTC receive edict	Ma-ch'i's son to be sent to the northwest
(T) Shang-yü Nei-ko[a] 9/3/26	PLCHTC to submit recommendations (*i-tsou*)	Ordered to recommend how many men to be selected for military service from each province; troop allocations
(T) 11808 Hsu Jung 9/5/12	Rescript sent memorial to PLCH Ch'u to file and discuss appropriate sections	Shipping grain to western Kansu
(T) 13052 Hsien-te and Huang T'ing-kuei memorial; rescript 9/5/16	PLCHTC to be informed	Tibetan and Mongol lamaism
Chu-p'i yü-chih 9:5756 Mai-chu 9/12/6	Rescript sent memorial to PLCHTC to discuss	Troop allocations for and defense of localities in Hupei
(T) Diary 10/3/2	PLCHTC receive edict (PLCCTC in *Shih-lu*)	Military supplies and weapons for the northwest
(T) Diary 10/3/16	PLCHTC receive edict (PLCCTC in *Shih-lu*)	Two high officials, Wu Li-pu and Pa-t'e-ma, being sent to train the Mongol Cha-sa-k'e troops
(T) Diary 10/7/25	PLCHTC receive edict (in *Shih-lu* as edict to Grand Secretariat, *Nei-ko*)	Imperial bodyguard, Ha-t'ai, ordered to the front
(T) 7793 Li Wei; rescript 10/9/4	PLCHTC to deliberate	Chihli military preparedness problems
(B) Lu-fu 2188-11 Chang Kuang-ssu 10/10/4	Memorial turned over to PLCH Ch'u	Attached slip inserted in the memorial; sending troops to help O-erh-t'ai

Continued on next page

Retrieval	Activity	Topics
(B) IFT YC11/spring	Most discussers in this volume are the PLCHTC	
(B) IFT 29–30 O-erh-t'ai and others; discussion memorial 11/1/17	Rescript on base ordered, PLCHTC to deliberate	Prices of horses for return to Tibet
(B) IFT 35–37 11/1/20	Rescript on base ordered, PLCHTC to deliberate	Fodder needed for horses in Kansu military encampments by spring (no grass would be available until the new growing season)
(B) IFT 39; rescript on base 11/1/21	Base turned over to PLCH	Yang-lien; horses
(B) IFT 41–62; rescript 11/1/24	PLCHTC to deliberate	Military personnel
(B) IFT 91–92; rescript 11/2/12	PLCHTC to deliberate	Request for *taotai* for Sian; personnel to be appointed for An-hsi
(B) IFT 53–54; lateral communication 11/7/11	PLCHTC[b] cited as a former agency that dealt with the problem that is now to be submitted to the PLCCTC	Illness of a dismissed official sent to northwest to serve as an ordinary soldier
(B) IFT 175–77; discussion 11/9/6	PLCHTC ordered to discuss the base memorial	Request of permission for official to conduct investigation at the front
(B) IFT 23[c] 11/10/17	Discussion memorial ordered turned over to the Chün-hsu ch'u to keep on file as well as to inform the appropriate governor	Troop rations

[a] For comment on another Yung-cheng Shang-yü Nei-ko usage, see Chapter 4, note 49.

[b] One of the terms in this entry was originally written *Pan-li Chün-chi*; the *chi* was crossed out, and the item then continued to read *hsu ta-jen ch'u*. The record book is a Ch'ien-lung–period copy, and the cross-out suggests that the copyist was proceeding according to habit and noted his mistake as soon as he had written it.

[c] This reference, late for mentions of the PLCHTC, is not phrased in the standard fashion and does not describe the high officials' usual activities of discussing and recommending (instead it consigns the cited document for filing). It may denote not the high officials but the Military Finance Section, the staff that was most frequently ordered to maintain files.

APPENDIX C
Names of High Officials of the Yung-cheng Period, *Pan-li Chün-hsu ta-ch'en* and *Pan-li Chün-chi ta-ch'en*

The following table lists those high officials whose names have come to light in the various sources available to me. This expands on the usual lists of early "grand councillors" supplied in sources such as the *Ch'ing-shih* (CS below), Liang Chang-chü's *Shu-yuan chi-lueh* (SYCL below), and the *Ch'ing-tai chih-kuan nien-piao* (CKNP below). In what follows I have also used another important source: the lists (rosters) of those named in the headings of the early court letters. Although the inner deputies supervised these high officials, the deputies were not part of the high officials group and accordingly are not included here.

The curious may wonder why the court letter rosters (CLR below) fail to list the members from YC10 and after whose names did appear in the *Ch'ing-shih*. Unfortunately, by YC10 it had become the practice for the court letter rosters to name only the deliberation manager (or sometimes two discussion managers), usually an inner deputy, rather than all participants to the deliberation (see Table 2 in Chapter 3).

Names that appear only once in a document (as opposed to a compilation) are omitted from the table. These include Chu Shih, La-(?)she, and O-shan. The SYCL also inconclusively lists So-chu, Na-yen-t'ai, Hsing-kuei, and Shuang-hsi in positions that they may have held as early as the Yung-cheng period. In the absence of specific dates and other confirming information, these names are also omitted.

Name	Date of First Reference (*YC*)	Source			
		CLR	CS	SYCL	CKNP
Yin-t'ai	8/12/28	×			
Cha-pi-na	8/12/28	×			
A-ch'i-t'u	8/12/28	×			
T'e-ku-t'e	8/12/28	×			
Hai-wang[a]	9/9/8	×		×	
Mang-ku-li[b]	9/9/8	×	×	×	
Feng-sheng-e[c]	9/9/8	×			
Ha Yuan-sheng	10/10		×		
Ma-lan-t'ai	11/2		×		×
Fu-p'eng	11/4		×		
No-ch'in[d]	11/11		×	×	×
Pan-ti[d]	11/11		×		

[a] Hai-wang is listed in the *Ch'ing-shih* but with a date after Yung-cheng's death. His listing in *Shu-yuan chi-lueh* (SYCL) is also of that date (although the SYCL gives no specific dates for this period).

[b] Mang-ku-li's placement in the *Ch'ing-shih* is after Yung-cheng's death.

[c] Note the anomalous position of Feng-sheng-e, who may at times have served as an inner deputy (see Chapter 3). In the *Ch'ing-shih* table, Feng-sheng-e's placement is after Yung-cheng's death.

[d] Both No-ch'in and Pan-ti were named in the SYCL clerks' tables, the former entering duty as a clerk in YC11, the latter in YC11/8. They may have become true members of the high officials' group only later. But see also Fu Tsung-mao's work, where No-ch'in is included in the "grand councillors" of the Yung-cheng period; *Ch'ing-tai Chün-chi ch'u*, pp. 148–49.

Inner-Court Manchu Clerks
of the Yung-cheng Period

The most complete tables of Grand Council clerks are to be found in Liang Chang-chü's compilation on the Grand Council (*Shu-yuan chi-lueh*, referred to as SYCL below). These begin with the appointment of Shu-ho-te late in YC8 (early 1731). Comparison of Liang's tables with other early lists and mentions, however, particularly those in Manchu-language archival sources, suggests that Liang was unable to obtain accurate information about the early years of the Manchu side. In the chart below, the Manchu clerks attached to various Grand Council antecedent organizations are given in the order of their first appearance of other sources; all dates are from the Yung-cheng period unless otherwise marked.

There are thirty-six names in all. Although thirty-two of these were listed in the Manchu clerks section of the SYCL, only twenty-four were included in the Yung-cheng–period section. Apparently so little was known about the other eight (many do not have precise dates of entry on duty, banner information, examination or previous post status, or other facts usually noted for clerks in the SYCL) that they were only vaguely shown as having come on duty at various times early in the Ch'ien-lung reign. Eleven additional names were culled from Manchu sources of the Yung-cheng period: four of these were not named in other sources; seven were listed but with a Ch'ien-lung–era start. Some of the discrepancies may derive from the fact that the early clerks were assigned to various areas or committees in the inner court whose records do not survive. In particular, those serving as clerks in the high officials' group (from whose records most of my additional identifications were made) may not have been generally known in other parts of the inner court. Apparently their names were written down much later.

The chart is significant because it reveals a substantial preponderance of Manchu clerks in comparison with Chinese in the Yung-cheng–era inner-court groups, an imbalance not so noticeable in the SYCL list. In addition, the fact that several of the Manchus now have to be removed from the Ch'ien-lung lists means that there was a proportionately larger growth of Chinese clerks in the early Ch'ien-lung period than has hitherto been apparent. Names of clerks listed only in the early Manchu sources with no corresponding appearance elsewhere are enclosed below in brackets. Men who joined on a Yung-cheng date that was after the death of the Yung-cheng Emperor have been regarded as Ch'ien-lung–period clerks and have not been listed.

Name	Early Manchu Source Date	(B) IFT Date	SYCL Listing and Date, If Any
Shu-ho-te		8/12/26	8/12
Ch'ang-chün			8 (no date)
Ming-shan (Mingshan)	8/12/26	9/2/25	9/2
Ming-te (Minde)	8/12/26		after CL9
Chao-hui		9/1/22	9/1
Ya-erh-ha-shan		9/2/2	9/2
Chi-lan-t'ai		9/6/4	9/6
A-ssu-ha		9/7/2	9/7
Pao-ning (Booning)	9/8/2		after 13/11
[Tungeme]	9/8/2		
Ch'ung-lu (Cunglu)	9/8/5		after CL9
Su-leng-e (Surrenge)	9/8/5		?10
Te-k'e-chin (Dekjin)	9/8/10		after CL9
Tung-han (Donghan)	9/8/10		after 13/11
Fo-ts'un (Fot'sun)	9/9/2		?10
T'ang-wu-li (Tanggūri)	9/9/2		?10
Te-hsing (Dehing)	9/11/10		?10
San-tsan-pao (Sangt'sangboo)	9/11/16		after CL9
[Teman] (also Demin)	9/11/19		
Shu-hsiu (Shusio)	9/11/27		after CL6
Shuo-shan (Surshan)	9/12/5	CL2/8/11	CL2/8
Fu-liang		10/10/11	10/10
Chio-huo-t'o			10?
Sun-cha-ch'i			10?
So-no-mu			10?
Yang-chu			10?
Kua-lan-t'ai			10?
Kuan-pao			10?
Chan-chu			10?
Ta-su		11/1/21	11/1
O-jung-an			11/5
O-lun			11/5
Pan-ti			11/8
No-ch'in			11 (no date)
Su-ch'ung-a		13/1/26	13/1

sources: Manchu Chün-wu I-fu tang (Beijing) YC8/12–9/8, YC9/8–12; I-fu tang (Beijing) CL2/12/11, pp. 353–55; *Shu-yuan chi-lueh* 16/1–3b; Yeh Feng-mao, *Nei-ko hsiao-chih* (Ch'ing printed ed., 1836), 11a–b.

APPENDIX E
Interim Council Editorial
Committee Members

The following chart shows the pattern of appointments of Interim Council members who headed the editorial committees of the large number of official publications under way in the Interim Council era. One or more council members held supervisory positions at the top of nearly all the editorial boards. Of course, these posts were concurrent and did not mean that council members spent their days on editorial work; council members were probably responsible for overall policy while men lower down did the actual work. In the right-hand column of names, the top line shows the highest editorial echelon and the next line gives the second highest; names of Interim Council members are underlined. In some instances full information about a compilation was not available, but the work's title has nevertheless been listed to show the diversity of the Interim Council's editorial concerns. Even when council members were not named to a top supervisory post, the Interim Council frequently made recommendations and drafted edicts on these publications.

All archival sources are from Beijing unless otherwise noted. All dates are from the Ch'ien-lung period unless marked "YC." *Chüan* and page numbers are at the end of each source entry. For a key to the abbreviations, see pp. 300–301.

Source Documents	Publication Title	Interim Council Members in the Editorial Committees' Two Top Echelons
SYT-FP YC13/12/1 165; CLSL 8/2; HTSL ·049/14b	Pa-ch'i Man-chou shih-tsu t'ung-p'u (Eight Banner clans)	O-erh-t'ai Fu-min, Hsu-yuan-meng
Chang T'ing-yü nien-p'u 4/1b 1/1/14	Yü-tieh (Imperial clan genealogy)	O-erh-t'ai, Chang T'ing-yü, Fu-p'eng (Prince P'ing) Hung-chou (Prince Ho) Fang Pao
SYT-FP 1/6/16 257–59; ECCP 236	Ch'in-ting Ssu-shu wen (Model examination essays)	O-erh-t'ai, Chang T'ing-yü, Chu Shih
Chang T'ing-yü nien-p'u 4/7 1/7/9; IFT 1/7/5 67–68 and 2/4/5 137–38; CLSL 21/1–2 1/6/16 and 22/23b; ECCP 236, 603	San-li i-shu (Commentaries on the three classics on rites) When printed, consisted of three works: Chou-kuan i-shu; I-li i-shu; Li-chi i-shu;	
HTSL 1049/14	Jih-chiang Li-chi chieh-i (Commentaries on the Book of Rites)	
Work begun CL1–6, completed CL21. IFT 1/7/5 67–68 and 2/4/5 137–38; HTSL 1049/14; ECCP 805; (T) SYT-FP 47/6/24 683	Ta Ch'ing t'ung-li (Compendium on ceremonies)	The Interim Council and the board ordered jointly to compile
SYT-FP 2/5/28 37; CLSL 43/18; HTSL 1049/·4b; ECCP 102, 318, 603	Shou-shih t'ung-k'ao (Treatise on Agriculture)	O-erh-t'ai, Chang T'ing-yü
YCSL Kao chüan 4b–5; HTSL 1049/12b–13b, edict of YC13/10	Yung-cheng Shih-lu (Veritable Records)	O-erh-t'ai Chang T'ing-yü, Fu-min, Hsu Pen, San-t'ai Same as Yung-cheng Shih-lu
HTSL 1049/13b, edict of CL1	Yung-cheng Sheng-hsün (Imperial Exhortations)	
SYT-FP 1/10/5 153; HTSL 1049/13b–14 IFT 1/6/28 55–56; 2/7/4 9–11; 2/J9/7 199–200; and 2/11/7 297[a]	Kuo-shih (Official history drafts) Lü-li (Compendium of laws)	O-erh-t'ai Interim Council members involved

Publications whose editing and printing began in an earlier reign but continued during the Interim Council era

ECCP 6, 453, 603, 718	Pa-ch'i t'ung-chih (Compendium on the Eight Banners)	O-erh-t'ai
ECCP 919	Shang-yü pa-ch'i (Edicts to the Eight Banners)[b]	Same as Yung-cheng Shih-lu
ECCP 919	Shang-yü ch'i-wu i-fu (Deliberations on Eight Banner affairs)	Same as Yung-cheng Shih-lu
ECCP 919	Yü-hsing ch'i-wu tsou-i (Memorials on Eight Banner affairs)	Same as Yung-cheng Shih-lu
YC CPYC preface edict, YC10/3/1, and postface edict, CL3/2/4	Yung-cheng Chu-p'i yü-chih (Palace memorials and vermilion rescripts)[c]	O-erh-t'ai, Chang T'ing-yü
ECCP 919; (T) IFT 25/3/26, pp. 53–54	Yung-cheng Shang-yü Nei-ko (Edicts issued through the Grand Secretariat)	Same as Yung-cheng Shih-lu
IFT 1/12/21 394. See YCSL 9/26 YC1/7/25 and CLSL 9/35b–36 SYT-FP YC13/11/15 71	Ming-shih (Official history of the Ming)	Chang T'ing-yü
	I-t'ung-chih (Comprehensive Geography of the Empire)	
(T) Ch'i-chü chu YC13/1/23; ECCP 792 and passim. See also HTSL 1049/14b	Huang-Ch'ing wen-ying (Collected court literature)	O-erh-t'ai, Chang T'ing-yü
K. Ch'en, Buddhism in China, 451	Chinese Tripitaka	

[a] For earlier Lü-li (these were revised approximately every five years), see Ta-Ch'ing li-ch'ao Shih-lu (Yung-cheng) 11/26b–27.

[b] The several Yung-cheng edict compilations were put together without the establishment of a separate editorial office. They were done out of the Veritable Records Office (Shih-lu kuan), which is why O-erh-t'ai, Chang T'ing-yü, and the others have been listed as editors; Fang Su-sheng, Ch'ing Nei-ko k'u-chu chiu-tang 1/24.

[c] The Yung-cheng Chu-p'i yü-chih was first published in YC10 (1732), but the memorials and responding rescripts for that edition obviously could not cover the entire reign. The complete edition was ordered proofread on CL3/2/4 (1738 March 23) and was printed in the following month; see Chu-p'i yü-chih postface edicts. We know that it was being worked on during the Interim Council era; see Shang-yü tang fang-pen (Beijing) CL1/11/1, p. 217.

The Work of the Grand Council Manchu Division (*Man-pan*) as Shown by the Topics of One Sample Month of Manchu Palace Memorials Early in the Ch'ien-lung Reign

The following lists the subjects of the Manchu-language palace memorials in one sample month, CL11/12 (1747 January 11–February 18). This month was chosen because it had by far the longest listing of memorials—a total of sixty-five—of any month of that year. The source is the Manchu Division's reference file list, composed as the memorials arrived in the capital. The file list groups memorials by month (no more precise dating is available) and supplies the name and rank of the chief memorialist and a summary of the topic. (Although memorialists were named in the original list, in the list below names are omitted and only ranks are supplied.) The memorialists ranged from princes, grand councillors, grand secretaries, and generals to lesser beings on the frontier such as banner, Sheng-ching, and customs post officials. Occasionally metropolitan agency officials may also be identified. The lowest-level person named in the two available years of this record (CL11, 1746; and CL14, 1749), was a board second-class secretary (rank 6A). The earlier of the two lists contained 413 memorials for the thirteen-month year, an average of thirty or so per month. A few of the memorials were submitted on behalf of others (*tai-tsou*). In some cases the laconic descriptions of the originals have had to be unsatisfactorily reproduced below.

Memorialist's Office	Topic
Censor	Advocates holding certain banner land income in public accounts to draw interest and later be given to banner members
Tibet deputy lieutenant-general	Tibet harvest Thanking emperor for gifts of glassware, porcelain (on behalf of another) Thanking emperor for gift of a necklace (on behalf of the Dalai Lama) Thanking emperor for gift of clothing and hats (on behalf of another) Plot against Polonai Thanking emperor for bolts of fine cloth (on behalf of another) Snow
Te-erh-min	Request for audience
Lieutenant-general	Funds belonging to bordered blue Mongol banner
Duke	Request for a permanent post for his son
Prince	Opposition to preceding request
Tientsin lieutenant-general	Date he set out for audience in Peking; eliminating a post in accordance with board recommendation
Manchu general-in-chief at Ninghsia	Appointment problem because no one has completed the necessary three years in office
Kuei-hua lieutenant-general	Thanking emperor for imperial instructions
Kiangning general-in-chief	Thanking for banner appointment for son
Ch'ing-chou general-in-chief	Recommending that another be turned over to the board for consideration of punishment
Jehol deputy lieutenant-general	Request to invest horse tent fund money in a pawnshop Thanks for appointment to Ku-pei K'ou provincial commander-in-chief post
Ning-ku-t'a general-in-chief	Appointment vacancy Apprehension of a criminal Reporting date he set out for Peking for an audience Apprehension and disposition of criminals Request to build guard posts

Continued on next page

Memorialist's Office	Topic
	Request for authorization to arrest and try a case
	Accusation
Deputy lieutenant-general	Reporting on distribution of annual imperial gift of five thousand taels
	Request that certain criminals be sent to Manchuria to serve as slaves
	Request to live in Peking because of mother's age
Sheng-ching board vice president	Request for money for houses for people in flood areas
Hangchow deputy lieutenant-general	Thanks for temporary post
	Rain and snow
Board department director	Request for an administrative change
	Another administrative change request
Deputy lieutenant-general	Request to retire because of chronic illness
Board vice president	Request for change in lowest-level translated examinations
Duke	Thanking emperor for gift to son
Szechuan-Shensi governor-general	Report on trial and recommendation
Ta-sheng-wu-la (tribe in Manchuria) controller	Accusations
Deputy lieutnant-general	Sending a temporary replacement for his post
Hei-lung-chiang general-in-chief	Reporting death of a banner captain and asking if the man's younger brother should inherit the post
Cha-p'u deputy lieutenant-general	Training of troops
Beile	Thanks for appointing his son to the post of *an-ta*
	Thanking emperor for gift of the *Pa-ch'i t'ung-chih*
Ch'i-shih (man's name)	Thanking for temporary post of Jehol deputy lieutenant-general
Chen-hai general-in-chief	Asks to have certain official funds invested in a pawnshop
Prince	Bodyguard appointments

Memorialist's Office	Topic
Court of Mongolian Affairs	Reporting a natural calamity in a Mongol tribal area and requesting tax remissions
Grand secretary and others	Accusation
Feng-t'ien general-in-chief	Requests for seals for Sheng-ching officials
	Official investments in Sheng-ching pawnshops
	Appointment
	Administrative change in handling certain funds
	Hunting areas
	Investigation of bannermen who suffered from a natural disaster; requesting tax relief
	Request for increase in imperial tomb attendants
	Discussion of A-lan-t'ai's request for impeachment
	Certain deductions
	Imperial tomb guardian personnel
	Investigation of a man's background
Beile	Responding to request to explain why he broke the memorial regulations
	Reporting death of a deputy lieutenant-general
General-in-chief	Arrests of criminals

SOURCE: Tsou-che hao-pu (Beijing) CL11/12. I believe that this is essentially a Manchu record book, misfiled with Chinese-language archives because of the presence of so many Chinese characters in its list; see *Ch'ing Chün-chi ch'u tang-an mu-lu* compiled by Palace Museum, Bureau of Documents (Peiping, 1930), p. 11. Once the full run of Manchu-language holdings is available for research, additional volumes may come to light. I have seen references to volumes for other years; see, for instance, I-fu tang (Beijing) undated CL4/12/12, pp. 307–10, which speaks of entering a Manchu deliberation in the "register" (*hao-pu*).

Notes

The notes are intended to promote accessibility to both archival and published versions of a document. This requires giving priority to the archival versions, both because they are less easily traced and because publication data do not readily lead back to locations in the archives. Accordingly, for archival documents full information sufficient for an archival search has been supplied: archival number or group and date, memorialist, and page numbers, as appropriate. Such information will also usually suffice to scan the summaries and indexes of published volumes. Archival references are preferable as well because generally I used the archival originals rather than the published versions and in some cases the latter have been cut or changed in the course of publication. To give one example: the Manchu-language halves of the joint-language memorials (*Man-Han ho-pi tsou-che*) do not appear in the Taipei Palace Museum's magnificent twenty-seven-volume set of Yung-cheng palace memorials (*Kung-chung tang Yung-cheng ch'ao tsou-che*), with the result that Manchu imperial rescripts on the Manchu half of a joint-language memorial were also eliminated. Because I occasionally cite a Manchu rescript or other unpublished section in such published documents, the archival reference is preferable to the published one. (For an example of a Chinese memorial published without its Manchu component see the Chinese memorial with Manchu labels attached, (T) KCT-YC021280, YC3/3/1, Yin-k'u [Silver Treasury], listed under the Board of Revenue in the Museum index, and the Chinese version published with the Manchu labels obliterated in volume 4 of the Yung-cheng memorials, pp. 86–91.)

Western-style volumes have been distinguished from traditional Chinese string-bound works by the use of colons to separate volume and page number for the former and slashes to separate *chüan* and page for the latter. Only the verso (b) of Chinese pagination is specified; otherwise the recto side (a) is meant.

ABBREVIATIONS IN THE NOTES

Ch'ing Reigns

SC	Shun-chih	TK	Tao-kuang
KH	K'ang-hsi	HF	Hsien-feng
YC	Yung-cheng	TC	T'ung-chih
CL	Ch'ien-lung	KHsu	Kuang-hsu
CC	Chia-ch'ing	HT	Hsuan-t'ung

Volumes issued serially according to reigns are so marked; for example, the *Ta-Ch'ing li-ch'ao shih-lu* (SL) appears variously as:

KHSL   K'ang-hsi *Shih-lu*

YCSL   Yung-cheng *Shih-lu*

CLSL   Ch'ien-lung *Shih-lu*

CCSL   Chia-ch'ing *Shih-lu*

and so forth.

Other Published Books
(*see bibliography for full reference*)

CPYC   *Yung-cheng chu-p'i yü-chih*

CS   *Ch'ing-shih*

ECCP   Hummel, Arthur W., ed., *Eminent Chinese of the Ch'ing Period*

HT   *Ta-Ch'ing Hui-tien*, Kuang-hsu edition

HTSL   *Ta-Ch'ing Hui-tien t'u shih-li*, Kuang-hsu edition; other editions of the *Hui-tien* are identified by the reign in which they were issued

SYCL   *Shu-yuan chi-lueh*

Archival References

Beijing Number One Historical Archives references are preceded with a (B), the Taipei Palace Museum archival references are marked (T). In the few instances of references from archives other than these two institutions, the full name of the installation is supplied. Distinguishing between the two major archival institutions is useful because of the possibility of different paginations in duplicate copies of handwritten record books. The reader is cautioned, however, that duplicates are available for only some of the works; in most instances it will be best to consult the depository identified in the note. I have usually dated undated documents, particularly those in record books, by the next preceding document in the series or pages.

CPTC (B)	Chu-p'i tsou-che, palace memorials. Usually identified by date and the subject heading of the box in which they are filed. In Taipei this same type of document is known as Kung-chung tang (see KCT below).
IFT (T, B)	I-fu tang, Grand Council record book of discussion memorials.
KCT (T)	Kung-chung tang, the Taipei Palace Museum palace memorial collection. Individual documents are identified by reign abbreviations and the Museum's retrieval number. Dates are usually date of dispatch, not the date the document was received at court. Unless otherwise noted, imperial rescripts are in the original vermilion calligraphy and are not copies or revisions. Published versions are found under the title *Kung-chung tang [reign title] tsou-che.* In Beijing this same type of holding is known as Chu-p'i tsou-che (see CPTC above).
Lu-fu (T, B)	Chün-chi ch'u lu-fu tsou-che, Grand Council reference collection, chiefly palace memorial copies.
SSTC (T, B)	Sui-shou teng-chi, Grand Council document register.
SYT-FP (T, B)	Shang-yü tang fang-pen, square form of the Grand Council record book of ordinary matters. In Beijing this is simply called Shang-yü tang, but the two are identified in the same manner below because they are the same record series. Variant titles such as Hsun-ch'ang tang and Hsien-yueh tang are spelled out.
TP (B)	T'i-pen, routine memorials.
WCT (T, B)	Wai-chi tang, record book of copied provincial palace memorials.
YC SYT (T)	Yung-cheng Shang-yü tang; a special archival volume of edicts devoted to Prince Yin-hsiang.

Other archival references are supplied by title.

PROLOGUE

1. For a recent example of this kind of analysis, see Chi Shih-chia, "Ch'ien-lun Ch'ing Chün-chi ch'u yü chi-ch'üan cheng-chin," *Ch'ing-shih lun-ts'ung* 5 (1984): 180. For a review of the debate over founding date and changing nomenclature, see Pei Huang, "The Grand Council of the Ch'ing Dynasty: A Historiographical Study," *London School of Oriental and African Studies Bulletin* 48, no. 3 (1985): 506–9. There is a voluminous modern literature on what has been called the Yung-cheng–period founding of the Grand Council, followed by an almost complete blank on the details of its subsequent development in the Ch'ien-lung and later periods. For works focusing on

the Yung-cheng antecedents, see Chuang Chi-fa, "Ch'ing Shih-tsung yü Pan-li Chün-chi ch'u ti she-li," *Shih-huo yueh-k'an* 6, no. 12 (Mar. 1977): 1–6; Feng Erh-kang, *Yung-cheng chuan* (Beijing, 1985), chap. 7; Pei Huang, "A New Instrument of Autocratic Rule—The Grand Council," chap. 6 of *Autocracy at Work: A Study of the Yung-cheng Period, 1723–1735* (Bloomington, Ind., 1974); Li Tsung-t'ung, "Pan-li Chün-chi ch'u lueh-k'ao," *Yu-shih hsueh-pao* 1, no. 2 (Apr. 1959): 1–19; Tu Lien-che, *Kuan-yü Chün-chi ch'u ti chien-chih* (Canberra, 1963); and Silas H. L. Wu, *Communicaton and Imperial Control in China: Evolution of the Palace Memorial System, 1693–1735* (Cambridge, Mass., 1970), esp. chap. 7, "The Grand Council and the New Communication-Decision Structure." Professor Wu has also written an article in which he analyzes some of the major primary sources for the Yung-cheng period: "Ch'ing-tai Chün-chi ch'u chien-chih ti tsai chien-t'ao," *Ku-kung wen-hsien* 2, no. 4 (Oct. 1971): 21–45. For the small number of works treating the Council in a general fashion over the entire Ch'ing period, see the two articles named at the beginning of this note and Fu Tsung-mao's substantial study (whose archival base was largely limited to the Grand Council Reference Collection [*Chün-chi ch'u lu-fu tsou-che*] in Taipei), *Ch'ing-tai Chün-chi ch'u tsu-chih chi ch'i chih-chang chih yen-chiu* (Taipei, 1967); Ch'ien Shih-fu, "Ch'ing-tai ti Chün-chi ch'u," in *Ch'ing-shih lun-wen hsuan-chi,* comp. People's University Ch'ing Research Institute (Beijing, 1979), 1:473–83 (essay written 1962); Alfred Kuo-liang Ho, "The Grand Council in the Ch'ing Dynasty," *Far Eastern Quarterly* 11, no. 2 (Feb. 1952): 167–82; Li P'eng-nien et al., *Ch'ing-tai chung-yang kuo-chia chi-kuan kai-shu* (Harbin, 1983); Liu Tzu-yang, "Ch'ing-tai ti Chün-chi ch'u," *Li-shih tang-an* 1981, no. 2 (May 1981): 99–104; Liu Yat-wing, "The Ch'ing Grand Council: A Study of its Origins and Organization to 1861" (M.A. thesis, University of Hong Kong, 1966); and Teng Wen-ju and Wang Chung-han, "T'an Chün-chi ch'u," *Shih-hsueh nien-pao* 2, no. 4 (1937): 193–98. The last named exhibited great enterprise because an attempt was made to interview the late Ch'ing grand councillors and clerks surviving at the time it was written.

2. Conversation with Mr. Chuang Chi-fa, Aug. 1979. The earliest regular references that I have noted occur in retrospective views composed during the Ch'ien-lung period; see CLSL 355/1b–2, entry of CL14; Hsi Wu-ao, *Nei-ko chih* (completed 1766; repr. Shanghai, 1920), p. 3; Wang Ch'ang, "Chün-chi ch'u t'i-ming chi," in *Huang-ch'ao ching-shih wen-pien,* vol. 1 (Ch'ing ed. 1827; repr. Taipei, 1963), 14/19a–b; and Yeh Feng-mao, *Nei-ko hsiao-chih* (1836), p. 11. My research in the Beijing archives corroborated Mr. Chuang's observation: there are no sustained Yung-cheng–period references to a *Chün-chi fang.* In the terminological chaos of the times there were occasionally other usages; see, for instance, the reference to the *Pan-li Chün-hsu ch'u* in (B) Lu-fu 2188-11, YC10/10/4, Chang Kuang-ssu.

3. Silas H. L. Wu, *Communication and Imperial Control,* chap. 8, esp. pp. 84–86.

4. On the limited strength and scope of the late Yung-cheng period organization known in Chinese as "Chün-chi ch'u," see Tu, *Kuan-yü Chün-chi ch'u ti chien-chih,* p. 17; and Silas H. L. Wu, *Communication and Imperial Control,* p. 86.

5. Ch'ien Mu, *Chung-kuo li-tai cheng-chih te-shih* (Taipei, 1969). There is a translation of this work by Chün-tu Hsueh and George O. Totten under the title *Traditional Government in Imperial China: A Critical Analysis* (New York, 1982).

6. See Pei Huang, "The Grand Council" pp. 509–11; quotation p. 509.

7. The Grand Council was abolished on HT3/4/10 (1911 May 8) and the "Cabinet" (*Tse-jen Nei-ko*) set up in its place; *Hsuan-t'ung cheng-chi Shih-lu* 52/18ff (see under

Ta-ch'ing li-ch'ao shih-lu). But reality differed from appearance: the four members of the supposedly new cabinet were precisely those of the Grand Council at its demise; CS 4:2512; *Ch'ing-tai chih-kuan nien-piao*, comp. Ch'ien Shih-fu (Beijing, 1980), 1:156. Moreover, when I examined the Grand Council record books of the time at the Taipei Palace Museum I observed that following a short hiatus right after the abolition the record keeping had not changed: it was in the same form and in the same types of record books. The 1911 Grand Council volumes of the record book of telegrams, Tien-chi tang, for instance, now at the Palace Museum in Taipei, continued well beyond the moment of the supposed abolition and right up to Chinese New Year's Day of 1912. A break in the record series occurred after the first ten days of the summer quarter, on HT3/4/10 (8 May 1911), but then picked up again with the autumn quarter and continued with very fat volumes in Grand Council style for the rest of the Chinese lunar year. Thus the Grand Council may have been abolished in name, but its records and processes were maintained without change for the final eight months of the dynasty.

8. There are occasional references in the Ch'ien-lung *Hui-tien*; see, for example, Ch'ien-lung *Hui-tien tse-li* 2/6.

9. Chang T'ing-yü, *Ch'eng-huai yuan chu-jen tzu-ting nien-p'u* (Preface 1749; repr. Taipei, 1970), 3/6.

10. Yeh Feng-mao completed his work in CL30; Hsi's work was finished a little earlier. See Silas H. L. Wu, "Ch'ing-tai Chün-chi ch'u chien-chih ti tsai chien-t'ao," pp. 22–23.

CHAPTER 1. STRENGTHENING THE INNER COURT IN THE EARLY YUNG-CHENG PERIOD

1. The generally acknowledged Ch'ing reign years do not exactly correspond with a man's time as ruler. Yung-cheng, for instance, acceded to power not in 1723, the date that is usually given, but at the death of his father on KH61/11/13 (1722 Dec. 20). Years named by Yung-cheng's reign title began only with the first day of the following Chinese lunar year, YC1/1/1 (1723 Feb. 5). See the "Note on Technical Matters" at the beginning of this book.

2. *Ch'ing-tai ti-chen tang-an shih-liao*, comp. Ming-ch'ing Archives Bureau of the State Archives Board (Beijing, 1959), pp. 1–2; YCSL 97/15–16. For a later perspective on this earthquake, see CLSL 19/19b–20.

3. Other terms for the Grand Council include *Pan-li Chün-chi ch'u* and, for the grand councillors, *Chün-chi ta-ch'en* or *Pan-li Chün-chi ta-ch'en*.

4. Ho Ping-ti, "Salient Aspects of China's Heritage," in *China in Crisis*, ed. Ho Ping-ti and Tang Tsou (Chicago, 1968), pp. 20–21; Arthur F. Wright's comments in Ho and Tang, *China in Crisis*, p. 40; Ch'ien Mu, "Chung-kuo ch'uan-t'ung cheng-chih," in *Chung-kuo t'ung-shih chi-lun* ed. Cha Shih-chieh (Taipei, 1973), pp. 84–128; and idem, *Chung-kuo li-tai cheng-chih te-shih*, pp. 26–27. On the suitability of using the inner/outer-court framework to study the Grand Council, see Pei Huang, "The Grand Council," esp. pp. 35–36. Note the caution on the usefulness of this terminology in Hans Bielenstein, *The Bureaucracy of Han Times* (New York, 1980), p. 155.

5. Chang T'ing-yü, *Ch'eng-huai yuan tzu-ting nien-p'u* (hereafter cited as *Nien-p'u*), 2/23b–24; *Ch'ing-pai lei-ch'ao*, comp. Hsu Ho (1917; repr. Taipei 1966), vol. 1, Kung-

yuan sec., p. 1; (B) IFT CL25/5/22, pp. 17–58; HT 70/9b; HTSL 319/1ff.; *Yung-hsien lu*, comp. Hsiao Shih (Yung-cheng period; repr. Taipei, 1971), p. 155.

6. For mid-Ch'ing administrative organization, see Immanuel C. Y. Hsu, *The Rise of Modern China*, 3d ed. (New York, 1983), chap. 3, "Political and Economic Institutions." For an analysis of the Yung-cheng administration, see Pei Huang, *Autocracy at Work*. For most board and other terms I have used the generally accepted English translations provided in H. S. Brunnert and V. V. Hagelstrom, *Present Day Political Organization of China*, trans. A. Beltchenko and E. E. Moran (Shanghai, 1912), even though for the Six Boards other clearer translations exist, such as "Personnel" for "Civil Appointment" and "Justice" for "Punishments." The size of the late-Ming capital civil service has been estimated at two thousand; Ray Huang, *1587, A Year of No Significance: The Ming Dynasty in Decline* (New Haven, 1981), p. 53.

7. E-tu Zen Sun, "The Board of Revenue in Nineteenth-Century China," *Harvard Journal of Asiatic Studies* 24 (1962–63): 175–228; and Madeleine Zelin, *The Magistrate's Tael: Rationalizing Fiscal Reform in Eighteenth-Century Ch'ing China* (Berkeley and Los Angeles, 1984), pp. 16–17. For an account of the Board of Punishment's responsibilities, see Derk Bodde and Clarence Morris, *Law in Imperial China: Exemplified by 190 Ch'ing Dynasty Cases (Translated from the "Hsing-an hui-lan")*, with Historical, Social, and Juridical Commentaries (Cambridge, Mass., 1967), pp. 122–31.

8. On the Ming memorial system, see Silas H. L. Wu, "Transmission of Ming Memorials and the Evolution of the Transmission Network, 1368–1627," *T'oung-pao* 54, nos. 4–5 (1968): 275–87; and Chang Chih-an, "Ming-tai Nei-to ti p'iao-ni," *Kuo-li Cheng-chih ta-hsueh hsueh-pao* 24 (Dec. 1971): 143–56. For a contemporary description of how the routine memorial system operated in the Ch'ing, see (B) IFT CL3/6/24, pp. 277–79.

9. For the prescriptions that governed Grand Secretariat routing procedures, see (B) P'iao pu-pen shih-yang and books of a similar nature also held in the archives.

10. On the Peking gazette, see Roswell S. Britton, *The Chinese Periodical Press, 1800–1912* (Shanghai, 1933; repr. Taipei, 1966), pp. 1–15; and Jonathan Ocko, "The British Museum's Peking Gazette," *Ch'ing-shih wen-t'i* 2, no. 9 (Jan. 1973): 35–49.

11. See, for example, Sun, "The Board of Revenue," pp. 190–91; and Bodde and Morris, *Law in Imperial China*, p. 127.

12. On the Huang Shih-ch'eng, founded in Ming Chia-ching 13 (1534), see *Ming Shih-lu* (Nankang, 1964–66), intro., 1a–b; CL *Hui-tien tse-li* 2/4a–b; HTSL 14/36. On the Nei-ko ta-k'u, see Wang Kuo-wei, "K'u-shu lou chi," in *Wang Kuan-t'ang hsien-sheng ch'üan-chi* (Taipei, 1968), 3:1164–68; Hsieh Kuo-chen, *Ming-Ch'ing pi-chi t'an-ts'ung* (Shanghai, 1962), pp. 149–50; Wu Che-fu, "Kuo-li Ku-kung po-wu-yuan ts'ang-shu chien-chieh," *Chiao-yü yü wen-hua* 418 (Aug. 1974): 36; Hsu Chung-shu, "Nei-ko tang-an chih yu-lai chi ch'i cheng-li," in *Ming-Ch'ing shih-liao*, vol. 1 (repr. Taipei, 1972), pp. 5–7; *Ch'ing Nei-ko k'u-chu chiu-tang chi-k'an*, comp. Fang Su-sheng (Peiping, 1934), ts'e 1, maps; *Ch'ing-kung shu-wen*, comp. Chang T'ang-jung (Taipei, 1969), 3/8b–9; *Pei-p'ing Ku-kung po-wu-yuan Wen-hsien kuan i-lan* (Peiping, 1932), pp. 8–9, 16.

13. Chu Hsieh, *Pei-ching kung-ch'üeh t'u-shuo* (Changsha, 1938), p. 83. There were several sets of the *Veritable Records*, so the permanent storage described here did not make the work inaccessible.

14. Hsieh Kuo-chen, *Ming-Ch'ing pi-chi*, pp. 149–51; Fu Tzu-chün and Chu Hsiu-yuan, "Ming-Ch'ing tang-an kuan li-shih tang-an cheng-li kung-tso tsai ta-yueh-chin

chung," *Li-shih yen-chiu* 1959, no. 1 (Jan. 1959): 95. I thank Susan Naquin for sending me a copy of this last article.

15. The court diaries should not be mistaken for personal accounts of either the emperor or his officials. A very ancient form, supposedly they were compiled from the diarists' observations and handwritten records, but in fact by Ch'ing times much of their material derived from official copies of audience records.

16. *Ch'ing Nei-ko k'u-chu chiu-tang chi-k'an* 1/18–20; *Ming Shih-lu*, intro., 1a–b; *Ku-kung po-wu-yuan Wen-hsien kuan hsien-ts'un Ch'ing-tai Shih-lu tsung-mu*, ed. Chang Kuo-jui (Pei-ping, 1934), p. 11; Hsieh Kuo-chen, *Ming-Ch'ing pi-chi*, pp. 150–51; (T) KCT-YC021251, YC1/5/15, Board of Civil Office memorial. On the use of Ming archival sources for historical compilations, see Wolfgang Franke, *An Introduction to the Sources of Ming History* (Kuala Lumpur, 1968), pp. 15ff.

17. Ray Huang, *1587*, pp. 9, 75–77.

18. (T) SYT-FP CC8/3/29, p. 345; ibid. CC23/7/6, pp. 39–41. Inner-court arrangements on imperial tours reveal that there were two inner courts ranged in concentric circles of proximity to the imperial person. The outer circle was the "white cloth city" (*pai-pu ch'eng*), an area deemed equivalent to the Ch'ien-ch'ing Gate plaza between the Peking palace's Lung-tsung and Ching-yün gates. On tours the "white cloth city" had to be cordoned off, excluding idlers but admitting inner-court staffmembers and supply carts. The inner circle, the "yellow cloth city" (*huang-pu ch'eng*), was a tour's counterpart to the Forbidden City's residential areas for the emperor and his personal retinue in the northern part of the palace. On the *huang-pu ch'eng*, see also (B) SYT-FP YC1/1/8, p. 63.

19. *Kuo-ch'ao kung-shih hsu-pien*, comp. Ch'ing-kuei et al., (Peiping, 1932) 2/2–3, 4a–b, 6/1a–b, and 5b; CS 1:228; YCSL 4/13b; CCSL 315/4–6b; *Kung-chung hsien-hsing tse-li* (HF era), 1/13b–14b, citing an edict of CL10. Yung-cheng–period sources suggest that the inner court of that earlier era covered approximately the same space; see YCSL 64/1a–b; *Kuo-ch'ao kung-shih*, comp. Yü Min-chung et al. (repr. from a 1761 manuscript Taipei, 1970), 3/1. See also the retrospective analysis concerning the Yung-cheng inner court in Kung Tzu-chen, *Ting-an wen-chi pu-pien* (repr. Taipei, 1968), 4:312.

20. Figures for the number of eunuchs attached to the imperial palace are very high. One estimate of the late Ming, which may be heavily exaggerated, is one hundred thousand. Ray Huang (*1587*, p. 13) gives a more moderate but still high figure of twenty thousand for the late Ming. Ch'ing estimates are lower and range from three thousand under the Empress Dowager down to a few more than a thousand at the end of the dynasty; see Albert S. J. Chan, "Peking at the Time of the Wan-li Emperor (1572–1619), *International Association of Historians of Asia: Second Biennial Conference Proceedings* (Taipei, 1962), 2:126; Ch'ing Hsüan-t'ung, *From Emperor to Citizen: The Autobiography of Aisin-Gioro Pu Yi*, trans. W.J.F. Jenner (Beijing, 1979), 1:62. See also Preston M. Torbert, *The Ch'ing Imperial Household Department: A Study of Its Organization and Principal Functions, 1662–1796* (Cambridge, Mass., 1977), pp. 39, 174.

21. Chang Te-ch'ang, "The Economic Role of the Imperial Household in the Ch'ing Dynasty," *Journal of Asian Studies* 31, no. 2 (Feb. 1972): 244, 253; and Torbert, *Imperial Household*, pp. 101–2 and passim.

22. (B) IFT CL1/10/19, pp. 289–95, lists 465 bodyguards from the upper three banners and 88 from the Imperial Equipage Department (*Luan-i wei*), the latter being in charge of the emperor's travel outside the palace. See also YCSL 2/38b–39; (B) SYT-FP CL32/2/1, pp. 95–99; (T) SYT-FP CC19/6/7, pp. 103–19.

23. (T) SYT-FP CC24/10/3, p. 23; the eight duty groups of the Banner Vanguard Division were said to number more than six hundred. See also (T) IFT CL5/6/19, pp. 125–28.

24. For a valiant attempt to clear Yung-cheng of the centuries of charges against him, see Silas H. L. Wu, *Passage to Power: K'ang-hsi and His Heir Apparent, 1661–1722* (Cambridge, Mass., 1979). For insights on the Yung-cheng accession and a summary of the recent literature, see Thomas Fisher, "New Light on the Yung Cheng Accession," *Papers on Far Eastern History* 17 (Mar. 1978): 103–36.

25. T'ien Ku, *Man-Ch'ing wai-shih* (Taipei, 1971), pp. 23–24. That Yung-cheng might have had the opportunity to alter the will may be indicated by one account that states that he made several visits to his father in his last hours; see Meng Sen, *Ch'ing-tai shih* (Taipei, 1960), p. 478.

26. Lawrence D. Kessler, *K'ang-hsi and the Consolidation of Ch'ing Rule, 1661–1684* (Chicago, 1976), pp. 7–8.

27. Hsiao I-shan, *Ch'ing-tai t'ung-shih* (Taipei, 1967), 1:861–62; ECCP, pp. 926–27; Silas H. L. Wu, *Passage to Power*, pp. 179–86 and passim; Jonathan D. Spence, *Emperor of China: Self-Portrait of K'ang-hsi* (New York, 1974), pp. 123–39; YCSL 26/11b–13; CS 5:3558–60.

28. CS 5:3558–60; (B) SYT-FP YC1/2/11, p. 189.

29. ECCP, p. 927. On A-ch'i-na, see Chapter 2, n. 8, below.

30. Manchu rescript on (T) KCT-YC020610, YC1/10/21, Yin-ssu. The Manchu half of this memorial was not reproduced in the published edition. I thank Mr. Chuang Chi-fa for calling this memorial and its rescript to my attention and for giving me his preliminary translation of the rescript. On this point, see also Hsiao, *Ch'ing-tai t'ung-shih* 1:864; and YCSL 26/11b–13.

31. Hsiao, *Ch'ing-tai t'ung-shih* 1:865. Yin-ssu died in 1726; the Ch'ien-lung Emperor cleared him posthumously and readmitted his heirs to the imperial clan; see CS 1:129.5; and CLSL 1048/17b–19.

32. ECCP, pp. 930–31; KHSL 293/4b. For the story of Yung-cheng's detention of Yin-t'i, see Chuang Chi-fa, "Ch'ing Shih-tsung chü-chin shih-ssu a-ko Yin-t'i shih-mo," *Ta-lu tsa-chih* 49, no. 2 (Aug. 1974): 24–38.

33. For an account of the K'ang-hsi Emperor's pursuit of Galdan, see Spence, *Emperor of China*, pp. 17–22. For general background on the Mongol situation, see W. D. Shakapba, *Tibet: A Political History* (New Haven, 1967), pp. 125–39; Henry H. Howorth, *History of the Mongols from the Ninth to the Nineteenth Century* (London, 1875–88), 1:497–525.

34. Vermilion note, (T) KCT-YC000440, undated enclosure no. 7.

35. Vermilion writing, (T) KCT-YC000454, undated.

36. (T) YC SYT YC8/5/14, pp. 53–57. For an account of similar difficulties experienced by the K'ang-hsi Emperor, see Spence, *Emperor of China*, pp. 19–20.

37. (T) YC SYT YC8/5/14, pp. 53–57. See also YCSL 2/14b–15.

38. On this disaster and the interregnum that followed, see Ph. de Heer, *The Care-taker Emperor: Aspects of the Imperial Institution in Fifteenth-Century China as Reflected in the Political History of the Reign of Chu Ch'i-yü* (Leiden, 1986). On regencies, see Shan Shih-k'uei, "Ch'ing-tai li-shih tang-an ming-tz'u chien-shih," in *Ch'ing-tai tang-an shih-liao ts'ung-pien*, comp. Palace Museum Ming-Ch'ing Archives Office, vol. 3 (Peking, 1979), pp. 197–98.

39. For a contemporary description of how the routine memorials were processed, see (B) Lu-fu CL2 Nei-cheng CL2/3/29, Ch'en Shih-kuan.

40. CL *Hui-tien tse-li* 2/4b; KH17 notice in HTSL 1014/2a–bff.; (B) IFT CL3/6/24, pp. 277–79; Chang T'ing-yü, *Nien-p'u* 4/22b.

41. Hsi, *Nei-ko chih*, p. 6; Silas H. L. Wu, "Emperors at Work: The Daily Schedules of the K'ang-hsi and Yung-cheng Emperors, 1661–1735," *Tsing-hua Journal of Chinese Studies*, n.s., 8, nos. 1–2 (Aug. 1970): 214–15; YCSL 9/10–12; CLSL 70/14a–b, 1003/22–23; HT 2/5–9; HTSL 14/2b–3. For the regulations for composing the draft rescripts, see (B) P'iao pu-pen shih-yang and volumes with similar titles and the edict quoted in (T) KCT-YC013085, YC8/5/22, Hsien Te. See also (B) IFT CL1/2/13, p. 171. Despite the large numbers, secrecy was possible in the routine system; see the early (Shun-chih) mandate in HT 13/3 and the special injunctions in YCSL 54/23b–24.

42. HT 5/17; HTSL 703/13b–14, 1042/7b; YCSL 4/16b–17; (T) SYT-FP TK30/11/10, pp. 103–8; Chuang Chi-fa, "Ch'ing Shih-tsung yü tsou-che chih-tu ti fa-chan," *Kuo-li T'ai-wan Shih-fan ta-hsueh li-shih hsueh-pao* 4 (Apr. 1976): 198. For an imperial reprimand concerning an instance of surreptitious copying, see KHSL 278/2a–b.

43. YCSL 1/8b–9.

44. For the subsequent appointment of a prince of the blood of the third rank (*pei-le*) to the group at the assisting (*hsieh-pan*) level, see YCSL 19/6a–b.

45. See YCSL, passim, for the years of the council's operation. On appointments, for instance, see YCSL 15/9a–b. For a detailed example of one of the council's military discussions, see the "follow-up recommendations" (*hsun-i*) in YCSL 16/16a–b, 18a–21b. For an early military review, see YCSL 2/41a–b. For a discussion on famine, see YCSL 15/16. There is also much relevant information in the memorials of the era. For the fact that the council was to set policy and manage reviews of both civil and military appointments, see (T) KCT-YC021962, Board of Civil Office memorial of YC1/3/14, citing an edict (omitted from the *Shih-lu*) of KH61/12/15; and (B) SYT-FP YC1/3/4, p. 257.

46. Recommendations on military strategy, troop allocations, and related subjects were frequently also sought from the Deliberative Princes and Ministers; see, for example, YCSL 17/21b–24b. Other scattered instances of Yung-cheng's not using his Plenipotentiary Council for this type of subject include YCSL 6/19b–20 (provisions for military garrison provisions in China proper discussed by the boards of Civil Office, Revenue, and War); 9/8–9b (Board of Works discussion of the strategic and other considerations in setting up a new town of military colonists in Ch'ing-hai); 15/15 (Board of War agreeing with the Deliberative Ministers' views on rations for troops in northern Chihli province); 17/12b–14b (middle Kiangsu troops, boats, patrols, to be discussed by Lung-k'o-to, a council member, and two others, Chu Shih and Chang T'ing-yü). Discussions relating to appointments were also sometimes routed to other groups and combinations of groups and individuals: see, for example, YCSL 15/16a–b (Board of Punishments discussing penalties to be imposed for improper reporting of illegal activity, penalties that would directly affect the miscreant's prospects for promotion).

47. YCSL 6/19a–b.

48. YCSL 9/10–12; Yung-cheng *Shang-yü Nei-ko* YC2/3/12.

49. YCSL 13/10b–11.

50. See YCSL 29/10b–13, 30/7–9b, 31/18–21; and (B) SYT-FP YC1/2/11, p. 189.

On Lung-k'o-to's increasingly uncertain position at court, see the edict quoted in (T) KCT-YC011150, YC3/1/7, Chu Kang; and (T) SYT YC8/5/7, pp. 29–35.

51. YCSL 29/10b–13.

52. Chao I, *Nien-erh shih cha-chi* (repr. Taipei, 1973), 33/483; Charles O. Hucker, "Governmental Organization of the Ming Dynatsty." *Harvard Journal of Asiatic Studies* 21 (1958): 27–30; Lynn A. Struve, *The Southern Ming 1644–1662* (New Haven, 1984), pp. 1–14.

53. *Ming Shih*, as quoted in Shen Jen-yuan and T'ao Hsi-sheng, *Ming-Ch'ing cheng-chih chih-tu* (Taipei, 1967), 1:59; see also Ch'ien Mu, *Chung-kuo li-tai cheng-chih te-shih*, pp. 88–90.

54. Shen Jen-yuan and T'ao Hsi-shing, *Ming-Ch'ing cheng-chih chih-tu* 1:53–54.

55. T'ai-tsung *Shih-lu* 28/2–3; Hsiao, *Ch'ing-tai t'ung-shih* 1:501; YC *Hui-tien* 3/2; Wu Chen-yü, *Yang-chi chai ts'ung-lu* 1896; (repr. Taipei, 1968), 4/1.

56. CS 2:1357; Hsiao, *Ch'ing-tai t'ung-shih* 1:501; Hsu Chung-shu, "Nei-ko tang-an chih yu-lai chi ch'i cheng-li," 1:4b.

57. CS 4:2453–61.

58. (B) SYT-FP YC1/2/10, p. 185.

59. HT 2/1; HTSL 11/4b–5; (B) SYT-FP CL13/11/30, p. 369; CLSL 330/6–7; CLSL 1155/21a–b; YCSL 15/15b–16; (T) KCT-YC021255, YC2/7/2, Ma-ch'i and others. A reference to Chang T'ing-yü as "Associate Grand Secretary" (*Hsieh-li ta-hsueh-shih shih-wu*) is in YCSL 41/26b–27; the official history took no notice of this imperial aberration and recorded only the correct term; CS 4:2462.

60. CS 4:2461–63; HTSL 11/4b–5. The number of grand secretaries was not limited until the following reign when, in CL13, it was fixed at four: two Manchu and two Chinese; CLSL 330/6–7.

61. YCSL 93/12; CS 2:1357. Despite the increase in rank, the salaries of those grand secretaries who did not also hold board posts lagged behind those of other capital officials; see (T) SYT-FP CL53/7/2, p. 7. On the grand secretaries' pavilion designations, see *Ming hui-tien* 2/10–11; HT 2/1; Wang Shih-chen, *Ch'ih-pei ou-t'an* (1691; repr. Taipei, 1976), 1/2. Because the *Chung-ho tien* designation was never used, the *T'i-jen ko* honorific was substituted in CL11; (B) Nei-ko Man p'iao-ch'ien pu-pen shih-yang, *chüan* 2. Manchu grand secretaries also concurrently held a Deliberative Council title until CL56 (1792); CS 2:1358.

62. See the mentions in William Frederick Mayers, *The Chinese Government: A Manual of Chinese Titles, Categorically Arranged and Explained, with an Appendix* (Shanghai, 1897; repr. Taipei, 1970), p. 19; Hsiao, *Ch'ing-tai t'ung-shih* 1:224–25; Thomas Metzger, *The Internal Organization of Ch'ing Bureaucracy: Legal, Normative, and Communicative Aspects* (Cambridge, Mass., 1973), pp. 123–24.

63. Sun, "The Board of Revenue." Occasionally information appears in the Grand Secretary tables, the imperial annals (*pen-chi*), or the *Veritable Records* (*Shih-lu*) but these entries do not supply a full list. I have also drawn on information that memorialists provided at the head of their reports.

64. *Ming Hui-tien* 2/10–11; YC *Hui-tien* 3/5; (T) T'ai-tsung *Shih-lu* (1655 ed.), T'ien-tsung 5/7/8 (1631 Aug. 5), 9/11b–12b. But see David M. Farquhar, "Mongolian versus Chinese Elements in the Early Manchu State," *Ch'ing-shih wen-t'i* 2, no. 6 (June 1971): 17, where it is argued that the Ch'ing inherited the post from Mongol rather

than Ming practice. The fact is that for board superintendencies the Ming used grand secretaries and the early Ch'ing rulers used princes. But later on the Ch'ing used both.

65. Fu Tsung-mao, *Ch'ing-tai Chün-chi ch'u*, pp. 29–30.

66. Ibid., pp. 28–30, 38–39; CS 4:2453–61; KH *Hui-tien* 2/1. It seems likely that the CS board tables do not list all of K'ang-hsi's appointments of this type.

67. YC *Hui-tien* 3/5. On Yung-cheng's disappointment with his imperial relatives, see Yung-cheng *Shang-yü Nei-ko* YC2/5/22, p. 15.

68. On the advantages of ambiguity, see Metzger, *Internal Organization*, pp. 123–24.

69. I take the use of one of the several terms for "in charge of" (*pan-li, chien-li, tsung-li, kuan-li*, etc.) or "concurrently in charge [*chien*] of board president affairs," together with the omission of the name from the board presidents' list in the official board tables, to signify the existence of a superintendency. Further research may result in a refinement of this definition. For an example of the use of two of these terms in the same document in what is a clearly distinctive and hierarchical manner, see CLSL 4/16.

70. (T) KCT-YC020607, YC3/4/13, Yin-ssu et al; (T) KCT-YC020074, YC6/2/8, Ch'ang-shou et al.

71. CS 4:2607; YCSL 2/26. Lung-k'o-to was related to the new emperor by marriage: his aunt had been the K'ang-hsi Emperor's mother, and one of his sisters had been empress to K'ang-hsi.

72. YCSL 2/26b, 4/2. Fu-ning-an's and Chang P'eng-ko's board presidency responsibilities were no longer listed in the board tables after they were appointed grand secretaries; see CS 4:2607–9.

73. For an example, see (T) KCT-YC021977, YC1/9/13, Board of Civil Office.

74. Chang T'ing-yü, *Nien-p'u* 3/23b–25. Chang was relieved of the Board of Civil Office superintendency in CL13; see CS 1:149.1–2.

75. Chang T'ing-yü, *Nien-p'u* 2/17b. The policy of not holding highly trusted and able superiors responsible for the mistakes of subordinates was sometimes applied to other officials; see, for example, YCSL 87/2–3b.

76. Imperial edict quoted in (T) KCT-YC002868, YC12/1/3, Chang T'ing-yü. On administrative punishment, see Metzger, *Internal Organization*, p. 115.

77. Chang T'ing-yü, *Nien-p'u* 3/25b–26. For a similar imperial view on not punishing another high official for mistakes, see (T) KCT-YC006651, YC2/5/12, T'ien Wenching, and Chapter 6, n. 32, below. On leniency in official punishment, see Metzger, *Internal Organization*, pp. 236–37; and Fu Tsung-mao, *Ch'ing-tai Chün-chi ch'u*, p. 419.

78. Chang T'ing-yü, *Nien-p'u* 4/23b.

79. CLSL 181/4–5b.

80. CLSL 340/23b; CCSL 130/14–15.

81. For a discussion of the situation in the late-nineteenth-century Board of Revenue, see Marianne Bastid, "The Structure of the Financial Institutions of the State in the Late Qing," in *The Scope of State Power in China*, ed. Stuart R. Schram (New York, 1985), p. 53.

82. Hsiao, *Ch'ing-tai t'ung-shih* 1:880–881; YCSL 3/34–35, 4/32a–b, 25/13b–14b; (T) KCT-YC021987, YC2/2/8, Li Pu (Board of Civil Office); Frederic E. Wakeman, Jr., *The Great Enterprise: The Manchu Reconstruction of the Imperial Order in Seventeenth-Century China* (Berkeley and Los Angeles, 1985), 1:447. On Ming corruption, see ibid., "The Attack on Ming Abuses," 1:448–54. The Number One Archives in Beijing has a

separate fond (*ch'üan-tsung*) of Audit Bureau materials; see Cheng Li, "Ming-Ch'ing tang-an," *Ku-kung po-wu-yuan yuan-k'an* 1979, no. 1 (Feb. 1979): 13.

83. YCSL 3/34–35, 4/32a–b; (B) SYT-FP YC1/2/8, p. 171. The list of the bureau's top panel in *Yung-hsien lu* 1/91 is not correct; the author must have been thinking of the Plenipotentiary Council. On the *pu-fei*, see Zelin, *The Magistrate's Tael*, pp. 45, 77–78, and other references under "Board Fees" in her index.

84. Hsiao, *Ch'ing-tai t'ung-shih* 2:355. For discussions of specific bureau acts, see (T) KCT-YC020580, YC1/9/20, and (T) KCT-YC020608, YC1/9/20, both Yin-ssu memorials; and (B) SYT-FP YC1/2/8, p. 171, and YC1/3/20, p. 297.

85. (T) KCT-YC004896, YC1/11/15, Hsu Jung.

86. YCSL 25/13b–14b.

87. Hsiao, *Ch'ing-tai t'ung-shih* 2:355.

88. CS 1:118.1.

89. The Audit Bureau resembles what Arthur M. Schlesinger, Jr., has called an "emergency agency"; see *The Age of Roosevelt*, vol. 2: *The Coming of the New Deal* (Boston, 1958), p. 534.

90. HT 2/4b–5

91. YCSL 28/9a–b. On audiences, see Silas H. L. Wu, "Emperors at Work," passim.

92. YCSL 54/23b–24.

93. HTSL 703/14a–b, 1042/7b; HT 69/13. Early in the next reign the five-day limit was changed to ten days; HTSL 703/16a–b. See also Silas H. L. Wu, *Communication and, Imperial Control*, pp. 28–29.

94. Chang T'ing-yü, *Nien-p'u* 4/22b; (B) IFT CL24/10/7, p. 362; (B) SYT-FP CL26/5/1, p. 155.

95. HTSL 13/4a–b, 1042/2–3; see also HT 2/6a–b. Early in the Ch'ien-lung period further changes were made in this prohibition. For a list of errors in routine memorials which in later years could lead to reprimand rather than rejection of the report, see (B) Nei-ko Man p'iao-ch'ien t'ung-pen shih-yang, *chüan* 17. The Yung-cheng Emperor is thought by some to have established the Chancery of Memorials; see Hsiao, *Ch'ing-tai t'ung-shih* 1:867. For further information on the Chancery, see note 124 below.

96. HTSL 13/4b, 1042/4; Chü Te-yuan, "Ch'ing-tai t'i-tsou wen-shu chih-tu," *Ch'ing-shih lun-ts'ung* 3 (1982): 219 and n. 4; YCSL 85/21a–b; (B) IFT CL4/7/2, pp. 201–3; (B) IFT CL7/5/16, pp. 297–98, referring back to a YC11 document; *Kung-chung tang Yung-cheng ch'ao tsou-che*, comp. Palace Museum, Documents Section (Taipei, 1977–80), 27:431–32, undated memorial of Yang Ju-ku; see also YCSL 132/14–15 and HTSL 1014/1a–b. The second type of routine memorial, the *tsou-pen* form, was discontinued in CL13 (1748); see HTSL 13/6b.

97. YCSL 4/16b–17, 5/5b–6.

98. YCSL 87/2–3b; see also HTSL 1042/7a–b.

99. YCSL 90/13a–b.

100. On the Southern [Imperial] Study, see Silas H. L. Wu, "Nan shu-fang chih chien-chih chi ch'i ch'ien-ch'i chih fa-chan," *Ssu yü yen* 5, no. 6 (March 1968): 6–12. The study's members are listed in the *Tz'u-lin tien-ku*, a compendium on the Hanlin Academy, completed in 1806 and printed in 1887.

101. ECCP, pp. 64, 329; SYCL 13/21a–b; *Ch'ing-pai lei-ch'ao, Li-chih* sec., pp. 14–15; CC *Hui-tien* 3/10b; *Yung-hsien lu*, p. 65; Wu Chen-yü, *Yang-chi chai ts'ung-lu* 4/1; Li Tsung-t'ung, "Pan-li Chün-chi ch'u lueh-k'ao," pp. 3–4.

102. HT 3/9a–b; *Kuo-ch'ao kung-shih* 12/8b; *Ch'ing-pai lei-ch'ao, Kung-yuan* sec., 3–4.

103. *Tz'u-lin tien-ku* 63/1–6. There may have been one or two additional Manchus—some of the names are difficult to identify. In the Yung-cheng period the first Manchu to be appointed was O-le-shun, in YC11; see ibid., 63/6b–9.

104. ECCP, p. 64; Chao I, *Yen-p'u tsa-chi* (repr. Taipei, 1957), 2:52–53; Li Tsung-t'ung, "Pan-li Chün-chi ch'u lueh-k'ao" 3–4; (T) SYT-FP HF1/5/4, p. 27. See also *Ch'ing-pai lei-ch'ao, Kung-yuan* sec., 3–4. In the K'ang-hsi era, Wang Hung-hsu disguised his communications for the emperor by using the name of the study; see *Wen-hsien ts'ung-pien* (Taipei, 1968) 1:78; Chuang Chi-fa, "Ts'ung Ku-kung po-wu-yuan hsien-ts'ang kung-chung tang-an t'an Ch'ing-tai ti tsou-che," *Ku-kung wen-hsien* 1, no. 2 (Mar. 1970):46.

105. *Tz'u-lin tien-ku* 63/6–9.

106. YCSL 13/17b–18; CS 5:5035; *Tz'u-lin tien-ku* 63/8.

107. Yeh Feng-mao, *Nei-ko hsiao-chih*, p. 11b; (T) KCT-YC016172, YC10/9/13, Liu Yü-i; (T) SYT-FP CL44/2/4, p. 199; *Kuo-ch'ao kung-shih* 12/8b; *Kuo-ch'ao kung-shih hsu-pien* 6/1a–b; SYCL 13/12, 21a–b; ECCP, p. 55.

108. On the council's early history and membership, see Chao-lien, *Hsiao-t'ing tsa-lu* (Taipei, 1968), 2/10; Fu Tsung-mao, *Ch'ing-tai Chün-chi ch'u*, pp. 52–53; Yung-cheng *Shang-yü Nei-ko*, YC1/8/22, p. 8; Hsiao, *Ch'ing-tai t'ung-shih* 1:501, 867–68; I-keng, *Tung-hua lu chui-yen* (repr. Taipei, 1970), p. 23; Robert B. Oxnam, "Policies and Institutions of the Oboi Regency," *Journal of Asian Studies* 32, no. 2 (Feb. 1973): 271–73; Wakeman, *The Great Enterprise* 2:850–51.

109. Chao I, *Yen-p'u tsa-chi* 1:1; Fu Tsung-mao, *Ch'ing-tai Chün-chi ch'u*, pp. 58–64, 93–94, 115; Inaba Iwakichi, *Ch'ing-ch'ao ch'üan-shih* (Taipei, 1960), 43/51–52; KHSL passim; Wu Chen-yü, *Yang-chi chai ts'ung-lu*, 4/1; *P'ing-ting Chun-ka-erh fang-lueh, Ch'ien-p'ien, chüan* 8.

110. See Fu Tsung-mao, *Ch'ing-tai Chün-chi ch'u*, p. 112.

111. CS 5:3995, 4008, 4098, for example.

112. Yung-cheng *Shang-yü Nei-ko*, YC1/8/22, p. 8; YCSL 47/13a–b; (T) KCT-YC019384, YC5/12/18, Sai-leng-e; ECCP, p. 305; Manchu rescript on (T) KCT-YC020607, YC3/4/13, Yin-ssu and others.

113. The term "competitive administration" is borrowed from Schlesinger, *The Coming of the New Deal*, pp. 528, 531–32.

114. For some examples of the variety of discussion assignments concerning military appointments, see YCSL 2/29b–30 (Deliberative Council); YCSL 3/40a–b (Plenipotentiary Council with a large number of others); (T) KCT-YC021962, YC1/3/14, Board of Civil Office (Plenipotentiary Council with the boards of Civil Office and War); YCSL 9/9–10 (Deliberative Council); YCSL 14/5b–6 (Deliberative Council); YCSL 20/5b–6 (Board of War); YCSL 20/7b (Board of War); and YCSL 25/9b–10b (Board of War). For examples of switching discussers of troop allocations, see YCSL 2/41a–b (Plenipotentiary Council on Ka-ssu troops); YCSL 11/19a–b (Plenipotentiary Council on Ch'ing-hai and Sinkiang); YCSL 13/1b–2b (Plenipotentiary Council on Mongol troop shifts); YCSL 17/21b–24b (Deliberative Council on Ch'ing-hai and Sinkiang troops); YCSL 25/8 (Board of War on Shensi frontier allocations); and, after the Plenipotentiary Council had been disbanded, YCSL 30/12–13b (Deliberative Council on Szechuan troops). For a variety of discourse on Manchu Banner garrisons, see YCSL 13/3b–4 (Plenipotentiary Council deliberating) and 90/10b–11b (first the Deliberative Council jointly with the Board of War, then separately to General O-erh-ta). For an example

of a memorial on Tibet sent to the Deliberative Princes and Ministers to discuss, see (T) KCT-YC018725, YC3/7/24, Shih Wen-cho. See also, for instance, the imperial rescript on (T) KCT-YC021879, YC4/12/30, Yueh Chung-ch'i, where Yung-cheng wrote that he had turned capital discussion of Tibetan matters over to the Deliberative Council. In the same rescript, however, he mentions discussing the problem with the I Prince and Yueh Chung-ch'i. Another vermilion comment from two years later reveals that the emperor consulted both the Deliberative Council and three stalwarts in the field—Cha-lang-a, Mai-lu, and Yueh Chung-ch'i—on a Tibetan problem; see vermilion enclosure to (T) KCT-YC000670, YC6/3/23, Cha-lang-a. The sources do not make clear if the background files worked up by one group were made available when another body was subsequently summoned to similar tasks, but later discussion memorials (*i-fu tsou-che*) frequently reviewed previous correspondence on a topic, so at least the memorials, if not the drafts and files, were probably passed on.

115. (B) IFT CL15/7/23, p. 455, referring to a joint deliberation (with the Board of Punishments) on the Lü Liu-liang case, YC7/12. (For an explanation of the case, see ECCP, pp. 551–52, and other entries traceable from its index.)

116. YCSL 88/6b–7b. On the possible connection between the Deliberative Council and the Grand Council founding, see Teng and Wang, "T'an Chün-chi ch'u," p. 194; Fu Tsung-mao, *Ch'ing-tai Chün-chi ch'u*, p. 115; Pei Huang, *Autocracy at Work*, p. 16. The Ch'ien-lung Emperor abolished the Deliberative Council (*I-cheng*) title in CL56; see CLSL 1389/26b–27. Nevertheless, it was revived in the second half of the nineteenth century for Prince Kung and others; see SYCL 13/14.

117. On the palace memorial system, see the basic work by Silas H. L. Wu, "The Memorial Systems of the Ch'ing Dynasty, 1644–1911," *Harvard Journal of Asiatic Studies* 27 (1967): 7–75; idem, *Communication and Imperial Control*, esp. chaps. 5–7; Jonathan D. Spence, "Ts'ao Yin as the Emperor's Secret Informant," chap. 6 of *Ts'ao Yin and the K'ang-hsi Emperor: Bondservant and Master* (New Haven, 1966); Chuang Chi-fa, *Ch'ing-tai tsou-che chih-tu* (Taipei, 1979), which incorporates most of his findings from his earlier published articles. Some of my findings appear with illustrations in "Ch'ing Palace Memorials in the Archives of the National Palace Museum," *National Palace Museum Bulletin* 13, no. 6 (Jan.–Feb. 1979): 1–21. For a comparison of the published and archival versions of the Yung-cheng documents, see my "The Secret Memorials of the Yung-cheng Period (1723–1735): Archival and Published Versions," *National Palace Museum Bulletin* 9, no. 4 (Sept.–Oct. 1974): 1–14.

118. *Wen-hsien ts'ung-pien* 1 : 78; Chuang, "Ts'ung Ku-kung po-wu-yuan hsien-ts'ang kung-chung tang-an t'an Ch'ing-tai ti tsou-che," p. 46. See also (T) KCT-YC003761, YC1/9/16, Fu-te. For some K'ang-hsi strictures on palace memorial secrecy, see KHSL 275/19b–22.

119. These rough estimates are based on the number of surviving K'ang-hsi palace memorials for the last thirteen years of the reign as reproduced in *K'ang-hsi ch'ao Han-wen chu-p'i tsou-che hui-pien* (Beijing, 1985), vols. 2–6, and, for the Yung-cheng period, statements in Chao-lien, *Hsiao-t'ing tsa-lu* 1/11b–12, and Yang Ch'i-ch'ao, *Yung-cheng ti chi ch'i mi-che chih-tu yen-chiu*, 2d rev. ed. (Hong Kong, 1985), pp. 195–96 ("Tsou-che shu-liang"). The K'ang-hsi figure is probably somewhat smaller than the number originally submitted because until Yung-cheng came to the throne there was no requirement that the palace memorials be returned to the capital for storage in the archives; see YCSL 1/26b. The Yung-cheng figure is calculated from the number of Yung-cheng

palace memorials published in the *Chu-p'i yü-chih* (eight thousand) combined with Chao-lien's estimate that the published memorials for the period constituted between 30 and 40 percent of the total.

120. (B) IFT CL1/2/13, p. 171.

121. Imperial edict quoted in (T) KCT-YC013085, YC8/5/22, Hsien Te. For an explanation of the reference to "the board," see Appendix A.

122. Silas H. L. Wu, "Memorial Systems," pp. 44–46; CLSL 1/18b–19, 34b–35b. See also (B) SYT-FP CL1/5/16, p. 142, which urged education commissioners to report. An edict from the end of the century claimed that Yung-cheng had extended the palace memorial privilege not only to circuit intendants but to prefects and subprefects too; CCSL 40/22–23. Pei Huang has found an instance of a palace memorial from a first-class subprefect; see his "Shuo 'Chu-p'i yü-chih,'" *Ta-lu tsa-chih* 18, no. 3 (Feb. 1959): 75. Instances of such lower-level reports were extremely rare.

123. Robert N. Weiss, "Flexibility in Provincial Government on the Eve of the Taiping Rebellion," *Ch'ing-shih wen-t'i* 4, no. 3 (June 1980): 3–4.

124. The exact date of the Chancery's founding is not known, but one modern scholar has placed it in the early Yung-cheng years; see Hsiao, *Ch'ing-tai t'ung-shih* 1:867–68. On the Chancery, see Shan Shih-yuan, "Ch'ing-kung tsou-shih ch'u chih-chang chi ch'i tang-an nei-jung," *Ku-kung po-wu-yuan yuan-k'an* 1986, no. 1 (Feb. 1986): 7–12ff.

125. (T) KCT-YC014726, YC5/8/10, O-erh-t'ai. For a similar example, see the rescript on (T) KCT-YC000440, YC7/5/9, Yueh Chung-ch'i, enclosure 2, in which Yung-cheng wrote: "I have heard that this man [the district magistrate T'ien Yü-chih] is far from being any good."

126. (T) KCT-YC018965, YC7/10/28, Fu-t'ai.

127. (T) KCT-YC011822, undated, Hsu Jung. See also the rescript on (T) KCT-YC012111, YC5/2/8, Chang T'ing-yü and others. On concealments in the editing of the Yung-cheng–period memorials, see my "Secret Memorials of the Yung-cheng Period." Except for the first memorial listed in the previous note above and the two cited in notes 133 and 136 below whose rescripts were revised for publication in order to conceal the imperial maneuvers, all the excerpts from the vermilion rescripts quoted in the text and cited in notes 125 through 137 were kept out of the published edition of Yung-cheng memorials (*Chu-p'i yü-chih*).

128. *Ch'ing-shih lieh-chuan* (Taipei, 1964), 14:38b–39; YCSL 96/4b–7. An example of this policy is explained by Kent Clarke Smith in his "Ch'ing Policy and the Development of Southwest China: Aspects of Ortai's Governor-Generalship, 1726–1731" (Ph.D. diss., Yale University, 1971), pp. 32–33. For other instances, see Yung-cheng *Shang-yü Nei-ko*, YC5/12/9, p. 9; and (T) KCT-YC016932, YC8/11/18, Chao Kuo-lin. It should be noted that a palace memorial rescript such as "Let the board consider and memorialize" (*Kai-pu i-tsou*) did not necessarily send the document for outer-court discussion. The resulting deliberations could have been limited to the inner-court members of the board's directorate; see the explanation of this process in Appendix A.

129. (T) KCT-YC003761, YC1/9/16, Fu-te.

130. YCSL 29/4b, 83/36b–38.

131. For one of many examples, see (B) IFT YC11/10/6, p. 9. For some exceptional instances when a palace memorial was rescripted to go directly to a board, see (T) KCT-YC020603, YC1/3/8, Nien Keng-yao; and (T) KCT-YC003519, YC13/5/11,

Ch'i-k'e-hsin. On the restrictions on the use of palace memorials for official administrative purposes during the Yung-cheng period, see Silas H. L. Wu, "Memorial Systems"; Chuang, "Ts'ung Ku-kung po-wu-yuan hsien-ts'ang kung-chung tang-an t'an Ch'ing-tai ti tsou-che," p. 44. I am indebted to Mr. Chuang Chi-fa for discussing this point with me at length.

132. For examples of using the palace memorial system to examine and work out proposals before they went into effect, see Zelin, *The Magistrate's Tael*, on working out the *yang-lien* schedules, chaps. 4, 5, and passim.

133. Rescript on (T) KCT-YC010774, YC2/9/4, Ch'en Shih-kuan. This rescript may be profitably compared with its revision in the CPYC 2:922–23, where the imperial order to rewrite the memorial for board consumption was entirely omitted.

134. Rescript (intended for O-erh-t'ai, to whom the I Prince's deliberation was being sent) on the face of (T) KCT-YC014708, YC4/4/26, Yin-hsiang. See also (T) KCT-YC017559, YC4/8/29, Huang T'ing-kuei, whose rescripted statement, "Palace memorials cannot be the basis [for action]," makes clear that the palace memorials could not be sent to a board for official action.

135. Imperial rescript quoted in (T) KCT-YC014726, YC5/8/10, O-erh-t'ai.

136. (T) Rescript on KCT-YC019217, YC1/5/9, K'ung Yü-hsun. Compare with the modified version of the rescript in CPYC 1:191–92, where the emperor's board bypass was made less explicit. For other examples of early Yung-cheng suppressions of information for a board, see (T) KCT-YC004623, undated Yin-ssu memorial, probably from YC1 or 2; and (B) SYT-FP, YC1/2/26, p. 235.

137. Rescript on (T) KCT-YC021863, YC4/11/12, Yueh Chung-ch'i. This memorial and its rescript are in the *wei-lu* prepared-copies section of the Taipei holdings. Although such documents must be used with caution, the point at issue here is not likely to have been less clearly put in the original. Indeed, the original, if ever found, will probably add to our insights into Yung-cheng's board bypass practices. For a later occasion when Yung-cheng overrode board objections based on regulations, see (T) Ch'i-chü chu YC9/2/1, Board of War deliberation of a Hukwang governor-general's recommendation.

138. YCSL 148/11b–12b; (B) IFT CL4/4/21, pp. 133–35 (talking about a Yung-cheng use of *t'e*); Ying-ho, *En-fu t'ang pi-chi* (1837), 1/29b; (T) KCT-YC015106, YC1/3/2, Yang Lin. For the military allocations, see (T) Pien-pei i-ch'ing tang, vol. 3, CL13/J7/16, pp. 111–12, explaining Yung-cheng–period practices. For another example, see (T) Ch'i-chü chu, YC8/7/8 (the YCSL 96/8b–9 version of this document is slightly cut). For other explanations of the meaning of *t'e*, see (B) IFT CL4/4/21, pp. 133–35; and Wang Ch'ang, "Chün-chi ch'u t'i-ming chi" 14/19–20b. *T'e* could also be employed in routine-system documents; see (B) P'iao pu-pen shih, Book 2 (Boards of Revenue and Rites), p. 13b; and CLSL 71/12b–13.

139. For an exceptional occasion when an individual named in a draft rescript saw the emperor's alteration, see Chang T'ing-yü, *Nien-p'u* 4/22b. Doubtless Chang's inner-court position allowed this special access.

140. Rescript on (T) KCT-YC019384, YC5/12/18, Sai-leng-e.

141. YCSL 82/6a–b, 105/5b–14. On the Ch'ing-hai campaign, see YCSL 15/5b; Hsiao, *Ch'ing-tai t'ung-shih* 1:853–54; Howorth, *History of the Mongols* 1:523–25. On Yueh Chung-ch'i's relation to Nien Keng-yao, see (T) KCT-YC019190, YC3/7/25, Li Ju-po.

142. One of these took place in YC5 (1727); see (T) KCT-YC000076, YC7/7/10, Yueh Chung-ch'i.

143. (T) KCT-YC021700, YC1/9/30, Yueh Chung-ch'i.

144. Edict of YC7/7/29 cited in (T) KCT-YC000220, YC8/5/30, Yueh Chung-ch'i. The edict is in YCSL 83/36b–38, but the emperor's praise of General Yueh is omitted, possibly because the general was in disgrace when the Yung-cheng *Shih-lu* was edited. (On this last point, see note 147 below.)

145. (T) KCT-YC018027, YC7/8/25, Yueh Chung-ch'i. See also General Yueh's memorials in *Kung-chung tang Yung-cheng ch'ao tsou-che* 13:483–95.

146. (T) KCT-YC000556, YC7/9/29, Yueh Chung-ch'i.

147. See, for example, (T) KCT-YC000592, undated document probably of late YC5, vermilion addenda and enclosures. Vermilion writings such as this are in the archives today because Yueh, obeying the edict to send back all imperial rescripts, returned all the extra loose pages of vermilion writing sent to him as well. Despite the faithful return of so many memorials, General Yueh's papers did not appear in the CPYC, probably because he was in disgrace by the time that work was compiled. Thus, for his memorials we are dependent on archival holdings; the Taipei Palace Museum has about 450 of his palace memorials, some in the form of specially prepared *wei-lu* copies. For an explanation of the latter, see Chapter 2, n. 52, above, and "Secret Memorials of the Yung-cheng Period," pp. 5 and 4, fig. 1.

148. (T) KCT-YC000257, YC8/4/22, Yueh Chung-ch'i.

149. (T) KCT-YC000440, YC7/5/9, Yueh Chung-ch'i, enclosure 4.

150. Ibid., enclosure 9.

151. Ibid., enclosure 8.

152. Edict quoted in (T) KCT-YC000210, YC8/4/22, Yueh Chung-ch'i.

153. (T) KCT-YC021686, YC7/12/7, Yueh Chung-ch'i.

154. (T) KCT-YC000571, YC5/3/25, Yueh Chung-ch'i.

155. (T) KCT-YC000490, YC5/3/9, Yueh Chung-ch'i.

156. Huang Pei, "Shuo 'Chu-p'i yü-chih,'" p. 76; (T) KCT-YC015690, YC1/7/6, Yang Ming-shih; (T) KCT-YC016591-1, undated greetings memorial, Wang Kuo-tung. The emperor's concern for the circular stain is explained by the fact that the act of his writing on a provincial official's memorial transformed an ordinary report into an imperial document that Wang might well fear to have desecrated.

157. (T) KCT-YC000440, YC7/5/9, Yueh Chung-ch'i, enclosure 3. Although the emperor's strong feelings at the snowfall may seem overdone, in fact north China's dry climate and the belief in the imperial responsibility for good harvests may well have justified imperial feelings of exultation. On the imperial preoccupation with auspicious days, see Reginald F. Johnston, *Twilight in the Forbidden City* (New York, 1934), pp. 167–68.

158. Vermilion addition to (T) KCT-YC000592, undated court letter in Yueh Chung-ch'i's packet. I have not been able to identify Chou K'ai-chieh, who may have caught the imperial fancy because his given name meant "path to victory." Yung-cheng frequently sought a man's eight characters; for other examples, see *Kung-chung tang Yung-cheng ch'ao tsou-che* 10:88–89, 252. Mr. Chao Chung-fu suggested to me that this sort of request may not have been as superstitious as it sounds and was probably Yung-cheng's way of asking for a full dossier on a man.

159. (T) KCT-YC000592, enclosure 2. The Zunghar depredations may be those

mentioned in the imperial rescript on (T) KCT-YC006033, YC8/11/28, O-erh-t'ai, or in (B) IFT CL1/9/6, pp. 201–3 (retrospective view of the Yung-cheng–period campaign). For another lengthy Yung-cheng epistle to Yueh Chung-ch'i, see (T) KCT-YC000454, undated piece of vermilion writing.

CHAPTER 2. YUNG-CHENG'S INNER-COURT ASSISTANTS: PRINCE AND GRAND SECRETARY

1. For an English-language biography of the prince, see ECCP, pp. 923–25. This biography, written without access to archival sources, nevertheless penetrates further than many more recent analyses to describe the prince's early central role in Yung-cheng's government. For genealogical information, see *Ai-hsin chüeh-lo tsung-p'u*, comp. Chin Sung-ch'iao (Fengtien, 1938), 1:51 and passim. For a sketch of the facts of Prince I's life, see *Ch'ing huang-shih ssu-p'u*, comp. T'ang Pang-chih (Taipei, 1968), 3/15a–b, or the official biography in CS 5:3561–62.

2. See, for example, the tables of grand councillors in CS 4:2486 and Fu Tsung-mao, *Ch'ing-tai Chün-chi ch'u*, p. 529, where Prince I is named at the head of the lists. The space under the prince's name in the latter's chart, however, is left blank and fails to offer details of the prince's supposed service. See also ECCP, p. 924, and Teng and Wang, "T'an Chün-chi ch'u," p. 194. For a contrasting view, see Silas H. L. Wu, *Communication and Imperial Control*, pp. 30, 173n.24. The prince's name was omitted from the table in SYCL 15/1.

3. YCSL 94/2b. On similar suspensions in the Ming, see Ray Huang, *1587*, p. 8.

4. Rescript on (T) KCT-YC000257, YC8/4/22, Yueh Chung-ch'i.

5. The "eight years" may be explained by the fact that although the prince helped at the center of government for only a little over seven years (until the early days of his final illness in late YC7 and early YC8), Yung-cheng's mourning statements were made following the prince's death at a moment when nearly eight years had passed.

6. (T) YC SYT, YC8/5/7, pp. 29–35; YC8/5/14, pp. 53–57; YC8/5/18, pp. 61–63. This volume of the Shang-yü tang, which covers the years YC1–8, is devoted to edicts—thirty-nine in all—about the prince. Roughly half of the edicts (particularly the early ones) are in the YCSL; a few others have been published elsewhere, but many seem to be available only in this unique archival volume (of which apparently no duplicate is in the Beijing archives). Although some of the edicts in this record book may have been generated from court discussions, some read as if they had been specially copied from Yung-cheng's own vermilion writing, a fact that is demonstrated in one edict where the emperor states, in enumerating the prince's virtues, "My brush cannot write them all down"; see (T) YC SYT, YC8/5/14, pp. 53–57.

7. (T) YC SYT, YC8/5/7, pp. 29–35. For a similar statement, see (B) Lu-fu, Nei-cheng section, Li-i subsection, document 2, YC8/5/9, imperial edict.

8. *A-ch'i-na* is said to be a derogatory Manchu word for "cur"; see ECCP, p. 927, and Hsiao, *Ch'ing-tai t'ung-shih* 1:862. (For another meaning, see Fu Lo-ch'eng, *Chung-kuo t'ung-shih* [Taipei, 1972], 2:677.) Nevertheless, I have found no Manchu specialist who acknowledges this meaning or can identify any other. A recent publication of the Manchu Section of the Number One Archives in Beijing admits that the meaning of this sobriquet has not yet come to light; see *Kuan-yü Chiang-Ning chih-tsao Ts'ao-chia*

tang-an shih-liao, comp. Palace Museum Ming-ch'ing Archives Office (Peking, 1975), p. 213.

9. (T) YC SYT, YC8/5/7, pp. 29–35.

10. Ibid. On Yueh Chung-ch'i as in league with Nien Keng-yao, see also KCT-YC019190, YC3/7/25, Li Ju-pai.

11. At his father's death late in 1722 Yin-hsiang was only thirty-six years old, with many older brothers in a stronger position to mount a challenge for the throne. For the prince's role during the K'ang-hsi years, see Silas H. L. Wu, *Passage to Power*, pp. 114, 124; and YCSL 13/21b–22.

12. YCSL 1/5, 1/10, 2/17b.

13. YCSL 1/8b–9.

14. YCSL 2/28. On the Three Treasuries, see Sun, "The Board of Revenue," pp. 188–89, there called "Three Storehouses"; and HTSL 181/1ff.

15. YCSL 3/34–35. In YC2 the tax arrears up to KH50 (1711) were said to have amounted to 941,600 taels and were remitted in the belief that they were not collectable; see YCSL 21/2b. On Prince I's accomplishments at the Board of Revenue, see YCSL 10/5b–6b, 98/8–9. For the Audit Bureau, see the discussion in Chapter 1.

16. For a detailed exposition and analysis of the Yung-cheng financial reforms, see Zelin, *The Magistrate's Tael*.

17. (T) YC SYT, YC8/5/14, pp. 53–57; YC8/5/25, pp. 75–80. The figure is also given in CLSL 60/4b–6. See also (B) SYT-FP, undated review of treasury (*k'u*) accounts of CL40/1/29, pp. 101–5, 107–9, whose figures show a drop in treasury reserves of nearly one-third from KH58 (1719) to KH60 (1721)—that is, from the reign high of 47,368,645 taels to 32,622,421 taels within three years. (The KH61 [1722] figures are missing from this list). By YC1 (1723) the total had fallen further to 23,711,920 taels, amounting to a drop of 50 percent in four years. The final Yung-cheng–reign figure of 34,530,485 taels is close to Chao-lien's estimate of 30 million; see Chao-lien, *Hsiao-t'ing tsa-lu* 1/8b–9. For a comment on how the late K'ang-hsi tax arrears were reported in one Ch'ing official publication, see my "Secret Memorials of the Yung-cheng Period," pp. 7–8. For a lower estimate of the outstanding debt, see Silas H. L. Wu, *Communication and Imperial Control*, p. 69, which cites a Board of Revenue treasury debt of only approximately 3,000 taels.

18. The two combined were known as *p'ing-yü fan-shih yin*, sometimes shortened to *p'ing-fan*. On *p'ing-yü*, see HTSL 20/2; and Zelin, *The Magistrate's Tael*, pp. 68–69. Readers should note that I have specified that this is the Yung-cheng Emperor's account of the financial shortages. It is possible that after Prince I's death facts were shaded to downplay the prince's role in what some contemporaries regarded as a harsh dragnet laid for unpaid taxes. The matter needs further investigation. These imperial recollections of how the tax arrears cases were argued and handled are at variance with other accounts; I find it significant that others have not stressed imperial conversations with Prince I on the subject of the financial reforms that instituted the nourish-honesty (*yang-lien*) payments.

19. (T) YC SYT, YC8/5/14, pp. 53–57. For another example of Yung-cheng's strict constructionist position on tracing tax debts, see the rescript on (T) KCT-YC018725, YC3/7/24, Shih Wen-cho; and YCSL 98/8–9. Prince I's role is corroborated in *Pei-chuan chi*, comp. Ch'ien I-chi (Taipei, 1974), 1/18b–19; Yung-cheng *Shang-yü Nei-ko*

YC4/6/15; and CLSL 60/4b–6. See also YCSL 21/2b. For another imperial diatribe against malfeasance in financial matters, see (T) KCT-YC009845, YC7/3/22, Ma Chi-hsun.

20. (B) TP 782 *tsou-hsiao* 0007, YC2/2/10, Yin-hsiang [Prince I] and others. Many other routine memorials of this type are in these files. Submission in both Manchu and Chinese was required for board deliberation (*i-fu*) memorials; the Chinese read from right to left and the Manchu text was placed on the other side, reading from left to right. The emperor might rescript such a memorial in either language.

21. (B) TP 783 *tsou-hsiao* 00013, YC4/7/22, Yin-hsiang and others.

22. (B) TP 782 *tsou-hsiao* 00006, YC2/2/5, Yin-hsiang and others.

23. (T) YC SYT, YC8/5/25, pp. 75–80.

24. Memorial of itemization (*t'iao-tsou*) summarized in YCSL 16/10a–b.

25. Hsiao, *Ch'ing-tai t'ung-shih* 1 : 870–71.

26. (T) KCT-YC004720, YC3/12/23, Yin-hsiang and others.

27. Enclosure to (T) KCT-YC014709, YC3/12/23, Yin-hsiang and others. I identify the enclosure as derived from the prince because it is on a capital discussion of a financial subject and the memorialist speaks of the discussers as "[the officials of] my board [*ch'en-pu*]." Both deliberations were probably returned to the capital together by a provincial official to whom they had been sent so he could ponder their advice.

28. *Ch'ing huang-shih ssu-p'u* 3/15a–b. Sometimes the prince's title for this post is given as *Tsung-li shui-li ying-t'ien shih*; see Hsiao, *Ch'ing-tai t'ung-shih* 1 : 869–70; and *Yung-hsien lu* 4/303–4. On the I Prince's water conservancy work, see Timothy Brook, "The Spread of Rice Cultivation and Rice Technology into the Hebei Region in the Ming and Qing," in *Explorations in the History of Science and Technology in China*, ed. Hu Tao-ching (Shanghai, 1982), p. 674.

29. Yung-cheng *Shang-yü Nei-ko* YC4/8/15. The grand secretary Chu Shih was sent to assist Prince I in the Chihli water conservancy post and suceeded to this task on the prince's death in YC8 (1730). On Chu Shih's role, see his biography in ECCP, p. 189; YCSL 48/22; and (T) KCT-YC020069, YC6/3/1, Yin-hsiang. For a Ch'ien-lung–period review of the Yung-ting flood project, see (B) IFT CL15/6/24, pp. 383–86. Local gratitude for the I Prince's water conservancy efforts was recorded in (T) KCT-YC007482, YC8/6/3, Shu Hsi; and in (T) KCT-YC019871, unsigned and undated discussion memorandum, probably from YC8.

30. The rule of avoidance stipulated that an official might not serve in his home province.

31. (T) KCT-YC018174, YC4/11/15, Li Fu.

32. (T) YC SYT YC1/11/25, pp. 1–2. Most of this edict is also in YCSL 13/21b–22, but only about a dozen of the words quoted here appear in the *Shih-lu* version, the emperor's attack on his brothers being deemed unsuitable for future *Shih-lu* readers.

33. For the horizontal tablet, see YCSL 46/25b–27. See also YCSL 30/34–35; and (T) YC SYT YC4/7/21, p. 21.

34. (T) YC SYT YC8/9/6, p. 105.

35. (T) YC SYT YC1/11/25, pp. 1–2. The same edict appears in abbreviated form in YCSL 13/21b–22, but the material quoted here is omitted.

36. For some examples, see YCSL 13/21b–22, 13/27a–b, 35/22a–b, 87/34a–b, 88/9a–b; (T) YC SYT YC8/6/14, pp. 89–92; and CS 5 : 3561–62.

37. (T) YC SYT YC3/9/13, p. 13. For two occasions on which the prince accepted imperial largesse, see YCSL 6/8 and 17/19.

38. (B) Lu-fu, Nei-cheng section, li-i subsection, 2, YC8/5/7.

39. YCSL 13/21b–22.

40. YCSL 105/5b–14; for other dates claimed as the start of the campaign, see also YCSL 82/6a–b; and (T) KCT-YC000737, YC7/11/16, Cha-lang-a. See also YCSL 81/12b–14b.

41. (T) KCT-YC000592, unsigned and undated draft court letter with long vermilion addendum. My dating is derived from internal evidence. For a retrospective account concerning the prince's ability to hold the line on military prices, see (B) IFT CL1/3/24, pp. 251–54.

42. (T) KCT-YC000618, YC6/9/2, Yung-cheng; *Ch'ing huang-shih ssu-p'u* 3/15b. The establishment of the new office is described in Chapter 4.

43. For one of many references to this kind of activity, see (T) KCT-YC000076, YC7/7/10, Yueh Chung-ch'i.

44. YCSL 16/10a–b.

45. Some of these improvements may have been those referred to in (B) TP 896 00875, YC12/7/3, Chang T'ing-yü. In addition, the fact that a review of Board of Revenue treasury contents undertaken half a century later yielded records for only twenty-six of the sixty-one years of the K'ang-hsi reign but found all of the Yung-cheng figures intact may have been due to the I Prince's Board of Revenue incumbency in the Yung-cheng period; see (B) SYT-FP undated Grand Council memorandum of CL40/1/19, p. 119. Prince I's responsibility for the campaign financial records at the Military Finance Section during the Yung-cheng period may also have resulted in the survival of figures for those expenditures. For such figures, see (B) Lu-fu, Chün-wu section, Chün-hsu subsection, 5, undated late–Yung-cheng list; and (B) SYT-FP undated Grand Council discussion of CL26/2/10, pp. 119–22.

46. (T) KCT-YC010970, YC6/9/undated (in the CPYC this is dated YC6/9/2), Li Lan; (T) KCT-YC011471, YC7/9/17, Mai-chu; (T) KCT-YC003975, YC7/9/29, Te-shou.

47. This was a secret military planning conference with General Yueh; see (T) KCT-YC021879, memorial dated YC4/12/30 but rescripted in YC5, Yueh Chung-ch'i.

48. (T) KCT-YC000592, datable by internal evidence to late YC5. In December 1985 I was permitted to examine the earliest surviving Chinese-language court letters in the Beijing Number One Archives Court Letter (T'ing-chi) file. There the two earliest documents were dated YC6 and both placed the prince at the head of the list of hearers. These three documents are the earliest surviving court letters I have found in both the Beijing and Taipei archives. There exist, however, earlier references to what may have been court letters—we cannot be sure without finding and examining the originals. For such a reference, see, for example, *Shih-liao hsun-k'an*, comp. Palace Museum [Peiping], Bureau of Documents (repr. Taipei, 1963), *T'ien-liu* sec., 16b–17b. This point is discussed in Chapter 3. The prince's role in the court letter system is made clear in the early entries of Table 2.

49. (T) KCT-YC006083, YC7/2/24, O-erh-t'ai. There are many references to the I Prince forwarding imperial edicts; for early examples from the first year of the reign, see *Chang-ku ts'ung-pien*, comp. Palace Museum [Peiping], Bureau of Documents, (repr. Taipei, 1964), p. 223; and (T) KCT-YC007321, YC1/8/24, Chi Tseng-yun.

50. *Li-tai ching-chi k'ao* (repr. Taipei, 1959), 3:6828; *Kuo-li Ku-kung po-wu-yuan p'u-t'ung chiu-chi mu-lu*, comp. Palace Museum (Taipei, 1970), p. 57.

51. (T) YC SYT, YC8/5/7, pp. 29–35.

52. *Yung-cheng chu-p'i yü-chih pu-lu tsou-che tsung-mu* (Peiping, 1930), passim. During the Ch'ing some of Chang's memorials were packed in files marked "not to be published" (*pu-lu*); others were listed as "not yet published [but intended for eventual publication]" (*wei-lu*). For an explanation of these terms, see my "Secret Memorials of the Yung-cheng Period," pp. 2–5. Fewer than twenty-five of Chang's memorials are now indexed in the Palace Museum's file of palace memorials, all but four of these from the Yung-cheng period. (There is no memorialist index for the Museum's Grand Council reference collection, so it is possible that some of Chang's later memorials might be tracked down there.) Other Chang memorials are to be found in the Number One Archives in Beijing, in the palace memorial, palace memorial copies (*lu-fu*), and routine memorial files, but none of these files have author indexes. Chang may have been excused from returning his palace memorials for archival storage; on this question, see (T) KCT-KH001467, YC1/1/26, Kao Ch'i-cho, which quotes a Yung-cheng edict of KH61/11/27 exempting four notables of that year from the general requirement of returning the palace memorials to the capital files. Although Chang was not one of the four, the emperor may later have awarded him the same distinction. A few of Chang's memorials appeared in his chronological autobiography and other publications of his writings.

53. On Chang's family background and career, see the biography of his father in ECCP, pp. 64–65; Lo Hsiang-lin, "The History and Arrangement of Chinese Genealogies," in *Studies in Asian Genealogy*, ed. Spencer J. Palmer (Provo, Utah, 1972), pp. 22–24; and Hilary J. Beattie, *Land and Lineage in China: A Study of T'ung-ch'eng County, Anhwei, in the Ming and Ch'ing Dynasties* (New York, 1979). Chang's own biography is in ECCP, pp. 54–56.

54. Sugimura Yūzō, *Kenryū kōtei* (Tokyo, 1961), p. 45; *Ming-Ch'ing li-k'e chin-shih t'i-ming pei-lu* (Taipei, 1969), K'ang-hsi sec., p. 68b. Observe how the information on his low examination rank is glossed over in *Ch'ing-shih lieh-chuan* 14/21b and other biographies of Chang. Chang did not conceal this in his own autobiography but forthrightly stated that he had placed 152d in the third class of the palace examination; see *Nien-p'u* 1/5b. For the normal appointment expectations of new *chin-shih* degree holders, see HTSL 72/1a–b; and John R. Watt, *The District Magistrate in Late Imperial China* (New York, 1972), p. 50. I thank Jonathan Spence for his comments on this point.

55. *Ch'ing-shih lieh-chuan* 14/21b. Although Chang was not a high-level imperial favorite in the K'ang-hsi period, his rise began in that era. See R. Kent Guy, "Zhang Tingyu and Reconciliation: The Scholar and the State in the Early Qianlong Reign," *Late Imperial China* 7, no. 1 (June 1986): 57–60.

56. (B) SYT-FP YC1/1/6, p. 59. On being an imperial tutor, see Johnston, *Twilight in the Forbidden City*, pp. 180–95.

57. YCSL 2/32b, 9/26; HTSL 1049/11–13b; *Ch'ing-shih lieh-chuan* 14/21b–22; *Kuo-li Ku-kung po-wu-yuan p'u-t'ung chiu-chi shu-mu*, pp. 42–43; *Ch'ing Nei-ko k'u-chu chiu-tang chi-k'an mu-lu* 1/24a–b. Although Chang was not head of the K'ang-hsi *Shih-lu* editorial board at first, he eventually guided the project to completion.

58. ECCP, p. 56. The completion of the K'ang-hsi *Shih-lu* was celebrated on YC9/12/20; see YCSL 113/17–18.

59. YCSL 9/10–11, 87/26–28b.

60. Manchu rescript on (T) KCT-YC020421, YC13/12/2, Chang T'ing-yü (the published version of this memorial is in *Kung-chung tang Yung-cheng ch'ao tsou-che* 25:471–72, though it omits the Manchu half along with the Manchu rescript); Chang, *Nien-p'u* 4/1b; CLSL 295/5b–6; list of editorial board at front of *Ch'ing T'ai-tsu Nu-erh-ha-ch'ih shih-lu* (Peiping, 1933); (T) KCT-YC020496, YC13/11/15, Chang T'ing-yü and others.

61. YCSL 9/26, 82/5–6b; CS 4:2486, 2609. For some of the memorials on the K'ang-hsi tax arrears for which Chang directed the deliberations, see (B) TP 783 *tsou-hsiao* 00014, YC4/9/15; 00015, YC4/9/17; 00016, YC4/9/17; and 00018, YC4/9/18.

62. CS 4:2461; but see the different rendering in *Ch'ing-tai chih-kuan nien-piao* 1:39, as well as in (T) KCT-YC004720, YC3/12/23, Yin-hsiang.

63. *Ch'ing-shih lieh-chuan* 14/22. In fact, when Chang was made *Pao-ho tien* Grand Secretary in YC6 (1728), one higher designation, the *Chung-ho tien* Grand Secretary, existed; see YC *Hui-tien* 3/2. The latter title as abolished in CL13 (1749) because it had never been used in either the Ming or the Ch'ing periods; see CLSL 330/6–7; (B) Nei-ko Man p'iao-ch'ien pu-pen shih-yang (Li-pu), CL11/12/14; CC *Hui-tien* 2/1.

64. Yeh, *Nei-ko hsiao-chih*, pp. 2a–b, 11.

65. This was Fu-min; see (T) Ch'i-chü chu YC10/7/25, summarized in YCSL 121/19a–b.

66. YCSL 41/26b–27. The list in CS 4:2612–13 omits Chang as Board of Revenue president after his elevation to the Grand Secretariat.

67. See the list of Board of Revenue directorate members and their titles in (T) KCT-YC014708, YC4/4/26, Yin-hsiang and others. See also YCSL 47/7b and the board tables in CS 4:2610ff.

68. YCSL 83/29a–b; Chang T'ing-yü, *Nien-p'u* 2/15b, 18–19b, 25b–27b, 3/10; Hsi, *Nei-ko chih*, 9b, 18a–b, 25b–27b, 3/10. For a similar example concerning O-erh-t'ai, see YCSL 115/16a–b.

69. Chang T'ing-yü, *Nien-p'u* 2/19b; YCSL 115/15–16.

70. Chang T'ing-yü, *Nien-p'u* 3/10–15; YCSL 135/7b–8, 136/2a–b.

71. Chang T'ing-yü, *Nien-p'u* 2/18a–b. Another example from YC13 avers that a stated willingness to accept dismissal was in accordance with regulations; see 3/25a–b.

72. Chang T'ing-yü, *Nien-p'u* 2/19.

73. Sugimura, *Kenryū kōtei*, pp. 45–46; CS 5:4035; *Ch'ing-shih lieh-chuan* 14/36a–b; Chang T'ing-yü, *Nien-p'u* 3/1b–3b; YCSL 131/1b–2b.

74. Chang T'ing-yü, *Nien-p'u* 2/20.

75. Ibid., 2/23b. Although several of these statements appeared in Chang's own autobiography, they were no idle boasts. Chang would have known that his autobiography would someday be published by his family; he could not have falsely claimed a close relationship with the emperor without endangering his descendants. For examples of other edicts that Chang handled alone, see (T) Ch'i-chü chu, YC10/7/25 and YC13/1/4.

76. Hsiao, *Ch'ing-tai t'ung-shih* 1:884.

77. Yeh, *Nei-ko hsiao-chih*, p. 11b.

78. Chao I, *Yen-p'u tsa-chi* 1:1–2, 4; Chang T'ing-yü, *Nien-p'u* 3/9. See also CS 4:4033; imperial edict of YC11 quoted in Chang T'ing-yü, *Nien-p'u* 2/36b; (T) KCT-YC016725, YC7/12/15, Cha-lang-a; (T) Diary YC9/2/2 and YC10/3/1. Despite the profusion of evidence attesting to Chang's central role as primary edict drafter during

the middle– and late–Yung-cheng years, there are many references to edicts masterminded by others as well, particularly by O-erh-t'ai and Feng-sheng-e; see rescript on
(T) KCT-YC003898, YC10/10/7, Pan Shao-chou; and the extensive discussion of this
point in Chapter 3 below. An edict of the Ch'ien-lung period also claimed that Chang
had been the chief drafter of the imperial edicts in the previous reign; see CLSL
486/16b–17b. The earliest reference to an edict with which Chang was involved,
probably in both the deliberation and the drafting, was dispatched to O-erh-t'ai in YC5;
see *Shih-liao hsun-k'an, T'ien*, sec. 6:16b–17b.

    79. *Ch'ing-shih lieh-chuan* 14/22.

    80. For dated evidence of an inner-court concern for making storage copies of the
palace memorials, see the imperial rescript on (T) KCT-YC005998, YC7/11/7, O-erh-
t'ai. (On the reference to "the board" in this, see Appendix A at the end of this book.)
But note the statement in *Wen-hsien t'e-k'an* (Peiping, 1935), p. 19, where YC8 is given
as the reference collection start, doubtless because no earlier items had survived to the
time that article was written. For an example of reference collection storage methods
that used Chinese characters as symbols to identify the monthly memorial packets, see
the storage slip still attached to (B) Lu-fu 2188-10, YC10/1/22, Yueh Chung-ch'i.

    81. For an example, see the rescript and the edict quoted at the beginning of (T)
KCT-YC016203, YC6/10/2, Hu Ying; and (T) KCT-YC009108, YC5/11/9, K'ung
Yü-p'u.

    82. Chang T'ing-yü, *Nien-p'u* 3/25; (T) Ch'i-chü chu YC13/1/23; ECCP, p. 792.

    83. YCSL 20/25b–26; YC *Hui-tien* list of editors and other works' lists of editorial
boards. Yung-cheng–period official publications were also hindered by a reduction in
the staff of the Hanlin Academy; see YCSL 12/16–17b.

    84. (T) YC SYT, YC8/5/14, pp. 53–57.

    85. ECCP, p. 54; CLSL 963/17–20. On Chang's receiving the Imperial Ancestral
Hall honor, see (B) IFT YC13/8/25, pp. 19–21.

CHAPTER 3. THE INNER-COURT IMPERIAL DEPUTIES

    1. See, for example, a random selection of some of the many early–Yung-cheng
committees empaneled from time to time for special tasks: five men appointed in
YC1 to read examination papers and recommend how the candidates should be
appointed: Lungkodo, Chang T'ing-yü, Chang Po-hsing, Teng-te, and Chu Shih,
YCSL 13/17b–18; three men appointed in YC2 to consider troop allocations in Suchow:
Lungkodo, Chu Shih, and Chang T'ing-yü, YCSL 17/12b–14b; four men appointed
in YC5 to draft an edict to be sent to O-erh-t'ai: Ma-ch'i, Fu-ning-an, Chu Shih, and
Chang T'ing-yü, *Shih-liao hsun-k'an, T'ien* sec., 66b–67b. For comments on these early
committees and a view that differs slightly from that presented here, see Silas H. L. Wu,
Communication and Imperial Control, pp. 80, 173*n*.25. But for the fact that he was frequently
ill, Chu Shih might have been called on more regularly in these years; see (T) KCT-
YC000758, undated Chu Shih memorial of around YC6/5. In (T) YC SYT YC8/5/25,
pp. 75–80, it is said that Prince I was aided by Chang T'ing-yü and Chiang T'ing-hsi
in clearing the financial accounts and that Chu Shih was also occasionally involved.
For a later gathering in which Chu Shih participated, see the roster of the court letter
sent to O-erh-t'ai cited in (T) KCT-YC006033, YC8/11/28, O-erh-t'ai.

    2. For some of the many examples of these imperial expressions, see the imperial

rescripts on *Kung-chung tang Yung-cheng ch'ao tsou-che* 10:251–2 (YC6/4/15, Yueh Chung-ch'i); (T) KCT-YC021603, YC6/9/16, Yueh Chung-ch'i; (T) KCT-YC000300, YC7/6/3, Yueh Chung-ch'i; (T) KCT-YC000327, YC7/6/3, Yueh Chung-ch'i; (T) KCT-YC00076, YC7/7/10, Yueh Chung-ch'i; (T) KCT-YC017523, YC7/7/24, Huang T'ing-kuei; and (T) KCT-YC007920, YC7/9/22, Hsien-te. Yung-cheng occasionally used other appellations, such as "court officials" (*t'ing-ch'en*); see (T) KCT-YC000293, YC7/7/10, Yueh Chung-chi. Although none of the foregoing identifies "the grand secretaries" or "the others" as the grand secretaries Chang T'ing-yü and Chiang T'ing-hsi, the fact that these two were repeatedly grouped together—frequently with a third person such as Prince I or Ma-erh-sai—for both edict drafting and deliberations indicates that the "grand secretaries" and "other" references are indeed to these two. On Yung-cheng's use of "the board," see Appendix A of this book.

3. (T) YC SYT YC8/9/6, p. 105.

4. *Pei-chuan chi* 22/18; (B) Court letters of YC10/8/1 and 3. (These court letters are not reproduced in the *Shih-lu*.) I was first able to examine the Beijing archives' court letter holdings—which proved to be essential to the findings of this chapter—in the autumn of 1985; I am grateful to Philip A. Kuhn for alerting me to the fact that by 1985 these materials had been sorted and were being made available for research, and to Yale University's A. Whitney Griswold Fund for contributing to the research and travel expenses of the trip. On the background to the Su-chou conversations with Cha-lang-a, see (B) Lu-fu 2161-2, YC10/7/24, Cha-lang-a.

5. For the Board of Revenue directorate, see Chapter 2 above. See also, for example, (T) KCT-YC011847, YC3/8/16, Yin-hsiang and others. See also Figure 4 and CS 4:2610–13. On the early deputies' Board of Revenue connection, see Fu Tsung-mao, *Ch'ing-tai Chün-chi ch'u*, pp. 122–23. On Yung-cheng's concern for the complexities of Board of Revenue work, see YCSL 10/5b–6b. For a biography of Chiang T'ing-hsi in English, see ECCP, pp. 142–43.

6. (T) KCT-YC014709, YC3/12/23, Yin-hsiang (Prince I) and others.

7. YCSL 105/5b–14 specifies that the teamwork of the I Prince "and others" on "military finance" began in YC4 (1726). Other references do not make the date so clear; see YCSL 81/12b–14b, 82/5–6b; (T) KCT-YC000737, YC7/11/16, Cha-lang-a. One set of surviving northwest campaign financial records, which the combined Board of Revenue team might have been responsible for, dates from YC5; see (B) SYT-FP undated memorandum, CL26/2/10, pp. 119–22. Some have taken the YC4 teamwork reference as the Grand Council founding date; for an example, see Li Tsung-t'ung, "Pan-li Chün-chi ch'u lueh-k'ao," pp. 4–5.

8. (T) KCT-YC007376, YC6/1/19, Chi Tseng-yun. (The court letter, described as a *lai-tzu*, contained an edict dated YC5/12/23.)

9. (T) KCT-YC000592, undated but from internal evidence estimated to be from late YC5; (T) KCT-YC021953, YC5/10/21, Yueh Chung-ch'i; (T) KCT-YC021521, YC6/5/4, Wang T'ang.

10. (B) Court letter, YC6/5/6.

11. YCSL 81/12b–14b.

12. Ma-erh-sai (sometimes Marsai), inheritor of the dukedom of his famous grandfather T'u-hai—who had himself been a grand secretary and general in the K'ang-hsi era—was appointed grand secretary on YC6/8/7; see YCSL 72/8a–b, CS 4:2462. The exact beginning of his inner-court service is not clear; being a grand secretary would

not necessarily have required inner-court attendance. On YC7/5/10 Yung-cheng honored Prince I, Chang T'ing-yü, and Chiang T'ing-hsi for their inner-court service without mentioning Ma-erh-sai (YCSL 81/12b–14b), but this may have been because he had started too recently to have been honored so soon; alternatively, in view of his later disgrace, the *Veritable Records* entry may have been edited to omit his name. His official biography gives YC8 as the earliest date of his inner-court participation in military campaign supervision—at that time he was jointly engaged with Chang T'ing-yü and Chiang T'ing-hsi; see CS 5:4097; also CS 4:2486 and Chang T'ing-yü, *Nien-p'u* 2/22a–b. Archival sources, however, suggest earlier inner-court responsibilities. Yüeh Chung-ch'i spoke of having received a court letter from the I Prince and Ma-erh-sai during YC7/1; reference in (T) KCT-YC000309, YC7/9/29, Yüeh Chung-ch'i. Cha-lang-a cited a court letter dated YC7/6/6 for which Ma-erh-sai had been lead drafter along with the other two grand secretaries; reference in (T) KCT-YC009754, YC7/11/4, Cha-lang-a. Another archival reference dates a court letter in which Ma-erh-sai was involved to YC7/11/16; see (T) KCT-YC016725, YC7/12/15, Cha-lang-a.

13. Yeh, *Nei-ko hsiao-chih*, pp. 1b, 2a–b, 9b–10b, 11a–b, 16a–b. See also Hsi Wu-ao's description of the inner deputies' inner-court status in *Nei-ko chih*, pp. 3–4. During the late Ming and Ch'ing, grand secretaries were frequently called "prime ministers"; note, for example, the title of the work listing the Ch'ing grand secretaries with brief biographies of each, *Hsi-ch'ao tsai-fu lu* (Record of prime ministers of the glorious dynasty), comp. P'an Shih-en (n.p., 1838). For a classic statement of the Grand Secretariat origin of the Grand Council, see Chao I, *Yen-p'u tsa-chi* 1:1. Without the Board of Revenue analysis, many of the documents of the time cannot be correctly understood; see Appendix A of this book. The analysis presented here has benefited both from the ground-breaking work on the sources by Silas H. L. Wu and my own subsequent archival access in both Taipei and Beijing.

14. Ma-erh-sai did not do well at the front. In YC11 he was court-martialed and executed in front of the army for failures in campaign leadership; see ECCP, p. 265.

15. Chang T'ing-yü, *Nien-p'u* 3/9b. The notice in SYCL 2/1a–b that as of YC10/2 Chang T'ing-yü and O-erh-t'ai were to be "in charge of military affairs" (*pan-li chün-chi shih-wu*) may well refer to O-erh-t'ai's new appointment at about this time. For biographic information on O-erh-t'ai, see ECCP, pp. 601–3; Smith, "Ch'ing Policy"; and Hsiao, *Ch'ing-tai t'ung-shih* 1:883–84. For information about some of O-erh-t'ai's writings, see Wang Shan-tuan, "Yung-cheng chu-p'i tsou-che lueh-shu," in *Wen-hsien chuan-k'an* (Peiping, 1944), *lun-shu* sec. pp. 63–64.

16. This Feng-sheng-e is not to be confused with another eighteenth-century figure who had the same Manchu name (rendered differently in Chinese characters) and who is the man described in ECCP, p. 221. For the characters of the man referred to here, see the index-glossary at the end of this book. Early in YC9, Feng-sheng-e succeeded to the new title of "Heroic and Sincere Duke of the Highest Degree" (*Ch'ao-teng Ying-ch'eng kung*), an honor that had probably just been posthumously bestowed on his famous ancestor Yang-ku-li (Yangguri) in support of the grandson's new inner-court position; YCSL 104/18. For Yangguri, see ECCP, pp. 898–99.

17. For Manchu-language discussions headed by Feng-sheng-e, see (B) Manchu Chün-wu IFT, vols. for YC8 and 9. These volumes show that during YC9/8–9 after Ma-erh-sai left for the front, Feng-sheng-e directly succeeded to one of his most important responsibilities: managing the Manchu-language deliberations. At first both Ma-

erh-sai and Feng-sheng-e headed various rosters; then after 9/9/8 all rosters were headed by Feng-sheng-e; see (B) Manchu *lu-fu* memorial, *Nei-cheng chih-kuan* category, of YC9/11/5, a court discussion of Mongol horses for campaign use with Feng-sheng-e in charge. For Feng-sheng-e's role managing the Chinese-language discussions, see (B) IFT YC11/2. For Feng-sheng-e's name at the head of the rosters of the Chinese-language court letters, see the court letters beginning in YC9/9/8 in Table 2 at the end of this chapter and in (B) Lu-fu 2188-5 (reference to a document of YC9/10/1), 2188-7 (YC9/10/7), 2188-8 (YC9/11/14), 2188-10 (YC9/12/14), and 2188-12 (YC10/12/12). Unfortunately, nearly all the Chinese-language deliberation and court letter rosters in which Feng-sheng-e was involved list only the leading figure and refer to subordinates not by name but only with the dismissive phrase "and others"; my scan of the Manchu records likewise failed to turn up the names of subordinate parties to the deliberations.

18. YCSL 124/2.
19. YCSL 159/19b–20.
20. (T) Ch'i-chü chu, YC13/10/8.
21. The CS official tables distinguish clearly between the inner deputies and the next echelon, for the inner deputies are not usually identified—in the manner of the high officials—as having had a primary assignment as "High Officials in Charge of Military Finance (or Strategy)" (*Pan-li chün-chi ta-ch'en*). O-erh-t'ai's appointment, for instance, which was made after the high officials had come into being, is described as "handling military matters" (*pan-li chün-chi shih-wu*); the name of the high officials' (or strategists') group was not used; CS 4:2486. An earlier notice in the same table speaks of Chang T'ing-yü's inner-court appointment as "the imperial order to handle military finance in secret" (*ming mi-pan chün-hsu i-ying shih-i*), and of Chiang T'ing-hsi's similarly (*mi-pan chün-hsu shih-i*); CS 4:2486. For some of the notices clearly identifying others as attached to the next echelon (*tsai Pan-li Chün-chi ch'u hsing-tsou*) rather than to the inner deputies, see for example Ha-yuan-sheng (YC10/10–11): CS 4:2486, 5:4104; Ma-lan-t'ai (YC11/2): CS 4:2486; Fu-p'eng (YC11/4–7): CS 4:2486; No-ch'in (YC11/11 or 12): CS 4:2486, 5:4116, YCSL 137/12b; Pan-ti (YC11/11): CS 4:2486, 5:4206. The CS distinctions should be heeded: those tables were compiled during the Ch'ing, the early ones probably during the eighteenth century. By ignoring these, compilers of tables other than those in the official history have greatly confused our understanding of the Yung-cheng situation; see Fu Tsung-mao, *Ch'ing-tai Chün-chi ch'u*, pp. 529–35; and *Ch'ing-tai chih-kuan nien-piao* 1:136. Although Liang Chang-chü's compendium wisely omitted most of the second level of advisers for the Yung-cheng period, the factual information in his tables for the beginning years is so sparse as to be almost useless; see SYCL 2/1, 15/1, 15/5. See also Chang T'ing-yü, *Nien-p'u* 3/23b, where it is related that when in YC11 the emperor distributed inkstones to the High Officials in Charge of Military Strategy (*Pan-li Chün-chi ta-ch'en*), his son Chang Jo-ai received one but Chang T'ing-yü did not, thus showing that the two men did not belong to the same group. For further information on this point, see Chapter 4, n. 51.

22. There appear to be no conveniently grouped archival sources for studying K'ang-hsi–period documents of deliberation, whether of the routine or the palace system. When I was at the Number One Archives in Beijing I was told that the K'ang-hsi files are not so organized and there are "no record books of deliberation documents [I-fu tang] of any kind for the period"; conversation with Mr. Liu Kuei-lin, Oct. 1980. Moreover, almost none of the surviving provincial palace memorials of the last five years

of the K'ang-hsi reign was rescripted for deliberation; see *K'ang-hsi ch'ao Han-wen chu-p'i tsou-che hui-pien*, vol. 8. Deliberations from officials attached to capital offices were permitted only from KH51 (1712) (Silas H. L. Wu, "Memorial Systems," p. 42), but the practice appears to have developed slowly.

23. Many statements of the K'ang-hsi and Yung-cheng eras claim that provincial palace memorials were submitted directly to the emperor without advance screening at the capital. The inner deputies were frequently asked to scan and advise before the capital deliberations went to the emperor.

24. For some of many examples, see the imperial rescript on *Kung-chung tang Yung-cheng ch'ao tsou-che* 11:360–63, YC6/9/16, Yueh Chung-ch'i and Hsi-lin. The rescript explains that the deliberation is being sent to Yueh. See also the rescripts on (T) KCT-YC012111, YC5/2/8, Chang T'ing-yü and others; and on (T) KCT-YC000299, YC7/7/16, Yueh Chung-ch'i.

25. I am grateful to Mr. T'ang Jui-yü of the Taipei Palace Museum for allowing me to examine this box. The box contains memorials now numbered (T) KCT-YC019792–19910, originally packet (*pao*) 518, in crate (*hsiang*) 77. The box, larger than the memorial caskets used for communicating via memorial messenger, measures 1 foot long, $6\frac{1}{4}$ inches wide, and $6\frac{1}{2}$ inches high; it had two hinges and a lock (the keys are now missing). Although most of the items in the box are undated, cross-checking permits a tentative date of YC6–10. Despite the inscription on the box, in using these documents I have not assumed that all emanated from the I Prince—some are clearly of too late a date. Of the few slips identifying the authors, most named Prince I "and others," or individuals such as Chang T'ing-yü, Chiang T'ing-hsi, and Ma-erh-sai. There was also one slip submitted by Yin-t'ai "and others," and one attributable to O-erh-t'ai.

26. On the northwest, see (T) KCT-YC019834, 19837, 19841, 19877, 19884, 19903, and 19905, for example; on the southwest, (T) KCT-YC019878, 19879, 19902—all unsigned, undated.

27. On prices, see (T) KCT-YC019805; on taxes, (T) KCT-YC019850, 19866; on water conservation, (T) KCT-YC019853, 19871; on grain shipments, (T) KCT-YC019842; and on *yang-lien* payments, (T) KCT-YC019792, 19833, 19885, 19891, 19901—all unsigned, undated.

28. On the sea god temple, see (T) KCT-YC019819; on tomb sacrifice costs, (T) KCT-YC019804; on local magistrate appointments, (T) KCT-YC019849; and on examination travel expenses, (T) KCT-YC019840—all unsigned, undated.

29. (T) KCT-YC019842, unsigned, undated.

30. (T) KCT-YC019853, 19871, unsigned, undated. For the base, see (T) KCT-YC019069, YC8/1/10, K'ung Yü-hsun.

31. (T) KCT-YC019877, unsigned, undated.

32. (T) KCT-YC000618, YC6/9/2, Yueh Chung-ch'i. The second enclosure should be read first. Although the enclosures were neither signed nor dated, their form is the same as the other "memorialized comments" in the box of inner-circle memoranda. When imperially authorized, these recommendations of inner-circle officials had the force of an imperial edict and were dispatched to provincial officials with the expectation that they would be obeyed. Thus sometimes the rescripts on discussion reviews have to be read with care; in many instances they addressed not the authors of the memorial of

deliberation but the provincial officials to whom the recommendation was about to be sent.

33. On the meaning of "fold" and for an explanation of the physical characteristics of memorials, see my "Ch'ing Palace Memorials," frontispiece.

34. (T) KCT-YC019892, unsigned, undated; KCT-YC008879, Yang K'un, YC7/4/ no day. Although Yang K'un's memorial appears in the Yung-cheng *Chu-p'i yü-chih* 7:4225–26, Yang's citation of the YC6/8 edict was not included.

35. (T) KCT-YC019802, unsigned, undated; KCT-YC008877, Yang K'un, YC7/4/ no day.

36. (T) KCT-YC019895, unsigned, undated; KCT-YC017297, Yang K'un, YC7/4/ no day. For assistance in deciphering the imperial scribbles and scrawls in the rescripts of this and the following memorials, I thank Wang Ching-hung, Librarian at the Palace Museum.

37. (T) KCT-YC019894, unsigned, undated; (T) KCT-YC008878, YC7/4/no day, Yang K'un. For other similar pairs of base memorial and deputies' considerations in the archives, compare (T) KCT-YC011799, YC7/11/20, Hsu Jung, and its enclosure; (T) KCT-YC009761, YC7/12/11, Cha-lang-a and Wu Ko, and the discussion, (T) KCT-YC019832, undated deliberation on Ma-erh-sai and others; and (T) KCT-YC017860, YC7/11/20, Wang Shih-chün, and its deliberation, (T) KCT-YC019840, undated and unsigned. I have not been able to discover Wei Ching-kuo's transgression. Late in the K'ang-hsi reign he was appointed Hukuang provincial commander-in-chief; CS 1:113.2. By early Yung-cheng times he held a military post in Chihli.

38. Edict of YC10/3/1 in preface to the CPYC.

39. (T) KCT-YC000592, Yueh Chung-ch'i, dated only by the month and day, "12/10," but probably YC5/12/10. There may have been court letter prototypes written in Manchu, but the evidence is far from conclusive. For a possible ancestor, see (B) SYT-FP YC1/2/24, p. 117, which possesses some court letter features and which may originally have been in Manchu. The Manchu-language record books of court letters date only from YC11 (but the titles of other Manchu record books that no longer survive suggest that their edicts on the northwest campaign may well have been court letters); see (B) Ch'ing-ch'a ko-tang chi-tsai pu.

40. See Table 2 at the end of this chapter. At the beginning of YC3 the emperor announced that he had two ways of communicating his views to the provinces: the board might transmit an edict or he could write a secret rescript; see YCSL 29/14b–15. The passage is difficult to interpret: possibly Yung-cheng's reference to "the board" signifies edicts discussed with the officials of any appropriate board; but the term may indicate that he was already using his two or three favorites in the Board of Revenue directorate. Despite this entry, however, early references to what may be court letters or their prototypes lack some of the characteristics of the developed form of this type of edict. See, for example, *Shih-liao hsun-k'an* 36–37, which quotes an imperial decree of YC5/4/26 dispatched to the governor-general O-erh-t'ai and possesses a roster of four high dignitaries: the grand secretary Ma-ch'i, Fu-ning-an, Chu Shih, and Chang T'ing-yü. Although the form and terminology are not exactly the same as in the later court letters, neither were these completely worked out in other early examples.

41. Rescript on *Kung-chung tang Yung-cheng ch'ao tsou-che* 17:410–12, YC8/12/29, Yueh Chung-ch'i.

42. The closing formula was *Ch'in-tz'u tsun-chih chi-hsin ch'ien-lai*. Other designations included *mi-cha* (YCSL 87/18b–19), *mi-yü* (rescript on [T] KCT-YC000257, YC8/4/22, Yueh Chung-ch'i), and *mi-tzu* ([T] KCT-YC009754, YC7/11/14, Cha-lang-a). *T'ing-chi* seems to be a later designation. The characters *tzu* and *chi* were used very freely in the terminological flux of the Yung-cheng period. On one occasion Yung-cheng even referred to his own rescript as a *tzu* (*Chang-ku ts'ung-pien*, pp. 77b–78), yet elsewhere he used the same character to designate the new edict form. For a later document from the Taipei archives that was only a letter sent to the Grand Council by a high official yet is called a *tzu-chi*, the term often used for court letters, see (T) CCT-CL007889, CL17/12/20. Other documents from the Yung-cheng and later periods show *tzu-hsin*, *tzu-chi*, and *chi-tzu* also used to describe not imperial communications but ordinary letters between officials or family members. See, for example, the references in (T) KCT-YC007607, YC4/10/25, Li Wei; (T) KCT-YC011525, YC7/9/17, Mai-chu; (T) KCT-YC013373, YC8/6/3, Kao Ch'i-cho; (T) KCT-YC019878, unsigned and undated; (T) KCT-YC016172, YC10/9/13, Liu Yü-i; (T) KCT-YC020597, YC1/5/3, Nien Keng-yao; (T) I-tsou tang CL15/9/16, pp. 31–32; and (T) CCT-CC047732, enclosure to CCT-CC047731, CC21/6/7. Further evidence of the informality of the lateral communication feature of the court letters can be observed at the end of the earliest Beijing example, dated YC6/5/6, where a short homily on upright official behavior followed directly after the end of the edict. Because its text was not elevated one space, however, we know that it was not part of the edict; accordingly, it must have been added by the roster officials—the I Prince and Chang T'ing-yü. Thus, even though the term *tzu-chi* was employed, the earlier documents referred to in Silas H. L. Wu's *Communication and Imperial Control* (p. 81, bottom paragraph) were not true court letters but were probably prototypes or early forms from when some sort of new inner-court edict system was being worked out. Those cited from the *Chang-ku ts'ung-pien*, pp. 39–42, were short directives received and transmitted by eunuchs; these short messages do not possess the characteristics of true court letters: there is no evidence that a group of edict drafters discussed them with the emperor, made drafts of the edicts, and then submitted them to the emperor for review, or that they were imperially corrected. The document that Professor Wu cites from Antonio Sisto Rosso, *Apostolic Legations to China of the Eighteenth Century* (South Pasadena, Calif., 1948), pp. 307–9, has as its addressees not provincial officials but missionaries. I have examined this document in the Wason Collection at Cornell University and find that it in no way resembles the archival court letters. I am grateful to Dr. Diane Peruschek, then Curator of the Wason Collection, for allowing me to inspect this document. Court letter forms were said to have been fixed by Chang T'ing-yü; see Chao I, *Yen-p'u tsa-chi* 1 : 3–4. Note that there was a special form, not illustrated in this book, for lower-level court letters to the provincial lieutenant governors and judicial commissioners; for an example, see (T) KCT-YC003898, YC10/10/7, P'an Shao-chou.

43. For one of many examples of a vermilioned court letter, see (B) Court letter of YC10/11/11, addressed to Huang T'ing-kuei and Hsien-te. A court letter edict with more than one addressee whose draft had been subjected to vermilion amendments would of course have to be sent to some addressees as copies rather than in the original. In this case the vermilion additions might be incorporated in the copies, or they could be deemed intended for only one addressee and omitted from the other copies. For an example of the latter, see (T) KCT-YC016724, YC7/12/15, Cha-lang-a, which quotes

back much of (T) KCT-YC000469, YC7/11/18; only parts of the vermilion addition from the original court letter, however, most of which was meant only for Yüeh Chung-ch'i, were quoted in Cha-lang-a's version. For an example of a Yung-cheng–period generally circulated court letter, see the reference in (T) KCT-YC009754, YC7/11/14, Cha-lang-a. The edict mentioned in (T) KCT-YC019849, unsigned and undated memorandom, may also have been of this type.

44. For an example of a memorial that quotes a vermilion addition to a court letter, calling it "vermilion edict" (*chu-p'i yü-chih* in this case), see (T) KCT-YC000172, YC7/12/27, Yüeh Chung-ch'i, quoting from the vermilion addition on the face of (T) KCT-YC000469, edict of YC7/11/18.

45. YCSL 87/18b–19. There is a longer version in Yung-cheng *Shang-yü Nei-ko*, same date.

46. Yung-cheng frequently added "specially edicted" (*t'e-yü*), meaning that the edict was not to be precedent-making, at the end of a court letter; for an example, see the court letter quoted in *Kung-chung tang tsou-che Yung-cheng ch'ao* 17:42–44, YC8/9/24, Cha-lang-a. For a fuller explanation, see Chapter 1, n. 138, above.

47. Reference to a court letter dated YC5/12/23 referred to in (T) KCT-YC007376, YC6/1/19, Chi Tseng-yun; (B) Court letter, YC6/5/6.

48. Archival versions of Yung-cheng–period court letters are to be found in both Taipei and Beijing. With one exception, the eighteen surviving Taipei court letters are all fairly early, beginning in late YC5 and running only through YC9. All but one of the Taipei examples were dispatched to General Yüeh Chung-ch'i and returned by him for storage with his palace memorials. The far larger number (forty-six) of Yung-cheng–period Chinese-language original court letters in Beijing are stored in packages known as "Palace Court letter packets" (Kung-chung t'ing-chi pao), for which there are twenty for the Yung-cheng reign, the earliest dated YC6. In addition, the *Veritable Records* and contemporary documents such as palace memorials have many references to court letters whose originals cannot at present be located. Neither repository possesses any K'ang-hsi–era court letters nor any originals in Manchu. Beginning in CC2 (1797), grand councillors' names were omitted from the court letter rosters; see *Ch'ing-ch'ao Hsu Wen-hsien t'ung-k'ao* (1921; repr. Taipei, 1965), 5:8774.

49. YCSL 87/26–28b. See also the discussion of this point in Chapter 2.

50. (T) KCT-YC000463, YC9/3/5, Yüeh Chung-ch'i. For another example, see (B) Court letter of YC11/10/4, which cites the "recommendations of court officials" (*t'ing-ch'en i*) that Cha-lang-a consult with others and decide which rebels should be executed at the front and which brought to the capital. Yung-cheng frequently spoke directly to the capital-based edict roster members in these edicts, particularly when instructing them to dispatch the message, as in: "You [pl.: *erh-teng*] are to send this court letter...." That discussion by experts was behind court letter drafts is further attested by the court letters based on deliberations of the Miao Council, a committee formed late in the Yung-cheng reign to oversee the campaign against the Miao in the southwest. For examples, see YCSL 118/7b–8 and adjacent documents.

51. Fu Lo-shu, *A Documentary Chronicle of Sino-Western Relations (1644–1820)* (Tucson, 1966), 1:151, 2:495n.425, 512n.49. Cha-pi-na is not named in the rosters after YC9 because he died in that year. For a reference to a lost court letter bearing the name of still another participant, O-shan, in the drafting discussions, see (T) Ch'i-chü chu YC9/1/14, edict on sending money to the northwest front. (O-shan was about to be sent

on a mission to the northwest.) A shortened version of this edict is in YCSL 102/13b–15. One roster for a court letter that has not survived, but is mentioned in another report, named Chu Shih in addition to the three inner deputies of the day, Ma-erh-sai, Chang T'ing-yu, and Chiang T'ing-hsi; (T) KCT-YC006033, YC8/11/28, O-erh-t'ai.

52. L. Petech, *China and Tibet in the Early XVIIIth Century: History of the Establishment of Chinese Protectorate in Tibet* (Leiden, 1972), p. 23; CS 1:109.6; (T) KCT-TC000592, undated court letter sent to Yüeh Chung-ch'i; YCSL 117/10; (B) Manchu Hsun-ch'ang IFT YC9/7/2, discussion headed by A-ch'i-t'u; (B) Court letter of YC10/1/26; and (T) SYT-FP CL52/1/25, p. 121. In YC10, A-ch'i-t'u was cashiered and exiled on the frontier.

53. CS 4:2603–21; and YCSL 133/6b. See also Fu Lo-shu, *A Documentary Chronicle* 1:124, 151, 165–6; 2:495*n*.425, 520*n*.96. T'e-ku-t'e was cashiered in YC11; YCSL 133/6b.

54. CS 5:4053; YCSL 2/27a–b, 40; ECCP, p. 12. At the end of his life the Yung-cheng Emperor appointed Mang-ku-li to the Office of Military Strategy, but he was dropped as soon as the Ch'ien-lung Emperor came to the throne; CLSL 5/42a–b.

55. CS 4:2619–24; YCSL 95/10b. See also (B) IFT YC11/7/2, pp. 3–4; and (T) KCT-YC020508, YC13/9/28, Hai-wang.

56. (T) KCT-YC000470, YC8/12/28.

57. YCSL 116/2b.

58. Tu Lien-che, *Kuan-yü Chün-chi ch'u*, pp. 17–18. See also Fu Tsung-mao, *Ch'ing-tai Chün-chi ch'u*, pp. 340ff., where the section on the Yung-cheng court letters is based on assumptions derived from his observation of the Ch'ien-lung–period tie between the Grand Council and this type of document. Before the award of the seal in YC10, a court letter was usually entered in the *Veritable Records* as "Edict to the Grand Secretaries" (*Yü Ta-hsüeh-shih teng*); after the seal had been granted, the new nomenclature "Edict to the High Officials in Charge of Military Strategy" (*Yü Pan-li Chün-chi ta-ch'en*) was usually employed. For an example from before the granting of the seal, compare (B) Court letter of YC10/1/28, marked drafted by "O-erh-t'ai and others," and YCSL 114/15a–b, where the same edict was headed "Edict to the Grand Secretaries." Even the first court letter discussed by the enlarged roster that included the high officials, (T) KCT-YC000470, was marked in the *Veritable Records* as an edict to the grand secretaries; see YCSL 101/19b–20. But there were exceptions, particularly in works not scrutinized and made uniform by the *Veritable Records* editors. Compare, for instance, the various terms used to refer to the early court letter (T) KCT-YC000469, YC7/11/18. Although the roster of its archival version named "the I Prince and others," in its *Veritable Records* version it was rendered as "Edict to the Grand Secretariat" (*Yü Nei-ko*; YCSL 88/17-18b), while a memorialized reference to the same edict called it "a lateral communication from the Board of Revenue" (*Hu-pu tzu*, probably meaning that it was drafted or discussed by the Board of Revenue triumvirate, Prince I, Chang T'ing-yü, and Chiang T'ing-hsi); (T) KCT-YC016724, YC7/12/15, Cha-lang-a. For other usages of this sort, see (T) KCT-YC000066, YC7/12/7, Yüeh Chung-ch'i; and (T) KCT-YC000226-1, YC8/6/19, Yüeh Chung-ch'i. Compare also the imperial edict of YC9/11/6 in the *Veritable Records*, where this edict is identified as "Edict to the Grand Secretaries," with the Yung-cheng *Shang-yü Nei-ko* version, which was headed "Edict to the High Officials in Charge of Military Strategy"; YCSL 112/6b–8. This was doubtless as confusing to officials of the time, when the system was being worked out, as it is to us

today; see YCSL 116/6. Although after the seal was granted most court letters were ascribed in the *Veritable Records* to the high officials (*Pan-li Chün-chi ta-ch'en*), on occasion the old nomenclature persisted.

59. This is discussed more fully in Chapter 4.

60. On the various types of Grand Secretariat edicts, see John K. Fairbank and Ssu-yü Teng, "On the Types and Uses of Ch'ing Documents," in *Ch'ing Administration: Three Studies* (Cambridge, Mass., 1961), pp. 75–76, for a general list, with definitions in the pages that follow. On the Grand Secretariat's preparation of responses to the routine memorials, see (B) P'iao pu-pen shih-yang and similar volumes.

61. See, for example, the references in (T) KCT-YC004255, YC6/10/22, Ch'un Shan and T'e-k'e-teng; and (T) KCT-YC000221, YC8/6/6, Yueh Chung-ch'i.

62. Enclosure in (T) KCT-KH001364, KH49/J7/14, Chao Hung-hsieh and Fan Shih-ch'ung. A translation of this edict appears in Rosso, *Apostolic Legations*, p. 287.

63. Rosso, *Apostolic Legations*, pp. 138 and n. 41, 158, 160, 161 and n. 31, and many other references to the four in the index.

64. Spence, *Ts'ao Yin and the K'ang-hsi Emperor*, p. 104n.89.

65. As in, for example, Rosso, *Apostolic Legations*, p. 336.

66. But note that forms differed for lower-ranking officials; see the final comment in note 42 above. For other documents that may have been prototypes, refer to those listed at the end of Appendix A, n. 6.

67. See, for example, (T) Ch'i-chü chu, YC8/7/10, YC8/10/11, YC9/2/1.

CHAPTER 4. THE INNER-COURT SUBORDINATE STAFFS SET UP FOR THE ZUNGHAR CAMPAIGN

1. (T) YC SYT YC8/5/25, pp. 75–80.

2. Vermilion writing, (T) KCT-YC000592, undated court letter in Yueh Chung-ch'i's packet, enclosure 2.

3. YCSL 81/12b–14b (this was YC7/5/10).

4. See Chapter 1 above.

5. For the literature on this and related points, see the Prologue, note 1. The office name that I translate "Military Finance Section" is rendered "Office of Military Supplies" in Silas H. L. Wu, *Cummunications and Imperial Control*, p. 87. Occasionally even the archival records betray confusion in writing the Chinese term; see, for example, *Chün-hsu ch'u* in (B) IFT YC11/10/17, p. 23; *Chün-hsu chü* in (B) IFT YC11/7/7, p. 45; and the emperor's rescripted *Pan-li Chün-hsu ch'u*, (T) KCT-YC011808, YC9/5/12, Hsu Jung, used in place of *Chün-hsu fang*.

6. Rescript on (T) KCT-YC019384, YC5/12/18, Sai-leng-e.

7. (T) I-tsou tang CL22/6/25, p. 216. There are, however, several other estimates for the expenses of this campaign. See the different figures supplied in (B) Lu-fu, Chün-wu category, Chün-hsu subcategory, 5, undated list (nearly 91 million taels); (T) Pien-pei i-ch'ing tang, CL13/J7/16, pp. 111–17 (66 million); (B) SYT-FP undated memorandum of ca. CL24/11/1, p. 392 (more than 54 million), and ibid., CL26/2/10, pp. 119–22 (66 million taels). The differences seem to depend in part on types of expenditures counted as military and the varied sources of funds dispatched to the front, but the matter needs further study. Thus, although two sources give the figure of

66 million taels, it is not clear that the calculations are based on the same kinds of computations. Moreover, the sum of 130 million may well be too high; the cost of the Second Chin-ch'uan War, a campaign of approximately the same duration fought later in the eighteenth century, was estimated at "not less than" 70 million taels; CLSL 1005/6b–8b. For a detailed analysis of the costs of other mid-Ch'ing military campaigns, see Susan Naquin, *Millenarian Rebellion in China: The Eight Trigrams Uprising of 1813* (New Haven, 1976), pp. 359–61n.194.

8. (T) KCT-YC000068, YC7/12/7, Yueh Chung-ch'i; (B) IFT YC11/1/24, pp. 41–62; YC11/9/19, pp. 213–21; YC12/4/30, p. 52; YC12/6/7, pp. 97–98; YC12/7/20, pp. 45–49; YC12/8/13, pp. 85–86. For later views, see (B) SYT CL26/4/6, pp. 25–26; CL26/5/18, pp. 227–28. On scorched-earth tactics, see Yung-cheng's account of Prince I's views in the vermilion addition to (T) KCT-YC000592, undated court letter; and (B) Lu-fu 2188-12, YC10/12/12, Cha-lang-a.

9. (B) IFT YC11/9/12, pp. 187–89; YC12/4/4, pp. 19–20; YC12/5/23, pp. 79–80.

10. (B) IFT YC11/7/9, p. 51; YC12/7/13, pp. 17–18; YC11–12 passim; (T) KCT-YC00059, YC7/12/7, Yueh Chung-ch'i.

11. (T) KCT-YC000059, YC7/12/7, Yueh Chung-ch'i.

12. (B) IFT YC11/2/27, pp. 121–25; YC11/7/22, pp. 79–80; (B) T'i-pen 286 00051, undated, Liu Yü-i; (T) KCT-YC000289, YC7/11/12, and (T) KCT-YC000068, YC7/12/7, both Yueh Chung-ch'i.

13. (T) KCT-YC000297, YC7/7/16, and (T) KCT-YC000059, YC7/12/7, both Yueh Chung-ch'i; (T) KCT-YC016727, YC8/1/4, Cha-lang-a and Wu Ko; (B) IFT YC11/1/17, pp. 29–30.

14. (B) IFT YC11/1/17, pp. 29–30; YC11/2/27, pp. 121–25; YC11/9/19, pp. 213–21; YC11/10/27, pp. 25–26. For shipping methods, see ibid., YC11/2/20, pp. 111–17.

15. (T) KCT-YC000327, YC7/6/3, Yueh Chung-ch'i; (B) IFT YC11/9/4, pp. 165–69; YC11/9/14, pp. 191–94; YC12/7/13, pp. 19–21; YC12/7/20, pp. 45–49.

16. (T) KCT-YC021859 YC4/11/12, Yueh Chung-ch'i; (B) IFT YC11/2/20, pp. 111–17; YC11/8/4, pp. 103–4; YC12/5/28, pp. 89–90; YC13/10/9, pp. 253–54.

17. (T) KCT-YC000022, YC7/2/1, Yueh Chung-ch'i.

18. (B) IFT YC11/9/22, pp. 225–26.

19. (T) KCT-YC000220, YC8/5/30, Yueh Chung-ch'i; YCSL 83/36b–38.

20. (B) IFT CL1/3/29, pp. 251–54, reviewing some earlier prices. On the problems of profiteering from inflation, see (T) KCT-YC010461, YC5/3/19, Mai-chu. On board commissions, see Chapter 1 above.

21. YCSL 98/8–9. For a handwritten example of the suspicion with which Yung-cheng regarded certain of his high officials in the northwest, see the imperial comment on the cover of (T) KCT-YC000469, YC7/11/18, draft edict. Despite Yung-cheng's precautions, the campaign spawned an enormous number of financial malfeasance cases that dragged on well into the next reign, with correspondence back and forth between court and provincial governments; see (T) Ch'i-chü chu YC13/9/27; (B) SYT-FP CL14/6/6, p. 347; and (B) IFT YC13/9/1, pp. 75–76, discussing the impeachment of a previously trusted provincial military finance officer. See also the various edicts quoted in (T) KCT-YC020423, YC13/11/18, O-erh-t'ai and others.

22. (T) KCT-YC000309, YC7/9/29, Yueh Chung-ch'i; see also *Kung-chung tang Yung-cheng ch'ao tsou-che* 13:483–95, a YC7/6/28 series of Yueh Chung-ch'i memorials. The pass was the Chia-yü Kuan.

23. The figure for YC5 was 244,394 taels; for YC6, 4,659,536 taels; and for YC7, 8,120,870; (B) SYT-FP undated document of CL26/2/10, pp. 119–22.

24. Inquiry of 9 Oct. 1980 addressed to Mr. Liu Kuei-lin of the Number One Archives in Beijing. These records appear not to have survived despite the fact that those of the Audit Bureau (*Hui-k'ao fu*) and other small staffs were preserved. Even a request for Yung-cheng–era Board of Revenue materials and an examination of the Ch'ing-period Grand Council inventories of Manchu materials yielded nothing. The loss of so many documents once regarded as so important that the emperor himself gave instructions to have them copied and preserved is difficult to explain. Possibly they were used in the early–Ch'ien-lung–period malfeasance cases; possibly they were destroyed because of the prospect of such use.

25. (T) KCT-YC020499, YC13/9/22, Prince Yin-li, Chang T'ing-yü, and Hai-wang. In 1980–81, thinking that another archival version might contain a processing note that would shed further light on this important memorial, I searched the Beijing archives for a record book or *lu-fu* copy but turned up nothing; thus, the Taipei original appears to be the only surviving version of this crucial document.

26. Yeh, *Nei-ko hsiao-chih*, p. 11. Weng Tsao's name appears in the early list of Grand Council clerks; see SYCL 18/1b.

27. (B) IFT YC11/7/7, pp. 45, 47; YC11/10/1, pp. 1–2, 3; YC11/11/27, pp. 53–54; YC13/9/8, p. 95. See also CLSL 3/34–35b. The last archival reference to the *Hu-pu Chün-hsu fang* is (B) IFT YC13/9/8, p. 95. A *fang* was an office designated for underlings; see Hsi, *Nei-ko chih*, p. 2.

28. Fu Tsung-mao appears to be the earliest modern writer to have clearly understood this early Board of Revenue connection; see his *Ch'ing-tai Chün-chi ch'u*, pp. 122–28.

29. The Military Finance Section's exact founding date is not certain; contemporary official pronouncements appear not to have survived. The memorial of Yin-li and others supplied only the founding year (YC7; 1729); see note 25 above. Some of those who take the founding of the Military Finance Section to be the founding date of the Grand Council base their argument on YCSL 82/5–6b (which is dated YC7/6/10) and CS 4 : 2486 and specify the month of YC7/6.

30. On the emperor's and others' references to "the board," see Appendix A.

31. (B) IFT YC13/10/1, pp. 181–83.

32. (B) T'i-pen 772, *ping-ma* category 00009, YC7/7/19, Chang T'ing-yü and others; (B) T'i-pen 896, 00875, YC12/7/3, Chang T'ing-yü and others. On some of the later cases arising from the campaign, see (B) IFT YC13/9/1, pp. 75–76; and (B) SYT-FP CL14/6/6, p. 347.

33. CLSL 3/34–35b, describing Yung-cheng's policies and the Military Finance Section's work. See also (T) KCT-YC000297, YC7/7/16, Yueh Chung-ch'i; and (B) IFT YC11–12, passim. For a description of late–K'ang-hsi–era malfeasance in reporting prices, see (B) IFT CL1/3/24, pp. 251–54. For a description of regular outer-court Board of Revenue methods of checking provincial accounts, see Zelin, *The Magistrate's Tael*, pp. 13–17.

34. (B) IFT YC11/10/1, pp. 1–2.

35. (T) KCT-YC000297, YC7/7/16, and (T) KCT-YC000066, YC7/12/7, both Yueh Chung-ch'i; and CLSL 3/34–35b.

36. (T) KCT-YC000067, YC7/12/7, Yueh Chung-ch'i; (B) IFT YC11/12/2, p. 67; YC12/5/19, pp. 69–70; YC12/8/22, pp. 97–98.

37. Rescript on (T) KCT-YC000309, YC7/9/29, Yueh Chung-ch'i.

38. YCSL 83/36b–38; (B) IFT YC11/11/27, pp. 53–54; and two Yueh Chung-ch'i memorials: (T) KCT-YC000043, YC7/3/30; and the rescript on (T) KCT-YC000066, YC7/12/7. A refinement on these arrangements was the "simplified accounting" register (*chien-ming ch'ing-ts'e* or *huang-ts'e*), which was to be sent to Yueh Chung-ch'i on the front lines so he might do further checking based on his knowledge of the accounts; see two Yueh Chung-ch'i memorials: (T) KCT-YC000309, YC7/9/29; and (T) KCT-YC000220, YC8/5/30. Other frontier finance officials could also be called on to check the accounts before these were forwarded to the capital.

39. Rescript on (T) KCT-YC000067, YC7/12/7, Yueh Chung-ch'i.

40. (B) IFT YC11–12, passim. For an example concerned with the Miao campaign, see (B) T'i-pen 896 000837, YC13/10/28, Chang T'ing-yü and others.

41. See, for example, (B) T'i-pen 772, *ping-ma* category 00011, YC10/11/2, Liu Yü-i; and 773, *ping-ma* category 00017 and 00018, YC12/3/28, Shih I-chih and others (Shih was temporarily assigned to the Shensi governorship and military finance affairs). See also CLSL 3/34–35b, which seems to be reporting on the late–Yung-cheng–period situation.

42. See, for example, (B) T'i-pen 773, *ping-ma* category 00027, YC13/2/28, O-erh-t'ai and others; and 896, 000887, YC13/10/28, Chang T'ing-yü and others.

43. (B) IFT YC11/11/25, pp. 45–46. See also (B) IFT YC12/9/18, pp. 129–30; YC13/10/9, pp. 253–54.

44. See, for example, (T) KCT-YC016754, YC8/5/29, Cha-lang-a; (B) IFT YC11/9/12, pp. 187–89; YC11/11/25, pp. 45–46; YC12/8/17, pp. 87–88; (T) YC *Shang-yü Nei-ko*, YC9/3/26.

45. (T) Ch'i-chü chu ts'e YC9/1/14 and 9/1/24; (T) Pien-pei i-ch'ing tang CL13/J7/16, pp. 111–17; slip ordering the document turned over to the Boards of Revenue and War inserted in (B) Lu-fu 2162-3, YC10/5/19, Liu Shih-ming; (B) T'i-pen 772, *ping-ma* category 0009, YC7/7/19, Chang T'ing-yü and others (this last is not a routine memorial prepared by the inner-court directorate; its memorialists included outer-court department directors, assistant directors, and secretaries); (B) IFT YC11/11/26, pp. 51–52; YC12/4/3, pp. 13–14; "Yung-cheng mo-nien po-fang chu-fang kuan-ping hsiang-hsu shih-liao," *Li-shih tang-an* 1986, no. 3 (Aug. 1986): 13–16. On early board handling of military purchases, see (B) IFT CL3/11/6, pp. 331–35 (discussing a YC1 situation). Many notices of "board" action, however, refer to the inner-court components of the board directorates and their staffs; see Appendix A.

46. (B) IFT YC13/10/9, pp. 253–54; CL3/11/12, pp. 479–81 (the latter discusses a case dating from YC10).

47. Yung-cheng later regretted having halted the campaign and confessed that it had been a "great error" and that he was "filled with remorse"; rescript on (T) KCT-YC000221, YC8/6/6, Yueh Chung-ch'i.

48. See Table 2 at the end of Chapter 3. The earliest surviving court letter with an enlarged roster was dated YC8/12/28. For another early reference, see (T) Ch'i-chü chu ts'e YC9/1/13. There is additional evidence of a new record book series dating from YC8/12; see (B) Manchu Chün-wu IFT, which begins YC8/12/26. In the Ch'ing inventories, the copying of Manchu documents for the Grand Council reference collection (*Chün-chi ch'u lu-fu tsou-che*) was said to have started in YC8/12, again the date of

the High Officials' appearance; see (B) Man Chün-chi tang-an tsung-mu cheng/fu pen ping yueh-che. The earliest surviving Chinese-language *lu-fu* memorial bears a YC9/2/2 date; (B) Lu-fu 2158/2, Yueh Chung-ch'i. But the earliest (B) Manchu Yueh-che tang begins in YC8/2, rather earlier than the enlargement of the court letter rosters. I was not able to examine these volumes individually in order to determine their relationship (if any) to the high officials.

49. Although there are records of some early uses of the term *Pan-li Chün-chi ta-ch'en*, these can be shown to be retrospective interpolations. See, for example, Yung-cheng *Shang-yü Nei-ko*, YC9/11/6; a YC9/1 reference in (B) T'i-pen 786, 00051, undated memorial of no earlier than YC11 (because of its references to accounts for YC10), Liu Yü-i; and the citation of a YC9 discussion memorial in (B) IFT YC12/6/26, pp. 109–10. The new terminology had come into use by the time these references were composed or, in the case of the published work, by the time they were edited. Thus, the presence of the successor term in these later citations should be viewed as instances of reading back and applying contemporary terms to earlier situations. In other words, I have not found the later term used authentically in documents of a genuine YC9 date.

50. See, for instance, (B) Chinese IFT volume for YC11/Spring, in which both titles were used, but the earlier one much more than its successor, which only appeared twice (pp. 1–3, 25). For a single document that used both titles, showing how one title had succeeded the other, see (B) IFT 11/7/11, pp. 53–54. This shift in nomenclature is the only evidence I have found for the widely popular metamorphosis-thesis of Grand Council origins. A phrase resembling the strategists' title was rendered in the Manchu title of a record book dating from YC8/12; see (B) Manchu Chün-wu i-fu tang (or Gisurefi wesimbuha dangse—cooha-i nashūn-i baita) for YC8/12–9/7.

51. (B) IFT for YC11–13, passim. O-erh-t'ai's name appears regularly in these volumes except when he was away from the capital, at which point Feng-sheng-e usually replaced him. (On the role of Feng-sheng-e, see the discussion in Chapter 3, n. 17, and related text.) The Manchu record books also supply information on this point. (B) Manchu Hsun-ch'ang IFT (An-i jergi baita gisurefi wesimbuha dangse), for YC9–10, lists Ma-erh-sai and Feng-sheng-e for all the YC9 memorials, with the exception of one discussion led by A-ch'i-t'u. Later O-erh-t'ai's name dominates. There are many instances of the emperor's ordering the High Officials in Charge of Military Finance (or Strategy) to deliberate and the reply memorial being headed by O-erh-t'ai or another Manchu inner deputy; see, for example, (B) YC11/1/17, pp. 29–30, where the high officials (*Pan-li Chün-hsu ta-ch'en*) were ordered to deliberate and O-erh-t'ai headed the response; and (B) IFT YC11/1/5, pp. 1–3, where the discussers were O-erh-t'ai "and others" but the order to deliberate was addressed to the High Officials in Charge of Military Strategy (*Pan-li Chün-chi ta-ch'en*). On the differentiation between the inner deputies and high officials, see Yeh Feng-mao, who observed "the inner Grand Secretaries sitting to the east and the high officials to the west" (*Nei-ko hsiao-chih*, p. 11b), and Hsi Wu-ao, who likewise distinguished between the two groups by averring that the inner grand secretaries "had not yet [become] men of the Military Finance Section [or, as he probably meant the term, the High Officials in Charge of Military Finance]" (*Nei-ko chih*, p. 5). For more on this important distinction, see Chapter 3, n. 21; and Silas H. L. Wu, *Communication and Imperial Control*, pp. 86, 174n.28.

52. See the discussion of the court letter rosters in Chapter 3 and Table 2.

53. Curators at the Number One Archives were helpful in autumn of 1985 in searching for material to identify all parties to the Manchu-language deliberations. I am told, however, that not all the Manchu materials have been sorted. For information on Ch'ien-lung's participation in the Miao Council, see CS 1:128.2 and the references in Harold L. Kahn, *Monarchy in the Emperor's Eyes: Image and Reality in the Ch'ien-lung Reign* (Cambridge, Mass., 1971), p. 110.

54. (B) Manchu Chün-wu IFT for YC8/12–9/7 and 9/8–12; and (B) Manchu Hsun-ch'ang IFT for YC9–10, passim. The later Chinese-language record books do not yield a similar bonanza of names. The SYCL possesses the most reliable published list, but see comments on its usefulness in the following note.

55. For other names, see Appendix D; (B) IFT CL2/12/11, pp. 353–55; SYCL 16/1–2 and 18/1. Shu-ho-te, Ya-erh-ha-shan, Wu Yuan-an, and Chiang Ping, for instance, are said to have worked for the inner deputies (Yeh, *Nei-ko hsiao-chih*, p. 11), but their names were mixed in with others on retrospective lists of early Grand Council clerks. I have found many mistakes in the early lists' entrance-on-duty dates: frequently the duty can be proved to have started long before the date given. See also Wang Ch'ang, "Chün-chi ch'u t'i-ming chi" 14/19. For the names of clerks who probably served too early to be regarded as having been associated with the high officials, see *Chün-chi chang-ching t'i-ming*, comp. Wu Hsiao-ming (1828; repr. Taipei, 1970), *fu-lu*, p. 16, which suggests that Wu Yuan-an and Yao P'ei-i belonged to an "earlier generation" of staff members. Possibly they served as staff for Prince I or the earliest inner grand secretaries.

56. YCSL 131/3. By his father's account, Chang Jo-ai was brought on to attend and learn from his father, in which case he would have begun as a clerk to the inner deputies rather than the high officials; Chang T'ing-yü, *Nien-p'u* 3/6. Nevertheless, he soon came to be regarded as a member of the high officials' group; ibid., 3/23b.

57. Thus, in the middle of YC7 the Hupei governor Ma Hui-po was yanked out of Wuchang and sent to the battle staging area at Su-chou in the far northwest "to be in charge of western front military finance" (*pan-li hsi-lu chün-hsu*); YCSL 82/10. At the same time, the acting Shen-Kan governor-general, Cha-lang-a, and his two governors were also given military finance responsibilities; YCSL 83/36b–38. Soon after this the Kansu lieutenant governor, K'ung Yü-p'u, was also deputed to a nearby backup post at Kan-Liang at the western end of the Kansu Corridor to handle military supply; YCSL 88/16a–b. In the following year, Cha-lang-a, ordinarily in residence at Lanchow, was shifted westward to Suchou to replace Ma Hui-po and handle western-front military finance; (T) KCT-YC009781, YC8/10/26, Cha-lang-a. Circuit intendants might also be involved; the *taotai* Wang T'ang was in charge of military finance in his area for many years; (T) KCT-YC021521, YC6/5/4, Wang T'ang; YCSL 131/9a–b; (B) IFT YC11/7/22, pp. 79–80; YC11/7/27, pp. 85–90. As the campaign intensified at the beginning of YC9 (1731) the regular staffs of the various northwest civil officials were augmented with sixteen men selected in imperial audience for assignment to various Shensi and Kansu yamen to assist with "military finance"; (T) Ch'i-chü chu, YC9/1/14. See also (B) T'i-pen 786 *tsou-hsiao* 00058, undated review probably of YC13/9–12; and (B) IFT CL2/3/18, pp. 103–4, which recapitulates the Yung-cheng–period career of one provincial military finance official.

58. *Ch'ing-shih lieh-chuan* 16/20; see also CS 4:2894–95; and *Ch'ing-tai chih-kuan nien-piao* 2:1395.

59. Compare YCSL 102/3 and the same edict in (T) Ch'i-chü chu for YC9/1/6, for example.

60. When in 1985 I asked the curators at the Number One Archives for the Manchu court letters of the Yung-cheng period I was told that none survived. (The packets of court letter originals, in contrast with the "Record Book of Court Letters," *T'ing-chi tang*, were not separately noted in the eighteenth-century Grand Council inventories.) Nevertheless, because of the language preferences of many of the commanders in the field, much of the military correspondence had to be in Manchu; see Yeh, *Nei-ko hsiao-chih*, p. 11. Additional Manchu documents may come to light in the future. Even the Chinese general Yueh Chung-ch'i—most of whose correspondence was in Chinese —had occasionally to deal with Manchu documents; see (T) KCT-YC000170, YC9/1/3, Yueh Chung-ch'i; and (T) KCT-YC000462, YC9/9/8, court letter to Yueh Chung-ch'i. The latter mentions translating a northern-front Manchu document into Chinese for Yueh to read.

61. See my "Books of Revelations: The Importance of the Manchu Language Archival Record Books for Research on Ch'ing History," *Late Imperial China* 6, no. 2 (Dec. 1985): 27–29; *Ch'ing Chün-chi ch'u tang-an mu-lu*, Yung-cheng sec., p. 1. Moreover, the Grand Council's own inventories of its record books do not indicate any Chinese-language record books before YC11. See, for example, (B) Han-k'u tang-an cheng-pen ch'ing-ts'e; and (B) Han Chün-chi tang-an tsung-ts'e.

62. Manchu-language record books that later come to be regarded as Grand Council books and were inventoried in the Grand Council's periodic enumerations of their archival holdings begin in YC8. With the exception of some Manchu-language K'ang-hsi records concerning Russia and two Chinese volumes that were probably retained in storage in what later became the Grand Council holdings, no trace of any earlier items in these series appears in the council's eighteenth- and nineteenth-century inventories. The Manchu records inventoried for YC8 included packets of memorial copies (the first packet ran from YC8/12 to 9/6) and record books with the following titles: Chün-wu i-fu (this is the one that begins in YC8/12); Chün-wu shang-yü; Chün-wu tsou-che; Hsun-ch'ang shang-yü; Chün-wu ming-fa (covering YC8/3–9/6); and Yueh-che, the last sometimes additionally called Hsun-ch'ang, with another parallel one called Chün-wu (first volume running from YC8/2 to 10/J5). For YC9, all the above titles were listed and in addition the following: Chun-ka-erh, Pei-lu chün-wu, E-lo-ssu, Hsun-ch'ang tsou-che, and Hsun-ch'ang i-fu. Other inventories simply group a large number of titles to cover the years YC8–13, so it is difficult to be sure which ones derive from the earlier years; see (B) Man Chün-chi tang-an tsung-mu cheng/fu pen ping yueh-che. For the inventories that supplied the information here, see those referenced in the list of inventories in the bibliography of this book. For the identification of campaign discussion memorials (and therefore the record book copies) as the high officials' responsibility, see (B) IFT YC13/8/26, p. 27. Just because a record book was inventoried during the Ch'ing is no guarantee that it survives today; in 1985 when I sought these volumes at the Number One not all were available. There were some earlier record books of the same titles that were not inventoried as part of the Grand Council records; see the mentions of Chün-wu IFT and Tsa-hsiang tsou-che in *Kung-chung tang Yung-cheng ch'ao tsou-che* 25:633–34, undated list probably of YC3 or YC4. Probably the high officials did not maintain all the Manchu record books of the time; those labeled "ordinary" (*hsun-ch'ang*) may derive from the inner deputies' offices, but this is difficult to ascertain

without the opportunity for direct examination of these records. Other types of Manchu-language records, such as those emanating from the Eight Banners or the Imperial Household, formed parts of other series and are not included in this analysis.

63. (B) IFT CL21/10/10, pp. 203–4. The YC11–13 Chinese-language record books also contain many references to documents translated from the Manchu; see (B) IFT YC11/8/22, pp. 159–60; YC12/7/13, pp. 19–21, 23–25; CL1/6/13, pp. 17–20.

64. See (B) Manchu Chün-wu IFT, passim; and, for a specific example, (B) IFT YC11/2/12, pp. 91–92. This point is also discussed in Chapter 3 above.

65. YCSL 116/2b. Note that the date of this important document as rendered in Silas H. L. Wu's *Communication and Imperial Contral*, p. 89, needs correction. For more information on the seal, see (B) IFT YC11/12/3, p. 79; and Wu Chen-yü, *Yang-chi chai ts'ung-lu* 4/1b.

66. (B) IFT CL1/7/24, pp. 101–3, and CL1/8/4, pp. 121–22, recall the frenzied activity in the military sphere in YC10–11. On how court letters were reproduced in the *Shih-lu* before and after the casting of the seal, see Chapter 3, n. 58.

67. For example, see the many lateral communications in (B) IFT YC11–13. These appear to have been written in Chinese. There were earlier Manchu-language record books of lateral communications. The responsibility for communications continued after Yung-cheng's death; see (B) IFT YC13/9/1, p. 73. On changes surrounding the new seal, see chapter 3, n. 58.

68. Imperial rescript on (T) KCT-YC016743, YC7/9/18, Cha-lang-a; (B) IFT YC13/8/26, p. 27, reviewing practices of the previous reign; (T) KCT-YC019846, unsigned and undated inner deputies' memorandum, probably from YC7 or 8; YCSL 96/4b–7.

69. The court letters also show the high officials' concern with the northwest; see the court letter data in Table 2, and (T) Ch'i-chü chu for YC9–13, passim. On troop allocations, see (B) IFT YC12/8/13, pp. 85–86. The high officials deliberated troop assignments all over the empire, doubtless because this required coordination.

70. (B) IFT YC11/9/2, pp. 161–62.

71. Reference to the outer storage area is in (B) Han Chün-chi tang-an tsung-ts'e.

72. Yeh, *Nei-ko hsiao-chih*, p. 11b, which also describes another office at the Summer Palace; *Ch'ing-kung shu-wen* 3/25b. Nearly all writers agree that the early arrangements were simple and unpretentious; for a recent statement, see Liu Wei, "Chün-chi ch'u yü Chün-chi chih-fang," in *Chin-tai ching-hua shih-chi*, ed. Lin K'e-kuang et al. (Beijing, 1985), p. 128.

73. For titles, see the Manchu inventories referenced in the bibliography. Despite the presence of the inner deputies' names at the head of the deliberations in these albums, I regard these record books as primarily derived from the high officials. (See Chapter 3.) See the notice dating from two days after Yung-cheng's death that averred that "all military matters on the two fronts had been turned over to the High Officials in Charge of Military Strategy to discuss"; (B) IFT YC13/8/26, p. 27, and the explanation of this point in Chapter 3 above. Accordingly, the record books containing copies of those discussions belonged to the High Officials.

74. YCSL 40/2b.

75. Tu Lien-che and Silas H. L. Wu have also made this point; see Tu, *Kuan-yü Chün-chi ch'u*, p. 17; and Wu, *Communication and Imperial Control*, p. 86.

CHAPTER 5. INNER-COURT TRANSFORMATION
UNDER THE INTERIM COUNCIL, 1735–38

1. CLSL 355/1b–2. The proposal was submitted by the censor Feng Yuan-ch'in. The censor's use of the name *Chün-chi fang* (rather than *Chün-chi ch'u*) to describe the council of his own times represents one of the earliest uses of this term that I have seen. The first Chin-ch'uan campaign was fought against the aborigines of western Szechuan in CL13–14 (1748–49).

2. For an eighteenth-century description of the *Shu-mi yuan*, see *Hsu T'ung-chih* (repr. Taipei, 1954), p. 4041. On the history of the *Shu-mi yuan* itself, see Edmund H. Worthy, "The *Shu-mi yuan*: From Privy Commission to Bureau of Military Affairs," chap. 5 of his Ph.D. dissertation, "The Founding of Sung China, 950–1000: Integrative Changes in Military and Political Institutions" (Princeton University, 1976). I am grateful to Dr. Worthy for sending me this chapter of his dissertation. According to Worthy, the *Shu-mi yuan* title is usually translated differently according to the various roles the council played over time, "Palace Council" being common usage for the T'ang version and "Bureau of Military Affairs" his choice for the Sung body (p. 214). On the *Shu-mi yuan* of the T'ang, see Denis Twitchett, "Introduction" to *The Cambridge History of China*, vol. 3: *Sui and T'ang China 589–906*, ed. Denis Twitchett (New York, 1979), part 1, p. 20, as well as references on pp. 544 and 634. The title was also employed during the Five Dynasties (907–60).

3. CLSL 355/1b–2. The involvement of eunuchs in the T'ang council may also have been a factor in the title's lack of appeal in the Ch'ing.

4. Later in the eighteenth century the historian Chao I also found the Grand Council comparable to the *Shu-mi yuan*; see his *Yen-p'u tsa-chi* 1:3 and *Nien-erh shih cha-chi* 22/291–92.

5. For the determination of the name, see (B) IFT YC13/8/24, p. 7. A literal translation of the title would be "Princes and High Ministers in Charge of [Government] Affairs." YC1 was the first time this title had been used in the Ch'ing; see Shen and T'ao, *Ming-Ch'ing cheng-chih chih-tu* 2:44–45.

6. The Grand Council was abolished just before the end of the dynasty, on HT3/4/10 (1911 May 8), and the Cabinet (*Tse-jen Nei-ko*) was set up in its place; see *Hsuan-t'ung cheng-chi Shih-lu* 52/18ff. See the comments on the abolition in the Prologue, including note 7.

7. See Nurhaci as quoted in Robert B. Oxnam, *Ruling from Horseback: Manchu Politics in the Oboi Regency, 1661–1669* (Chicago, 1975), p. 22.

8. On earlier regencies see Shen and T'ao, *Ming-Ch'ing cheng-chih chih-tu* 2:44; Wakeman, *The Great Enterprise* 1:158–60, 297–98; and ECCP, passim. Although a mourning period was loosely described as lasting three years, this was because its stretch of twenty-five or so months went into a third year; see Arthur Waley, *Three ways of Thought in Ancient China* (Garden City, N.Y., 1956), p. 94.

9. Oxnam, *Ruling from Horseback*, pp. 1, 15–20, 47–49, 50ff., and his Appendix 1, pp. 205–7; Kessler, *K'ang-hsi*, chap. 2, esp. pp. 20–21.

10. YCSL 159/19b–20; CLSL 1/9a–b; ECCP, pp. 331, 925. Prince I (Yin-hsiang), the thirteenth brother and ablest member of the faction, had already died in the middle of the reign; see Chapter 2 above.

11. The Yung-cheng Emperor appears to have been unusual in the history of the Ch'ing monarchy in that he selected the members of two transition councils, his own and his son's. The usual procedure would have been for K'ang-hsi to have made the earlier set of appointments, but for some reason (possibly the suddenness of the K'ang-hsi Emperor's death) this was not done; see YCSL 1/8b–9.

12. YCSL 159/19b–20; CLSL 1/9a–b; (B) SYT-FP YC13/8/23, p. 5. Chang's proficiency in Manchu may have been one of the reasons why he received this appointment and honor; see the discussion of this point in Chapter 2, n. 60, and related text. On the award of the Imperial Ancestral Temple honor, see (B) IFT YC13/8/25, pp. 19–21; CLSL 1/15b–16b; ECCP, pp. 55–56; Hucker, *A Dictionary of Official Titles in Imperial China* (Stanford, 1985), item 6188.

13. CLSL 1/18b; (T) KCT-YC020420, YC13/12/17, Lai-pao and others. The description of Pan-ti's and So-chu's positions—"follow [instructions]...for assignment [of duties]"—suggests their slightly lower status, below the top echelon. For continued distinctions between the Interim Council and the Office of Military Strategy up to the date of the final amalgamation, see some of the many examples in (B) IFT YC13/8/26, p. 27; (B) SYT-FP YC13/8/25, p. 49; and (B) IFT YC13/9/8, pp. 91–92. On Chu Shih's appointment, see CS 1:128.6. Chu Shih's status is not entirely clear. On the very day that Yung-cheng died, the new emperor recalled Chu from water conservancy duty in the south to take over an unspecified post in the capital; (B) IFT YC13/8/26, p. 23, citing the YC13/8/23 edict; CS 1:128.4. Chu's Interim Council appointment was announced about ten days later, on YC13/9/4; CLSL 2/14. On memorials of this period, Chu listed himself as "adjunct" (*hsieh-pan*); (T) KCT-YC020415, YC13/11/15. Moreover, his name was not included in a list of highest Interim Council members who submitted a memorial on YC13/9/7; (B) IFT YC13/9/7, pp. 83–84. But despite these indications of adjunct status, Chu appears to have held an anomalous intermediary position—higher than other adjunct members but slightly below those of the top echelon. For instance, when on YC13/9/13 Interim Council members were honored, Chu Shih was listed in the same group as the top four, but his honor was a little different. The two princes were given a "permanent" grant of double salary; O-erh-t'ai and Chang T'ing-yü were awarded the sixth hereditary rank, *Ch'ing-che tu-yü*; but Chu received the seventh, *Ch'i-tu-yü*; CS 1:128. Nevertheless, Chu did receive a reward, whereas other adjunct members such as Pan-ti and So-chu were ignored. Possibly Chu had to be less favored because he had not been named to the council by the Yung-cheng Emperor; see Ch'ien Shih-fu, "Ch'ing-tai ti Chün-chi ch'u," p. 474. Further evidence of Chu Shih's being at a lower level than O-erh-t'ai or Chang T'ing-yü in this period lies in the fact that he was rarely listed with them as edict drafter; see (T) Ch'i-chü chu for these months, passim. But because of his high position Chu was awarded a sixty-*chien* house, moving expenses, and permission to keep his country villa; (B) IFT YC13/10/17, p. 293; (B) SYT-FP YC13/9/21, p. 149; CLSL 3/12b. Chu Shih did not live to the end of the Interim Council term but died in the autumn of CL2; CLSL 35/5b. On his descendants, see (T) SYT-FP CL41/7/22, p. 157; (T) KCT-CC004575, CC4/5/8, Chang Ch'eng-chi.

14. (T) KCT-YC020499, YC13/9/22, Yin-li, Chang T'ing-yü, and Hai-wang. (Most of this document is translated near the beginning of Chapter 4.) A memorial of about this time shows that the three top Board of Revenue members—the superintendent and the two board presidents—were all members of the Interim Council; (T) KCT-YC020500, YC13/9/20, Yin-li and others. The last archival mention of the

Military Finance Section is dated (B) IFT YC13/9/8, p. 95. (The later mention in CLSL 3/34–35b, dated YC13/9/27, refers to an earlier situation.) For a reference to a Board of Revenue (but probably inner-court) memorial very likely resulting from the reversion of files, see (B) IFT CL1/3/24, Interim Council.

15. CLSL 5/42a–b. The High Officials in Charge of Military Strategy (*Pan-li Chün-chi ta-ch'en*), or the Office of Military Strategy (*Chün-chi ch'u*), are still mentioned in the sources during the months just before this group was amalgamated with the others. See, for example, its joint deliberations with the Interim Council cited in (B) IFT and SYT-FP for YC13/8 and 9, passim: e.g., (B) SYT-FP YC13/9/17, pp. 136–39; (B) IFT YC13/10/9, pp. 253–54, 255–56; (T) Ch'i-chü chu YC13/9/23. Continuity between the Office, the Interim Council, and the Grand Council is evident from statements in (B) IFT CL2/11/29, pp. 325–28; and (B) IFT CL3/11/12, pp. 479–81. The reader should be aware that the (B) SSTC references to the "Grand Council" (*Chün-chi ch'u*) during CL1–2 should not be taken to mean that the Office of Military Strategy had not been disbanded. The SSTC for the early Ch'ien-lung years (CL1–4) is not an original but was constructed in the late 1920s out of the remaining Grand Council reference collection holdings by enthusiastic archivists at the Bureau of Documents (*Wen-hsien kuan*); see the inscription on the front cover of the CL1 SSTC; Chang Te-tse, "Chün-chi ch'u chi ch'i tang-an," in *Wen-hsien lun-ts'ung* (Peiping, 1936), *Lun-shu* sec., p. 70; and *Wen-hsien t'e-k'an, pao-kao* sec., p. 19. Similarly, the (T) Ch'ang-pien tang for these years employs another misleading term, not because it was created in Bureau of Document days (it was composed during the Ch'ien-lung period) but because it used the term *Chün-chi* not to refer to the Office of Military Strategy or the Grand Council but to guide users to the Office of Military Strategy (later Grand Council) reference files (*Chün-chi ch'u lu-fu tsou-che*). Those who argue for a Yung-cheng–period founding for the Grand Council frequently claim that the Grand Council continued right through the mourning period and beyond; see, for example, Chi, "Ch'ien-lun Ch'ing Chün-chi ch'u," pp. 181–82.

16. Before coming onto the Interim Council, Hsu Pen may have been attached briefly to the old Office of Military Strategy; CLSL 5/8b.

17. CLSL 5/42a–b; (B) IFT CL1/1/10. According to the *Veritable Records*, the Miao Council had been founded on YC13/5/25; YCSL 156/15a–b. Before that, the Office of Military Strategy handled Miao as well as northwest affairs. After the young Ch'ien-lung was enfeoffed as the Pao Prince in YC11, he was ordered to concern himself with military policy and the Miao frontier; CS 1 : 128.2. The parallel existence of the Interim Council and the Miao Council up to the latter's dissolution is attested in (B) IFT YC13/8/30, pp. 53 54; (B) SYT-FP YC13/9/21, pp. 151–52; and (T) Ch'i-chü chu YC13/9/24. The last archival mention of the Miao Council before its dissolution is (B) IFT YC13/9/27, pp. 173–74. On the Miao Council, see Tu, *Kuan-yü Chün-chi ch'u*, pp. 17, 19.

18. (B) SYT YC13/11/19, p. 85; YC13/11/24, p. 123.

19. On the inner deputies, see Chapter 3 above.

20. Compare SYCL 16/1ff. and 18/1ff. with (B) IFT CL2/12/11, pp. 353–55. See also (B) IFT CL2/11/29, pp. 325–28. The names of some Manchu clerks appear in the Manchu record books (B) Chün-wu IFT and (B) Hsun-ch'ang IFT from YC9 and 10, passim; these frequently suggest earlier dates for entrance on duty than appear in the SYCL. See the explanation at the beginning of Appendix D. Another name, Chang

Pao-ch'uan, not supplied in these sources, is to be found in *Chung-ho yueh-k'an shih-liao hsuan-chi* (Taipei, 1970), 1:1.

21. CS 1:128.5; CLSL 1/9b. See also CS 1:289.0; CLSL 4/17.

22. Information from how Chang listed himself on memorials of the era, as in (T) KCT-YC020499, YC13/9/22; KCT-YC020511, YC13/10/28; KCT-YC020492, YC13/11/8; and KCT-YC020496, YC13/11/15. Toward the end of the first year of the reign, a second Board of Civil Office superintendency was awarded to Ch'ing-fu; CS 1:131.1.

23. CS 1:128.5; CLSL 2/1b–2. Prince Chuang did not remain long in this post, and the Board of Works superintendency was later given to Mai-chu; CS 1:130.0. The Kuo Prince (Yin-li) had previously superintended the Board of Revenue during YC12; (B) T'i-pen 783, 00026, YC12/4/12, Prince Kuo and others.

24. (T) KCT-YC020410, YC13/10/3, Yin-lu (the Chuang Prince) and four others described as "in charge of the Imperial Household" (*Tsung-kuan Nei-wu-fu*).

25. CLSL 4/16, 5/12–13. Yin-hsi was shortly relieved of his Imperial Library responsibilities and replaced by the Ho Prince; (B) IFT YC13/10/27, pp. 327–28.

26. CLSL 5/12–13. For other nonprincely superintendencies created during the Interim Council period, see CS 1:129.4 (Sun Chia-kan at the Board of Civil Office, YC13/11/18) and CS 1:129.6 (Fu-nai at the Board of War, YC13/12/15).

27. CLSL 26/15a–b; (B) SYT-FP CL3/1/20, p. 23. Yin-li was let go in gentle fashion, being first advised to take care of his health and attend to business in his residence, safe from the winter weather, and only later dismissed.

28. YCSL 74/17a–b; Fu Tsung-mao, *Ch'ing-tai Chün-chi ch'u*, p. 29.

29. For the best examples, see (T) Ch'i-chü chu ts'e for this period, passim. For some other examples, see (B) IFT YC13/8/23, p. 1 (with the Kuo Prince); (B) SYT-FP YC13/11/2, p. 15 and passim; (B) SYT-FP CL1/5/16, p. 142 and passim; CLSL 8/9b–10b, 13/13a–b. For evidence from the years after the end of the Interim Council, see (T) Chi-hsin tang for CL3/9/1 and 3/9/12. Other sources show that the two former deputies frequently shouldered deliberation assignments; see, for example, (B) IFT CL3/2/28, pp. 59–61. Although it would be helpful to examine surviving court letter records to obtain names of edict drafters, some of these are defective for the kind of analysis presented here. The (T) record book of court letters Chi-hsin tang (for CL2/6–12), for instance, cannot be used: it contains a mixture of different types of edicts but not one true court letter. (I believe it is an early Shang-yü tang.) The Beijing Chi-hsin tang series was not inaugurated until CL3/9/1 and has a notice in the front of that volume stating clearly that it is the first of a new series. The (T) Pien-pei i-ch'ing tang for these years likewise contains no court letters. The interesting question of the exact role of the princes in these years could be further researched in Beijing materials that I have not been able to examine. There are hints in the sources that the princes were occasionally involved in significant work; see, for example, CLSL 3/17a–b.

30. See the several Ch'ien-lung–period volumes at the Number One Archives with titles such as Liu-ching pan-shih tang and Liu-ching jih-chi tang. There was a similar pattern for left-in-the-capital appointments in the late–Yung-cheng reign. An imperial tomb visit at the beginning of YC11 left Yin-lu, Yin-li, O-erh-t'ai, and Chang T'ing-yü in charge at the capital—again, the two princes and the two inner deputies of that time; see Chang T'ing-yü, *Nien-p'u* 2/28. But there were also tours when princes were not given this responsibility; see CCSL 132/8a–b, for example. Following the Interim

Council era, the real work of the left-in-the-capital group continued to be directed by "the grand secretaries": O-erh-t'ai and Chang T'ing-yü.

31. But see CLSL 62/5b, which shows that on CL3/2/4 Prince Chuang (Yin-lu) became superintendent of the Court of Colonial Affairs (*Li-fan yuan*). The princes also frequently discussed matters of imperial family interest; see, for example, (B) IFT CL7/3/26, pp. 123–25. Princes sometimes had a role in palace security; see, for example, (B) SYT-FP YC13/8/23, p. 7. In general, however, the princes lost ground over the course of the Ch'ien-lung and Chia-ch'ing reigns. A Chia-ch'ing edict specified that princes were to avoid contact with the grand councillors; CCSL 76/20b–22.

32. S. N. Eisenstadt, *The Political Systems of Empires* (New York, 1969), pp. ix, xiv–xv, 21, 133.

33. See SYCL *chüan* 16–19, passim.

34. Cited in (B) IFT CL1/12/6, pp. 349–50.

35. (B) IFT CL1/12/6, pp. 349–50. I was not able to locate the original memorial or the initial board investigation of the problem.

36. (B) SYT-FP CL1/11/30, p. 267.

37. (B) IFT undated document probably of CL1/12/19, pp. 399–400. This report covers CL1–12. Unfortunately, comparable paper use reports for the Yung-cheng–period inner-court staffs have not come to light.

38. CLSL 40/35b–36; HTSL 249/5b–6.

39. (B) IFT CL1/6/20, pp. 27–30; CLSL 21/8–9b.

40. (B) IFT CL1/8/9, pp. 141–42; CL1/8/16, pp. 145–52; CLSL 25/1b–2. The force of the imperial largesse was slightly mitigated the following year when the doubled portion of the salary, known as the "benevolent payment" (*en-feng*), was no longer permitted immunity from monetary penalties levied against officials convicted of malfeasance; CLSL 40/35b–36.

41. (B) SYT-FP YC13/8/24, p. 21; CLSL 1/15b.

42. (B) IFT YC13/9/24, pp. 159–60. See also (B) IFT CL1/2/7, p. 147.

43. (T) KCT-YC005858, CL1/1/11, Yung-t'ai. Many of the base memorials of this period that were considered by the Interim Council were censors' suggestions; see (B) IFT CL2, passim. A cangue was made of several heavy wooden boards with a hole cut in the middle and was worn around the miscreant's neck. The punishment offered both a heavy weight to be carried and the inconvenience of being unable to look down at what one was doing with one's hands or feet.

44. (B) IFT CL1/1/17, pp. 35–36.

45. (T) KCT-YC005624, YC13/10/6, Weng Tsao.

46. (B) IFT YC13/8/20, p. 43.

47. (B) IFT CL2/9/3, pp. 137–38.

48. (B) IFT YC13/8–10; CL1–2/11, passim.

49. (B) IFT YC13/10/25, pp. 313–14.

50. CLSL 6/10a–b.

51. (T) KCT-YC020415, YC13/11/15, Yin-lu. In the fashion of outer-court capital memorials, this is a joint-language Manchu-Chinese memorial (*Man-Han ho-pi*) and received its imperial rescript in Manchu on the Manchu half (not reproduced in *Kung-chung tang Yung-cheng tsou-che* 25:409–11). The rescript read *Gisurehe songkoi obu*, equivalent of the Chinese "Recommendation approved" (*I-i*). The calculation by which the so-called Nine Ministers (*Chiu-ch'ing*) became forty-four in number is illus-

trated in the Ch'ien-lung *Hui-tien*, where the nine offices involved were listed: the Six Boards plus the Censorate, the Transmission Office, and the high court. Each of these bodies' full ministerial level (*t'ang*) participated; CL *Hui-tien* 3/2b.

52. (T) IFT CL5, undated entry, pp. 95–99, citing the CL1 case. See also (B) SYT-FP CL2/1/17, p. 13; CLSL 23/16–21. The case concerned Wang Shih-chün; see ECCP, p. 720.

53. CLSL 3/17a–b.

54. (B) SYT-FP CL2/4/13, p. 143. The edict is described as emanating from the Grand Secretariat (*Nei-ko feng shang-yü*). I take this to mean that it was publicly promulgated (*ming-fa*) and not that it was actually drafted on the Grand Secretariat premises at a distance from the emperor and the inner court. The key fact is that it was recorded in an Interim Council record book, probably drafted by the council's grand secretaries, O-erh-t'ai and Chang T'ing-yü.

55. See, for example, (B) SYT-FP CL1/9/22, p. 121; this edict on the appointment of Chun-t'ai is described as a Board of Civil Office draft (*Li-pu feng shang-yü*), but its placement in an Interim Council record book indicates that the draft was drawn up under Interim Council direction, in this case probably by the Interim Council Board of Civil Office superintendent, Chang T'ing-yü. This reasoning will indicate how other operations apparently undertaken by one of the boards might be interpreted when the organizations in question possessed inner-court superintendents. See, for example, CLSL 7/6a–b, which is described as a Board of War deliberation; but the Interim Council member O-erh-t'ai was superintendent of that board, and he may well have drafted this edict as he did so many others. See the argument presented in Appendix A.

56. Waley, *Three Ways of Thought*, pp. 94–98; CLSL 1048/17b–19, 1489/18–22. For an account of the Ch'ien-lung succession that emphasizes different problems, see Guy, "Zhang Tingyu and Reconciliation."

57. For the palace memorial correspondence on the new "nourish-honesty" schedules, see Zelin, *The Magistrate's Tael*.

58. Conversation with Professor Madeleine Zelin, 15 June 1981. For background on the silver-meltage fee, see Hsiao, *Ch'ing-tai t'ung-shih* 1:355–56, which also gives details of the Yung-cheng Emperor's insistence that the topic be reported secretly and his reluctance to make public (through the routine system or a publicly promulgated edict) his approval of this surcharge.

59. Although a direct survey of palace memorials of the era would be best for presenting topics being reported in the palace memorial system by the Interim Council era, there is unfortunately no readily available assemblage of all palace memorials of the times. The Taipei palace memorial holdings for this period are seriously deficient; see the table in my "Ch'ing Palace Memorials," pp. 16–17, noting particularly the opening years of the Ch'ien-lung reign, which may be read in the first three columns of the table. But the mainland holdings are not much more satisfactory because so many palace memorials and their reference copies are closed to the view of foreigners; see my "An Archival Revival: The Qing Central Government Archives in Peking Today," *Ch'ing-shih wen-t'i* 4, no. 6 (Dec. 1981): 99. The (B) SSTC volumes for this era were put together in the early Republic and do not supply a complete list. Some topics taken up by the council may be gleaned from the summaries in (T) Ch'ang-pien tang for these years.

60. See sources listed in the preceding note.

61. (B) Nei-ko Wai-chi mu-lu, earliest section (for CL1/3). The Wai-chi tang, an archival record found in both Beijing and Taipei, contains palace memorials turned

over (*chiao*) to the Grand Secretariat for transmission to various boards. The clue character *chiao* usually appears on the face of the reference collection (*lu-fu*) copy of the memorial as well as in the logbook (the Sui-shou teng-chi tang). So far as I have been able to ascertain, the volumes of the Wai-chi tang begin in CL1 and no comparable system was used in the Yung-cheng era. See also *Ch'ing Nei-ko k'u-chu chiu-tang chi-k'an, ts'e* 1, p. 43b; and Chuang Chi-fa, review of *Communication and Imperial Control* by Silas H. L. Wu, *Ta-lu tsa-chih* 41, no. 8 (Oct. 1970): 25. I am also indebted to Mr. Chuang for his discussion of this problem with me. For an exceptional use of the old Yung-cheng *chü-t'i-lai* formula, see (B) SSTC CL1/1/25, pp. 6–7. Occasionally a similar form was employed to prescribe waiting for the fuller account that would be reported in a routine memorial; see, for example, (B) IFT CL20/3/20, p. 91.

62. See (B) IFT YC13/8, passim, esp. 13/8/23–30. pp. 3–54. (The YC IFT from just before Yung-cheng's death are missing. The (B) YC13 IFT usually described as covering the eighth and ninth months of YC13 in fact begins with YC13/8/23, the day of Yung-cheng's death.) Other changes in record series that took place early in the new reign include a special new record to track military topics, the Pien-pei i-ch'ing tang. The new series was necessary because the Shang-yü tang had now been expanded to general rather than only military coverage.

63. See my "Books of Revelations." One of the new titles of Manchu-language records introduced either after Yung-cheng's death or beginning with CL1 was a record book on Interim Council affairs (*Tsung-li shih-wu tang*); (B) Man Chün-chi tang-an tsung-mu cheng/fu pen ping yueh-che.

64. HTSL 1049/1ff.

65. YCSL 115/15–16; ECCP, p. 56. The *Shih-lu* editing frequently resulted in omissions, sometimes for the sake of condensation to manageable compass, sometimes for elegance of expression, and sometimes for face-saving purposes. For an example of differences between an archival and a *Shih-lu* document of this era, compare (B) SYT-FP CL1/6/16, pp. 257–59, and CLSL 21/2–3.

66. On the publication history of the Yung-cheng *Chu-p'i yü-chih*, see my "Secret Memorials of the Yung-cheng Period." See also enclosure in (T) KCT-YC016033, YC9/1/10, Li Wei; and ECCP, p. 919.

67. Kenneth K. S. Ch'en, *Buddhism in China: A Historical Survey* (Princeton, 1964), p. 451; ECCP, p. 919; David M. Farquhar, "Emperor as Bodhisattva in the Governance of the Ch'ing Empire," *Harvard Journal of Asiatic Studies* 38, no. 1 (June 1978): 5–34.

68. *Ch'ing Nei-ko k'u-chu chiu-tang chi-k'an, ts'e* 1, pp. 23a–b. The compiler, Fang Su-sheng, describes the memorial as having been submitted by the Grand Secretariat (Nei ko), which probably means the two chief inner-court grand secretaries, O-erh-t'ai and Chang T'ing-yü. The memorial talked about being in the midst of finishing the work on the Yung-cheng *Veritable Records*. Since that compilation was completed in CL6, the memorial was probably submitted a year or two earlier. On the problem of holdovers from the Yung-cheng period, see CLSL 6/29a–b.

69. *Ch'ing Nei-ko k'u-chu chiu-tang chi-k'an, ts'e* 1, pp. 23a–b. On work on board regulations, see (B) IFT CL1/6/28, pp. 55–56; CLSL 2/1b–2. On a publications office set up inside the Board of Rites rather than separately, see (B) IFT CL2/4/5, pp. 137–38.

70. YCSL Piao *chüan* 4b–5; CLSL 4/14b–15.

71. *Ch'ing Nei-ko k'u-chu chiu-tang chi-k'an, ts'e* 1, pp. 18, 20.

72. (B) IFT CL1/3/19, pp. 237–42.

73. (B) SYT-FP CL1/10/5, p. 153; HTSL 1049/13b–14; CLSL 28/10a–b.

74. (B) IFT CL3/10/25, pp. 459–65, referring to ongoing work; (B) SYT-FP CL1/6/17, pp. 263–64. See also Hsiao, *Ch'ing-tai t'ung-shih* 5:15.

75. R. Kent Guy, *The Emperor's Four Treasuries: Scholars and the State in the Late Ch'ien-lung Era*, Harvard East Asian Monographs, no. 129 (Cambridge, Mass., 1987); Benjamin A. Elman, *From Philosophy to Philology: Intellectual and Social Aspects of Change in Late Imperial China*, Harvard East Asian Monographs, no. 110 (Cambridge, Mass., 1984), pp. 13–17.

76. On the importance of publications projects to the livelihood of scholars, see (B) SYT-FP YC13/11/15, pp. 69–70. The government was aware of a surfeit of scholars eager to be employed. Early in the Yung-cheng period there had been more than two hundred men employed as compilers and correctors at the Hanlin Academy. By the early Ch'ien-lung period only seventy-five occupied such Hanlin posts, but the investigation reporting this fact does not make clear if this number included those who were busily employed on the capital's many publications projects; (B) IFT CL7/4/14, p. 197. See also Pamela Kyle Crossley, "*Manzhou yuanliu kao* and the Formalization of the Manchu Heritage," *Journal of Asian Studies* 46, no. 4 (Nov. 1987): 761–90.

77. Guy, "Zhang Tingyu and Reconciliation," pp. 52–53.

78. (B) IFT CL1/2/13, p. 171.

79. (B) Lu-fu CL2 Nei-cheng, CL2/3/29, Ch'en Shih-kuan.

80. (B) IFT CL2/4/4, pp. 133–35.

81. (B) IFT CL2/11/27, pp. 319–21. On the three years being twenty-five months, see note 8 at the beginning of this chapter.

82. CLSL 57/5b–6b.

83. Ibid.

84. CLSL 57/6b. The Chuang Prince, the Kuo Prince, and the P'ing second-degree Prince were dropped from the council, as was Hsu Pen. O-erh-t'ai, Chang T'ing-yü, No-ch'in, Hai-wang, Na-yen-t'ai, and Pan-ti continued, with Chang T'ing-yü the only Chinese until until Hsu Pen was brought back on the following year. See CS 4:2487.

85. (B) IFT undated item probably of CL3/2/23, pp. 53–55.

CHAPTER 6. THE STRUCTURE OF THE EIGHTEENTH-CENTURY GRAND COUNCIL

1. CLSL 57/6b.

2. See, for example, (T) Pien-pei i-ch'ing tang, vol. 1, CL1/2–5/12; the first mention of the Grand Council is on p. 183. Other records such as the Shang-yü tang fang-pen and the I-fu tang also continued without change at this point, most of the changes having occurred following the death of the Yung-cheng Emperor; see Chapter 5, n. 62.

3. Although there was a push at the end of the Yung-cheng period and the beginning of the following reign to issue administrative codes (*tse-li*) for the Six Boards and other offices at the capital, the Grand Council was exempted from any formal codification of its processes. There was no description of Grand Council regulations in the *Hui-tien* until the Chia-ch'ing edition of CC23 (1818), and even at that point, although the *Hui-tien* had a short *chüan* of statutes (*chüan* 3), there were no corresponding precedents in the precedents section (*shih-li*); Fu Tsung-mao, *Ch'ing-tai Chün-chi ch'u*, p. 144 (on this point, see also Prologue, n. 8). Because of their informal nature, Grand Council positions were

not described in the *Li-tai chih-kuan piao* (1784), even though the council had been in existence for almost fifty years when that work was published. During the eighteenth century occasional edicts described some Grand Council procedures, but the assembling and publishing of information about council procedures had to wait until Liang Chang-chü's *Shu-yuan chi-lueh* (SYCL) appeared in the nineteenth century. There is a small (fewer than twenty-five double pages) archival compendium of regulations, (B) Chün-chi ch'u kuei-chih chi-tsai (one *ts'e* in box 3/2365), which has some material not in the SYCL.

4. Liang came on duty as a Grand Council clerk in CC23 (1818) from a position as second-class secretary at the Board of Rites; SYCL 18/25.

5. Because the K'ang-hsi Emperor had ruled sixty-one years (1661–1722), out of considerations of filial piety Ch'ien-lung determined not to exceed that length. Accordingly, at the end of the sixtieth year of his reign, on Chinese New Year's Day 1796 (CC4/1/1), he abdicated the throne. Nevertheless, he continued to run the government until his death three years later, using the title Supreme Abdicated Emperor (*T'ai-shang Huang-ti*). During this period he rescripted all but a handful of the palace memorials; see my "Imperial Notations on Ch'ing Official Documents in the Ch'ien-lung (1736–1795) and Chia-ch'ing Reigns (1796–1820) [Part One]," *National Palace Museum Bulletin* 7, no. 2 (May–June 1972): 1–13. As a result of Ch'ien-lung's continued dominance in the government, within the palace the abdication years were sometimes referred to not by the Chia-ch'ing reign title but as "Ch'ien-lung 61, 62, and 63." For an example see *Shih-liao hsun-k'an*, p. 118.

6. (B) SSTC for CL7/8 (1742), pp. 157–80; and (B) SSTC CL55/11, pp. 255–330. These figures were assembled fairly randomly from a sampling of thirty-day months when the emperor was not likely to be on tour. There was a decline at the very end of the reign: the figures for the thirty-day month of CL7/10 are higher than those in the text — 191 provincial memorials for the month, averaging 6.37 per day; lower figures than at the end of the reign can be found in Ch'ien-lung's declining years — 312 for the month and 10.4 per day in CC1/5, for example; (B) SSTC CL7/10, pp. 202–24; (T) SSTC CC1/5, pp. 169–351. For the Yung-cheng Emperor's own account of the numbers of palace memorials he saw each day (he estimated twenty to thirty, sometimes fifty to sixty), see YCSL 96/4b–7. An oft-cited set of early-Ming figures (for the routine system, of course) is 1,660 documents concerning 3,391 separate matters in one ten-day period, which works out to nearly 5,000 documents per month and seems extraordinarily high, even for the routine system; Hucker, "Governmental Organization of the Ming," p. 28. The comparable figures for one early–Hsien-feng month of palace memorials were 643 provincial memorials for the thirty-day month, 21.43 per day; (B) SSTC HF3/3, pp. 303–477. Part of the reason for the record of increases shown in the SSTC may be that the rationalization of reporting that took place during the Ch'ien-lung reign came to require separate covering documents and enclosures for certain topics, with the result that SSTC document-counts may produce figures inflated only by the new reporting requirements and not by real increases. Figures for precise rates of increase are thus difficult to obtain. For this reason I have included other kinds of paper counts to supplement the SSTC calculations. I have not employed the Grand Council's own annual reports on paper use because those reported amounts received from the Board of Revenue and not the exact amounts used; without an indication of the number of sheets left over from the previous years those figures tell little.

7. *Ch'ing Chün-chi ch'u tang-an mu-lu,* comp. Palace Museum, Bureau of Documents (Peiping, 1930), pp. 7, 8, 13. Two volumes per year was the rule until TK7 (1827), when there was a change to one volume per quarter. Of course, the number of pages in each volume should also be taken into consideration when measuring these increases. The earliest volumes were smaller than the later ones; those for CL7 and 10 were under two hundred pages but were written in cursive script that would have taken up more space if done in a clear hand. By CL20 and 21 (1755 and 1756) individual volumes—each still covering an entire year—had about four hundred pages. Toward the end of the reign the half-year volumes had almost four hundred pages. The single volumes for each quarter in the early Hsien-feng period hovered around five hundred pages.

8. Table in my "Books of Revelations," p. 29.

9. The record book of deliberations (I-fu tang) is a good example. Although not all volumes survive, apparently four were originally compiled for the year YC12, one for each season. Late in the Ch'ien-lung reign the seasons were still the guiding principle for the major divisions, but the volumes had become so fat that there had to be two per season, and when copies were made there was often a further division into months.

10. HTSL 320/18b–20; ECCP, p. 917. The Chancery of Memorials (*Tsou-shih ch'u*) and not the Grand Council oversaw palace memorial storage, but the council processed these documents when they were part of the government's current information system. On the council's archives, see Chapter 7, note 113, and related text. The proportionately longest *Veritable Records* of the dynasty was compiled for the T'ung-chih reign (1861–74) and averaged 10.7 *chüan* per year.

11. (B) IFT CL2/12/2, p. 339; (T) Chün-chi ch'u wen-i tang CL43/5/29, pp. 5–6, 7–8. See also (T) Wen-i tang CL57/2, pp. 9–10.

12. SYCL 14/12b–14b. The grand councillors took their early morning meal with the others; the later meals of the day were served at the Military Archives Office, apparently without the councillors; SYCL 14/10.

13. Usually the size of the Military Archives Office reflected the number of publication projects it was overseeing. The highest figures I have found were in (B) Cho-fan tang CL46/4, p. 20, which named 141 persons on duty. Another high figure of 138 persons was cited in the same series for CL43/2, pp. 3–8. But earlier years sometimes show relatively low figures, as the basic complement of 41 in CL26; (B) Cho-fan tang CL26/3/1, pp. 4–7. See also other volumes of this record book.

14. The errand runners were variously known by the Manchu terms for "attendants" (*pai-t'ang-a* and *su-la*) or affectionately in Chinese as "young'uns" (*hsiao yao-erh*). Many of the "young'uns" served for their entire lives, continuing to be hailed by the diminutive in their sixties; see Teng and Wang, "T'an Chün-chi ch'u," p. 197.

15. CS 4:2487–97, Grand Council tables. My figure of an average of 6.95 councillors per year over the course of the Ch'ien-lung reign and the three abdication years was obtained by excluding councillors whose tenure overlapped with their successors in any one year; otherwise the averages would have been even higher but slightly inaccurate. In the busy thirty-year period CL13–42 in the middle of the reign, the average reached 7.5 councillors per year. The longest lists in the tables are years showing 12 councillors (CL13) and 10 or 11 councillors (CL19 and 41), but usually when this happened several councillors were out of the capital on military or investigative missions. During the K'ang-hsi period the numbers of grand secretaries fluctuated in similar

fashion; see CS 4:2445-61. The number of grand secretaries was limited to four, two Manchu and two Chinese, in CL13; HTSL 11/4b-5. During Chia-ch'ing's personal rule (CC4-25), the number of councillors averaged about 4.5; CS 4:2497-2500. For the average length of time individual men served as grand councillors, see Metzger, *Internal Organization*, app. 6, pp. 435-36.

16. This figure includes those at the twelve tables, the number of grand councillors, and a rough calculation of those off duty on any one day: 16 to 20 clerks and probably some underlings whose duty schedules and numbers are not clearly understood. I have not been able to calculate the full extent of the vast outer-court bureaucracy. Well over 200 men worked at the Hanlin Academy in the Yung-cheng period; YCSL 12/16-17b. In the same era there were 143 clerks (*chung-shu*) at the Grand Secretariat; YC *Hui-tien* 2/1b. Middle-level Six Board posts included 57 Chinese (*Han*) second-class secretaries; (B) IFT CL2/6/24, pp. 381-88.

17. CLSL 284/10-11b; SYCL 13/16a-b; (B) IFT CL7/6/11, pp. 29-30.

18. The three sent to Szechuan in CL13 were No-ch'in, Pan-ti, and Fu-heng, while Kao Pin was sent to Shantung; CS 4:2489; CLSL 332/10-11.

19. SYCL 16/3b-4b, 18/3a-b. Twenty-four additions to the body of clerks meant a sizable new complement; even at the end of the dynasty the total number of Grand Council clerks legally permitted at one time came to only thirty-two (half Manchu and half Chinese).

20. *Pei-wu* could also be used to refer to the entire council. On the terms *Pei-wu* and *Nan-wu*, see *Chung-ho yueh-k'an shih-liao hsuan-chi* 1:1. At first the grand councillors and clerks had only a few rooms in a wooden building, probably in the Imperial Household area west of the Lung-tsung Gate. They are thought to have moved to more spacious quarters in CL12 (1747). For some of the many references on these offices, see SYCL 14/10a-b, 22/7; *Chün-chi chang-ching t'i-ming*, postscript by the compiler, Wu Hsiao-ming, pp. 1-3; Wu Chen-yü, *Yang-chi chai ts'ung-lu* 4/2b; Fu Tsung-mao, *Ch'ing-tai Chün-chi ch'u*, p. 450; Shan Shih-yuan, "Ku-kung Chün-chi ch'u chih-fang," *Wen-wu* 1960, no. 1 (Jan. 1960): 41-43; Yeh, *Nei-ko hsiao-chih*, p. 11b-12b; *Kuo-ch'ao kung-shih* 3/7a-b. For an illustration of the interior reconstructed probably according to Kuang-hsu times, see *Ch'ing-tai kung-t'ing sheng-huo*, comp. Wan I, Wang Shu-ch'ing, and Lu Yen-chen (Hong Kong, 1985), illus. 82 and 83. The name of the Grand Council clerks' office, located to the south of the councillors' premises and therefore known as the "Southern Quarters" (*Nan-wu*), can sometimes be used to identify its documents and activities when these were noted with references to "these quarters" (*pen-wu*) or "the southern quarters" (*nan-wu-che*). For the location of the council offices, see Map 1.

21. *Ch'ing-kung shu-wen* 3/25b; *Ch'ing Nei-ko k'u-chu chiu-tang chi-k'an* 1/22.

22. I am indebted to Professor Harold Shadick for his elucidation of this matter (conversation of 10 Apr. 1979). For instances of the broader use of *chün* to signify "affairs of state" in terms such as *chün-kuo chi-wu*, *chün-kuo*, and *chün-chi*, see *Hsu t'ung-chih* 1:4040; *T'ai-tsung shih-lu* 63/20-22 (and as explained in Fu Tsung-mao, *Ch'ing-tai Chün-chi ch'u*, p. 23); YCSL 2/24b-26, 29/4b; Hsi, *Nei-ko chih*, p. 4. For a CC10 (1805) edict's denial of an assertion that the name referred narrowly to military affairs, see CCSL 144/4b-5. See also Hsiao, *Ch'ing-tai t'ung-shih* 1:867; and Tu, *Kuan-yü Chün-chi ch'u*. Although it is tempting to speculate that the YC11 name change was conferred in anticipation that there would later be an opportunity for the inner-court staffs' amalgamation and

expansion of their role, in which case a title better than "military finance" would be desirable, I have found no solid evidence of any such long-range plotting. The council's name was frequently rendered *Pan-li Chün-chi ch'u*. Variants were also used, such as *Pan-li Chün-chi shih-wu fu*; (B) Lu-fu, Chün-wu category, *chün-hsu* subclass, 5, YC13/10/9. In Manchu the council's name was *Cooha-i nashūn-i ba*, a title that unmistakably conveys the early military connotation. The eighteenth-century Annamese court, desiring to install a faithful imitation of the Central Kingdom's high privy council, misunderstood the meaning of the council's name and conferred titles with military connotations on its own civil councillors; see Alexander B. Woodside, *Vietnam and the Chinese Model: A Comparative Study of Nguyen and Ch'ing Civil Government in the First Half of the Nineteenth Century* (Cambridge, Mass., 1961), pp. 96–100.

23. For exceptions, see Brunnert and Hagelstrom, *Present Day Political Organization*, p. 128; and Hucker, *Dictionary of Official Titles*, item 1735, where the translation is "Council of State." The Chinese *ch'u*, meaning "office," is not often applied to capital agencies and usually denotes an inferior body or subordinate office. Its use for the Grand Council is sometimes helpful in identifying council documents where the term "this office" (*pen-ch'u*) is employed; see the editor's explanatory note in *Ch'ing-kung shu-wen* 3/25b. Other terms such as "inner-court high privy officials" (*shu-ch'en*) and "eminences" (*ta-jen* or *ta chün-chi*) were also used to designate the councillors; see, for example, (B) SSTC CL14/10/7, p. 286. In the eighteenth century, councillors were said to be "attached" (*hsing-tsou*) to the council, but sometimes a new man would be given the designation "attached on probation" (*hsueh-hsi hsing-tsou*); see SYCL 13/3a–b; Ying-ho, *En-fu t'ang pi-chi* 1/29; Ch'en K'ang-ch'i, *Lang-ch'ien chi-wen* (1880; repr. Taipei, 1968), 2/1b; Li P'eng-nien et al., *Ch'ing-tai chung-yang kuo-chia chi-kuan k'ai-shu*, p. 61. In the late nineteenth century, the Deliberative Council (*I-cheng wang ta-ch'en*) title was revived and used concurrently for Prince Kung when he headed the Grand Council; see (T) Kung-chi pei-k'ao, vol. *yuan-hsia*; SYCL 13/2; (T) SSTC TC3/7/4, p. 23.

24. (B) Chi-hsin tang CL3/9/1, p. 1. A court letter in CLSL 25/20a–b dated CL1/8/26, for instance, is headed in the old way: "Edict to the grand secretaries." This fails to suggest the Interim Council origin of the draft, which is clear from the archival version (in what was to become a Grand Council record series); (B) SYT-FP CL1/8/26, pp. 55–56. Uncertainty about titles and names continued well into the new reign.

25. (B) IFT CL8, passim. For another example, see (B) IFT CL7/6/12, pp. 33–38, where the grand secretaries were ordered to investigate and the grand councillors responded. See also Hsi, *Nei-ko chih*, p. 5.

26. In (B) CHT CL4/7/26, pp. 43–44, O-erh-t'ai and Chang T'ing-yü were titled "Grand councillor and grand secretary" (*Pan-li Chün-chi ta-ch'en ta-hsueh-shih*), but in other documents of the times the Grand Council title was frequently omitted. In the second and third decades of the reign, however, the Ch'ien-lung Emperor began to direct more memorials to the "grand councillors"; see, for example, (B) IFT CL16 and CL24, passim.

27. On the leading grand councillor position, see SYCL 13/2; and Fu Tsung-mao, *Ch'ing-tai Chün-chi ch'u*, pp. 229–33. In the nineteenth century a second-in-command appeared, known as *Pang ling-pan*; see Teng and Wang, "T'an Chün-chi ch'u," p. 194. For other terms for the council leader, such as *shou-hsi* and *k'uei-hsi*, see Ch'ien Shih-fu, "Ch'ing-tai ti Chün-chi ch'u," 1:475. Other eighteenth-century sources refer to the leading grand councillor as "prime minister." See, for example, Chao I, *Yen-p'u tsa-chi*

1:4–5. One modern author has also called these men "prime ministers" (*k'uei-shou*); Li P'eng-nien et al., *Ch'ing-tai chung-yang kuo-chia chi-kuan k'ai-shu*, pp. 60–61.

28. CS 4:2487–96. The two Ch'ien-lung–period Chinese ranking councillors were Liu T'ung-hsun in CL37–38 (1772–73) and Yü Min-chung in CL39–44 (1774–79); CS 4:2448–49.

29. The leading grand councillor is listed first in the year-by-year rankings of the official history tables; CS 4:2486–2512.

30. SYCL 13/1a–b.

31. Chao, *Yen-p'u tsa-chi* 1:4–5. According to a twentieth-century description, the morning audience was known as the "early conversation" (*tsao-mien*); Teng and Wang, "'l'an Chün-chi ch'u," p. 195. I have not seen this usage in eighteenth-century accounts.

32. CLSL 336/24b–25. Note the similar waivers of the Yung-cheng Emperor cited in Chapter 1, nn. 75–80, and related text.

33. (B) SYT-FP CL13/12/12, pp. 427–28; CLSL 328/42b–45. For another list of officials whom Ch'ien-lung found especially trustworthy, see *Kung-chung hsien-hsing tse-li* (Kuang-hsu ed.), 1/28–29b.

34. *Ch'ing-ch'ao Hsu Wen-hsien t'ung-k'ao* 5:8774, edict of CC2/9.

35. Teng and Wang, "T'an Chün-chi ch'u," pp. 194–95; Fu Tsung-mao, *Ch'ing-tai Chün-chi ch'u*, pp. 231–32, 569ff. For the hierarchy within the grand secretaries' ranks, see YC *Hui-tien* 3/2 (for the old-style list) and HT 2/1.

36. CS 4:2494–97. On the ranking of A-kuei and Ho-shen, see also the comment at the end of the following note.

37. The councillors' internal rankings were probably decided by the date of their appointment to the council, with ambiguous situations resolved by the monarch. Each year's hierarchy is to be found in the tables of the official Ch'ing history, CS 4:2486–2512. An alternative ranking scheme is provided for many years in the archival Ch'ing History Office (Ch'ing-shih kuan) tables, compiled in the Republican era; (T) Chün-chi ta-ch'en nien-piao. In one of these volumes (no. 724), Ho-shen is consistently ranked ahead of A-kuei in the late–Ch'ien-lung–period list.

38. For some examples, see (B) SYT-FP CL32/11/7, pp. 129–30; (B) IFT CL20/12/8, p. 93. In periods when there were two dignitaries with the same surname, personal names were nevertheless avoided. See, for example, the Grand Secretariat instruction book (B) P'iao pu-pen shih, Book 2, Board of Rites "Tan-ch'ien i-i" sec., where a "Southern Liu" (*Nan Liu*) is named, distinguishing Liu Lun, who was from Kiangsu, from Liu T'ung-hsun, who hailed from Shantung; SYCL 15/5b.

39. On the appointment of grand secretaries, see HT 3/3a–b; CLSL 330/6-7, Hsi, *Nei-ko chih* 3a–b. I have not found examples of the Board of Civil Office lists that Hsi describes.

40. Chi, "Ch'ien-lun Ch'ing Chün-chi ch'u," p. 182. In the official regulations the process is described as involving "special appointments" (*t'e-chien*), meaning that it was handled without creating precedents; HT 3/1. For an archival record of an edict announcing a grand councillor appointment, see (B) SYT-FP CL13/9/30, p. 201.

41. CS 4:2497. The story appears in Wu's official biography in CS 6:4475–76. Note that it is differently portrayed in the *Veritable Records* (CCSL 19/17b–18), where it is claimed that need for more Chinese on the Grand Council was the reason for the appointment. The sources do not explain why Ch'ien-lung was summoning his grand councillors in the middle of the night. Wu was awarded a good alternative post: Chihli

lieutenant governor. On the grand councillors' availability to the emperor, see the petulant edict in CLSL 292/12b–13.

42. HT 3/1. The regular Ch'ing bureaucracy consisted of eighteen ranks numbered from 1–9, with two subranks at each step. For an explanation of official ranks, see Hucker, *Dictionary of Official Titles*, pp. 4–5.

43. See the ECCP biographies of these men. Note, however, that Fu-heng's biography entirely fails to mention that he ever served as a grand councillor, let alone as the ranking councillor for twenty-one years.

44. ECCP, pp. 72–74. On Chao-hui's Grand Council appointment, see (B) IFT CL25/3/10, p. 44.

45. See the list of designations for Pan-ti in *Ming-Ch'ing tang-an ts'un-chen hsuan-chi*, comp. Li Kuang-t'ao (Taipei, 1959), memorial illustrated on 1:230–38.

46. CCSL 53/22a–b, for example.

47. Prince Kung served briefly on the Grand Council in HF3 (1853) and became ranking member in TC1 (1862), stepping down in KHsu10 (1884); CS 4:2504–08. See note 23 above. Other princes served later, at the end of the dynasty.

48. SYCL 16/5b; CS 4:2493, 2495–99. For a list of fathers and sons who served as grand councillors up to the Tao-kuang period, see Ying-ho, *En-fu-t'ang pi-chi* 1/30. The appointment of relatives is best understood in the framework of the Chinese high regard for the male family line in which an individual was esteemed as part of the continuum; see Frank Ching, *Ancestors: 900 Years in the Life of a Chinese Family* (New York, 1988), p. 91.

49. Fu Tsung-mao, *Ch'ing-tai Chün-chi ch'u*, table p. 336n.202.

50. Ying-ho, *En-fu-t'ang pi-chi* 1/5.

51. Fu Tsung-mao, *Ch'ing-tai Chün-chi ch'u*, pp. 159, 500–501. A better distribution was achieved in the Chia-ch'ing reign: in fifteen years (out of twenty-five) a balance was maintained (51 percent of the time); in six years there were more Chinese than Manchus (24 percent); and in four years there were more Manchus than Chinese (16 percent); ibid., p. 160. Fu's calculations were assembled on the basis of the tables of grand councillors in his book (pp. 529–683), whereas I have drawn on those in the official Ch'ing history, CS 4:2486–2512. During the Ch'ien-lung reign, particularly in the early years, the shortage of Manchus with *chin-shih* degrees was keenly felt; see, for example, (B) IFT CL13/8/18, p. 213. See also SYCL 15/1–3; and Ying-ho, *En-fu-t'ang pi-chi* 1/30, where Ying-ho speaks of the small number of Manchu and Mongol grand councillors of the Ch'ien-lung reign who held the *chin-shih* degree and names others from the Chia-ch'ing reign. See Chapter 8, n. 45, below. For information concerning the early Ch'ing Grand Secretariat, see Hsieh Pao-chao, *The Government of China (1644–1911)* (London, 1966), p. 74n.

52. CS 4:2487. For a penetrating analysis of the significance of growing Chinese influence in the council on one occasion, see Guy, *The Emperor's Four Treasuries*, pp. 69–70. Nevertheless, the council's Manchu preponderance appears to have persisted through much of the nineteenth century as well. See, for example, John K. Fairbank, *Trade and Diplomacy on the China Coast: The Opening of the Treaty Ports 1842–1854* (Cambridge, Mass., 1964), 1:85.

53. CCSL 49/14–15, 130/14–15; and Fu Tsung-mao, *Ch'ing-tai Chün-chi ch'u*, pp. 188–202. On the board superintendents, see Chapter 1 above, pp. 35–41.

54. CLSL 1017/2a–b; CS 4:2493–94, 2670.

55. CLSL 1017/2a–b. On this point see note 108 below and accompanying text.

56. SYCL 15/5–7b; Wei Hsiu-mei, "Ts'ung-liang ti kuan-ch'a t'an-t'ao Ch'ing-chi Pu-cheng-shih chih jen-shih ti-shan hsien-hsiang," *Chin-tai shih yen-chiu so chi-k'an* 2 (June 1971): 517; Guy, *The Emperor's Four Treasuries*, p. 90; CLSL 16/7–10. On the early Ch'ing, see Frederic Wakeman's finding concerning a preponderance of Shantung men in the central government in *The Great Enterprise* 1:436–47.

57. See Philip A. Kuhn, *Rebellion and Its Enemies in Late Imperial China: Militarization and Social Structure, 1796–1864* (Cambridge, Mass., 1970), pp. 12–13.

58. *Chiu-tien pei-cheng*, comp. Chu P'eng-shou (Taipei, 1968), pp. 29–30. The four *ching-lueh* were Chang Kuang-ssu (not a grand councillor), who was sent to take charge of the Miao frontier late in YC13; No-ch'in, dispatched to the Chin-ch'uan front in CL13; Fu-heng, appointed to replace No-ch'in later the same year; and Fu-heng, gazetted to the Burma campaign in CL34. The title was at the same level as Field Marshal (*Ta-chiang-chün*); see *Ch'ing-tai wen-hsien mai-ku lu*, comp. Chao Tsu-ming (Taipei, 1971), p. 283. Hucker's explanation that during the Ch'ing this official was in charge of Green Standard forces is mistaken; see his *Dictionary of Official Titles*, item 1234. For another possible eighteenth-century *ching-lueh* appointment, see CLSL 284/19a–20b, but the use of the term here seems verbal and does not make clear that Ch'ing-fu actually held the high title.

59. (B) SYT-FP CL13/10/19, p. 25; CL14/1/3, pp. 3–4; CS 1:149.8.

60. CLSL 1002/40.

61. CS 4:2493–94. The four were A-kuei, Feng-sheng-e, Fu-k'ang-an, and Ming-liang.

62. ECCP, pp. 7–8.

63. (B) IFT CL13/12/10, pp. 408–12; CLSL 335/2b.

64. (B) SYT-FP CL14/1/17, pp. 33–35. The archival version of this edict shows that it was personally received (*mien-feng*) by the Chuang Prince and others.

65. For a list of the offices and ranks from which the grand councillors were appointed, see Fu Tsung-mao, *Ch'ing-tai Chün-chi ch'u*, pp. 167–69. On Ming central government officials' lack of field experience, see Ray Huang, *1587*, p. 50.

66. Depositions (*kung*) were not usually copied into the record books destined for outer-court use or for the History Office, nor were they sent out of the council by any other route. Thus, today these valuable documents are usually available only in the Grand Council archives, just as during the Ch'ing they were made available only to members of the central government's most politically reliable group, the Grand Council and its staff.

67. For example, (B) SYT-FP CL32/5/14, p. 268; (T) Chiao-pu ni-Hui tang CL49/5/26, p. 171.

68. L. Carrington Goodrich, *The Literary Inquisition of Ch'ien-lung* (1935; repr. New York, 1986), pp. 34, 52, and passim; Guy, *The Emperor's Four Treasuries*. (T) SYT-FP CL44/7/1, p. 3; CL46/12/14, p. 340; and CL47/12/10, pp. 207–9 contain some examples of the many Grand Council memorials on scanning, burning, and so forth. Many of these books were first stored in the Military Archives Office in the palace in Peking, the crates so numerous that some had to be left out in the courtyard; see (T) SYT-FP CL43/5/17, pp. 361–62. After the fall of the Ch'ing, a considerable number still reposed there, having never been burned at all. Many of these were later taken to Taiwan.

69. ECCP, p. 917. The task of compiling the Yung-cheng Emperor's rescripts and edicts into publishable editions, for example, would have required considerable discretion and could only be entrusted to the highest inner-court confidants.

70. See my "Secret Memorials of the Yung-cheng Period." For an account of similar activities in the Ming, see de Heer, *The Care-taker Emperor*, p. 138.

71. Teng and Wang, "T'an Chün-chi ch'u," p. 197; Chao I, *Yen-p'u tsa-chi* 1:5–6. Occasionally when people attempted to get at the emperor through the grand councillors, these high officials were forced to explain such suspicious invasion of their isolation. See, for example, the account of a petition presented to Shu-ho-te by a minor member of the Censorate, (T) SYT-FP CL41/7/23, pp. 585–91. Chao I may have been describing a Grand Council isolation that was characteristic only of the first half of the Ch'ien-lung reign, up to the time of his departure from the council. See also the stories told in Guy, *The Emperor's Four Treasuries*, pp. 72, 84–85.

72. As suggested by Teng and Wang, "T'an Chün-chi ch'u," p. 195.

73. See Chang T'ing-yü, *Nien-p'u.* The work's first and very brief mention of the High Officials in Charge of Military Strategy appears on 3/6. As far as we know, no record was kept of Grand Council discussions. By contrast, see the comments on the highly confidential memoranda of T'ang and Sung deliberations known as the "Records of Current Government" (*Shih-cheng chi*) in Wolfgang Franke, "The Veritable Records of the Ming Dynasty (1368–1644)," in *Historians of China and Japan*, ed. W. G. Beasley and E. G. Pulleyblank (London, 1961), p. 65.

74. A *Wen-ch'eng kung* [*A-kuei*] *nien-p'u*, comp. Na-yen-ch'eng (1813; repr. Taipei, 1971). The archives, however, contain a large number of these missing memorials. Even though the grand councillors forbore to describe council proceedings, some of the council's clerks—Chao I, Wang Ch'ang, Ch'eng Chin-fang, and above all Liang Chang-chü—have left helpful descriptions. (For references, see the bibliography.)

75. (B) IFT CL1/12/6, pp. 349–50; BH 129; Fu Tsung-mao, *Ch'ing-tai Chün-chi ch'u*, pp. 188–94; Ch'ien Shih-fu, "Ch'ing-tai ti Chün-chi ch'u," 1:475 and n. 3. Ming grand secretary appointments were concurrent right through to the end of that dynasty; see Ch'ien Mu, *Chung-kuo li-tai cheng-chih te-shih*, p. 90. In the early Ch'ing, the grand secretaries possessed concurrent titles as board presidents; KH *Hui-tien* 2/1.

76. *Ming-Ch'ing shih-liao* (Taipei, 1972), 9.10:907b–8, 9.8:755a–b. For other lists of councillors' concurrent posts, see the list for Le-pao in (T) SYT-FP CC19/J2/2, pp. 29–30; and one for Sai-shang-a in (T) SYT-FP HF1/3/9–10, pp. 83, 89, 95.

77. (B) IFT CL23/4/8, pp. 80–88.

78. (B) IFT CL16/J5/13, pp. 79–80.

79. For example, (B) IFT CL25/10/5, pp. 177, 179–80. One of the Chia-ch'ing reforms stipulated that the grand councillors were not to work on board matters at the council premises. This stricture seems designed not to prevent expansion of council activities but rather to preserve council confidentiality by ruling against board personnel coming to the council offices to pick up board work; CCSL 76/20b–22.

80. See (B) IFT CL13/10/28, p. 321, and the related document of CL13/11/19, p. 377; (B) IFT CL13/11/20, pp. 387–88; (B) IFT CL20/2/3, p. 21.

81. See the KH *Hui-tien* explanation of compilation procedures (*fan-li*) and 2/2b–3; (B) IFT CL1/12/7, pp. 367–71; HTSL 1049/1. The procedures for the court diaries are described in HTSL 1055–56.

82. (B) IFT CL6/7/6, pp. 273–75; CL6/8/5, p. 345; CL9/3/2, pp. 67–68; CL25/5/

22, pp. 57–58; (B) SYT-FP CL4/5/10, p. 105; CL55/4/19, p. 197; (T) Hsun-ch'ang tang CL55/1/27, pp. 189–90; YC *Hui-tien* 2/13; HT 3/9a–b. But compare the Hanlin handling of certain in-service testing in CC8; (T) SSTC CC8/3/5, p. 185.

83. Note that even at the end of the dynasty the official regulations placed much of the official publications work in the Hanlin Academy because the Grand Council positions remained concurrent and unofficial; see HT 70/4b–7; HTSL 1049/13bff. Many of the works listed under the Hanlin in the *Ta Ch'ing Hui-tien* were actually edited under Grand Council auspices, particularly during the Ch'ien-lung period. In Chia-ch'ing times some were moved back under the supervision of outer-court academicians.

84. See, for example, (B) IFT CL16/5/7, p. 11. On another occasion the councillors reported that they had drafted the rescript "in accordance with regulations" (*chao-li*); (B) IFT CL20/5/7, pp. 155–56.

85. (B) SYT-FP CL13/11/29, pp. 357–61; CLSL 330/29b–30. Of course, many draft rescripts were still composed in the Grand Secretariat, but when the emperor revised one (*kai-ch'ien*), the Grand Council paid special attention to the document; see, for example, (T) SYT-FP CL55/6/21, p. 417. Many Grand Secretariat edicts were handled in the inner court at a far earlier date; there are some examples from the Yung-cheng period. See also the (T) record book labeled Chi-hsin tang but containing publicly promulgated edicts, for example, one of CL2/9/26. In the early nineteenth century Kung Tzu-chen observed that the Grand Council grand secretaries did not deal with the routine memorials (*Ting-an wen-chi* 4 : 311ff.), but this should probably be taken to mean that in general the routine memorials were processed in the outer court; nevertheless, numerous archival examples exist of inner-court handling. See also (T) SYT-FP CL52/12/1, p. 435.

86. (T) SYT-FP CC8/6/25, p. 159.

87. (T) Hsun-ch'ang tang CL55/1/23, pp. 151–63.

88. CLSL 350/6b–7; (B) SYT-FP CL46/9/11, p. 330; SYCL 13/16.

89. For example, (B) P'iao t'ung/pu-pen shih-yang.

90. For example, see the grand councillors' report to the emperor that they had investigated certain Board of Works accounts by asking the board about them. The board replied to the Grand Council, and the council in turn wrote out and submitted an entirely new communication on the subject to the emperor, so that the board's explanation did not directly reach Ch'ien-lung; (T) I-tsou tang CL22/5/30, pp. 186–87. See also (T) SYT-FP CL47/12/24, pp. 371–72, in which the council handed in the list received from the Board of Works but at the same time wrote its own summary for imperial perusal. (T) SYT-FP CL49/5/3, p. 284, shows a similar document in which the Grand Council acted as intermediary in summarizing certain previous memorials. (T) SYT-FP CL51/10/6, p. 145, shows the grand councillors summarizing an important K'ang-hsi–period case the emperor had asked about, at the same time submitting the original routine memorial in which it had first been reported. The outer-court reply to the request for information does not appear in the correspondence I examined.

91. (T) SYT-FP undated entry of CL50/1/16, pp. 83–99; CLSL 1223/1b–2; (T) SYT-FP CL52/7/10, p. 55. For the *k'ou-hun* cases, see (T) SYT-FP CL55/4/4, pp. 21–22; and (T) SYT-FP CC10/9/18, pp. 209–12. An idea of the myriad topics subject to Grand Council consideration has been provided in Chapter 5, but that list is almost certainly not complete. Without an inspection of the full run of Manchu-language materials—something that has not yet been possible—the likelihood of omissions is

high. A general overview of council responsibilities is available in Li P'eng-nien et al., *Ch'ing-tai chung-yang kuo-chia chi-kuan k'ai-shu*, pp. 61–63.

92. The surviving Grand Council working ledgers track a miscellany of areas: the use of various kinds of seals (for which see [T] Yin-hua pu), names of those reporting for duty each day ([T] Chih-pan tang), expenses for meals taken at the council premises ([B] Cho-fan tang), and many aspects of communications management. The (T) Lai-wen tang listed but did not copy lateral communications and recorded the ciphers (particular individual ways of signing) of the outer-court messengers who came to the council to receive the documents; the process is described in *Chung-ho yueh-k'an shih-liao hsuan-chi* 1:5. Two late-nineteenth-century indexes, (T) Kung-chi pei-k'ao and (T) Nei-che tsung-mu, furnished a rough index by listing some of the palace memorials under subjects of interest. For additional descriptions of Grand Council daybooks and ledgers, see SYCL 22/6a–b; and Chang Te-tse, "Chün-chi ch'u chi ch'i tang-an."

93. (T) SYT-FP CL52/2/20, p. 222. For illustrations of the green-headed tallies, as well as of the red-headed sticks used for members of the imperial clan, see *Ch'ing-tai kung-t'ing sheng-huo*, illus. 75.

94. HT 4/1–2; (T) KCT-YC021966, YC2/1/26, Lung-k'e-to and four other Board of Civil Office officials; *Ch'ing-kung shu-wen* 4/34; *Ch'ing-pai lei-ch'ao*, vol. 1: *Ch'ao-kung lei*, pp. 6–7. Manchu and Mongol inscriptions might be prepared by the Court of Colonial Affairs; (T) Chiao-p'ien tang CC25/8/26, p. 51.

95. (B) SYT-FP undated entry of CL32/2/1, pp. 93–94; CL47/1/3, pp. 19–20 plus attached list pp. 21–23; (T) SYT-FP CL49/4/28, p. 237; HF1/5/28, pp. 245–46. The list in the second item shows the type of information the emperor got on the green-headed tallies: the man's name, rank, banner, age, examination, first post, later post, length of time in office, and a four- or five-character evaluation. For punishments, see (T) SYT-FP CC23/12/21, pp. 239–45; Tai Chün-yuan, the grand councillor in question, was also president of the Board of Civil Office at the time.

96. (T) SYT-FP CL52/12/9, p. 495; CL52/2/20, p. 222.

97. (B) IFT CL9/12/13, pp. 345–46; (T) SYT-FP CL43/4/10, p. 77; CLSL 1054/16b–17; *Ch'ing-shih lieh-chuan* 28/38b. The regulations for these systems are in HT 3/2b. In CL6 (1741), for example, when the Hunan governor sought grain price adjustments for Miao frontier areas because they were so distant from the established granaries, Ch'ien-lung sent the memorial to the board for its recommendation, at the same time asking the grand councillors to keep the memorial on hand and to remind him when the board reply arrived. The board deliberations—presumably based on regulations and precedents—recommended rejecting the governor's request. Nevertheless, after reviewing the board response the emperor authorized the price adjustments urged in the original memorial. Thus, the emperor initially sought support in the empire's regulations and his board's interpretations but then was willing to override recommendations that did not agree with his views—in this instance probably because of a desire to honor the request of a trusted provincial official; see (B) IFT CL6/7/12, pp. 291–92.

98. For example, (B) IFT CL6–10 vol., CL10/4/3, pp. 385–88; (B) IFT CL13/11/8, p. 345. For a description of the inner deputies' similar services for the Yung-cheng Emperor, see Chapter 3 above.

99. (B) IFT CL6/5/21, p. 219.

100. (B) Chu-p'i tsou-che, Nei-cheng category, Chih-kuan subcategory, CL7/2/1, Yang Hsi-fu.

101. (B) IFT CL8/2/26, p. 19.

102. HT 3/9a–b.

103. (T) SYT-FP CL41/2/29, p. 271. An example of accompanying guidance is supplied in (T) SYT-FP CL55/4/23, p. 263. This kind of document could also be submitted in Manchu; see (T) SYT-FP CC25/11/2, p. 36. Not all appointments were handled by this method, however, as certain provincial appointments, apparently at all levels, were handled in the routine system with the edicts drafted in the Grand Secretariat; see (T) SYT-FP CC7/12/25, p. 289. There were also edicts prepared with blanks for naming a position rather than a man, called *k'ung-ch'ueh yü-chih*; see, for example, (B) IFT CL16/3/17, p. 195. For a description of a routine-system model for this kind of prepared form, see Hsi, *Nei-ko chih*, p. 6. In the routine system this kind of document was sometimes called a "slip with a blank for a name" (*k'ung-ming ch'ien* or *k'ung-ming p'iao-ch'ien*); see (B) P'iao pu-pen shih, Book 2 (Hu and Li boards), p. 3b. Two types of these forms—one for appointments and one for money—filled in by the Chia-ch'ing Emperor are illustrated in color on the back cover of my "Imperial Notations on Ch'ing Official Documents."

104. (B) IFT CL16/5/7, p. 9. For other examples, see (T) IFT CL5/2/29, p. 27; and (T) SYT-FP CL52/10/17, p. 123.

105. (T) SYT-FP CL55/4/27, p. 287; CLSL 1353/36b–37. Other examples are in (T) IFT CL5/7/11, p. 185; and (T) SYT-FP CC17/9/25, p. 263.

106. (T) SYT-FP CC12/10/27, pp. 211–13, 231–32.

107. (T) SYT-FP CL55/6/4, pp. 261–64.

108. (B) SYT-FP CL26/12/27, pp. 386–97.

109. The archives are filled with materials concerning the frequent imperial tours. Those that have been used in preparing this section are (B) IFT CL20/9/25, pp. 23–24; CL21/10/27, pp. 207–15; CL21/12/23, pp. 253–64; (B) SYT-FP CL32/2/1, pp. 95–99; and (T) SYT-FP CL41/1/29, pp. 75–76. On the imperial tours of the Ch'ien-lung period, see Harold L. Kahn, "The Politics of Filiality: Justification for Imperial Action in Eighteenth Century China," *Journal of Asian Studies* 26, no. 2 (Feb. 1967): 197–203. On financial rewards to some of the high-level members of tours, see CLSL 10/6–7.

110. In the autumn of 1985 I examined examples of this kind of material on display in a special Huang-shih ch'eng exhibit in Beijing.

111. On the dismissed officials, see, of many discussions in the archives, (T) I-tsou tang CL22/6/18, pp. 221–22; and (T) SYT-FP CL41/8/2, p. 223. The late–Chia-ch'ing–period regulations on how the council handled the dismissed officials are supplied in SYCL 14/3a–b. One late-Ch'ing record book is exclusively concerned with this problem: it is the (T) Wen-wu ch'a-pan fei-yuan tan-tang. On how Sun Shih-i won advancement as a result of an imperial tour interview, see (B) SYT-FP CL40/3/27, pp. 352–53.

112. See, for example, (T) SYT-FP CL51/4/29, p. 259.

113. Compare (T) SYT-FP CL54/11/1, p. 251, with the (T) Ch'i-chü chu entry for the same day. The archives contain several examples of this sort of cover-up for the benefit of inner-court patronage. Compare (T) SYT-FP CL41/10/14, pp. 93–94; CL54/7/17, p. 15; and CL55/5/4, p. 373, with the related (T) Ch'i-chu chü entries for the same days. (The first example, concerning a Grand Council noted names list for prefects and *taotais*, has no equivalent listed in the Diary under its date.) The earliest reference to a Grand Council noted names list that I have found is in (B) IFT

CL20/12/26, p. 111. For an example of the handling of a different kind of noted names list long before the Grand Council's founding, see (T) Ch'i-chü chu KH35/2/10, where eleven grand secretaries and subchancellors discussed the matter in what was apparently a large public audience (*Ch'ien-ch'ing men t'ing-cheng*). That the grand councillors were allowed some patronage opportunities early in the reign, but along with other high officials, is suggested by the list of men they were permitted to recommend for promotion in (B) IFT CL13/8/13, pp. 199–204.

114. CCSL 181/29–30. The possibility of a similar problem of Grand Council as opposed to board lists for prefect vacancies is suggested in (B) IFT CL23/4/24, pp. 128–30. On the Grand Council responsibility for managing appointments, see HT 3/3–5 (this is the same in the Chia-ch'ing *Hui-tien*) and SYCL 13/18a–b, 20a–b. For a description of the situation as it probably was handled toward the end of the dynasty, see Teng and Wang, "T'an Chün-chi ch'u," p. 196. On a question of Ho-shen's dubious use of a noted names list, see CCSL 37/34b.

115. (T) SYT-FP CL43/1/27, p. 177; see also (B) Lu-fu, *chih-kuan* sec., undated list in the CL40 box. The difference between the noted names lists at the beginning and the end of the Ch'ien-lung reign is suggested by comparing the foregoing with CLSL 21/20b, an edict concerning the Board of Civil Office noted names list for first- and second-class subprefects and district magistrates. By the end of the reign, however, sometimes the Grand Council was handling such positions as these; (T) SYT-FP CL55/11/12, p. 13. I believe that the council's use of its own noted names lists was but one way in which it was able to influence imperial appointments; this matter needs further study.

116. Exceptions to the in-and-out-in-one-day practice were regularly noted; see, for example, (B) SSTC CL20/1/2, p. 1.

CHAPTER 7. GRAND COUNCIL SUBORDINATE ORGANIZATIONS

1. On the Tsungli Yamen, see Immanuel C. Y. Hsu, *China's Entrance into the Family of Nations: The Diplomatic Phase, 1858–1880*, Harvard East Asian Monograph no. 5 (Cambridge, Mass., 1960); and S. M. Meng, *The Tsungli Yamen: Its Organization and Functions* (Cambridge, Mass., 1970). On the relationship between the Grand Council and the Tsungli Yamen, see (T) SYT-FP KHsu15/2/15, pp. 117–21; HFSL 340/9a–b; and Teng and Wang, "T'an Chün-ch'u," p. 196. The council did have other minor subordinate offices; one of these, the Secret Accounts Bureau (*Mi-chi ch'u*), which prospered for about twenty years at the end of the Ch'ien-lung reign, will be described in Chapter 8.

2. The Manchu *janggin* is derived from Mongolian and rendered *chang-ching* in Chinese. Although it had a military meaning (and has been equated with the Chinese *chiang-chün*, "general"), when employed for the Grand Council clerks it was equivalent to the Chinese *ssu-yuan* and could be used interchangeably for both Manchu and Chinese clerks. Thus, the terms *chang-ching* and *ssu-yuan* do not denote two different groups in the Grand Council as declared in Alfred Kuo-liang Ho, "The Grand Council in the Ch'ing Dynasty," p. 172. I have even seen the usage "Chinese *chang-ching*"; see, for example, (T) SYT-FP CC10/10/1, p. 7. The term "staff official" (*kuan-yuan*) is also sometimes used for these men. Other terms for the clerks were "middle-level staff-members of the central government" (*shu-ts'ao* or *shu-shih*) and "little Grand Council"

(*hsiao Chün-chi*); see Liang Chang-chü, comp. *Ch'eng-wei lu* (1875), 13/2; and Teng and Wang, "T'an Chün-chi ch'u," pp. 193–96. After their appointment they were said to be "attached to the Grand Council" (*tsai Chün-chi ch'u hsing-tsou*); for an example see (T) SYT-FP CC25/2/13, pp. 103–4. The unwary should not confuse the Manchu *janggin* in titles of Sinkiang and other frontier officials with the Grand Council usage; although the characters used for these titles were the same, nevertheless the two were different; for the former, see Brunnert and Hagelstrom, *Present Day Political Organization*, pp. 724, 874; and HT 3/5. See also the entry under *janggin* in Ferdinand D. Lessing, comp. *Mongolian-English Dictionary* (Bloomington, Ind., 1973). Compared with the very ancient history of the term used for the Grand Secretariat clerks (*chung-shu*), which in one form reached back more than a thousand years, the *chang-ching* term of Manchu-Mongolian origin was a relative newcomer; see *T'ung-chih* (repr. Shanghai, 1935), 1:657. Along with other middle-level servitors, the Grand Council clerks used special terms: they referred to themselves as *chih* and called the documents they wrote *pin*.

3. See, for one of many possible examples, the notice of Chiang Ping's being sent for reward for two memorials offering his views, in (B) SYT-FP CL1/2/25, p. 170; see also note 54 below and its accompanying text. Note also the important role played by four Grand Council clerks in the Hundred Days Reform of 1898, when they served as the "executives of reform," the link between K'ang Yu-wei and the emperor; Immanuel Hsu, *The Rise of Modern China*, p. 374.

4. A good example of the detailed regulations applied to outer-court appointments in the eighteenth century in contrast with the informality of Grand Council clerk selections is in (T) SYT-FP CL47/10/6, p. 51.

5. SYCL 13/5b–6; (T) SYT-FP CL45/11/20, pp. 277–78; see also Wang Ch'ang, "Chün-chi ch'u t'i-ming chi" 14/19–20b. Of course, the concurrent-post requirement meant that all clerks had to meet the specifications for their original posts; see (T) KCT-YC021983, YC2/4/5, Lung-k'e-to and others (on examinations); (T) SYT-FP CL45/11/30, pp. 277–78 (on going through the triennial Great Accounting as members of their original staffs). In 1906, the Grand Council clerkships were made official and the clerks no longer had to come onto the council from concurrent posts. Clerk lists usually show the original agencies; see SYCL 16–19, passim. In the Yung-cheng period, some Manchu clerks appear to have received appointment to the inner court without a concurrent post; see Appendix D and the lists in its sources. Occasionally this could still happen in the Ch'ien-lung reign, although efforts were made to obtain a concurrent post as soon as possible; see, for example, (B) SYT-FP CL40/5/19, p. 253; (T) SYT-FP CL46/7/9, p. 77. Clerks were paid by the salaries appropriate to their concurrent, not their Grand Council, posts. Not much information about the salaries has come to light. One CL40 notice reviewed the promotion of a Grand Secretariat secretary (*chung-shu*) (rank 7B) who had been paid 90 taels of salary (*feng-yin*) per year. With additional amounts for expenses, his annual total was 248 taels. He was being promoted to second-class secretary (*chu-shih*) (6B) at the Board of Punishments, for which he would receive 120 taels of basic salary and enough in expense reimbursements to bring him up to about 250 taels per year; (B) Ho-t'u-li tang CL40/J10/27. On basic salary levels, see HTSL 249/1a–b. Two men sent to the front in the Yung-cheng period to be attached to Yueh Chung-ch'i's staff, one of whom shortly became an inner-court clerk, received 200 taels each from the provincial treasury as well as other rations; (T) KCT-YC000170, YC9/1/3, Yueh Chung-ch'i. Of course, funds would have to be made available to the

Grand Council for expenses (in contrast to wages); see CLSL 896/18a–b; SYCL 14/10, 12. It is worth noting that the basic salary figures given in the Ho-t'u-li tang reference are twice the amounts provided in Chang Chung-li's study (*The Income of the Chinese Gentry* [Seattle, 1962], p. 12, table 1); this suggests that Chang's work failed to take into account the CL2 doubling of capital-level salaries (on which see Chapter 5 above). For examples of some of the many eighteenth-century grand councillors' requests to appoint clerks, see (B) SYT-FP CL4/2/20, p. 218; (T) SYT-FP CL41/10/28, p. 183; CL46/7/9, p. 77.

6. On the desirability of appointments related to board experience, see SYCL 1/16b–17. See also CLSL 302/4b–5; and Adam Yuen-chung Lui, "The Practical Training of Government Officials Under the Early Ch'ing, 1644–1795," *Asia Minor* 16, nos. 1–2 (1971): 84–85. For an example of Grand Council clerks in action, involved in board work, see *Ming-Ch'ing shih-liao* 10:950b–51 and other similar references in note 54 below. Not surprisingly, these included several clerks from the boards of Civil Office and Revenue. There is evidence that some Grand Council clerk spots were reserved for certain outer-court agencies, so that a memorandum might speak of a "Grand Secretariat clerk" (*chung-shu*) vacancy on the council clerks' roster; see, for example, (T) SYT-FP CL43/5/20, p. 395; TK2/4/3, p. 29.

7. SYCL 13/5b–6.

8. Ibid. See also Ying-ho, *En-fu t'ang pi-chi* 1/29b, where the author points out that these appointments were made under special dispensation (*t'e-chih*) and were not to be a precedent for future action.

9. The policy is mentioned in (T) SYT-FP KHsu15/2/15, pp. 117–21, but an exception may be found under the name of Yuan Ch'eng-ning, appointed in CL57; SYCL 16/13b. I have not been able to discover the reason for this proscription. There may also have been a rule against censors holding concurrent posts in the council; *Ch'ing-ch'ao hsu Wen-hsien t'ung-k'ao* 5:8773. An exception is related in (B) IFT CL1/12/6, pp. 349–50. After promotion, Hanlin members were not permitted to serve as council clerks; see Yao Yuan-chih, *Chu-yeh t'ing tsa-chi* (repr. Taipei, 1969), 1/15b. Other proscriptions on service as clerks are given in Wu Chen-yü, *Yang-chi chai ts'ung-lu* 4/2a–b.

10. YCSL 131/3; see also 131/1b–2b; Chang T'ing-yü, *Nien-p'u* 3/6; CS 6:4207. A proscription against high officials' brothers and sons serving in any capacity on the council is said to derive from the Chia-ch'ing period, but it was already mentioned in a work based on eighteenth-century observations; see Wang Ch'ang "Chün-chi ch'u t'i-ming chi" 14/19. The Chia-ch'ing proscription was lifted very soon after Tao-kuang came to the throne; see SYCL 13/9b–10b.

11. See the clerk lists for the Ch'ien-lung period in SYCL 16 and 18. Some well-known father-and-son clerk pairs were Kung T'i-shen, father of Kung Li-cheng (whom he adopted; the latter was in turn the father of Kung Tzu-chen, who was rejected for a clerkship); and Hui-ling, father of Kuei-fen; see SYCL 16/7b, 11b, 16b; 18/8, 13; and Judith Whitbeck, "The Historical Vision of Kung Tzu-chen (1792–1841)" (Ph.D. diss., University of California, Berkeley, 1980), pp. 12–13. In the eighteenth century there were also some brothers who served: Cha-k'e-sang-a and Cha-la-sang-a, for instance. The Chia-ch'ing reforms changed the possibility for concurrent service by relatives in one's immediate family; see CCSL 239/8a–b; CS 6:4584.

12. (B) IFT CL14/4/10, pp. 283–84. See also the reliance on the Nine Ministers described in (T) KCT-YC021973, YC1/8/6, Board of Civil Office memorial. On ap-

pointments to some of the posts that might lead to Grand Council clerkships, see (B) IFT CL1/5/17, pp. 415–16.

13. (B) Chün-chi ch'u kuei-chü chi-tsai, p. 4; CCSL 38/1–2. In CC18 (1813), limits were suggested on the numbers of candidates the capital agencies might propose for council clerkships; CCSL 271/16b–17b.

14. (B) Chün-chi ch'u kuei-chü chi-tsai, p. 4; HT 3/5a–b; "Ch'i Wen-tuan [Chün-tsao] shu-t'ing tsai-pi i-kao," in *Ch'ing-tai chang-ku chui-lu* (Taipei, 1974), p. 117.

15. CCSL 271/16b–17b.

16. SYCL 15/5–6b.

17. SYCL 16/1–17/6b, 18/1–19/9. In addition to the figures given in the text, in the first period twenty-five Chinese clerks and in the second period twenty-four had irregular examination routes. This meant that they had only passed a lower examination, had inherited examination status, or had been specially awarded a degree so that they could take up a certain position. During the Ch'ien-lung reign the *chin-shih* examination quotas were greatly reduced: from 344 members of the CL1 (1736) class to 81 members in CL58 (1793), the last regular class of the reign; see *Ch'ing-tai ting-chia lu*, comp. Chu P'ei-lien (Taipei, 1968), pp. 16–17. The four Manchus who distinguished themselves in the first period were O-erh-t'ai's relations O-jung-an and O-lun (both *chin-shih*) and A-kuei and Cheng-ts'e (*chü-jen*); SYCL 15/2b and 16/2, 7b. In the second period, Wen-hai achieved a *chü-jen* degree; SYCL 17/6. On the difficulties of finding Manchus who had come up through the examination system, see (B) IFT CL13/8/18, p. 213. On Chinese clerks' examination achievement, see the following note.

18. SYCL 16–19 (Grand Council clerk tables), passim. See the story of Pi Yuan later in this chapter. During the Ch'ien-lung reign, the Chinese clerks who achieved first place (*chuang-yuan*) included Liang Kuo-chih, Chuang P'ei-yin, Chin Pang, Pi Yuan, and Wu Hsi-ling. The clerks Mei Li-pen and Chu Ch'ung-kuang won second place (*pang-yen*), and Chao I and Shen Ch'ing-tsao won third (*t'an-hua*); SYCL 18, passim. On Manchu clerks' examination achievement, see the previous note.

19. After the situation was regulated, exceptions were sometimes made. In CC21 (1816), for example, Chiang Feng-t'ai, son of a district magistrate who had died as a result of the 1813 Eight Trigrams uprising, was rewarded out of consideration for his family's suffering and given a post as second-class secretary (rank 6B) at the Board of Works. A few months later he was brought on the Grand Council as a clerk. At the time that his candidacy for a board position was discussed, one of the board documents pointed out that the proposed appointment "was not in line with regulations." Nevertheless, said the report, "the father's achievement was so valorous that we must not be bound by the rules." Chiang was brought into the clerk body under the honorary licentiate (*yin-sheng*) designation. The exception made for him involved giving him a supernumerary (*e-wai*) position, making him the ninth man in his group; CCSL 319/5–6; (T) SYT-FP CC21/11/14, pp. 95-97; SYCL 18/5; Naquin, *Millenarian Rebellion*, p. 133.

20. CCSL 38/1–2. See also Yao, *Chu-yeh t'ing tsa-chi* 1/25. On the importance of character and deportment, see CCSL 271/16b–17b.

21. Kung Tzu-chen, as translated by David Nivison in his "Protest Against Conventions and Conventions of Protest," in *The Confucian Persuasion*, ed. Arthur F. Wright (Stanford, 1960), p. 199; quoted by permission of the Stanford University Press. For a detailed study of Kung, see Whitbeck, "The Historical Vision of Kung Tzu-chen."

22. (B) IFT CL2/12/11, pp. 353–55. See also (B) IFT CL2/11/29, pp. 325–28, on the same subject; and the SYCL 6/1–2b entry, which is probably derived from these archival records.

23. (B) IFT CL13/12/10, pp. 408–12; (B) SYT-FP CL14/2/16, pp. 125–26; CLSL 335/2b. These sources are helpful because they list all the clerks on duty both in the capital and in Szechuan who were being recommended for rewards for services in support of the Chin-ch'uan war.

24. CLSL 896/18a–b. Because of wars, numbers continued to fluctuate in the nineteenth century; see the figure of sixty clerks for late in the dynasty supplied in Brunnert and Hagelstrom, *Present Day Political Organization*, item 129B.

25. *Ch'ing-ch'ao hsu Wen-hsien t'ung-k'ao* 5:8773. In KHsu32 (1906), the number of clerks was increased to thirty-six; SYCL 13/4b–5.

26. SYCL 13/4b; (B) Chün-chi ch'u kuei-chu chi-tsai, p. 3b. A detailed breakdown of members of the clerk group may be obtained from Liang Chang-chü's description of the clerks, SYCL 16–19, which lists the clerks by name, native place, education, date of entrance on duty, and highest later post. Liang's record supports the point concerning expansion of clerk numbers in the Ch'ien-lung reign, but Liang did not show date of departure from duty, which means that for most clerks it is difficult to know the actual length of service, the average length of their terms, or exactly how many clerks were serving at any one time. I have found many errors in the listings for the early years, particularly a failure to enumerate some of the Manchus who served on Yung-cheng's inner-court staffs. In addition, occasionally the archives mention clerks of the Ch'ien-lung period, whom Liang failed to list; see, for example, the case of Chi Ch'eng-chih cited in (T) SYT-FP CL46/7/9, p. 77. Another list of clerks is available in *Chün-chi chang-ching t'i-ming*, but this has even fewer names than Liang's. On the four supernumerary positions added to deal with the Taiping Rebellion, see (T) SYT-FP KHsu15/2/15, pp. 117–21 (reviewing the earlier situation); HF3/2/6, p. 71; HF3/2/11, p. 151.

27. (B) Chün-chi ch'u kuei-chü chi-tsai, p. 2b; SYCL 13/3b, 4b; 14/8, 10; 22/5a–b; Teng and Wang, "T'an Chün-chi ch'u," p. 195. Yeh Feng-mao stated that there was a clerk group head as early as YC11; see *Nei-ko hsiao-chih*, p. 11b. The position of assisting head may be a nineteenth-century refinement. In 1908, the clerks' leader was awarded rank 3B and the assistant leader rank 4B; CS 2:1358. On the leaders' duties, see Wu Chen-yü, *Yang-chi chai ts'ung-lu* 4/1b.

28. *Chung-ho yueh-k'an shih-liao hsuan-chi* 1:1. Liu Yat-wing believes that the Manchu clerks were the first to occupy the southern quarters (*nan-wu*); see his "The Ch'ing Grand Council," pp. 61–62. By the Kuang-hsu period the four subgroups had names: *Man t'ou-pan, Han t'ou-pan, Man erh-pan*, and *Han erh-pan*; see, for example, (T) KHsu4/3/8, pp. 127–30; KHsu15/2/8, pp. 49–52; KHsu18/1/4, pp. 41–44.

29. Chao I, *Yen-p'u tsa-chi* 1:7–8.

30. Taking the night shift was known as *kai-yeh pan*. In addition to the four men assigned to a shift, each duty group had a fifth man who served as leader (*ling-pan* or *ta-la-mi*); SYCL 14/8, 22/6b–7.

31. Chao I, *Yen-p'u tsa-chi* 1:7–8, 10.

32. Ibid.

33. SYCL earliest preface. For a contrasting lack of opportunity for access to the Grand Secretariat Great Treasury, see Juan K'uei-sheng, *Ch'a-yü k'e-hua* (eighteenth-

century memoirs; repr. Taipei, 1976), 2/1b. Liang's compendium, while useful and revealing, is hardly voluminous. But the openness displayed by this clerk writing in the early Tao-kuang era stands in marked contrast with the secrecy and reticence of earlier times.

34. *Li-tai hsiao-shuo pi-chi hsuan (Ch'ing)* (Hong Kong, 1958), 3:771–72. On typical schedules of the mid-Ch'ing emperors, see Silas H. L. Wu, "Emperors at Work."

35. SYCL 14/7b–8. The sixteen clerks who accompanied the imperial tour received a special payment, called *pang-t'ieh yin*, of twenty taels for the spring tour and fifty taels for the longer autumn tour; SYCL 14/12b–14b. Council tour duty groups were noted in the Sui-shou teng-chi.

36. SYCL 22/7a–b.

37. Ibid.

38. For some of the many possible examples of these terms in the (T) SSTC, see CC13/4/2, p. 181; CC24/9/9–10, pp. 214–15; and TK3/9/24–26, pp. 244–45. For an example of a reference to an imperial tour encampment, see (T) SSTC CC8/8/23, p. 140.

39. Observations from the Beijing and Taipei SSTC, Ch'ien-lung and Chia-ch'ing reigns.

40. See, for example, (B) IFT CL13/9/12, pp. 253–54; and (T) SYT-FP, tag pasted on the top of CL47, Hsia vol., p. 265.

41. CLSL 1223/6–8.

42. Note, however, that some concern for routine-system efficiency was expressed in the volumes of (T) Hu-k'e shih-shu, where each month's routine-system communications were tallied in terms of totals of the various items, with the numbers completed and not completed separately noted; see, for example, the entries under CL20/1/30. For delays or potential halts in the routine system, see p. 29 and related notes.

43. Chao I, *Yen-p'u tsa-chi* 2:44–45. This is an appropriate point at which to thank Ms. Chang Lin-sheng (Leslie Chang) of the Taipei Palace Museum for introducing me to the pleasures of Chao I and reading some passages with me.

44. For a different interpretation of this same account, see David S. Landes, *Revolution in Time: Clocks and the Making of the Modern World* (Cambridge, Mass., 1983), pp. 50–52. In this connection it is appropriate to recollect Arthur Koestler's presentation of premodern notions of time, in which peasants needing to take a train would simply go to the railroad station early in the day and wait until the train arrived; see *Darkness at Noon* (New York, 1948), p. 190.

45. Chao I, *Yen-p'u tsa-chi* 1:7; *Chün-chi chang-ching t'i-ming*, postscript p. 1b. I am indebted to Chao Chung-fu and Ju Deyuan, two men of Manchuria, for explaining to me the valuable properties of Korean paper (*kao-li chih*), which they had observed still in use in Manchuria in the twentieth century. Mr. Wu Yü-chang, retired curator at the Taipei Palace Museum, informed me that when he reported for duty when the Museum opened in Peiping in 1925 he was assigned an office in the clerks' building, where the windows still contained the old paper; only at this point was it replaced with glass. For additional references on the Grand Council offices, see Chapter 6, n. 20.

46. (T) P'ing-ting Chun-ka-erh wen-i tang CL23/2–24/12; (T) Chün-chi ch'u wen-i tang CL57/10, pp. 11, 13. I have heard it suggested, though not proved definitively, that the grand councillors frequently worked at home, which all the more suggests that the comforts of coal and ice may have been ordered for the clerks' offices.

47. For a more detailed description of the different kinds of documents for which the clerks were responsible, see SYCL 22/6a–b.

48. Chao I, *Yen-p'u tsa-chi* 1:7. A standard memorial box measured approximately 11 inches by 5 inches; just the length of a memorial but not long enough to rest the wrist.

49. Teng and Wang, "T'an Chün-chi ch'u," p. 196.

50. Chao I, *Yen-p'u tsa-chi* 1:5–6.

51. See, for example, (T) SYT-FP CC8/J2/11, p. 101; CC12/10/25, p. 177; CC21/2/11, pp. 125–26.

52. (T) SYT-FP TK30/11/10, pp. 103–8.

53. (T) KCT-CC004671, Kuan-yü, CC5/2/28, and its enclosure.

54. For the compiler of the briefing book, K'ang Shao-yung, see *Hsu pei-chuan chi* (repr. Taipei, 1974), 16/1a–b. For Wu Hsiao-ming's advice on two military campaigns, see CS 6:4585. For some memorials showing that Grand Council clerks participated in deliberations as part of the memorializing roster of their boards, see *Ming-Ch'ing shih-liao* 10:950b–51, 954b–55b, 963b–64b. The clerk Wang Ch'ang also claimed that clerks gave important advice; see his "Chün-chi ch'u t'i-ming chi" 14/19b.

55. SYCL 22/5a–b.

56. SYCL 20/16. This is explained in Chü Te-yuan's article "Ch'ing-tai ti pien-nien t'i tang-ts'e yü kuan-hsiu shih-shu," *Ku-kung po-wu-yuan yuan-k'an* 1979, no. 2 (May 1979): 37. Each day the surnames of the two duty clerks who wrote up the SSTC were appended to the account; the fact that these were Chinese names suggests that this particular duty was the responsibility of Chinese clerks.

57. On the document register, see Chuang Chi-fa, Introduction to "Pen-yuan tien-ts'ang Ch'ing-tai tang-an mu-lu," *Ku-kung wen-hsien* 2, no. 4 (Sept. 1971): 81; and my "Ch'ing Documents in the National Palace Museum Archives. Part One. Document Registers: The *Sui-shou teng-chi*," *National Palace Museum Bulletin* 10, no. 4 (Sept.–Oct. 1975): 1–17. Further information on this record book appears in *Chung-ho yueh-k'an shih-liao hsuan-chi* 1:5. The earliest Sui-shou teng-chi, which is now held in the Beijing Number One Archives, is dated CL7 (1742). Of course, this may not originally have been the earliest; others may be lost. For a list of some of the other Grand Council daybooks and registers (*mu-lu lei*) maintained by the clerks, see Shan Shih-yuan, "Ku-kung po-wu-yuan Wen-hsien kuan so-ts'ang tang-an ti fen-hsi," in *Chung-kuo chin-tai ching-chi shih yen-chiu* 2, no. 3 (May 1934): 276.

58. (T) SSTC CC3/12/22, p. 254; HF3/3/1, p. 304. For other kinds of measures taken for the sake of secrecy, see note 63 below.

59. SYCL 22/6a–b. For a list of the Grand Council Chinese-language record books, see *Ch'ing Chün-chi ch'u tang-an mu-lu*, passim, and the fuller lists in the Grand Council's archival inventories and the notebooks compiled by the Number One Archives in Beijing.

60. *Ch'ing Chün-chi ch'u tang-an mu-lu*, pp. 1–6, record books listed in the *tsung-mu* section; Shan Shih-yuan, "Ku-kung po-wu-yuan Wen-hsien kuan so-ts'ang tang-an ti fen-hsi," pp. 276–77; and "Ch'en-lieh wen-wu tsung-mu," in *Wen-hsien t'e-k'an*, Ch'en-lieh tsung-mu sec., p. 69. Some of these were duplicate copies; many derived from the nineteenth century. Of course, not all 150 were being maintained simultaneously by the end of the Ch'ing.

61. See my "Books of Revelations," p. 29.

62. SYCL 14/16; for the A-kuei memorial of CL43/5/16 that discussed the copying program, see (T) Chün-chi ch'u wen-i tang, p. 1.

63. Even some of the top secret (*mi-hsing ch'en-tsou*) palace memorials could also be seen by a Grand Council clerk when the time came to copy them for the Grand Council reference file (*Chün-chi ch'u lu-fu tsou-che*), although there was a precaution of not letting such materials circulate to the lower-level personnel at the Military Archives Office; SYCL 22/6. The clerks would probably not have had access to materials whose content was concealed in or entirely omitted from the Sui-shou teng-chi. See, for example, SYCL 1/15–16b, edict of CC10/6/29, which mentions a secretly sealed memorandum (*tsou-p'ien mi-feng*) handed in by Ying-ho. The SSTC for that date does not list this document, which requested a special audience to lodge a complaint against another grand councillor; its contents, thus, were probably not made generally available to council members, and certainly not to the clerks. Occasionally a grand councillor would seal and store a document temporarily in order to safeguard confidentiality. For an example, see (T) SYT-FP and SSTC for TK3/6/9, pp. 79 and 422, respectively.

64. CLSL 274/12a–b.

65. (T) SYT-FP CL44/11/2, p. 148. On the clerks' duties on the imperial tours, see SYCL 14/7b–8.

66. See, for example, (B) IFT CL13/9/30, p. 281; CL13/12/10, pp. 408–12, on the clerks who worked on the first Chin-ch'uan campaign in Peking and at the front; SYCL 14/12b–14b, on the use of large numbers of clerks in the second Chin-ch'uan campaign of CL36 (1771). Other eighteenth-century sources also speak of Grand Council clerks' involvement in military campaigns; see, for example, (T) SYT-FP CL54/2/1, pp. 127–28. According to a later complaint, sometimes officials not on the Grand Council nevertheless attempted to take council clerks with them when deputed outside of Peking, perhaps to take advantage of their experience and council connections; see CCSL 73/18a–b.

67. (B) Ho-t'u-li tang CL43/12/26. For the biography of the Board of Punishments official Chiang Sheng, see CS 6: 4455–56.

68. (T) Chiao-pu ni-Hui tang CL49/8/16, pp. 227–46.

69. Ibid., pp. 187–91. (This record book has a large number of depositions at this point.)

70. Chao I was the author of *Huang-ch'ao wu-kung chi-sheng*, an account covering seven of the Ch'ien-lung military campaigns, two of which he took part in; ECCP, p. 76. Examples of military campaign records composed or edited by Grand Council clerks include Chao I and Wang Ch'ang, *P'ing-ting Liang Chin-ch'uan fang-lueh*, and Chu Hsueh-ch'in et al., *Chiao-p'ing Yueh-fei fang-lueh*, the official account of the suppression of the Taiping rebels. Chu became a Grand Council clerk in HF8 (1859); see SYCL 19/7. The eighteenth-century clerk Kuan Shih-ming wrote an account of traveling in the imperial retinue when the emperor led the autumn hunts, *Hu-pi ch'iu-hsien chi-shih*; see Li Tsung-t'ung, *Shih-hsueh kai-yao* (Taipei, 1968), pp. 291–92. Two clerks wrote accounts of the Grand Council itself: Liang Chang-chü compiled the *Shu-yuan chi-lueh*, and Wu Hsiao-ming was responsible for the shorter *Chün-chi chang-ching t'i-ming*. Another work on the same subject, Wang Ch'ang's "Chün-chi ch'u t'i-ming chi," seems to have survived in part, its preface being available in *Huang-ch'ao ching-shih wen-pien* 14/19–20b. On this last work and its unavailability even in Ch'ing times, see SYCL 22/4a–b.

71. Chao I, *Yen-p'u tsa-chi* 1:4–5. Chao I was Wang Yu-tun's clerk and doubtless heard this story from him.

72. Ibid., p. 2; Teng and Wang, "T'an Chün-chi ch'u," p. 196.

73. ECCP, p. 75.

74. Chao I, *Yen-p'u tsa-chi* 1:6. A *li* equals about one-third of a mile.

75. Ibid., pp. 7–8.

76. Chao I's tale is an unofficial reminiscence. In official accounts the clerks are rarely portrayed as playing such an important role in edict drafting; see, for example, SYCL 22/6b. Many of the most useful sources on the Grand Council clerks were framed by clerks themselves, with, one suspects, a desire to emphasize the clerks' importance, perhaps sometimes at the expense of fact. Li Tsung-t'ung found that during the Kuang-hsu–period negotiations with Russia, the grand councillors themselves drafted the treaty cables to keep their content secret from the clerks; see his *Shih-hsueh kai-yao*, p. 293. On the clerks' role in edict drafting, see also CCSL 132/10a–11b; and Chao-lien, *Hsiao-t'ing tsa-lu* 7/18–19.

77. (B) SYT-FP CL40/6/9, pp. 329–30. For similar instances, see (T) SYT-FP CL46/8/7, p. 626; TK4/7/5, p. 45. In many of the archival examples that I have come across, the recommendation of a light administrative punishment frequently resulted in no punishment at all. On light administrative punishment, see Metzger, p. 115.

78. (T) I-tsou tang CL22/10/10, pp. 273–74. Chao I had probably not been covering up the instance of dubious behavior at the provincial level, for he had made a copy of another document—a lateral communication sent to the council—reporting the same information. For a similar instance, see (T) SYT-FP CC19/12/23, pp. 551–52. In CL40 (1775), another clerk was expelled from the council for errors in copying; this unusually heavy punishment may have reflected a desire to get rid of the man anyway; (B) SYT-FP CL40/5/12, p. 215.

79. (T) SYT-FP CL46/7/16, pp. 250–52. Another example of maps being taken away from the council is described in SYCL 1/18a–b.

80. SYCL 1/20b–21b. The case is briefly described in ECCP, pp. 541–42.

81. (T) SYT-FP CC7/9/24, p. 251.

82. (B) SYT-FP CL40/6/9, pp. 329–30.

83. Sometimes an accusation against a clerk did not result in punishment. In CC17 (1812), the emperor exonerated two clerks for giving presents in response to the provincial treasurer's personal command. The imperial marginalia added to the court letter on the subject said that this sort of thing was "unavoidable"; (T) SYT-FP CC17/8/27, pp. 199–201.

84. Wang Ch'ang, "Chün-chi ch'u t'i-ming chi" 14/19b.

85. As indicated, for example, in (T) Chiao-pu ni-Hui tang CL49/5/15, p. 75; (T) SYT-FP CL47/4/30, p. 289; CL55/11/1, p. 2.

86. *Chün-chi chang-ching t'i-ming*, postscript p. 1b.

87. Chao I, *Yen-p'u tsa-chi* 1:7.

88. This story comes from the writing of Hung Liang-chi, as cited in Li Tsung-t'ung, *Shih-hsueh kai-yao*, pp. 289–90. The rest of the story is that two other clerks who were also about to take the examination had taunted Pi Yuan beforehand because, they said, his "fair to middling" calligraphy gave him little hope of a top placement in the morrow's examination. Claiming that they would have a better chance, they withdrew to review, leaving Pi Yuan on duty.

89. (B) IFT CL25/6/21, pp. 91–92; SYCL 18/4b–5. In addition to the standard biographies of Pi Yuan, see also Chao-lien, *Hsiao-t'ing tsa-lu* 7/13b–14.

90. For rewards for clerks, see (B) IFT CL2/11/29, pp. 325–28; (T) Chiao-pu ni-Hui tang CL49/7/14, p. 51, and (T) Chiao-pu tang CC7/12/17, pp. 77–78. Rewards were most commonly given following a period of exhausting council service, such as on a military campaign or for the heavy rounds of duty necessary to the massive projects of document copying that took place at the council every five years (after the middle of the nineteenth century, every three years). For documents on clerks' promotions, see (B) IFT CL13/6/7, pp. 17–19; (B) SYT-FP CL47/9/24, p. 437, (T) SYT-FP CC25/11/18, p. 242. Grand councillors also sought to have their clerks given small promotions at their concurrent posts, to provide them slightly higher stipends while they continued to serve at the council; see (B) IFT CL23/10/22, pp. 271–72. That Grand Council clerkships were regarded as positions in which promising young men would be trained for higher posts is made clear in SYCL 13/9b–10b.

91. Teng and Wang, "T'an Chün-chi ch'u," p. 198.

92. SYCL 14/16. A few clerks served only a year or less before moving on to higher rank; see SYCL 18/5 (Chu Ch'ung-kuang and Chung Feng-san, both of whom served less than a year).

93. (T) SYT-FP CL52/11/17, p. 305. For examples of men who served again after an interruption, see (B) CL32/4/12, p. 69; (B) SYT-FP CL40/3/27, pp. 352–53; and (T) SYT-FP CC25/2/13, pp. 103–4. Some returnees came back after punishment and having been degraded to a level that allowed them to serve at the council once more; see, for example, the case of Chiang Ping, (B) IFT CL23/4/11, p. 110.

94. (T) SYT-FP CL46/12/2, pp. 157–58.

95. Chao I, *Yen-p'u tsa-chi* 1:3n., 2:43; see also SYCL 22/4a–b. For an analysis of Chao I's view of the role of the Grand Council, see Quinton G. Priest, "Portraying Central Government Institutions: Historiography and Intellectual Accommodation in the High Ch'ing," *Late Imperial China* 7, no. 1 (June 1986): 27–49.

96. Wang Ch'ang, "Chün-chi ch'u t'i-ming chi" 14/19b.

97. CCSL 25/32b–34; see also (T) CCT-CL029103, CC33/12/10, plus its Board of Civil Office discussion of 12/19.

98. (B) and (T) SSTC, passim.

99. For *pan* 班 used to refer to both the Chinese and the Manchu clerks' groups, see SYCL 13/11a–b. Sometimes the term "Manchu quarters" (*Man-wu*) is used instead of *Man-pan*, the former being a term we can be sure refers to the Manchu clerks; see *Chung-ho yueh-k'an shih-liao hsuan-chi* 1:1; and Chapter 6, n. 20. The term *Man-wu* appears to have been used more late in the dynasty; see, for example, (B) SSTC HF3/3/14, p. 382; (T) SSTC TC9/6/7, p. 181.

100. (B) and (T) SSTC, passim.

101. For information on some of the surviving Tsou-che hao-pu, see *Ch'ing Chün-chi ch'u tang-an mu-lu*, p. 11. One of the inventories of Manchu archival holdings, the (B) Man Chün-chi tang-an tsung-mu cheng/fu ping yueh-che, states that there once were twenty volumes, called Yueh-che hao-pu, during the Ch'ing, covering the period CL1–19. The other eighteen volumes may yet come to light when the Manchu materials are thoroughly sorted.

102. (B) Tsou-che hao-pu CL11/7, p. 60.

103. Ibid., CL14/3, p. 25.

104. Ibid., CL11/4, p. 31; CL14/10, p. 93; see also (T) SYT-FP CL45/2/24, p. 273.

105. SYCL 14/16b, 23. There were other Grand Council and inner-court facilities for handling translations, in particular the Inner Manchu-Chinese Translation Office (*Nei Fan-shu Fang*) set up chiefly to translate edicts from one language to the other. It is not clear when this office was founded. An edict of CL22 (1757) ordered that edicts to be translated were to be sent to the Grand Council, with the translators selected from the council; CS 2:1358; CC *Hui-tien* 3/12b–13; HT 3/11b; *Kung-shih hsu-pien* 54/1b–2; and Chuang Chi-fa, "Shang-yü tang," *Ku-kung wen-hsien* 3, no. 2 (Mar. 1972): 67.

106. CLSL 5/40a–b. See also the YC4 notice on regular translation of Grand Secretariat edicts addressed to the boards in the CL *Hui-tien tse-li* 2/21b–22. The HTSL 15/20a–b also has this, but without the indication that only board edicts were being discussed.

107. YCSL 87/2–3b; (T) IFT CL5/3/26, pp. 53–54. Nearly two million items written in Manchu survive in the Number One Archives in Beijing; conversation with Mr. Liu Ching-hsien, 23 June 1981. At the time of our conversation the work of sorting and arranging these documents had not been completed.

108. In CL32, the arrangements for an imperial tour that was to take place by boat revealed just how heavily Manchu the inner-court inner circle was. Accompanying the emperor in a flotilla that would keep up with him every day were five chamberlains of the imperial bodyguard, two grand councillors (one of whom was Chinese), eleven Manchu attachés in the imperial suite, and twenty-five bodyguards—in other words, an inner circle of more than forty men, only one of whom was Chinese; (B) SYT-FP undated CL32/2/1, pp. 95–99.

109. YCSL 1/29b–31. I am indebted to my colleague and friend Ju Deyuan for assistance on these points. In 1980–81 I ran across a good example of the Manchu-language dominance in frontier matters when I attempted to help Dr. Alynn Nathanson locate archival materials on the Chingünjav Rebellion, which she was studying for her Ph.D. dissertation, "Ch'ing Policies in Khalka Mongolia and the Chingünjav Rebellion of 1756" (University of London, 1983). I found no Chinese-language documents in any of the appropriate archival finding lists and with Dr. Nathanson's help learned that the many Manchu documents photographed in the Beijing archives in the 1950s and translated into Mongol for publication in N. Ishjamts, comp., *Mongolyn ard tümnii 1755–1758 ony tusgaar togtnolyn zevsegt temtsel*, Studia Historica Instituti Historiae Academiae Scientarum Republica Populi Mongoli (Ulaanbaatar, 1962), vol. 3, fasc. 3, represented the bulk of the reporting on the affair.

110. (T) Hsun-ch'ang tang CC4/11/10, pp. 127–29.

111. See Brunnert and Hagelstrom, *Present Day Political Organization*, item 139, which mistakenly places this organization "under the supervision and control of the Grand Secretariat," an error that has been repeated by others. In the *Collected Statutes and Precedents*, the Military Archives Office itself is correctly described as a Grand Council subsidiary (HT 3/10a–b), but many of its products, the campaign histories for instance, are then described under the Hanlin section of the *Hui-tien* because, it is said, the Hanlin received the order to compile; HTSL 70/4–6b; see this echoed in W. A. P. Martin, *Hanlin Papers* (London, 1880), p. 26. Nevertheless, many other records survive to assure us that the campaign histories and other works, too, were compiled not in the Hanlin but on the premises of the Military Archives Office, possibly supervised by a Hanlin grand councillor. See the discussion of the office's Grand Council connections in note

118 below. For some late-nineteenth-century accounts of Grand Council management of campaign history matters, see (T) Chiao-pu tang TC8/3/12 (unpaginated); (T) SYT-FP KHsu15/1/14, pp. 93–96; SYCL 12/9–14b. I thank Robert Jenks for the first of these three references.

112. The dossiers of transactions with Russia (E-lo-ssu tang and variant titles) appear to be one of the few specialized archival records maintained in the K'ang-hsi inner court. So far as we know these survived to the twentieth century; see Shan Shih-yuan, "Ku-kung po-wu-yuan Wen-hsien kuan so-ts'ang tang-an ti fen hsi," p. 276. There is a Chinese-language version of this record dating from the Hsien-feng period; see Chang Te-tse, "Chün-chi ch'u chi ch'i tang-an," p. 72. Probably the Manchu versions had to be handled in the inner court; see notes 107–10 above and their accompanying text.

113. For an illustrated copy of the Yung-cheng edict requiring return of the palace memorials, see my "Ch'ing Palace Memorials," p. 9.

114. Document copying is said to have begun in YC7 or 8 (1729–30); for an imperial order, see, for example, the imperial rescript on (T) KCT-YC000022, YC7/2/1, Yueh Chung-ch'i. For one of the inner deputies' many assurances that they had made a copy (for the reference collection), see (T) KCT-YC019819, undated unsigned memorandum. Some of the YC7 copied documents survived to the twentieth century; see "Cheng-li Chün-chi tang-an chih ching-kuo," *Wen-hsien t'e-k'an* (Peiping, 1935), pp. 18–19. Today the earliest item in this holding of the Beijing archives is (B) Lu-fu 2158-1, YC7/4/29, an imperial edict with vermilion corrections; most of the documents preserved, however, date from YC8.

115. See the Ch'ing archival managers' own inventories of these materials; (B) Man Chün-chi tang-an tsung-mu cheng/fu pen ping yueh-che and (B) Ch'ing-ch'a ko-tang chi-tsai pu.

116. Most K'ang-hsi–era editorial work was carried out in the outer court, probably at the Hanlin; YCSL 12/16–17b. But the three campaign histories of that era were probably compiled in the inner court under the supervision of grand secretaries assigned there. The fact that these campaign histories touched on sensitive border and rebellion affairs made them unlikely candidates for outer-court editorial attention. The head compiler of the earliest of the K'ang-hsi campaign histories, *P'ing-ting San-ni fang-lueh* (Official history of the Three Feudatories campaign, completed 1686), was Le-te-hung, who at times was the second-ranking grand secretary and therefore may well have served in K'ang-hsi's inner court. Although the editorial board for the *P'ing-ting Shuo-mo fang-lueh* (Official history of the campaign against Galdan, completed 1708) was first headed by the grand secretary Wen Ta, who at the end of his life was the ranking grand secretary and therefore certainly attached to the inner court, it was completed under the direction of the Hanlin and Southern [Imperial] Study—that is, inner court—member Chang Yü-shu; see ECCP, 65–66; *Tz'u-lin tien-ku* 63/1a–b. The *P'ing-ting Lo-ch'a fang-lueh* (Official history of the [K'ang-hsi–period] campaign against Russia [Amur River valley dispute]; in *Kung-shun t'ang ts'ung-shu, ts'e* 21) was originally written in Manchu and may be derived from the inner-court archival records on dealings with Russia mentioned above. Its compilers' names are not known, but its sensitive subject again suggests inner-court editorial work. Fang Su-sheng (p. 23) mentions two additional works of the K'ang-hsi era written in the military campaign history style, one on pirates and one on Chahar; I have not been able to examine either of these.

117. This was the *P'ing-ting Chun-ka-erh fang-lueh*. Many of those involved in its compilation were grand councillors: Fu-heng, the editor-in-chief; Liu T'ung-hsun; Yin-chi-shan; Yü Min-chung; and Chao-hui; see ECCP, p. 253.

118. CLSL 335/1b–2b, 338/16–17b. The copy related to the latter in *Ming-Ch'ing shih-liao* 10 : 929b–30b states that the chief memorialist was Chang T'ing-yü. See also *Ch'ing Nei-ko k'u-chu chiu-tang chi-k'an* 1/22b. The grand councillors probably acquired their overlordship of the campaign histories from concurrent positions as grand secretaries, as the grand secretaries are listed as having had this responsibility in earlier reigns; YC *Hui-tien* 2/3. Both Chang T'ing-yü and Lai-pao were grand secretaries at the time they proposed the establishment of the Military Archives Office.

119. (B) IFT CL15/1/22, pp. 35–36; HT 3/10b–11; SYCL 14/23; Teng and Wang, "T'an Chün-chi ch'u," p. 196. For the Grand Council submissions of finished work, see (B) Ko-shu chin-ch'eng tsou-che tang and (B) Pao-hsiao chin-shu tang.

120. *Ch'ing Nei-ko k'u-chu chiu-tang chi-k'an* 1/22b; *Ch'ing-kung shu-wen* 3/25b. The building, now torn down, was close behind the Imperial Printing Establishment (Wu-ying tien), to the north. For a map location, see Wu Ch'ang-yuan, *Chen-yuan shih-lueh* (1788; repr. Taipei, 1972), 1/32a–b, and Map 1 above.

121. My earliest reference to the archives subsection is in the (T) Chün-chi ch'u wen-i tang, CL43/5/29; see also (T) SYT-FP CL49/4/30, pp. 261–62, which refers to a Manchu and Chinese Archival Section (*Man-Han tang-fang*). For the titles of the servitors, see (B) Cho-fan tang. On the contents of the Military Archives Office holdings, see (T) SYT-FP CC23/7/24, pp. 233–34; Chang Te-tse, "Chün-chi ch'u chi ch'i tang-an," p. 82; "Ch'en-lieh shih wen-wu tsung-mu, in *Wen-hsien t'e-k'an, Ch'en-lieh tsung-mu* sec., p. 70. The archival records of the Military Archives Office are sufficiently large to rate separate categorization in the Ming-Ch'ing archives in Beijing; see Cheng Li, "Ming-Ch'ing tang-an," p. 13.

122. The earliest form of this type of record book is the (T) P'ing-ting Chun-ka-erh wen-i tang (Lateral communications record book [of the Military Archives Office set up to compile] the campaign record on the Zunghar suppression), with documents dating from CL23 (1758).

123. HT 3/9; (T) Chün-chi ch'u wen-i tang CL44/5, pp. 29–30. For recent general reviews of Grand Council archival curatorship and the state of these archives today, with further bibliographical references, see my "Ch'ing-tai Chün-chi ch'u ti tang-an kuan-li chih-tu—kuan-liao t'i-chih ch'uang-hsin chih-i yen-chiu" (Ch'ing Grand Council archival curatorship: A study of bureaucratic innovation), trans. Ch'en Kuo-tung, in *Ming-Ch'ing tang-an yü li-shih yen-chiu: Chung-kuo ti-i li-shih tang-an kuan liu-shih chiu-nien chi-nien lun-wen chi* (The Ming-Ch'ing archives and historical research: Papers in commemoration of the sixtieth anniversary of [the founding of] the Number One Archives of China), ed. The Number One Archives of China (Beijing, 1988), 2 : 643–68 (paper originally presented at the Ming-Ch'ing Research Symposium, Beijing, Oct. 1985), and "Chung-kuo tang-an chi ch'i-chung ti Mei-kuo shih tzu-liao" (Chinese archives and their materials on U.S. history), trans. Liang K'an, *Tang-an hsueh ts'an-k'ao* (Journal of archival studies), nos. 16–17 (Dec. !986): 2–17 (translation of "Archive Materials in China on United States History," in *Guide to the Study of United States History Outside the U.S. 1945–1980*, ed. Lewis Hanke [White Plains, N.Y., 1985], 1 : 504–66). The Chinese versions of these articles were published under my Chinese name, Pai Pin-chü.

124. Chang Te-tse, "Chün-chi ch'u chi ch'i tang-an," p. 82.

125. (T) SYT-FP TK3/7/22, pp. 229–30; *Ch'ing Nei-ko k'u-chu chiu-tang chi-k'an* 1/22–24b. The list of Ch'ien-lung–period campaign histories is too long to reproduce here; see ibid., 1/22a–b. For a fuller exploration of eighteenth-century publications than is possible here, see my "History as Mirror: Through the Looking-Glass and into Wonderland with the Ch'ien-lung Emperor" (paper presented at the American Historical Association, Dec. 1982).

126. Franke, *Introduction*, pp. 4–7.

127. On the *P'ing-ting Lo-ch'a fang-lueh*, see note 116 above.

128. I thank Professor Tu Wei-yun for discussing these points with me.

CHAPTER 8. THE CHIA-CH'ING REFORMS
OF THE GRAND COUNCIL, 1799–1820

1. For English-language accounts of the Ho-shen case, see Knight Biggerstaff's biography of Ho-shen in ECCP, pp. 288–90; David Nivison, "Ho-shen and His Accusers: Ideology and Political Behavior in the Eighteenth Century," in *Confucianism in Action*, ed. David S. Nivison and Arthur F. Wright (Stanford, 1960), pp. 209–43; Susan Mann Jones, "Hung Liang-chi (1746–1809): The Perception and Articulation of Political Problems in Late Eighteenth Century China" (Ph.D. diss., Stanford University, 1971; E. Backhouse and J.O.P. Bland, *Annals and Memoirs of the Court of Peking* (repr. Taipei, 1970), pp. 343–71 (this offers translations of many of the primary documents); Kahn, *Monarchy in the Emperor's Eyes*, pp. 248–59; and A. E. Grantham, *A Manchu Monarch: An Interpretation of Chia Ch'ing* (London, 1934), chaps. 1 and 2. For an analysis of certain major published primary sources on the Ho-shen case, see Knight Biggerstaff, "Some Notes on the *Tung-hua lu* and the *Shih-lu*," *Harvard Journal of Asiatic Studies* 4, no. 2 (July 1939): 110–13. For an unusual set of published primary sources on the late Ho-shen era, see *Chia-ch'ing san-nien T'ai-shang huang-ti Ch'i-chü chu* (Diary of the activities of the Abdicated Emperor [Ch'ien-lung]), in *Chia-ch'ing* 3 [1798], ed. Chu Hsi-tsu (Peiping, 1930). Ho-shen's bodyguard post was at the Ch'ien-ch'ing Gate. The Palace Museum in Taipei holds the final draft of Ho-shen's official biography made for the official Ch'ing history; I am grateful to Wu Che-fu for making a copy available to me.

2. Hsiao, *Ch'ing-tai t'ung-shih* 2:212.

3. CCSL 37/46b–51b. On Ho-shen's wealth, see Shang Ch'üan, "Ch'ing-tai Ho-shen tsai-ching chia-ch'an k'ao-shih" (unpublished manuscript); I thank Mr. Yang Nai-chi of the National Architectural History Institute for lending me his copy and also for taking me through Ho-shen's villa.

4. Backhouse and Bland, *Annals and Memoirs*, p. 367 *n.*; Li Chien-nung, *Chung-kuo chin-pai-nien cheng-chih shih* (Shanghai, 1948), pp. 10–11. Li also estimated Ho-shen's estate to be the equivalent of ten times the seventy million tael annual income of the Chinese empire at the time. For schedules of Ho-shen's confiscated wealth, see *Shih-liao hsun-k'an*, pp. 97ff.

5. CCSL 37/46b–51b. The pavilion was the Ning-shou Kung.

6. CCSL 39/32b–34.

7. These records, the Mi-chi tang, appear in the Grand Council inventory of its Manchu materials, (B) Man-k'u tang-an ts'ao-pen ch'ing-ts'e (which shows two vol-

umes for CL51), (B) Ch'ing-ch'a ko-tang chi-tsai pu (one volume for CC1), and (B) Man Chün-chi tang-an tsung-mu cheng/fu pen ping yueh-che; some items appear in the Bureau of Documents' published listing, *Ch'ing Chün-chi ch'u tang-an mu-lu*, pp. 9, 21. One volume of the archival survivals, covering roughly CL58 and 59, was published in *Wen-hsien ts'ung-pien* 2:733–49. The Palace Museum in Taipei has four volumes, one each for CL40–50, CL53–57, CL58–60, and CC1. The four volumes in Beijing cover CL51–53, CL58, and CL60 and at present appear to be part of the Chinese-language holdings (Box 2247). Note that there are other archival volumes by this title, but these are not related to the late–Ch'ien-lung Secret Accounts Bureau; one (2247-5) dates from the T'ung-chih period. The earliest records of the Secret Accounts Bureau may have been kept in volumes also used for other purposes, with separate records set up only once a large number of documents warranted that. See, for example, the redemption fine notice in (B) Ho-t'u-li tang CL43/12/3.

8. This is the position taken by Torbert, *The Ch'ing Imperial Household Department*, pp. 117–20. On the office as separate from other Grand Council workplaces, see Chao-lien, *Hsiao-t'ing tsa-lu* 7/16b–17b. On the relation to the Grand Council, see Chuang Chi-fa, "Kuo-li Ku-kung po-wu-yuan tien-ts'ang Ch'ing-tai tang-an shu-lueh," *Ku-kung chi-k'an* 6, no. 4 (Summer 1972): 61.

9. See, for example, (T) Mi-chi tang CL57/10/15, pp. 263–64; and (T) SSTC, passim, for the appropriate dates.

10. For an English-language description of the Secret Accounts Bureau, see Chang Te-ch'ang, "The Economic Role of the Imperial Household," pp. 264–65.

11. See, for example, (T) Mi-chi tang CC1/2/3, pp. 19–23. The vermilion comments were specially noted in these records.

12. (T) Mi-chi tang, passim.

13. (T) SSTC from CC4 on, passim.

14. CCSL 37/28b–29b, 47b; 38/14.

15. CCSL 37/48b, 40/14b–15b; see also CCSL 37/15–16b. This charge was not emphasized, doubtless to forestall the notion that this kind of malefaction might be easily repeated. The problem of Ho-shen's influence and the faithfulness of the edict drafts is discussed in Meng Sen, *Ch'ing-tai shih*, pp. 273–77. The imperial emendations on various edicts on the Ho-shen case are shown in *Shih-liao hsun-k'an*, pp. 97–100, 127–31, 149–53, 262–66.

16. CCSL 37/27a–b, 38/9a–b. There are several additional references to this male-faction. For instance, there was an imperial rescript on (T) KCT-CC004489, CC3/12/16, Fu-ch'ang, which warned, "As for the Grand Council sealed copies [*fu-feng*], these are prohibited for all time." This rescript is illustrated is my "Imperial Notations on Ch'ing Official Documents," frontispiece. See also Fairbank and Teng, "Types and Uses of Ch'ing Documents," p. 26*n*.52.

17. CCSL 37/9b–10, 48b.

18. (T) SSTC CC1–3, passim; SYCL 22/5b. Among the palace memorials of this era I found only one inexplicably delayed because it seemed to have taken two and a half months to come from Canton; perhaps it arrived and was returned for reformulation; (T) KCT-CC003622, CC3/1/9, Ch'ang-fu.

19. SYCL 13/1.

20. See, for example, (B) IFT CL2/4/21, pp. 231–32; CL6/9/11, p. 365; CL13/12/1, p. 401; (T) SYT-FP CC10/12/16, p. 267. In the Yung-cheng period, instructions given

in audience had to be written out and submitted to the emperor so that he could be sure that only the views he wished to have disseminated were going into circulation; see, for example, (T) KCT-YC000471, YC8/10/15, Yueh Chung-ch'i.

21. When Manchu grand councillors were appointed, the emperor was routinely asked if they should be permitted to read the Chinese-language as well as the Manchu memorials; this question was no longer asked after the beginning of the Tao-kuang period, at which point all grand councillors were permitted to see all the palace memorials, SYCL 13/2b–3. See also HT 3/1b.

22. CCSL 37/27a–b. See also note 16 above.

23. See, for example, (T) Hsun-ch'ang tang CL49/10/16, p. 183; (T) SYT-FP CL51/6/6, pp. 558–59; CL52/11/26, p. 415; CL55/5/23, p. 151. Although I have not often seen this in periods other than the Ho-shen era, occasionally other examples appear; see, for instance, (B) IFT CL4/9/28, p. 257.

24. The years CC1–3 were in reality the last three years of the Ch'ien-lung reign; see Chapter 6, n. 5.

25. CCSL 37/27b, 32ff.

26. The emperor's permission for suicide by strangulation (hanging) was a compassionate gesture. Death by strangulation was preferred to any sort of execution involving dismemberment (such as beheading) because of the belief that one's body should be returned intact to one's parents and ancestors at death.

27. CCSL 37/27b, 38/2b–7; CS 4:2497. For Fu-ch'ang-an's biography, see ECCP, p. 249; and CS 5:4121.

28. Those restored were Tai Chü-heng, Na-yen-ch'eng, and Fu-sen, who had been dismissed the previous year; Tung Kao, who had gone into mourning in CC2 (1797); and Ch'ing-kuei, who had last served on the council in CL58 (1793); see CS 4:2496–97. Prince Ch'eng's position as Grand Council leader is not shown in the official Ch'ing tables (CS 4:2497) because he acquired the post after the beginning of one year and stepped down before the beginning of the next. The fact is noted, however, in his official biography, CS 5:3568. At the time that Prince Ch'eng stepped down on CC4/10/22 (1799 Nov. 19), the edict anounced that having princes on the Grand Council "does not accord with the basic principles of our Empire"; CCSL 53/22a–b. Later in the nineteenth century, the rule against having princes on the Grand Council was quietly abandoned. Prince Kung served as the ranking councillor in the early years of the Hsien-feng reign and again for the entire T'ung-chih period and through KHsu10 (1884); CS 4:2504, 2505–8. Other princes served later in the dynasty. As we know, the edict's statement was a misrepresentation of the facts when applied to Chia-ch'ing's father's reign, as two princes had served on the Interim Council at the beginning of the reign and other imperial relatives had figured importantly on the council during the remainder of the century. See the discussion of this subject in Chapter 5 above.

29. CCSL 37/27b–28.

30. CS 4:2694.

31. CCSL 38/7b–9, 46/4b; CS 6:4458; Susan Mann Jones and Philip A. Kuhn, "Dynastic Decline and the Roots of Rebellion," in *The Cambridge History of China*, vol. 10: *Late Ch'ing, 1800–1911*, pt. 1, ed. John K. Fairbank (New York, 1978), p. 108. The memory of the Kansu case of two decades earlier, when large numbers of officials were executed and many others dispatched into exile, may have lingered as a warning against rooting out every last malefactor. For a brief description of the Kansu case, in which

an appropriation of approximately one million taels for famine relief found its way into the pockets of the provincial officials charged with handling local relief, see ECCP, p. 100. The relief background for understanding the case has been investigated in Pierre-Étienne Will, *Bureaucratie et famine en Chine au 18ᵉ siècle* (Paris, 1980).

32. CCSL 37/46b–51b has the indictment. For other accusations, see CCSL 37/32–36.

33. CCSL 37/46b–47, 38/3–4b.

34. CS 5:2141.

35. (T) SYT-FP CC7/2/24, pp. 117–22. There is an incomplete version (about two-thirds) in SYCL 1/10–12. Although the archival version of this document that I used was a copy, the emperor's vermilion addition to the draft was marked.

36. SYCL 13/6b–9.

37. CCSL 181/29–30.

38. See the discussion of the noted names list near the end of Chapter 6.

39. SYCL 1/17.

40. On the rescript, see note 16 above. See also Hsieh Pao-chao, *The Government of China*, pp. 85–87, for the view that the Chia-ch'ing reforms were designed to break the power of the Grand Council and that they were put through by the emperor on the advice of censors.

41. Although, as has previously been mentioned, superintendency appointments are difficult to trace, the Ch'eng Prince Yung-hsing appears to have been the last board superintendent of the early Chia-ch'ing reign.

42. CCSL 130/14–15. Board superintendencies were revived later in the nineteenth century.

43. CCSL 132/8a–b.

44. Ying-ho, *En-fu t'ang pi-chi* 1/5.

45. SYCL 15/1–4b. In the 1830s when Ying-ho assembled his recollections on his experience in the Grand Council and other aspects of his life, he listed the Manchus and Mongols from before his own time who had held the *chin-shih* degree, been members of the Hanlin Academy, and served on the Grand Council. In the entire three-quarters of a century covered he was able to identify only three Manchu and Mongol *chin-shih* degree holders who had become grand councillors: Yin-chi-shan, who joined in CL13 (1748); Meng-lin, who began in CL21 (1756); and Na-yen-ch'eng, who began in CC3 (1798). But within the thirty-three years of his own times he identified five such men who became grand councillors: himself in CC9 (1804), Kuei-fang in CC18 (1813), Mu-chang-a in TK7 (1827), his son K'uei-chao in TK17 (1837), and Wen-ch'ing in TK17 (1837). Ying-ho triumphantly concluded his discussion by pointing out that the contemporary phenomenon of five Manchu and Chinese Hanlin scholars serving together on the Grand Council was something that "has never happened before"; Ying-ho, *En-fu t'ang pi-chi* 1/30; CS 4:2489ff.

46. These figures were compiled from the tables in CS 4:2487–2500; see Chapter 6, n. 15. It must be remembered that many of the councillors on duty during the Ch'ien-lung (but not the Chia-ch'ing) period would have been out of the capital serving as generals at the front or carrying out special investigative missions. In compiling these statistics I have computed the Ch'ien-lung reign as having lasted sixty-three years, through CC3 (1798), and the Chia-ch'ing era as having begun only in CC4 (1799), when Chia-ch'ing succeeded to personal rule. These topics could be studied further by

using the draft tables (*piao*) and notes prepared by the State History Office (*Kuo-shih kuan*) during the Ch'ing and redrafted by the Ch'ing History Office (*Ch'ing-shih kuan*) after the fall of the Ch'ing (both held at the Palace Museum in Taipei).

47. Rescript on (T) KCT-YC006651, YC2/5/12, T'ien Wen-ching.

48. On punishment, see Guy, *The Emperor's Four Treasuries*, pp. 95–104.

49. (T) SYT-FP CC7/2/24, p. 120.

50. Metzger, *Internal Organization*, p. 115. The documents show that the court or the emperor had an opportunity to supply a hint of the eventual recommendation desired. Thus, if *ch'a-i* was designated, the likely result was no punishment at all. If, however, *yen-chia i-ch'u* was suggested in the court's directive, the recommendation was likely to be harsh.

51. (T) SSTC CC10/12/26, p. 478; (T) SYT-FP CC10/2/5, pp. 73–74; CC10/12/6, pp. 111–12; CC10/12/10, p. 161. I have selected these examples from the same month to show the frequency of such notices. Although there were similar notices in the Ch'ien-lung period, the equivalent record books of that era have far fewer entries of this type.

52. (T) SYT-FP CC13/3/3, p. 19. I have not found any Chia-ch'ing–period instances of the most serious instruction, *yen-chia i-ch'u*, applied to the grand councillors' offences. On punishment of inner-court officials, see pp. 40–41 above.

53. On the tallies, see Chapter 6, nn. 93–96 and related text.

54. *Tsung-kuan Nei-wu fu t'ang hsien-hsing tse-li* (1853), 1/2–3; CCSL 76/20b–22; SYCL 14/8b; Yao Yuan-chih, *Chu-yeh t'ing tsa-chi* 1/14b. In CC6 (1801), it was decided that the supervising censor would not be required to attend at the Summer Palace and had to be on duty only in the city (SYCL 14/9b–10)—further evidence that this reform was particularly designed to deal with board spying at the Grand Council, since board staffmembers would not have been regularly showing up at the Summer Palace. The surveilling censor at the capital was abandoned almost immediately after Tao-kuang came to the throne; SYCL 14/10. In CC8 (1803), similar rules were enacted for the imperial tour to prevent idlers from approaching the tents where government business was being carried on (in what was known as the "White Cloth Area" [*Pai-pu ch'eng*], said to correspond with the inner court, and the "Yellow Cloth Area" [*Huang-pu ch'eng*], said to correspond to the Peking palace's innermost precincts where the emperor resided); (T) SYT-FP CC8/3/29, p. 345. These warnings had to be repeated in CC23; see (T) SYT-FP CC23/6/7, pp. 39–41.

55. Chao I, *Yen-p'u tsa-chi* 1:6.

56. HFSL 21/15–17. The same edict, with a few more phrases and items, appears in (T) SYT-FP TK30/11/10, pp. 103–8.

57. Li Tsung-t'ung, *Shih-hsueh kai-yao*, p. 289. The Grand Council windows were small by modern standards: 44 inches wide by 32 inches high. On the windows, see Chapter 7, n. 45 and related text.

58. ECCP, p. 805. The Grand Council *chüan* in the Chia-ch'ing *Hui-tien* is almost identical to its counterpart in the Kuang-hsu *Hui-tien*, 3/1–12b. For the clerks' compilations, see the appropriate entries under their names in the bibliography. Wu became a clerk in CC18, Liang in CC23; SYCL 18/14b–15.

59. For the presents, see HT 3/5b–9b; edict drafting received short shrift in 3/2–3. The reader of this book will note that the *Hui-tien* Grand Council *chüan* has not often been cited in this study; it simply was not useful.

60. On the Ch'ien-lung–period treatment of clerks, see Chapter 7 above.

61. For example, three of the earliest Grand Council clerk appointments—of Chang Jo-ai, O-jung-an, and O-lun, in YC11 (1733)—were of sons and nephews of Chang T'ing-yü and O-erh-t'ai; YCSL 131/3. Kung Tzu-chen claimed that Chang T'ing-yü and O-erh-t'ai brought ten clerks into the organization; see Teng and Wang, "T'an Chün-chi ch'u," p. 195.

62. CCSL 38/1–2.

63. See ibid.; and a slightly fuller version in *Ch'ing-ch'ao hsu Wen-hsien t'ung-k'ao* 5:8773. In CC11, arrangements were made to retain a man who had been serving as a replacement by calling him a "supernumerary" (*e-wai hsing-tsou*); SYCL 13/4b. The supernumerary post also served as a trial appointment. Usually men taken on by this means stepped into the next available vacancy. See (T) SYT-FP CL54/11/16, pp. 309–10; KHsu10/3/26, p. 227. In HF11, when the Tsungli Yamen was set up, a special group of supernumerary Grand Council clerks was created to serve concurrently at the new office; SYCL 13/106. By the end of the dynasty the number of clerks permitted may have risen further; see Chapter 7, n. 24; and Li P'eng-nien et al., *Ch'ing-tai chung-yang chi-kuan*, p. 64.

64. CCSL 38/1–2.

65. SYCL 13/6. This stricture was apparently put through because the censors' ranks, 5A and 5B, were considered too high for the clerks to hold concurrently, not because there were objections to the council having Censorate ties. After this time clerks could also not hold concurrent posts in the Supervisorate of Imperial Instruction or the Transmission Office; see Wu Chen-yü, *Yang-chi chai ts'ung-lu* 4/2a–b.

66. SYCL 1/16b–17.

67. Yao Yuan-chih, *Chu-yeh t'ing tsa-chi* 1/15.

68. CCSL 271/16b–17b.

69. "Ch'i Wen-tuan [Chün-tsao] shu-t'ing tsai-pi i-kao," in *Ch'ing-tai chang-ku chui-lu*, p. 117; SYCL 17 and 19, passim. On another instance for selecting Manchu clerks for the Grand Council, see (T) Chiao-p'ien tang CC23/4/26, pp. 196, 200, 201–8, 228–30, where matters preliminary to the imperial audience were being handled by the Manchu Section. Out of fifty-five examined, sixteen did sufficiently well in the examination and were otherwise well qualified so as to be selected for audience; nine eventually served as clerks, see SYCL 16/17, 17/1–2.

70. (T) SYT-FP CC10/10/29, pp. 393–95; CCSL 271/16b–17b. In this case the emperor appears to have largely followed the order of a list of thirty-one Chinese brought to audience as part of the clerk selection process. If the imperial choices had been made on an entirely uninfluenced basis we should expect an approximately equal number of selections from each section of the list. But in fact, by dividing the list in four parts we find that six men were chosen from the first eight names, six from the second eight, three from the third, and two from the last (of seven names only). Such a dwindling proportion suggests that the order of names in the list as composed for the emperor represented the grand councillors' preferences, which then strongly, but not entirely, guided the emperor when he made his selections.

71. There is a suggestion that in the Ch'ien-lung period some critics argued against nepotism; see, for example, Wang Ch'ang, "Chün-chi ch'u t'i-ming chi" 14/19.

72. SYCL 13/7; CCSL 239/8a–b. For the archival documents, see (T) SYT-FP CC10/10/24, pp. 319, 331–35, 337.

73. SYCL 13/9b-10b; see also Yao Yuan-chih, *Chu-yeh t'ing tsa-chi* 1/15b; and the statements of Ku Ch'un cited in his biography, CS 6:4584.

74. *Kung-chung hsien-hsing tse-li* 1/36-37; SYCL 13/12.

75. CCSL 73/18a-b.

76. CCSL 132/8a-b.

77. SYCL 14/12b-14b; (B) IFT CL13/9/30, p. 281. The sum had traditionally been paid over by the Imperial Household, which now protested and asked that it be returned.

78. (T) SYT-FP CC18/12/16, pp. 79-80; CC18/12/17, pp. 81, 83-85. These entries list the thirty-three Grand Council clerks of the time and stipulate rewards for their service during the campaign to suppress the Eight Trigrams rebellion. All the clerks were rewarded in this distribution of imperial favors. Eight received "special honors" (*ts'ung-yu i-hsu*), and the other twenty-five received ordinary rewards (*i-hsu*).

79. Various forms of the Ta-yuan tzu-ti tang are listed in *Ch'ing Chün-chi ch'u tang-an mu-lu*, pp. 19-20, 28, 41, as well as in the Tsung-mu section, the earliest dated CC11. Scattered volumes of the Chia-ch'ing and Tao-kuang era were also listed in (B) Man-k'u tang-an ts'ao-pen ch'ing-ts'e, which shows that these records were Manchu Section compilations. Their *Ch'ing Chün-chi ch'u tang-an mu-lu* listing derives from their mixed content of Chinese and Manchu entries, with the result that at some point archival sorters pulled various of them for the Chinese holdings. The fact that the examples I saw were probably not the earliest examples is explained by this dispersion. Moreover, the inventories, which list no entries from before the Chia-ch'ing era, show that at an early date there was no longer any continuity in the survivals. These records tended to disappear, possibly because they were not particularly valued, possibly because they may have contained information that someone wished to dispose of. Earlier a similar type of information appeared in other record books; see below, note 83.

80. (T) Ta-yuan tzu-ti tang CC11/2, pp. 34-35. Although these are Manchu names, they appear to be in the Chinese style. The fact that there are different generational characters in the treasurer's and the others' names may indicate a different mother.

81. For an exception, note that in CC10 it had been decided that the second brother listed would not be required to resign his Grand Council clerkship on account of his older sibling's higher post because he had come on duty before the new regulation had gone into effect; (T) SYT-FP CC10/10/24, p. 337.

82. (T) Ta-yuan tzu-ti tang CC20, p. 107.

83. Some of the Ch'ien-lung-period lists appear in the Chia-ch'ing-period Ta-yuan tzu-ti tang; see, for instance, CC20, pp. 109, 111-13, which contains copies of CL50 and 55 appointment lists. Three similar lists appear in what might seem to be an inappropriate record book, (B) Liu-ching pan-shih tang CL49/2/16, pp. 25-29.

84. *Ch'ing Chün-chi ch'u tang-an mu-lu*, tsung-mu sec., p. 3, lists fifty-eight volumes, all from the nineteenth century; see pp. 20-21, 28-29, 34-35, 58, 68. The earliest examples are dated CC7-9; earlier volumes may be lost or this aspect of the reforms may not have been instituted until this time. I have found no indication that this kind of record series existed in the Ch'ien-lung period. The Tao-kuang volumes are also listed in (B) Man-k'u tang-an ts'ao-pen ch'ing-ts'e. The volumes that I have seen contain a mixture of Chinese and Manchu, which explains why although these should have been stored with Manchu-language holdings, they were listed in the finding list for Chinese-language record books, the *Ch'ing Chün-chi ch'u tang-an mu-lu*, and are held with Chinese-

language materials in the Taipei Palace Museum. Their placement in the Manchu inventory of the Ch'ing period and their omission from the document register (SSTC), which indexed only what were regarded as documents in the Chinese category, make clear that these were regarded as Manchu-language materials. Consultation of the Manchu archives, once they are sorted, may shed more light on the situation.

85. For example, (T) Chiao-p'ien tang CC25/4/23, p. 40.

86. On the "avenue of words," see Lloyd E. Eastman, *Throne and Mandarins: China's Search for a Policy During the Sino-French Controversy, 1880–1885* (Cambridge, Mass., 1967), pp. 20–21.

87. CCSL 54/4–6.

88. CCSL 40/22–23; see also Chapter 1, n. 122. For an excellent summary of the rules for reporting under the Palace Memorial system, see Silas H. L. Wu, "Memorial Systems," pp. 25–26, 61–62n.49. There is also some information in Metzger, *Internal Organization*, app. 5, pp. 433–34.

89. For one such rare example, see (T) KCT-CC004580, CC4/5/11, Ha-tang-a and Yü Ch'ang.

90. Weiss, "Flexibility in Provincial Government," pp. 3–4.

91. Fairbank, *Trade and Diplomacy* 1 : 189–95.

92. CCSL 61/24a–b.

93. CCSL 103/24b–25.

94. Ibid.

95. (T) SYT-FP CC10/12/2, p. 25.

EPILOGUE

1. CS 4:2486.

2. Li Tsung-t'ung, "Pan-li Chün-chi ch'u lueh-k'ao," pp. 4–5.

3. Silas H. L. Wu, *Communication and Imperial Control*, pp. 86–92.

4. There are indications that certain areas of inner-court secrecy became less well managed as time wore on. Personnel reports, for instance, became less frank and more standardized, losing the spontaneity and directness that had candidly identified good and bad candidates for the Yung-cheng Emperor (described in Chapter 1). See, for example, the personnel report contained in (T) KCT-CC003519, CC3/12/15, Liang K'en-t'ang. An edict deploring a serious breach of inner court confidentiality is to be found in CLSL 963/17–20.

5. (B) IFT CL23/12/11, p. 299.

6. (T) SYT-FP HF3/2/6, p. 71.

7. See the discussion of this important point in Chapter 6, pp. 186–90.

8. See Chapter 6, n. 83.

9. Pamela Kyle Crossley, "*Manzhou yuanliu kao* and the Formalization of the Manchu Heritage," *The Journal of Asian Studies* 46, no. 4 (Nov. 1987): 762–90; my "History as Mirror." See also the information on publications in Chapters 5, 6, and 7 above.

10. On the change in the *Lü-li* editorial boards, compare YCSL 9/22 and 11/26b–27 and Interim Council deliberations in (B) IFT CL1/6/28, pp. 55–56; CL1/8/11, p. 133; CL2/J9/7, pp. 199–200; CL2/11/7, p. 297. See also the Interim Council entry under *Lü-li* in Appendix E.

11. CLSL 332/1b–3b. It is often said that even in the palace memorial system New Year's Day was held sacred and free of work, a fact that was auspiciously marked by a notice in the Sui-shou teng-chi that read: "Peaceful without official business" (*T'ai-p'ing wu-shih*). Although I have observed this comforting maxim inscribed in the early SSTC, by the nineteenth century the formula was honored more in the breach as the exigencies of rebellion and invasion denied even that one day to the frenzied servitors of the inner court.

12. (B) IFT CL15/1/29, p. 55. For a list of occasions on which the routine system was required to halt, see HT 2/5–6. On the closing of the seals, see Bodde, *Annual Customs and Festivals*, p. 95.

13. Lynn A. Struve, *The Southern Ming 1644–1662*, pp. 2–7, 14, and bibliographical references; conversation with Professor Struve, 17 Jan. 1989.

14. See, for example, (B) SYT-FP undated Grand Council memorandum of CL32/12/3, p. 261.

15. See, for example, (B) SYT-FP undated Grand Council memorandum of CL32/2/1, pp. 93–94.

16. YC11/12/20 document as reported in (B) CPTC CL24/4/27, Nei-cheng, ch'i-t'a.

17. SYCL 12/9–14b. For some Ch'ien-lung–period submissions, see the volumes of (B) Pao-hsiao chin-shu tang.

18. See, for example, the famous essay by Kung Tzu-chen, "Shang Ta-hsueh-shih" (On the grand secretaries), in his *Ting-an wen-chi* (repr. Taipei, 1968), 4:311–22.

19. Harold Wechsler, *Mirror to the Son of Heaven: Wei Cheng at the Court of T'ang T'ai-tsung* (New Haven, 1974), pp. 22–24. There is a considerable literature on the supposed increase in imperial absolutism since the T'ang-Sung era; for a succinct statement of the arguments, see Frederick W. Mote, "The Growth of Chinese Despotism: A Critique of Wittfogel's Theory of Oriental Despotism as Applied to China," *Oriens Extremus* 8 (1961): 1–41.

20. The K'ang-hsi Emperor as quoted in Chu Chin-fu, "Ch'ing K'ang-hsi shih-ch'i chung-yang chüeh-ts'e chih-tu yen-chiu," *Li-shih tang-an* 1987, no. 1 (Feb. 1987): 80.

21. I have not seen any of the appropriate eighteenth-century volumes and believe that they have probably disintegrated and disappeared over time. Nevertheless, the (B) P'iao pu/t'ung pen shih and related volumes, which I date to the Tao-kuang period, contain many Ch'ien-lung–era prescriptions; the earliest entry in the Tao-kuang series, for instance, was YC5 (1727). The booklets that I saw were arranged by board, with an average of 60 pages per board, or 360 pages for all six. This suggests that as of the early Tao-kuang period there may have been as many as 720 pages in several *ts'e* to be consulted by those who wrote the draft rescripts. By the late nineteenth century the content had expanded with many more volumes in separate categories.

22. See my "Imperial Notations on Ch'ing Official Documents in the Ch'ien-lung and Chia-ch'ing Reigns, Part Two, "*National Palace Museum Bulletin* 7, no. 3 (July–Aug. 1972): 4–5.

23. See, for example, (B) IFT YC13/8/28, p. 39; (B) SSTC CL50/3/9, p. 110; (T) SSTC CC3/12/26, p. 262; (T) KCT-CC 004407, CC3/11/16, Ssu-ma T'ao and Wo-shih-pu.

24. On the court letter edicts, see Chapter 3 above.

25. (T) KCT-YC000592, vermilion enclosure 2.

26. See the analysis of the practice of heading the court letter edicts with rosters of those consulted in Chapter 3 above, pp. 106–9.

27. *Ch'ing-ch'ao Hsu Wen-hsien t'ung-k'ao* 5:8774, reading *ni* for *i*.

28. For an explanation of the monarch's power to act independently and charismatically, see Philip A. Kuhn, "Political Crime and Bureaucratic Monarchy: A Chinese Case of 1768," *Late Imperial China* 8, no. 1 (June 1987): 80–104. There is no question that imperial independence in decision making was possible, but the varieties described by Kuhn were unusual. The eighteenth-century SSTC shows that in nearly all instances Ch'ien-lung approved his capital officials' written recommendations.

29. Richard E. Neustadt, *Presidential Power: The Politics of Leadership* (New York, 1960), pp. 6, 112.

30. This argument is explored in greater detail in my "Vermilion Brush: The Grand Council Communications System and Central Government Decision Making in Mid Ch'ing China" (Ph.D. diss., Yale University, 1980), particularly chap. 8.

APPENDIX A.   ANALYSIS OF "THE BOARD" NOTICES IN YUNG-CHENG–PERIOD DOCUMENTS

1. For two of many examples, see the Yueh Chung-ch'i memorials (T) KCT-YC000059, YC7/12/7, and (T) KCT-YC000068, YC7/12/7, both of which concern military supplies for the front and whose rescripts speak of "the board," in the former case turning the memorial over to "the board" and in the latter addressing an order to "the board." For a Cha-lang-a example, see (T) KCT-YC016727, YC8/1/4.

2. On the use of *Chü-t'i-lai*, see Chapter 1, nn. 130–33 and related text.

3. The six men in this case consisted of a superintendent, two Chinese (but no Manchu) board presidents, and three vice presidents, whose names appeared in the roster of memorialists (see Figure 4); (T) KCT-YC014708, YC4/4/26, Yin-hsiang (Prince I) and five others.

4. Ibid.

5. (T) KCT-YC014709, YC3/12/23, Yin-hsiang (Prince I) and five others. Some instances of palace memorials being sent to outer-court boards occurred early in the reign, before the *chü-t'i lai* formula had been generally prescribed (there were also some examples of *chü-t'i lai* in the K'ang-hsi palace memorials). See, for example, *Nien Keng-yao tsou-che* 1:4–5, YC1/5/8, Nien Keng-yao.

6. (T) KCT-YC016724, YC7/12/15, Cha-lang-a, which quotes (T) KCT-YC000469, court letter of YC7/11/18 addressed to General Yueh and drafted by "Prince I and others"; apparently a copy was sent to Cha-lang-a. The character *tzu* here is different from the court letter usage (in *tzu-chi*) and signifies a lateral communication enclosing an edict, in the manner of a court letter. A similar instance spoke of a "Board of Revenue communication" (*Hu-pu tzu*), was on a military finance topic, and stated that board officials (*pu-ch'en*)—surely the directorate or the inner deputies—had considered the problem; (T) KCT-YC000066, YC7/12/7, Yueh Chung-ch'i. Another example is in (T) KCT-YC000226-1, YC8/6/19, Yueh Chung-ch'i, which mentions receiving a *Hu-pu tzu* containing an imperial edict on a military campaign topic. See also (T) KCT-YC000220, YC8/5/30, Yueh Chung-ch'i, which quotes an edict that appears to have been a court letter. (This was presented in abbreviated form in YCSL 83/36b–38, where it was misidentified as an "Edict to the Board of War." The content of the edict

concerned military finance details of the sort that the Board of Revenue deputies would have discussed with the emperor and then dispatched in a court letter.) Yung-cheng's rescript on (T) KCT-YC000300, YC7/6/3, Yueh Chung-ch'i, informed Yueh that "this [military finance] matter was also turned over to the I Prince and others [and] there was a decree which the board was promulgating." By now we may surmise that these edicts sent in Board of Revenue lateral communications were court letters drafted by the imperial deputies. There are earlier examples of the use of Board of Revenue lateral communications to send imperial commands. *Kung-chung tang Yung-cheng ch'ao tsou-che* 8:821–22, YC5/9/4, Yueh Chung-ch'i, refers to a "board communication" (*pu-tzu*) on a late-YC3 military topic that had been discussed by the Deliberative Council. (T) KCT-YC020075, edict on flood relief for Hunan, dated YC5/7/13 and marked "Edict drafted by the Board of Revenue" (*Hu-pu feng shang-yü*), was not described with the character *tzu*, nor did it possess other characteristics of the developed court letter form. Without the originals it is difficult to ascertain the exact nature of these references; they may have been court letter prototypes whose drafting was supervised by the early inner deputies.

7. (B) IFT YC11/11/27, pp. 53–54. Other references to the "Board of Revenue's Military Finance Section" are scattered through these records; see, for instance, (B) IFT YC11/7/7, p. 45; YC11/12/2, p. 67.

8. (T) KCT-YC020499, YC13/9/22, Yin-li, Chang T'ing-yü, and Hai-wang.

9. *Kung-chung tang Yung-cheng ch'ao tsou-che* 11:360–63, YC6/9/16, Yueh Chung-ch'i and Hsi-lin, with enclosed deliberation slip (*i-che*) of the type identifiable as composed by the inner deputies. Many others rescripts of the day directly named the inner deputies instead of using "the board" shorthand; see, for example, (T) KCT-YC000327, YC7/6/3, Yueh Chung-ch'i.

10. Edict of YC7/7/29 cited at length in (T) KCT-YC000220, YC8/5/30, Yueh Chung-ch'i. Part of the edict appears in YCSL 83/36b–38. The explanation provided here refutes Silas H. L. Wu's claim that as long as General Yueh asked that matters be turned over to the board, this signified that the Military Finance Section had not yet been founded; see his "Ch'ing-tai Chün-chi ch'u," p. 29, and the imperial rescript, which he cites, on (T) KCT-YC000289, YC7/11/12, Yueh Chung-ch'i. On the pre–Military Finance Section situation, recall the Chapter 3 description of the inner deputies' YC6 review of General Yueh's mathematics for horse and cart purchases, pp. 104–5.

11. The quotations are from (T) KCT-YC020499, YC13/9/22, Yin-li, Chang T'ing-yü, and Hai-wang.

Bibliography of Works Cited

ARCHIVAL WORKS

Because many archival record series were copied during the Ch'ing, some of the surviving duplicates are variously divided between Beijing and Taipei. Although the notes specify, with either (B) or (T), the location of the particular source that I used for the research in question, source installations have been omitted from this bibliography of archival sources lest the reader be misled into thinking that a series consulted in one place is not available in the other. (Moreover, the versions frequently have different paginations and occasionally slightly different content.) The translations of archival series titles offered below are tentative and in some instances summarize content rather than providing a literal rendering. Manchu-language items are listed under their Chinese-language titles, just as they were inventoried in Ch'ing times and have to be retrieved today.

Grand Council Records

Chi-hsin tang 寄信檔 (Record book of court letters)

Chiao-p'ien tang 交片檔 (Record book of lateral communications)

Chiao-pu ni-Hui tang 剿捕逆回檔 (Record book of the [late–Ch'ien-lung] campaign against the Moslems)

Chiao-pu tang 剿捕檔 (Record book of military campaigns [against internal rebels])

Ch'ing-ch'a ko-tang chi-tsai pu 清查各檔記載簿 (Record book for noting various archival holdings [a council inventory record])

Cho-fan tang 桌飯檔 (Record book of tables of food [served at the Grand Council])

Chu-p'i tsou-che 硃批奏摺 (Palace memorials [Beijing holdings; at the Taipei Palace Museum these documents are known as Kung-chung tang, which see below])

Chün-chi ch'u kuei-chü chi-tsai 軍機處規矩記載 (Notation of [some] Grand Council regulations)

Chün-chi ch'u wen-i tang 軍機處文移檔 (Record book of Grand Council lateral communications [dispatched from the Office of Military Archives, *Fang-lueh kuan*])

Han Chün-chi tang-an tsung-ts'e 漢軍機檔案總冊 (Archival inventory of the Chinese Grand Council holdings)

Han-k'u tang-an cheng-pen ch'ing-ts'e 漢庫檔案正本清冊 (Inventory record of archival originals in the Chinese-language holdings)

Hsun-ch'ang tang 尋常檔 (Record book of ordinary matters [a variant title for the Shang-yü tang—fang-pen, which see below])

I-fu tang 議覆檔 (Record book of discussion memorials [Note that the Manchu holdings contain several subtypes: Manchu Chün-wu I-fu tang 軍務議覆檔 (Record book of Manchu-language discussion memorials on military matters) and Manchu Hsun-ch'ang i-fu tang 尋常議覆檔 (Record book of Manchu-language discussion memorials on ordinary affairs)])

I-tsou tang 議奏檔 (Record book of discussion memorials)

Kung-chi pei-k'ao 公記備考(Notebook recording topics of concern)

Kung-chung tang 宮中檔 (Palace memorials [Taipei Palace Museum holdings; in Beijing these documents are known as Chu-p'i tsou-che, which see above])

Kung-chung t'ing-chi pao 宮中廷寄包 (Beijing files of court letter packets [the Taipei holdings in this category are filed in the Kung-chung tang, which see above])

Lai-wen tang 來文檔 (Record book of lateral communications)

Lu-fu 錄副 (Memorial packet copy of a palace memorial [holdings also sometimes known as Chün-chi ch'u lu-fu tsou-che 軍機處錄副奏摺; there are also Manchu language holdings of this series])

Man Chün-chi tang-an tsung-mu cheng/fu pen ping yueh-che 滿軍機檔案總目正/副本並月摺 (General archival inventory of the Manchu Grand Council holdings, [including] originals, copies, and memorial packets)

Man-k'u tang-an ts'ao-pen ch'ing-ts'e 滿庫檔案草本清冊 (Inventory of record book copies in the Manchu-language holdings)

Mi-chi tang 密記檔 (Record book of secret accounts)

Nei-che tsung-mu 內摺總目 (List of capital palace memorials under predetermined categories)

Pao-hsiao chin-shu tang 報銷進書檔 (Reports on planned publications submitted [to the emperor])

Pien-pei i-ch'ing tang 邊備夷情檔 (Record book of the northwest military campaign)

P'ing-ting Chun-ka-erh wen-i tang 平定準噶爾文移檔 (Record of lateral communications concerning the [publication of the official history of the] Zunghar campaign) [dispatched from the Office of Military Archives (*Fang-lueh kuan*); see Chün-chi ch'u wen-i tang above]

Shang-yü tang—fang-pen 上諭檔 — 方本 (Record book of imperial edicts [and other materials]—square form) In Beijing the term *fang-pen* is not used.

Sui-shou teng-chi tang 隨手登記檔 (Register [of documents] as they came to hand [the Grand Council logbook])

Ta-yuan tzu-ti tang 大員子弟檔 (Record book of the sons and younger brothers of high officials)

Tien-chi tang 電寄檔 (Record of telegraphed edicts)

Tsou-che hao-pu 奏摺號簿 (Record of [stored Manchu-language] palace memorials and storage symbols)

Wen-i tang 文移檔 (Record book of [Grand Council] lateral communications [see Chün-chi ch'u wen-i tang above])

Wen-wu ch'a-pan fei-yuan tan-tang 文武查辦廢員單檔 (Record book of lists of dismissed officials under investigation [for possible reinstatement in office])

Grand Secretariat Records

Nei-ko Man p'iao-ch'ien pu-pen shih-yang 內閣滿票籤部本式樣 (Prescriptions for drawing up Manchu draft rescripts for routine capital memorials)

Nei-ko Man p'iao-ch'ien t'ung-pen shih-yang 內閣滿票籤通本式樣 (Prescriptions for drawing up Manchu draft rescripts for routine provincial memorials)

P'iao pu-pen shih-yang 票部本式樣 (Prescriptions for drawing up draft rescripts for routine capital memorials)

T'i-pen 題本 (Routine memorials)

Others

Ch'i-chü chu 起居注 (Diaries of imperial actions and speech)

Ho-t'u-li tang 和圖利檔 (Record book of lateral communications, [an Imperial Household record])

Hu-k'e shih-shu 戶科史書 (Copies of routine-system memorials circulated to the office of the Board of Revenue junior metropolitan censor)

Shang-yü tang 上諭檔 (Record book of imperial edicts)

PUBLISHED WORKS

In the following bibliography, the capital of the Ch'ing empire is identified as "Peking." For works appearing during the Republic (1912–49), however, the same city is noted as "Peiping," and "Beijing" is used to describe the capital since 1949. The two palace museums existing after 1949 are individually identified by their location in either Beijing or Taipei.

A Wen-ch'eng kung [*A-Kuei*] *nien-p'u* (Chronological Biography of A-kuei). Compiled by Na-yen-ch'eng. 34 *chüan.* 1st ed. 1813; repr. Taipei: Wen-hai, 1971.

Ai-hsin chüeh-lo tsung-p'u (Genealogy of the Aisin-gioro clan). Compiled by Chin Sung-ch'iao. 8 vols. Fengtien, 1938.

Arlington, L. C., and William Lewisohn. *In Search of Old Peking.* Peking: Henri Vetch, 1935.

Backhouse, E., and J. O. P. Bland. *Annals and Memoirs of the Court of Peking.* 1st ed. 1914; repr. Taipei: Ch'eng-wen, 1970.

Bartlett, Beatrice S. "An Archival Revival: The Qing Central Government Archives in Peking Today." *Ch'ing-shih wen-t'i* 4, no. 6 (Dec. 1981): 81–110.

——— [Pai Pin-chü]. "Archive Materials in China on United States History." In *Guide to the Study of United States History Outside the U.S. 1945–1980*, edited by Lewis Hanke, 1: 504–66. White Plains. N.Y.: Krause International, 1985. (Translated by Liang K'an and published in *Tang-an hsueh ts'an-k'ao* [Journal of archival studies], nos. 16–17 [Dec. 1986]: 2–17, as "Chung-kuo tang-an chi ch'i-chung ti Mei-kuo shih tzu-liao" [Chinese archives and their materials on U.S. History].

————. "Books of Revelations: The Importance of the Manchu Language Archival Record Books for Research on Ch'ing History." *Late Imperial China* 6, no. 2 (Dec. 1985): 25–36.

————. "Ch'ing Documents in the National Palace Museum Archives. Part One. Document Registers: The *Sui-shou teng-chi.*" *National Palace Museum Bulletin* 10, no. 4 (Sept.–Oct. 1975): 1–17.

————. "Ch'ing Palace Memorials in the Archives of the National Palace Museum." *National Palace Museum Bulletin* 13, no. 6 (Jan.–Feb. 1979): 1–21.

———— [Pai Pin-chü]. "Ch'ing-tai Chün-chi ch'u ti tang-an kuan-li chih-tu—kuan-liao t'i-chih ch'uang-hsin chih-i yen-chiu" (Ch'ing Grand Council archival curatorship: A study of bureaucratic innovation). Translated by Ch'en Kuo-tung. In *Ming-Ch'ing tang-an yü li-shih yen-chiu: Chung-kuo ti-i li-shih tang-an kuan liu-shih chou-nien chi-nien lun-wen chi* (The Ming-Ch'ing archives and historical research: Papers in commemoration of the sixtieth anniversary of [the founding of] the Number One Archives of China), ed. The Number One Archives of China, 2:643–68. Beijing: Chung-hua shu-chü, 1988. (Paper originally presented at the Ming-Ch'ing Research Symposium, Beijing, Oct. 1985.)

————. "History as Mirror: Through the Looking-Glass and into Wonderland with the Ch'ien-lung Emperor." Paper presented at the American Historical Association, Dec. 1982.

————. "Imperial Notations on Ch'ing Official Documents in the Ch'ien-lung (1736–1795) and Chia-ch'ing (1796–1820) Reigns." *National Palace Museum Bulletin* 7, no. 2 (May–June 1972): 1–13, and no. 3 (July–Aug. 1972): 1–13.

————. "Ruling in Late Imperial China: Evidence from the Memorials of Discussion and Recommendation." Paper presented at the New England Conference of the Association for Asian Studies, Yale University, 15 Nov. 1986.

————. "The Secret Memorials of the Yung-cheng Period (1723–1735): Archival and Published Versions." *National Palace Museum Bulletin* 9, no. 4 (Sept.–Oct. 1974): 1–12.

————. "The Vermilion Brush: The Grand Council Communications System and Central Government Decision Making in Mid Ch'ing China. Ph.D. diss., Yale University, 1980.

Bastid, Marianne. "The Structure of the Financial Institutions of the State in the Late Qing." In *The Scope of State Power in China*, edited by Stuart R. Schram. New York: St. Martin's Press, 1985.

Beattie, Hilary J. *Land and Lineage in China: A study of T'ung-ch'eng County, Anhwei, in the Ming and Ch'ing Dynasties.* New York: Cambridge University Press, 1979.

Bielenstein, Hans. *The Bureaucracy of Han Times.* New York: Cambridge University Press, 1980.

Biggerstaff, Knight. "Some Notes on the *Tung-hua lu* and the *Shih-lu.*" *Harvard Journal of Asiatic Studies* 4, no. 2 (July 1939): 101–15.

Bodde, Derk, and Clarence Morris. *Law in Imperial China: Exemplified by 190 Ch'ing Dynasty Cases (Translated from the "Hsing-an hui-lan"); with Historical, Social, and Juridical Commentaries.* Cambridge, Mass.: Harvard University Press, 1967.

Bredon, Julie. *Peking.* Shanghai: Kelly and Walsh, 1931.

Britton, Roswell S. *The Chinese Periodical Press, 1800–1912.* 1st ed. Shanghai: Kelly and Walsh, 1933; repr. Taipei: Ch'eng-wen, 1966.

Brook, Timothy. "The Spread of Rice Cultivation and Rice Technology into the Hebei Region in the Ming and Qing." In *Explorations in the History of Science and Technology in China*, edited by Hu Tao-ching. Shanghai: Chinese Classics, 1982.

Brunnert, H. S., and V. V. Hagelstrom. *Present Day Political Organization of China.* Translated by A. Beltchenko and E. E. Moran. Shanghai: Kelly and Walsh, 1912. (First published in Russian, 1910.)

Chan, Albert, S.J. "Peking at the Time of the Wan-li Emperor (1572–1619)." In *International Association of Historians of Asia: Second Biennial Conference Proceedings*, 2: 119–47. Taipei: IAHA, 1962.

Chang Chih-an. "Ming-tai Nei-ko ti p'iao-ni" (The advisory functions of the cabinet in the Ming dynasty). *Kuo-li Cheng-chih ta-hsueh hsueh-pao* 24 (Dec. 1971): 143–56.

Chang, Chung-li. *The Income of the Chinese Gentry.* Seattle: University of Washington Press, 1962.

Chang-ku ts'ung-pien (Collected historical records). Compiled by the Bureau of Documents, National Palace Museum [Peiping]. 1st ed. 1928–29 in 10 *ts'e*; repr. Taipei: Kuo-feng, 1964.

Chang Te-ch'ang. "The Economic Role of the Imperial Household in the Ch'ing Dynasty." *Journal of Asian Studies* 31, no. 2 (Feb. 1972): 243–73.

Chang Te-tse. "Chün-chi ch'u chi ch'i tang-an" (The Grand Council and its archives). In *Wen-hsien lun-ts'ung, Lun-shu* (Articles) sec. 2, pp. 57–84. Peiping, 1936.

Chang T'ing-yü. *Ch'eng-huai yuan chu-jen tzu-ting nien-p'u* (Autobiography [of Chang T'ing-yü]). 6 *chüan*. Preface dated 1749; repr. Taipei: Wen-hai, 1970.

Chao I. *Nien-erh shih cha-chi* (Commentaries on the twenty-two standard histories). Last preface dated 1801; repr. Taipei: Le-t'ien, 1973.

———. *Yen-p'u tsa-chi* (Miscellaneous notes). 4 *chüan*. Ch'ing printed ed.; repr. Taipei: Chung-hua shu-chü, 1957.

Chao-lien. *Hsiao-t'ing tsa-lu* (Miscellaneous notes on mid-Ch'ing history). 10 *chüan* composed 1814–26; repr. in 2 vols., Taipei: Wen-hai, 1968.

Ch'en K'ang-ch'i. *Lang-ch'ien chi-wen* (Miscellaneous notes). Ch'ing printed ed. 1880 in 12 *chüan*; repr. in 4 vols., Taipei: Ch'eng-wen, 1968.

Ch'en, Kenneth K. S. *Buddhism in China: A Historical Survey.* Princeton: Princeton University Press, 1964.

"Ch'en-lieh shih wen-wu tsung-mu" (Exhibition list of documents and articles in the Palace Museum [Peiping] in 1936). In *Wen-hsien t'e-k'an, Ch'en-lieh tsung-mu* sec., pp. 1–96. Peiping: Palace Museum, Bureau of Documents, 1935.

Cheng Li. "Ming-Ch'ing tang-an" (The Ming-Ch'ing archives [in Beijing]). *Ku-kung po wu-yuan yuan-k'an* 1979, no. 1 (Feb. 1979): 11–20.

"Cheng-li Chün-chi ch'u tang-an chih ching-kuo" (The process of putting the Grand Council archives in order). In *Wen-hsien t'e-k'an, Pao-kao* (Announcements) sec., pp. 17–21. Peiping: Palace Museum, 1935.

Chi Shih-chia. "Ch'ien-lun Ch'ing Chün-chi ch'u yü chi-ch'üan cheng-chih" (A brief discussion of the Ch'ing Grand Council and totalitarian government). *Ch'ing-shih lun-ts'ung* (Collected essays on Ch'ing history) 5 (1984): 179–91.

Chia-ch'ing san-nien T'ai-shang huang-ti Ch'i-chü chu (Diary of the activities of the abdicated emperor [Ch'ien-lung] in Chia-ch'ing 3 [1798]). Edited by Chu Hsi-tsu. Peiping: Peking University, 1930.

Ch'ien-lung ching-ch'eng ch'üan-t'u (Map of the capital city in the Ch'ien-lung period).

Originally drawn ca. 1750; 1st printed Peiping: Nihon Kōain (Japan China Board, North China Division), 1940.

Ch'ien Mu. "Chung-kuo ch'uan-t'ung cheng-chih" (China's traditional government). In *Chung-kuo t'ung-shih chi-lun* (Collected essays on Chinese history), ed. Cha Shih-chieh. Taipei: Ch'ang Ch'un-shu, 1973.

———. *Chung-kuo li-tai cheng-chih te-shih* (History of Chinese political institutions). Taipei: San-min, 1969. (In English as *Traditional Government in Imperial China: A Critical Analysis*. Translated by Chün-tu Hsueh and George O. Totten. New York: St. Martin's Press, 1982.)

Ch'ien Shih-fu. "Ch'ing-tai ti Chün-chi ch'u" (The Ch'ing Grand Council). In *Ch'ing-shih lun-wen hsuan-chi* (Selected articles on Ch'ing history). Compiled by the People's University Ch'ing Research Institute. Beijing: Jen-min ta-hsüeh, 1979.

Ch'in-ting Ssu-shu wen (Imperially authorized collection of model examination essays). Compiled by Hung-chou and Fang Pao. 41 *chüan*. Preface dated 1739.

Ching, Frank. *Ancestors: 900 Years in the Life of a Chinese Family*. New York: Fawcett Columbine, 1988.

Ch'ing-ch'ao hsu Wen-hsien t'ung-k'ao (Supplement to the Encyclopedic Institutional History of the Ch'ing). Compiled by Liu Chin-tsao. 14 vols. Compiler's preface dated 1921; repr. Taipei, 1965.

Ch'ing Chün-chi ch'u tang-an mu-lu (Catalog of [record books in] the Grand Council archives). Compiled by Palace Museum, Bureau of Documents. Peiping, 1930.

Ch'ing Hsüan-t'ung. *From Emperor to Citizen: The Autobiography of Aisin-Gioro Pu Yi*. Translated by W.J.F. Jenner. 2nd ed. 2 vols. Beijing: Peking Foreign Languages Press, 1979. (1st ed. 1964.)

Ch'ing huang-shih ssu-p'u (Genealogies of the Ch'ing Imperial House in four parts). Compiled by T'ang Pang-chih. 1st ed. 1923; repr. Taipei: Wen-hai, 1968.

Ch'ing kung-shih and *Ch'ing kung-shih hsu-pien*. see *Kuo-ch'ao kung-shih*, etc.

Ch'ing-kung shu-wen (Informal history of the Ch'ing palace). Compiled by Chang T'ang-jung. 6 *chüan*. Last preface dated 1937; repr. Taipei: Wen-hai, 1969.

"Ch'ing Nei-fu ts'ang ching-ch'eng ch'üan-t'u nien-tai k'ao" (An inquiry into the date of the map of the capital city held in [the archives of] the Ch'ing Imperial Household). In *Wen-hsien t'e-k'an*, Pao-kao (Announcements) sec., pp. 37–38. Peiping: Palace Museum, Bureau of Documents, 1935.

Ch'ing Nei-ko k'u-chu chiu-tang chi-k'an (Compilation concerning the materials stored in the Grand Secretariat Great Treasury). Compiled by Fang Su-sheng. 6 *ts'e*. Peiping: Palace Museum, Bureau of Documents, 1934.

Ch'ing-pai lei ch'ao (Miscellaneous historical comments arranged in categories). Compiled by Hsu Ho. 12 vols. 1st ed. 1917; repr. Taipei: Commercial Press, 1966.

Ch'ing-shih (History of the Ch'ing dynasty). 8 vols. Taipei: Kuo-fang yen-chiu yuan, 1961. Cited as CS.

Ch'ing-shih lieh-chuan (Official biographies [prepared] for the Ch'ing history). 10 vols. 1st ed. Shanghai, 1928; repr. Taipei: Chung-hua, 1964.

Ch'ing-shih lun-ts'ung (Collected essays on Ch'ing history). Compiled by the Chinese Academy of Social Sciences. Beijing: Chung-hua shu-chü, yearly from 1979.

Ch'ing-shih wen-t'i (The study of Ch'ing history). English-language journal appearing irregularly 1964–1985; in June 1985 name changed to *Late Imperial China*.

Ch'ing-tai chang-ku chui-lu (Selected materials on the Ch'ing period). Taipei: San-jen hang, 1974.

Ch'ing-tai chih-kuan nien-piao (Chronological tables of Ch'ing officials). Compiled by Ch'ien Shih-fu. 4 vols. Beijing: Chung-hua, 1980.

Ch'ing-tai kung-t'ing sheng-huo (Life in the Ch'ing Forbidden City). Compiled by Wan I, Wang Shu-ch'ing, and Lu Yen-chen. Hong Kong: Commercial Press, 1985.

Ch'ing-tai ti-chen tang-an shih-liao (Archival materials on earthquakes in the Ch'ing period). Compiled by Ming-Ch'ing Archives Bureau of the State Archives Board. Beijing: Chung-hua shu-chü, 1959.

Ch'ing-tai ting-chia lu (Record of the Ch'ing examination system). Compiled by Chu P'ei-lien. Taipei: Chung-hua, 1968.

Ch'ing-tai wen-hsien mai-ku lu (Collected materials of the Ch'ing period). Compiled by Chao Tsu-ming. Taipei, 1971.

Ch'ing T'ai-tsu Nu-erh-ha-ch'ih shih-lu (The Veritable Records of the Ch'ing founding emperor). Peiping: Palace Museum, Bureau of Documents, 1933. (Ch'ien-lung–period version, Min-kuo typeset edition.)

Chiu-tien pei-cheng (Miscellaneous information about Ch'ing officials). Compiled by Chu P'eng-shou. 5 *chüan*. Postface dated 1941; Taipei: Wen-hai, 1968.

Chu Chin-fu. "Ch'ing K'ang-hsi shih-ch'i chung-yang chüeh-ts'e chih-tu yen-chiu" (A study of the central government decision-making system of the K'ang-hsi period). *Li-shih tang-an* 1987, no. 1 (Feb. 1987): 80–88.

Chu Hsieh. *Pei-ching kung-ch'üeh t'u-shuo* (Illustrated description of the palace in Peking). Changsha: Commercial Press, 1938.

Chü Te-yuan [Ju Deyuan]. "Ch'ing-tai ti pien-nien t'i tang-ts'e yü kuan-hsiu shih-shu" (The Ch'ing chronologically organized archival record books and official historical writing). *Ku-kung po-wu-yuan yuan-k'an* 1979, no. 2 (May 1979): 34–44.

———. "Ch'ing-tai t'i-tsou wen-shu chih-tu" (The memorial system of the Ch'ing period). *Ch'ing-shih lun-ts'ung* (Collected essays on Ch'ing history). (1982): 218–38.

Chuang Chi-fa. "Ch'ing Shih-tsung chü-chin shih-ssu a-ko Yin-t'i shih-mo" (An account of Ch'ing Shih-tsung's detention of his fourteenth brother, Yin-t'i). *Ta-lu tsa-chih* 49, no. 2 (Aug. 1974): 24–38.

———. "Ch'ing Shih-tsung yü Pan-li Chün-chi ch'u ti she-li" (Yung-cheng and the founding of the Grand Council). *Shih-huo yueh-k'an* 6, no. 12 (Mar. 1977): 666–71.

———. "Ch'ing Shih-tsung yü tsou-che chih-tu ti fa-chan" (The development of the palace memorial system in the Yung-cheng period). *Kuo-li T'ai-wan Shih-fan ta-hsueh li-shih hsueh-pao* 4 (Apr. 1976): 197–220.

———. *Ch'ing-tai tsou-che chih-tu* (The palace memorial system of the Ch'ing period). Taipei: Palace Museum, 1979.

———. "Kuo-li Ku-kung po-wu-yuan tien-ts'ang Ch'ing-tai tang-an shu-lueh" (Brief description of the Ch'ing archives housed in the Palace Museum [Taipei]). *Ku-kung chi-k'an* (Palace Museum quarterly) 6, no. 4 (Summer 1972): 57–66.

———. Introduction to "Pen-yuan tien-ts'ang Ch'ing-tai tang-an mu-lu." *Ku-kung wen-hsien* (Ch'ing documents at the Palace Museum [Taipei]), 2, no. 4 (Sept. 1971): 81.

———. "P'ing-chieh Wu-chu 'Ch'ing-ch'u tsou-che chih-tu chih fa-chan'" (Review of Silas Wu's *Communication and Imperial Control in China: Evolution of the Palace Memorial*

System, *1693–1735*), *Ta-lu tsa-chih* 41, no. 8 (Oct. 1970): 21–28.

———. "Shang-yü tang" (Description of the archival record book known as the Shang-yü tang). *Ku-kung wen-hsien* 3, no. 2 (Mar. 1972): 67–68.

———. "Ts'ung Ku-kung po-wu-yuan hsien-ts'ang kung-chung tang-an t'an Ch'ing-tai ti tsou-che" (Discussion of Ch'ing memorials based on the National Palace Museum collection of Ch'ing documents). *Ku-kung wen-hsien* 1, no. 2 (Mar. 1970): 43–53.

Chün-chi chang-ching t'i-ming (List of Grand Council clerks). Compiled by Wu Hsiao-ming. 1st ed. 1828; repr. Taipei: Wen-hai, 1970.

Chung-ho yueh-k'an shih-liao hsuan-chi (Selected historical materials from the Chung-ho monthly). 2 vols. Taipei: Wen-hai, 1970.

Crossley, Pamela Kyle. "*Manzhou yuanliu kao* and the Formalization of the Manchu Heritage." *Journal of Asian Studies* 46, no. 4 (Nov. 1987): 761–90.

Eastman, Lloyd E. *Throne and Mandarins: China's Search for a Policy During the Sino-French Controversy, 1800–1885.* Cambridge, Mass.: Harvard University Press, 1967.

Eisenstadt, S. N. *The Political System of Empires.* New York: Free Press, 1969.

Elman, Benjamin A. *From Philosophy to Philology: Intellectual and Social Aspects of Change in Late Imperial China.* Harvard East Asian Monogaphs, no. 110. Cambridge, Mass.: Harvard University, Council on East Asian Studies, 1984.

Eminent Chinese of the Ch'ing Period (1644–1912). Edited by Arthur W. Hummel. 1st ed. 1943; repr. Taipei, 1967. Cited as ECCP.

Fairbank, John K. *Trade and Diplomacy on the China Coast: The Opening of the Treaty Ports 1842–1854.* 2 vols. Cambridge, Mass.: Harvard University Press, 1964.

Fairbank, John K., and Ssu-yü Teng. "On the Types and Uses of Ch'ing Documents." In *Ch'ing Administration: Three Studies.* Cambridge, Mass.: Harvard University Press, 1961. (Originally published in *Harvard Journal of Asiatic Studies* 6, no. 1 [Jan. 1940]: 1–71.)

Farquhar, David M. "Emperor as Bodhisattva in the Governance of the Ch'ing Empire." *Harvard Journal of Asiatic Studies* 38, no. 1 (June 1978): 5–34.

———. "Mongolian versus Chinese Elements in the Early Manchu State." *Ch'ing-shih wen-t'i* 2, no. 6 (June 1971): 15–22.

Feng Erh-k'ang. *Yung-cheng chuan* (Biography of Yung-cheng). Beijing: Jen-min ch'u-pan she, 1985.

Fisher, Thomas S. "New Light on the Yung Cheng Accession." *Papers on Far Eastern History* 17 (Mar. 1978): 103–36.

Franke, Wolfgang. *An Introduction to the Sources of Ming History.* Kuala Lumpur: University of Malaya Press, 1968.

———. "The Veritable Records of the Ming Dynasty (1368–1644)." In *Historians of China and Japan,* edited by W. G. Beasley and E. G. Pulleyblank. London: Oxford University Press, 1961.

Fu Lo-ch'eng. *Chung-kuo t'ung-shih* (General history of China). 2d ed. 2 vols. Taipei: Ta Chung-kuo t'u-shu kung-ssu, 1972.

Fu Lo-shu. *A Documentary Chronicle of Sino-Western Relations (1644–1820).* 2 vols. Tucson: University of Arizona Press (for the Association for Asian Studies), 1966.

Fu Tsung-mao. *Ch'ing-tai Chün-chi ch'u tsu-chih chi ch'i chih-chang chih yen-chiu* (Functions and organization of the Grand Council of the Ch'ing period). Taipei, 1967.

Fu Tzu-chün and Chu Hsiu-yuan. "Ming-Ch'ing tang-an kuan li-shih tang-an cheng-li kung-tso tsai ta-yuch-chin chung" (The work of arranging the historical documents in the Ming-Ch'ing Archives during the Great Leap Forward). *Li-shih yen-chiu* 1959, no. 1 (Jan. 1959): 95–96.

Goodrich, L. Carrington. *The Literary Inquisition of Ch'ien-lung*. 2d ed. New York: Paragon Books, 1986. (1st ed. 1935.)

Grantham, A. E. *A Manchu Monarch: An Interpretation of Chia Ch'ing*. London: George Allen and Unwin, 1934.

Guy, R. Kent. *The Emperor's Four Treasuries: Scholars and the State in the Late Ch'ien-lung Era*. Harvard East Asian Monographs, no. 129. Cambridge, Mass.: Harvard University, Council on East Asian Studies, 1987.

———. "Zhang Tingyu and Reconciliation: The Scholar and the State in the Early Qianlong Reign." *Late Imperial China* 7, no. 1 (June 1986): 50–62.

Heer, Ph. de. *The Care-taker Emperor: Aspects of the Imperial Institution in Fifteenth-Century China as Reflected in the Political History of the Reign of Chu Ch'i-yü*. Leiden: E. J. Brill, 1986.

Ho, Alfred Kuo-liang. "The Grand Council in the Ch'ing Dynasty." *The Far Eastern Quarterly* 11, no. 2 (Feb. 1952): 167–82. (Reprinted in *China: Enduring Scholarship Selected from the Far Eastern Quarterly—The Journal of Asian Studies, 1941–1971*, edited by John A. Harrison. Tucson: University of Arizona Press, 1972.)

Ho, Ping-ti. *Studies on the Population of China, 1368–1953*. Cambridge, Mass.: Harvard University Press, 1959.

Ho, Ping-ti, and Tang Tsou, eds. *China in Crisis*. Vol. 1, Book 1: *China's Heritage and the Communist Political System*. Chicago: University of Chicago Press, 1968.

Howorth, Henry H. *History of the Mongols from the Ninth to the Nineteenth Century*. 3 vols. in 4. London: Longmans, Green, 1875–88.

Hsi-ch'ao tsai-fu lu (Record of prime ministers of the glorious [Ch'ing] dynasty). Compiled by P'an Shih-en. 1 chüan. 1838.

Hsi Wu-ao. *Nei-ko chih* (An account of the Grand Secretariat). Ca. 1766; Shanghai: Po-ku chai, 1920.

Hsiao I-shan. *Ch'ing-tai t'ung-shih* (Complete history of the Ch'ing). 5 vols. 1st ed. 1928–31; Taipei: Commercial Press, 1967.

Hsieh Kuo-chen. *Ming-Ch'ing pi-chi t'an-ts'ung* (Collected notes on Ming-Ch'ing history). Shanghai: Chung-hua, 1962.

Hsieh Min-ts'ung. *Ming-ch'ing Pei-ching ti ch'eng-yuan yü kung-ch'üeh chih yen-chiu* (A study of the city walls and palaces of Peking in the Ming and Ch'ing periods). Taipei: Hsüeh-sheng shu-chü, 1980.

Hsieh Pao-chao. *The Government of China (1644–1911)*. 1st ed. 1925; London: Frank Cass, 1966.

Hsu Chung-shu. "Nei-ko tang-an chih yu-lai chi ch'i cheng-li" (The history of the Grand Secretariat archives and their arrangement). In *Ming-Ch'ing shih-liao* (Historical materials from the Ming and Ch'ing periods), vol. 1. Repr. Taipei: Academia Sinica, Institute of History and Philology, 1972.

Hsu, Immanuel C. Y. *China's Entrance into the Family of Nations: The Diplomatic Phase, 1858–1880*. Harvard East Asian Monograph no. 5. Cambridge, Mass.: Harvard University Press, 1960.

———. *The Rise of Modern China*. 3d ed. New York: Oxford University Press, 1983.

Hsu pei-chuan chi (Supplement to the collected epitaph biographies). Compiled by Miao

Chi-sun. Preface dated 1910; repr. Taipei, 1974.

Hsu t'ung-chih (The augmented encyclopedia of political history). Compiled by Chi Huang. Compilation ordered 1767; repr. Taipei, 1954.

Hsuan-t'ung cheng-chi shih-lu. Part of the *Ta-ch'ing li-ch'ao shih-lu*, covering the last reign of the dynasty.

Huang, Pei. *Autocracy at Work: A Study of the Yung-cheng Period, 1723–1735.* Bloomington: Indiana University Press, 1974.

———. "The Grand Council of the Ch'ing Dynasty: A Historiographical Study." *London School of Oriental and African Studies Bulletin* 48, no. 3 (1985): 502–15.

———. "Shuo 'Chu-p'i yü-chih'" (Discussion of the [published] vemilion rescripts [of the Yung-cheng Emperor]). *Ta-lu tsa-chih* 18, no. 3 (Feb. 1959): 75–80.

Huang, Ray. *1587, A Year of No Significance: The Ming Dynasty in Decline.* New Haven: Yale University Press, 1981.

Hucker, Charles O. *A Dictionary of Official Titles in Imperial China.* Stanford: Stanford University Press, 1985.

———. "Governmental Organization of the Ming Dynasty." *Harvard Journal of Asiatic Studies* 21 (1958): 1–66. (Reprinted in *Studies of Government Institutions in Chinese History*, edited by John L. Bishop. Cambridge, Mass.: Harvard University Press, 1968.)

Hui-tien and *Hui-tien shih-li* and *tse-li.* See under *Ta-ch'ing hui-tien.*

I-keng, comp. *Tung-hua lu chui-yen* (Supplement to the *Tung-hua lu*). Preface dated 1844; repr. Taipei: Wen-hai, 1970.(Part of the *Chia-meng hsüan ts'ung-shu*, 1st printed 1935.)

Inaba Iwakichi. *Ch'ing-ch'ao ch'üan-shih* (Complete history of the Ch'ing dynasty). Translated from the Japanese. First Chinese ed. 1914; repr. Taipei: Chung-hua shu-chü, 1960.

Ishjamts, N., comp. *Mongolyn ard tümnii 1755–1758 ony tusgaar togtnolyn zevsegt temtsel* (The armed struggle of the Mongolian people for independence, 1755–1758). Studia Historica Instituti Historiae Academiae Scientarum Republica Populi Mongoli, vol. 3, fasc. 3. Ulaanbaatar, 1962.

Johnston, Reginald F. *Twilight in the Forbidden City.* New York: D. Appleton–Century, 1934.

Jones, Susan Mann. "Hung Liang-chi (1746–1809): The Perception and Articulation of Political Problems in Late Eighteenth Century China." Ph.D. diss., Stanford University, 1971.

Jones, Susan Mann, and Philip A. Kuhn. "Dynastic Decline and the Roots of Rebellion." In *The Cambridge History of China*, vol. 10: *Late Ch'ing, 1800–1911*, edited by John K. Fairbank. New York: Cambridge University Press, 1978.

Ju Deyuan. See Chü Te-yuan.

Juan K'uei-sheng. *Ch'a-yü k'e-hua* (Miscellaneous chats at tea). 18th cent.; repr. Taipei: Commercial Press, 1976.

Kahn, Harold L. *Monarchy in the Emperor's Eyes: Image and Reality in the Ch'ien-lung Reign.* Cambridge, Mass.: Harvard University Press, 1971.

———. "The Politics of Filiality: Justification for Imperial Action in Eighteenth-Century China." *Journal of Asian Studies* 26, no. 2 (Feb. 1967): 197–203.

K'ang-hsi ch'ao Han-wen chu-p'i tsou-che hui-pien (Combined [Beijing and Taipei] edition of the K'ang-hsi-reign Chinese-language palace memorials). Compiled by the Number One Archives of China. 8 vols., 3,119 docs. Beijing: Tang-an ch'u-pan she, 1985.

Kessler, Lawrence D. *K'ang-hsi and the Consolidation of Ch'ing Rule, 1661–1684.* Chicago:

University of Chicago Press, 1976.

Koestler, Arthur. *Darkness at Noon.* New York: New American Library, 1948.

Ku-kung po-wu-yuan Wen-hsien kuan hsien-ts'un Ch'ing-tai Shih-lu tsung-mu (List of Ch'ing Veritable Records held by the Palace Museum). Compiled by Chang Kuo-jui. Peiping: Palace Museum, Bureau of Documents, 1934.

Ku-kung po-wu-yuan yuan-k'an (Palace Museum journal [Beijing]). Quarterly from Feb. 1979 (with two issues in 1959 and 1960).

Ku-kung wen-hsien (Ch'ing documents at the National Palace Museum) [Taipei]. Quarterly, 1969–73.

Kuan-yü Chiang-Ning chih-tsao Ts'ao-chia tang-an shih-liao (Historical materials from the archives concerning the Ts'ao family of the Chiang-Ning textile factory). Compiled by Palace Museum, Ming-Ch'ing Archives Office. Beijing: Chung-hua shu-chü, 1975.

Kuang-hsu Shun-t'ien fu-chih (Kuang-hsu–period gazetteer of the city of Peking). Compiled by Miao Ch'üan-sun. Ch'ing printed ed., 1886.

Kuhn, Philip A. "Political Crime and Bureaucratic Monarchy: A Chinese Case of 1768." *Late Imperial China* 8, no. 1 (June 1987): 80–104.

———. *Rebellion and Its Enemies in Late Imperial China: Militarization and Social Structure, 1796–1864.* Cambridge, Mass.: Harvard University Press, 1970.

Kung-chung hsien-hsing tse-li (Current regulations in use in the palace). 4 *chüan.* Kuang-hsu printed ed.

Kung-chung tang Yung-cheng ch'ao tsou-che (Palace memorials of the Yung-cheng period). Compiled by the Palace Museum, Documents Section. 27 vols. Taipei: Palace Museum, 1977–80.

Kung-shih and *Kung-shih hsu-pien.* See *Kuo-ch'ao kung-shih* and *Kuo-ch'ao kung-shih hsu-pien.*

Kung Tzu-chen. *Ting-an wen-chi* (Collected works [of Kung Tzu-chen]). 4 vols. Repr. Taipei: Commercial Press, 1968. (First printed variously in the late nineteenth century; includes *Ting-an wen-chi pu-pien,* 4 *chüan* in vol. 4.)

Kuo-ch'ao kung-shih (History of the Ch'ing imperial palace). Compiled by Yü Min-chung et al. 36 *chüan* in 2 vols. Repr. Taipei: Kuo-ch'ao Kung-shih, 1970. (First published Peiping: Palace Museum, 1925, from a Ch'ien-lung–period manuscript; preface dated 1761.)

Kuo-ch'ao kung-shih hsu-pien (Continuation of the history of the Ch'ing imperial palace). Compiled by Ch'ing-kuei et al. 100 *chüan* in 12 *ts'e.* Peiping: Palace Museum, 1932. (From a Chia-ch'ing–period manuscript.)

Kuo li Ku-kung po-wu-yuan p'u-t'ung chiu-chi mu-lu (Catalog of oridinary [Ch'ing and Republic] books in the Palace Museum [Taipei]). Taipei: Palace Museum, 1970.

Landes, David S. *Revolution in Time: Clocks and the Making of the Modern World.* Cambridge, Mass.: Harvard University Press, 1983.

Late Imperial China. Edited by James Lee and Charlotte Furth. Pasadena: Society for Qing Studies, twice yearly from 1985.

Lessing, Ferdinand D., comp. *Mongolian-English Dictionary.* Bloomington, Ind.: Mongolia Society, 1973.

Li Chien-nung. *Chung-kuo chin-pai-nien cheng-chih shih* (The political history of China in the last one hundred years). Shanghai: Commercial Press, 1948.

Li P'eng-nien et al. *Ch'ing-tai chung-yang kuo-chia chi-kuan kai-shu* (Outline of Ch'ing central-government agencies). Harbin: Heilungkiang People's Publishing Co., 1983.

Li Tsung-t'ung. "Pan-li Chün-chi ch'u lueh-k'ao" (A brief investigation of the founding of the Grand Council). *Yu-shih hsueh-pao* 1, no. 2 (Apr. 1959): 1–19.

————. *Shih-hsueh kai-yao* (The study of history). Taipei: Cheng-chung, 1968.

Li-shih tang-an (Historical archives) [Beijing]. Quarterly from Feb. 1981.

Li-tai ching-chi k'ao (Assemblage of the Ching-chi k'ao sections [on literature and publication] of the *Wen-hsien t'ung-k'ao* and its subsequent editions). Compiled by Ma Tuan-lin et al. 4 vols. in 2. Repr. Taipei: Hsin-hsing, 1959.

Li-tai hsiao-shuo pi-chi hsuan (Ch'ing) (Selections from fiction and belles lettres [Ch'ing]). Hong Kong: Commercial Press, 1958.

Liang Chang-chü, comp. *Ch'eng-wei lu* (Miscellaneous notes.) 32 *chüan.* 1875.

————, comp. *Shu-yuan chi-lueh* (Materials on Grand Council history). See under title.

Liu Tzu-yang. "Ch'ing-tai ti Chün-chi ch'u." *Li-shih tang-an* 1981, no. 2 (May 1981): 99–104.

Liu Wei. "Chün-chi ch'u yü Chün-chi chih-fang" (The Grand Council and the Grand Council office). In *Chin-tai ching-hua shih-chi* (Capital city historical remains of the modern period), compiled by Lin K'e-kuang et al. Beijing: People's University Press, 1985.

Liu, Yat Wing. "The Ch'ing Grand Council: A study of Its Origins and Organization to 1861." M.A. thesis, University of Hong Kong, 1966.

Lo Hsiang-lin. "The History and Arrangement of Chinese Genealogies." In *Studies in Asian Genealogy*, edited by Spencer J. Palmer. Provo, Utah: Brigham Young University Press, 1972.

Lui, Adam Yuen-chung. "The Practical Training of Government Officials Under the early Ch'ing, 1644–1795." *Asia Minor* 16, nos. 1–2 (1971): 82–95.

Martin, W. A. P. *Hanlin Papers: Essays on the Intellectual Life of the Chinese.* London: Trübner, 1880.

Mayers, William Frederick. *The Chinese Government: A Manual of Chinese Titles, Categorically Arranged and Explained, with an Appendix.* 1st ed. Shanghai: Kelly and Walsh, 1987; repr. Taipei: Ch'eng-wen, 1970.

Meng, S. M. *The Tsungli Yamen: Its Organization and Functions.* Cambridge, Mass.: Harvard University Press, 1970.

Meng Sen. *Ch'ing-tai shih* (History of the Ch'ing period). Taipei: Cheng-chung, 1960.

————. *The Internal Organization of Ch'ing Bureaucracy: Legal, Normative, and Communication Aspects.* Cambridge, Mass.: Harvard University Press, 1973.

Ming-Ch'ing li-k'e chin-shih t'i-ming pei-lu (Chin-shih examination classes of the Ming and Ch'ing periods, with brief biographical notices). Taipei: Hua-wen, 1969.

Ming-Ch'ing shih-liao (Historical materials from the Ming and Ch'ing periods). 15 vols. 1st ed. 1930–57; repr. Taipei: Academia Sinica, Institute of History and Philology, 1972.

Ming-Ch'ing tang-an ts'un-chen hsuan-chi, ch'u-chi (Selected materials from the Ming-Ch'ing archives: Documents of the late Ming and the early Ch'ing dynasties photographically reproduced). Vol. 1. Compiled by Li Kuang-t'ao. Taipei: Academia Sinica, Institute of History and Philology, 1959.

Ming hui-tien (Collected statutes of the Ming dynasty). 40 vols. Taipei: Commercial Press, 1968.

Ming Shih-lu (Veritable Records of the Ming Dynasty). 117 vols. Repr. Nankang: Academia Sinica, Institute of History and Philology, 1964–66.

Mote, Frederick W. "The Growth of Chinese Despotism: A Critique of Wittfogel's Theory of Oriental Despotism as Applied to China." *Oriens Extremus* 8 (1961): 1–41.

Naquin, Susan. *Millenarian Rebellion in China: The Eight Trigrams Uprising of 1813*. New Haven: Yale University Press, 1976.

Nathanson, Alynn. "Ch'ing Policies in Khalka Mongolia and the Chingünjav Rebellion of 1756." Ph.D. diss., University of London, 1983.

Neustadt, Richard E. *Presidential Power: The Politics of Leadership*. New York: John Wiley, 1960.

Nien Keng-yao tsou-che (The Palace memorials of Nien Keng-yao). 3 vols. Taipei: Palace Museum, 1971.

Nivison, David S. "Ho-shen and His Accusers: Ideology and Political Behavior in the Eighteenth Century." In *Confucianism in Action*, edited by David S. Nivison and Arthur F. Wright. Stanford: Stanford University Press, 1959.

———. "Protest Against Conventions and Conventions of Protest." In *The Confucian Persuasion*, edited by Arthur F. Wright. Stanford: Stanford University Press, 1960.

Ocko, Jonathan. "The British Museum's Peking Gazette." *Ch'ing-shih wen-t'i* 2, no. 9 (Jan. 1973): 35–49.

Oxnam, Robert B. "Policies and Institutions of the Oboi Regency." *Journal of Asian Studies* 32, no. 2 (Feb. 1973): 265–86.

———. *Ruling from Horseback: Manchu Politics in the Oboi Regency, 1661–1669*. Chicago: University of Chicago Press, 1975.

Pei-ch'ing li-shih ti-t'u chi (Historical maps of Peking). Compiled by Hou Jen-chih. Beijing: Beijing ch'u-pan she, 1985.

Pei-chuan chi (Collected epitaph biographies). Compiled by Ch'ien I-chi. 1st ed. in 160 *chüan*, n.p.: Chiang-su shu-chü, 1893; repr. Taipei: Bank of Taiwan, 1974.

Pei-p'ing Ku-kung po-wu-yuan Wen-hsien kuan i-lan (On the Ch'ing archives held by the Palace Museum, Peiping). Compiled by the Ku-kung po-wu yuan (Palace Museum). 1 *ts'e*. Peiping: Palace Museum, 1932.

Petech, L. *China and Tibet in the Early XVIIIth Century: History of the Establishment of Chinese Protectorate in Tibet*. Leiden: E. J. Brill, 1972.

P'ing-ting Chun-ka-erh fang-lueh (Record of the pacification of the Zungars). Compiled by Fu-heng et al. 171 *chüan*. Palace ed., 1772.

P'ing-ting liang Chin-ch'uan fang-lueh (Campaign record of the suppression of the two Chin-ch'uan). Compiled by A-kuei et al. 136 *chüan*. Palace ed., completed 1779–80, printed 1800.

P'ing-ting Lo-ch'a fang-lueh (Official history of the [K'ang hsi period] campaign against Russia). In *Kung-shun t'ang ts'ung-shu, ts'e* 21 (4 *chüan*), edited by P'an Tsu-yin. Late Ch'ing woodblock ed.

P'ing-ting San-ni fang-lueh (Official history of the Three Feudatories campaign). Compiled by Le-te-hun et al. Completed 1686; repr. Taipei: Chung-hua, 1970.

P'ing-ting Shuo-mo fang-lueh (Official history of the campaign against Galdan). Compiled by Chang Yü-shu. Completed 1708.

Priest, Quinton G. "Portraying Central Government Institutions: Historiography and Intellectual Accommodation in the High Ch'ing." *Late Imperial China* 7, no. 1 (June 1986): 27–49.

Rikubu seigo chūkai (A guide to the terminology of the Six Boards). Tokyo: Taian, 1962.

Rosso, Antonio Sisto. *Apostolic Legations to China of the Eighteenth Century*. South Pasadena,

Calif.: P. D. and Ione Perkins, 1948.

Schlesinger, Arthur M., Jr. *The Age of Roosevelt*. Vol. 2: *The Coming of the New Deal*. Boston: Houghton Mifflin, 1958.

Schram, Stuart R., ed. *The Scope of State Power in China*. London: School of Oriental and African Studies, University of London, 1985.

Shakabpa, W. D. *Tibet: A Political History*. New Haven: Yale University Press, 1967.

Shan Shih-k'uei. "Ch'ing-tai li-shih tang-an ming-tz'u chien-shih" (Explanation of the terminology of the Ch'ing archives). In *Ch'ing-tai tang-an shih-liao ts'ung-pien* (Historical materials selected from the Ch'ing archives), compiled by the Palace Museum, Ming-Ch'ing Archives Office, 3:195–202. Beijing, 1979.

Shan Shih-yuan. "Ku-kung Chün-chi ch'u chih-fang" (The Office of the Grand Council in the Palace Museum). *Wen-wu* 1960, no. 1 (Jan. 1960): 41–43.

——. "Ku-kung po-wu-yuan Wen-hsien kuan so-ts'ang tang-an ti fen-hsi" (Archives in the library of the Palace Museum [Peiping]). *Chung-kuo chin-tai ching-chi shih yen-chiu* 2, no. 3 (May 1934): 270–80.

——. "Ch'ing-kung Tsou-shih ch'u chih-chang chi ch'i tang-an nei-jung" (The operation of the Ch'ing palace Chancery of Memorials and the contents of its archival records). *Ku-kung po-wu-yuan-k'an* 1986, no. 1 (Feb. 1986): 7–12.

Shang Ch'üan. "Ch'ing-tai Ho-shen tsai-ching chia-ch'an k'ao-shih" (An inquiry into the estate of Ho-shen). Unpublished undated manuscript, probably ca. 1936.

Shang-yü Nei-ko (Edicts of the Yung-cheng Emperor promulgated through the Grand Secretariat). 159 *chüan*. Peking: Palace eds., 1731 and 1741.

Shen Jen-yuan and T'ao Hsi-sheng. *Ming-Ch'ing cheng-chih chih-tu* (Ming-Ch'ing political organization). 2 vols. in 1. Taipei: Commercial Press, 1967.

Shih-liao hsun-k'an (Historical materials published thrice monthly). Compiled by the Palace Museum, Bureau of Documents. Peiping: Palace Museum; repr. Taipei: Kuo-Feng, 1963.

Shu-yuan chi-lueh (Materials on Grand Council history). Compiled by Liang Chang-chü. 28 *chüan* in 2 vols. Taipei: Wen-hai, 1967. (Reprint of the 1823 [Ch'ing] ed. as amended by Prince Kung and republished in 1875.) Cited as SYCL.

——. 28 *chüan*. Ch'ing printed ed., 1875.

Smith, Kent Clarke. "Ch'ing Policy and the Development of Southwest China: Aspects of Ortai's Governor-Generalship, 1726–1731." Ph.D. diss., Yale University, 1970.

Spence, Jonathan D. *Emperor of China: Self-Portrait of K'ang-hsi*. New York: Alfred A. Knopf, 1974.

——. *Ts'ao Yin and the K'ang-hsi Emperor: Bondservant and Master*. New Haven: Yale University Press, 1966.

Struve, Lynn A. *The Southern Ming 1644–1662*. New Haven: Yale University Press, 1984.

Sugimura Yūzō. *Ken-ryū kōtei* (The Chien-lung Emperor). Tokyo: Nigen sha, 1961.

Sun, E-tu Zen. "The Board of Revenue in Nineteenth-Century China." *Harvard Journal of Asiatic Studies* 24 (1962–63): 175–228.

——, ed. and trans. *Ch'ing Administrative Terms: A Translation of the Terminology of the Six Boards, with Explanatory Notes*. Cambridge, Mass.: Harvard University Press, 1961.

Ta-Ch'ing Hui-tien (Collected statues of the Ch'ing period [K'ang-hsi, Yung-cheng, Ch'ien-lung, and Chia-ch'ing editions, the latter two with precedents, *Tse-li* in the first and *Shih-li* in the second]). Peking: Palace eds., 1690, 1732, 1767, and 1818.

Ta-Ch'ing Hui-tien t'u shih-li (Collected statutes, illustrations, and precedents of the

Ch'ing dynasty [Kuang-hsu edition of 1899]). 100, 270, and 1,220 *chüan* in 24 vols. Repr. Taipei: Ch'i-wen, 1963. Cited as HT and HTSL.

Ta-Ch'ing li-ch'ao shih-lu (The veritable records of the Ch'ing dynasty). (Composed following each Ch'ing reign.) 96 vols. Repr. Taipei: Hua-lien, 1964. Cited as KHSL, YCSL, CLSL, CCSL.

Ta-Ch'ing shih-ch'ao sheng-hsun (Imperial instructions from ten reigns of the Ch'ing dynasty). 20 vols. Repr. Taipei: Ta-ta, 1965.

Ta-lu tsa-chih (Continent magazine). [Taipei]. Semimonthly from July 1950.

T'ai-tsung *shih-lu.* See *Ta-ch'ing li-ch'ao shih-lu.*

Teng Wen-ju (Shih-hsi) and Wang Chung-han. "T'an Chün-chi ch'u" (On the Grand Council). *Shih-hsueh nien-pao* (Historical annual) 2, no. 4 (1937): 193–98.

T'ien Ku. *Man-Ch'ing wai-shih.* Taipei: Kuang-wen, 1971.

Torbert, Preston M. *The Ch'ing Imperial Household Department: A Study of Its Organization and Principal Functions, 1662–1796.* Cambridge, Mass.: Harvard University Press, 1977.

Tsung-kuan Nei-wu fu t'ang hsien-hsing tse-li (Regulations of the Imperial Household). 5 *chüan* in 4 *ts'e.* Ch'ing printed ed., 1853.

Tu Lien-che. *Kuan-yü Chün-chi ch'u ti chien-chih* (On the establishment of the Grand Council). Canberra: Australian National University, Centre of Oriental Studies, 1963.

Tun Li-ch'en. *Annual Customs and Festivals in Peking.* Translated and annotated by Derk Bodde. 1st English ed. Peiping: Henri Vetch, 1936; repr. Hong Kong: Hong Kong University Press, 1965.

T'ung-chih (Historical essays). Compiled by Cheng Ch'iao. 200 *chüan.* Repr. Shanghai: Commercial Press, 1935.

Twitchett, Denis. Introduction to *The Cambridge History of China,* vol. 3: *Sui and T'ang China, 589–906,* pt. 1, edited by Denis Twitchett. New York: Cambridge University Press, 1979.

Tz'u-lin tien-ku (Compendium of materials relating to the Hanlin Academy). 64 *chüan.* Completed 1806; printed 1887.

Wakeman, Frederic E., Jr. *The Great Enterprise: The Manchu Reconstruction of the Imperial Order in Seventeenth-Century China.* 2 vols. Berkeley and Los Angeles: University of California Press, 1985.

Waley, Arthur. *Three Ways of Thought in Ancient China.* Garden City, N.Y.: Doubleday, 1956.

Wang Ch'ang. "Chün-chi ch'u t'i-ming chi" ([Preface to] a record of Grand Council personnel). In *Huang-ch'ao ching-shih wen-pien* (Collected essays on statecraft), vol. 1. Ch'ing ed. 1827; repr. Taipei: Kuo-feng, 1963.

Wang Kuo-wei. "K'u-shu lou chi" (Notes from my library). In *Wang Kuan-t'ang hsien-sheng ch'üan-chi* (Complete works of Wang Kuo-wei), 3:1164–68. Taipei: Wen-hua, 1968.

Wang Shan-tuan. "Yung-cheng chu-p'i tsou-che lueh-shu" (Description of the rescripted memorials of the Yung-cheng emperor). In *Wen-hsien chuan-k'an, Lun-shu* (Articles) sec., pp. 63–64. Peiping: Palace Museum, 1944.

Wang Shih-chen. *Ch'ih-pei ou-t'an* (Miscellaneous notes). 26 *chüan* in 2 vols. 1691; repr. Taipei: Commercial Press, 1976.

Watt, John R. *The District Magistrate in Late Imperial China.* New York: Columbia

University Press, 1972.

Wechsler, Howard J. *Mirror to the Son of Heaven: Wei Cheng at the Court of T'ang T'ai-tsung*. New Haven: Yale University Press, 1974.

Wei Hsiu-mei. "Ts'ung-liang ti kuan-ch'a t'an-t'ao Ch'ing-chi Pu-cheng-shih chih jen-shih ti-shan hsien-hsiang" (A quantitative analysis of the careers of provincial treasurers in the late Ch'ing). *Chin-tai shih yen-chiu so chi-k'an* 2 (June 1971): 505–33.

Weiss, Robert N. "Flexibility in Provincial Government on the Eve of the Taiping Rebellion." *Ch'ing-shih wen-t'i* 4, no. 3 (June 1980): 1–42.

Wen-hsien chuan-k'an (Special publication on archival documents). Peiping: Palace Museum, 1944. (Reprinted in *Wen-hsien ho-chi*, which see.)

Wen-hsien ho-chi (Collection of three earlier [Palace Museum, Peiping] publications on archives and archival documents: *Wen-hsien t'e-k'an* [1935], *Wen-hsien lun-ts'ung* [1936], and *Wen-hsien chuan-k'an* [1944]). Taipei: T'ai-lien Kuo-feng, 1967.

Wen-hsien lun-ts'ung (Collected essays on archival documents). Peiping: Palace Museum, 1936. (Reprinted in *Wen-hsien ho-chi*, which see.)

Wen-hsien t'e-k'an (Special publication on archival documents). Peiping: Palace Museum, 1935. (Reprinted in *Wen-hsien ho-chi*, which see.)

Wen-hsien ts'ung-pien (Collected historical documents). Issued serially in 43 nos., Peiping: Palace Museum, 1930–37; repr. in 2 vols., Taipei: Kuo-feng, 1968.

Wen Wu (Cultural artifacts) [Beijing]. Journal from 1950; 1950–58 under title *Wen Wu ts'an-k'ao tzu-liao* (Research materials for cultural artifacts); did not publish 1967–71.

Whitbeck, Judith. "The Historical Vision of Kung Tzu-chen (1792–1841)." Ph.D. diss., University of California, Berkeley, 1980.

Will, Pierre-Étienne. *Bureaucratie et famine en Chine au 18ᵉ siècle*. Paris: Mouton/École des hautes études en sciences sociales, 1980.

Woodside, Alexander Barton. *Vietnam and the Chinese Model: A Comparative Study of Nguyen and Ch'ing Civil Government in the First Half of the Nineteenth Century*. Cambridge, Mass.: Harvard University Press, 1971.

Worthy, Edmund H. "The Founding of Sung China, 950–1000: Integrative Changes in Military and Political Institutions." Ph.D. diss., Princeton University, 1976.

Wu Ch'ang-yuan. *Chen-yuan shih-lueh* (Description of Peking and environs). 16 *chüan* in 2 vols. 1788 woodblock ed.; repr. Taipei: Wen-hai, 1972.

Wu Che-fu. "Kuo-li Ku-kung po-wu yuan ts'ang-shu chien-chieh" (Introduction to the rare books in the National Palace Museum). *Chiao-yü yü wen-hua* 418 (Aug. 1974): 30–36.

Wu Chen-yu. *Yang-chi chai ts'ung-lu* (Notes from the Yang-chi studio). 26 plus 10 *chüan* in 2 vols. Preface dated 1896; repr. Taipei: Wen-hai, 1968.

Wu Hsiao-ming, comp. *Chün-chi chang-ching t'i-ming* (List of the Grand Council Clerks). See under title.

Wu, Silas Hsiu-liang. "Ch'ing-tai Chün-chi ch'u chien-chih ti tsai chien-t'ao" (A reappraisal of the establishment of the Grand Council under the Ch'ing). *Ku-kung wen-hsien* 2, no. 4 (Oct. 1971): 21–45.

———. *Communication and Imperial Control in China: Evolution of the Palace Memorial System, 1693–1735*. Cambridge, Mass.: Harvard University Press, 1970.

———. "Emperors at Work: The Daily Schedules of the K'ang-hsi and Yung-cheng Emperors, 1661–1735." *Tsing-hua Journal of Chinese Studies*, n.s., 8, nos. 1 and 2 (Aug. 1970): 210–27.

————. "The Memorial Systems of the Ch'ing Dynasty, 1644–1911." *Harvard Journal of Asiatic Studies* 27 (1967): 7–75.

————. "Nan-shu fang chih chien-chih chi ch'i ch'ien-ch'i chih fa-chan" (The founding and early development of the Southern [Imperial] Study). *Ssu yü yen* 5, no. 6 (Mar. 1968): 6–12.

————. *Passage to Power: K'ang-hsi and His Heir Apparent, 1661–1722.* Cambridge, Mass.: Harvard University Press, 1979.

————. "Transmission of Ming Memorials and the Evolution of the Transmission Network, 1368–1627." *T'oung-pao* 54, nos. 4–5 (1968): 275–87.

Yang Ch'i-ch'iao. *Yung-cheng ti chi ch'i mi-che chih-tu yen-chiu* (The Yung-cheng Emperor and his secret memorial system). 2d ed., rev. Hong Kong: San-lien, 1985.

Yang Nai-chi. "Ch'ien-lung ching-ch'eng ch'üan-t'u' k'ao-lüeh" (Study of the Ch'ien-lung–period map of the capital city [Peking]). *Ku-kung po-wu yuan yuan-k'an* 1984, no. 3 (Aug. 1984): 8–24.

Yao Yuan-chih. *Chu-yeh t'ing tsa-chi* (Miscellaneous notes from the bamboo leaf pavilion). 8 *chüan* in 2 vols. 1st ed. 1893; repr. Taipei: Wen-hai, 1969.

Yeh Feng-mao. *Nei-ko hsiao-chih* and *Nei-ko ku-shih* (Notes on the Grand Secretariat). Each 1 *chüan*. Ch'ing printed ed., 1836.

Ying-ho. *En-fu t'ang pi-chi* (Miscellaneous notes). 2 *chüan*. Ch'ing printed ed., 1837.

Yü Ying-shih. *Li-shih yü ssu-hsiang* (History and thought). Taipei: Lien-ching, 1976.

Yung-cheng chu-p'i yü-chih (Vermilion endorsements [and palace memorials] of the Yung-cheng period). 10 vols. Taipei, 1965. (Reprint of Ch'ing ed.) Cited as CPYC.

Yung-cheng chu-p'i yü-chih pu-lu tsou-che tsung-mu (List of palace memorials designated not to be published in the *Yung-cheng chu-p'i yü-chih*). Peiping: Palace Museum, Bureau of Documents, 1930.

"Yung-cheng mo-nien po-fang chu-fang kuan-ping hsiang-hsu chih-liao" (Materials on military supplies sent to garrison troops in the late Yung-cheng period). *Li-shih tang-an* 1986, no. 3 (Aug. 1986): 13–16.

Yung-cheng Shang-yü Nei-ko. See under *Shang-yü Nei-ko.*

Yung-hsien lu (Records of the Yung-cheng reign). Compiled by Hsiao Shih. Composed in the Yung-cheng period; repr. Taipei: Wen-hai, 1971.

Zelin, Madeleine. *The Magistrate's Tael: Rationalizing Fiscal Reform in Eighteenth-Century Ch'ing China.* Berkeley and Los Angeles: University of California Press, 1984.

GLOSSARY-INDEX

Mourning period, Confucian, 155–56, 168,
199, 238, 258, 267, 339 n8
Mu-chang-a 穆彰阿, 374 n45
mu-lu lei 目錄類, 364 n57. *See also* Registers

Na-yen-ch'eng 那彥成, 186, 373 n8, 374 n45
Na-yen-t'ai 納延泰, 143, 173, 178, 287,
346 n84
Nan-chai 南齋. *See* Southern [Imperial] Study
nan-mu 楠木, 234
Nan shu-fang 南書房. *See* Southern [Imperial]
Study
Nan-wu 南屋. *See* Southern Quarters
nan-wu-che 南屋者, 349 n20
Naquin, Susan, xiii, xvi, 15, 305 n14
nei 內, 92
nei chung-t'ang 內中堂. *See* Grand secretaries
Nei fan-shu fang 內繙書房. *See* Translation
Office, Inner Manchu-Chinese
Nei-ko 內閣. *See* Grand Secretariat
Nei-ko feng shange-yü 內閣奉上諭, 344 n54
Nei-ko hsueh-shih 內閣學士, 202
Nei-ko ta-k'u 內閣大庫. *See* Great Treasury of
the Grand Secretariat
Nei-ko Wai-chi mu-lu 內閣外紀目錄, 344 n61
nei-t'ing 內廷. *See* Inner court
Nei tsou-shih ch'u 內奏事處. *See* Chancery of
Memorials
Nei-wu-fu 內務府. *See* Imperial Household
Department
Nei-yu 內右 Gate, 249
Neustadt, Richard (*Presidential Power*), 276
ni-p'iao 擬票. *See* Draft rescripts
nien-fu 年富, 248
Nien Keng-yao 年羹堯, 57, 70
Nine Ministers, 20, 154, 188, 202, 273,
343 n51, 360 n12
No-ch'in 訥親, 94, 143, 148, 174, 175, 176,
182–83, 185, 217, 218, 223, 346 n84,
349 n18, 353 n58
Northern Quarters, 173, 349 n20
Northwest campaign, 2, 26–27, 28, 56–58,
60–64, 69, 105, 106, 110, 120–34, 154,
157, 173; advisers for, 130–31, 132; cost of,
121–22, 331 n7; documents of, 96, 102,
226, 323 n7, 325 n17, 370 n122; financing
of, 73, 91, 97; and Grand Council, 218,
259; history of, 51; Prince I and, 76–77;
renewal of, 85, 111, 128. *See also* Military
Finance Section; Military Strategy
Section
Nourish-honesty payments, 91, 98, 99, 100,

133, 150, 155, 156, 317 n18, 326 n27,
344 n57
Nurhaci 努爾哈赤, 25, 47, 81, 139, 163,
339 n7

O-erh-t'ai 鄂爾泰, 128, 129, 130, 202, 279,
340 n13, 342 n30, 361 n17, 376 n61; as
grand councillor, 175, 176, 346 n84,
350 n26; as grand secretary, 344 n54,
345 n68, 350 n26; and military affairs, 127,
324 n15, 325 n21; and palace memorials,
280, 322 n78, 326 n25, 327 n40, 330 n58,
355 n51, 344 n55; and publication boards,
87, 160, 163; recalled from Southwest, 69,
78, 79; and transition council, 139, 141,
143, 144, 145, 148, 155, 157, 167, 173; and
Yung-cheng, 40, 41, 54, 85, 88, 90, 93, 96
O-jung-an 鄂容安, 202, 361 n17, 376 n61
O-le-shun 鄂樂舜, 311 n103
O-lun 鄂倫, 202, 361 n17, 376 n61
O-shan 鄂山, 287, 329 n51
Oboi Regency, 141
Office of Military Archives, 11, 172, 200,
207, 213, 225–28, 348 nn12, 13; and
campaign histories, 173, 184, 368 n111;
establishment of, 370 n118; and Grand
Council, 259, 260, 265, 369 n111; location
of, 132, 226, 370 n120; records of, 227,
353 n68, 370 nn121, 122; and secret
memorials, 365 n63
Office of Military Strategy, 137, 138, 143,
174, 202, 302 n2, 330 n54, 339 n1, 340 n13,
341 n15; and Grand Council, 2, 8, 121,
134; granting of seal for, 131–32, 330 n58,
338 nn65, 66
Official History of Four Reigns, 163
Official History of Three Reigns, 163
Opium War, 1, 252
Outer court, 3–7, 19, 20–23, 28, 127–28, 228;
bribery in, 42; communications in, 4,
21–22, 43–46, 127, 199, 224, 231; and
Grand Council, 196–99, 232, 239,
253–55, 269, 359 n4; map of, 14–15;
opposition to inner-court growth, 164–66;
problems of, 28–30; publications, 22–23.
See also Communications; Inner court;
Memorials, routine

Pa-erh-k'u-erh 巴爾庫爾 (Barkul in
Sinkiang), 57, 58
pa-tzu 八字. *See* Eight characters
Pai Huang 白潢, 42, 59